Time Out

Chicago

Penguin Books

PENGUIN BOOKS

Published by the Penguin Group
Penguin Books Ltd, 27 Wrights Lane, London W8 5TZ, England
Penguin Books USA Inc., 375 Hudson Street, New York, New York 10014, USA
Penguin Books Australia Ltd, Ringwood, Victoria, Australia
Penguin Books Canada Ltd, 10 Alcorn Avenue, Toronto, Ontario, Canada M4V 3B2
Penguin Books (NZ) Ltd, 182-190 Wairau Road, Auckland 10, New Zealand

Penguin Books Ltd, Registered Offices: Harmondsworth, Middlesex, England

First published 2000
10 9 8 7 6 5 4 3 2 1

Colour reprographics by Westside Digital Media, 9 Bridle Lane, London W1
and Precise Litho, 34-35 Great Sutton Street, London EC1
Printed and bound by Cayfosa-Quebecor, Ctra. de Caldes, Km 3 08 130 Sta, Perpètua de Mogoda, Barcelona, Spain

Edited and designed by
Time Out Guides Limited
Universal House
251 Tottenham Court Road
London W1P 0AB
Tel + 44 (0)20 7813 3000
Fax + 44 (0)20 7813 6001
Email guides@timeout.com
www.timeout.com

Editorial

Editor Will Fulford-Jones
Deputy Editor Sophie Blacksell
Consultant Editor Mike Michaelson
Listings Editor Chris Barsanti
Proofreader Tamsin Shelton
Indexer Julie Hurrell

Editorial Director Peter Fiennes

Series Editors Ruth Jarvis, Caroline Taverne
Deputy Series Editor Jonathan Cox

Design

Art Director John Oakey
Art Editor Mandy Martin
Senior Designer Scott Moore
Designers Benjamin de Lotz, Lucy Grant
Picture Editor Kerri Miles
Deputy Picture Editor Olivia Duncan-Jones
Picture Admin Kit Burnet
Scanning & Imaging Dan Conway, Chris Quinn
Ad make-up Glen Impey

Advertising

Group Advertisement Director Lesley Gill
Sales Director Mark Phillips
Advertisement Director, North American Guides
Liz Howell (1-808 732 4661/1-888 333 5776 US only)
Advertising in the US co-ordinated by *Time Out New York*
Alison Tocci (Publisher), Tom Oesau (Advertising
Production Manager), Claudia Pedala (Assistant to
the Publisher)

Administration

Publisher Tony Elliott
Managing Director Mike Hardwick
Financial Director Kevin Ellis
Marketing Director Gillian Auld
General Manager Nichola Coulthard
Production Manager Mark Lamond
Production Controller Samantha Furniss
Accountant Bridget Carter

Features in this guide were written and researched by: Introduction Will Fulford-Jones. **History** Victoria Cunha.
Chicago Today Dave Chamberlain. **Architecture** Chad Schlegel. **Fictional Chicago** Chris Jones & Gillian Darlow,
Mike Michaelson. **Media** Joshua Green (*My kind of town* Will Fulford-Jones). **Sightseeing** Sara Burnett, Dave Chamberlain,
Will Fulford-Jones, Joshua Green, Chris Jones & Gillian Darlow, Mike Michaelson, Chad Schlegel; *Museums reviewed*
by Allison Stewart (*Making the world go round, Radio days* Sam Jemielity; *A view to a thrill, Resting in peace* Chad
Schlegel). **Chicago by Season** Ben Cannon. **Accommodation** Sophie Blacksell, Will Fulford-Jones, Mike Michaelson.
Restaurants Mike Michaelson (*Slices of life* Sam Jemielity). **Bars & Pubs** Sara Burnett, Dave Chamberlain, Will
Fulford-Jones, Joshua Green, Chad Schlegel (*The missing links, Screen test* Dave Chamberlain; *Gardens of Eden*
Joshua Green). **Shops & Services** Elizabeth Lenhard, Todd Savage. **Art Galleries** Allison Stewart. **Children** Cyndee Miller.
Film Ben Cannon. **Gay** Matthew Michael Wright. **Music** Dave Chamberlain. **Nightlife** Matthew Michael Wright (*House
parties* Frank Broughton). **Sport** Joshua Green, Sam Jemielity (*The ivy leagues, My kind of town* Will Fulford-Jones).
Theatre, Dance & Comedy Chris Jones (Theatre, Dance, *Being John Malkovich, Base camp Chicago*); Mark Bazer
(Comedy, *My kind of town*). **Trips Out of Town** Mike Michaelson (*Milwaukee* Will Fulford-Jones). **Directory** Chris Barsanti,
Sophie Blacksell, Will Fulford-Jones. **Further Reading** Will Fulford-Jones, Mike Michaelson.

The Editor would like to thank the following: Sophie Blacksell, Pat Burrell, Dave Chamberlain, Simon Chappell, Isaac Davis,
Sarah Guy, Wendy Haase at the Greater Milwaukee Convention & Visitors' Bureau, Kevin Hudson, Ruth Jarvis, Brother Jones,
Heidi Kooi at the Chicago Office of Tourism, Rebekah McVitie, Mike Michaelson, Seth Mindel at the Chicago Transit Authority,
Amy Mohme, Rootle Pootle, Ros Sales, Chad Schlegel, Glynis Steadman, Natalie Van Straaten at *Chicago Gallery News*,
Patricia Sullivan at the Chicago International Press Center, Caroline Taverne, Jeff Thornton.

The Editor flew to Chicago with United Airlines (UK reservations 0845 844 4777/US reservations 1-800 241 6522/
www.unitedairlines.com).

Maps by JS Graphics, 17 Beadles Lane, Old Oxted, Surrey RH8 9JG. Public transport maps used courtesy of the CTA.

Photography by Paul Avis except: page 3 Mary Evans Picture Library; pages 4, 6, 9, 11, 13, 14, 16, 17, 19, 20, 22 , 225,
226 and 232 Corbis; page 5 Hulton Getty; page 34 Tony Gibson; pages 37 and 39 Kobal Collection; page 216 William
Burlingham; page 218 George Saint George; pages 220 and 222 Mike Rosley; page 241 Lynn Goldsmith/Corbis; pages 246,
261 and 262 Terry W Phipps; page 250 Reagan Home; pages 263, 264, 266 and 270 GMCVB; page 274 Wisconsin Dells
Visitors' and Convention Bureau; page 274 Scott Witte. The following photographs were supplied by the featured
establishments: pages 26, 106, 115, 185, 217, 221, 249, 257, 266 and 272.

Contents

Introduction

It's big. Christ, is it ever big. Sure, it's the birthplace of the skyscraper, the business centre of the Midwest and the convention capital of the world, but nothing quite prepares you for its vastness. On a cloudy day – and there are many, more's the pity – some of the buildings in the Loop don't seem to be grounded so much as suspended from the sky, or perhaps even holding it up. But on a sunny summer's afternoon, these selfsame buildings resemble rockets in mid-takeoff, launching to who knows where, but getting there in some style.

But, perversely, when you get a little closer up, it doesn't seem quite so daunting. Sure, it's bustling and hustling, urban and urbane, rough and ready, alive and kicking – all the stuff a great city should be, in other words – but it's somehow more than that. Much more. It's got some mammoth buildings, a rattling public transportation system and some areas you shouldn't enter without a police escort, but it's also got an idyllic beach (a few blocks from the main shopping stretch), an unmanageably large park and some of the friendliest locals you're likely to meet in any city, let alone one of this sprawling size and scale.

Granted, most cities come with similarly charming contradictions. But here, the contradictions are the very point. It's the lovely summer sun and the demoralising cold of winter. It's the idyllic, unspoiled calm of Lake Michigan next to the aggressively modern skyline. It's the Cubs setting attendance records at Wrigley Field with a team that's too painful to watch. It's the rumble of the El and the tranquility of Grant Park. These contradictions – and many more besides – are what differentiates the place from, say, New York, where the buildings are brash but the people are, too; or Boston, where everything is just a little too nice for its own good. They're what keeps the place moving, preserves its vitality. Taking the best bits from both ends of the spectrum, it's a small town masquerading as a city. Or a city masquerading as a small town. Or both. Whatever.

It's also a City of Big Shoulders (© Carl Sandburg). The Windy City (though this nickname has less to do with the breezes off Lake Michigan and more to do with the fatuous spoutings of local politicos in days of yore). Hustlertown (less said the better). The Pride of the Rustbelt (evocative, if hardly attractive). The City That Works (yep). The Second City (with apologies to the now more populous but far less interesting Los Angeles). Oh, and it's also, according to a song named for the city itself, 'a toddling town'. Whatever *that* means.

Of course, no catchy nickname can really hope to capture the essence of this most fascinating of cities, let alone do it any kind of justice. But spend any amount of time here, and you'll at least agree with the greatest singer of the 20th century. For as Francis Albert Sinatra put it so zestfully, 'Chicago is my kind of town'. Here's hoping it's yours, too.

ABOUT TIME OUT GUIDES

The first edition of the *Time Out Chicago Guide* is one of the expanding series of *Time Out* guides produced by the people behind London and New York's renowned listings magazines. Our team of writers, all residents of Chicago, have been tearing around town like men and women possessed to bring you the lowdown on this most windy of cities. From the grandest of museums to the lowest-down and dirtiest of bars, not one of the proverbial stones has been left unturned. The result, we think, is the definitive guide to this definitively American city.

THE LIE OF THE LAND

Chicago is a terrifically easy place to get around. The city works, like many American cities, on a grid system, with street numbers corresponding to a fairly simple pattern.

Ground zero from a street-numbering point of view is at the corner of State Street, which runs north to south, and Madison Street, which runs east to west, in the Loop. All north-south streets north of Madison are prefixed with 'N', with the others prefixed 'S'; all east-west streets east of State are prefixed 'E', with the rest prefixed 'W'.

The numbering of the streets works outwards from these points, with each 800 measuring one mile. Thus, 800 N Clark Street is a mile north of Madison, 1600 S Michigan Avenue is two miles south of Madison, 200 E Wacker Drive is a quarter of a mile east of State and so on.

There is an online version of this guide, as well as weekly events listings for more than 30 international cities, at www.timeout.com.

Throughout this guide, we've listed full street addresses with a nearest cross-street. The maps at the back of the book are also marked with many points of interest and block-numberings every half-mile (for example, 'N Halsted Street 800W', and 'W Belmont Avenue 3200N').

ESSENTIAL INFORMATION

For all the practical information you might need for visiting the area – including emergency numbers, websites, useful numbers for business travellers and conventioneers, and full details of the local transport system – turn to the Directory chapter at the back of this guide. It starts on page 276.

THE LOWDOWN ON THE LISTINGS

Above all, we've tried to make this book as useful as possible. Addresses, phone numbers, websites, transport information, opening times, admission prices and credit card details are all included. However, owners and managers can change their arrangements at any time and we'd strongly advise you to phone ahead to check opening times and the like. While every effort and care has been made to ensure the accuracy of the information contained in this guide, the publishers cannot accept responsibility for any errors it may contain.

PRICES & PAYMENT

In the listings given for the majority of venues, we have noted which credit cards are accepted, using the following abbreviations: American Express (**AmEx**), Diners Club (**DC**), Discover (**Disc**), MasterCard (**MC**) and Visa (**V**). Please note that other cards may also be taken.

For each restaurant, we have listed the range of prices for main courses. For several of the chapters in the Arts & Entertainment section of the book, we have instead given a range of ticket prices in the introduction that you might reasonably expect to pay, as many of these rates are subject to frequent change.

In all cases, the prices we've supplied should be treated as guidelines, not gospel. Fluctuating exchange rates and inflation can cause charges, in shops and restaurants particularly, to change rapidly. If prices vary wildly from those we've quoted, ask whether there's a good reason. If not, go elsewhere. Then please let us know. We aim to give the best and most up-to-date advice, so we always want to know if you've been badly treated or overcharged.

TELEPHONE NUMBERS

The Chicago region boasts a multitude of telephone area codes. To be precise, there are five: the majority of numbers listed in this guide fall into the 312 and 773 area codes, with area codes 847, 708 and 630 covering the suburbs.

When dialling from a number within the same area code – for example, when dialling a 312 number from a number that also has a 312 prefix – there's no need to dial the code: simply dial the last seven digits of the phone number. When dialling from outside the area you're calling – for example, when calling a 773 number from a number with a 312 prefix – dial 1 first, then the ten-digit number as listed in the guide.

MAPS

At the back of this guide are a series of maps that detail much of central Chicago, as well as an overview map of the city, a map relating to the Trips Out of Town chapter and maps of the CTA system. Many of Chicago's main attractions, from museums and architecturally renowned buildings to theatres and sporting stadia, have been marked on the map. Everything else listed in the guide has been map-referenced to these maps. In addition, there is a map of central Milwaukee in the Trips Out of Town chapter on page 268.

LET US KNOW WHAT YOU THINK

We hope you enjoy the *Time Out Chicago Guide* as much as we enjoyed putting it together and we'd like to know what you think of it. We welcome your tips for places to include in future editions and take notice of your criticism of our choices. There's a reader's reply card at the back of this book, though if you prefer, you can also email us on chicagoguide@timeout.com.

Sponsors & advertisers

We would like to stress that no establishment has been included in this guide because it has advertised in any of our publications and no payment of any kind has influenced any review. The opinions given in this book are those of *Time Out* writers and entirely independent.

In Context

DEFENSE
FORT DEARBORN STOOD ALMOST ON THIS SPOT.
AFTER AN HEROIC DEFENSE IN EIGHTEEN
HUNDRED AND TWELVE THE GARRISON TOGETHER
WITH WOMEN AND CHILDREN WAS FORCED TO EVACUATE
THE FORT LED FORTH BY CAPTAIN WELLS. THEY
WERE BRUTALLY MASSACRED BY THE INDIANS
THEY WILL BE CHERISHED AS MARTYRS IN
OUR EARLY HISTORY
ERECTED BY THE TRUSTEES OF THE
B F FERGUSON MONUMENT FUND
1928

History

More than three centuries separate Louis Jolliet and 'Joliet' Jake Blues. Quite a lot happened in between.

The Paris of the Midwest, the Second City, the City of Big Shoulders, the Wild Onion, Hustlertown and the Windy City. All monikers, at one time or another, of Chicago, which currently houses three million people within its borders. A great American city, it lives and thrives because of the people who, one by one, contributed their unique vision to its growth and development in its brief yet undeniably turbulent history.

IN THE BEGINNING
Missionary Father Jacques Marquette and cartographer Louis Jolliet were the first to explore the lower Lake Michigan region. In 1673, the pair attempted to follow the Mississippi and its tributaries as far as possible to the north-east. Chartered and funded by the governor of latter-day Quebec, Marquette and Jolliet's party travelled to the native village of Kaskaskia (near what is now Utica, Illinois) on the Illinois River before proceeding north-east on the Des Plaines River.

After reaching what the Native Americans who lived in the area called 'Checagou' (believed to translate as 'wild onion', which grew in the area), the explorers floated on down the Chicago River to Lake Michigan before heading north to Green Bay in the fall of 1673. After that successful trip, Marquette returned to the area in 1674 and spent the winter as a temporary resident of what would later become known as Chicago before returning to Kaskaskia in the spring. He died the same year; Jolliet never returned to the area again.

The first permanent non-native resident of Chicago, Jean Baptiste Point du Sable, came to the area three decades before Fort Dearborn was established in 1804. The well-educated son of a French father and white mother, the black du Sable married a Potawatomie native named Catherine, and established a fur trading post at the mouth of the Chicago River as early as 1772. During the Revolutionary War, du Sable was suspected of being an enemy sympathiser and was briefly imprisoned at a military outpost, but returned to the Chicago River area in 1779. A year later, he sold his property to a fur trapper, who in turn sold it to John Kinzie, a trader eventually nicknamed the 'Father of Chicago'. Du Sable, meanwhile, moved to Peoria, Illinois and lived there for the next ten years, before heading to St Charles, Missouri, where he died in 1818. He is commemorated in the name of the **Du Sable Museum of African-American History** (*see page 88*).

THEY FORT THE LAW
Fearful of further trouble after the Revolutionary War, the government decided a military presence was necessary in the area, and so Fort Dearborn was built in 1803 at what is now the south end of the Michigan Avenue Bridge. Then the major western US Army garrison in the country, complete with a stockade and two blockhouses, it occupied a strategic point near the lower (southern) end of Lake Michigan on the south side of the Chicago River across from Jean Baptiste Pointe du Sable's cabin.

Sure enough, the US were soon at war with the British, and by the summer of 1812, tensions between soldiers and natives (who were bought off by the British) were at an all-time high. Despite efforts to appease the Potawatomie native leaders, it was clear to Captain Nathaniel Heald, who was then in charge of Fort Dearborn, that evacuating the fort's residents was imperative for their safety. Accompanied by an escort of friendly Miami natives from Indiana led by Captain William Wells, the entire garrison began its journey along the lakefront, but was ambushed by rifle-bearing natives. Heald and his wife were taken prisoner, but almost all of the others who were attempting to leave the fort were executed; in all, 53 settlers and natives died. Not content with their destruction, the Potawatomies returned three days later and burnt the fort.

> **'Despite several setbacks, Gurdon S Hubbard's prosperity mirrored that of his adopted hometown.'**

Soon after, though, things returned to normal, and the area started trading again. John Kinzie, who had established his base in Chicago by 1804 and fled the city during the Fort Dearborn Massacre, returned in 1816 and resumed his trading activities, though never to the extent or with the same success that he had enjoyed before the attack. However, his descendants continued to make themselves known through their various civic and

industrial ventures in the remaining years of the 19th century, and today's Kinzie Street, which lies just to the north of the Chicago River, stands as testimony to his influence on the development of the city.

Another early settler, Gurdon S Hubbard, arrived from Montreal in 1818, the same year that Illinois joined the union as a state, and quickly established a successful fur trade route from Danville, Illinois to Chicago nicknamed 'Hubbard's Trail'. Later, Hubbard bought an American Fur Company franchise and reaped plenty of financial rewards. Established in 1808 by German immigrant John Jacob Astor, the American Fur Company grew to rival established Canadian fur and dry goods trading companies that did business with the Native Americans and other settlers. The success of the American Fur Company had made its founder the richest man in America at the time of his death in 1848.

By the time Chicago was officially incorporated as a town in 1833, Hubbard had settled permanently in Chicago, and went about diversifying his interests into meatpacking, shipping, insurance and real estate. Despite several setbacks, Hubbard persevered, and his own prosperity mirrored that of his adopted hometown. When he died in 1886, aged 87,

Cyrus McCormick. *See page 6.*

Chicago's population numbered three-quarters of a million people, compared to just a couple of hundred at the time Hubbard had first settled in the city.

PIONEER CHECKPOINT

In 1825, the Erie Canal opened, linking the Hudson River – and, thus, the East Coast – with Buffalo, New York (on Lake Erie, one of the Great Lakes). The canal opened travel and commerce into Illinois, a significant development that favoured Chicago's growth, especially with regard to those pioneers coming from more populous areas in the east. A prime example was William Ogden, a transplanted Yankee who came west in 1835 to sell a parcel of land for a family member, but who stayed and became mayor of Chicago just two years later. The famed meatpacking mogul Philip Armour also moved to Chicago from Milwaukee after the Civil War ended, and earned millions selling barrels of pork. Armour employed refrigerated train cars for shipping fresh meat, expanded the use of animal by-products, and diversified into other businesses to widen his empire. And yet another entrepreneur, Cyrus McCormick – after whom **McCormick Place** (*see page 87*) is named – also found Chicago to be most hospitable to his Virginia-bred sensibilities. McCormick, who went on to invent the grain reaper, even borrowed money from Ogden to build his factory. During his time in

Key events

1673 Father Jacques Marquette and Louis Jolliet discover what later becomes Chicago.
1779 Jean Baptiste Point du Sable becomes the first permanent resident of area.
1812 53 settlers are killed by natives in the Fort Dearborn Massacre.
1818 Illinois receives statehood.
1837 Chicago incorporates as a city; William Ogden is elected its first mayor.
1847 The Chicago River and Harbor Convention is held to promote waterway commerce.
1848 The Illinois-Michigan Canal is completed, increasing trade opportunities; the Chicago Board of Trade is established.
1850 Northwestern University opens its doors.
1860 Abraham Lincoln is nominated as Republican presidential candidate in Chicago at the Wigwam convention.
1871 The Chicago Fire destroys $200 million worth of property and claims over 250 lives.
1872 The first mail-order catalogue business is begun by Aaron Montgomery Ward.
1879 The Chicago Academy of Fine Arts (later the Art Institute of Chicago) is incorporated.
1886 The Haymarket labour riot takes place, with eight policemen and four civilians killed.
1889 Social reformer Jane Addams opens the settlement centre known as Hull House; architect Frank Lloyd Wright builds his own residence in Oak Park with a loan from mentor Louis Sullivan.
1891 Theodore Thomas establishes the Chicago Orchestra (later the Chicago Symphony Orchestra).

1892 The first elevated train service in Chicago is offered to commuters in the central district.
1893 The World's Columbian Exposition opens, drawing huge crowds.
1894 Pullman train employees, inspired by labour rights leader Eugene V Debs, strike for improved working conditions.
1900 Chicago River is made to run backwards towards the Mississippi for sanitary purposes.
1903 A fire at the Iroquois Theatre kills 600, prompting national safety laws for public buildings.
1907 Essanay Studios on W Argyle Street contracts Charlie Chaplin, Gloria Swanson and Ben Turpin for films.
1909 Daniel Burnham, city visionary, unveils his comprehensive and park-filled Plan of Chicago.
1915 The Eastland pleasure vessel capsizes in the Chicago River, killing 812.
1919 Race riots rage in July: 38 die.
1920 Eight Chicago White Sox players, including 'Shoeless' Joe Jackson, are banned from baseball for life after they fixed the 1919 World Series in what became known as the 'Black Sox' scandal.
1921 The Field Museum of Natural History opens.
1924 Leopold and Loeb are sentenced to life in prison for murder.
1926 National radio broadcasts of Amos 'n' Andy, Fibber McGee and Molly and other popular shows start to originate from Chicago.

Chicago, McCormick became active in Democratic politics, and ran unsuccessfully for Congress in 1864.

Another person from Yankee stock who shaped Chicago was Long John Wentworth, twice Republican mayor, six-term Democratic US Congressman, editor of the city's first newspaper, all-round egotist and bon vivant. He stood six foot six inches (1.98 metres) tall, weighed in excess of 300 pounds (136 kilogrammes) and had a reputation for grand living. Wentworth's newspaper, the *Chicago Democrat*, advocated the candidacy of Andrew Jackson as opposed to Abraham Lincoln (from Illinois), but merged with its rival the *Chicago Tribune* in 1861, when the Civil War broke out.

In addition, Wentworth was an early antagonist of vice, and it was he, along with Scottish-born detective Allan Pinkerton – the man behind Chicago's first private detective agency – who tried to put a lid on the town's growing reputation for lawlessness. Police raids commissioned by Wentworth on the city's red-light districts were unsuccessful, though, and he spent the rest of his post-political life quietly on a farm in suburban Summit. Pinkerton, though, was appointed a deputy sheriff in 1852, and eventually expanded his agency's influence into government by providing assistance to the Union Army at President Lincoln's request. Pinkerton also published numerous detective novels between 1874 and 1884.

1929 Seven bootleggers are executed by Al Capone's gang in the St Valentine's Day Massacre.
1933 The Century of Progress World's Fair opens, as does the Museum of Science and Industry; Mayor Anton Cermak is killed by a gunman intending to shoot President-elect Franklin D Roosevelt in Miami.
1934 The FBI's most wanted criminal, 'Public Enemy Number One' John Dillinger is shot and killed behind the Biograph movie theatre in Lincoln Park.
1942 Physicist Enrico Fermi conducts successful nuclear chain reaction experiments at the University of Chicago.
1953 Hugh Hefner publishes the inaugural monthly issue of *Playboy* in December.
1954 The Lyric Opera company is established at the Lyric Theatre, with a mostly Italian repertoire.
1955 Mayor Richard J Daley is elected for the first of six consecutive terms; O'Hare International Airport opens in October; the first McDonald's restaurant is opened by Ray Kroc in suburban Des Plaines.
1958 A fire at Our Lady of the Angels school kills three nuns and 87 children.
1959 The first ever Second City cabaret show takes place; Chicago becomes an ocean port with the opening of the St Lawrence Seaway.
1966 Richard Speck kills eight student nurses on the West Side.
1967 A blizzard in January closes down the city with 22 inches of snow; Riverview, a favourite North Side amusement park for 63 years, closes.
1968 Riots take place after the assassination of Martin Luther King, Jr; the Democratic

National Convention in August is marred by violence.
1969 The Chicago Seven conspiracy trial (Abbie Hoffman, Jerry Rubin et al) takes place; two radicals die in a Black Panther raid.
1971 Union stockyards close after 105 years of continuous livestock trading.
1973 Sears Tower, then the world's tallest building, opens in May.
1976 Mayor Richard J Daley dies in office.
1978 Police excavate John Wayne Gacy's home on the North West Side, finding 29 bodies.
1979 *The Blues Brothers* is filmed in the city; an American Airlines DC-10 crashes near O'Hare Airport, claiming 273 lives.
1986 The Chicago Bears routs the New England Patriots 46-10 to win their first Super Bowl.
1987 Mayor Harold Washington, the first black mayor of Chicago, dies while in office in November.
1988 Lights are finally installed at the Cubs' Wrigley Field ballpark, allowing for night games.
1989 Richard M Daley, son of Richard J Daley, is elected mayor of Chicago.
1992 The Chicago River floods underground tunnels, causing $1 billion of damage to offices in the city.
1994 The United Center opens.
1995 Temperatures top 100 degrees for five straight days in July, killing 550 people.
1996 Michael Jordan and the Chicago Bulls win their sixth NBA championship.
1999 Over 200 decorated bovine statues are displayed throughout the city as part of the 'Cows on Parade' outdoor exhibit.

TRAINS AND BOATS AND PLAINS

In 1837, a country-wide economic depression, known as the Panic, threatened to put a lid on Chicago's growth. However, the Panic also coincided with Chicago achieving official city status for the first time, and in the following years things slowly but surely picked up again. In 1848, two projects were completed that were to signal the beginnings of spectacular growth in the city: the first telegraph line reached the city, radically improving communications, and, more importantly, the Illinois-Michigan Canal was finally completed, almost two decades after work on it had begun.

> ## 'Because of its central location and existing trade connections, Chicago became a crucial checkpoint for railway commerce in the US.'

The canal created a connection with vessels sailing to and from the Atlantic Ocean via the Great Lakes. The previous year, the River and Harbor Convention held in Chicago had promoted waterway trade to thousands of attendees, many of whom hailed from the east. The event simultaneously began Chicago's long tenure as a host city for national and international conferences and meetings.

Furthermore, the same savvy investors soon became aware of the city's potential as a railway hub. Because of its central location and existing trade connections, Chicago indeed became a crucial checkpoint for railway commerce in the US. Soon livestock, lumber, grain and other goods were speedily transported through Chicago at previously unheard of quantities. As a consequence, more and more industries established their headquarters on the south-western shores of Lake Michigan rather than at rival city St Louis, Missouri on the banks of the Mississippi River, 300 miles (483 kilometres) to the south-west.

By 1856, Chicago had become the largest railroad centre in the country. The Chicago and Northwestern Railroad had been the first to cross the Mississippi River, but other rail companies, such as the Chicago and Galena Railroad, the Illinois Central and the Chicago and Alton Railroad, all expanded the networks of trade. Coming at the juncture of such rapid technological development, the Civil War also spurred Chicago's population growth, as the more northerly city surpassed St Louis. Indeed, St Louis's port on the Mississippi was blockaded by Navy vessels for the duration of the conflict, constricting trade movement, and Chicago benefited hugely: by 1870, its population had topped 300,000.

Another industry that reaped great rewards from the burgeoning railway network was that of steel manufacturing. South Chicago – situated along the banks of Lake Michigan at the mouth of the Calumet River – became home to a number of blast furnaces, which set the stage for further growth. By the turn of the century, steel production in the area accounted for fully 50 per cent of the entire domestic output. Employment of immigrant, unskilled labour in the mills was also a major factor in the growth and development of Chicago's extreme south-east neighbourhoods.

In fact, by 1870, more than half Chicago's population was foreign-born, with Germans, Irish, Bohemians and Scandinavians representing a majority of the immigrant groups. The rapid, unplanned population growth in the city led to the construction of cheap, wooden buildings: lumber was easy to come by at the time, and inexpensive, too. A lack of housing codes, especially in those districts where large numbers of immigrants resided, set the stage for problems in sanitation, schooling and law enforcement. In the fall of 1871, a number of fires had taken their toll in and around the city, but no one would have guessed that a conflagration of such fury and force was imminent.

FIRING THE IMAGINATION

On 8 October 1871, a fire broke out adjacent to an immigrant neighbourhood that bordered the central business district. Spreading quickly to the north-east, the blaze gained momentum and was not slowed even upon reaching the south branch of the Chicago River. By the time the fire finally had burnt itself out in Lincoln Park several miles to the north, it had left an unprecedented level of destruction in its wake (*see opposite* **You stupid cow**). But Chicago retained much of its human and business resources, and relief efforts soon gave way to rebuilding ventures funded by eastern banks. After a few years, taller, fireproof buildings stood proudly in the downtown sector, beckoning architects to develop the already-existing elevator buildings into what were later termed 'skyscrapers' (for the development of skyscrapers, *see chapter* **Architecture**).

All this may have been of scant consolation at the time to Potter Palmer, the first merchant prince of Chicago. A Quaker by birth, Palmer had opened a dry goods business on Lake Street in 1852, employing none other than the young Marshall Field as an assistant (Palmer was later

You stupid cow

The Chicago Fire, which lasted from 8 to 10 October 1871, was the defining moment in the city's burgeoning growth in the second part of the 19th century. All Chicagoans know the legend of how Mrs O'Leary's cow kicked a lantern over in a residential neighbourhood on the near South West Side, but few remember that over three square miles (777 hectares) of land were charred, 17,000 buildings were burned and 300 lives were lost. Through its rebuilding efforts in the years after the conflagration, Chicago made its presence felt as a survivor despite – or even because of – this devastating setback to its momentum.

Several factors – a drier than usual summer, a massive amount of wooden constructions (including roadways, amazingly) and convection whirls called 'Fire Devils' that enabled the blazes to leap over rivers once they'd started – all contributed to the horrific inferno. Over the good part of two nights and one day, Chicago's citizenry fled with only their most essential possessions, with few buildings surviving the devastation from Taylor Street north to Fullerton and from the Chicago River east to Lake Michigan.

First-hand accounts of the conflagration were recounted in newspapers all over the country after the blaze ended. The 98,000 people who'd been left homeless by the fire were given succour by the outpourings of charity from many other American cities and abroad (Great Britain, for example, contributed books for a makeshift public library housed in an unused water tank). The downtown business district merchants, bloodied but unbowed, wasted no time in obtaining loans and hiring rebuilding crews to construct new, fireproof buildings.

A mere 12 months after the fire, 300 new structures had been erected, and as early as

1879, Chicago hosted a Midwest trade exposition to celebrate its growth since the disastrous blaze and its optimism about future industriousness and business promise. In fact, without the fire, Chicago would probably not have had either the opportunity or incentive to rebuild itself in such dramatic fashion: today, the city boasts perhaps the finest collection of architecture in the US. And though the tale is probably apocryphal – it's now believed that a gentleman by the name of Daniel Sullivan started the fire by accident – we prefer to believe it's all thanks to Mrs O'Leary's cow.

to build Field's first store for him and his partner, Levi Leiter). By 1871, his enterprises had grown so much that Palmer owned vast swathes of real estate in the city; so much, in fact, that he lost some 95 buildings on State Street in the fire.

Only a few months prior to the blaze, the 44-year-old bachelor had wedded 21-year-old Bertha Honore (originally of Louisville, Kentucky) and given her the 225-room **Palmer House Hotel** as a wedding gift. The building was levelled in the fire, but, undaunted by the setback, Palmer soon rebuilt it as a fireproof structure using insurance loans.

Bertha came to carry out her social and philanthropic ventures from a grand mansion on fashionable Astor Street, which later became the heart of the city's 'Gold Coast.' Built on what was marshland, the massive structure came to be known as 'Palmer castle' thanks to its crenellated walls and towering main parapet that resembled a Rhenish villa (it was torn down in 1950). From this grand setting, the

Palmers became the most celebrated hosts of not only Chicago's elite, but also visiting dignitaries, artists, politicians and even royalty. Bertha's art collection, consisting mostly of French Impressionist paintings, later formed the core of the **Art Institute**'s holdings from the era (*see page 51*). She also participated in promoting the city by heading the Columbian Exposition's Board of Lady Managers.

WATER, WATER EVERYWHERE

Another elemental problem, that of water, also needed to be addressed by the city planners following the fire. Despite the seemingly unlimited supply of freshwater provided by Lake Michigan, the polluting matter being dumped into the Chicago River in vast quantities was in danger of permanently befouling the city's drinking water supply. By 1879, the heavy rains that swept the filth further into the lake prompted such severe outbreaks of cholera and dysentery that state leaders formed the Chicago Board of Sewerage Commissioners. This board, and other local entities, studied the surrounding issues of the river's interdependence with the lake.

Subsequently, the groups proposed various plans to purify the river water and to halt the spread of disease. However, all the plans were costly and involved, and much debate ensued to decide upon a course of action. The eventual solution affected not only city residents but also those from downstate, since the plan involved forcing the river to flow not towards but away from the lake. Therefore, the sewage that had previously flowed unchecked into the clear waters of Lake Michigan would be redirected to the Mississippi River by means of a channel built to extend to a tributary in Lockport, Illinois. This channel, later known as the Sanitary and Ship Canal, was commissioned in 1889, and opened the following year against legal protests on behalf of the city of St Louis. Eventually, the suit was dropped when the water was deemed safe for consumption, as it reached its new destination in the south. With Chicago's water deemed safe for drinking, another important hurdle in the city's seemingly unstoppable growth had been passed.

WORKERS' PLAYTIME

However, it wasn't all plain sailing by any means, for the workers were getting restless. A nationwide railroad strike in the mid-1870s affected Chicago more than most, pitting out-of-work rioters against state militia units. During the strike, crowds assembled by the thousands to hear speeches espousing workers' rights. The mayor of Chicago issued warnings to those not affected by the walkout, especially women and children, to stay at home away from the out-of-control mobs. A number of protesters and civilians died in the violence in Chicago, which more or less mirrored the national climate as workers everywhere struggled to gain rights and power.

'It's partly thanks to William Rainey Harper that today's University of Chicago hospitals are among the best in their field.'

Another worker's revolt, the Haymarket Square riot of 1886, was a watershed moment in the struggle between self-described 'anarchist' workers and their bosses. On the night of 4 May, a public gathering in the square to protest against the treatment of workers at the McCormick Harvesting plant the previous day turned violent when a bomb was thrown into the crowd. Several people, including one police officer, were killed, and ten defendants were indicted. Of the eight that eventually stood trial, four were executed and three were pardoned, largely thanks to attorney John Peter Altgeld's efforts. The 'Haymarket martyrs', as they came to be known, inspired the socialist celebrations of workers in May that continue to this day.

SEATS OF LEARNING

1892 marked an important year in the educational life of Chicago, when William Rainey Harper became the first president of the University of Chicago. The holder of a PhD from Yale University, Harper had hoped to found an institution of higher learning in the Midwest nearer to or even in Ohio (his birthplace). But by convincing John D Rockefeller and local philanthropists such as the now wealthy Marshall Field of the importance of a university to the life of the city, Harper was able to realise his dream on a parcel of land at 57th Street and Ellis Avenue.

Harper was something of a progressive for his time, and envisioned his university offering an equal education for both men and women students, a university press that stood ready to disseminate its teachings throughout the country, and the use of a quarter system to allow for greater flexibility among the schedules of faculty and staff. And though Harper's premature 1906 death from cancer at the age of 49 came prior to the establishment of a medical school at the campus, it's perhaps partly thanks to his quest for excellence that today's University of Chicago Hospitals, as well as its other schools and divisions, are counted among the very best in their field. The university eventually played a key role in the development of nuclear energy when, in 1942, a team led by Enrico Fermi built the first ever nuclear reactor, an event that led to the Manhattan Project and the first atomic bomb.

SOCIAL EXPERIMENTS

By the early post-Civil War years, George Pullman's sleeping and dining train cars were the standard for the industry. The size of his factories, located in a number of major cities including Detroit and San Francisco, testified to the fact that his innovations had revolutionised rail travel. However, Pullman was searching for a way to reduce the unrest among his workers, and in so doing hit upon the idea of a planned community, an idea that had already been tried in England. His vision for a self-contained industrial city was realised over 3,000 acres (1,215 hectares), which he purchased in Lake Calumet to the south of Chicago.

At Pullman City, designed by Solon S Beman, employees were ensconced within a residential system that was expected to generate a profit just as did the Pullman factory. Despite the decent local amenities – such as a park, a church, a hotel, a theatre, a library, churches, relatively comfortable houses and assorted shops – workers were expected to pay higher rents for their living quarters than those outside the district. They also had to walk to the edge of Pullman City for a drink at a tavern: the whole of the 'town' was dry.

In 1894, disgruntled Pullman employees staged a strike that dragged on as their employer stubbornly refused to compromise. After a number of stalemated weeks, the American Railway Union's president, Eugene V Debs, intervened on behalf of the workers, thereby instigating a boycott of Pullman train cars across the nation. Violence, rioting and several deaths ensued, before President Grover Cleveland threatened to send in federal troops to replace the police militia that had been involved in keeping the peace up until that

A local artist depicts the **Haymarket riots**.

point. Eventually, in July, the strike was broken and the Pullman plant reopened in August with a substantial percentage of new workers.

Even when criticised by members of his own family for his behaviour towards employees, Pullman never conceded to the opposition. When he died three years later in 1897, he was buried at **Graceland Cemetery** under tons of asphalt to stop resentful workers desecrating his body (*see page 80* **Resting in peace**). In 1899, the town of Pullman was annexed to Chicago, and in 1971 the district was designated a national landmark known for well-preserved examples of row housing and the Hotel Florence, a *grande dame* that hosted Ulysses S Grant, Todd Lincoln and other notables.

Not far from Pullman City, on the near-South Side, a different kind of social experiment was brought to fruition. In 1889, Jane Addams founded **Hull House**, America's first settlement centre, at 800 S Halsted Street (*see page 78*). Addams had visited Toynbee Hall in London, and decided to start her own version of the scheme, providing day-care facilities, an employment office and assorted other social services to an embattled and deprived local community made up mostly of immigrants and living in abject squalour. To her credit, Addams extended Hull House's ventures regarding the poor and illiterate into the community at a grass-roots level; eventually, the centre grew to encompass 12 buildings, including a dining hall, a nursery, a gymnasium, a residence hall and an art gallery.

Unafraid of controversy, Addams constantly wrestled with the city's political entities, which she viewed as inadequate in their response to the needs of the neighbourhoods, particularly with respect to sanitation and health. Her allies in this venture included other early feminist activists, such as Dr Alice Hamilton and Julia Lathrop, but Addams was also adept at gaining the assistance of young men and women, some of whom resided at the settlement centre and who contributed their time and energy to its efforts at social reform. During Addams's tenure at Hull House, she enlisted the aid of the existing social power base to achieve her objectives. With co-founder Ellen Gates Starr, Addams – the 1931 recipient of the Nobel Peace Prize for her humanitarian, feminist and internationalist work – contributed one of the most enduring and comprehensive human rights organisations to a city that, at the turn of the century, had a population of over one and a half million.

Held just 22 years after the Chicago Fire of 1871, the World's Columbian Exposition was a prime opportunity for Chicago to showcase its growth and civic pride. This exposition kicked off a renaissance of popular culture in Chicago that extended into the next century, and which expanded the leisure activities of residents and visitors to encompass dance halls, movie palaces, nightclubs, amusement parks and vaudeville shows. All these forms of entertainment became popular and accessible both in the city's downtown and in its neighbourhoods. *See opposite* **Fairs' fare**.

SODOM AND TOMORROW

At the end of the 19th century, the Levee district took corruption and decadence to a new level in the history of Chicago. Located in the First Ward, the inhabitants of the Levee included gamblers, johns, drunks, prostitutes and penny-ante criminals. However, its denizens took second place to the colourful brothels themselves: the Everleigh Club (run by sisters Minna and Ada), Freiberg's dance hall, the Library, the House of All Nations and the Opium Den, among others. It could be argued that these establishments were the norm for an 'open' city like Chicago, yet for such activity to flourish, favours had to be granted and eyes had to look the other way more often than not.

On the legislative front, 'machine' politics and ward 'bosses' were becoming the standard among the various districts. In more prosperous neighbourhoods, fancy balls were held as political party fundraisers, made popular in the First Ward by Chicago aldermen Michael 'Hinky Dink' Kenna and John 'Bathhouse' Coughlin. These two unscrupulous politicians had a knack for entertaining others while lining their own pockets with illicit lucre from businesses grateful for their favours.

Eventually, the moral adversaries of the goings-on in the Levee were prompted to put an end to the lawlessness once and for all. A Vice Commission appointed by the mayor enabled enforcers to shut down brothels based on the lost taxable income to the city. After the renowned Everleigh Club closed its doors, the rest of the Levee's institutions were systematically raided until both patrons and proprietors wearied of the law's interference.

One of the beneficiaries of Kenna's and Coughlin's largesse was Charles Tyson Yerkes. A broker by trade, he left his Philadelphia home under a cloud of controversy after a scandal involving city bonds, but not before investing in railroads and transit interests. In 1882, he settled in Chicago and began to buy favours from the aldermen in a bid to gain control of the city's streetcar lines. Using stockholders' money to pay himself first while investors went without, he systematically expanded his activities into ownership of trolley cars and elevated train car lines.

But finally, the 'traction king', as Yerkes was by then known, stepped too far over the line. In 1895, his political cohorts introduced a bill in the state legislature that would extend Yerkes's transit franchise for another 50 years, with no additional compensation to the city. Even though the bill was passed, it was repealed after two years of massive public protest. Yerkes eventually tired of the fray in Chicago and moved to London, where he played a role in the development of that city's subway system. Some 42 years after his death in 1905, the Chicago Transit Authority was created as a municipal agency to oversee the various mass transportation entities (bus, rail, train) in the city, which it still does to this day.

INSULLATION

Another powerful man who left his impression on Chicago through his business dealings and philanthropy was utilities magnate Samuel Insull. After emigrating from Britain to the United States in 1881 as inventor Thomas Edison's assistant, Insull quickly proved his worth by increasing Edison's domestic business fourfold, and became president of the Chicago Edison Company in 1892. Insull also left his mark on the city's transportation by his role as one of the forces behind the inter-urban railroads that connect Chicago to its suburbs, a train system now known as the Metra.

Through his hard work, ambition and dedication, Insull set a sterling example for other entrepreneurs hoping to strike it rich. In his day-to-day dealings, he treated workers fairly in exchange for their loyalty and respect, but his passion after hours was for the opera. During the 1920s, his patronage of the Chicago Opera Company surpassed even those of staunch supporters like Harold Fowler McCormick and his wife Edith Rockefeller (John D's youngest daughter). Insull proposed to build a brand new opera house for Chicago that would be financially supported by offices also contained within the building (much like Adler and Sullivan's **Auditorium Building**, built between 1886 and 1889; *see pages 25 & 53*). Soon, Insull had the support of other major arts patrons, but he still insisted on taking ownership of the entire project, hiring the respected architectural firm of Graham, Anderson, Probst and White to design the structure.

The **Civic Opera House** building (*see pages 55 & 215*) was completed in 1929, shortly after the stock market crash. The irony, of course, was that Insull's empire began to fall apart even as his magnificent new structure welcomed its first patrons through its doors. After losing all of his companies, he travelled to

Fairs' fare

Chicago has hosted two successful world's fairs, both of which came at extremely opportune moments in the city's history. The first, the World's Columbian Exposition, was held between May and October of 1893, and ostensibly commemorated the 400th anniversary of Christopher Columbus's discovery of the New World in 1692 (albeit a year late). However, it also gave the city a chance to show off just how far it had come since the Chicago Fire of 1871 had razed vast swathes of the city to the ground. As visitors discovered, it had come a very long way indeed.

The main planner for the fair was Daniel Burnham, who enlisted the talents of Frederick Law Olmsted, designer of New York's Central Park. Olmsted envisioned a fair that separated park-like areas, most notably the Midway Plaisance – a court of grandly imposing buildings in the classic style surrounding a statue-filled pool – from the amusement attractions. Present-day Jackson Park, located on the city's South Side – not far from the **Museum of Science and Industry** (*see page 88*), another structure originally created for the fair – and the replica of the Statue of the Republic by Daniel Chester French that stands within it, act as today's reminders of the grand and glorious 'White City' that thrilled over 25 million attendees.

At the World's Columbian Exposition, 46 nations provided 250,000 displays in its various halls, and many notable artists – including Mary Cassatt, Auguste Saint-Gaudens and Louis Sullivan – contributed works. The first ever Ferris wheel, standing 250 feet (76 metres) tall and featuring 36 cars that each could hold up to 60 people, was built for the fair, and remained on the Midway for the next two years until it was moved to St Louis for the Louisiana Purchase Exposition of 1904 (the Ferris wheel now on Navy Pier, opened in 1995, is a replica of this original; *see page 65*). The most

financially successful attraction, though, was the 'Streets in Cairo' section that featured an exotic dancer named Little Egypt.

The second fair, the Century of Progress, was held 40 years after the first, and stayed open for two consecutive summers (1933 and 1934). The exposition, marking the centennial of Chicago's incorporation as a city, was also built adjacent to the lakefront, though further to the north and much nearer to the city's central business district. Another connection to the earlier fair came with the appointment of Daniel Burnham's two sons Hubert and Daniel as architect and secretary respectively to the board of trustees.

Many major corporations, including the Ford Motor Company and *Time* magazine, hosted individual pavilions at their own cost, though most of the funding came from private sources and through memberships sold to the general public. In addition to the art deco architectural theme throughout, popular attractions included a Sky Ride that enabled patrons to visit 600-foot (183-metre) tall observation towers and to ride in cars suspended 200 feet (61 metres) above the ground. Interestingly, another dancer rose to fame during this fair. A burlesque performer from Kansas City, Sally Rand, gained prominence during her popular fan dance shows for which she garnered the princely sum of $75 per week.

The profits from the two-year exposition aided some of the arts organisations involved in preserving the fair's exhibits, including the Museum of Science and Industry (originally built for the earlier Columbian Exposition), the **Adler Planetarium** (*see page 57*) and the South Park Corporation (later taken over by the Chicago Park District). However, the Balbo column (1600 South, just east of Lake Shore Drive), commemorating Italian General Balbo's transatlantic flight to Chicago in 1933, is the only structure that remains from the Century of Progress fair.

Crime & the city

No history of Chicago is complete without tales of its underworld connections, and particularly those that thrived during the early part of the 20th century. Enacted as a law by Congress on 16 January 1920, Prohibition set the stage for bootlegging and rampant political graft. Predictably, organised criminals seized the liquor ban as an irresistible opportunity to add to their coffers. In the Windy City, saloons had traditionally been the territory of established Irish syndicates, but patterns of immigration made the newer wannabes from the Mediterranean countries – most notably, Italy – hungry for a piece of the action. These Italian networks, which became known as 'La Cosa Nostra', quickly rose to prominence as ruthless and dangerous adversaries to the Irish and Jewish criminal families that dominated cities such as New York and Chicago.

Bar none, the city's most infamous criminal was Al 'Scarface' Capone. A native of Brooklyn, Capone came to Chicago in 1920 during Prohibition and made his mark through the consolidation of power from another Italian crim, Diamond Jim Colosimo. Colosimo ran a string of brothels along with a famous restaurant, the Four Deuces at 2222 S Wabash Avenue, to keep up appearances. Capone was not content to stay in Colosimo's shadow for long, and eventually his rivalry with other established Chicago gangs involved in illegal liquor distribution turned bloody.

Along with Johnny Torrio, another crime boss of ill repute, Capone sought the favours of powerful politicos, and even financed the successful Chicago mayoral campaign of William 'Big Bill' Thompson in 1927. The violence among respective factions trying to control the booze rackets continued to escalate, and by 1929, there were debts to settle on a grand score. Capone was taking no chances. On the morning of St Valentine's Day, seven members of the Bugs Moran gang were gunned down in cold blood by four counterfeit cops, later discovered to be Capone's henchmen. Capone had ordered the hit, and while the feds couldn't pin the killings on him, he was convicted of tax evasion two years later and sent to Alcatraz for eight years. After that, Capone fell ill from the effects of syphilis and became an underworld nonentity. He died in 1947.

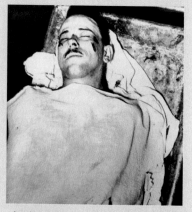

Another crook and killer, John Dillinger, arrived on the Chicago stage in the Depression of the 1930s, living under the alias 'Jimmie Lawrence'. Dillinger had earlier participated in a shootout in a Wisconsin resort town in which one federal agent had died; J Edgar Hoover, then head of the FBI, granted Dillinger the rare honour of being Public Enemy Number One, as much to create a media event as for his own desire for power. A woman named Anna Sage agreed to lead the agents to Dillinger after a promise of a payoff, and the stage was set for the downfall of America's most wanted.

On the evening of 22 July 1934, Dillinger, Sage and another woman reputed to be Dillinger's girlfriend, Polly Hamilton, exited the **Biograph Theatre** (*see page 195*) after a screening of the Clark Gable flick *Manhattan Melodrama*. The Biograph, which still stands near the intersection of Fullerton, Lincoln and Halsted Avenues in Lincoln Park, had been surrounded by agents while Dillinger's last entertainment had played, and as he walked out with the two women, Public Enemy Number One was shot – along with two innocent bystanders – from the rear and fell dead in the alleyway adjacent to the theatre. Morbidity reigned supreme in the aftermath of the shooting: passers-by soaked handkerchiefs in Dillinger's blood, and crowds hoping for a glimpse of the infamous criminal's body – which is pictured above – flocked to the morgue the next day.

Europe for a brief respite, before returning to the States to withstand court proceedings regarding fraud and embezzlement, among other charges. After being acquitted in three separate trials, Insull died of a heart attack in a Paris subway in 1938 with less than a dollar's worth of change in his pocket. With the Civic Opera House, Insull left a fond legacy to the citizens of his adopted city, but one that was all the more bittersweet for his meteoric rise and subsequent downfall.

PAYING THE BILL

On the political front, the father-and-son mayoral legacies of Carter Harrison I and II dating back to the 1870s left large shoes to fill as far as the office itself was concerned. The 24th mayor of Chicago, Harrison senior (a five-term mayor) was the presiding official during the time of the rebuilding after the Chicago Fire of 1871, as well as during the World's Columbian Exposition. The success of the Expo brought Chicago to the forefront of national pride. 'Our Carter', as Harrison was fondly known, was a political fixture through some of Chicago's greatest challenges and triumphs. Later, Harrison junior, the 30th mayor of Chicago and the first to be born in the city, showed himself to be even more reform-minded than his father. Also winning five terms in office, he was known for his fair dealings with immigrant and minority groups, and was successful in closing down the prostitution houses of the Levee district during his tenure at City Hall.

But there were some personalities up to the task of filling the Harrisons' shoes, one of which was William Hale 'Big Bill' Thompson, three-time mayor of Chicago. Thompson was an athlete, a scion of a real estate business family and a powerful friend to less-than-upstanding citizens, including Al Capone. Furthermore, he was a popular if none-too-bright politician, and came to power as the Republican candidate for mayor. Thompson won the mayoral election in 1915 for the first time, but lost his second campaign (for US Representative) a mere three years later.

In 1919, he was re-elected mayor of Chicago, but though he was an enthusiastic recipient of many minority votes, his passivity during the Chicago Race Riots that same year may have hurt his chances for re-election for a further consecutive term. In the summer of 1919, an isolated incident at one of Chicago's beaches set off five days of rioting between whites and blacks, leaving over 35 people dead and hundreds more injured.

Things escalated with the death of black teenager Eugene Williams, who drowned at the segregated 29th Street beach on 27 July 1919

after a reputed confrontation between blacks and whites prevented him from coming ashore. Tragically, his death was the spark that set alight a series of violent racial confrontations and retaliations in the city. When word got out about Eugene's death, the story soon changed, claiming that he had been stoned to death and prompting such fury among blacks that they retaliated wherever they could. After several attempts to quell the violence without additional force, Mayor Thompson consented to ask the governor of Illinois for the assistance of state troops. Eventually, 5,000 men were summoned to keep the peace, marking the event as the worst ever outbreak of racial tensions in Chicago at that time. When coupled with Thompson's pro-German stance during World War I, an ill-timed tactic that may have cost him his popularity with all but Chicago's sizeable German population, the reasons for his fall from grace become obvious.

> ## 'Thompson's administration lost control of the city to criminals, the most infamous of whom was Al Capone.'

After another unsuccessful mayoral campaign against the well-respected William E Dever, Thompson won the city election again in 1927, but during his administration, the city lost control of the town to criminals, the most infamous of whom was Al Capone. There were 62 bombings in the city in 1928 attributed to the Mob, mostly directed against reform leaders. Thompson's building campaigns, including beautification of public works such as streets and bridges, were probably the best thing about his administrations. However, his stubborn refusal to give up politics even after two more defeats in the mayoral campaigns and one way-out attempt to gain the governorship of the state in 1936 by forming a party of his own – the Union Progressives – was typical of the careerist politician and limelight addict he had become.

THE GREAT MIGRATION

In the years leading up to the Race Riots of 1919, the African-American population of the city had increased rapidly. In what became known as the Great Migration, huge numbers of African-American residents of states such as Alabama, Arkansas, Louisiana, Georgia, Mississippi, Tennessee and Texas moved north in the years between the 1890s and World War I. By 1910, New York, Chicago and Philadelphia claimed fully one-quarter of northern black residents.

Various reasons for the movement of so many families and individuals from the South are generally cited: the problems of low crop prices, racial discrimination and hatred (most notably the Ku Klux Klan) in the South, and the temptation of higher wages, better education and the chance for a new beginning without the shadow of slavery in the North. In time, migration clubs, church networks and other agencies were formed to specifically assist those making the transition. The migration also brought other pressing issues, such as abusive working conditions, inadequate housing, discrimination and poverty, to the forefront of the Chicago social agenda.

Indeed, social, political and popular effects of the migration were evident. Ida B Wells, a noted black writer and civil rights advocate, created the Negro Fellowship League in 1908, providing lodgings, assistance in finding employment, and a reading room with periodicals from both northern and southern cities. In politics, Mayor William Thompson successfully cultivated black constituents by having black politicians speak to them on his behalf. And in the near-South Side neighbourhood known as Bronzeville, many black artists, writers and entertainers along with businessmen and entrepreneurs made their presence known, much as in New York's Harlem. Louis Armstrong, Nat 'King' Cole, Scott Joplin and publishing magnate John H Johnson were just a few of Bronzeville's more famous residents.

CRIMES AND MISDEMEANOURS

The city's inhabitants were riveted in 1924 by a celebrated crime case involving two privileged Jewish students who attended the University of Chicago. Richard Loeb, 17, and Nathan Leopold, 18, were convicted of the senseless murder of a 14-year-old boy named Bobby Franks, traced by a typed note that demanded that $10,000 be dropped off at the victim's parents's home, and a pair of eyeglasses found near Franks's body. Leopold and Loeb were admitted homosexual lovers, which added a lurid aspect to a case that titillated the public and presaged the media circuses of the Lindbergh baby kidnapping, the Manson murders and the trial of OJ Simpson.

The criminals' illustrious defender in the courts, Clarence Darrow, was able to obtain a sentence of life imprisonment instead of execution. A writer named Meyer Levin later turned the case into a story called *Compulsion*, for which Loeb unsuccessfully attempted to sue Levin for invasion of privacy; Alfred Hitchcock's *Rope* was also based around the tale. Loeb later died in a prison attack in 1936, while Leopold moved to Puerto Rico in 1958 upon achieving parole, where he lived until his death in 1971.

PROHIBITION AND DEPRESSION

On 16 January 1920, the Prohibition Era in the United States began when Congress ratified the 18th Amendment banning the manufacture and sale of alcohol. Many factors had led to the

Lovers **Leopold and Loeb** shocked the city with their murder of a 14-year-old boy in 1924.

Chief Yippie **Abbie Hoffman**. *See page 18*.

and his fellow agents conducted their attempts to gather evidence that would imprison gangsters with booze-running rings, such as Capone, Dion O'Banion and others.

In the later 1920s and early 1930s, or so some historians have theorised, the Depression itself acted as a force for the repeal of the 18th Amendment. This was because of the changes it produced in American society, and the accompanying political and economic shifts that it brought about in the social structure. When, in 1933, almost three-quarters of convention delegates voted to pass the 21st Amendment repealing Prohibition, it was clear that the individual states would again gain control of the regulation and taxation of alcohol, and that the public sale of 'demon rum' would again be legal across the nation.

During the Depression, more changes in the city's immigrant population base, and subsequently in Chicago politics, occurred. Anton 'Tony' Cermak, a Czech coal miner's son and street vendor, became mayor in 1931, defeating Thompson by the largest margin ever in the history of city elections. Cermak tried to balance the city budget by reducing the swelled payrolls left by his predecessor and applying for federal relief, but due to the poor economy, the existing fiscal problems were immense. Worse was to follow when, in 1933, Cermak was struck by an assassin's bullet intended for President Franklin D Roosevelt. At the time of the shooting, Cermak was visiting Roosevelt in Miami to parlay with the president about federal assistance to Chicago under the 'New Deal'. Though Cermak lingered for over two weeks, the gunshot wound proved to be fatal, and the Italian immigrant assassin, Guiseppe Zangara, was later executed.

After World War II, Chicago benefited from a huge economic boom. Still growing, its population topped 3.6 million in 1950, and affluence was everywhere, as people began to move from the city to the newly created suburbs. Five years later, the city was to reach a turning point in its history with the election of one of the most famous American city mayors of the century.

passing of the amendment, but Chicago's involvement in the days prior to the amendment came chiefly through Frances Willard, an Evanston resident. In 1874, Willard founded and presided over the Women's Christian Temperance Union, whose membership (which eventually peaked at 175,000) advocated the complete prohibition of liquor as a means to protect the American family against the harmful effects of alcohol abuse. The temperance movement gained momentum in the post-World War I years, culminating in its followers obtaining signed pledge cards from untold numbers of people. The pledge of temperance was a factor in the political climate that fuelled the need for alcohol restrictions, first at the community and state levels, then at the federal level.

It can be argued that the well-intentioned ideals of the 18th Amendment caused unbearable hypocrisy within American society, corruption at all levels of government, and an astounding death toll linked to the alarming crime rate. Certainly, Chicago played a large part, with Al Capone's crime empire leading the bootleggers and ensuring that the local police force looked the other way thanks to some attractive payoffs. Capone's nemesis, US marshal and special Prohibition task force agent Eliot Ness, and his band of cohorts were later termed 'the Untouchables' for their resistance to bribery attempts on behalf of the Mob. From a tiny office on Wabash Street, Ness

OUR DALEY BREAD
In 1955, **Richard J Daley** won his first of six consecutive terms as mayor (*see page 19* **My kind of town**). Skilled in the machine politics tradition through his chairmanship of the Cook County Democratic party since 1953, Daley was an Irish-Catholic Democrat who gained the favour of minority and working class voters by his straight talk and get-the-job-done attitude. His mettle, though, would be severely tested by the city's challenges during the next two

decades: a corrupt police force, spiralling crime and racial tension, the latter epitomised by the civil unrest that was triggered by the assassination of activist and civil rights leader Dr Martin Luther King, Jr.

King had come to Chicago several times during the mid-1960s, and with each visit he had pointed up more of the problems faced by the urban minority community. Inadequate housing, job discrimination, school overcrowding, poverty and illiteracy were just a few of the issues with which King hoped to deal. However, he was met with scorn by less evolved whites, even after several meetings with Daley in a bid to set up a Citizens Advisory Committee to address racial tensions.

When King announced his intention to take up residence in a slum building in the Lawndale neighbourhood, the owners of the structure promptly took him to court. Various rallies and marches led by King in predominantly white neighbourhoods led to police intervention to quell any potential violence. This set the stage for the widespread burning and looting of white-owned businesses that occurred predominantly in black neighbourhoods on the West Side immediately following King's death in April 1968. To mitigate the chaos, Daley called in the National Guard, but it was only the beginning of a turbulent year, which culminated in a national PR disaster for Daley and his administration.

RIOT POLICE

The Democratic National Convention of 1968, held in Chicago, was to be another test for Daley and his reputation for toughness in the face of forces beyond his control. Anti-war protesters had come to the city in their hundreds – not, though, in their thousands, as the organisers had originally hoped – to celebrate the 'Festival of Life' sponsored by the self-described Yippies, and threatened to create mayhem for the political delegates attending the convention. However, it wasn't the demonstrators who proved to be violent: rather, it was Daley's men in blue, the Chicago Police, who caused much of the trouble. During the convention, national television broadcast the melées between the 'pigs' and the 'flower children', at the expense of the city's reputation. Daley stuck with his increasingly indefensible hard line, and was not swayed when distinguished members of the press disagreed with his minions' treatment of the protestors.

Subsequently, the scapegoating of several protestors from the previous summer's demonstrations became a famous 1969 federal court case later termed the 'Chicago Eight' trial. Indicted for conspiring to cause riots, the recalcitrant defendants – including Abbie Hoffman, Tom Haydn and Bobby Seale – found themselves at the centre of the controversy, and made the most of it by hiring brash New Yorker William M Kunstler as their attorney. A parade of well-known witnesses, frequent outbursts against the court and the colourful personalities of those on trial made for lively coverage in the press. Moreover, certain aspects of the case reflected concerns about the Vietnam War felt by many across the nation. A seasoned though embattled judge, Julius J Hoffman, presided over the 100-day trial and its 175 counts of contempt, which ended with the defendants being acquitted on the charge of inciting riots; in 1972, it was established that the FBI, with the complicity of Judge Hoffman, had bugged the offices of the defendants' attorneys.

Another confrontation between police and radicals occurred late in 1969, when the Weathermen's 'Days of Rage' were fashioned after ambushes by the Black Panther party. The Weathermen, later termed the 'Weather Underground', were an offshoot radical subgroup of the Students for a Democratic Society (SDS) who advocated armed overthrow of US governmental entities to atone for the country's exploitation of foreign nations and its military action in Vietnam. In October 1969, the Weathermen's members vandalised property and openly attacked uniformed police officers in areas of the Loop and the Gold Coast. These skirmishes between civilians and uniformed cops occurred mostly on the North Side and in the Civic Center.

By the time the violence had ceased, dozens of police and demonstrators had been injured in the battles. Unfortunately, the constructive gains of these bloody protests were few, and it may have been symbolic that the leader of the Chicago chapter of the Black Panther party, Fred Hampton, died in a police raid that very December. Racial problems in the city continued well into the following decade and, for better or worse, in Chicago and other cities many white residents chose to leave for the suburbs in a phenomenon termed 'white flight'.

THE CULTURE CLUB

The arts, and especially theatre, took off in Chicago after the turbulent 1960s. Along Lincoln Avenue and in other North Side locations, the now legendary Organic, Wisdom Bridge, Victory Gardens and St Nicholas theatres, in addition to the more established **Goodman** (*see page 236*) and **Second City** (*see page 244*), produced such important contributors to the medium as playwright David Mamet, actors William Petersen, Joe

My kind of town The Daleys

Richard J Daley and Richard M Daley. Boss and bureaucrat. Machine politics and public relations. The unique imprimatur of an Irish-Catholic father-son mayoral combination separated by a 13-year run of other mayors during the late '70s and '80s is the stuff of urban legend in Chicago. Together, the pair have surpassed the notoriety of a previous father-son combination who were elected mayors of Chicago in 1878 and 1908 respectively, and who also shared the same name (Carter Harrison): indeed, the legacy of the Daleys towers over the Chicago political world, dominating any analysis of the town's history and future.

An only child born in the city's southwest Bridgeport neighbourhood, Richard J Daley (pictured) spent most of his life in public service. He joined the Cook County Clerk's office early on, and there learned how collegial networks of influence – most often ruled by race or religion rather than socio-economic status – functioned with respect to governmental entities. In the meantime, he set about producing a large family of his own (eventually numbering five children) with his wife Eleanor ('Sis'), a tireless helpmate on the campaign trail and, later, a loyal and dedicated first lady of Chicago.

As all Chicagoans know, Daley senior was an influential, opinionated, life-long politico who reigned for over two decades (1955 until 1976) in City Hall. His influence, particularly with the infamous Chicago Democratic machine, was instrumental in the outcome of wider elections, particularly that of John F

Kennedy's successful presidential campaign of 1960. A consummate dealmaker, Richard J shared his views and emotions with sometimes laudatory, occasionally disastrous results: his admonition to 'shoot to kill' those curfew-breakers who carried arson materials during the riots that followed the assassination of Martin Luther King, Jr, for example, was long remembered by the public as reactionary and inhumane. Nearly as legendary are Daley's malaprops: 'Chicago is reaching for higher and higher platitudes' is not an atypical example, though it pales next to his declaration that, 'The police are not there to create disorder, they are there to preserve disorder.'

Richard M Daley, Chicago mayor since 1989, is a somewhat more subdued leader than his late father. The third son of the elder Daley, Richie's two brothers William and John have also had illustrious careers in public service. Roots aside, though, Daley junior is just as much a dyed-in-the-wool outspoken civic booster as his father. His management style is involved yet centrist, and he has been hugely successful in his attempts to bring Chicago to the forefront as an international city during the past decade. This has been accomplished mostly through grand building campaigns, though two notable failures were his bid to build a third airport on the South East Side in Lake Calumet, and a plan to construct a $2-million casino on the lakefront near the central business district.

The younger Daley has transformed the city in many other ways, mostly for the better. City-wide community policing programmes, the beautification of streets and mass transit terminals through greenery and renovation, the reduction of business taxes to encourage new building development on behalf of private companies, and infrastructure repairs to major thoroughfares and bridges are all testament to his foresight, while the elevation of women and minorities to positions of influence within his administration is also to be applauded.

Richard M Daley can't go on for ever, though it occasionally feels like he might. But when he does decide to call it a day, don't expect to have heard the last from the family: children Nora (born 1973), Patrick (b 1975) and Elizabeth (b 1983) will doubtless be waiting in the wings...

Mantegna and Dennis Franz, and director Robert Falls. Later, the **Steppenwolf Theatre** (*see page 237*) added to the Chicago-based star roster with the likes of John Malkovich, Joan Allen, Gary Sinise and Frank Galati.

Meanwhile, to avoid the high costs of New York, film directors and producers were also starting to view Chicago as a place to make movies while at the same time cutting expenses by utilising the local union and non-union talent base. Robert Altman was one of the more influential directors in the 1970s to film a major studio effort here with *A Wedding*, parts of which were made in Oak Park and along the North Shore. In 1980, *The Blues Brothers* came with a distinct hometown flavour, as did another memorable effort from the same year, *Ordinary People*, based on the Judith Guest novel and featuring a young Timothy Hutton. Tom Cruise did a dance in his skivvies and rode the El with Rebecca DeMornay in 1982's unforgettable *Risky Business*, while John Hughes got in on the act with *The Breakfast Club*, *Pretty in Pink*, *Ferris Bueller's Day Off* and the record-breaking blockbuster *Home Alone*. All of this film industry activity was eventually co-ordinated by the Chicago Film Office, a division of the Mayor's Office of Special Events. Currently, the agency does its part to bring in millions of dollars' worth of work yearly for local film and television crews and actors.

DALEY PART II

City politics were far from dormant after Richard J Daley's death in 1976. Three years later, a woman heavily connected to the Democratic organisation made a successful bid in the mayoral race. Jane Byrne, a protégé of Daley's, ran against incumbent mayor Michael Bilandic in 1979 and won by 17,000 votes. Her effort was helped by Chicago's largest ever snowfall that season – 82 inches in all – with which Bilandic was ill equipped to deal. Byrne proved to be up to the task of surface gestures, such as festivals and parades for the constituency, but her tactics behind closed doors were often strident and inconsistent.

The next mayoral primary saw Byrne, Richard M Daley (son of Richard J) and a black candidate named Harold Washington in a three-way heat for the Democratic nomination. After winning the 1983 primary, Washington went on to become Chicago's first black mayor, and over the next four years battled long and hard with the city council. Washington's death of a heart attack in 1987 while still in office marked another political milestone for Chicago in that his replacement, former alderman Eugene Sawyer, was also black. Sawyer ran for

Mayor Harold Washington, who died in office.

mayor in 1989, but was defeated by Richard M Daley in the first of his three (so far) consecutive terms.

Chicago's status as an industrial city may be long gone, but it's regaining the prosperity that illuminated its early history. The transformation of the Loop in the 1970s into a financial capital helped, as has the burgeoning convention industry responsible for thousands of jobs in the service industry. The recent era has seen city beautification, notable public works, huge private investment in new commercial buildings and residential space, and the emergence of Chicago as a truly world-class city.

But without a doubt, the mainstay of Chicago's prosperity and growth throughout the last several hundred years has been its 'I Will' spirit. By balancing its natural, cultural and civic resources and celebrating its diversity, Chicago's residents take pride in the motto 'Urbs in Horto' ('city in a garden'). And just like real gardens, sometimes seeming disasters only serve to make the plants grow stronger.

▶ For more on **architecture**, see page 24.
▶ For more on **movies filmed in Chicago**, see page 36.

Chicago Today

If you ever want to scare a Chicago politician, tell him you came to see Al Capone 'stuff'.

Chicago in the roaring '20s and Depression '30s, and the faces of those who graced and disgraced the city – Al Capone, John Dillinger, Baby Face Nelson – is an image that has stuck with the Windy City for 70 years. It's also the image every mayor has tried to erase from the minds of tourists. Gangsterland Chicago is a compelling mix of fact and myth: Eliot Ness chasing Capone down the street in a Hudson Super-Six, tommy-guns blazing. Unfortunately for city officials who've fruitlessly tried to banish that very image, one of the coolest things about Chicago is the opportunity to visit the spots where the gunplay really happened.

Luckily for the locals, present-day Chicago isn't quite as scary as the town of Capone's era. The city is currently in a perpetual state of redevelopment, continuing a trend started several decades ago. As well as developments on the near-North Side, downtown Chicago is expanding to the west, north and south, usurping land reserved for industrial corridors, housing projects and skid rows.

But perhaps Chicago's most interesting modern drama is one that's been running even longer: the ongoing political soap opera. The city that gained worldwide notoriety for its political corruption in days of yore is presently the domain of Richard J Daley. The son of Richard M, who reigned from 1955 until his death in 1976 (it was about the only way he was going to relinquish office), Daley *fils* presides over Chicago with an iron – if occasionally clumsy – fist, and operates a less corrupt version of machine politics in an attempt to keep the aldermen from fragmenting. Harold Washington's legacy may have faded, but its spirit lives on in the person of Daley.

CRIME AND PUNISHMENT

He may be the city's most recognisable celebrity, but Al Capone didn't do the city any favours by establishing the country's largest organised crime ring. John Dillinger didn't help much either. And though both men died before World War II, the image of Chicago as a crime-ridden

urban landscape has been difficult to shake off. Unfortunately, the rest of the century has hardly changed the perceptions of the public at large.

In 1966, Richard Speck killed eight nurses in a drunken rampage, an incident called the 'crime of the century' at the time by Cook County Coroner Andrew Toman. Condemned to die in the electric chair, the state's voiding of the death penalty in 1971 resulted in his sentence being commuted to life imprisonment. Speck remained out of sight and out of mind until after his death in 1991, when TV reporter Bill Kurtis got hold of videotapes that showed him (Speck, not Kurtis) involved in drug and sex orgies in jail. Needless to say, state officials were not pleased, especially when the tapes were aired on a national news show.

Just a few years later, another grim Chicago tale hit the headlines. Between 1975 and '78, John Wayne Gacy murdered 33 young boys, burying them under the floorboards and lawn of his Norwood Park house. In 1994, Gacy was put to death at the Stateville Correctional Center, though the damage to the city's image had already been wreaked. Even more harm had been done back in 1968, though, as hordes of protesters at the Democratic National Convention were beaten, gassed, maced and brutalised by Chicago police. The abomination was seen on national TV, and embarrasses the city – especially Mayor Daley, whose father was mayor at the time – even today.

Serial killer **John Wayne Gacy**.

'Richard J Daley presides over Chicago with an iron – if occasionally clumsy – fist.'

Chicago has been largely spared from nastiness on a national-headline-making scale over the past 20 years. As is the case across the United States, most crime has decreased since 1990: according to the Chicago Police, crime in the city has decreased by an average of 1.2 per cent every year since 1990 (murder, however, fluctuates, mostly as a result of gang-related incidents). Several incidents in the late 1990s, though, caught the national spotlight, and show that all is not sunshine and roses yet. And like the rest of the country, Chicago has a sizeable gang presence: while the Mafia has all but disappeared, violence remains in the form of drive-by shootings, carried out in the name of protecting neighbourhood dominance.

Mayor Daley has taken radical steps to reduce crime, enacting anti-loitering laws (since declared unconstitutional), lobbying for harsher penalties for possession of illegal firearms, fully supporting federal penalties for hate crimes and keeping a watchful eye on the city's police. He

was the impetus behind the Safe Neighborhoods Act of 1994, which made possession of an illegal firearm a felony rather than just a misdemeanour, though in early 2000, Illinois State lawmakers were attempting to repeal the act, opening the doors for as many as 2,000 inmates to be released. Daley has encountered opposition from downstate lawmakers under the sway of National Rifle Association (NRA) lobbyists, but he stands firm in his commitment to erasing Chicago's image as Capone's city.

WHAT'S OLD IS NEW

Beginning in the late 1980s, Chicago – and, specifically, downtown Chicago – has undergone a renaissance of expansion and redevelopment. The beautification of the city has not been without its detractors, however, as the expansion has often come at the expense of the city's poor.

Several near-downtown landmarks reveal the city's dedication to increasing tourism. The area that contains the **Field Museum**, the **Adler Planetarium** (itself tagged for $40 million worth of improvements) and the **Shedd Aquarium** was recently blessed with a multi-million dollar renovation, and has since been dubbed **Museum Campus** (*see page 57*). More prominently, the expansive, 2.2 million-square foot (204,600 square metres) concrete giant just south of Museum Campus has morphed into **McCormick Place**, North America's largest convention centre and host to more than four million visiting professionals each year.

And when the millions of conventioneers are done work for the day, many choose to head for **Navy Pier** (*see page 65*). For years, it was appreciated only by walkers, joggers and strolling romantics, who loved the breeze and lakeside vistas, before benefiting from a nine-figure refurb in the early 1990s. It's now a spick-and-span tourist hotspot replete with a skyline-dominating Ferris wheel, boutiquey-type shops, a skating rink, museums, a theatre and a load of boat docks. The pier and McCormick Place bring in over $5 billion each year to the state in revenues. And then there's the $110-million **Symphony Center**, the poshing-up of **Grant Park**… will it ever end?

It's not all good news, however. Problems lie to the west, where the presence of Cabrini-Green, once one of the city's largest and most dangerous housing projects, has prevented the city from usurping the prime real estate that sits under Chicago's magnificent skyline. The residents of Cabrini-Green are fighting the city's voucher programme (Section 8) that scatters residents of public housing and moves them into mixed-income, private accommodation. The battle has raged since the beginning of the 1990s, but though the residents have fought hard, the Chicago machine is slowly moving them out; in early 2000, Cabrini-Green was only 20 per cent occupied.

The future of Chicago development lies in the hands of city lawmakers and the state legislature. In addition to the Cabrini-Green controversy, Meigs Field, a small airport that mostly serves businessmen and lawmakers, was also the centre of a heated conflict. Mayor Daley wanted the airstrip, located on a small isthmus on the lake, turned into a park, but then-Governor Jim Edgar rallied support for Meigs and forced the airstrip to remain open. The expiry of the state's lease in 2002 will no doubt intensify the debate as to how the land should be used. Trouble is also brewing over the building of a new Chicago Bears stadium to replace Soldier Field after the McCaskey family, who control the team, threatened to move it to the suburbs – or, worse, Indiana – unless the city kick in the cash towards either renovation or funding for a new stadium. And why not? After all, it's how the White Sox got their new ballpark.

POLITICS AS USUAL
Some little-known trivia: Chicago's nickname, the Windy City, was coined not because of the blasting gales that come off Lake Michigan, but rather because of its politics, and specifically the blustering wind that emanates from local politicians. Bear that in mind as you're walking down Lake Shore Drive trying hard not to get blown down a neighbouring street.

As the major population centre of Illinois, Chicago and its mayor exert a large degree of influence on the state's political landscape.

Though this dominance means the city benefits from hefty allowances of federal and state dollars, it also draws resentment among state lawmakers from outside the city. State politics aside, Chicago's political scene is tinged with scandal and is often under the watchful eye of federal investigators. Through it all, Mayor Daley has remained devoid of controversy, though at times it has come perilously close to his office.

> **'Politicians are constantly besieged by scandal, from ghost-payrolling family members to strong-arming campaign donations.'**

The 1990s were dominated by Operation Silver Shovel, a federally sponsored investigation into widespread corruption among a veritable jigsaw puzzle of aldermen and other city officials. Repercussions from Operation Silver Shovel still resonate almost a decade into the investigation. And then there was the 'scofflaw' incident, during which it was revealed that over a million dollars in parking tickets picked up by city employees remained unpaid. Though the city machine made extensive efforts to make the scofflaws pay up, locals collectively groaned at yet another example of city employees abusing the system.

More recently, City Treasurer Miriam Santos was convicted of harassing would-be campaign donors for money. Santos was re-elected despite the allegations, but she was convicted and sentenced to three years in a federal prison shortly afterwards (her sentence was subsequently overturned). The city's politicians are constantly besieged by some scandal or another, from ghost-payrolling their family members for no services provided to city officials strong-arming campaign donations. In fact, it has become very difficult to surprise Chicagoans, no matter how much of their money the dodgy politicos have taken.

But despite its image as a corrupt city full of tommy-gun toting gangsters and crime-infested housing projects, Chicago is forging into the new millennium on an encouraging note. Violent crime is down, economic and geographic expansion is bringing in valuable tourist dollars, and the ethnic diversity and nightlife have never been better. Granted, Chicago is by no means perfect, but it is attacking its problems head-on and working towards a better standard of life for what is fast becoming, once again, a truly great city.

Architecture

Though not everyone gets it, no visitor can dare miss it:
Chicago's skyscape is the most stunning in the US.

Other metropolises lay claim to having more buildings per square mile, perhaps rightly. Of late, others have boasted that they have the tallest skyscrapers. Chicago, though, can claim the most dynamic, architecturally significant collection of edifices in the world. Here, it's quality, not quantity, though the latter was obviously not far from some architects' minds.

Though boat tours offer a fine perspective on the city's architecture, Chicago's dramatic skyline is, perhaps, best viewed from the window of a plane circling overhead, where one can clearly observe the point at which the still blue waters of Lake Michigan suddenly give way to glittering spikes of steel jabbing skyward. You could say that the skyline is a metaphor for the city itself: a jarring spectacle of industry and ingenuity rising from middle America. Oh, and not a little stunning, too.

BRIGHT SPARKS
The story of Chicago's ascent from ramshackle Midwestern berg to world-class architectural showcase began in 1871, with what undoubtedly seemed like the end for those who lived in the city at the time. On the night of

8 October, a fire broke out in the barn behind the home of Patrick and Catherine O'Leary on the city's Near West Side and raced north and east. When the conflagration finally burned itself out two days later, much of the city was reduced to smouldering ruins.

While many theories exist about what caused the fire – from Mrs O'Leary's much-maligned cow (see page 9 **You stupid cow**) to a fiery meteorite – most will agree that poor urban planning was ultimately to blame. At the time, the city was a veritable tinderbox: two-thirds of the city's 60,000 buildings were made of wood, while of the city's 60-odd miles of paved streets, most were covered with wooden planks. Add to that the city's crowded conditions and lack of fire codes, and, with hindsight, disaster was all but inevitable. The fire, though, was the spur for the city to rebuild itself with dramatic immediacy and effect.

THE CHICAGO SCHOOL
Refusing to be beaten by the tragedy, the city fathers were determined to rebuild their city to greater glory. Once the rubble was cleared away, scores of architects converged on the city,

drawn by the idea of a clean slate, a city without an established, confining architectural heritage.

Among them was Louis Sullivan. Born and educated in Boston, Sullivan arrived in Chicago in 1873 and went to work for Dankmar Adler, a German émigré with an established architectural firm. Despite – or, more likely, because of – their differences in personality, the two worked well together, Sullivan's erratic moods and artistic hauteur tempered by Adler's sober professionalism. Sullivan, along with a handful of noteworthy contemporaries including William LeBaron Jenney and Daniel H Burnham, would help define what eventually came to be known as the Chicago School style of architecture.

The Chicago School's biggest innovation was the use of an interior steel structure to distribute and carry the weight of a building. Previously, constructing taller buildings meant thickening the load-bearing exterior masonry walls to support the weight of upper floors. The result was frequently a squat, fortress-like structure, such as the **Auditorium Building** (50 E Congress Parkway, at S Wabash Avenue): designed by Adler and Sullivan and completed in 1889, it combined a 4,200-seat auditorium with office space and a hotel. Owned by Roosevelt University since 1946, the Auditorium Theatre remains one of the city's premier theatre and music venues. Catch a Broadway-style show to get a view of the spectacular interior, with its dramatic arches, gilded plater reliefs and rows of sparkling electric lights.

The **Fine Arts Building** (410 S Michigan Avenue, at E Van Buren Street), constructed by Solon Spencer Beman in 1885 as a showroom and factory for Studebaker carriages, is another classic example of load-bearing masonry construction, as is the **Monadnock Building** at 53 W Jackson Street, at N Dearborn Street. Designed by Burnham and John Welborn Root in 1891, the hulking Monadnock was the last skyscraper to be built from solid masonry construction. Most experts agree that the first official 'skyscraper' to use a steel skeletal frame was the Home Insurance Building, constructed seven years earlier by Jenney at LaSalle and Adams streets. Don't bother looking for it, though: this influential structure was demolished in 1931.

> **'You could say the skyline is a metaphor for the city itself: a jarring spectacle of industry and ingenuity.'**

Chicago School buildings are tall and rectangular with flat roofs, and often made up of three distinct elements: base, rise and capital. Their grid-like steel structure is often recognisable on the structure's outer surfaces. With the steel frame taking care of the heavy lifting, exterior walls are opened up for windows and other non-load bearing materials,

Adler and Sullivan's revolutionary **Auditorium Building**, completed in 1889.

Size doesn't matter.
Okay, just kidding…

For more than two decades, Chicago was the home of the tallest building in the world. It seemed only fitting, since this is the city that invented the art form. But sadly, as Asia came to dominate the world economy in the late 20th century, it was only a matter of time before the Far East would make a run at that quintessential American icon, the skyscraper. And ever since their city was emasculated by the 1,483-foot (452-metre) Petronas Towers, built in Malaysia in 1996, Chicagoans have suffered from an acute case of – our apologies to Dr Freud – Skyscraper Envy.

Many, in fact, are in denial, and argue that the Sears Tower is technically still the tallest structure in the world. According to rules set by an international panel of 'experts', the broadcast towers that top most tall buildings are not considered part of the structure, and as such are not included in a building's height: this is why the Sears' broadcast masts are not counted in its measurement. However, the Petronas's ornamental spires were designated as part of its superstructure, and, as such, are fair game. Regardless of what the experts say, though, Chicagoans find some consolation in the fact that, antennae aside, the Sears Tower still has the highest occupiable floor. So there.

To end all debate on the matter, Chicago has set its sights on officially reclaiming its World's Tallest designation. In 1999, the city approved plans for the construction of a 112-storey skyscraper at **7 S Dearborn Street** (pictured). Though still at the planning stage, the building would soar to a height of 1,537 feet (468 metres). Add on the antennae, and it will reach a total height of 2,000 feet (610 metres), the maximum height allowed by Federal Airline Administration regulations.

The multipurpose building will comprise office and retail space, 350 residential units and parking facilities. Designed by Adrian Smith of Skidmore, Owings & Merrill LLP – the folks who brought you cloudbursting phalluses the Sears Tower and the John Hancock – the building's floors will diminish in size toward the top of the structure, cantilevered out from a visible cement core. Faced with stainless steel and reflective green-tinted glass, the plans resemble nothing if not a futuristic Christmas tree.

While 7 S Dearborn would save Chicago's rep in architectural circles, the supposed motivation behind the construction is the need for additional platforms from which to broadcast digital TV signals. The higher the antennae, the better the signal, and with the transmission spaces at both the Sears and the Hancock spoken for, something needs to be done to keep up with the digital revolution. It's no surprise, then, that one of 7 S Dearborn's biggest backers is a consortium of local TV stations, the Chicago Digital Broadcasters Committee. If 7 S Dearborn ever makes it from blueprint to sidewalk, it will be the first mixed-use building constructed specifically as a platform for digital broadcasting. It will also boast the highest residential units in the world.

But who are they kidding? This is all about size. Indeed, the developers had better get busy: Chicago's return to the top could be short-lived, for developers in Australia, China and India all have announced plans for their own contenders in the World's Tallest international pissing contest. The race is on, but for now, ours is bigger than yours. Ner-ner-ner-ner-ner.

The **Monadnock Building**, the last masonry-constructed skyscraper. *See page 25.*

most often light-coloured terracotta. Buildings constructed in the Chicago School style avoid unnecessary ornamentation in favour of utilitarian simplicity: it was, after all, Chicago School heavy-hitter Sullivan who declared that 'form follows function'.

The **Reliance Building**, at the intersection of State Street and Congress Parkway, is a classic example of Chicago School innovations. Built in 1894 by Burnham along with Root and Charles Atwood, the soaring Reliance makes use of a Chicago School mainstay, the oriel window: a protruding bay window that runs the length of the building, underscoring its soaring verticality. With its abundance of large plate glass windows, the Reliance presaged the future of the modern-day skyscraper. Also typical of the style is Sullivan's **Carson Pirie Scott Building** (1 S State Street, at Madison Street), which makes use of another common design element, the Chicago Window, one large pane of glass flanked by two smaller opening windows.

But when the World's Columbian Exposition (aka the World's Fair) came to Chicago in 1893 (*see page 13* **Fairs' fare**), Burnham was tapped to oversee the construction of the buildings in which the exhibits were to be housed. However, the popularity of his gleaming white Beaux Arts classical constructions changed the course of architecture in the early 20th century, effectively – and ironically – outmoding the reigning Chicago School in the process.

Carson Pirie Scott, at State and Madison.

The stunning **Lake Shore Drive Apartments**.

Burnham's 'White City' was levelled when the Columbian Exposition ended, and the area was eventually paved over to create Meigs Field, a small lakefront airstrip. Burnham is now best remembered for a contribution that lasted a little longer: the 1909 Chicago Plan, which mapped out the city's development. In addition to traffic-relieving bi-level thoroughfares around the downtown area (such as Wacker Drive, which hugs the south bank of the Chicago River), Burnham's plan minimised lakefront development, a shrewd move that resulted in the expansive lakefront parks that stretch from the South Side to the northern suburbs.

'I don't want to be interesting. I want to be good.' Mies van der Rohe

THE INTERNATIONAL STYLE

By the 1920s, Chicago School was old hat, and American architects began looking to Europe for inspiration. It eventually arrived in 1938 in the shape of Ludwig Mies van der Rohe, one of the leading proponents of the International Style that would eventually be further popularised by Frank Lloyd Wright (*see pages 30-31* **The Wright stuff**).

This new style of architecture was founded in Germany but borrowed heavily from the strident simplicity of the Chicago School, ultimately carrying it to new extremes. Buildings in the International Style feature cubic shapes, long horizontal bands of glass called 'ribbon windows', low, flat roofs, and open floorplans divided by movable screen walls. Often coloured white, these buildings, usually constructed from glass, steel and concrete, are devoid of ornamentation and regional characteristics. The emphasis is on the horizontal plane, even – perhaps perversely – in skyscrapers.

After serving as director of the Bauhaus from 1930 to 1933, Mies van der Rohe came to America, where he became a professor of architecture at the Armour Institute (later renamed the Illinois Institute of Technology) in 1938. Only a year later, he redesigned the campus, creating a handful of simple yet striking buildings that demonstrated his affection for steel-framed glass and cubic abstraction, not to mention a willingness to make his buildings adaptable to suit the changing needs of the occupants. While they may lack frills, Mies van der Rohe's buildings are of unquestionable versatility and functionality. 'I don't want to be interesting,' the master architect, who soon became the champion of this new aesthetic in Chicago, once commented. 'I want to be good.'

Chicago offers several other opportunities to admire Mies van der Rohe at the peak of his powers. Upon their completion in 1951, the stunning **Lake Shore Drive Apartments** (860-880 N Lake Shore Drive, at E Chestnut Street) were light years ahead of their time. A classic example of the International Style, the state-of-the-art 26-storey twin towers were an instant commercial and critical success. The **Federal Center**, meanwhile, is the unofficial name of a grouping of buildings constructed between 1964 and 1975 at 200 S Dearborn Street (at W Adams Street). You'll immediately recognise Mies van der Rohe's signature curtain wall of glass, supported by steel black I-beams that support individual panes, emphasising the building's internal skeletal structure. The plaza at the centre of the complex is home to Alexander Calder's famous *Flamingo* sculpture from 1974. The abstract red bird provides a colourful contrast to the solid black walls of the surrounding buildings. The grey granite used to pave the plaza continues uninterrupted into the lobby, creating a feeling of openness and flow.

The 52-storey **IBM Building** (300 N Wabash Avenue, at E Wacker Drive) was begun in 1969 and completed after Mies van der Rohe's death in 1969 by one of the architect's associates. The architect, who told students that 'God is in the detail', lavished careful attention on every aspect of his creations, even going so far as to design the furniture for them. The building's voluminous glass-walled lobby – a Mies van der Rohe staple – is decorated with his chrome and leather Barcelona chairs, designed for an exposition in 1929.

OTHER LOCAL FAVOURITES

While the Chicago School and International Style defined Chicago's architecture in the early years – and continue to influence the work of modern architects – these styles are only a small part of the city's architectural legacy. Many other buildings in a variety of styles are certainly worth checking out.

One of the city's most unusual buildings is the **Tribune Tower** (435 N Michigan Avenue, at E Hubbard Street). The design for the headquarters for the city's largest newspaper, the *Chicago Tribune*, was chosen after a contest held in 1922. The winning entry was the New York duo of Howell and Hood's limestone-clad 456-foot (139-metre) Gothic tower, complete with flying buttresses at its ornate crown, that still stands in all its glory today. Embedded in the walls around the entrance to the Tower are artefacts from significant structures around the world, from the Great Pyramids at Cheops to Notre-Dame Cathedral.

Just across the Magnificent Mile is the **Wrigley Building** (400 N Michigan Avenue, at E Kinzie Street), a massive wall of a building

The bouncer at the **Tribune Tower**.

The gum-coloured **Wrigley Building** dominates the view over the Michigan Avenue bridge.

Looking down from the **Sears Tower**.

that rises majestically over the Chicago River. The white terracotta that covers the building starts off cream-coloured at street level, but gets lighter towards the top of the structure. At

night, when the façade is illuminated by giant floodlights, the *trompe l'oeil* gives the building a glorious, glowing aspect. West of the Wrigley Building, on the north bank of the river – 300 N State Street, at the Chicago River – are the 61-storey 'corncob' twin towers of the **Marina City** apartment complex. Constructed of reinforced concrete, the individual floors of each tower are cantilevered out from the main core, which houses elevator shafts and garbage chutes. A theatre venue constructed between the two towers in 1966 is currently occupied by the House of Blues.

The **Sears Tower** (233 S Wacker Drive, at W Adams Street) is undoubtedly the most famous skyscraper in Chicago, if not the world. Formerly the world's tallest building – it was unseated by the Petronas Towers in Kuala Lumpur, Malaysia, in 1996 – the 1,454-foot (443-

The Wright stuff

Ask John Q Public who the world's greatest architect is or was, and chances are he'll reply 'Frank Lloyd Wright'. Even the most casual observer of popular culture is aware of the importance of Wright's contributions to modern architecture, even if they've never seen his work. Strange, that, considering the Chicago-based architect made his most lasting contributions to the art form not by building grandiose public buildings or flashy skyscrapers, but rather by constructing isolated residences for rich suburbanites, shuttered to the prying eyes of the common man. The fact that the homes he built so greatly altered norms of residential construction is a testament to his genius. That his once-revolutionary design elements are now taken for granted bears witness to the prophetic prescience of his designs.

Raised in Wisconsin, Wright arrived in Chicago in the years following the Great Fire and went to work in the offices of Adler and Sullivan, where he was assigned to the firm's residential design department. Eschewing the Beaux Arts style popular at the time, Wright's residential designs had much in common stylistically with the International Style of architecture, which was taking hold in Europe around the end of the century.

In 1893, though, Wright was fired from Adler and Sullivan for moonlighting and set up his own practice at his home in suburban Oak Park, Illinois, which he shared with his wife Catherine Tobin and six children. At his home studio, Wright spent the next decade defining

what would come to be known as the Prairie Style. Among the results of his labours are the 25 homes the architect designed for his Oak Park neighbours, such as those at nos.1019, 1027 and 1031 W Chicago Avenue and at nos.210, 318 and 333 N Forest Avenue. All can still be seen today, with both guided and self-guided tours available from the **Frank Lloyd Wright Home & Studio**.

Both of Wright's parents belonged to the Unitarian Church, which encourages followers to approach religion through nature along with science and art, disciplines that reveal the underlying principles of God's universe. Indeed, Wright's respect for natural elements and precise geometry is apparent in his designs. Prairie Style homes, most constructed of light-coloured brick and stucco, are low, ground-hugging, rectangular structures with broad gabled roofs, sweeping horizontal lines and open, flowing floor plans. Most importantly, perhaps, they blend in with their surroundings, imitating the wide open, flat topography of the Midwest plains. Common features include enclosed porches, stout chimneys and overhanging eaves.

metre) black aluminum and amber glass tower clearly owes a debt to the International Style with its chunky, cubist proportions. At 1,127 feet (344 metres), the **John Hancock Center** (875 N Michigan Avenue, at E Chestnut Street) is second only to the Sears on the Chicago skyline. Vaguely pyramid-shaped, the building gradually tapers from street level to its top floor. The building's distinctive, visible X-shaped structural supports evenly distribute the enormous weight of the building and help it resist the tremendous forces of wind at its higher elevations.

One of the world's tallest multi-purpose buildings, the Hancock is occupied by retail outlets and restaurants on its lower floors, and office space and condominiums on the upper floors, while the building even boasts its own post office and supermarket. The top floor is occupied by an exclusive (but of course) bar/restaurant and a slightly less exclusive observatory. For more on this pair, *see page 56* **A view to a thrill**.

While the International Style Federal Center pushed the boundaries of what a government building should look like, the dome-shaped **State of Illinois Building** (100 W Randolph Street, at N Clark Street) blew them away when it was completed in 1985. Despite its stridently modern appearance, the building pays subtle homage to traditional government buildings, with its abstract suggestion of the traditional cupola. The main attraction, though, is the wonderful 230-foot (70-metre) atrium created by the rotunda; ample lighting, exposed elevator shafts and mechanics, and reflective surfaces create a vibrant sense of movement.

Wright left his home studio in 1909 and sold the property in 1925. By 1974, the building had been so abused and altered by subsequent owners that it barely resembled the architect's original design. That year, the Frank Lloyd Wright Home and Studio Foundation was formed to acquire the home and studio, oversee a $3-million restoration that returned the property to its 1909 appearance, and open it to the public as a museum and education centre.

One of the last designs to come out of Wright's Oak Park studio was the **Robie House** (pictured), located near the University of Chicago on the city's South Side. In 1909, Wright began work on the private residence of Chicago industrialist Frederick C Robie, a project the architect would later proclaim 'the cornerstone of modern architecture'.

The Robie House was indeed a departure from the norm, and upon its completion in 1910, nonplussed observers likened the house to a steamship. A masterpiece of the Prairie Style, it featured dramatic horizontal lines, emphasised by steel-reinforced beams that extended 20 feet (six metres) past the walls; daring cantilevered surfaces; expansive stretches of glass; and Wright's signature open floorplan. Inside, Wright used patterned glass doors and walls to eliminate the traditional 'room as a box' aesthetic and maximise flow and light. Despite the fact that many were slow to accept its genius, the property eventually came to significantly alter the course of American residential design.

The Robie House remained a private residence until 1926, when it was sold to the Chicago Theological Seminary. For the next 40 years, ownership changed hands repeatedly; in 1957, it narrowly escaped demolition. Six years later, it was donated to the University of Chicago which, in 1992, joined forces with the Home and Studio Foundation and the National Trust for Historic Preservation to restore the house and maintain it as a museum.

When asked what his best building was, the self-aggrandising Wright answered, 'My next one.' It seems that he was right. If not his best, at least one of his most famous buildings, New York City's Guggenheim Museum, was the last he designed before his death in 1959. Indeed, Wright designed notable buildings all over the world, but, luckily for visitors, the city where he got his start remains the best place to see the man working at the peak of his career.

Frank Lloyd Wright Home & Studio
951 W Chicago Avenue, at N Forest Avenue (708 848 1976/78/www.wrightplus.org). CTA Harlem/Lake. **Tours** 11am, 1pm, 3pm Mon-Fri; every 15 mins 11am-3.30pm Sat, Sun. **Admission** $8; $6 concessions.

Robie House
5757 S Woodlawn Avenue, at E 58th Street (708 848 1976/78/www.wrightplus.org). Metra 59th Street. **Open** 11am, 1pm, 3pm Mon-Fri; every half-hour 11am-3.30pm Sat, Sun. **Admission** $8; $6 concessions.

When you're up, don't look down: the **John Hancock Center**.
See page 31.

Oh, and don't miss...

● Take a gander at the **Amoco Building** (200 E Randolph Street), and marvel not only at how the 80-storey structure was built, but also at how on earth they managed to completely re-panel the entire exterior when the marble that once graced it started to fall off a decade after it was completed.
● Pet the lions guarding the entrance of the **Art Institute of Chicago** (S Michigan Avenue, at E Adams Street), a grand old building designed by Shepley, Rutan and Coolidge in the late 19th century.
● Art deco is alive and well at the stunning **Chicago Board of Trade** (141 W Jackson Boulevard).
● The **Chicago Cultural Center** (78 E Washington Boulevard) will probably be your first stop anyway, but take time to enjoy the wonderful staircases.
● Like curves? You'll adore the **First National Bank** (bounded by E Madison Street, S Dearborn Street, E Monroe Street and S Clark Street).
● If you didn't know who James R Thompson was before – a former governor of Illinois, since you ask – you'll remember him for a while after catching sight of the startling

glass frontage of the **James R Thompson Center** (100 W Randolph Street).
● Pay tribute to the guy who first stumbled upon the city by taking in the decorative panels at the front of the **Marquette Building** (140 S Dearborn Street).
● The birds that once called 209 S LaSalle Street home have long gone, leaving the **Rookery** – designed by Burnham, with a Lloyd Wright atrium – in peace.
● The name is so-so, but **333 W Wacker Drive** (guess where it is) makes up for it with a stunning plain glass frontage: curved to imitate a curve in the river by which it sits, it changes colour as the reflections on it alter.

The enormous **Merchandise Mart**, situated by the river at N Wells Street, was the largest building in the world when it was completed in 1931. The building's dramatic waterfall-style limestone façade rises 25 storeys above the Chicago River, with sculptures of the busts of some of America's leading merchants, including Marshall Field, A Montgomery Ward and Frank W Woolworth, lining the riverfront esplanade. The building was commissioned by Marshall Field to house the department store's wholesale operation, along with those of other furniture and interior design shops. It was sold to the Kennedy family in the years following the Depression, though a 1991 renovation created a public mall on the first two floors.

If you have access to a car or don't mind a short train ride, make a day trip to the **Baha'i House of Worship**, just north of the city in Wilmette, Illinois, near Northwestern University. Completed in 1953, the Baha'i House was the first temple of the Baha'i faith built in the western hemisphere. Surrounded by quiet gardens, the breathtaking, gleaming white dome-like structure is covered with rich lacy ornamentation and inscribed with verses

from the Baha'i Writings. A visitors' centre offers additional information and maps. To get there, take the Red line north to Howard, then get the Purple line north to Linden and walk three blocks east. Arriving by car from the south, take Lake Shore Drive north to the Sheridan Road exit, then continue north on Sheridan to Linden Street.

The buildings discussed in these pages, along with many others, are highlighted by a variety of architectural walking and boat tours offered by several local organisations all year round. By far the most illuminating come courtesy of the terrific **Chicago Architecture Foundation** (312 922 8687/922 3432/www.architecture.org): it offers all manner of walking and bus tours and, during the summer, several boat and bike tours each day. If you want to get the stories behind the architecture in the city, told with a rare panache and enthusiasm, head here first.

▶ For more on **architecture in the Loop**, see page 57.
▶ For more on **architectural tours**, see page 82.

Fictional Chicago

It's Sandburg's 'City of the Big Shoulders', but it's also
David Mamet's muse and home to the brothers Blues.

Literary Chicago

In 1914, **Carl Sandburg** stared out at the
bloody stockyards of his home city and saw a
'Hog Butcher for the World' (*Chicago Poems*,
1916). Sure, the restaurants now are hip, the
buildings scrape the sky, yuppies rule the
yacht-infested lakefront and condos are pushing
out the meatpackers. But when it comes to the
fictional image of Chicago in literature,
Sandburg set in place an all-purpose metaphor
of blue-collar brawn and grit that neither
seismic historical change nor a city perpetually
concerned with bolstering its public image can
ever entirely banish.

Born in Galesburg, Illinois and a leader of the
so-called 'Chicago Renaissance' of arts and
letters, Sandburg wrote about a city where the
workers' shoulders were outsized. He told of
women with painted faces who lured farm boys;
he spoke of a hardbitten town where tools were
made, where wheat was stacked, and where the
railroads seemed to handle all of America's

freight, both actual and metaphorical.
Sandburg's Chicago may have been strong,
proud and alive but it was irrefutably coarse.
This, after all, was a city where you could read
hunger on a man's face.

Sandburg was not the only brave soul who
committed the stench of the stockyards to
paper. In 1916, the Baltimore-born **Upton
Sinclair**'s brutal novel *The Jungle* spoke of
spoiled meats, acrid acids and dangerous vats
of lard in the Chicago stockyards. If there is one
image that has pervaded Chicago's place in
20th-century literary history, it's the city's
identity as a worker's town.

In the 1930s and '40s, **Nelson Algren** – *The
Man With the Golden Arm*, *Walk on the Wild
Side*, *The Neon Wilderness* – set about achieving
a youthful ambition: to become the closest thing
to Maxim Gorky that America had produced.
And it wasn't too hard to persuade readers and
publishers that he was living in just the right
socially apocalyptic spot in which to sell his
writings about the lower depths of urban life.

Algren's Chicago had achieved more industrial prowess and political might than Sandburg could ever have thought possible. And thanks to the wealth of the industrials and their status-hungry wives, culture was winning over carcasses. But Algren still saw a 'city on the make', and adroitly positioned himself as a scribe of the impoverished. So when Simone de Beauvoir began an affair with this self-styled poet of the addict, prostitute, murderer and prisoner, the Parisian sophisticate was slumming it in a big way. And when Algren brought Ms de B to Chicago to live in his one-room apartment in the Polish section of town, the feminist found herself hanging out around police line-ups and strip joints rather than drawing rooms and cafés.

The sex, say de Beauvoir's recently published letters, was great. But in the end, Sartre and the South Bank won out over Polish sausage. And Algren – and, by extension, his Chicago – felt betrayed for the rest of his life. He'd surely forgotten his own published words of advice: 'Never sleep with someone whose problems are greater than your own.' A steak-sized chip on the shoulder is a vital part of the literary consciousness of the Second City, so the pain probably did Algren some good. Anyway, the image of Chicago as a worker's town lasted far longer than any possible affair with an aesthete.

The literature of hard graft can be found in the works of **Studs Terkel**, the living poet laureate of Chicago grit and paradox, and an author best known for his five books of oral history that include *Working* and *The Good War*. He may have been born in New York, but Terkel is adored in an adopted hometown he once described as a 'city of hands', as distinct from all those other pretentious cities of paper.

In fact, the only kind of paper that Chicago really respects is newsprint. From **Ben Hecht** and **Charles MacArthur**'s colourful 1928 Broadway pageant, *The Front Page*, to the mythology surrounding late *Chicago Tribune* columnist **Mike Royko**, broadsheet wordsmiths have always commanded a special kind of respect. After all, it's writing in the form of honest daily labour. Or perhaps it's just because the ink comes off on your hands.

Chicagoans have never placed much separation between labour and art, and, as a result, the divide between writer and the regular Joe or Jane in the street is far less pronounced than in other literary centres. As legions of the city's literary figures have acknowledged (with varying degrees of affection or dismay), no one has much time for literary awards, writer's circles, aesthetic movements or other fanciness. And writers have usually had to leave town before they started making any real money.

This house style – call it a city style – has resulted in native literary types that just don't seem to fit. You'll experience the real **Ernest Hemingway** in Key West, not in the Chicago suburb of Oak Park where he was born in 1899: he never had the city in his soul. Far less reasonably, uncharitable souls said the same of Canadian-born **Saul Bellow**, a long-time Chicago-based author, professor and winner of the 1976 Nobel Prize for Literature, when he moved to Boston in the late 1990s. The town's most noted playwright lives in Boston, too, but his Chicago identity is far more secure.

When he was writing his early dramas and living on the North Side, **David Mamet** spent his days driving a cab. His singularly clipped and profanity-laden style of dialogue may have reflected the new urban vibe of the 1970s and 1980s, but Mamet's Chicago was still a town of workers, even if the collars had all turned white from fear. Adrift and in agony, the lost souls in *Sexual Perversity in Chicago* copulate more from desperation than reckless abandon. If Sandburg's Hog Butchers had a 1980s equivalent, it was surely the hapless losers pedalling swampland from their Chicago office in *Glengarry Glen Ross*. Sales represented the rump of the American dream and Chicago was the place to make the cut.

Mamet's crowd, of course, rarely ventured south of downtown. Chicago's large African-American population and segregated urban divide has made the city a popular flashpoint for America's long series of agonised literary wails over the horrors of racism.

In the historically pivotal 1959 drama *A Raisin in the Sun*, Chicagoan **Lorraine Hansberry** depicted heaven for Mama, Walter Lee and the other hard-working Youngers as a new house on Clybourn Avenue on the white side of town. And when **Richard Wright** came up to Chicago from Mississippi in the 1930s and imagined a young and innocent black man (Bigger Thomas) from Chicago charged with the murder of a white woman in *Native Son*, he fictionalised a scenario that would play out for real countless times in his adopted city in the years that followed.

Gwendolyn Brooks, poet laureate of Illinois and a resident of Chicago since the age of one month, would have understood Bigger Thomas's agonies. 'Swing low swing low sweet sweet chariot,' Brooks wrote in her poem *DeWitt Williams on his way to Lincoln Cemetery*, 'he was nothing but a plain black boy.'

When poet **Marc Smith**, originator of Chicago's famous poetry slam, looks out at post-Sandburg, postmodern Chicago, he sees wheat traders with suntans, players with railroads and a City of Big Business Ventures. In their leisure time, such folks likely read the artful bestselling thrillers of **Scott Turow**, a Chicago author-lawyer who writes on the train on his way into work. So did the glorification of the worker go west with the new information age?

Actually, fictional Chicago has always been shot through with paradox. **Hugh Hefner** published the seemingly Californian *Playboy* magazine here in the prosaic Midwest – though the Bunny was a semi-mythical creature without geographic referent – and, in the 1910s, **Harriet Monroe**'s *Poetry* magazine specialised in TS Eliot and Ezra Pound, spawning its own literary movement. Chicago never could be reduced to hogs and social anguish, though two other early works, **Theodore Dreiser**'s *Sister Carrie* (1900) and **James T Farrell**'s *Studs Lonigan* trilogy (1932-35), come with plenty of the latter.

But in today's mosaic, Turow's book jackets share local-interest shelf space with **Sandra Cisneros**'s progressive *The House of Mango Street*, while the locally filmed movie *Love Jones*, a celebration of Chicago's poetry scene, showcased a poet, percussionist and activist named Reggie Gibson. 'God,' wrote this literary Chicagoan with an eye for both the musical past and the freedoms of the present, 'is a blooz man.'

Chicago on film

An over-stimulated bulldog took a mouthful out of the lead actor's arse during the 1896 filming of *The Tramp and the Dog*, the first movie ever shot in Chicago. In the following primitive years, **'Colonel' William Selig** produced a slew of silent westerns, romances and animal adventures (he kept a menagerie of exotic animals and didn't hesitate to kill a few of them when the plot so demanded). As Selig's career flourished, so did those of his local competitors. **L Frank Baum**'s Oz Films produced the first screen version of his *The Wizard of Oz*, which featured Oliver Hardy making another fine mess as the Tin Man.

Several African-American film companies, including Foster Photoplay and Birth of a Race Photoplay, tried to redress racial stereotypes prevalent in mainstream film production. Director **Oscar Micheaux**, whose posthumous fan club includes Spike Lee and Julie Dash, is now lauded for his Chicago-borne creations, including a three-hour epic entitled *The Homesteader*; *Within Our Gates*, an initially censored attack on mob lynchings; and *Body and Soul*, which marked the 1924 film debut of Paul Robeson.

At the top of Chicago's huge silent film industry, however, was the Essanay Film Manufacturing Company. Founded by **George Spoor** and former Selig western star **Gilbert**

'Bronco Billy' Anderson, Essanay introduced such talents as gorgeous Gloria Swanson, heart-throb Francis X Bushman, cross-eyed vaudevillian Ben Turpin and Wallace Beery, perhaps film's first cross-dresser.

The most famous of Essanay's actors, though, was **Charlie Chaplin**, who commanded the highest weekly salary known to the 1914 film industry: a whopping $1,250. *His New Job*, starring Chaplin and Swanson, was shot entirely in Chicago and released in 1915, just shortly before a perpetually pissed-off Chaplin returned to California. The Essanay studios still stand, though somewhat remodelled, at 1333-45 Argyle Street, the current home of St Augustine College. But the lousy weather and the lure of Hollywood fame ultimately put an end to the Chicago film studios, and by the beginning of World War II, Chicago was little more than a location shoot; or, when budgets were tight, a city to be recreated on California sound stages.

Based on an unsolved murder, *Call Northside 777* brought Jimmy Stewart to 1947 Chicago as a reporter struggling to help a wrongly accused man. With similar persistence, Cary Grant survived his narrow escape from a mercenary crop duster only to confront a suspicious Eva Maria Saint at the Ambassador East Hotel in Alfred Hitchcock's *North by Northwest* (1959). The film version of *Native Son*, in which author Richard Wright himself played Bigger Thomas, juxtaposed downtown glitter with the dreary life on the South Side. And though *The Front Page* (1931) and its 1940 remake *His Girl Friday* created a fake Chicago in California, a young Sidney Poitier actually showed up here in 1961 to star in *A Raisin in the Sun*. Chicago also had its share of twisted cult hits, including the cerebrally grim and artsy *Mickey One* (1965), in which Warren Beatty played a comedian pursued by mobsters and his own imagination (hard to know which is scarier), and *The Gore-Gore Girls* (1972), made by Herschell Gordon Lewis, the 'Godfather of Gore'.

Filming slowed further during the mayoral term of the infamous **Richard J Daley**, after he was reputedly angered by footage used by director Haxell Wexler in *Medium Cool*, which blended fact with fiction in its tale of a television cameraman's coverage of the 1968 Democratic National Convention and the ensuing riots. To punctuate the drama, the activist director sent his actors and camera crew deep into the actual fray in Grant Park to film several brutal scenes. *Medium Cool* led to an unofficial mayoral ban on co-operation with filmmakers. Even for ready cash, permits were suddenly tough to snag.

Jake, Elwood and **Mayor Jane Byrne** changed all that. A cornball story that had the besuited brothers Blues careening through

John Belushi and Dan Aykroyd go on a mission from God in *The Blues Brothers*.

Chicago in an effort to save their childhood orphanage, *The Blues Brothers* was filmed in the city in 1979 and released the following year. Chicago-bred director **John Landis** placed a never-ending series of car crashes, shopping malls and unscheduled R&B performances in the paths of John Belushi and Dan Aykroyd. Though it died at the box office, it proved a watershed for movie-making in Chicago: ever since, the city has been courting Hollywood with all the limited charm that current Mayor Richard M Daley can muster. An incorrigible film buff who apparently harbours few of his father's grudges, 'Hizzoner' has supported a flurry of filming in Chicago, including *Ordinary People*, *The Color of Money*, *The Untouchables*, *Wayne's World* and, more recently, *My Best Friend's Wedding* and *Never Been Kissed*.

Chicago's cavernous museums and its nightmarish housing projects have also provided ample fodder for horror. A brain-sucking monster lurked in the basement of the **Field Museum** (*see page 57*) in *The Relic* (1996); *Candyman* (1992) munched at Cabrini Green; and parts of *Damien: Omen II* (1978) and *Flatliners* (1990) were set in the **Museum of Science and Industry** (*see page 88*). Elsewhere, *Risky Business* (1983), the finally-getting-laid-thanks-to-a-friendly-call-girl story that gave the world Tom Cruise, is memorable mostly for a midnight El 'ride' with Rebecca DeMornay. CTA sex was never the same.

It gets worse, though. For among many other sins, Chicagoan **John Hughes** inflicted the so-called Brat Pack on an unsuspecting world. The careers of such barely pubescent actors as Molly Ringwald, Ally Sheedy, Judd Nelson, Andrew McCarthy and Matthew Broderick were launched by the acne-riddled Hughes films *Sixteen Candles*, *The Breakfast Club*, *Weird Science* and *Ferris Bueller's Day Off*, while future child litigant Macauley Culkin was *Home Alone* in Chicago's poshest suburbs. (Ugly kid: who could blame the parents?)

On location

- The urban expanse known as **Daley Plaza** (50 W Washington Boulevard; *see page 49*) has been home to everything from befuddled Neanderthals in *The Naked Ape*, to Elizabeth Shue in *Adventures in Babysitting*, to the National Guardsmen, tanks and 500 extras on the lookout for John Belushi and Dan Aykroyd in *The Blues Brothers*.
- For a holier *Blues Brothers* moment, check out the **Pilgrim Baptist Church** (3235 E 91st Street), scene of soul-stirring celluloid preaching by James Brown.
- The **Drake Hotel** (140 E Walton Place; *see page 101*) attracts a cosmopolitan crowd: Cary Grant, James Mason and Eva Marie Saint all graced the lobby during Alfred Hitchcock's *North by Northwest*; Julia Roberts plotted against precious Cameron Diaz in *My Best Friend's Wedding*; and Tom Cruise awaited *Risky Business* girl-for-hire Rebecca DeMornay in the hotel's Palm Court.
- Another hotel, the **Chicago Hilton & Towers** (720 S Michigan Avenue; *see page 101*) dates back to 1927 and has provided settings for *The Package*, *My Best Friend's Wedding*, *Home Alone II: Lost in New York* and *US Marshals*. However, it's probably best known for its role in *The Fugitive*, where its Grand Ballroom, three-storeyed laundry room and towering rooftop provided the backdrop for Harrison Ford's athletic escapade.
- Remember the baby carriage that careened, slow-mo, down a marble staircase during the signature Brian De Palma shoot-out between Eliot Ness (Kevin Costner) and Al Capone's lackeys in *The Untouchables*? Well, the same location where that was shot, gorgeous **Union Station** (210 S Canal Street; *see page 55*), was also the final destination of the runaway train *Silver Streak*, which crashed through a model of the terminus in the 1976 movie of the same name.
- Beware dark and dank **Lower Wacker Drive**, which is replete with murderers (*Henry: Portrait of a Serial Killer*) and car chases (*Primal Fear* and *Thief*).
- Similarly, **Lake Shore Drive** has been the site of many high-speed escapades, including the Porsche-driving, pimp-eluding scene in *Risky Business*, the demolition derby finale of *The Blues Brothers*, and illicit Ferrari cruising in *Ferris Bueller's Day Off*.
- The prosthetics lab of **Cook County Hospital** (1835 W Harrison Street) helped Harrison Ford begin his search for the one-armed wife-killer in *The Fugitive*. However, exterior shots of the hospital show up regularly on *ER*.
- *Backdraft* incinerated the former **Cuneo Press Building** (455 W Cermak Street), rousing Kurt Russell and his buddies from their headquarters at the **Chinatown Fire Station** (4195 S Archer Avenue).
- The **Maxwell Street District Police Station** (943 W Maxwell Street) provided the exterior for the *Hill Street Blues* cop shop in the show's opening credits.
- In *About Last Night*, Rob Lowe and Demi Moore completed their sexual preliminaries at **Mother's** (26 W Division Street). Non-fictional one-night stands remain a speciality of the bar.
- And finally, Paul Newman taught Tom Cruise the tricks of the trade at pool halls all across town in *The Color of Money*. To trace their potting adventures, visit **FitzGerald's** (6615 Roosevelt Road; *see page 208*), **Chicago's Finest Billiards** (6414 S Cottage Grove), the **Ginger Man** (3740 N Clark Street; *see page 157*), **Chris's Billiards** (4637 N Milwaukee Avenue; *see page 231*), and whatever is left of **St Paul's Billiards** (1415 W Fullerton Avenue), where Cruise's character got his pretty features rearranged.

Hughes chooses to make his films here because he's from Chicago. And as the city's actors, writers and directors have gained Hollywood clout, more folks have been bringing the cameras home. A product of the South Side, **Andrew Davis** has shot all his films in Chicago, including *The Package* (1989), a political thriller starring Gene Hackman; *The Fugitive* (1993) with wrongly accused Harrison Ford; and *Chain Reaction* (1996), featuring the unlikely Keanu Reeves as a smart scientist. Many Chicago-trained actors also come home to

develop new films, such as happened with John Cusack's recent vehicle *High Fidelity* (2000).

Sometimes, even clout-less Chicago movies have broken out of the pack, especially if the critics **Roger Ebert** and the late **Gene Siskel** lent their weight. Such was the case with the highly acclaimed *Hoop Dreams*. Filmed over four years by Chicago resident Steve James and released in 1994, the basketball documentary followed the lives of two African-American boys, both of whom aspired to NBA greatness. A similar surprise was the success of the

Clockwise from top left: *My Best Friend's Wedding, Risky Business, Backdraft, The Fugitive, The Color of Money, The Untouchables.*

chilling *Henry: Portrait of a Serial Killer* (1986), which launched the careers of director **John McNaughton** and producer **Steven A Jones**.

TV shows such as *Married with Children, The Bob Newhart Show* and *Good Times* hinted at Chicago locales, but never left the sunshine. They've always got the snow machines running full blast in LA when they film *ER* – don't they know it's occasionally summer here? – but at least both *ER* and *Chicago Hope* film their bloodcurdling crash scenes in Chicago: look for cars shattering plate-glass windows and the like.

But since various network shows died premature deaths, *Early Edition* – where the newspaper arrives one day early and allows the hero to change the future – was the only network series filmed entirely in Chicago in early 2000. But this dumb endeavour is no threat to the Great Queen of Chicago Media. For from her Harpo Studios on the near-West Side, **Oprah Winfrey** dictates tastes, makes careers and has more significance in Hollywood than all of the Chicago silent movie pioneers put together.

Media

Tenacious newspapers, non-essential sports radio and the most notorious TV talk shows in the States.

Chicago has a storied newspaper history that dates back to the city's inception in the early 19th century. The classic image of the hard-drinking, chain-smoking, grizzled city editor practically originated here, and for years Chicago had numerous newspapers that competed for readers and attention. Both the late, great columnist Mike Royko and reporter/playwright Ben Hecht (who co-wrote *The Front Page*) only added to the city's reputation as a hack's paradise, a reputation onto which it has managed to cling to this day.

Like all American cities, though, Chicago has seen many of its daily newspapers decline or disappear in recent years, as readers turn increasingly to television and the internet for news and information. But the city can still lay claim to one of only a few remaining newspaper wars in the country, as the *Chicago Tribune* and the *Chicago Sun-Times* go head-to-head each day in a battle for readership. Recently, weekly newspapers have also started to thrive, becoming particularly valuable sources of arts and entertainment news, listings and criticism.

Despite the relative decline in the newspaper industry, Chicagoans still take their news seriously, and the famously corrupt city politics never fails to provide entertaining and outrageous stories. While proper newsstands have dwindled in all but a few downtown areas, newspaper boxes dot the city and are never further away than the nearest street corner.

PRESS
Founded in 1847, the **Chicago Tribune** is the reigning daily newspaper, and offers extremely broad coverage of national and foreign news, politics, arts and suburban issues. It's also one of the most powerful papers in Illinois, if not the US, especially since its dominating merger with the *Los Angeles Times* in March 2000.

For the first half of the 20th century, the paper was run by a maverick, right-wing editor and publisher, Colonel Robert McCormick. It's since become more respectable, and is now the more liberal-leaning of the two major dailies. While in theory it competes with the *Sun-Times*, the *Trib*, as it's commonly known, is widely considered the better paper. It gives more coverage to the suburbs, which the *Sun-Times* all but ignores, and offers plentiful regional sports and arts coverage. It's also the local paper to invest in if you're after foreign news; though its international coverage isn't exactly gigantic, a copy of the *Trib* is arguably better value than an overpriced and outdated imported rag. Another asset of the *Trib* is its fine entertainment-led 'Friday' supplement.

The *Trib* has been especially active in synergising its print, radio, internet and television holdings, and has put many of its resources into non-newspaper media. Nationally, however, it's still considered a second-tier paper, so those looking for the best newspaper in town will want to pick up the special Midwest edition of the *New York Times*.

The **Chicago Sun-Times** is the tabloid competitor to the *Trib*, though it's been in sharp decline of late. Now owned by a Canadian conglomerate, the paper has a conservative editorial page. But profits seem to have trumped quality as the newspaper's goal: though it offers the occasional slice of gritty reporting on city politics and thorough coverage of Chicago's sports teams, most news stories are squeezed into a few paragraphs, and the paper's bulk is due mainly to department store ads. At 35¢, though, it is at least cheaper than the *Trib* by a whopping 15¢.

Those hoping for news from home won't find it in the *Sun-Times*: unless the US happens to be bombing your country, that is, in which case you can expect a paragraph or two on the event. Coverage of the arts is particularly weak, with notable exceptions being a funny television critic (Phil Rosenthal), an acerbic music scribe (Jim DeRogatis) and a nigh-on legendary movie hack (Roger Ebert, who presented a weekly movie show with the late *Trib* crit Gene Siskel for years). Like the *Trib* and its 'Friday' rag, the *Sun-Times* offers a weekend pull-out section which is worth a look.

The **Daily Herald** and the **Daily Southtown** round out Chicago's dailies, but neither attempts to compete with the *Trib* or *Sun-Times* inside the city. The *Herald* publishes zoned suburban editions, while the *Southtown*, as its name indicates, concerns itself only with the southernmost area of the city.

The **Chicago Reader** is the dominant free weekly newspaper, and is a must-have for visitors and locals alike. For precisely that reason, it's often difficult to track down a copy after the paper is published on Thursday: if you can't find one in the numerous yellow newspaper boxes the *Reader* scatters around town, check inside the doorway of the nearest local business for a stack of copies.

The *Reader* offers excellent coverage of music, movies, theatre and art, and has the most comprehensive and reliable events listings. It also gives nuanced coverage to the many movie festivals held in the city, and offers particularly good tips for underground music shows. The news section of the paper specialises in lengthy human interest pieces that many folks find tedious (it's famous for once running a 19,000-word story on bees, for example). But it does offer a from-the-ground-up perspective of many neighbourhoods and a welcome alternative view of the community.

Newcity is Chicago's other alternative weekly freesheet, and is available in many bars and shops, and from orange boxes on street corners. While it doesn't compete with the *Reader* in terms of quality or quantity, it's certainly not without its merits. Written in more of an undergraduate, first-person style, *Newcity* offers a variety of annual specials on stuff like eating out and movies, a quarterly literary supplement (curiously absent in the *Reader*) and the occasional off-the-beaten-track newsy gem. It, too, features movie, music and theatre listings, though its arts criticism is a little spotty.

> ## 'The classic image of the hard-drinking, chain-smoking, grizzled city editor practically originated here.'

The **Onion** is certain to startle anyone who isn't already familiar with its immensely popular website (www.theonion.com). If nothing else, it's welcome evidence that satire isn't dead in America, as proven by headlines such as 'Clinton Feels Nation's Pain, Breasts' and 'Pope Admits "God Ain't Said Shit To Me"'. More than that, though, it's also devastatingly funny. In addition to the humour, it provides excellent coverage of music and movies, deadly accurate cut-through-the-bullshit reviews, and a 'Savage Love' sex advice column. It's available for free in most bars and convenience stores downtown, and is not to be missed.

The rest of the street-corner boxes are filled with a variety of other weekly, fortnightly and monthly freesheets. A few are specific to the neighbourhood in which they're found, while others – such as gay weeklies the **Windy City Times** and the **Chicago Free Press**, the latter of which was founded in 1999 by disillusioned ex-staff of the former – are targeted at certain communities. The bizarre fortnightly rag, **Barfly Newspaper**, also comes into this category.

My kind of town Jerry Springer

You could always blame Phil Donahue, but only if you were desperate for a scapegoat. It'd be like blaming Henry Ford when you get woken up in the middle of the night by a squealing car alarm. And though Geraldo Rivera upped the daytime ante a tad, he can hardly be held accountable. Nope: when it comes to taking responsibility for Chicago's leading talk-show host, you have to give the man himself his due. Mr Jerry Springer – for it is he – *Time Out* salutes you. Kinda.

Born in 1944 in – of all places – London, Springer and his family emigrated to New York five years later. After studying political science at New Orleans's Tulane University, Springer journeyed to Chicago and completed a law degree in 1968. A stint as a campaign aide to Bobby Kennedy followed, after which Springer moved to Cincinnati and made some political headway there. So much so, in fact, that he was elected the city's mayor by a landslide in 1977.

By the early 1980s, he'd graduated to television work as a political reporter on a Cincinnati TV station, soon being appointed managing editor and chief news anchor and going on to win a clutch of Emmys for his work at local level. But then, in 1991, came an offer he couldn't refuse. An offer to host his own daily talk show. In Chicago.

And that's where the fun starts. We find it hard to believe that there's anyone out there who hasn't seen the *Jerry Springer Show*, but just in case you've been hiding under a rock for the last decade, the show goes something like this. Transsexual/obese hooker/ philandering grandmother/ comically mulleted trailer park dweller (delete as applicable) enters stage left. Lets Springer and baying audience in on bizarre secret: sleeping with partner's mother, sleeping with own mother, is a man but boyfriend doesn't know it, that sort of thing. Unknowing person to whom guest number one has done wrong enters

stage right. Discovers secret. Much cursing, chair-throwing and general hypertension. Repeat several times. Cue Springer, with smarmy, lowest-common-denominator moralising pay-off. Roll credits. Bob, as they say, is your uncle.

There's no doubt, of course, that as well as being considerably smarter than those who appear on his show each day, Jerry Springer is a very smart man in his own right. For one thing, he's managed to put his knack for bullet-dodging learned during his stint in politics to good use in his TV career, succeeding in placing himself above the fray he presides over daily with a mix of self-deprecation, braggadocio, charm and factual bet-hedging. To those outraged interviewers who have the balls to tell him that his show is trash, he invariably shrugs and replies that yes, it is, isn't it? He's even gone so far as to

tell one reporter that if he were you, he probably wouldn't watch it either. Springer is sensible and savvy enough not to even attempt to defend the indefensible.

But most tellingly, he's shrugged off accusations that the guests on his show are paid actors and/or fakers with the semantic aplomb of a seasoned politico. At one stage, the Chicago City Council was so concerned about the violence on the show that it took the unprecedented and entirely ludicrous step of inviting Springer to appear before them to justify it. '[The violence] seems real to me,' he told the council. 'The people are real, the stories are real, and when they are wrestling, it looks like it's real. But the show is produced.' Precisely the sort of comment, in other words, that was immortalised in *All The President's Men* as a 'non-denial denial'.

Of course, it could be that the public doesn't care whether it's real or not: after all, with episodes that boast titles such as 'I Married A Horse!', it's all too easy to doubt the show's veracity. In which case, as Springer himself cheekily pointed out afterwards, the council succeeded only in plugging his show by bringing him to court for a televised inquisition.

He's not untouchable, mind. *Ringmaster*, a movie based on the life of Springer – co-produced by the man himself, in a rare outward show of vanity – died on its arse critically and commercially. He was alleged to have enjoyed a three-in-a-bed session in a hotel with a 21-year-old blonde and her 28-year-old stepmother, both of whom had been guests on his show. His stint on WMAQ as an editorialising TV news commentator came to an abrupt end after just a week. And perhaps most damagingly, the same station later dropped Springer's daytime show after pressure from local religious groups, though it's since found a new home on WFLD.

Yet despite all these setbacks, and despite the fact that the ratings-grabbing violence on the show has fallen away following a stern edict from the studio that owns it, the rise and rise of Chicago's most notorious, most comical and most watched talk-show host looks set to continue. Go Jerry. Go Jerry.

● *Tickets for* The Jerry Springer Show *are available on 312 321 5365.*

Chicago magazine, priced at $3.99, is the only monthly publication of note in the city, and looks thoroughly drab from the outside. However, the journalism is surprisingly good for a city magazine: such publications are often little more than super-sponsored city guides, but *Chicago* magazine does run consistently interesting features on the city's most powerful and important people. And if you should be looking for a decent restaurant, its anonymous critics are always trustworthy.

Other monthlies, all of them freesheets available from a street corner near you, include **Chicago Social**, mainly a vehicle for advertisers and society photographers but with occasional features on interesting restaurants and businesses; **Chicago Women**, which is self-explanatory and unexceptional; and **UR Chicago**, an entertainment paper that, though sparky, pales in comparison to its two weekly competitors. **Streetwise** is written and sold by the homeless (it costs $1, though it's customary to give the vendor a little extra), while those on the outs with their spouse may like to pick up **Chicago Divorce** ($3.95); only, as they say, in America. And no piece on Chicago media would be complete without mention of **Playboy**: founded in Chicago by Hugh Hefner, it's still based here and is bigger than ever.

Visitors suffering from the dearth of international news should head for one of the city newsstands or a major bookstore, where they can pick up foreign newspapers and magazines. **City Newsstand** (4018 N Cicero Avenue; 773 545 7377) is arguably Chicago's best and largest, but it's a little bit out of the way on the city's North West Side. However, if you can make it up there, you'll likely find what you're looking for. The stand carries a variety of out-of-town and international newspapers along with some 6,000 magazines, many of which hail from abroad. Unfortunately, bookstores, which have coffeeshops and comfortable reading areas, and which also don't mind if you read without buying, are slowly taking over the market from the stands. Shame.

Bookstore-wise, the best selection of international reading can be found at the Magnificent Mile branch of **Borders**. Its international offerings include the UK's *Guardian*, Spain's *El País* and Sweden's *Dagens Nyheter*, among others. Sunday papers typically arrive on Wednesday, and can be enjoyed in the third-floor coffeeshop. A second Borders, all the way up in Lake View on N Clark Street, offers a similar selection. The new **Barnes & Noble** on N State Street has a less thorough selection of international news, but does carry the major papers from France, Britain and Germany.

TELEVISION

Chicago is the country's third-largest media market, and is home to numerous TV stations. In addition to affiliates of the four major broadcast networks – **WLS-Channel 7** (ABC), **WMAQ-Channel 5** (NBC), **WBBM-Channel 2** (CBS) and **WFLD-Channel 32** (Fox) – Chicago has both a local cable station (**CLTV-Channel 11**) and a national one (**WGN-9**).

But for all its size and apparent importance, television in Chicago offers little bang for its considerably large advertising buck. News shows are virtually indistinguishable and tend toward sensational coverage. Fox is particularly guilty of this, though NBC briefly usurped it in an ill-fated move by hiring Jerry Springer as a commentator (*see page 42* **My kind of town**). And while Chicago's sports teams once commanded the airwaves, the declining fortunes of the Bulls, Bears and Blackhawks – as well as the long-suffering Cubs and White Sox – have resulted in a general malaise towards televised sports, the exception being a Sammy Sosa at-bat on WGN.

Only Chicago's talk shows seem to be thriving. In Chicago, Oprah Winfrey is queen, though she's recently been topped in the ratings by Springer and also has competition from fellow locals Jenny Jones and Montel Williams. But the best local programming can be found on public television (**WTTW-Channel 11**). The channel features the finest local show around: *Wild Chicago*, a low-budget masterpiece that spotlights the quirky, eclectic, unusual and hilarious around the city. The half-hour show is broadcast on Fridays at 10pm (repeated on Sundays at 10.30pm), and is full of great ideas with which to occupy the following afternoon.

RADIO

Like any major American city, Chicago has a wide variety of radio programming, with a particular emphasis on sports-talk radio. And also like any major American city, corporate owners are taking over the airwaves and causing most of the smaller, more interesting stations to disappear. The major FM rock stations are bland and practically indistinguishable, with **WXRT** (93.1 FM), **WKQX** (101.1 FM) and **WTMX** (101.9 FM) the main offenders. Oldies may care to tune to **WUBT** (103.5 FM), **WJMK** (104.3 FM), while fans of classic and '80s rock can take their pick between **WXXY** (103.1 FM), **WXCD** (94.7 FM), **WLUP** (97.9 FM) and **WCKG** (105.9 FM), the Chicago outlet for Howard Stern's morning rantings. Adult contemporary sounds can be found all over the dials: the major stations are the comically monikered **WIND** (560 AM), **WMAQ** (670 AM), **WLIT** (93.9 FM) and **WNUA** (95.5 FM).

There is, thankfully, still some variety on the Chicago airwaves, particularly on the many college stations. Try Northwestern University's **WNUR** (89.3 FM); Columbia College's **WCRX** (88.1 FM); **WDCB** (90.9 FM) from the College of DuPage; Loyola University's **WLUW** (88.7 FM); the University of Chicago's **WHPK** (88.5 FM); St Xavier University's **WXAV** (88.3 FM); and **WUIC** (89.5 FM) from the University of Illinois at Chicago. But to get an earful of what Chicago's most famous for, tune into any sports radio station. The newest is ESPN's **WMVP** (1000 AM), but there are also **WSCR** (1160 AM) and **WJK** (94.3 FM) for those who like to listen to illiterate Chicago men shout at each other about how much the Bulls suck.

For sheer curiosity value, don't miss the Moody Bible Institute's radio station **WMBI** (90.1 FM) and the exceptional **WBEZ** (91.5 FM), Chicago's public radio station. In addition to National Public Radio shows, it regularly features famous Chicago author and activist Studs Terkel on *Eight Forty-Eight*, broadcast from 9.30am to 11am, Monday to Friday.

> ## 'Listen to illiterate Chicago men shout at each other about how much the Bulls suck.'

INTERNET

Chicago is a wonderfully wired city. If you know where to point your browser, it's easy to scout things out from practically anywhere in the world. In deference to America's more famous technology havens – Silicon Valley in California and Silicon Alley in New York City – Chicago has dubbed itself the 'Silicon Prairie'. The name fits.

Proper cybercafés, where patrons sip coffee while paying to surf the net, are rarer in Chicago than in other cities, apparently because the economy won't support them. This might sound alarming to the tech-savvy traveller, but it's actually good news: there are so many places in town that offer free internet access that cybercafés aren't necessary. If you're downtown and quick off the mark, you're in luck: the **Chicago Public Library** has multiple locations that offer free internet access to anyone. Bear in mind, however, that a 30-minute limit is strictly enforced.

▶ For more on **bookshops**, see page 162.
▶ For more on the **gay press**, see page 204.
▶ For more on the **internet**, see page 285.

Sightseeing

Feature boxes

Sightseeing

From the top of the Sears Tower to the tip of Lincoln Park, Chicago has plenty of sights for sore eyes.

The Loop

In Chicago, all routes lead to the Loop. The heart of 'the city that works', it's here that business and politics converge – sometimes in the same room – alongside world-famous architecture, beautifully restored theatres, a multitude of museums and a re-awakened shopping district. Named after the cable cars that 'looped' around downtown during the area's first heyday in the 1880s, the Loop today – bounded by the Chicago River to the north, Grant Park to the east, Congress Parkway to the south and Clinton Street to the west – is experiencing a comeback of sorts, with new commercial venues and high-end condos bringing a 24-hour life of sorts.

Still, the area is quieter on evenings and the weekends than other, more tourist-populated areas, and on any given weekday, travellers are likely to be outnumbered by politicos and local nine-to-fivers. Easily accessible by major roads, buses, subways and the elevated train – which still travels an overbearing path similar to that trailed by the now-extinct cable cars – the Loop and its surrounds are anchored by Chicago classics like the Sears Tower, the Art Institute, old City Hall and Grant Park, future home to the city's multi-million-dollar Millennium Park.

The **Mercantile Exchange**. *See page 48.*

Neighbourhood watch

THE LOOP The financial and business centre of Chicago, the Loop stretches south from the Chicago River to Congress Parkway, and covers the area west to Union Station and Clinton Street.

SOUTH LOOP As you'd expect, really: the South Loop falls just below the Loop, and covers the area from Congress Parkway down to Roosevelt Road between the Chicago River and Lake Michigan.

MUSEUM CAMPUS South and east of the South Loop on the edge of Burnham Park and Lake Michigan stand three museums, from which this area takes its name: the Shedd Aquarium, the Adler Planetarium and the Field Museum.

NEAR NORTH Another self-descriptive area name, the Near North area covers the wedge of Chicago stretching north from the Chicago River to Chicago Avenue, and stretching east from the north branch of the river to the lake. It's here you'll find the shopping of the **Magnificent Mile**, some superbly posh hotels and hundreds of eateries. Within the confines of Near North, the blocks west of Clark Street are known as **River North**, an area home to plenty of art galleries and other cultural hotspots. The area east of Michigan Avenue, **Streeterville**, is where you'll find Navy Pier, among other attractions.

GOLD COAST Swanky in the extreme, the Gold Coast sits proudly between Chicago

Sears Tower

Probably more than any other landmark, the
Sears Tower symbolises Chicago, making its
skyline easily distinguishable from any other.
Built in 1974, it made headlines as the world's
tallest building until Malaysia upped the ante in
1996. At 1,454 feet (443 metres) – 110 storeys,
plus protruding antennae – it's still America's
tallest building, not to mention one of the city's
most popular attractions.

Designed by the Chicago firm of Skidmore,
Owings & Merrill LLP, nine steel tubes of
varying heights form the frame of the black
aluminium and glass-covered building. Only
two of the tubes continue all the way to the top,
giving the structure a multi-tiered look. From
the Skydeck Observatory on the 103rd floor,
visitors can take in a panoramic view that on a
clear day can take in as many as four states.
Nearly 15,000 people visit the Sears Tower each
day, either for work or pleasure, and more than
100 elevators carry them up and down (it takes
just one minute to make the trip from the
visitors' centre to the Skydeck). Tickets for the
observatory can be bought in the atrium off
Wacker Drive, where you'll also find Universe,
a 33-foot (10-metre) high sculpture by
Alexander Calder representing the sun, a
pendulum and three flowers. In the case of
heavy fog, catch a glimpse of what you're
missing in the free short film *Over Chicago. See
also page 56* **A view to a thrill**.

Just south of the Sears Tower is the **311 S
Wacker Building**, on Wacker Drive at W
Jackson Boulevard. Known by most Chicagoans
as 'that bright castle-looking thing next to the

What's the time, **Marshall Field**? *See p49.*

Sears Tower', the structure actually holds the
distinction of being the tallest reinforced
concrete building in the world. It has an exterior
of glass and pink granite surrounded by a
neatly landscaped yard: at night, the crown of
the 65-storey structure is lit up like the top of a
Christmas tree, making the building skyline-
defining in its own way. Inside, a vaulted
atrium and fountain leads to the Yvette
Wintergarden, where live music can be
heard nightly.

Sears Tower

*233 S Wacker Drive, at W Jackson Boulevard (312
875 9696). CTA Quincy.* **Open** *Mar-Sept* 9am-11pm
daily; *Oct-Feb* 9am-10pm daily. **Admission** $8.50;
$5.50-$6.50 concessions; $24 family (2 adults + 3
children). **Credit** Disc, MC, V. **Map** p305 G12.

LaSalle Street

East of Wacker Drive sits S LaSalle Street, a
smaller version of New York's Wall Street,
commonly referred to as the financial district of

Avenue and North Avenue to the east of Clark
Street. This is where you'll find the most
prohibitively expensive real estate in the city,
but also, in an ironic twist, the nastiest,
naffest bars in the city down near the
intersection of State and Division.
OLD TOWN A historic area just north of the
Gold Coast that contains many fine bars, the
eminently visitable Chicago Historical Society
and an alarming amount of yuppies.
LINCOLN PARK Taking in part of the huge
park from which it takes its name, the area
known as Lincoln Park also includes DePaul
University and plenty of great nightlife. In the
last decade, it's become one of the city's
most desirable addresses.

LAKE VIEW Stretching north from Diversey
Parkway to Irving Park Road, Lake View is an
increasingly lively neighbourhood that
encompasses Boystown, Chicago's main gay
and lesbian drag, and **Wrigleyville**, a name
coined by real estate types to signify the area
around Wrigley Field.
WEST SIDE Though Chicago stretches a long
way west, the area referred to in this guide as
the West Side includes the headily ethnic
locales of **Pilsen**, **Greektown**, **Little Italy**
and **Ukrainian Village**.
HYDE PARK Dominated by the University of
Chicago, this South Side neighbourhood is
also home to some splendid museums and
the rather lovely Washington Park.

the Midwest. Of course, this didn't mean a damn thing to the birds who once nested in the run-down temporary City Hall at no.209. When the current masonry structure was built in 1888, the birds' presence was remembered in the new name of the building, the **Rookery**. Two rooks at the LaSalle Street entrance still serve as characterful reminders, though a 1991 renovation ensured there is nothing dilapidated about the Rookery today. A spiral staircase climbs to the top floor of the building, and the lobby walls, redesigned by Frank Lloyd Wright in 1905, are lined with marble.

Back to finance, though, and a block south on LaSalle is one of the largest cogs in Chicago's money machinery. In 1848, a group of merchants founded the **Chicago Board of Trade** to regulate the grain futures market (*see page 52* **Making the world go round**). Today, the art deco building erected in 1930 is still the spot where deals are made for corn, wheat, soybeans, government bonds, gold and silver. On the outside of the building, sculptures of men holding wheat and corn loom over an entrance, while a 30-foot (9.1-metre) statue of Ceres, the Roman goddess of agriculture, sits appropriately atop the roof. Traders can be seen in action from a fifth floor visitors' centre overlooking the pits.

An addition to the Board of Trade was built in 1980, connecting the building via a pedestrian bridge to the **Chicago Board Options Exchange** and creating the largest contiguous trading floor space in the United States. Groups of ten or more can tour the facility, with a fourth-floor viewing room available for individuals or groups of any size.

Continuing south on LaSalle, the **One Financial Place** building (440 S LaSalle Street, at W Congress Parkway) stands above the Eisenhower Expressway. Traffic heading in or out of the Loop literally drives under the building, through arches that serve as stilts. Built in 1985 and designed by the same architects who drew the Sears Tower, it's home to the top-rated **Everest** restaurant (*see page 129*) and the Midwest Stock Exchange, the second-largest exchange in the US.

Head north-west of the Sears Tower for another glimpse of the seemingly mad business of commodity trading at the **Chicago Mercantile Exchange**. On two separate trading floors, men and women jump up and down, hollering and waving frantic hand signals as they negotiate the futures and options on foreign currencies, gold and pork bellies. Visitors' galleries – complete with educational videos to help you understand just what the hell is going on – are located above each floor.

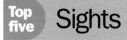

Top five | Sights

Art Institute of Chicago
Museums don't get much better than this. See page 51.

John Hancock Observatory
The Sears Tower is taller, but here's where you'll find the better views. See page 63.

Lincoln Park
A zoo, a theatre, a mausoleum... What more could you ever want? See page 72.

Museum Campus
Three great museums and a lovely lakeside view. See page 57.

Navy Pier
Everyone else goes there, and it's no surprise. See page 65.

Chicago Board Options Exchange
400 S LaSalle Street, at W Van Buren Street (800 678 4667/www.cboe.com). CTA LaSalle (Blue, Brown/Orange/Purple). **Open** 8.30am-3.15pm Mon-Fri. **Map** p305 H13.

Chicago Mercantile Exchange
30 S Wacker Drive, at W Madison Street (312 930 8249). CTA Washington (Brown/Orange/Purple). **Open** *tours* 8am-3.15pm Mon-Fri. **Map** p305 G12.

State Street

... Or 'State Street, that great street', the stuff songs are made of. Closed to traffic in 1979 to form a pedestrian mall, the stretch that made Frank Sinatra sing was reopened to vehicles in 1996. A $25-million facelift widened the streets, added landscaping and historic streetlights, and helped restore the activity that disappeared during the time the street was shut off to traffic.

Top on the list of landmarks on State is **Marshall Field's** (*see page 165*), which opened at a different location in 1852 but which has occupied its current site since 1868, despite being twice destroyed by fire (once in the Chicago Fire of 1871, and again in 1887). The store's selection of goods has grown over the years, following Marshall Field's philosophy of 'Give the lady what she wants', and today offers 75 acres (30 hectares) of merchandise in more than 400 departments.

In 1992, a $115-million, five-year renovation programme gave new life to the historic building, the second-largest department store in the United States. A Tiffany mosaic dome

Sightseeing

(c1907) still stands high above one atrium, and the historic clock at State and Randolph Streets, the inspiration for a Norman Rockwell painting that graced the cover of the *Saturday Evening Post* on 3 November 1945, still keeps perfect time; indeed, the original Rockwell hangs inside the store, near the seventh-floor visitors' centre. During the holidays, crowds line up around the building to take in the store's animated window displays.

Block 37, the public park across from Marshall Field's between E Randolph and E Washington Streets, is home to a free outdoor ice rink – **Skate on State** (*see page 232*) – during the winter months. This block was once slated to be redeveloped as another shopping centre. But when the deal and development fell through, and with the office buildings that once stood there already demolished, the city decided to dedicate the area for some much-needed green space. In the summer, the block hosts a worthy arts programme for high school students in the city.

North of Marshall Field's on State is the **Chicago Theatre** (*see page 239*). You can't miss the red vertical marquee of this former movie house, which first opened in 1928 and which today plays host to a variety of musical shows and concerts. Look south on State from Block 37, meanwhile, and you'll be face-to-face with one of Chicago's greatest restoration projects in recent history, the **Reliance Building/Hotel Burnham** (*see page 113*). Built in 1895, the Reliance Building was once one of the more elegant early Chicago skyscrapers, but years of neglect left it in disrepair. In 1994, the city bought the building and restored the grime-covered terracotta exterior to lily white. Then, in October 1999, the former office building reopened as the rather pleasant Hotel Burnham, named after famed architect Daniel Burnham, whose firm designed the building.

Carson Pirie Scott, another of Chicago's largest department stores (*see page 165*), sits to the south of Marshall Field's. Designed by Louis Sullivan in 1899, it was one of the architect's last Chicago commissions. The building stands out because of its rounded entrance and cast-iron window panels. And just off State Street at Monroe is the **Shubert Theatre**, built in 1904 and home to some of the biggest Broadway shows to visit Chicago (*see page 239*).

Chicago Theatre
175 N State Street, at E Lake Street (312 443 1130). CTA Lake, State or Washington (Red). Open box office 10am-6pm (8pm on performance nights) Mon-Fri. Tickets varies. Credit AmEx, MC, V. Map p305 H11.

Shubert Theatre
22 W Monroe Street, at S State Street (312 977 1700). CTA Monroe (Blue, Red). Open box office 10am-6pm Mon-Fri; 10am-4pm some Sats. Tickets varies. Credit AmEx, MC, V. Map p305 H12.

Randolph Street

Chicago's politics – and that of much of the surrounding area – play out in the buildings along a stretch of Randolph Street between LaSalle and Dearborn Streets. Immediately noticeable for the way it fails to blend in with its surroundings is the **James R Thompson Center**. Named after the former governor who commissioned it, the building has more than its fair share of glass and mirrors, exterior panels of red, white and blue, and a dominant salmon colouring.

Thompson called it 'a building for the 21st century' when it was dedicated in 1985, but now that the new century is upon us, most Chicagoans consider it an abomination. The interior, however, does have some redeeming features. Offices circle an indoor atrium, skylights flood the granite floor and glass elevators shoot visitors to the top of the 17-storey building. Retail stores and a food court occupy the lower levels, while state offices line the other floors. Outside the building, at the corner of Clark and Randolph, is Jean Dubuffet's black and white sculpture *Monument with Standing Beast*.

City Hall and the **County Building** (Cook County, that is) take up the block bounded by Randolph, Washington, Clark and LaSalle. The fifth floor is home to the city's mayor and city council; indeed, on good days, a meeting of the Chicago city council can be the best show in town. Over the years, performances have included screaming aldermen jumping on top of their desks, jeering crowds and even an appearance from talk-show host Jerry Springer (*see page 42* **My kind of town**). Council meetings are held every two weeks and are open to the public: call 312 744 3081 for details.

Across the street from City Hall stands the **Daley Center**, named after Chicago's long-time mayor (and father to the current mayor) Richard J Daley. Cook County's court system also has its headquarters in this rust-coloured high-rise, but the building is perhaps best known for the sculpture by Picasso that graces its plaza. No one knows for certain what the sculpture – invariably referred to only as 'the Picasso' – is supposed to represent, though the most educated guesses say it's a woman's head.

The building itself was erected in 1965, and the sculpture followed in 1967. The city's official Christmas tree is put up each year in the Daley

664 N. Michigan Avenue
Chicago, IL 60611
312.664.3939
www.terramuseum.org

Hours:
Tues 10am to 8pm
Wed–Sat 10am to 6pm
Sun noon to 5pm

Above (detail):
Charles Demuth,
Welcome to Our City,
1921, oil on canvas,
25 1/8 x 20 1/8 inches,
Terra Foundation for the Arts,
Daniel J. Terra Collection,
1993.3.

TERRA MUSEUM *of* AMERICAN ART

Center plaza, which also plays host to concerts (every weekday of the year at noon, rain or shine), farmers' markets and the occasional protest throughout the year. An eternal flame has burned in the plaza for nearly three decades in memory of the nation's war dead.

James R Thompson Center

bounded by W Lake Street, N Clark Street, W Randolph Street & N LaSalle Street (312 814 6667). CTA Washington (Brown/Orange/Purple). **Open** 8.30am-6pm Mon-Fri. **Map** p305 H11.

Richard J Daley Center

bounded by W Randolph Street, N Dearborn Street, W Washington Boulevard & N Clark Street (312 443 5500). CTA Washington (Blue, Brown/Orange/Purple, Red). **Open** 8am-4.30pm Mon-Fri. **Map** p305 H12.

Grant Park

East of the Loop along Lake Michigan is **Grant Park**, which stretches from Randolph to Roosevelt between Michigan Avenue and the lake. Built on landfill in the 1920s, the park's 220 acres (89 hectares) are home to the **Petrillo Music Shell**, annual festivals such as the **Taste of Chicago** (*see page 92*) and two rose gardens. Unfortunately, it's also nationally known as the site of riots during the 1968 Democratic National Convention. A $230-million Millennium Park is scheduled to be built in Grant Park's north-west corner by 2001, complete with newly commissioned sculptures and a band shell designed by Frank Gehry, the architect behind the Guggenheim Museum in Bilbao, Spain. The new band shell, which will be topped with curling ribbons of steel, is expected to have seating for 4,000, with the lawn accommodating another 3,000 people.

Today, Grant Park's most recognisable feature is **Buckingham Fountain** (in operation from 1 May until mid-October), a gift to the city in 1927 from the family of Clarence Buckingham, a trustee and benefactor of the Art Institute. The fountain, which was modelled after the fountain at Versailles only to twice its size and which uses more than a million gallons of water, symbolises Lake Michigan and is surrounded by a pool edged by four bronze sea horses representing Michigan, Illinois, Minnesota and Wisconsin, the four states that border the lake. Framed by more than 5,000 rose bushes, the pink marble fountain is lit in the evening, making it a popular attraction.

Smack bang in the centre of Grant Park, two lions – animated versions of whom roar at Bulls fans prior to games on a local TV station – guard the entrance to the **Art Institute of Chicago**, one of Chicago's most magnificent edifices and one of the world's great museums.

Going up... **City Hall**. *See page 49.*

Opened in 1879 as a school and museum, the Art Institute grew into a world-famous museum known for its collections of Impressionist and post-Impressionist paintings. Among the most famous pieces are Picasso's *The Old Guitarist*, Seurat's *A Sunday on La Grande Jette – 1884* (which Ferris Bueller ogled at on his day off), Edward Hopper's *Nighthawks* and Grant Wood's *American Gothic*, though the museum also holds numerous Van Goghs, Magrittes, Matisses, Whistlers, Homers, Monets and Renoirs. Less celebrated but equally worthy are the Asian, medieval, modern and Renaissance art collections, while other diversions include a faithfully rebuilt model of the old Chicago Stock Exchange, a sculpture garden, a paperweight collection, and Kraft's Education Center, which has dozens of games to keep children interested during what could well be a whole day's visit.

Just north of Grant Park along Michigan Avenue sits the **Carbide & Carbon Building** (230 N Michigan Avenue, at S Water Street). Designed in 1929 by the sons of city planner Daniel Burnham, the green terracotta tower is trimmed in gold leaf, while the building also has a base of polished granite and an awe-inspiring lobby of marble with glass ornamentation. Slightly south on Michigan Avenue is the **Stone Container Building**

(150 N Michigan Avenue, at E Randolph Street), built in 1983 and home to Yaacov Agam's aluminium sculpture, *Communication X9*. It's an appropriate name, since this is the first Chicago building to be wired throughout for computer use.

Meanwhile, to the east on Randolph Street is the **Amoco Building** (200 E Randolph Street, at N Columbus Drive). The second-tallest building in Chicago, it was formerly known as the Standard Oil building. *Sounding*, a 1975 sculpture by Harry Bertoia, stands in a reflecting pool in the building's lower level plaza. The **Prudential Building** (130 E Randolph Street, at N Stetson Avenue) to the west displays an exterior form of the Rock of Gibraltar, the company's trademark. The building was the tallest in the city for about a decade after it was built in 1955.

Art Institute of Chicago

111 S Michigan Avenue, at W Adams Street (312 443 3600). CTA Adams or Jackson (Red). **Open** 10.30am-4.30pm Mon, Wed-Fri; 10.30am-8pm Tue; 10am-5pm Sat; noon-5pm Sun. **Admission** $8; $5 concessions; free under-5s; all free Tue. **Credit** AmEx, DC, Disc, MC, V. **Map** p305 J12.

Michigan Avenue

Though it's the stretch of Michigan Avenue north of the river that's known as the Magnificent Mile, Michigan Avenue in the Loop

Making the world go round

A statue of Ceres, the goddess of agriculture, sits placidly atop the 45-storey **Chicago Board of Trade**, the world's oldest and largest futures exchange. Formed in 1848 by 82 traders in order to stabilise the grain trade, the CBOT set a new world volume record in 1998 with over 281 million contracts traded. Inside, the huge trading floor – the Money Pit – is anything but placid. Trading in the Pit, so called because of its amphitheatrical shape, operates on an 'open outcry' system: each trader shouts out the price and quantity of the commodity he is selling to prospective buyers, using hand signals to clarify and firm up deals. How stressful is the pit? Well, consider that in 1996, the US Military sent marines into trading pits at the New York Mercantile Exchange to learn all about split-second decision-making.

Adding to the bizarre nature of this financial war zone, CBOT traders are required to wear ties and jackets, but they don't go for your average Ralph Lauren blue blazer. Instead, the exigencies of quick movements and perspiration led to the evolution of the trading vest: an invariably outlandish, garish cross between hunting vest and rodeo clown garb, tricked out with a name badge and ID card. Members of the same brokerage firm wear the same colour jackets for easy identification in the tense, make-or-break madness of the Pit. With all the torn-up contracts littering the floor, you'd be forgiven for thinking the Super Bowl Bears just had a ticker-tape parade through the building. But what's all the fuss about?

Futures, that's what. Futures are legally binding agreements to buy or sell a commodity some time in the future, and everything is standardised (quality, time of delivery, location, etc) except price. Bottom line: this forward pricing helps businesses manage risk. A full explanation would be impossible here, though should you be sufficiently interested, take a visit to the CBOT's fifth floor Agricultural Visitors' Gallery, which has an observation window that provides front-row seats to this make-or-break world. There's a guided tour that runs every half-hour, with a much more complete explanation of futures trading, plus there's a worthwhile CBOT video, 'A Window on Futures'. If you're more of the self-help type, there are also taped explanations of market principles in ten languages. Try Chinese: you'll probably have about as much chance of understanding the action below.

Better yet, leave the tour part to the high school kids and hang out at the observation window for as long as possible to enjoy showtime down on the floor. See if you can pick out the guy who just made $70,000 on corn, or just lost $100,000 on soybeans. You won't feel so guilty next time you buy a $1 lottery ticket.

Chicago Board of Trade

Agricultural Visitors' Center, Fifth Floor, 141 W Jackson Boulevard, at S LaSalle Street, The Loop (312 435 3590). **Open** 8am-2pm Mon-Fri; *tours* every half-hour 9am-1.30pm (reservations required for groups of ten or more). **Map** p305 H13.

is scarcely any less lovely. A grand, open street that opens out into Grant Park, it's densely packed with buildings and sights of no little cultural interest.

The **Chicago Cultural Center**, a block-long building that sits proudly on Michigan between Randolph and Washington, was built in 1897 and offers a great deal for the architectural and design connoisseur: two Tiffany domes, a grand marble staircase, several glass mosaics and, on its exterior, a wool cloth displaying the names of famous authors. Art exhibitions, lectures and free concerts are held here on a regular basis, and it's an invaluable resource for cultural information: anyone seeking tourist information, theatre, dance, choral programmes or a wealth of cultural exhibits will find it here.

Be sure not to miss the **Museum of Broadcast Communications** while you're here. As well as offering lectures, simulcasts and Smithsonian-esque television relics – including pieces from the set of the famed 1960 Kennedy/Nixon presidential debate – you can also read the news (and pick up a video of your efforts), listen to your favourite radio legends, hear instant replays of the greatest moments in sports in the Sportsman's Café, and sit in the audience for a live radio broadcast. The AC Nielsen, Jr Research Center archives contain 10,000 television shows, 50,000 hours of radio, 9,000 television commercials and 2,500 hours of radio. How's that for channel surfing?

Close by is the **Hellenic Museum & Cultural Center**. Dedicated to the preservation of Greek culture, it derives many of its pieces from the collections of local Greek families. Impressively instructive in relating the history of Greeks in America and in Chicago in particular, the Hellenic Museum is in the midst of fundraising for a planned research facility and library to be built elsewhere in the city.

Located in a storefront right off the Magnificent Mile, the **Chicago Athenaeum** is a privately owned museum of architecture and design, the only independently operating facility of its kind in the country. Featuring examples of everything from industrial design (household appliances, china, etc) and graphic design (artful packaging) to film and photo archives, the Athenaeum's collection of both local and international design is impressive, and its gift shop divine.

The **Symphony Center** (see page 217), located just across the street from the Art Institute, is home to the Chicago Symphony Orchestra. Made up of three wings connected by a central rotunda, the facility encompasses the 1904 Orchestra Hall, home to more than 200 concerts per year, a park, a restaurant, a store

and an education and administration wing. There's also ECHO, a rather clunky acronym for the Eloise W Martin Center of the Chicago Symphony Orchestra, a hands-on learning centre for children and adults. The six-storey building underwent a multi-million-dollar restoration that was completed in 1997, just as its resident band have gone from strength to strength under the baton of the mighty Daniel Barenboim (see page 216 **My kind of town**).

Down the block from the Symphony Center is the **Santa Fe Building** (224 S Michigan Avenue, at E Jackson Boulevard), designed in 1904 by Daniel Burnham. Inside the building is the marvellous **Chicago Architecture Foundation**, which offers lectures and more than 50 tours covering Chicago on foot, bus and bicycle. Dedicated to furthering public interest in architecture, the foundation offers a wealth of exhibits detailing the rich architectural heritage of the city, and also sells guidebooks, maps, toys and children's books alongside an exhibition gallery. However, the jewel in its crown are the boat tours it operates, which provide more interesting insights into the city's stunning architecture than you thought possible. When it comes to taking a boat tour down the river – and every visitor to Chicago should – then accept no imitations. See page 82 **Tours**, and chapter **Architecture**.

The **Fine Arts Building** at 410 S Michigan Avenue once housed the showrooms of the Studebaker Company, which in 1895 was showing carriages rather than cars. In 1889, it was converted into a theatre on the first floor and studios on the upper floors, and the words 'All Passes – Art Alone Endures' were carved just inside the entrance. Music practice rooms and offices now surround an interior courtyard and an operator runs the creaky old elevators. Frank Lloyd Wright had a studio here at one time, as did L Frank Baum of Wizard of Oz fame. The first floor was converted to the **Fine Arts Theatre** in 1992, and today shows art, foreign and independent films over four screens (see page 198).

The **Auditorium Building**, a stone's toss away from the Fine Arts Building, is sometimes billed as the building that put Chicago on the cultural map. It was conceived in 1885 just as the city was gearing up for the World's Columbian Exposition of 1893. In 1889, President Benjamin Harrison dedicated the theatre, which was designed by Louis Sullivan and Dankmar Adler as the first home of the Chicago Opera Company, though it also went on to house the Chicago Symphony Orchestra prior to the opening of Orchestra Hall. During World War II, though, it was converted into a servicemen's centre, and the massive stage area

Sightseeing

was used as – of all things – a bowling alley. And in 1946, nearby Roosevelt University bought the entire building and renovated a 400-room hotel into offices and classrooms.

However, in 1960 the Auditorium Theater Council was formed and raised $3 million for the building's restoration; it reopened in 1967. (This fundraising eventually led to a legal battle in 1996 over whether it should be the council or the university that controlled the theatre's pocketbook.) It's now on the National Register of Historic Places, and plays host to touring productions of shows such as *Les Misérables* and *Miss Saigon*. Tours of the building can be arranged.

Auditorium Building

430 S Michigan Avenue, at E Congress Parkway (312 922 4046/tours 312 431 2354). CTA Harrison or Library. **Open** *theatre box office* 10am-6pm Mon-Sat; *tours* by appointment. **Tickets** *theatre* $12-$100. **Credit** AmEx, DC, MC, V. **Map** p305 J13.

Chicago Architecture Foundation

224 S Michigan Avenue, at E Jackson Boulevard (312 922 3432/www.architecture.org). CTA Adams or Jackson (Red). **Open** 9am-7pm daily. **Map** p305 J12.

Chicago Athenaeum

6 N Michigan Avenue, at E Madison Street (312 251 0175). CTA Madison. **Open** 11am-6pm Tue-Sat; noon-5pm Sun. **Admission** $3; $2 concessions. **Credit** AmEx, MC, V. **Map** p305 J12.

Chicago Cultural Center

78 E Washington Boulevard, at N Michigan Avenue (312 346 3278). CTA Randolph or Washington (Blue, Red). **Open** 10am-7pm Mon-Wed; 10am-9pm Thur; 10am-6pm Fri; 10am-5pm Sat; 11am-5pm Sun. **Admission** free. **Map** p305 J12.

Hellenic Museum & Cultural Center

Fourth Floor, Atlantic Bank Building, 168 N Michigan Avenue, at E Randolph Street (312 726 1234). CTA Lake, State or Randolph. **Open** 10am-4pm Mon-Fri. **Admission** *suggested donation* $4. **Credit** MC, V. **Map** p305 J11.

Museum of Broadcast Communications

Chicago Cultural Center, 78 E Washington Boulevard, at N Michigan Avenue (312 629 6000). CTA Randolph or Washington (Blue, Red). **Open** 10am-4.30pm Mon-Sat; noon-5pm Sun. **Admission** free. **Map** p305 J12.

West Loop

The **Civic Opera House**, put simply, is a lovely building. Home to the Lyric Opera since 1950 and located by the river at S Wacker Drive and W Madison Street, the Civic houses a lavish art deco auditorium adorned in red and orange with gold leaf accents; with a capacity of over

3,500, it's the second-largest opera house in the country. Renovated in 1996, the 1929 building still has the terracotta and bronze forms of a trumpet, lyre and the masks of tragedy and comedy on its interior and exterior walls (*see page 215*).

The Loop extends west over the Chicago River to encompass the **Citicorp Center**, home to the **Richard B Ogilvie Transportation Center** (aka Northwestern Station; 500 W Madison Street, at N Canal Street) and the former Northwestern Atrium Center. Further south, **Union Station** (210 S Canal Street, at W Adams Street; 312 655 2385) lays easy claim to the title of Chicago's most famous train station. A baby carriage was caught in a shoot-out on the steep stairway from Canal Street to the waiting area in Brian De Palma's 1987 movie *The Untouchables*, though in real life, it's a far less outrageous place. Thousands of riders pass through the station daily on Amtrak and suburban commuter trains, as sunlight streams through skylights ten storeys high and onto the columns and statues lined up inside the station, which was built in 1925 and restored in 1992.

Not even this part of town has escaped the vogue for sculpture. Outside the Social Security Administration Building at 600 W Madison Street, catch a glimpse of Claes Oldenburg's sculpture *Batcolumn*, a 100-foot (30.5-metre) high baseball bat that cynics maintain is nothing more than the largest phallic statue on earth. Cross back over the river to see *Dawn Shadows*, a black steel sculpture at 200 W Madison Street. Designed in 1983 by Louise Nevelson, it was inspired by the elevated train tracks that rise above it.

Inner Loop

Rising 400 feet (122 metres) above ground, the **Chicago Temple** is known as the 'Chapel in the Sky'. The headquarters of the First United Methodist Church of Chicago has an eight-storey spire visible only from a distance, a sanctuary and office space.

On an exterior first level wall, a series of stained-glass windows depict the church's history in Chicago. Joan Miró's 93-foot (28-metre) tall sculpture *Chicago* sits in a small plaza to the east. It's one of a great many sculptures in the Loop and one of the best. Just a couple of blocks away is another outstanding piece of city art: Marc Chagall's 70-foot (21-metre) long mosaic *The Four Seasons*, which stands in the **First National Bank Plaza** (bounded by Dearborn, Clark, Monroe and Madison). It's a popular spot with picnickers, musicians and artists in warm weather.

Sightseeing

A view to a thrill

Spend any time in downtown Chicago and you'll realise this city is full of spectacular vistas, most of which take in the mightily impressive architecture of the city. Some of them are free for the gawking, while others will cost you a small admission fee.

As you may well be aware, the **Sears Tower Skydeck** tops most tourists' lists. For a few bucks, you can take a 20mph-elevator ride to the top and take in views that can stretch 80 miles in all directions. Before you go, make sure the skies are clear: in inclement weather, the top half of the building is typically sheathed in thick clouds, while crisp, cold winter days offer the best visibility. Try and arrive before noon to beat the droves of elementary school field trips and bus-borne tour groups. And don't panic if you feel the floor moving: on windy days, the building tends to sway in the breeze, as evidenced by the water sloshing around in the observation deck toilet bowls.

However, superior to the Sears Tower's Skydeck is the **John Hancock Center's Signature Room at the 95th.** Thanks to the Hancock's location in the thick of things on Michigan Avenue, the views from the restaurant and bar are more dynamic than those from the Sears, way down in the Loop. If dinner in the Signature Room is too rich for your blood (entree prices range from $23 to $30, after all), you can hang with the rest of the tourists.

Ironically, the bar's biggest attraction, its spectacular views, are also its biggest liability. What should be the world's coolest cocktail lounge is packed with Hawaiian shirt-clad tourists and giddy, boisterous

---

Head a block east on Monroe and stop in the **Palmer House Hilton**, if only to marvel at the elegant lobby. Up one flight of stairs, the posh room has murals on the ceiling, exquisite furniture and lush carpeting, all reminiscent of the fine hotels once common in this area (*see page 103*). A block further south on Adams is another holdover from days or yore: the **Berghoff** restaurant (*see page 129*). Built in 1872, it served as an outdoor beer garden for the World's Columbian Exposition, and today is one of only two buildings with cast-iron fronts still left in the city (the other is the **Page Brothers Building** at 177 N State Street, at E Lake Street).

Chicago Temple

77 W Washington Street, at N Clark Street (312 236 4548/www.chicagotemple.org). CTA Washington (Blue, Brown/Orange/Purple, Red). **Open** *Sanctuary* 7am-7pm daily; *tours* 2pm Mon-Sat; after noon service Sun; *services* 9am, noon. **Map** p305 H12.

South Loop

When the 16-storey **Monadnock Building** was erected in 1891, at 53 W Jackson Boulevard, at S Dearborn Street, it was the tallest and heaviest load-bearing structure in the world. Today, it's still the world's tallest all-masonry building, and in order to support the great weight, the building's walls are six feet (1.8 metres) thick at the base and thin out as the building rises.

The top 16 floors of the **Metropolitan Correctional Center**, a triangular-shaped building at 71 W Van Buren Street, house federal prisoners and suspects awaiting trial. Windows on those floors can be only five inches wide, the maximum size allowed by the Federal Department of Corrections – so small that no bars are required – and a total of 44 prisoners can be held here at one time. Administrative offices occupy the bottom 11 floors, so don't worry if the windows there look a little large.

Welcome respite comes courtesy of the **Harold Washington Library Center**, named after Chicago's first African-American mayor and located at the southern tip of the Loop on State Street. The second-largest public library in the world, it houses more than two million volumes. Built in 1991 of granite and brick with a terracotta exterior, the building blends in with its long-standing neighbours, borrowing details from some of Chicago's most famous structures. Inside is a 400-seat auditorium theatre, an 18,000-square-foot (1674-square-metre) children's library, the Chicago Blues Archives, and the Jazz, Blues and Gospel Hall of Fame.

South and east of the library – right by the **Museum of Contemporary Photography**, in fact (*see page 187*) – is the **Spertus Museum**. Created to reflect the rich diversity of Jewish culture, the Spertus offers an impressive collection of artefacts from all over the world, including ancient Torah scrolls.

Harold Washington Library

400 S State Street, at W Congress Parkway (312 747 4999/www.chipublib.org). CTA Jackson (Blue, Red) or Library. **Open** 9am-7pm Mon, Tue; 11am-7pm Wed, Fri, Sat; 9am-5pm Thur; 1-5pm Sun. **Map** p305 H13.

suburbanites on their annual foray into the Big City. Still, don't be a snob: sit and have a drink. It's sure to be the best $6 Miller Lite you've ever had. Keep one eye on your glass and the other on that soon-to-be-vacated table closer to the windows. If you stay long enough, you'll eventually work your way towards the best seats in the house.

Visitors with wheels – or enough money to luxuriate in a cab – can enjoy two very different but equally incredible views of the skyline: travelling north up **Lake Shore Drive** from the South Side, with Gold Coast high-rises to your left and the sapphire expanse of Lake Michigan to the right; or heading south on the **Kennedy Expressway** between the Fullerton on-ramp and the Loop. Get off at the Ogden exit and head for **La Borsa** (375 N Morgan Street, at E Kinzie Street), a hip Italian restaurant in a shabby-chic warehouse district, where you can sip a nice Chianti on the patio with the north–south spread of the

city providing a thrilling backdrop. Failing that, head over to **Navy Pier**, where for a few bucks you can buy a seat on any one of a variety of tour boats for an hour-long sightseeing excursion on Lake Michigan.

It doesn't end there, either. While passing over the **Michigan Avenue Bridge** in the heart of the downtown shopping district, look west up the river into the heart of the city. Or when knocking about the Theatre District, take a detour over to **LaSalle Street**, where the high-rises that line both sides of the narrow street create a kind of urban canyon that terminates at the art deco-style Chicago Board of Trade building. And if in you're Greektown, head to the **Pegasus** restaurant (*see page 131*) and grab a drink on the rooftop terrace for some terrific views of the skyline.

Of course, you don't have to go searching for spectacular views in Chicago. Keep your eyes peeled: around every corner, sometimes when you least expect it, they'll find you.

Spertus Museum

Spertus Institute of Jewish Studies, 618 S Michigan Avenue, at E Harrison Street (312 322 1747). CTA Harrison. **Open** 10am-5pm Mon-Wed, Sun; 10am-8pm Thur; 10am-3pm Fri. **Admission** $5; $3 concessions. **Map** p305 J13.

Museum Campus

No prizes for guessing what the dominant attractions are around these parts. The area in question – a small pocket of culture south of the Loop, near Soldier Field – was only christened in the late 1990s, after Lake Shore Drive was shunted away from the lake. The three attractions – the Adler Planetarium, the Shedd Aquarium and the Field Museum – that had long called the area home finally became more accessible to pedestrians, who can now skip merrily between the three without risking being turned into roadkill by the passing traffic.

Any comprehensive tour of Chicago's museums really ought to start at this large, grassy quad. A veritable ground zero of Chicago tourism, the Museum Campus is equivalent to a mid-sized city park in area and holds the nation's oldest planetarium, largest aquarium and one of the world's finest anthropological resource centres. Get off the El at Harrison and take a slight detour via the **Buckingham Fountain** (*see page 51*); you'll be left with a 20-minute walk down to the museums along the lake path, which on a sunny day is among the loveliest strolls in the city.

The 1930 building that holds the **Adler Planetarium** is a 12-sided architectural marvel, each side representing a sign of the zodiac. It's home to the dome-topped Sky Theatre, where star shows are played out daily, and the Gravitation Station, which lets visitors experiment with mass, speed and distance to create their own model of the solar system on a computer. A recent $40-million facelift added the StarRider Theatre (an interactive, virtual-reality voyage of discovery 'into space'), four new exhibition galleries and Galileo's, a café with incomparable view of the skyline. A 3D tour of the Milky Way galaxy explores Earth's role in the universe, while the museum also holds one of the world's largest collections of historically significant scientific instruments; like the rest of the museum, it's interactive, interesting and kid-friendly without being dumbed-down.

The **Field Museum of Natural History** opened as part of the World's Columbian Exposition in 1893 as the Columbia Museum of Chicago. It was renamed after philanthropist and department store magnate Marshall Field in the early 1900s, and moved into its jaw-droppingly multi-storeyed location soon after. A must-see for anyone visiting Chicago, the museum is one of the most impressive natural science centres in the world, with a wealth of biological and anthropological exhibits and a world-class on-site research facility. One of the world's largest T-Rex dinosaurs, dubbed 'Sue' by museum workers, is newly on display alongside the famed (stuffed) lions of Tsavo, the man-eating creatures made famous in the

The **Lyric Opera**: where fat ladies (and gentlemen) sing. *See page 55.*

Michael Douglas movie *The Ghost and the Darkness*. Kid-friendly exhibits abound, but adults will be similarly entranced.

And as if those two aren't enough to be going on with, Museum Campus is also home to arguably the best aquarium in the country. The **John G Shedd Aquarium** is housed in a beautiful, circular lakefront building that holds every conceivable kind of fish and water mammal, as well as underwater cameras and a host of other high-tech devices that allow visitors to get closer to life underwater than ever before. But it's the education-oriented Oceanarium that is the facility's true gem. Penguins, dolphins, otters, seals and whales are shown in approximations of their natural habitat, and the water shows, in which trainers coax the mammals into a series of non-degrading jumps and dives, are a must-see for any city visitor. Tickets for the Oceanarium are available from Ticketmaster (312 559 0200); try and buy ahead of time, as it does get very busy.

Adler Planetarium

1300 S Lake Shore Drive, at E Solidarity Drive (312 322 0590/www.adlerplanetarium.org). CTA Roosevelt/State or Roosevelt/Wabash. **Open** 9am-5pm Mon-Thur; 9am-9pm Fri; 9am-6pm Sat, Sun. **Admission** *museum* $5; free Tue; *shows* $5. **Credit** AmEx, Disc, MC, V.

Field Museum of Natural History

1400 S Lake Shore Drive, at E Roosevelt Road (312 922 9410/www.fieldmuseum.org). CTA Roosevelt/

State or Roosevelt/Wabash. **Open** 9am-5pm daily. **Admission** $7; $4 concessions; free under-3s, all on Wed. **Credit** AmEx, Disc, MC, V. **Map** p305 J14.

John G Shedd Aquarium

1200 S Lake Shore Drive, at E McFetridge Drive (312 939 2438/www.sheddnet.org). CTA Roosevelt/State or Roosevelt/Wabash. **Open** *Sept-May* 9am-5pm Mon-Fri; 9am-6pm Sat, Sun; *June-Aug* 9am-6pm daily. **Admission** *Tue-Sun* aquarium & oceanarium $11; $9 concessions; free under-3s. *Mon* aquarium free; oceanarium $6; $5 concessions. **Credit** AmEx, Disc, MC, V. **Map** p305 K14.

Near North

North of the Chicago River and – though it's extremely ill-defined – east of Clark Street, the River North entertainment district lures visitors with an almost dizzying array of bars, restaurants and galleries. The stretch of Michigan Avenue known as the Magnificent Mile is all about shopping, shopping, shopping. East of Michigan Avenue is Streeterville, home to Navy Pier, the Museum of Contemporary Art and an array of hotels. Together, these three neighbourhoods make up the area known as Near North, the hub of Chicago consumerism in every imaginable way.

Settled by Irish immigrants in the 1840s, **River North** was a largely industrial area until the end of World War I, when many of the factories began to fail; soon, buildings were snatched up for use as warehouses. The area hit bottom during the 1950s, when even the stately old homes were converted into low-rent apartments. But by the 1970s, a turnaround was occurring, as abandoned buildings were transformed into artists' studios and late-night dance clubs, and entertainment venues opened at a furious rate. These days, the area's so brightly lit and its streets so populated in the wee small hours of the morning that it's sometimes hard to tell what time it is.

The affluent **Magnificent Mile** and **Streeterville** have likewise climbed to their current status from rather humble beginnings. More than a century ago, much of the area was covered with water. When a thug from Milwaukee named Captain George Wellington Streeter grounded his boat on a sand bar between Oak Street and Chicago Avenue in the late 1880s, he claimed the land as his own and promptly began collecting money from building contractors to dump their trash there. Soon, the area now known as Streeterville grew to nearly 200 acres (89 hectares) of shacks and saloons. The courts ordered Streeter's removal and the burning of the shanties in 1918, and wealthy settlers who made the Near North area their home throughout the 19th century eventually laid claim to the area. It is now home to some of the city's most beautiful homes and expensive real estate. Indeed, the **John Hancock Center** today towers on the spot rumoured to have been the location of Captain Streeter's own shanty.

River North & surrounds

Low rents attracted artists and developers to the huge, empty warehouses in River North in the 1970s. Easily converted into studios, galleries, shops and restaurants, the buildings today form one of the hippest neighbourhoods in Chicago. The area between Chicago, Orleans, Erie and Wells known as the **River North Gallery District** – and SuHu, after the streets on which most of the galleries are found (Superior and Huron) – contains more than 65 art galleries, all of which welcome casual visitors. Most galleries are closed on Mondays; Friday nights are generally the nights for new show openings. *See chapter* **Art Galleries** and pick up a copy of *Chicago Gallery News* at the Water Tower visitors' centre for more information.

The area's popularity with young artists is nothing new. Lambert Tree, a lawyer and philanthropist, built **Tree Studios** at 4 E Ohio Street, at N State Street as an affordable home for Chicago artists in 1894. Galleries and art-supply stores filled the lower level, with 17 studios in the upper level surrounding a courtyard behind Tree's home. Most of the city's best-known artists have lived or worked here. Nowadays, artists share the space with the **Medinah Temple Association**, whose main building stands where Tree's home stood. The faces of Lambert and his wife Ann can be seen in carvings near the Ohio Street entrance.

Though there are a number of galleries in the area, there aren't too many museums. The main exception is the first and only museum of its kind in the country: the **Peace Museum**, co-founded by a former US Ambassador to UNICEF. A non-profit educational and cultural centre, it contains a large collection of anti-war memorabilia, including photos, quilts, paintings, a manuscript from Bono of U2 and one of John Lennon's guitars, donated by Yoko Ono.

Several blocks south-east stands the former nemesis of Chicago's criminal contingent. **Courthouse Place** (54 W Hubbard Street, at N Dearborn Street), the former Cook County Courts building, was built in 1892 as the second county courts facility (the first was torn down because it was too small, which unintentionally speaks volumes about the city's crime problems at the time). Courthouse Place is now an office building, but if the walls could talk they would surely tell some of the greatest legal stories of the city's history: that of the impassioned performance in 1924 of famed attorney Clarence Darrow, say, which saved convicted murderers Nathan Leopold and Richard Loeb from a certain death sentence (*see page 16*). Carl Sandburg was a reporter here in the 1920s, as was Ben Hecht, co-author of *The Front Page*.

As if by way of contrast, the area also provides much of interest for the religious. The large brick **Moody Bible Institute** is home to hundreds of Christian students, who study for religious careers. The Moody Bookstore, also located here, is Chicago's largest Christian bookstore, selling a huge selection of Christian music and compact discs, Bibles and books on family, faith, finances and marriage.

In a city predominantly populated by Catholics, **Holy Name Cathedral** has served as the cathedral of the Catholic Archdiocese of Chicago for more than a century. Built between 1874 and 1875, more than 5,000 people attended the Victorian Gothic cathedral's dedication and parade. Pope John Paul II visited here in 1979, and Luciano Pavarotti and the Chicago Symphony Orchestra have performed in the sanctuary, notable for its ornate wooden ceiling and huge organ loft. A funeral mass for Harry Caray, the beloved long-time broadcaster for the Chicago Cubs, was celebrated here in 1998.

North-east of Holy Name Cathedral sits the **Quigley Seminary & St James Chapel**, often referred to as 'a jewel' for its perfect

Sightseeing

acoustics and 14 stained-glass windows, which contain more than half a million pieces of glass. The seminary is named after Chicago's Archbishop James Quigley, who established a school in 1905 to prepare boys for the priesthood. Designed in 1917 and 1925, the Gothic buildings and courtyard were modelled after the Sainte-Chapelle in Paris. Tours of the chapel are held four days a week; call ahead to book your spot.

And then there's the **Episcopal Cathedral of St James**, first built in 1857 and rebuilt in 1875 following the Chicago Fire of 1871. The unusual interior walls of the cathedral are pure Arts and Crafts, decorated with stencil patterns in more than 20 colours; you'd never guess it by looking at the traditionally Gothic exterior. Originally dreamt up by a New York architect in 1888, the designs were restored in 1985. It's Chicago's oldest Episcopal church.

Back down by the water stands a monument to consumerism that rivals any on the Magnificent Mile. Originally built in 1931 as showrooms and a wholesale office for Marshall Field, the **Merchandise Mart** is the one of the largest buildings in the United States, second only to the Pentagon with 4.2 million square feet (390,000 square metres) of floor space. Field sold the building to Joseph P Kennedy of the famed political family when the Mart hit financial hard times in the 1930s, and it was Kennedy who had the compellingly freakish Merchandise Mart Hall of Fame installed in 1953, commemorating retail titans such as Marshall Field, Edward A Filene and FW Woolworth. Today, though most of the Merchandise Mart's 600-plus showrooms are open only to merchants and designers, they still manage to attract around 10,000 visitors a day;

The Terra way

Operating out of a storefront location on the Magnificent Mile, the comparatively little-known **Terra Museum of American Art** has long been neglected in favour of splashier museums like the Art Institute. However, the Terra offers one of the country's greatest collections of American art, centring largely upon Impressionists like Mary Cassatt, with a similarly impressive repository of art from early 20th-century masters like James Whistler and Winslow Homer.

The Terra Museum was founded in the Chicago suburb of Evanston in 1980 by Daniel J Terra, a former United States Ambassador at Large for Cultural Affairs under Ronald Reagan, and an avid collector of art. The museum moved to its present, compact Michigan Avenue location in 1987, where it was promptly ignored both by tourists and by locals. Indeed, tens of thousands of people still pass by the Terra Museum every day without realising it even exists.

From the outside, the marbled façade of the Terra may seem unexceptional, but it holds more than 700 paintings, prints and sculptures, including works by Cole, Church, Wyeth and John Singer Sargent. Later 20th-century stars like Edward Hopper and Georgia O'Keefe are also well represented. Morse's famed *Gallery of the Louvre* hangs here, too, as does one of the world's most comprehensive collections (69 pieces, at the last count) of work by Maurice and Charles Prendergast.

The multi-levelled museum vaguely recollects, however inadvertently, the Guggenheim museum in New York City. Like the Guggenheim, the Terra's collections can be viewed from many levels at once, though the narrow design of the Terra – which came courtesy of Booth/Hansen in 1987 – was likely born of necessity, given the building's location on high-toned, built-up Michigan Avenue.

Before his death, Daniel Terra also opened the excellent Musée d'Art Americain in Giverny, France, with the stated purpose of bringing American culture to the presumably resistant French. Run by the Terra Foundation, the Musée is a sister museum of sorts to the Terra, and is similarly focused on educating often-reluctant natives about the enduring value of American art and artists.

In keeping with its goal of making access to art affordable and unintimidating, the American outlet of the Terra Museum also offers a great series of family programmes and guest lecturers. It also may be the only museum in Chicago that gives free access to teachers and veterans.

Terra Museum of American Art

664 N Michigan Avenue, at E Erie Street (312 664 3939). CTA Grand. **Open** 10am-8pm Tue; 10am-6pm Wed-Sat; noon-5pm Sun. **Admission** $7; $3.50 concessions; free students, under-14s, teachers, veterans, all on Tue & 1st Sun of month. **Credit** AmEx, MC, V. **Map** p306 J10.

A bunch of art at the **Tree Studios**. *See page 59.*

tours of the showrooms are available, though the lower two levels have been open to the public as a retail shopping mall since 1991.

Head two blocks east, and you'll be reaching for your camera. No, not another mammoth skyscraper or major architectural achievement, but rather the hysterically huge Quaker Oats box that fills the lobby of the **Quaker Oats Building** (321 N Clark Street), designed in 1987. A block away, though, and you'll be under the spectacular **Marina City** towers at 300 N State Street, known throughout town as the Corncobs (it'll be obvious why). The towers house trapezoid-shaped apartments on the top 40 floors, with the lower 20 used for parking. Designed as 'a city within a city' in 1959, the complex combines residential use with entertainment: the **House of Blues** *(see page 209)*, **AMF Marina City Lanes** *(see page 228)* and several restaurants are all located in the same development.

A little further north on Kinzie Street, and you'll catch sight of a monstrous sign reading 'Holy Cow!'. As any baseball fan will know, that was the signature cry of Cubs broadcaster Harry Caray, whose restaurant, imaginatively named **Harry Caray's** *(see page 132)*, carries on serving burgers and the like even though the man himself died in 1998. The Flemish Gothic building, designed in 1895, looks like it belongs amid the windmills of Amsterdam. Inside, the bar is 60 feet, six inches long – the distance from the pitcher's mound to home plate – and

the entire bar joins in to sing *Take Me Out to the Ballgame* every night at 7.30pm, a tribute to Harry and his trademark routine during seventh-inning stretch at Wrigley Field.

Slightly further north-east from here is North Bridge. Part bona fide area – it's ostensibly bounded by Michigan, Hubbard, State and Ontario – and part facile buzzword, it's where you'll find some of Chicago's glitziest and swankiest tourist spots. **ESPN Zone** *(see page 147)* and **DisneyQuest** *(see page 192)* are just two of the many attractions here that will keep the kids happy for hours. If not days.

Episcopal Church of St James
*65 E Huron Street, at N Wabash Avenue (312 787 7360). CTA Chicago (Red). **Open** services 12.10pm Mon, Tue, Thur, Fri; 12.10pm, 5.30pm Wed; 9am Sat; 8am, 9am, 11am Sun. **Map** p306 H10.*

Holy Name Cathedral
*735 N State Street, at E Superior Street (312 787 8040). CTA Chicago (Red). **Open** 6am-6pm Mon-Fri. **Map** p306 H10.*

Merchandise Mart
*between N Wells Street & N Orleans Street, along the Chicago River (312 644 4664). CTA Merchandise Mart. **Open** tours noon Mon-Fri. **Map** p306 G11.*

Moody Bible Institute
*150 W Chicago Avenue, at N LaSalle Street (bookstore 312 329 4352). CTA Chicago (Brown/Purple, Red). **Open** bookstore 8am-7pm Mon-Fri; 9am-6pm Sat. **Map** p306 H10.*

Peace Museum

314 W Institute Drive, at N Franklin Street (312 440 1860). CTA Chicago (Brown/Purple). **Open** 11am-5pm Tue-Sat. **Admission** *suggested donation* $3.50; $2 concessions. **Map** p306 G9.

Quigley Seminary & St James Chapel

831 N Rush Street, at E Pearson Street (312 787 9343). CTA Chicago (Red). **Open** 7.30am-4pm Mon-Fri. **Map** p306 J9.

Magnificent Mile

Opened at the south end of Michigan Avenue in 1920, the Michigan Avenue Bridge was a boon to the area north of the Chicago River, making access to the Loop that much easier for residents and businessmen. A plaque at the south-east end of the bridge commemorates Fort Dearborn (the military outpost from which the city developed), while bronze bricks in the sidewalk on the south-east corner of Wacker Drive and Michigan Avenue mark the spot where the fort's actual walls once stood. Four sculptures on pylons along the bridge represent major Chicago events: the city's exploration by Jolliet and Marquette, trader Jean Baptiste Point du Sable's settlement, the massacre at Fort Dearborn in 1812 and the rebuilding following the Chicago Fire of 1871. (For details of these events, *see chapter* **History**.) However, stand on the bridge as the sun sets on a summer's day and it's unlikely you'll notice any of them, such is the stunning view from the bridge itself.

Not even the **Chicago Sun-Times** building, west of Michigan Avenue along the river and designed to resemble a steel barge, can ruin the vista. The smaller of Chicago's two competitive daily newspapers (*see page 41*), the tabloid prides itself on its aggressive reporting, not the beauty of its building; probably a smart move, considering the competition across the street. The design for **Tribune Tower**, home to the *Chicago Tribune*, was selected in 1922 by then-publisher Colonel Robert McCormick from a field of international entries. The Gothic tower houses the daily newspaper (*see page 40*), the *Tribune*-owned WGN radio station – the call-sign letters stand for World's Greatest Newspaper – and CLTV, Chicago's local television news station, also *Tribune*-owned. Scattered about the first floor exterior of the building are stones that have been reputedly pirated from landmarks around the world by *Tribune* foreign correspondents. Among them are chunks from the Alamo, St Peter's Basilica, Westminster Abbey, the Berlin Wall and the Parthenon.

The headquarters of the Wrigley chewing gum company are located across the street from Tribune Tower in the **Wrigley Building** (400 N Michigan Avenue). A brightly illuminated white terracotta building designed by the same architects who created Union Station and the Merchandise Mart, the Wrigley Building has

These shoes were made for walking among the upscale shops of the **Magnificent Mile**.

Corn, anyone? **Marina City**. *See page 61.*

stood at the base of Michigan Avenue since 1922. The clock tower was based on a similar tower on the cathedral in Seville, Spain.

While Michigan Avenue has its share of breathtaking architecture, the main reason most people flock here is to shop. The seemingly endless row of upscale stores on the Magnificent Mile – as nicknamed by developer Arthur Rubloff in 1947 – doesn't disappoint. From the five-storey Crate & Barrel at the corner of Erie Street to Burberry's, Tiffany & Co, Borders Books and Niketown, the streets are lined with places to drop heavy loads of cash. It is easy to miss the **Terra Museum of American Art** tucked among the glitzy stores and art deco towers (*see page 60*).

One Magnificent Mile (home to Polo Ralph Lauren) is the first of several malls between Oak Street and the river. Others include **Water Tower Place** at no.835; **900 N Michigan Avenue**, where you'll find Bloomingdale's; and **Chicago Place** at no.700, site of the Chicago branch of Saks Fifth Avenue. And just east of Michigan on Oak Street is Chicago's equivalent of Rodeo Drive, complete with the most upscale designer boutiques, including Versace, Betsey Johnson and Barney's. For more on the retail delights of the Magnificent Mile, *see chapter* **Shops & Services**.

The **Water Tower** and **Chicago Water Works** (formerly known as the Pumping Station) on Michigan Avenue just north of Chicago Avenue were two of the few structures to survive the Chicago Fire of 1871. Built to resemble medieval castles, the buildings were once responsible for pumping more than 70 gallons of water to city residents each day. When Oscar Wilde visited the city in 1882, he described the tower as 'a castellated monstrosity with pepper boxes stuck all over it'. That doesn't stop people from gathering in the small plaza around the building, a favourite spot for amateur musicians and artists looking for a little spare change. A visitors' centre located inside the Water Tower offers all kinds of useful information, while the Chicago Water Works also houses a restaurant, a gift shop and an animated 'Honest' Abe Lincoln.

Standing proudly near the tip of N Michigan Avenue, around the point where the already posh Near North melds into the even posher Gold Coast is the **John Hancock Center** (875 N Michigan Avenue, at E Delaware Place; 312 751 3681), a little – well, smaller – brother to the Sears Tower but the reigning king of the Mag Mile. The criss-cross braces that form the outer frame of the 1,107-foot (337-metre) tall building were designed to keep the structure from swaying in the heavy winds that blow off Lake Michigan. While the Hancock is about 300 feet (91 metres) shorter than the Sears Tower, many Chicagoans favour the Hancock's observation deck because of its view of the Loop – including the Sears Tower – and its proximity to the lake. Oh, and the fact that it's got a bar at the top. *See page 56* **A view to a thrill**.

High-speed elevators whisk visitors to the 94th floor Skydeck Observatory and open-air skywalk 1,000 feet (305 metres) above the ground, from where you can see for 80 miles (129 kilometres) and across four states on a clear day. An 80-foot (24.4-metre) History Wall outlines significant moments in Chicago's past, while the virtual reality Windows on Chicago lets you tour more than 80 sites at the push of a button. Visit the Signature Room restaurant on the 95th floor or Images Lounge on 96th to wine and dine while enjoying the same breathtaking view, though prepare to take out a second mortgage once you've seen the prices. Much of the building is residential, while lower levels and the sunken plaza house the **Chicago Architecture Foundation** shop (*see page 176*), other gift and clothing stores and the Cheesecake Factory, a full-service restaurant. Guess what the house speciality is.

Across the street from 'Big John' is the **Fourth Presbyterian Church**, built in 1914. One of the church's prominent members

TimeOut

'THE GREATEST LONDON AUTHORITY'

designed the parish house and the fountain in the adjacent ivy-trimmed courtyard, the site of occasional outdoor concerts and a peaceful retreat from the often maddening strip. This is the congregation's second church, built after its first was destroyed by the Chicago Fire; the congregation had celebrated its first service in the original church at Grand and Wabash just hours before the fire broke out.

The **Drake Hotel** (*see page 101*) has played host to the rich and famous since its opening in 1920. It was designed to resemble a Renaissance palace: a gorgeous second floor lobby welcomes guests to the more than 500 plush rooms, while the first floor is lined with small retail shops. Located inside are the Cape Cod Room and Coq D'Or, a dark lounge known for knock-'em-dead Martinis and swanky live piano music.

Chicago Sun-Times
401 N Wabash Avenue, at the Chicago River (312 321 3251). CTA Grand, Lake or State. **Open** *tours* Tue-Thur (call for reservations).* **Map** p306 H11.

Fourth Presbyterian Church
126 E Chestnut Street, at N Michigan Avenue (312 787 4570). CTA Chicago (Red). **Open** 9am-5pm Mon-Fri; 9am-4pm Sat; 9am-8pm Sun. **Map** p306 J9.

John Hancock Observatory
865 N Michigan Avenue, E Delaware Place (1-888 875 8439). CTA Chicago (Red). **Open** 9am-midnight daily. **Admission** $8.75; concessions $6-$6.75; free under-4s. **Credit** Disc, MC, V. **Map** p306 J9.

Tribune Tower
435 N Michigan Avenue, at E Illinois Street (312 222 2116). CTA Grand, Lake or State. **Open** *tours* call for reservations. **Map** p306 J11.

Water Tower & Chicago Water Works
163 E Pearson Street, at N Michigan Avenue (312 744 2400). CTA Chicago (Red). **Open** 7.30am-7pm daily. **Map** p306 J9.

Streeterville

The artistic jewel in the hotel-heavy area east of Michigan Avenue is undoubtedly the excellent **Chicago Museum of Contemporary Art**. Founded in 1967 by patrons who felt the **Art Institute** (*see page 51*) was too conservative for avant-garde exhibitions, the museum moved to this $46-million building in 1996, where works by artists like Franz Kline, Andy Warhol, Alexander Calder and René Magritte are displayed in four naturally lit barrel-vaulted galleries overlooking the lake. The 220,000-square-foot (20,460-square-metre) facility boasts a collection that runs to more than 7,000 pieces, a studio/classroom, a theatre, an art library, an outdoor sculpture garden, a café and gift shop, and is well worth a visit.

It certainly stands in stark contrast to one of Chicago's most popular attractions, which reaches out a half-mile into Lake Michigan at Grand Avenue. **Navy Pier** hasn't always been the glittering tourist façade it is today, however. It was built as a commercial shipping pier in 1916, but became more or less deserted when most commercial ships were re-routed to a South Side pier instead. The US Navy occupied the pier during World War II, and the 50-acre (20.25-hectare) site also served as the first campus for the University of Illinois at Chicago.

However, in 1995, the city completed a massive four-year renovation of the pier, which today is home to a 15-storey **Ferris wheel**. A ride costs $3 and the fabulous view, especially at night, just about makes it worth sitting through the appalling commentary. There's also an **IMAX cinema** (*see page 198*), a six-storey glass atrium with a botanical garden, a 38-piece hand-painted musical carousel, more than a dozen restaurants, a beer garden and the **Skyline Stage** (312 595 7437), where outdoor concerts are held in spring and summer. Various sculpture exhibitions take place on the pier all year, and, in winter, an open-air ice rink is put up alongside the wheel. Retail shops, a festival hall and grand ballroom are located inside. In late 1999, the eye-catching **Chicago**

The **Water Tower**. *See page 63.*

Navy Pier: when man invented the wheel, this was perhaps not what he had in mind.

Shakespeare Theater (*see page 235*) opened here, with the fascinating **Smith Museum of Stained Glass Windows** following suit in February 2000. The US's only stained-glass museum, it offers pieces from the likes of Louis Comfort Tiffany, Frank Lloyd Wright and John LaFarge. It's open during the same hours as the pier (*see page 67*) and offers free admission; for more information, call 312 595 5024.

Navy Pier is something of a tourist ghetto, to be honest, but is redeemed spectacularly by both the views and the fact that it's not always rammed with visitors: time your visit carefully, and you'll be seduced by the calm and the fresh breeze whipping in at the end of the pier. If you're feeling more energetic, take a ride on one of the boats that dock along the south side of the pier (appropriately named Dock Street): most offer trips up and down the shore throughout the day and evening. It's also a great place for kids: young 'uns are especially taken with the hands-on activities in the **Chicago Children's Museum** (*see page 190*), perhaps the best attraction on Navy Pier. With everything from interactive Tinker Toy displays to exhibits extolling the virtues of tolerance, it's exhaustive and invaluable. Kids can play on slides, make dams, visit the small aquarium and the animal exhibits and learn about nature and dinosaurs.

Just outside Navy Pier to the north, off Lake Shore Drive, is **Olive Park**, a quiet green space with room for picnicking. The small **Ohio Street Beach** is located to the immediate west,

and offers great views of the skyline. A tiny sculpture garden honouring Jane Addams is also located here. The clover-shaped high-rise towering near the park houses the Lake Point Tower condos at 505 N Lake Shore Drive.

Further south is **North Pier** (435 E Illinois Street, at N Lake Shore Drive; 312 836 4300) home to a multitude of bars and restaurants, retail stores, offices and, increasingly, condominiums. Sit outside and watch boats come and go along the Chicago River. At the eastern end of the pier is the **Centennial Fountain and Arc**, commemorating the city's Water Reclamation District. An arc of water shoots out of the fountain and into the river – and sometimes onto passing boaters – every hour on the hour for ten minutes between 10am and 2pm, and 5pm and midnight from 1 May until 1 October.

Close by at Columbus and Illinois is the **NBC Tower**. Built in 1989, it was designed to blend in with the 1920s and '30s art deco skyscrapers that surround it, but the illuminated peacock atop the building's spire gives it away. Two of the nation's trashiest talk shows – those hosted by Jerry Springer and Jenny Jones – are taped here in the WMAQ studios, while the **NBC Store** at N Columbus Drive (*see page 176*) does a brisk trade in memorabilia with the peacock emblem and Springer stuff. Alongside the NBC Tower, between the river and the Tribune Tower, is **Pioneer Court**, a neat plaza lined with trees and fountains.

Museum of Contemporary Art

220 E Chicago Avenue, at N Mies van der Rohe Way (312 280 2660/www.mcachicago.org). CTA Chicago (Red). **Open** 10am-8pm Tue; 10am-5pm Wed-Sun. **Admission** $7; free-$4.50 concessions. **Credit** AmEx, DC, Disc, MC, V. **Map** p306 J9.

Navy Pier

600 E Grand Avenue, at Lake Michigan (312 595 7437/www.navypier.com). CTA Grand/29, 65, 66 bus. **Open** 10am-8pm Mon-Thur; 10am-10pm Fri, Sat; 10am-7pm Sun. **Map** p306 K10.

NBC Tower

454 N Columbus Drive, at E Illinois Street (312 836 5555). CTA Grand. **Open** 9am-6.30pm daily. **Map** p306 J11.

Gold Coast

A visitor to Chicago in the early 1900s once gazed at the Gold Coast's elaborate mansions and noted, 'They are of different sizes and styles. All are attempts to create something impressive.' Nearly a century later, many of those buildings still stand, but nobody is 'attempting' anything: today, the neighbourhood – bounded by Chicago and North Avenues, Clark Street and the lake – is home to Chicago's high-society set, titans of business, and young up-and-comers. Oh, and the Roman Catholic Archbishop.

An entrepreneur named Potter Palmer was the first to settle in the Gold Coast in 1882. Palmer built a $250,000 'mansion to end all mansions' along Lake Shore Drive, and others followed suit, building gigantic homes and luxury high-rise apartment buildings just off Lake Michigan that remain prominent even today. Sadly, Palmer's Castle, as it was dubbed, was torn down in 1950 to make way for the high-rise apartment complex still standing at 1350 N Lake Shore Drive.

In the midst of the stately homes and grand high-rises is the bustling area around Rush and Division Streets. Since the 1920s, Rush Street has had more bars and restaurants per square foot than any other stretch in Chicago. The block along Division between Rush/State and Dearborn Streets, especially, is popular with out-of-town guests, conventioneers and singles (or singles-for-a-night). Late at night, the streets flood with people and the scene can get a little

Sightseeing

Radio days

No one has chronicled Chicago life – or American life – in the past century quite like **Studs Terkel**, perhaps the pre-eminent interviewer of our time. Is that claim too grandiose? Well, consider that the 1934 University of Chicago Law School graduate hosted the Studs Terkel Show on Chicago radio station WFMT-FM every day for more than 40 years. By his final show, in 1997, Terkel had compiled 5,000 reels and 7,000 hours of interviews with some of the age's most influential figures: Marcel Marceau, Louis Armstrong, Janis Joplin, Nelson Algren, Arthur Miller, Toni Morrison, Simone de Beauvoir, Tennessee Williams, James Baldwin, Bruno Bettelheim, Danny Kaye and numerous other celebrated types.

Over the years, Terkel published his observations – culled from interviews on the show as well as additional reportage – in 13 books, including the Pulitzer Prize-winning *The Good War: An Oral History of World War II*. Despite the world-renowned figures he interviewed, Terkel turned to the Everyman, the working stiff or man or woman on the street,

MY AMERICAN CENTURY
Studs Terkel
FOREWORD BY ROBERT COLES

for insight into American life, as shown in his books *Hard Times: An Oral History of the Great Depression* and *Working: Talking to People About What They Do All Day & How They Feel About What They Do*.

Since more or less retiring from radio in 1997, Terkel has dedicated himself to the **WFMT/Studs Terkel Archive Project**. The sound recordings, most of which have never been transcribed, comprise a rich history of the second half of the 20th century. For a taste of Terkel's famed interviewing prowess, visit the **Chicago Historical Society** (*see page 71*) and their permanent exhibit, 'On the Paper Trail', where you can listen to audio of the blue-collar scribe's 1965 interview with community activist Florence Scala, about an uprooted neighbourhood on Chicago's Near West Side.

While the preservation of Studs' 6,000-plus interviews is an ongoing process, the society plan to make a selection of the interviews available to the public during late 2000, with others becoming available in the future.

Oak Street Beach (*see page 69*). It's slightly warmer in summer.

out of hand. When the Chicago Bulls won the NBA title in 1996, for example, people celebrated here by tipping over cars and starting small fires. Rest assured, though: as the Bulls aren't in danger of winning anything in the foreseeable future, such an event is unlikely to reoccur at any time soon.

Near Lincoln Park

To be honest, you'd expect there to be at least one stupendously posh school in the Gold Coast, and the **Latin School of Chicago** doesn't disappoint. With a high school student body of about 400, it is one of the city's most expensive and highest-rated private schools. Catch a glimpse of the privileged few in the large brick building at 59 W North Avenue on the edge of Lincoln Park.

Nearby, the **International Museum of Surgical Science**, two blocks east and one block south, depicts the history of surgery in dizzying – and sometimes nauseating – detail, with exhibits filling 32 rooms in a landmark 1918 building. An iron lung, old, *Marathon Man*-like dental equipment, antiquated x-ray machines and a copy of Napoleon's death mask are just a few of the delights contained within. Just as entrancing are the turn-of-the-century apothecary shop and the exhibits on plastic surgery, x-rays and anaesthesiology. It's the ideal destination for anyone wanting to know how holes were drilled in skulls in the old, pre-

anaesthetic days. Outside the building is *Hope and Help*, a sculpture of a doctor tending to an ill patient.

International Museum of Surgical Science

1524 N Lake Shore Drive, at E North Avenue (312 642 6502). CTA Clark/Division/72, 73, 151 bus. **Open** 10am-4pm Tue-Sat. **Admission** $5; $3 concessions. **Map** p307 H7.

Astor Street District

More than 300 buildings in the Astor Street District are listed on the National Register of Historic Places; a walk down the tree-lined streets is like a step back in time. The **Patterson-McCormick Mansion** at Burton Place and Astor Street was commissioned by former Chicago mayor and *Tribune* editor Joseph Medill as a gift to his daughter, Mrs Robert Patterson, in 1892, and once played host to lavish high-society parties, and kings and queens. In 1927, industrialist Cyrus McCormick bought the home and built an addition that doubled the mansion's size. The house was restored in 1979 and today has been converted into condominiums.

The **Roman Catholic Archbishop of Chicago** still has his private residence at 1555 N State Street, the oldest building in the Astor Street Historic District. Much of the associated land was sold as the surrounding neighbourhood was built up, but the Queen Anne-style home, built in 1880, still remains. The painstakingly landscaped building consists of two and a half storeys of red brick and limestone, topped with steeply pitched roofs and 19 chimneys.

Returning to Astor Street and heading south to the 1400 block, nearly all the homes are significant for their architecture, if not for their beauty alone. Architect David Adler designed the house at **1406 N Astor Street** in 1922 for Joseph T Ryerson, long-time chairman of the board for Inland Steel. William D Kerfoot, a prominent developer known as the first man to begin rebuilding in the city's business district after the Chicago Fire of 1871, was the first to live in the home at **1425 N Astor Street** when it was built in 1895. **Charnley House**, located at 1365 N Astor Street, was built in 1892 according to designs by Frank Lloyd Wright, then a 25-year-old draughtsman for the firm of Adler & Sullivan.

In 1894, the house just off Astor at **36 E Schiller Street** was built for five-term Chicago mayor Carter Henry Harrison, Jr, whose father – also a five-term mayor – was killed during the 1893 World's Columbian Exposition. The second owner of the home, still a private residence, was William Wrigley, Jr. In the centre of the neighbourhood is **Goudy Square Park**, named after prominent Chicago attorney William C Goudy. Residents raised $350,000 in 1990 to build the children's playground area.

Oak Street Beach & surrounds

Founded by a group of society women that included the wife of meatpacking titan Ogden Armour, Jane Addams and Gwetholyn Jones, the **Three Arts Club** was intended as a refuge for young women studying painting, drama or music in the 'wicked city'. Built in 1914 to resemble a Tuscan villa, the four-storey building is a Chicago landmark and the only club of its kind still in existence (in their day, similar clubs could be found in Paris, New York and London). Today, the original three arts have expanded to include interior design, architecture and fashion. Visitors – including men – are welcome to tour the first floor recital room, the library, the sitting room, the tearoom and dining room.

Cut along Goethe Street – stopping, if you're thirsty, for a drink in the splendidly louche **Pump Room** (*see page 148*) – and head across to the lake. Three blocks south you'll find the **Lake Shore Drive Synagogue**, which has been called the city's 'most magnificent' for the ornate stained-glass windows that line the interior. The structure, built in the late 1800s, is open to visitors.

A little further south from there – along Lake Michigan off Oak Street – is **Oak Street Beach**, the place where Chicago's beautiful people go to sun, swim and be seen. Considered

Washington Square, the city's first ever public park. *See page 70.*

Ommmmmmmmmmmmmmmmmm... The **Midwest Buddhist Temple**. *See page 72.*

the Riviera of Chicago's shoreline, the area attracts legions of scantily clad men and women, Rollerbladers, cyclists, runners and walkers. In summer, volleyball nets are put up and vendors sell food, drinks and the occasional souvenir. Pedestrian access is through underpasses located across from the Drake Hotel at Michigan Avenue and Oak Street.

Cut back along Walton Street for several blocks until you reach a green space. This is **Washington Square**, Chicago's first public park. Bounded by Delaware Place, Walton, Dearborn and Clark Streets, the park has been the location of numerous spirited protests over the years: in the 1850s, for example, a group of German beer hall owners held demonstrations here against the city's increased liquor-license fees, while in the 1920s, it was a frequent soapbox spot for radical speakers on Sunday evenings. The park tends to be calmer today.

Overlooking the square is the stunning **Newberry Library**, Chicago's research library for the humanities, which was founded in 1887 at the bequest of Walter L Newberry, a pioneer Chicago banker and land speculator who wanted a library to 'serve the city he loved and helped to build'. The library's non-circulating collections are rich in European and American history, literature, genealogy and cartography. It also houses an impressive collection of Thomas Jefferson's letters, acts as home to the Chicago Genealogical Society and hosts seminars, lectures and concerts. Anyone

who isn't an archivist or a scholar won't find much to do, but the building itself, designed by Henry Ives Cobb and completed in 1893, is worth a stop: free tours are conducted on Thursdays at 3pm and Saturdays at 10.30am.

Lake Shore Drive Synagogue
70 E Elm Street, at N Lake Shore Drive (312 337 6811). CTA Clark/Division. **Open** hours vary; call ahead. **Map** p307 J8.

Newberry Library
60 W Walton Street, at N Clark Street (312 943 9090). CTA Clark/Division. **Open** 8.15am-5.30pm Mon; 8.15am-7.30pm Tue-Thur; 8.15am-5.30pm Fri-Sat. **Admission** free. **Map** p306 H9.

Three Arts Club
1300 N Dearborn Street, at W Goethe Street (312 944 6250). CTA Clark/Division. **Open** *first floor* 7am-11pm Mon-Fri; hours vary Sat, Sun. **Map** p307 H8.

Old Town

Once a working class, predominantly German neighbourhood, Old Town over the past century has grown into a diverse shopping and entertainment area, while still managing to maintain much of its historic charm. Home to a mix of long-time residents, young professionals and eccentric artists, the neighbourhood boasts the legendary Second City comedy club and the Old Town Triangle District, placed on the National Register of Historic Places in 1984.

Before the Chicago Fire of 1871 pushed hundreds of German immigrants north from their homes to Old Town, the stretch of land between North, Armitage, Larrabee and Clark was known as the 'cabbage patch' because it was little more than a patchwork of gardens and cow pastures. When the German population grew and shops sprouted up in the area, North Avenue became known as 'German Broadway'. As the years passed, however, many Germans moved further north, and other ethnic groups moved into Old Town.

The development of the Cabrini-Green housing project along Division Street in the late 1950s lowered rents in the surrounding area, changing the face of Old Town's south-west corner. Today, the high-rises of this notorious area are slowly being evacuated and boarded up – and the area around it developed for pricey townhouses and condominiums – but the Cabrini neighbourhood is still best avoided by tourists and others unfamiliar with the area.

A restoration campaign inspired largely by the artists who moved into Old Town's lower-income areas in the late 1950s is today credited with restoring the vitality the neighbourhood still enjoys. In 1977, the Old Town Triangle was declared a Chicago landmark, helping raise property values and prompting a flood of renovations, new developments and shopping and entertainment venues, especially along Wells and Armitage Streets.

Local tradition dictates that if you can hear the bells of **St Michael's Church**, you're in Old Town. Built in the centre of the neighbourhood in 1869 on land donated by early beer baron Michael Diversey, the church was partially gutted by the Chicago Fire two years later. At the time, a *Tribune* reporter commented that the structure's remains were the 'most impressive ruins on the North Side'. The Germans rebuilt the massive Romanesque church in just one year, and in 1888 hired a New York artist to restore the interior and place a steeple at the top of the church tower; the four-sided clock that sits there today was added a year later. By 1892, St Michael's Church had become Chicago's largest German parish.

Inside the brick building is a carved wooden altar and glorious stained-glass windows; outside are stone columns of varying heights and several roofs with intricate brickwork. The five bells in the tower each weigh between 2,500 and 6,000 pounds (1,133 and 2,778 kilogrammes), making them audible from quite a distance.

Founded in 1852 and dedicated to the preservation, dissemination and interpretation of Chicago history, the **Chicago Historical Society** is Chicago's oldest cultural institution.

The society's brick Georgian building, built here in 1932, houses permanent exhibits that include Chicago's first locomotive, the Illinois Pioneer Life Gallery – where costumed docents demonstrate early crafts – and the popular diorama room, where the exhibits make up a Chicago History 101.

There are artefacts from the Chicago Fire of 1871 and the Civil War on display, as well as the nation's largest 19th-century women's costume collection, the table upon which Abraham Lincoln signed the Emancipation Proclamation and the bed in which he died, George Washington's inaugural suit and Al Capone's mugshot. Modern extensions to the original building house a gift shop and the Big Shoulders Café, which does a fine Sunday brunch with live jazz. The Chicago Historical Society also hosts excellent tours of the city's neighbourhoods throughout the year.

Across the street from the Historical Society sits the gargantuan **Moody Church**, built in 1925 with seating for 4,000 in the main sanctuary and balcony. The non-denominational Protestant church was founded by evangelist Dwight L Moody, a Boston shoe salesman who came to Chicago to minister to poor homeless children. Today, it's one of the largest Protestant churches in the country. The lack of interior columns means that everyone has an unobstructed view of the services, which are broadcast via radio and television around the world. The church is affiliated with the **Moody Bible Institute** (*see page 59*).

Improvisational comedy theatre **Second City** (*see page 244*) doesn't quite hold 4,000; far from it, in fact. However, it has produced scores of famous actors and comedians since Mike Nichols, Elaine May and a group of friends founded the club in 1959. Among the most well-known are John Belushi, Ed Asner, Alan Arkin, Bill Murray (*see page 241* **My kind of town**) and Shelley Long. The satirical comedy, then performed by a half-dozen cast members on an empty stage with few props or costumes, quickly caught on. In 1967, a touring company was formed, and in the early 1970s a second Second City was opened in Toronto, which eventually gave the world SCTV, Dan Aykroyd, John Candy and the beloved Gilda Radner.

These days, the cast still follows the same format: performing several skits and then asking the audience to participate as they improvise on various themes. The theatre has two stages with performances happening simultaneously: occasionally a cast member hops over and joins in on one show after finishing his or her first. The name 'Second City', incidentally, was borrowed from a rather disparaging article about Chicago that appeared in the *New Yorker* in the early 1950s. The theatre is located inside Piper's Alley, an enclosed mall that was home to the Piper family bakery in the late 1800s. Also included in the building is a movie theatre, several small shops and a Starbucks.

Nestled among a neighbourhood of close brick homes is the strikingly simple **Midwest Buddhist Temple**. Built by one of the many Japanese immigrants who settled in Old Town in the 1940s and '50s, the temple's walls and pagoda-like roof stand atop a one-storey concrete base; a gold Buddha is one of the few objects inside the temple. The congregation, about 80 per cent Japanese, hosts a festival each year to introduce the neighbourhood to Japanese culture, dance, music and food.

Chicago Historical Society
1601 N Clark Street, at W North Avenue (312 642 4600). CTA Sedgwick. **Open** 9.30am-4.30pm Mon-Sat; noon-5pm Sun. **Admission** $5; $1-$3 concessions. **Credit** AmEx, DC, Disc, MC, V. **Map** p307 H7.

Midwest Buddhist Temple
435 W Menomonee Street, at N Hudson Avenue (312 943 7801). CTA Sedgwick. **Open** call ahead. **Map** p307 G7.

Moody Church
1630 N Clark Street, at W North Avenue (312 943 0466). CTA Sedgwick. **Open** 8.30am-5pm Mon-Fri; 12.15pm tours Sun.

St Michael's Church
1633 N Cleveland Avenue, at W North Avenue (312 642 2498). CTA Sedgwick. **Open** 9am-8.30pm Mon-Fri; 9am-noon Sat. **Map** p307 G7.

Crilly Court

Crilly Court, one block west of busy N Wells Street, tucked between W St Paul Avenue and W Eugenie Street, bears the name of Daniel F Crilly, a South Sider who bought the block and then put in a street of his own. Between 1885 and 1893, Crilly built rowhouses on the west side of the block and four-storey apartment buildings on the east side, above the doors of which he carved the names of his four children, Edgar, Oliver, Isabelle and Erminnie. Edgar renovated all of the buildings some 50 years later, closing off the back alleys to form a series of courtyards. The restoration was one of the first in the Old Town Triangle area, and the younger Crilly is credited with leading the way in the historical preservation of the locale.

Several homes in the immediate area of Crilly Court have their own historic significance. The small private residence at

216 W Menomonee Street is believed to have been a 'fire relief cottage', one of the homes built by the city following the Great Fire to provide shelter to homeless residents. Built at a cost of about $75, some of the homes were also used to serve food and distribute clothing.

The 1872 frame house at **1802 N Lincoln Park West**, meanwhile, is one of only a handful of wooden farmhouses left in the area. Further north are two other frame houses built in the early 1870s for the Frederick Wacker family, prominent German brewers. Frederick's son Charles, a member of Chicago's planning commission for 17 years and the namesake of Wacker Drive, lived in the carriage house at **no.1836**, while his father lived at the Swiss chalet-style residence at **no.1838**. Frame houses like these are uncommon in the area because of the restrictions on building materials the city imposed after the Chicago Fire of 1871. Just down the street, the rowhouses at **1826-34 N Lincoln Park West** were designed by Adler and Sullivan from 1884 to 1885: displaying Louis Sullivan's love of geometric ornamentation, they're rare examples of his early residential work. All of the homes are now private residences.

Lincoln Park

The two words 'Lincoln Park' come with a variety of meanings. Depending on context, they could refer to the largest metropolitan park in the United States, which runs along Lake Michigan from North Avenue (around the 1600 N block) all the way north to Hollywood Avenue (the 5700 N block). They could also be used to describe the increasingly desirable residential neighbourhood bordered roughly by Armitage to the south and Diversey to the north and which includes the DePaul University campus, along with residential and commercial zones that extend all the way west to the north branch of the Chicago River. But then again, some locals and most cab drivers consider Lincoln Park to be the area around the zoo, including North and South Pond and the greens that surround them. All very confusing.

The park

Lincoln Park – as in the park – was established in the 1860s, after the sprawling cemetery that once stood here was cleared. The bodies went north to Graceland and Rosehill cemeteries (*see page 80* **Resting in peace**), apart from that of hotelier Ira Couch. His family went to court to prevent the city moving their beloved's grave;

One of the resolutely old-fashioned frame houses in Old Town.

they succeeded, hence the **Couch Mausoleum** that stands near the junction of LaSalle Drive and Clark Street.

Couch aside, the park soon became a popular attraction among locals while, at the same time, the area to the west became more densely populated as European immigrants moved in. Though the surrounding area has had its ups and downs, the park itself has remained steadfastly popular.

The most visited attraction in the area by far is the **Lincoln Park Zoo** (*see also page 189*), the nation's oldest zoo and one of a dwindling number that don't charge admission. It's open 365 days a year, and houses more than 1,000 species of animal. Among other things, the zoo is a world leader in gorilla breeding, with more than three dozen born here since 1970.

The zoo itself is fairly compact, with shady paths that wind between exhibits, so it isn't difficult to see everything in an afternoon. The biggest draws are the Kovler Lion House, the Great Ape House and the African elephants, though visitors to the latter exhibit should make it a point to be alert at all times. Signs posted along the fence warn spectators that elephants occasionally hurl objects from their pen. What the signs – and most guidebooks – fail to mention is that the 'objects' in question are lumps of their own dung. There are few sights more startling – or, to be frank, hilarious – than that of the unwary visitor who is successfully targeted by a disgruntled elephant.

In front of the zoo's main entrance – at 2200 N Stockton Drive – is a famous statue of President Abraham Lincoln, after whom the park and zoo are named. **'The Standing Lincoln'**, as it is known, is the oldest monument to Lincoln in existence, and is widely considered the most important work of 19th-century sculptor Augustus Saint-Gaudens, who sculpted another Lincoln – this one seated – that resides in Grant Park.

Just to the north of the main entrance is the lush **Shakespeare Garden**, which contains a variety of flowers and plants mentioned in the Bard's plays. The garden also houses a bronze bust of the playwright that dates back to 1894, and the Bates Fountain, also designed by Saint-Gaudens and a popular cooling destination in the summertime. The broad lawn leads to the **Lincoln Park Conservatory**, a three-acre (1.2-hectare) Victorian greenhouse that was erected in 1892. The conservatory is divided into four sections: the Palm House, the Fernery, the Tropical House and the Show House, which hosts four major displays each year. The warm, tropical setting allows plants from all over the globe to flourish. It also allows frozen travellers a welcome opportunity to thaw in colder seasons, and admission is always free.

Across Fullerton Avenue to the north is the new **Peggy Notebaert Nature Museum**, which was launched with a great fanfare in the autumn of 1999. The airy, $31-million, 73,000-square-foot (6,740-square-metre) structure is an impressive sight nestled along the edge of the newly revitalised North Pond: it's shaped like ancient sand dunes. Yet despite the respect accorded it as the museum of the Chicago Academy of Sciences, there is surprisingly little of interest for the $6 admission fee. Granted, the Butterfly Haven, a soaring, brightly lit habitat for 600 indigenous Illinois butterflies, is pleasant on a sunny day: stand and admire the view – and the snazzy indoor waterfall – while butterflies flit around and occasionally land in your hair. The other main exhibit, City Science, is a behind-the-scenes look at what kind of germs, bugs and rodents populate the typical Chicago dwelling. The most attractive part of the museum, however, is the outdoor pond and walkway that can be enjoyed for free, leaving the $6 admission fee to be invested in a good lunch instead.

The best way to enjoy Lincoln Park is a simple stroll along its many paths, which offer excellent views of the city centre, the lake, and acres of playing fields, ponds and park benches that attract locals from all over Chicago in warmer weather. For those hoping to cover a little more ground, there are half a dozen bicycle shops along the park's edge that rent by the day or by the hour. Alternatively, paddleboats are for rent at a South Pond kiosk for $9 an hour during boating season (15 May to 15 October), and right next door is the historic **Café Brauer** (2021 N Stockton Drive; 312 280 2724), which serves ice-cream and snacks.

Chicago Academy of Sciences Peggy Notebaert Nature Museum

2430 N Cannon Drive, at W Fullerton Avenue (773 755 5100). CTA Fullerton. **Open** *Sept-May* 10am-5pm Mon, Tue, Thur-Sun; 10am-8pm Wed; *June-Aug* 10am-6pm Mon, Tue, Thur-Sun; 10am-8pm Wed. **Admission** $6; $3-$4 concessions; free under-3s, all on Tue. **Credit** AmEx, Disc, MC, V. **Map** p308 H5.

The neighbourhood

Lincoln Park only really began to take off as a residential neighbourhood in the 1970s when previously dilapidated properties were renovated to splendid effect; it is now a sought-after address among the young and the restless. For visitors interested in Chicago's history of organised crime, however, Lincoln Park is a legendary destination. Just west of the zoo on N Clark Street is the site of the infamous St Valentine's Day Massacre. On 14 February 1929, Chicago godfather Al Capone sent a team of gangsters disguised as policemen to the garage of rival gang leader George 'Bugs' Moran. Capone's men announced a bust, and lined Moran's gang up against a wall as if they were going to pat them down. The seven men complied and were promptly executed with submachine guns. As luck would have it, Moran had overslept and so avoided death. But the incident ruined him and solidified Capone's ascendance to the top of Chicago's powerful organised crime world.

Winter in **Lincoln Park**, as the city of Chicago looks on in the distance.

Today, the garage, which was located at 2122 N Clark Street, is gone. But the incident still resonates in the neighbourhood. A stunning photograph of the slaughter hangs in the back room of the **Clark Bar** (*see page 152*), while the **Chicago Pizza & Oven Grinder Company** across the street at no.2121 (773 248 2570) tells the full tale of the St Valentine's Day Massacre on the back of its menus.

Several blocks to the north-west is the sight of another fabled gangland killing. John Dillinger, who rivals Capone as a crime legend in Chicago, was fatally shot outside the **Biograph Theatre** by FBI agents on 22 July, 1934. Legend has it that agents were acting on a tip provided by Anna Sage, a Romanian madam hoping to avoid extradition.

On the evening of his death, Sage accompanied Dillinger and his girlfriend to the theatre to watch a movie, wearing a red dress as a signal to the agents. As he later exited the Biograph, Dillinger was gunned down. His execution was witnessed by a crowd of bystanders, many of whom dipped their skirts and handkerchiefs in his blood. For months afterwards, blood-soaked cloth could be purchased on the streets of Chicago, though Sage didn't invest in any: she was paid $5,000 and immediately deported to Romania. For more on both Capone and Dillinger, *see page 14* **Crime and the city**; for more on what happened to Dillinger before he arrived in Chicago a wanted man, *see page 255* **Trips Out of Town**.

The Biograph still shows movies (*see page 195*), though gangster attendance is notably diminished. However, Dillinger's spirit lives on: each year on the anniversary of his death, fans meet in the upstairs room of the **Red Lion Pub** (*see page 155*) across the street, then follow a bagpipe procession to the scene of the outlaw's grizzly death.

These days, Lincoln Park is far more sedate, though it is a lively area for night-time funseekers, many of whom are students at **DePaul University**. The **Bars & Pubs** chapter gives the full lowdown on after-hours entertainment in the neighbourhood. On the off-chance that Lincoln Park itself didn't provide enough green pleasantness, then be sure to pop by **Oz Park**. The park takes its name from the seminal Judy Garland-starring movie, whose author L Frank Baum lived in Chicago. It's guarded by an adorable Tin Man statue and features the requisite yellow brick road. There's no sign of the Wicked Witch: she's dead, of course, though our enquiries as to whether it was Capone, Moran or Dillinger who saw her off yielded nothing in the way of new evidence.

Lincoln Park Zoo. *See page 73.*

Lake View

Prior to 1889, Fullerton Parkway formed Chicago's northern boundary. Above Fullerton lay the sparsely populated, rural Lake View Township, which stretched from Fullerton north to Devon, and from the lake west to Western Avenue. In 1889, the area was annexed by the city.

Today, only the southernmost portion of the former Lake View Township retains the name, the northern reaches having been carved into the present-day neighbourhoods of Wrigleyville, Roscoe Village, Andersonville, Edgewater, Buena Park, North Center, St Ben's, Lincoln Square and Uptown. Lake View quickly developed as a residential and entertainment district, with high rents keeping factories away.

Indeed, north-east Lake View Township, known today as Uptown, was a playground for gangsters like Al Capone and John Dillinger, who appreciated the anonymity afforded by hanging out in 'the sticks'. The **Green Mill** cocktail lounge and jazz club (*see page 158*) was a popular haunt back in the day, and was even operated by Al Capone in the '20s. The former speakeasy, which helped launch the career of Billie Holiday, still attracts an artsy, hip crowd.

The first Northern European immigrant to Lake View was a Swede named Conrad Sulzer, who arrived in 1836, sparking an influx of Scandinavians and Germans whose influence remains to this day. The neighbourhood is still home to many German-American families, and German restaurants abound. The epicentre of Teutonic culture is Lincoln Square, at the intersection of Lincoln and Western Avenues, where you can shop for home-made Bratwurst at **Meyer's**, an authentic Old World deli, or buy imported soaps, lotions and herbal homeopathic remedies at the **Merz Apothecary**. Lincoln Square is also the site of the annual **German-American Festival**, held every September (*see page 94*).

The face of the area was changed forever in 1914 with the construction of Wrigley Field, now, as then, the home of the **Chicago Cubs** (*see page 255*). Originally known as Weeghman Park, the Friendly Confines, with its ivy-covered walls and hand-operated scoreboard, has become an American icon recognised around the world.

It was at Wrigley Field, during the third game of the 1932 World Series, where Babe Ruth reputedly pointed to the bleachers and proceeded to pound Charlie Root's next pitch several hundred feet in that direction (no matter

Lincoln Park Conservatory. *See page 73.*

that the veracity of the 'Called Shot' is extremely doubtful, to say the least; it adds to the myth and legend of the place). In 1941, the Cubs became the first team in the major leagues to provide pipe organ music through its stadium. It was also here that Ernie Banks hit his 500th career home run on 12 May 1970; where Pete Rose nailed his 4,191st career hit in 1985, tying Ty Cobb's record for the most in baseball history; and where Sammy Sosa broke Roger Maris's fabled home run record in 1998, though his 66 dingers were topped by St Louis Cardinal Mark McGwire's 70 in the same year. The pinstriped flags that fly from the left- and right-field foul poles bear the numbers of two of the greatest players ever to wear the Cubs uniform: Ernie Banks, no.14, and Billy Williams, no.26.

On 8 August 1988, Wrigley became the last major league ballpark to add lights, a $5-million renovation that scandalised old-timers. Still, tradition has been maintained with the Cubs' inability to win. And if you can't get game tickets, then try the 90-minute tour of the park, which includes the press box, the visitors' clubhouse, the Stadium Club, the bleachers, Cubs security, the Cubs clubhouse, the dugout and the field itself. For more on the Chicago Cubs, *see pages 226-7* **The ivy leagues**.

Perhaps Lake View's most prized possession is the obvious one: its lakefront, which includes the northern end of Lincoln Park. During the summer, the park offers a multitude of outdoor activities on or around its exercise course, jogging paths, tennis courts and expansive grassy fields.

Lake View's most recent change of identity began in the '70s, when climbing property values in Lincoln Park resulted in the northward migration of young professionals. Slightly sleazy south Lake View began a slow but deliberate gentrification that resulted in higher rents and the opening of upscale boutiques and eateries.

Today, Lake View is an upscale neighbourhood with just enough grit to keep things interesting. The south-east portion, referred to by locals as 'Boystown' for its large gay population, is the shopping and dining centre of the neighbourhood, with expensive clothing stores, home decorating shops and restaurants peacefully co-existing with tattoo parlours and sex shops.

Along with a number of gay bars and dance clubs (*see pages 201-2*), the culture of Boystown is defined by some unique shops: the **Unabridged Bookstore** (*see page 205*) features an expansive collection of alternative lifestyle titles and has readings by authors popular with gay readers; the **Alley, Flashy**

The **Biograph Theatre** (*see page 75*). Try not to get shot on your way out.

Trash and **Ragstock** (*see pages 167-72*) sell cool duds to club kids who hang out in the neighbourhood; while **Uncle Fun** (*see page 193*) offers a demented selection of bizarre knick-knacks, greetings cards, vintage kitsch and gag gifts. There's plenty doing nightlife-wise, too: both Lake View and Wrigleyville are characterised by some excellent bars and club venues, including the **Metro**, perhaps the city's best live music venue, and **Schubas Tavern**, a little out of the way at Southport and Belmont but well worth making a detour for. For both, *see page 210.*

Around the corner at the intersection of Belmont and Sheffield is the 1912 **Vic Theater**, a former vaudeville house that boasts marble staircases, a large balcony, ornate mouldings and excellent acoustics. It's found deserved fame for its regular **Brew & View** movie nights (*see page 196*), where entry is a mere $4 and beers can be had for a couple of quarters. Perhaps understandably, the audiences tend to get loud and drunk, often speaking dialogue along with the actors, so if you're looking for a highbrow cinematic experience, you're better off heading north up Southport Avenue to the **Music Box Theatre**.

Built in 1929 in the style of the great cinemas of the day, the Music Box bills itself as 'Chicago's year-round film festival,' and with good reason: it's the city's leading purveyor of underground, independent American and foreign language movies. Seeing a flick at the

Music Box is an event, both because of the high calibre of the films shown here, and because of the over-the-top Italian Renaissance-inspired architecture. At the time of its construction, the Music Box, with seating for 800 patrons, was considered small compared to competing movie theatres, but the emphasis, then as now, was on atmosphere; it was even built with an orchestra pit in case the newfangled talkies flopped and silent film accompaniment was required.

Since its renovation in 1983, it has found a niche as a first-run art theatre, showing an average of 300 films every year over two theatres. The main theatre, seating 750, uses *trompe l'oeil* paintings of garden walls to create the illusion of sitting in an outdoor courtyard. The spectacular scene is completed by the ceiling, which is painted blue and covered with twinkling stars and moving cloud formations. The second theatre, with seating for 100, was added in 1991 to extend the runs of popular films and allow for more specialised films that draw smaller audiences. For more information, *see page 198.*

Merz Apothecary
4716 N Lincoln Avenue, at W Lawrence Avenue (773 989 0900). CTA Western. **Open** 9am-6pm Mon-Sat. **Credit** AmEx, Disc, MC, V.

Meyer
4750 N Lincoln Avenue, at W Lawrence Avenue (773 561 3377). CTA Western. **Open** 9am-9pm Mon-Sat; 10am-5pm Sun. **Credit** MC, V.

Museums you may have missed

Balzekas Museum of Lithuanian Culture

6500 S Pulaski Street, at W 65th Street, South Side (773 582 6500). CTA Pulaski (Orange)/53, 63 bus. **Open** 10am-4pm daily. **Admission** $4; $1-$3 concessions.

Founded in 1966 by Stanley Balzekas, Jr, the Museum of Lithuanian Culture has been in its present South Side location – an old, converted hospital – since 1986. Committed to both education about and preservation of Lithuanian history, the museum has an exhaustive collection of artefacts culled from various Lithuanian families throughout the city and the world. Folk art, suits of armour and an impressive collection of high-calibre Lithuanian amber are just some of the treasures to be found here.

Ernest Hemingway Museum

200 N Oak Park Avenue, at W Ontario Street, Oak Park (708 848 2222/ www.hemingway.org). CTA Oak Park. **Open** 1-5pm Thur, Fri, Sun; 10am-5pm Sat. **Admission** $6; $4.50 concessions; free under-5s.

One of the nation's many Hemingway museums, this one focuses on the iconic author's early years. Hemingway spent much of his childhood in this Chicago suburb, for which, if anecdotal evidence is to be believed, he did not have an overwhelming fondness. Nevertheless, this museum holds a wealth of Hemingway relics, most of which date from the author's childhood and teens. A tour of the author's nearby boyhood home is also available.

Leather Museum & Archives

6418 N Greenview Avenue, at W Devon Avenue, Far North (773 761 9200). CTA Loyola. **Open** 10am-5pm Mon-Fri. **Admission** free.

Wrestling with the **International Museum of Surgical Science** (*see page 68*) for the dubious honour of Chicago's Oddest Museum, the Leather Archives moved to this sweeping old North Side theatre building in February 2000. Devoted to preserving the shared heritage of the leather/S&M/ bondage/fetish community, the on-site archives, which may be the world's largest, have been used by Kinsey researchers and the television show *20/20*, to name just a couple. Created under the aegis of Chuck Renslow, who also started the nation's first leather bar, the museum holds a large collection of books and erotic art, some of it by well-known names such as Robert Mapplethorpe.

West Side

In the late 1880s, German, Irish, Russian, Greek and Eastern European immigrants streamed into the industrial and residential area that now forms three distinct and fascinating Chicago neighbourhoods: **Little Italy**, **Pilsen** and **Greektown**. Given the area's working-class heritage, well-preserved historical sites are not found on every corner around here. But for the adventurous modern visitor, these gritty but vibrant neighbourhoods offer a chance to explore and experience kitsch-free Chicago communities. While care should be exercised around here, especially after dark, the best way to explore these neighbourhoods is to set out on foot along their main streets.

A decent starting point is the **Jane Addams Hull House Museum** on Halsted Street between Polk and Taylor Streets. Founded as a social settlement house in 1889 by Jane Addams and Ellen Gates Starr, Hull House became a world-famous centre for urban research and arts education, and a focal point for the women's labour union movement, the fight for immigrants' rights and social reform. In 1931, Addams became the first American woman to win the Nobel Peace Prize. With some of the original furnishings intact in its two-building complex – one of which is a landmark 1856 mansion that would be worth a look even without its social history – the heady Hull House exhibits provide an in-depth introduction to the American labour movement and the social issues faced by immigrant populations that settled on Chicago's near West Side.

These days, the Hull House's two historic buildings seem strangled by the brutalist architecture of the **University of Illinois at Chicago** (UIC) campus, built in the 1960s as a sprawling and devastating interruption to the historic neighbourhoods that surround the school. A casual eye may have difficulty discerning the university's laudable recent attempts to soften its concrete landscape by adding trees and grassy medians throughout the busy campus.

Martin D'Arcy Museum of Art

*Cudahy Library, Loyola University, 6525
N Sheridan Road, at W Arthur Avenue,
Far North (773 508 2679). CTA Loyola.*
Open *Sept-Apr* noon-4pm Tue-Sat.
Admission free.

Named after the British scholar who presided
over a similar collection at Oxford and located
within the grounds of a leading Jesuit seat of
learning, the Martin D'Arcy Museum houses
Loyola University's large collection of
medieval, Renaissance and baroque art.
Open since 1969, it concentrates on pieces
from the years AD 1100 to 1750. Among
the delights contained within are important
works from artists such as Tintoretto and
Bellini, while there are also impressive
selections of both French and Italian
furnishings and jewellery.

Spiritual Museum

*New Age Psychic Center, 4328 N Lincoln
Avenue, at W Montrose Avenue, Far North
(773 478 2410). CTA Wilson.* **Open** 11am-
5pm Mon-Wed, Fri-Sun. **Admission** $5; $1.50
concessions.

This small museum on the North Side,
curated by psychic Mike Kurban, holds a
wealth of spooksome objects, including
voodoo dolls, Polaroids of ghosts and a
mirror in which you can see your aura.
No, really. The shop has a wide selection
of paranormalia.

Swedish American Museum Center

*5211 N Clark Street, at W Foster Street, Far
North (773 728 8111). CTA Berwyn.* **Open**
10am-4pm Tue-Fri; 10am-3pm Sat, Sun.
Admission *suggested donation* $4; $2
concessions; free under-12s.

Preserving Swedish heritage in the Swede-
heavy neighbourhood of Andersonville for
almost 25 years, the Swedish American
Museum Center began in a small log cabin,
moving to its present location in 1987. This
24,000-square foot (2,232-square-metre)
space, christened by His Royal Majesty Carl
Gustaf XVI of Sweden, contains a permanent
exhibition space, a gallery of rotating exhibits, a
gift shop, library and meeting space.

Vietnam War Museum

*954 W Carmen Avenue, at N Sheridan Road
(773 728 6111). CTA Argyle.* **Open** 11am-
3pm Sat, Sun. **Admission** free.

This admittedly sombre, little-known
Uptown museum is one of the city's most
worthy, and not nearly as grim as it sounds.
Dedicated to instructing the average citizen
about the everyday horrors faced by
American soldiers in Vietnam, this museum
contains newspapers and uniforms from
the period, and cages in which actual
American prisoners of war were held.
Many of the artefacts were donated by the
soldiers themselves.

Just a couple of blocks south of the Hull
House lies the now-decayed area that gave birth
to the Chicago blues. The **Maxwell Street
Market**, formerly on Halsted Street between
Roosevelt Road and W 14th Street, was
officially founded more than 100 years ago by
European Jewish immigrants who manned
pushcarts, stalls and storefronts to sell
inexpensive goods to neighbourhood residents.
The flea market grew over the years, and by the
1940s and 1950s, when the blues scene erupted
in the area, was providing gospel, jazz and
blues performers with a regular venue for
experimentation, performance and potential
discovery by roving talent scouts.

The original storefronts, most now
abandoned, still stand at the old market site by
and on Halsted Street. The music, too, may have
moved elsewhere, but a visit affords resonant
nostalgia, especially if accompanied by the
city's cheapest Chicago-style hotdogs. However,
this is a crime-ridden corner of the city that
should only be visited in daylight hours, and
even then with care.

The multi-ethnic Maxwell Street Market has
now been relocated half a mile east to Canal
Street. The low-priced Sunday offerings remain
wide and varied, with the array of toys, shoes,
tools and thrift-store oddities – as well as
roasted corn, *churros, carne asada*, candies and
fresh fruit – creating a visual and sensual feast
that should not be missed. Still, residents
bemoan the city's recently stringent oversight,
which has greatly improved safety but made it
more difficult to easily retrieve hubcaps
cleverly removed from unlucky cars the
previous week. *See page 180.*

Jane Addams Hull House Museum

*University of Illinois at Chicago, 800 S Halsted
Street, at W Polk Street (312 413 5353). CTA UIC-
Chicago.* **Open** 10am-4pm Mon-Fri; noon-5pm Sun.
Admission free.

Little Italy

A stroll west from Halsted on Taylor Street
(along the south side of the UIC campus) leads
into Little Italy, a friendly neighbourhood

Resting in peace

The corner of Clark Street and Irving Park Road is perhaps the city's most prestigious address. Chicago's great and good all long to find a home here one day, and stop at almost nothing to ensure they'll be able to move in when their time comes. The catch? The corner of Clark Street and Irving Park is only a desirable address if you happen to be dead. For it's here you'll find **Graceland Cemetery**, a sprawling 120-acre (49-hectare) necropolis that is *the* place to hang out when your last breath has been well and truly drawn.

Boasting tombs and landscaping designed by Louis Sullivan, William LeBaron Jenney and other greats, Graceland was established in 1861. Everyone who was anyone in Chicago life is buried here, more or less, and it's easy to spend a day just wandering around the place taking in the history and thanking your lucky stars that you're not quite ready to join the residents just yet.

Perhaps the cemetery's most impressive grave is that of Potter and Bertha Honore Palmer. Potter was one of the prime movers in rebuilding Chicago after the fire of 1871 – hardly surprising, since he lost a load of property in the blaze – and now lies, with his wife, in a hilltop Greek-style temple overlooking Lake Willomere. The Palmers' bodies lie within two large granite sarcophagi, with inverted torches on the sides of the temple symbolising death for those who haven't quite got the message yet.

The grave of Marshall Field, buried here in 1906, is also an impressive affair. Field's resting place was designed by Daniel Chester French, who also designed the similar Lincoln Memorial in Washington, DC; here, it's the seated figure of Memory, not Abraham Lincoln, who watches over the retail magnate's grave.

Field was worth an estimated $100 million when he died, in stark contrast to Louis Sullivan, the master architect who designed the Auditorium Theatre and Carson Pirie Scott building. Sullivan fell on hard times when his designs fell out of favour, and died so flat-broke in 1924 that his estate did not allow for a grave marker. However, admirers of his work took up a collection and commissioned a black granite marker, ornamented with geometric designs, bearing a profile of the architect and, on the sides of the monument, the evolution of the skyscraper.

Before he died, Sullivan had designed the tombs of Martin Ryerson and Henry Harrison Getty. Ryerson's black granite tomb is capped with an Egyptian-style pyramid, while Getty's looks not unlike one of the architect's skyscrapers: a large cube decorated with geometric and floral patterns entered via one of Sullivan's trademark arches. Both deserve a closer look.

Sullivan is by no means the only architectural giant buried here. Ludwig Mies van der Rohe, proponent of the International Style of architecture in Chicago, was famous for uttering 'Less is more', so he'd undoubtedly approve of his gravestone: a simple granite marker with his name chiselled into it. Daniel Burnham, the architect who devised the Chicago Plan and designed the Reliance Building and the 'White City' of the 1893 World's Columbian Exposition, joined the party in 1912, finding a spot on an island in Lake Willomere, while William LeBaron Jenney, the architect credited with building the world's first skyscraper – Chicago's now-demolished Home Insurance Building – is also a permanent resident.

Elsewhere, you'll find William Hubert, founder of baseball's National League, buried under a baseball-shaped headstone, former mayor and *Chicago Tribune* publisher Joseph Medill, and George Pullman, creator of the Pullman train sleeping car. Pullman, buried here in 1897, lies in perhaps Graceland's most notorious plot. A ruthless businessman, he's best – or worst – remembered for ending Chicago's historic Pullman Strike in 1894 by firing the protesting workers. Worried that former employees would desecrate the grave, Pullman's family had his coffin encased in cement and buried safely beneath a large Corinthian column.

Graceland's office is just inside the main gate at the main entrance at Clark and Irving Park. There you can pick up a cemetery map and a copy of *A Walk Through Graceland Cemetery*, a publication of the Chicago Architecture Foundation, which highlights the cemetery's architecture and tells the stories of Graceland's most noteworthy residents.

Graceland Cemetery

4001 N Clark Street, at W Irving Park Road (773 525 1105). CTA Sheridan.
Open 8.30am-4.30pm daily.

where red sauce and meatballs fuel the local action. On hot summer nights, people drive in from the suburbs just to stand in line for the flavoured ices and snowballs at the long-established **Mario's Italian Lemonade** stand (*see* **Street food** *page 133*).

In a bizarre bit of urban planning, a decayed public housing project sits smack in the middle of Little Italy's Taylor Street promenade of restaurants and shops and necessitates some night-time caution. (As part of a controversial gentrification plan, the city is slowly demolishing such buildings and relocating the low-income residents.) But just west of the projects, Little Italy has a maze of residential side streets that reward exploration. Head north on Loomis to view the classic Chicago three-flats and stoops that line the street, and turn east on Lexington to enjoy the beautiful old homes that overlook **Arrigo Park**, a peaceful green that stands out amid this brick, stone and stucco landscape.

Back on Taylor Street, check out the **Scafuni Bakery** at no.1337 (312 733 8881). The wrinkled proprietresses serve up delicious fresh-baked cookies and pastries that should not, under any circumstances, be missed if you're in the area. Most things Italian – wine, fresh pasta, chocolates, meats, sausages, olive salads and espresso from the coffee bar up front – can be procured at the upscale **Conte di Savoia** grocery store at no.1438, while down the street at the fabled **Rosebud Café**, where the portions of home-made pasta are stomach-stretching, photos of *fedora*-sporting former regulars adorn the walls.

The **National Italian American Sports Hall of Fame** is being erected directly across Taylor Street from the new **Piazza DiMaggio**, a plaza dedicated to every Italian-American's favourite son, who died in 1999. The Hall of Fame is scheduled to be completed some time during 2001, and will feature such disparate treats as Mario Andretti's racecar and legendary Chicago Cubs announcer Harry Caray's glasses.

The gastronomic offerings of Taylor Street are capped off by the **Pompei Bakery** at no.1455 (312 421 5179), which serves up a culinary concoction called pizza strudel. The main attraction here, however, is the indoor mural celebrating the restaurant's founding family who all eerily display exactly the same face on a series of different bodies.

Rosebud Café

1500 W Taylor Street, at S Laflin Street (312 942 1117). CTA Polk. **Open** 11am-10.30pm Mon-Thur; 11am-11.30pm Fri; 5-11.30pm Sat; 4-10pm Sun. **Main courses** $5.95-$29.95. **Credit** AmEx, DC, Disc, MC, V.

Pilsen

If you return to Halsted Street and go south for a few blocks, you'll find 18th Street, which runs west to the centre of Pilsen. Now the largest Mexican and Mexican-American community in the Midwest, Pilsen was originally settled in the 19th century by German, Czech and Polish immigrants drawn to work on the railroads. By the late 1800s, industrialisation and the concomitant urban issues transformed the working class neighbourhood into a hub of labour activism. As the US immigrant quotas began to restrict the influx of Southern and Eastern Europeans in the 1920s, Pilsen gradually began to take on a Latino flavour. The murals on 18th Street, proclaiming 'Unidos Para El Progreso' and other ardent slogans, continue the area's activist tradition.

While a sizeable artistic community inhabits the blocks around the intersection of 18th and Halsted, the main commercial ebullience of Pilsen lies further west on 18th Street between Racine and Paulina, where street vendors and murals abound and salsa music pours out of passing vehicles. Additional points of interest include the left-leaning **Jumping Bean Café & Gallery** at no.1429 and the **Tortilleria Sabinas** factory (1509 W 18th Place), where you can watch through giant glass windows as the staff make tortillas in the back.

At the three-way intersection of Loomis, Blue Island and 18th Street sits **WRTE**, 90.5 FM Radio Arte. This local radio station, with only glass walls between its disc jockeys and the street, engages hapless pedestrians in one-way communication, broadcast by outdoor speakers on the sidewalk. Nearby on Ashland, **Rustico's Rancho Viejo** (1812 S Ashland Street, at 18th Street; 312 733 9251) inhabits a building that encapsulates the neighbourhood's ethnic history. Once a *sokol* (school) for Czech and Polish immigrants and then later a dance hall, this enormous artisans' store now sells a wide variety of Mexican crafts. Carved wooden furniture, Oaxacan figurines and vibrant paintings adorn the former stage, balcony and dancefloor.

Many people visit Pilsen just to see the well-known **Mexican Fine Arts Center Museum**, located on 19th Street just north of Ashland. Built to resemble Mayan architecture, this informal but instructive cultural centre explores the richness and breadth of Mexican and Mexican-American heritage through the visual arts, performance, dance and music. The Museum's annual Day of the Dead festival, which stretches from September to early December, is of particular interest. The centre is currently undergoing a major expansion, which is scheduled to be completed in April 2001.

Sightseeing

Tours

Chicago Architecture Foundation River Cruise

Tickets & information: Chicago Architecture Foundation, Santa Fe Building, 224 S Michigan Avenue, at E Jackson Boulevard, South Loop (information 312 922 8687/switchboard 312 922 3432/ Ticketmaster 312 902 1500/ www.architecture.org). **Tours** *late Apr-early June 11am, 1pm, 3pm Mon-Fri; hourly 11am-3pm Sat, Sun; mid-June-Sept hourly 10am-3pm daily, also 5pm Sat, 10am Sun; Oct 11am, 1pm, 3pm Mon-Fri; hourly 10am-3pm Sat, Sun.* **Tickets** $21. **Credit** AmEx, DC, Disc, MC, V. **Map** p305 J12.

The definitive river tour. Trained guides provide an informed commentary on the best Chicago architecture. Cruises depart from the Mercury Cruiseline Dock at the Michigan Avenue Bridge, and advance booking – through Ticketmaster, on 312 902 1500 – is highly recommended. For other Chicago Architecture Foundation Tours by foot, bike, bus or train, call the numbers above or visit their informative website at www.architecture.org. It details all manner of interesting, educational and entertaining excursions throughout the city, complete with prices, departure times and other essential information on these truly splendid tours.

Chicago Neighbourhood Tours

Chicago Cultural Center, 77 E Randolph Street, at Michigan Avenue, The Loop (312 742 1190/www.chgocitytours.com). CTA Randolph. **Tours** *10am Sat; special tours times & days vary.* **Tickets** $30; $27 concessions. **Credit** AmEx, MC, V. **Map** p305 J12.

The Chicago Office of Tourism offers these informative bus tours, which focus on a different Chicago neighbourhood each week, with visits to historical sites, museums and attractions. Special themed tours such as the 'Roots of Chicago Blues' are also available.

Chicago Trolley Company

Information 312 663 0260/ www.chicagotrolley.com. **Tours** *9am-5.30pm daily; winter 9am-4.30pm daily.* **Tickets** $18; concessions $8-$15; *two-day pass* $20. **Credit** AmEx, DC, Disc, MC, V

A hop-on/hop-off service that trawls the major sights. Knowledgeable guides indicate points of interest along the way. Tickets are only available on board.

Loop Tour Train

Tickets & information: Chicago Office of Tourism, Cultural Center, 77 E Randolph Street, at Michigan Avenue, The Loop (312 744 2400). CTA Randolph. **Tours** *every*

Mexican Fine Arts Center Museum

1852 W 19th Street, at S Damen Avenue (312 738 1503). CTA 18th Street. **Open** 10am-5pm Mon, Tue, Sun. **Admission** free.

Greektown

Bookended at Van Buren and at Monroe by the pseudo-Grecian columns that sprang up when Mayor Daley wanted to impress delegates to the 1996 Democratic Convention, Halsted Street suddenly becomes Greektown. Actual Greek residents may be thin on the ground – the University of Chicago has shunted most of them to the suburbs – but this is still the Midwest's biggest Hellenic commercial area. Cheap and cheerful Greek restaurants abound here, and an eclectic array of treats can be discovered at the local bakery, jewellery shop and the Panellinion butcher shop, which boasts a perpetual special on whole baby goats. The **Athenian Candle Company** (300 S Halsted

Street, at W Jackson Boulevard; 312 332 6988), with its own factory visible in the backroom, peddles floor wash charms to rid the house of temperamental spirits and dozens of dream books to charm good luck into one's future. The upstairs deck of the **Pegasus** eaterie (*see page 131*) offers stunning views of the downtown skyline.

One block from Halsted Street, on the other side of the freeway at Adams and Desplaines, sits **Old St Patrick's Church**, one of the first churches in America built primarily to serve Irish immigrants. Built in 1856 and decorated with beautifully muted stained glass windows, St Pat's is the oldest surviving church in Chicago and among the very few buildings that managed to survive the Chicago Fire of 1871.

Greektown's Halsted Street is one border of the newly trendy neighbourhood with the clumsy moniker, 'West Loop Gate'. Once known for its book warehouses, cookie factories and freshly made underwear, the formerly industrial

40mins 12.15-2.15pm Sat. **Tickets** free.
Map p305 J12.
Travel the El from Randoph station, while
guides from the Chicago Architecture
Foundation fill you in on local history.

Lake & river cruises

Countless operators offer cruises on Lake
Michigan departing from Navy Pier,
including Seadog (312 822 7200);
Shoreline (312 222 9328); Spirit of
Chicago (312 836 7899) and Ugly Duck
Cruises (630 916 9007). For tours of the
Chicago River, try Mercury (312 332 1353)
or Wendella Boats (312 337 1446).

Untouchables Tour

*610 N Clark Street, at W Ohio Street
(773 881 1195). CTA Grand.* **Tours**
10am Mon-Wed; 10am, 1pm Thur; 10am,
1pm, 7.30pm Fri; 10am, 1pm, 5pm
Sat; 11am, 2pm Sun. **Tickets** $22;
$16 concessions. **Credit** MC, V.
Map p306 H10.
The Untouchables Tour kicks off from the
Rock 'n' Roll McDonald's at 605 N Clark
Street, visiting the actual sites of some
of the city's biggest gangster shoot-'em-
ups, including the Dillinger murder and
the St Valentine's Day Massacre. Guides
in full costume provide all the gory
background details.

West Loop has quickly become one of the
hottest residential areas in town. Between
Halsted and Racine, Randolph Street is the
epicentre of the hip new loft and restaurant
developments that have sprung up. Whether or
not you eat there, be sure to check out the
psychedelic *Alice in Wonderland*-inspired WCs
at **Marche**.
At **Fulton Market**, two blocks north of
Randolph, there is a palpable tension between
this wholesale meatpacking district and the
encroaching population of gallery owners and
loftdwellers. Yet, on any weekday along Fulton
and Lake near Halsted, the pungent aromas and
the noisy bustle of truckers loading their vans
with frozen slabs of pork and beef help explain
why they call this the City of Big Shoulders.
West Loop entertainment options include the
chance to kvetch with Chicago's most famous
resident. At **Harpo Studios** on Washington at
Carpenter Street, visitors can book free tickets
to tapings of *Oprah* (a one- to two-month

advance reservation is recommended). And
while it's hidden away and not especially well-
known, the small **Museum of Holography** on
Washington at May Street is well worth your
attention. A little further west on Madison
Street, the huge **United Center** (*see pages 211
and 225*) houses the once-great Chicago Bulls,
the Blackhawks hockey team and numerous
popular music acts. Most sports fans see only
the arena – and maybe a bar – before heading
back to less interesting parts of town.

Harpo Studios

*1058 W Washington Boulevard, at N Carpenter Street
(Oprah reservations 312 591 9222). CTA Ashland
(Green) or Racine.* **Open** *ticket line* 9am-5pm Mon-Fri.

Marche

*833 W Randolph Street, at N Green Street (312 226
8399). CTA Clinton.* **Open** 11.30am-2pm, 5.30-10pm
Mon-Wed; 11.30am-2pm, 5.30-11pm Thur; 11.30am-
2pm, 5.30pm-midnight Fri; 5.30pm-midnight Sat;
5.30-10pm Sun. **Average** $16-$30. **Credit** AmEx,
DC, MC, V.

Museum of Holography

*1134 W Washington Boulevard, at N Racine Avenue
(312 226 1007). CTA Ashland (Green) or Racine.*
Open 12.30-5pm Wed-Sun; closed Mon, Tue.
Admission $2.50; free under-6s. **No credit cards**.

Old St Patrick's Church

*700 W Adams Street, at S Desplaines Street (312
648 1021). CTA Clinton (Blue) or UIC Halsted.*
Open 9am-5pm Mon-Fri.

Wicker Park & Bucktown

The Wicker Park/Bucktown/Ukrainian Village
area is an extension of Chicago's Milwaukee
Avenue corridor, a major diagonal thoroughfare
that served as a pathway of urban expansion
after the Chicago Fire in 1871. Originally a path
made by local Native Americans in order to
follow buffalo to the Chicago River prior to the
settling of Chicago, Milwaukee Avenue became
a plank-road thoroughfare that connected the
north-west farming areas to the core of the city.
Though the Milwaukee corridor has
historically been an artery of ethnic settlement,
its recent hipness, with its extensive nightlife and
artistic flavour, has attracted gentrification and
younger, whiter residents. As a result, the
borders of Wicker Park, Bucktown and Ukrainian
Village are far from rigid, each blossoming more
as real estate names rather than neighbourhood
titles. As a rule of thumb, beginning roughly
where Milwaukee Avenue meets the Kennedy
Expressway, the Milwaukee Avenue corridor
follows Chicago Avenue west up to Western

The Bulls sullying the memory of Jordan and Pippen in the **United Center**. *See page 83.*

Avenue, and then follows Milwaukee Avenue north until approximately Armitage. The southern portion is commonly perceived as **Ukrainian Village** or **West Town**, the central as **Wicker Park**, and the northern section – essentially, north of the Milwaukee/North/Damen intersection – as **Bucktown**.

The development of the area is a microcosm of Chicago's ethnic settlement. Though Wicker Park and Bucktown predominantly house young professionals and those Hispanics who haven't been pushed further west by rising housing costs, the area was originally settled by Germans after the Chicago Fire. They built stately houses – many of which still exist – in the area around the plot of recreational land that is the actual Wicker Park. Ukrainian Village was settled primarily by Poles, Ukrainians and Russians, and remains one of the city's largest bubbles of East Slavic population, though it's not hard to notice the influence of Hispanic – specifically, Puerto Rican and Mexican – cultures, too.

Up until 1992, Wicker Park was widely considered to be one of Chicago's most dangerous neighbourhoods, but the poshing-up has smoothed out some of the locale's rougher edges and made it destination number one for Chicago's young professionals and artistic types.

Ukrainian Village & Lower Wicker Park

Any tour of Wicker Park and Ukrainian Village begins at the south-west corner of Milwaukee Avenue and Augusta, where the **Polish Roman Catholic Union of America** stands. This is the home of the oldest Polish fraternal organisation, founded, as the sign says, in 1873: one of the founders, Vincent Barzynski, was a vital figure in the development of Chicago's Polish community.

It's also home to the **Polish Museum of America** (founded in 1961), the largest and oldest ethnic museum in America. The museum boasts an enormous library and cultural and historical archive, as well as occasional films, lectures, concerts and scholarly conclaves. Chicago contains a higher concentration of people of Polish descent than anywhere else outside Poland, and the museum serves as an ersatz community base. It contains a fine, post-Impressionist collection of Polish art as well as Gabinet Paderewskiego, an exhibit devoted to Polish royalty.

A block to the west and north stands the **Northwestern University Settlement House** (1400 W Augusta Boulevard, at N Noble Street), homebase of the organisation founded by sociologist Charles Zeublin. A lesser-known cousin of Jane Addams' **Hull House**, it played a critical role in the development of social service. The building was designed by architect Irving K Pond, who earned a name as a developer of settlement houses, and the building still houses social service organisations.

Further north-west, the three-way intersection of Milwaukee, Division and Ashland marks the Polonia Triangle, known throughout the city's history as Polish Downtown and the one-time heart of Polish Chicago. The large white terracotta building that's now a TK store was once the home of *Dziennik Zwiazkowy*, Chicago's largest Polish-language daily newspaper, as well as the Jan Smulski Bank Polski. Just to the east of here, at 1520 W Division Street is a large grey building that once housed the Polish National Alliance, the largest fraternal Polish organisation in the country.

On the corner of Evergreen and Noble stands the gigantic **St Stanislaus Kostka**, completed in 1881 and home to Chicago's first Polish-Catholic congregation. Modelled after a church in Krakow, Poland, St Stanislaus Kostka boasted one of the United States's largest congregations – believed to be close to 5,000 families – at the turn of the nineteenth century. The church was dedicated and served by Vincent Barzynski until his death in 1899.

One block north of the church is Blackhawk Street, which will take you back to Ashland. Though redevelopment has reared its ugly head here, there are still a few pre-20th-century homes built during the height of the area's economic prosperity. The oldest homes are easily distinguished by the fact that they are built below sidewalk level, an oddity resulting from an 1850 decision by the city to raise sidewalks in order to facilitate better drainage. The heart of the Ukrainian Village, though is further west. At the south-west corner of Haddon and Leavitt stands the **Holy Trinity Orthodox Cathedral**, the first Orthodox and Greek Rite church to drop anchor in the community. Founded in 1892 by Carpatho-Ukraine immigrants in 1892 as St Vladimir's Russian Orthodox Church, it was redesigned by Louis Sullivan to resemble a Slavic church. Czar Nicholas II donated $4,000 towards the construction. The new church was consecrated in 1903 and was designated a place of worship and a cathedral by the Russian Orthodox Church in 1923. In 1976, it was added to the National Register of Historic Places and was assigned Chicago Landmark status in 1979.

A couple of blocks away, on the north-east corner of Oakley and Cortez, is **St Volodymyr's Ukrainian Orthodox Cathedral**. Built in 1911, it marks the proper entrance to Ukrainian Village and was the first religious institution formed by local Ukrainians in the area.

Head south on Oakley until Rice, where you can't miss the huge, Byzantine-styled **St Nicholas Ukrainian Catholic Cathedral**, modelled after the cathedral in Kiev. Originally completed in 1915 and renovated in 1975, it was founded by Uniate Catholics, who hailed from Galicia and the Carpatho-Ukraine. St Nicholas was the community centre of Ukrainians until 1968, when a split in the parish over use of Gregorian and Julian calendars divided the congregation and sent many to the SS Volodymyr & Olha church. The interior of St Nicholas is among Chicago's most elaborate, with ornate paintings and carpentry dominating the interior cupolas and imparting a distinctive Byzantine flavour.

The rest of the splintered parish can now be found at **SS Volodymyr & Olha Church**, a modern-Byzantine edifice with golden cupolas and a gigantic mosaic in front depicting the conversion of the Ukraine to Christianity in AD 988 by St Volodymyr. The church is a piece of living history where the Eastern Rites are still practised and services are conducted in traditional Ukrainian.

A little north on Chicago Avenue, among authentic Ukrainian and Russian businesses, stands the diminutive but worthwhile **Ukrainian Institute of Modern Art**, which does exactly what you might expect.

Holy Trinity Orthodox Cathedral

1121 N Leavitt Street, at W Haddon Street (773 486 4545). CTA Damen (Blue). **Open** by appointment. **Map** p310 B9.

Polish Roman Catholic Union of America & Polish Museum of America

984 N Milwaukee Avenue, at W Augusta Boulevard (773 384 3352). CTA Chicago (Blue). **Open** 11am-4pm daily. **Admission** *suggested donation* $3; $1 concessions.

St Nicholas Ukrainian Catholic Cathedral

2238 W Rice Street, at N Oakley Boulevard (773 276 4537). CTA 49, 50, 66 bus. **Open** by appointment.

St Stanislaus Kostka

1351 W Evergreen Avenue, at N Noble Street(773 278 2470). CTA Division. **Open** by appointment.

St Volodymyr's Ukrainian Orthodox Cathedral

2250 W Cortez Street, at N Oakley Avenue (773 278 2827). CTA 49, 50, 66 bus. **Open** by appointment. **Map** p310 B9.

Sightseeing

SS Volodymyr & Olha Ukrainian Catholic Parish
739 N Oakley Boulevard, at W Superior Street (773 276 3990). Bus 49, 50, 66. **Open** 9am-4pm daily.

Ukrainian Institute of Modern Art
2320 W Chicago Avenue, at N Oakley Boulevard (773 227 5522/www.brama.com/uima). Bus 66. **Open** noon-4pm Wed, Thur, Sat, Sun.

Wicker Park & Bucktown

From the institute, it's a walk east down Chicago and north up Ashland to Milwaukee Avenue. Head north-west up Milwaukee and once you pass Wood Street, you'll be on one of the city's hippest nightlife corridors.

At the maddening three-way intersection of Milwaukee, North and Damen stands the **Northwest Tower**, a 12-storey art deco building completed just before the Depression in 1929 by the architectural firm Holabird & Root. The one-time centre of Wicker Park's business, the Northwest Tower – aka the Flatiron Building – was virtually empty by 1970, but a restoration plan in 1984 has again filled the building with offices and businesses. Many of the neighbourhood's numerous art galleries are also to be found near this intersection. For a taster of what's in the area, *see chapter* **Art Galleries**.

South of the intersection, just off Damen, is Pierce Street, lined with fine examples of the large homes built in the area by earlier German and Polish residents. At **2141 W Pierce** stands a house adorned with an Orthodox cross on top: built in the late nineteenth century, it was once the home of the archbishop of the Russian Orthodox Holy Virgin Protection Church. The **Gingerbread House** (2137 W Pierce, at N Leavitt Street) was built in 1888 by Herman Weinhardt, a German merchant responsible for making Wicker Park a German enclave in the 1870s. Across the street at no.2138 stands the **Padrewski House**, built in 1886 and originally called the Runge-Smulski House, but renamed after the famous Polish pianist who reputedly entertained a crowd from the porch.

Slightly south on Damen, you'll find the plot of land that gives the area its name: **Wicker Park**, originally donated to the city by German Protestants Charles and Joel Wicker in 1870. A word of warning: occasionally, the northern border of Wicker Park (along Wicker Park Street) is lined with gang-affiliated drug dealers. Don't hassle them, and they won't hassle you.

Further across, on Claremont Street just north of North Avenue, is the **Pedro Albizu Campos Museum of Puerto Rican History & Culture**. Named after Puerto Rican

The **Gingerbread House** on Pierce Street.

liberation activist Campos, this museum hosts a collection of art by Puerto Rican and Puerto Rican-American artists. There are also rotating exhibits and lectures.

Pedro Albizu Campos Museum of Puerto Rican History & Culture
1671 N Claremont Street, at W North Avenue (773 342 8023). CTA Western (Blue (NW)). **Open** noon-4pm Thur-Sun. **Admission** free. **Map** p310 A7.

South Side

Aside from those in **Hyde Park** (*see opposite*), you won't find too many attractions on Chicago's South Side, nor will you find the volume of nightlife that you'll have noticed north of the river. Much of the South Side is still something approaching a no-go area for visitors, and should not be entered lightly. However, there is an assortment of interesting spots scattered about the city south of Museum Campus: if nothing else, a trip south should provide a welcome contrast from the heady atmosphere found in the north of the city, where most holidaymakers spend most if not all of their time.

Of course, if you're here on business and, specifically, for a convention, you're likely to find yourself at **McCormick Place** (E 23rd

Street, at S Lake Shore Drive) for much of your stay. A gargantuan near-South Side site that's home to about 500 zillion conventioneers each year, it doesn't bear detailing in any great depth. Still, a few points are worth making: first, it's absolutely huge, with over two million square feet (186,000 square metres) of meeting space and excellent facilities; also, the massive conventions held here are the reason why mere vacationers have trouble finding a hotel room in Chicago; and finally, it's an absolute bugger to get back from at the end of the day. For more information, consult its website, www.mccormickplace.com, or call 312 791 7000.

Just north of McCormick Place is the Prairie Avenue Historical District, which is where you'll find some lovely examples of old Chicago architecture. **Clarke House** and its sister location, **Glessner House**, are two of the once-legendary neighbourhood's few surviving houses. During the late 1900s, before the city's shift in opulent living from the South to the North Side, this was the grandest part of town, home to many of the city's leading magnates and high-society types. Clarke House, a breathtaking Greek revival built in 1836, is the oldest house in the city and an impressive monument to the area's past glories. This despite the fact that it's had to be moved twice to avoid demolition; it now sits at 1855 S Indiana Avenue. Glessner House, built in 1887, was rescued in 1966 and is now a National Historic Landmark.

Tours of the pair begin at Glessner House, though while you're there, be sure to take a peek at the exteriors of the neighbouring houses, which include the **William B Kimball House**, the **Joseph G Coleman House** and the **Elbridge G Keith House**, all on S Prairie

Avenue at no.1801, no.1811 and no.1900 respectively. Ask nicely, and your guide will be able to fill you in on the intriguing history of the area and these houses in particular.

Also in this area is an invaluable though often overlooked museum, a tour of which invariably provides for a culturally educative experience after the deliciously grand architecture nearby. The **National Vietnam Veterans' Art Museum** holds a stock of over 500 works of art by close to 100 veterans. It's well worth a look. Also in the area, a few blocks away on Michigan Avenue, is the **Blues Heaven Foundation**, a shrine to Chicago's famous musical heritage (*see below* **Seein' the blues**).

Glessner House & Clarke House Mansion

1800 S Prairie Avenue, at E 18th Street (312 326 1480). CTA Cermak/Chinatown. **Open** *tours noon, 1pm, 2pm Wed-Sun.* **Admission** *one house $7; both houses $11; free Wed.* **Credit** MC, V. **Map** p304 J16.

National Vietnam Veterans' Art Museum

1801 S Indiana Avenue, at E 18th Street (312 326 0270). CTA Cermak/Chinatown. **Open** *11am-6pm Tue-Fri; 10am-5pm Sat; noon-5pm Sun.* **Admission** $5; $4 concessions. **Credit** MC, V. **Map** p304 J16.

Hyde Park

Though the locale surrounding the Adler Planetarium, the Shedd Aquarium and the Field Museum has claimed the word 'Campus' as part of its name (*see page 57*), it's fair to say that Hyde Park is far more deserving of such a moniker. For this implausibly pleasant little village – and village it near enough is – takes as

Seein' the blues

Chicago is, among other things, home to more blues legends, clubs and stories than anywhere besides Clarksdale, Mississippi and maybe Memphis. The former headquarters of the venerable Chess Records – aka the home of Chicago blues – is now a non-profit museum, and is as good a place as any to learn about Chicago's rich blues history. Tours of the **Blues Heaven Foundation** are comprehensive, erudite and, unlike a lot of museum tours, actually fun. Blues heroes like Willie Dixon (who set up the Blues Heaven Foundation to preserve the Chess legacy), Koko Taylor (whose long-ago classic *Wang Dang Doodle*

may as well be the Chicago national anthem) and Muddy Waters (who surely needs no introduction) recorded here, and their presence is felt in every corner of the building. Rock scholars may find the building's address already rings a bell: unsurprising, as the Rolling Stones recorded a song entitled *2120 South Michigan Avenue* after a session here.

Blues Heaven Foundation

2120 S Michigan Avenue, at E 21st Street (312 808 1286). CTA Cermak. **Open** noon-2pm Mon-Sat. **Admission** free (donations welcome). **Map** p304 J16.

its centrepiece the campus of the **University of Chicago**. As with most neighbourhoods whose dominant feature is a university, Hyde Park is at least partly defined by the students who call the area home for nine months of the year.

But while the students of DePaul University in Lincoln Park (*see page 75*) are, by and large, young and lively – a fact apparent enough from an early-evening trawl around some of the local bars – Hyde Park boasts more graduates than undergraduates. As a result, the area is rather more sedate and relaxed than its collegiate compatriot to the north, though there are bustling areas of activity around 53rd and 57th Streets. Not that it's all students around here: far from it, in fact. The areas to the south and west of the locale are shabby, to say the least, but Hyde Park itself is smart and decidedly middle class. It's also home to a number of fine museums and one truly great one.

The **Museum of Science & Industry** is itself reason enough to make the half-hour Metra journey down to this part of town. One of Chicago's most popular attractions, this interactive, kid-friendly museum is housed in an enormous turn-of-the-19th-century building by Jackson Park to the east of the university, and is an absolute marvel. Don't plan to be in and out of here in a hurry: there are thousands of exhibits to examine, including a German submarine you can walk through and a mock-up of a human heart that's over 20 feet (six metres) tall. Also among the permanent exhibits are a history of fast-food toys dating back to 1977 and an enterprise exhibit that includes a financial fast track you can actually climb. Gift shops and snack shops abound. There's an Omnimax theatre, too, though admission is separate and it's best to call ahead for tickets. And nearby is **Promontory Point**, a lovely spot on which to while away an hour or so in the company of a picnic and a close companion.

After such an all-encompassing experience, Hyde Park's other museums have a tough job competing. But compete they do. Head east on 58th Street into the body of the university itself – passing Frank Lloyd Wright's wonderful **Robie House** on the way (*see pages 30-1* **The Wright stuff**) – and you'll find something of a hidden gem. The University of Chicago's **Oriental Institute Museum** is a world-class showcase for the history, art and architecture of the ancient Near East. The museum's four galleries – Egyptian, Mesopotamian, Persian and Assyrian – are currently undergoing a lengthy renovation and are scheduled to reopen successively over the next few years. The already-open Egyptian gallery features an excavated statue of King Tut, along with a collection of ancient pottery, reliefs and a Roman-era mummy. When the rest of the museum has opened, it should be a stop on every visitor's itinerary. As it is, it's still worth a visit.

Two blocks north and one block west is the small but perfectly formed **David & Alfred Smart Museum**. Named after the founders of *Esquire* magazine, it boasts an impressive art collection as well as furniture designed by native son Frank Lloyd Wright and sculptures by Henry Moore and Degas. And west from there, in the sedate surroundings of Washington Park, is the **DuSable Museum of African American History**. With a stated mission to preserve and interpret the history and achievement of African-Americans, the DuSable Museum was founded in 1961 and named after Chicago's first permanent settler (*see page 4*). It is the nation's oldest African-American history museum and holds over 1,300 artefacts, including a sweeping collection of slave and civil rights memorabilia. The DuSable also hosts lectures, literary readings, art education programmes and dance performances.

While you're here, of course, you may want to check out the university itself. It operates free tours every Saturday at 10am (information on 773 702 8374), which makes for a pleasant diversion on a weekend morning. Whether you're on a tour or not, try and stop by the **Rockefeller Memorial Chapel**. A grand construction named after John D, who helped found the university, the chapel boasts some terrific stained-glass windows and a suitably grand carillon.

David & Alfred Smart Museum

University of Chicago, 5550 S Greenwood Avenue, at E 55th Street (773 702 0200). Metra 55th-56th-57th Street. **Open** 10am-4pm Tue, Wed, Fri; 10am-9pm Thur; noon-6pm Sat, Sun. **Admission** free. **Map** p311 X17.

DuSable Museum of African American History

740 E 56th Street, at S Cottage Grove Avenue (773 947 0600). CTA Garfield. **Open** 10am-5pm Mon-Sat; noon-5pm Sun. **Admission** $3; $2 concessions; free under-6s, all on Sun. **Credit** AmEx, Disc, MC, V. **Map** p311 X17.

Museum of Science & Industry

5700 S Lake Shore Drive, at E 57th Street (773 684 1414/www.msichicago.org). Metra 59th Street. **Open** 9.30am-4pm Mon-Fri; 9.30am-5.30pm Sat, Sun. **Admission** $7 adults; $3.50-$6 concessions; free under-2s. **Credit** AmEx, Disc, MC, V. **Map** p311 Z17.

Oriental Institute Museum

University of Chicago, 1155 E 58th Street, at S University Avenue (773 702 9507). Metra 59th Street. **Open** 10am-4pm Tue, Thur-Sat; 10am-8.30pm Wed; noon-4pm Sun. **Admission** free. **Map** p311 X17.

Chicago by Season

Fireworks, festivals, fairs and feasts: dozens of events make the Chicago year go round.

Chicago is a city that thrives on diversity and celebration, regardless of the time of year. The people, music, restaurants, nightlife and art that constitute the city's culture and define its style are celebrated daily on an individual basis, and annually across the city. Whether you're traversing the Magnificent Mile in the frozen heart of winter or digging your toes into the lakefront summer sand, there's bound to be an eruption of seasonal merriment near by.

Winter sees the start of hibernation for many Chicagoans, but it's also a season that transforms the concrete and steel façade of the city into a frosted and sublime panorama – a change demanding awe, as well as providing an impetus for festivity. The **Mayor's Office of Special Events** is the chief planner for most events; even when the city is enveloped by the freezing weather, it lays on a number of activities and festivities, catering to the throngs of seasonal shoppers on Michigan Avenue.

With the thawing of the last snowfall, though, the city bristles with awakened energy and the more boisterous festivities begin to take place. The spring and summer seasons teem with city- and neighbourhood-sponsored events, with scarcely a weekend neglected. The pillars of the summer roster are undeniably the series of music festivals in Grant Park, led by the

Grant Park Music Festival (*see page 90* **The sounds of summer**), and the **Taste of Chicago** (*see page 92* **Food, glorious food**), a gluttonous feast of Chicago's restaurants that's savoured by millions. However, **neighbourhood festivals** also abound during summer, and generally follow a predictable if entertaining pattern: live acts, local food and craft vendors, and lots and lots of beer.

Other summer essentials include the numerous parades that weave through the city streets, in which various ethnic groups take turns treading jubilantly through town and generally leaving a stream of bloated bars and spontaneous revelries in their wake. An assortment of art, book, flower and cultural fairs fill out the calendar of the warmer seasons.

INFORMATION

Admission to all the events listed here is free unless otherwise indicated. Be sure to contact the hosting organisation, the **Mayor's Office of Special Events** (312 744 3315) or the **Chicago Office of Tourism** (312 744 2499) for detailed information on scheduled events: many existing festivities may be subject to change and many new ones are regularly added throughout the year. See its website – www.ci.chi.il.us/SpecialEvents/index.html – for more details. The Chicago Office of Tourism offers a quarterly publication that contains a comprehensive catalogue of seasonal events and celebrations. Indispensable for the short-term visitor, it can be picked up at either of their downtown branches at the Chicago Water Works (163 E Pearson Street, at N Avenue, Near North/Magnificent Mile) and the Chicago Cultural Center (E Randolph Street, at N Michigan Avenue, The Loop).

Public holidays

If a holiday falls on a weekend, it is celebrated on the following Monday.

Dates

New Year's Day 1 Jan
Martin Luther King's Birthday 3rd Mon in Jan
Presidents' Day 3rd Mon in Feb
Pulaski Day 1st Mon in Mar
Memorial Day last Mon in May
Independence Day 4 July
Labor Day 1st Mon in Sept
Columbus Day 2nd Mon in Oct
Veterans Day 11 Nov
Thanksgiving Day 4th Thur in Nov
Christmas Day 25 Dec

Spring

St Patrick's Day Parade

Dearborn Street, from W Wacker Drive to W Van Buren Street, The Loop (information 312 744 3315). CTA any station in the Loop. **Date** 17 Mar. **Map** p305 H11-13.
A Chicago institution, in which gigantic balloons are ushered through town by verdant floats and festive Irish (and Irish-ish) folk. The Chicago River is dyed a suitably lairy green, and any pub that serves Guinness proclaims itself the spiritual home of the

party. The South Side, cradle of Chicago's Irish, is where the parties are the strongest: nary a barstool is left unattended from dawn to dusk.

Spring & Easter Flower Show

Garfield Park Conservatory, 300 N Central Park Boulevard, at N Lake Street, West Side (312 746 5100). CTA Kedzie (Green) or Kedzie-Holman. Lincoln Park Conservatory, 2400 N Stockton Drive, at W Fullerton Parkway, Lincoln Park (312 742 7737). CTA Fullerton. **Date** *late Mar-early Apr.* **Map** *Lincoln Park Conservatory p308 G5.*

Lincoln Park Conservatory and the Garfield Park Conservatory boast a collage of the first blooms to escape the icy hold of winter. The opening reception is held at the Garfield Park Conservatory on the Sunday, with refreshments, children's activities and music provided throughout the six-week run.

Art Chicago

Festival Hall, Navy Pier, 600 E Grand Avenue, at Lake Michigan (Art Chicago 312 587 3300/ www.artchicago.com). CTA Grand. **Date** *mid-May.* **Admission** *$10; $7 concessions; free under-10s. 3-day pass $20; 5-day pass $30;* **Credit** AmEx, DC, Disc, MC, V. **Map** *p306 K10.*

More than 200 galleries from over 20 countries pour their exhibits into the Festival Hall at Navy Pier. This world class exposition of visual art runs for five days beginning on Mother's Day weekend. During the fair, a shuttle bus transports visitors from Navy Pier to the city's art galleries in River North and the West Loop.

Mayor Daley's Kids & Kites Festival

Museum of Science & Industry, 5700 S Lake Shore Drive, at E 57th Street, Hyde Park (information 312 744 3315). Metra 55th-56th-57th Street or 59th Street. **Date** *May & Oct.* **Map** *p311 Z17.*

A surefire kid-pleaser, the Kitefest offers classes on designing, constructing and (of course) flying kites. Skilled flyers perform thrilling displays of aerial acrobatics on the lawn of the Museum of Science & Industry, while young 'uns howl as they get their strings all tangled up.

Summer

For details of the **Gay & Lesbian Pride Parade,** *see page 203* **The queer year.**

Neighborhood Summer Festivals

All over Chicago (information 312 744 3315). **Date** *May-Oct.* **Admission** *varies.*

Chicago's neighbourhoods take turns celebrating for a weekend in the summer. Streets are blocked off and local vendors provide meals, usually of the deep-fried or between-the-bun variety. A roster of local

The sounds of summer

During the summer months, Grant Park becomes the focus of Chicago's music scene, with several large festivals showcasing a variety of musical genres.

The backbone of the season is the **Grant Park Music Festival** (312 742 4763; www.grantparkmusicfestival.com), a summer-long series of free evening concerts by the Grant Park Symphony Orchestra at the Petrillo Music Shell. Founded in 1935 by the Chicago Park District, this is the only free, publicly funded, outdoor classical music festival in the States. In 2001, it will move to a state-of-the-art music pavilion in Chicago's Millennium Park, designed by Frank Gehry.

In early June, the **Gospel Festival** (information 312 744 3315) draws gospel musicians for three days of soulful jubilation. This is followed by the **Chicago Blues Festival** (information 312 744 3315), the behemoth of Chicago's summer musical festival family. The four-day event sees the best in local, national and international blues acts performing to huge and appreciative crowds. Good music is guaranteed from wherever a seat can be found or created.

The blues gives way to folk, bluegrass, Cajun and rockabilly during the **Country Music Festival** (information 312 744 3315) for two days in early July and, later in the summer, Grant Park swings to Latin, Cuban and salsa rhythms at the Latin music festival, **Viva! Chicago** (312 744 3370). The **Chicago Jazz Festival** (312 744 3370) brings some of the most acclaimed names on the jazz circuit to town at the end of August for four days of be-bop and swing. Less raucous than its bluesy big brother, the Jazz Fest features a splendid art fair replete with sculptures, jewellery, metalwork, pottery and paintings.

Rounding off the season, the **Celtic Fest Chicago** (information 312 744 3315) in September celebrates Celtic heritage from around the world, with traditional music and dance, Celtic food vendors, crafts, storytelling and poetry.

Grant Park

at E Jackson Drive & S Columbus Drive, The Loop. CTA Adams or Jackson (Red). **Map** p305 J12.

Deckchairs, picnics and the CSO: essential ingredients of the **Ravinia Festival**.

and national bands typically play on one or more stages. Expect to pay a stiff admission at the gate, but note that many neighbourhoods turn a portion of the proceeds over to charity or invest them in improving the conditions of their district. A full schedule can be obtained from the Mayor's Office of Special Events on the above number.

Ravinia Festival
Ravinia Park, at Green Bay & Lake Cook Roads, Highland Park (847 266 5100). Metra Ravinia. **Date** June-Sept. **Admission** *lawn* $8-$10; *reserved seats* $15-$50. **Credit** AmEx, DC, Disc, MC, V.
This idyllic North Shore music venue is home to the Chicago Symphony Orchestra during the summer. The CSO performs several times each week, with jazz and pop artists filling the roster. The priciest tickets are for the covered pavilion, which guarantees seats and views of the performers; however, the secret to truly experiencing Ravinia are the lawn seats, which invite picnicking and stargazing.

57th Street Art Fair
E 57th Street, at S Kimbark Avenue, Hyde Park (773 493 3247/www.57thstreetartfair.org). Metra 55th-56th-57th Street. **Date** 1st weekend in June. **Map** p311 Y17.
Galleries and individual artists submit their works to the discriminating eye of the jury and the roving eye of the public at the oldest art festival of its kind in the Midwest. The pieces on show are generally of a higher grade than those offered by the festival's other summer kin.

Printer's Row Book Fair
S Dearborn Street, between W Congress Parkway & W Polk Street, South Loop (312 987 9896). CTA Harrison or LaSalle (Blue). **Date** 1st weekend in June. **Map** p304 H13.
Printer's Row, once the wellspring of the city's publishing prosperity, rekindles its heritage once a year by offering a myriad of new and used books over a weekend in the South Loop. Over 170 of the nation's most diverse booksellers are represented, making this the largest literary festival in the Midwest.

Old Town Art Fair
N Lincoln Park West, at W Wisconsin Street, Old Town (information 312 337 1938). CTA Sedgwick. **Date** 2nd weekend in June. **Map** p308 G6.
This juried art fair in historic Old Town caters more to the thirsting rover than the discriminating art collector, but the neighbourhood- and people-watching potential is enormous.

Theatre on the Lake
2400 N Lake Shore Drive, at W Fullerton Avenue, Lincoln Park (312 742 7994). CTA 51 bus. **Date** mid-June-mid-Aug. **Admission** $10. **Credit** V. **Map** p308 H5.
Some of the best received Off-Loop theatre productions of the previous year are presented in a semi-outdoor theatre in Lincoln Park. Re-staged shows do not always match the quality of the original, but this is a charming way to spend a summer evening by the water. Tickets are a bargain at $10.

Food, glorious food

Proud locals often claim that Chicago's cuisine is one of the city's foremost attractions, and it would be difficult to find a taste bud that would disagree. Restaurants of all ethnic and stylistic origins riddle the sidewalks of Chicago, tempting the salivary glands of the roving masses with their savoury lures.

You could spend a lifetime in Chicago and only sample a portion of its 7,000 restaurants. This is exactly the quandary that Arnie Morton, owner of the celebrated Morton's Steak House, attempted to resolve when he organised the **Taste of Chicago** in 1980. He was looking to create a forum in which Chicagoans and visitors could sample menus from the city's restaurants without the expense of dining independently. The restaurants, of course, would benefit from the public exposure.

From humble beginnings, a veritable monster has grown. The Taste of Chicago currently consumes Grant Park for 11 summer days from late June until the 4 July weekend.

More than 70 restaurants stake tents along the park sidewalk and medians, churning their fodder out with wholesale efficiency. Chicago's elite restaurants have long turned up their noses at the feast, but those lower on the food chain easily fill the vacancies. A number of Chicago mainstays still participate, including **Ann Sather** (*see page 142*), the **Billy Goat Tavern** (*see page 146*) and **Original Gino's East** (*see page 138*), but the bulk of the roster consists of the tenuous celeb eateries, such as **Iron Mike's Grille** (*see page 119*) and **Harry Caray's** (*see page 132*), and neighbourhood start-ups vying for a more permanent slot.

The event has developed into something of a carnival. Towering inflatable beer cans bob lazily from atop distributor tents. Cash and credit vendors lurk at footpath junctions offering raffled prizes and promotional deals. Disc jockeys pontificate from broadcast booths like sideshow barkers. Free concerts are offered nightly, featuring a number of acts

Natsu Matsuri

Buddhist Temple of Chicago, 1151 W Leland Avenue, at N Broadway, Far North (773 334 4661). CTA Lawrence. **Date** last weekend in June. **Admission** free; $3 donation suggested.
Heralded as 'Chicago's longest running Japanese cultural festival', this celebration at the Buddhist Temple features a variety of Japanese food, music, dance, arts and crafts. Among the crowd favourites are a martial arts exhibition, a traditional tea ceremony and a haiku contest.

Andersonville Midsommerfest

N Clark Street, between W Foster Avenue & W Berwyn Street, Far North (773 665 4682). CTA Berwyn. **Date** June.
Once the home of Chicago's prominent Swedish community, the business district of N Clark Street all the way up in Andersonville is sequestered by maypole dancers, Swedes in colourful folk costumes and general revelry during this fun summer festival.

Independence Day Concert & Fireworks

Grant Park, The Loop (information 312 744 3315). CTA Adams. **Date** 3 July. **Map** p304-5 J11-14.
Huge crowds flock to Grant Park the day before Independence Day to sway to live bands, then turn their eyes to the sky for a spectacular fireworks display that manages to diminish the reach of the skyline. The display is best viewed from Grant Park and environs and along the nearby lakefront.

Race to Mackinac

Monroe Harbor, Lake Michigan, at 100 South, The Loop (Chicago Yacht Club 312 861 7777). CTA Adams. **Date** July. **Map** p305 K12.
The world's largest freshwater yacht race begins in Chicago's Monroe Harbor and ends 333 miles later at Mackinac Island, Michigan (*see p259*). The party the preceding night, which is open to the public, sees thousands of sailors spout their lore and reverence for the regatta.

Sheffield Garden Walk

N Sheffield Avenue, at W Webster Avenue, Lincoln Park (773 929 9255/www.sheffieldfestivals.org). CTA Armitage. **Date** July. **Map** p308 E5.
Lincoln Park's more genteel homes open their garden gates to crowds of admirers at this charming waste of a summer's day. Children are likely to be found soliciting homemade lemonade between stops and garden curators linger, primed with advice and pride. The walk also provides a peaceful retreat from the block party's more boisterous elements.

Venetian Night

Lake Michigan, from the Adler Planetarium, Museum Campus to Monroe Harbor, The Loop (information 312 744 3315). CTA Red or Green line between Monroe or Adams & Roosevelt/State or Roosevelt/Wabash. **Date** late July. **Map** p304-5 K12-14.
Boat owners celebrate their water-borne community by adorning their crafts with lights and parading them along the waterfront at twilight. A brilliant fireworks display concludes the event.

that are typically past their prime. The Taste Stage, a smaller set-up on Congress Parkway, provides a continuous calliope for the frenzy of people who circulate the footpath besieging the food stands.

It's the largest food festival in the world, with nearly four million attendees each year. Indeed, there are times when it can feel like all four million are in attendance at the same time. Visitors and residents with flexible hours can enjoy the event during its off-hours: weekdays just before lunch and during the afternoon. But the desk-tied are less fortunate: lunchtimes are congested affairs, with crowds of office-dwellers looking to break the cafeteria monotony, while the evenings are choked with hungry crowds. grappling with one another to find a queue for the next barbecued chicken leg or overpriced beer. Weekends are worse and are best avoided; 3 July is when attendance is the heaviest, though this is due at least in part to the spectacular fireworks display in the evening.

For those courageous enough to take on the event, comfortable shoes and sunscreen are musts: the event always seems to coincide with a horrific heatwave. Buy food tickets in advance at **Dominick's** (*see page* 174*):* you'll save a buck on each strip of ten with a Fresh Values Card and won't have to wait in line at the park – and distribute your party among separate vendor lines for maximum food-gathering effectiveness. And bring something with which to stake out your territory: a perishable blanket, spool of chicken wire or small Uzi will suffice. Otherwise, you'll find yourself standing throughout, wrestling with a paper plate, a drink and your rationale for choosing to attend.

Taste of Chicago

Grant Park, at E Jackson Drive & S Columbus Drive, The Loop (information 312 744 3315). CTA Adams or Jackson (Red). **Date** late June-early July. **Admission** free; ten food tickets $6. **Map** p305 J12.

Bud Billiken Day Parade & Picnic

From 39th Street, at S King Drive to Washington Park, at E 51st Street, Hyde Park (information 312 744 3315). CTA Indiana or 51st Street. **Date** 2nd Sat in Aug. **Map** p311 X16.
This African-American parade is the third largest parade in the nation. The patron, Bud Billiken, is associated with an ancient Chinese guardian angel of children. The parade begins on 39th Street and King Drive and proceeds south to Washington Park.

Gold Coast Art Fair

South-east of N State Street & W Division Street, Gold Coast (information 312 744 2400). CTA Chicago (Red). **Date** 2nd Sat in Aug. **Map** p306 H9.
Artists flood the blocks north of the Magnificent Mile hoping to chip away at the wealth that abounds in this neighbourhood. Dealers and roving artists line the blocks south-east from State and Division.

Chicago Air & Water Show

North Avenue Beach, from E Oak Street to W Diversey Parkway, Gold Coast, Old Town & Lincoln Park (information 312 744 3315). CTA Clark/Division. **Date** Aug. **Map** p307-8 J8-H4
Millions cram the lakefront to witness teams of air-craft and boats performing thrilling acrobatic exer-cises. The crowds are hellish, but the stunts are fun.

Chicago Carifete

Around the streets of Hyde Park (773 509 5079). CTA Garfield/Metra 59th Street. **Date** late Aug. **Map** p311.

This celebration of Caribbean culture includes a lively masquerade parade through the streets of Hyde Park. Costumed bands with steel drummers keep the procession in stride, while Caribbean cuisine and stalls offering cultural wares are also on hand.

Autumn

For details of the **Chicago International Film Festival**, *see page* 197 **Festivals**.

Around the Coyote

Galleries around N Damen Avenue, W North Avenue & N Milwaukee Avenue, Wicker Park/Bucktown (773 342 6777/www.aroundthecoyote.org). CTA Damen. **Date** Sept. **Map** p310 B7.
Around the Coyote offers a glimpse into the personal studios and galleries belonging to the artists who define the Wicker Park/Bucktown district. Art in all its mutations can be seen, and that which is tangible is usually for sale. The association also organises other events, including theatre and comedy, as part of the festival.

German-American Festival

4700 N Lincoln Avenue, at W Leland Avenue, Far North (847 647 9522). CTA Western. **Date** Sept.
Kind of a Diet Oktoberfest: it features all the ingre-dients of its Bavarian counterpart, with the notable exception of the stewed masses. The festival coin-cides with the Von Steuben Day Parade, which takes place in the Loop.

Berghoff's Oktoberfest

Berghoff Restaurant, 17 W Adams Street, at S State Street, The Loop (312 427 3170). CTA Adams or Monroe (Blue, Red). **Date** mid-Sept. **Map** p305 H12.

A raucous but consistently popular street festival held in front of the restaurant of the same name on W Adams Street in the Loop. This three-day beer fest comes complete with imported German bands and there are Bratwursts galore within easy stumbling distance. Just make sure you don't have to be up early the next morning.

World Music Fest Chicago

Various venues (312 742 1938/www.ci.chi.il.us). **Date** late Sept-early Oct. **Admission** free-$10. **Credit** varies.

A newcomer to the music festival family, this ten-day event showcases scores of musical ensembles from all ends of the globe, some traditional, some contemporary, some offering a fusion of various musics. Many events are free, though others are ticketed.

Columbus Day Parade

Dearborn Street, between W Wacker Drive & W Van Buren Street, The Loop (information 312 744 3315). CTA Clark. **Date** 2nd Mon in Oct. **Map** p305 H11-13.

A massive parade ensues on this national holiday, as locals celebrate in very jolly – and, in many cases, slightly alcoholic – fashion.

Chicago Marathon

Around Chicago (312 904 8000/ www.chicagomarathon.com). **Date** Oct. **Admission** *spectators* free; *national runners* $60; *international runners* $70. **Credit** MC, V.

One of the flattest and, therefore, fastest marathons in the world, Chicago's annual 26-miler sees thousands of spectators take to the streets to cheer on the human river that circulates downtown.

Day of the Dead

Mexican Fine Arts Center Museum, 1852 W 19th Street, at S Damen Avenue, South Side (312 738 1503). CTA 18th Street. **Date** 1 Nov.

A fine romance

The **Old St Patrick's Church** was one of the few structures left standing after the Chicago Fire of 1871. The flames miraculously expired two short blocks from the church steps, leaving the grand Romanesque cathedral intact. Most of its neighbours were consumed in the blaze, though, which made the church the oldest public building in Chicago and secured it a spot on the National Register of Historic Places.

The ensuing rebirth of downtown introduced the skyscraper, which gradually became the new temple for the masses. The neighbourhood that once cradled the church was replenished with businesses and parking lots, and when Father Jack Wall came to Old St Pat's in 1983, he found a sad and desolate building standing, nearly forgotten, on the corner of the Loop. Only 25 people attended his first Sunday sermon in a house that was built for thousands, and only four attendees were registered members. The institution was on the verge of closing down.

Father Wall launched a campaign to revive the ailing parish, targeting the young adults who populated the surrounding offices. The astute rector had witnessed the popularity of the numerous neighbourhood block parties held each summer and decided to create one in St Pat's neighbourhood. Nearly 5,000 people attended the first event in 1985, and the success fuelled subsequent parties, always held on the third weekend of July.

Ten years on, the festival was swelling with double the number of crowds that had participated in the original event. The money raised has helped with the much-needed restoration of the church and prompted a number of community outreach programmes, sustained by the church to this day. The crowds accumulated throughout the years have also helped boost the church's membership to its current register of over 2,500 households.

The festival now typically draws 20,000 attendees over its two-night run, which arguably validates its self-proclaimed moniker as the World's Largest Block Party. Upwardly-mobile young urbanites spill from the neighbouring offices at closing time and kick-start the revelry, with support coming from droves of suburbanites and city-dwellers informed of the event via radio and corporate sponsors. Desplaines Street from Madison to Adams, and Monroe Street from the Kennedy expressway to Jefferson Street, are blocked off for the event, and two concert stages, one for popular rock and another for jazz, are erected on the enclosed parking lots.

After 15 years, Father Wall still has a strong hand in the orchestration of the event and continues to make his voice heard in the welcoming pamphlet. 'This event is about coming together to celebrate,' writes the pastor, a fact all too apparent from the state of some of his guests as night draws in.

This traditional Mexican celebration honours the gone-but-not-forgotten with exhibits at the Mexican Fine Arts Center Museum, located in the heart of the largest Mexican community in the Midwest. Macabre art and other accoutrements are showcased.

Christmas Around the World

5700 S Lake Shore Drive, at E 57th Street (773 684 1414/www.msichicago.org). Metra 59th Street. **Date** mid Nov-early Jan. **Open** 9.30am-4pm Mon-Fri; 9.30am-5.30pm Sat, Sun. **Admission** $7 adults; $3.50-$6 concessions; free under-2s. **Credit** AmEx, Disc, MC, V. **Map** p311 Z17.

A cultural survey of the ways different communities celebrate Christmas fills up the Museum of Science & Industry in Hyde Park over the festive season. Diwali, Hanukkah, Kwanzaa and Chinese New Year are among the festivals spotlighted, with children from local schools supplying decorations for Christmas trees. Throughout the festival, there are theatre performances, concerts and dance events to jolly things along.

Magnificent Mile Lights Festival

N Michigan Avenue, from the Chicago River to E Oak Street (information 312 744 3315). CTA Chicago (Red) or Grand. **Date** late Nov. **Map** p306 J9-11.

Millions of twinkling white lights are laced along buildings and trees on Michigan Avenue, from Oak Street to the Chicago River. The lighting ceremony is followed by an ace fireworks display, with stage performances, a petting zoo and ice sculptures also on show. The crowds are dense, but the visual effect is sublime.

Holiday Tree Lighting Ceremony

Daley Plaza, W Washington Boulevard & N Dearborn Street, The Loop (312 744 3315). CTA Washington (Blue, Red). **Date** late Nov. **Map** p305 H12.

A giant 80-ft (25-m) tree constructed of numerous smaller evergreens is illuminated at Daley Plaza the night after Thanksgiving, usually around 4pm. Four giant toy sentries tower over onlookers and an enormous toy train roams the plaza's corner, adding to the skewed proportions of the whole event.

With such a dense concentration of partygoers, it is perhaps inevitable that strangers will come together.

And so it goes, for the World's Largest Block Party has acquired a reputation as the leading matchmaking event of the summer. Literally thousands of hopefuls from Chicago's burgeoning singles scene attend what is nothing if not an enormous love mart, buoyed by the knowledge that at least 60 couples have met at the block party and later married. The statistic even led local deity Oprah Winfrey to profile the event on her show, which only served to heighten its popularity. A number of Block Party mergers have walked up the aisle at Old St Patrick's Church to celebrate their happy day; the church now oversees nearly 200 weddings each year. The rate of subsequent Block Party divorces has not been recorded.

World's Largest Block Party

Old St Patrick's Church, 700 W Adams Street, at S Desplaines Street (312 648 1021). CTA Clinton (Blue). **Date** late July. **Map** p305 F12.

Dr Dolittle wannabes get the animals into the festive spirit at **Lincoln Park Zoo**.

Winter

Christkindlmart

Daley Plaza, W Washington Boulevard & N Dearborn Street, The Loop. CTA Washington (Blue, Red). **Date** late Nov-late Dec. **Map** p305 H12.

The German-American Chamber of Commerce converts Daley Plaza into a German-style market in the run-up to Christmas, with authentic German food and traditional art on offer. A preview of the event is held on Thanksgiving from 11am to 4pm.

Carol to the Animals

2150 N Cannon Drive, at W Webster Avenue, Lincoln Park (312 742 2000). CTA Fullerton. **Date** 2nd Sun in Dec. **Map** p308 H5.

Hordes of visitors roam Lincoln Park Zoo singing carols to the bewildered inmates in what is, on the face of it, the strangest idea ever concocted. Still, it's all very festive, and the creatures love it. We think.

Pre-Kwanzaa Celebration

South Shore Cultural Center, 7059 S Shore Drive, at E 71st Street, South Side (773 509 8080/312 747 2536). Metra South Shore. **Date** mid-Dec.

Kwanzaa is an East African word meaning 'first fruits of the harvest' and is a time for celebration in traditional African society. The South Shore Cultural Center marks the celebration with music, dance and a series of Afro-centric lectures and workshops.

Do-it-Yourself Messiah

220 S Michigan Avenue, at E Adams Street, The Loop (312 294 3000). CTA Adams. **Date** late Dec. **Open** *box office* 10am-6pm Mon-Sat; 11am-4pm Sun. **Credit** AmEx, DC, MC, V. **Map** p305 J12.

A Chicago tradition, in which local have-a-go types join the Chicago Symphony Orchestra in a rousing rendition of Handel's classic. Hallelujah!

Chicago Boat, Sports & RV Show

McCormick Place, E 23rd Street & S Lake Shore Drive, South Side (1-888 322 9922). Metra 23rd Street. **Date** late Jan. **Admission** $8; $6 concessions; free under-12s. **Credit** *groups only* MC, V.

An annual event at Convention Central showcasing the newest in commercial leisure vehicles for a well-moneyed crowd. A few weeks later (in mid-Feb), the car industry congregates here to get their motors running before heading out on the highway at the hugely popular ten-day **Chicago Auto Show** (630 495 2282/www.chicagoautoshow.com; tickets $8; $5 concessions).

Black History Month

Various venues (Chicago Historical Society 312 642 4600). **Date** Feb. **Admission** varies according to venue. **Credit** varies according to venue.

Exhibitions observing African-American heritage are rotated between Navy Pier, the Chicago Cultural Center and the Field Museum of Natural History throughout the month of February. The Chicago Historical Society also organises music concerts, film screenings, theatrical productions, art shows, ethnic dance performances and lectures by visiting scholars to complement the exhibitions.

Chinatown New Year Parade & Lion Dance

From W 24th Place, at S Wentworth Avenue to W Cermak Road, at S Princeton Avenue, Chinatown, South Side (312 225 6148/fax 312 225 1155). CTA Cermak-Chinatown. **Date** 1st Sun after Chinese New Year (early Feb).

Chinese New Year is celebrated with an array of festivities in the streets of Chicago's Chinatown. Included in the celebrations are parades, banquets, lion dances, traditional music and a steady fanfare of exploding firecrackers.

Consumer

Feature boxes

Accommodation

Wherever you lay your hat, that's your home. Assuming you can find anywhere to lay your hat, that is.

Chicago, like other great cities around the world, is a victim of its own popularity. The city is home to myriad hotels, many of which boast a vast number of rooms. However, despite the apparent surfeit of beds, many of the hotels in Chicago tend to book up months in advance.

Though the city is becoming increasingly popular as a holiday destination, the main reason for this perpetual 'no vacancies' state is the city's status as convention capital of the US. Convention block-bookings account for a vast number of Chicago hotel rooms at certain times of the year, and it's for this reason that it's advisable to book as far ahead as possible. Indeed, at peak convention season, hotels have been known to raise their prices above the advertised rack rates: the further you book in advance, the better off you're likely to be.

The chain gang

Many chains have other branches in and around the Chicago region – such as at O'Hare airport – which may prove useful if the downtown hotels are booked up at peak times. Call the 1-800 numbers below or log on to the websites for full details.
Best Western 1-800 780 7234/
www.bestwestern.com
Comfort Inn 1-800 228 5150/
www.comfortinn.com
Hilton 1-800 445 8667/www.hilton.com
Holiday Inn 1-800 445 8667/
www.holiday-inn.com
Hyatt 1-800 233 1234/www.hyatt.com
Marriott 1-800 228 9290/
www.marriott.com
Motel 6 1-800 466 8356/www.motel6.com
Radisson 1-800 333 3333/
www.radisson.com
Ramada 1-800 272 6232/www.ramada.com
Red Roof Inn 1-800 733 7663/
www.redroof.com
Ritz-Carlton 1-800 241 3333/
www.ritzcarlton.com
Sheraton 1-800 325 3535/
www.sheraton.com
Westin 1-800 937 8461/www.westin.com

Conversely, though, when there isn't a convention in town and it's not the middle of summer, you should be able to find a terrific deal on a room if you're prepared to spend an hour or so on the phone: up to 50 per cent off the rack rate in many cases. Many hotels also offer special weekend packages (shopping weekends and the like): always ask about availability when you call.

The expense-account nature of many of the hotel customers in Chicago means that there also aren't many options for travellers on a budget. If, for you, money is no object, then you'll be impeccably catered for by the city. But if you find that money is an object owned mostly by other people, then booking ahead becomes even more imperative. Unless, that is, you want to run the risk of sleeping on Lower Wacker Drive. Which is not a good idea, as anyone who's seen *Henry: Portrait of a Serial Killer* will know only too well.

The rates listed below are meant as a guide, and exclude the crippling hotel tax, which runs to 14.9 per cent on rooms and hotel services. All rates are exclusive of breakfast unless stated. We've also only listed those hotels within reasonable distance of downtown, though other chain hotels can be found further out of town (at O'Hare Airport, for example). For a list of 1-800 numbers and websites for the main hotel chains, *see* **The chain gang**.

BOOKING AGENCIES AND B&B

The **Illinois Reservations Service** (1-800 491 1800) provides a free room-hunting service for hotels within Chicago. If you cancel, you may be charged a booking fee depending on the hotel's policy. **Hot Rooms** (1-800 468 3500/773 468 7666/www.hotrooms.com) provides a similar service, though if you cancel, you will automatically be billed $25.

Bed and breakfast is also available in Chicago. If you'd rather avoid the big downtown properties, then B&B can be arranged in a myriad local properties through **Bed & Breakfast/Chicago** (1-800 375 7084/773 248 0005/fax 773 248 7090/www.chicago-bed-breakfast.com). In addition to organising reservations, it also owns and operates a Lincoln Park B&B property, the **Windy City Inn** (773 248 7058/www.chicago-inn.com).

For a taste of luxury, duck into **The Drake's** incredible lobby.
See page 101.

Deluxe

Chicago Hilton & Towers

720 S Michigan Avenue, at E Balbo Drive, South Loop, IL 60605 (1-800 445 8667/312 922 4400/ fax 312 922 5240/www.chicagohilton.com). CTA Harrison. **Rates** *single/double* $159-$314; *suite* $625-$725. **Credit** AmEx, DC, Disc, MC, V. **Map** p305 J13.
For a hotel so large – with 1,543 rooms, it's virtually a city within a city – this Hilton flagship does a commendable job of projecting style. Its vast, always-crowded public spaces are decorated with fine art, expensive flower arrangements and plush carpets and seating. A concierge level in the tower has its own check-in and a standard of pampering consistent with the hotel's premium prices. Kitty O'Shea's is a lively Irish pub where the brogues are real (thanks to an exchange programme with Ireland), while Buckingham's fine-dining restaurant offers prime beef and a notable collection of single-malt Scotch.
Hotel services *Air-conditioning. Bar. Beauty salon. Business services. Concierge. Disabled: adapted rooms. Gym. Limousine service. No-smoking floors. Parking. Restaurant. Swimming pool.*
Room services *Dataport. Mini-bar. Room service (7am-11pm). TV: VCR/cable.*

The Drake

140 E Walton Street, at N Michigan Avenue, Gold Coast, IL 60611 (1-800 553 7253/312 787 2200/ fax 312 787 1431/www.thedrakehotel.com). CTA Chicago (Red). **Rates** *single/double* $196-$395; *suite* $395-$2,050. **Credit** AmEx, DC, Disc, MC, V. **Map** p306 J9.
London has its Dorchester, New York its Plaza. Chicago, though, has the Drake. As icon hotels will, it attracts royalty (Princess Diana) and Hollywood (Julia Roberts in *My Best Friend's Wedding*). But mostly, this is a traditional 'old money' hotel favoured by Chicago socialites. Built in 1920, the Drake exudes style, with velvet seats on elevators, bowls of fresh fruit on each floor and rooms with graceful high ceilings and a full range of modern amenities. There are some 485 rooms and 50 suites; superb seafood is served in the **Cape Cod Room** (*see p140*) and harp music is performed in the classic Palm Court.
Hotel services *Air-conditioning. Babysitting. Bar. Business services. Concierge. Disabled: adapted rooms. Gym. Limousine service. No-smoking floors. Parking. Restaurant.* **Room services** *Dataport. Mini-bar. Room service (24hrs). TV: cable.*

Fairmont

200 N Columbus Drive, at E Lake Street, The Loop, IL 60601 (1-800 526 2008/312 565 8000/fax 312 856 1032/www.fairmont.com). CTA Lake or State. **Rates** *single/double* $179-$349; *suite* $600-$3,700. **Credit** AmEx, DC, Disc, MC, V. **Map** p305 J11.
Not only are these digs exceedingly comfortable – oversized bathrooms (equipped with mini TVs), separate dressing rooms, fluffy towelling robes – but they're easy to get to without trudging down long corridors: none of the Fairmont's 692 rooms and suites is more than four doors away from an elevator. This is the ultimate hotel for 'cocooning', given ultra-comfortable guestrooms and a variety of in-house attractions. Afternoon tea accompanied by piano music is served in the sunken lobby; the Art Deco Metropole lounge attracts top jazz performers; and at Primavera Ristorante, professional singers serve up opera, operetta and showtunes.
Hotel services *Air-conditioning. Bar. Business services. Concierge. Disabled: adapted rooms. Gym. No-smoking floors. Parking. Restaurant. Swimming pool.* **Room services** *Dataport. Mini-bar. Room service (24hrs). TV: cable.*

Four Seasons

120 E Delaware Place, at N Michigan Avenue, Gold Coast, IL 60611 (1-800 332 3442/312 280 8800/ fax 312 280 9184/www.fourseasons.com). CTA Chicago (Red). **Rates** *single* $425; *double* $465; *suite* $545. **Credit** AmEx, DC, Disc, MC, V. **Map** p306 J9.
You want style, comfort and class? You'll find them at this 343-room hotel that consistently makes critics' and travellers' 'best' lists. You'll get the idea of its decorous comfort as you explore public spaces decorated with Italian marble, glittering crystal and exquisite woodwork. Service is also a priority, with twice-daily maid service and a carafe of water delivered at turndown. Those in search of edibles and potables will find the acclaimed Seasons restaurant, a clubby cigar bar, and a lounge with a wood-burning fireplace, a waterfall and lovely views of the Magnificent Mile.
Hotel services *Air-conditioning. Babysitting. Bar. Business services. Concierge. Disabled: adapted rooms. Gym. No-smoking floors. Parking. Restaurant. Swimming pool.* **Room services** *Dataport. Mini-bar. Room service (24hrs). TV: VCR (on request)/cable.*

Hotel Inter-Continental

505 N Michigan Avenue, at E Grand Avenue, Near North, IL 60611 (1-800 628 2112/312 944 4100/ fax 312 944 1320/http://hotels.chicago.interconti.com). CTA Grand. **Rates** *single/double* $239-$409; *suite* $475-$2,000. **Credit** AmEx, DC, Disc, MC, V. **Map** p306 J10.
Architecture buffs love this 844-room hotel, built in 1929 as the Medinah Athletic Club, a luxury men's club. Get a tape deck from the concierge for a self-guided tour of eight floors that are a crazy textbook of styles, from French Renaissance to Byzantine. Visit Tarzan's swimming pool: an opulent Venetian-styled pool with stained glass and Majolica tile where Olympic gold medalist and movie Tarzan Johnny Weissmuller trained. The guestrooms here are also lavish, with rare woods, thick carpets and bedspreads that replicate a 19th-century French design. And though the nearby shops may be calling, don't miss afternoon tea with Devonshire cream tea.
Hotel services *Air-conditioning. Bar. Beauty salon. Business services. Concierge. Disabled: adapted rooms. Garden. Gym. Limousine service. No-smoking floors. Parking. Restaurant. Swimming pool.* **Room services** *Dataport. Mini-bar. Refrigerator. Room service. TV: VCR/cable.*

Consumer

Palmer House Hilton

17 E Monroe Street, at S State Street, The Loop, IL 60603 (1-800 445 8667/312 726 7500/fax 312 917 1707/www.chicagohilton.com). CTA Monroe (Blue, Red). **Rates** *single* $119-$349; *double* $149-$379; *suite* $450-$1,100. **Credit** AmEx, DC, Disc, MC, V. **Map** p305 H11.

On 26 September 1871, the first Palmer House opened to the public. Thirteen days later, it burned to the ground in the Chicago Fire. Undaunted, entrepreneur Potter Palmer raised the money to rebuild and the hotel was back in business by July 1873. As the longest continuously operating hotel in America, it's as modern as a state-of-the-art golf simulator, and as Victorian as the Florentine gilt and frescoes of its opulent lobby. The spectacular lobby ceiling has 21 individual oil paintings by a noted 19th-century muralist. Get your exotic cocktails at Trader Vic's, your bountiful buffets at the French Quarter and your live sports at the Big Downtown.

Hotel services *Air-conditioning. Babysitting. Bar. Beauty salon. Business services. Concierge. Disabled: adapted rooms. Gym. Limousine services. No-smoking floors. Parking. Restaurant. Swimming pool.* **Room services** *Dataport. Mini-bar. Room service (6am-2am). TV: VCR/cable.*

Ritz-Carlton Chicago

160 E Pearson Street, at N Michigan Avenue, Gold Coast, IL 60611 (1-800 621 6906/312 266 1000/fax 312 266 1194/www.fourseasons.com). CTA Chicago (Red). **Rates** *single/double* $360-$455; *suite* $510-$1,610. **Credit** AmEx, DC, Disc, MC, V. **Map** p306 J9.

Shoppers from adjoining Water Tower Place gladly set down their bags and take up a teacup or Martini glass here. The lavish lobby of the Ritz-Carlton is a soothing, restful place, with a massive skylight and bubbling fountain that provides a soft background for the many activities held in lobby bars and restaurants. Under the guidance of Sarah Steger, the Dining Room is one of the finest restaurants in town. Spacious guestrooms feature nine-foot ceilings, attractive green-and-red colour schemes, cherry-wood furnishings and marble bathrooms. Premier rooms on the 30th floor guarantee spectacular views of the city.

Hotel services *Air-conditioning. Babysitting. Bar. Beauty salon. Business services. Concierge. Disabled: adapted rooms. Gym. Limousine service. No-smoking floors. Parking. Restaurants. Swimming pool.* **Room services** *Dataport. Mini-bar. Refrigerator. Room service (24hrs). TV: VCR (on request)/cable.*

Sheraton Chicago

301 E North Water Street, at N Columbus Drive, Near North/Streeterville, IL 60611 (1-800 325 3535/ 312 464 1000/fax 312 329 6929/www.sheratonchicago.com). CTA Grand. **Rates** *single/double* $129-$429; *suite* $350-$650. **Credit** AmEx, DC, Disc, MC, V. **Map** p306 J11.

This 1.2 million-sq-ft (111,600-sq-m) behemoth catches the rhythms of the river it overlooks. A massive lobby with imported marble and rich wood accents has huge picture windows, while at Waves lobby piano bar, ceiling mirrors reflect the river and create a wave-like effect. Spectators is an upscale sports bar with comfortable green leather couches and views of the Centennial Fountain that, in warm-weather months, periodically arcs a jet of water across the river. At each end of the lobby are quiet, perpetual waterfalls in black granite, while the glass entrance doors mimic Frank Lloyd Wright.

Hotel services *Air-conditioning. Babysitting. Bar. Business services. Concierge. Disabled: adapted rooms. Garden. Gym. Limousine service. No-smoking floors. Parking. Restaurants. Swimming pool.* **Room services** *Dataport. Mini-bar. Refrigerator (on request). Room service (24hrs). TV: VCR (on request)/cable.*

Swissôtel

323 E Wacker Drive, at N Columbus Drive, The Loop, IL 60601 (1-800 654 7263/312 565 0565/ fax 312 565 9930/www.swissotel.com). CTA Lake or State. **Rates** *single/double* $169-$399; *suite* $459-$950. **Credit** AmEx, DC, Disc, MC, V. **Map** p305 J11.

This Swiss hotel (duh!) runs more like a Rolex than a cuckoo clock, though you will find homely touches: a huge bowl of chocolates at the registration desk, say, or the konditorei selling fresh-baked loaves and strudel. Otherwise, this triangular glass edifice is strictly high-tech, from its ergonomically designed furniture to a 42nd-floor state-of-the-art fitness spa that offers spectacular views (every room is designed to provide a lake or river view). Steak lovers will find prime beef at a branch of the famous Palm. In addition to Swissôtel's standard room rates, good-value weekend bed-and-breakfast packages can also be arranged.

Hotel services *Air-conditioning. Bar. Business services. Concierge. Disabled: adapted rooms. Garden. Gym. Limousine service. No-smoking rooms. Parking. Restaurant. Swimming pool.* **Room services** *Dataport. Mini-bar. Refrigerator. Room service (24hrs). TV: VCR/cable.*

Sutton Place

21 E Bellevue Street, at N Rush Street, Gold Coast, IL 60611 (1-800 606 8188/312 266 2100/fax 312 266 2141/www.suttonplace.com). CTA Clark/ Division. **Rates** *single* $189-$300; *double* $214-$325; *suite* $395-$870. **Credit** AmEx, DC, Disc, MC, V. **Map** p309 H9.

Built in 1988, Sutton Place is unashamedly modern. A series of Mapplethorpe photographs – commissioned for the hotel's opening – decorate the lobby and the rooms, which should give some idea as to the modish nature of the place. The rooms are all of uniform size, so you know what you're getting when you pick from the roomy kings, double doubles, junior suites (one room, with a large living area) and one of six penthouse suites. All boast modern, slightly hip decor, wonderfully deep baths with separate showers and, uniquely, stereo systems. This last aspect may explain why the place is popular with musicians from Bonnie Raitt to Maxwell, though it's made possible by the perfect sound-proofing (poured concrete).

Consumer

Hotel services *Air-conditioning. Bar. Business services. Concierge. Disabled: adapted rooms. Gym. Limousine service (7am-2pm). No-smoking rooms. Parking. Restaurant.* **Room services** *Dataport. Mini-bar. Refrigerator. Room service (24hrs). TV: VCR (on request)/cable.*

Talbott Hotel

20 E Delaware Place, at N Rush Street, Gold Coast, IL 60611 (1-800 621 8506/312 944 4970/fax 312 944 7241/www.talbotthotel.com). CTA Chicago (Red). **Rates** *single/double* $139-$229; *suite* $179-$329. **Credit** AmEx, DC, Disc, MC, V. **Map** p306 H9.
If this boutique hotel in a 1920s Gold Coast building is reminiscent of a small, upscale European hotel, it's for good reason. During a trip to Europe, owner Basil Kromelow was captivated by elegant, family-owned hotels with large sitting rooms and tea served by a fireside; duly inspired, he opened the Talbott in 1987. Guests take coffee by the fireplace or sip aperitifs at a sidewalk café as the world goes by. The stylish guestrooms have been refurbished with marble bathrooms and marble vanities with dual sinks.
Hotel services *Air-conditioning. Babysitting. Bar. Business services. Concierge. Disabled: adapted rooms. Limousine service. No-smoking rooms. Restaurant.* **Room services** *Dataport. Mini-bar. Room service (6am-10pm). TV: cable.*

Westin Hotel

909 N Michigan Avenue, at E Delaware Place, Gold Coast, IL 60611 (1-800 228 3000/312 943 7200/ fax 312 943 9347/www.westinmichiganave.com). CTA Chicago (Red). **Rates** *single* $169-$399; *double* $194-$424; *suite* $450-$1,500. **Credit** AmEx, DC, Disc, MC, V. **Map** p306 J9.
A massive refurb has spruced up guestrooms and public spaces at the former Hotel Continental, and added the 300-seat Grill on the Alley, operated by a Beverly Hills-based chain. Baseball fans request the Harry Caray room: a standard room (at standard rates) decorated with photographs of the beloved sports broadcaster and equipped with tapes of his commentaries. Kids enjoy stories over room telephones and Westin Kids' Club amenities.
The other Westin in Chicago, the **Westin River North**, offers fine business services and well-appointed if pricey rooms, perfectly suited to the expense-account traveller. Rates are similar.
Branch: Westin River North 320 N Dearborn Street, at the Chicago River, Near North/River North, IL 60610 (1-800 937 8461/312 744 1900/fax 312 527 2664/www.westinrivernorth.com). **Map** p306 H11.
Hotel services *Air-conditioning. Bar. Beauty salon. Business services. Concierge. Disabled: adapted rooms. No-smoking floors. Parking. Restaurant.* **Room services** *Dataport. Mini-bar. Refrigerator (on request). Room service (24hrs). TV: cable.*

Whitehall Hotel

105 E Delaware Place, at N Michigan Avenue, Gold Coast, IL 60611 (1-800 948 4255/312 944 6300/ fax 312 944 8522/www.whitehall-chicago.com). CTA Chicago (Red). **Rates** *single/double* $89-$319; *suite* $525-$1,250. **Credit** AmEx, DC, MC, V. **Map** p306 J9.

Anyone who visited Chicago in the 1970s may recall the cachet attached to this small luxury hotel and its private dining club. After being shuttered for several years, the Whitehall is again receiving guests to totally refurbished European-style rooms with mahogany armoires and Chippendale desks. The 221-room boutique hotel occupies a landmark building, developed in 1928 to house luxury apartments. The panelled lobby retains its English club look, though a stylish restaurant has supplanted the private dining club.
Hotel services *Air-conditioning. Bar. Business services. Concierge. Disabled: adapted rooms. Gym. Limousine service. No-smoking floors. Parking. Restaurant.* **Room services** *Dataport. Mini-bar. Refrigerator. Room service (24 hours). TV: VCR/cable.*

Expensive

Allerton Crowne Plaza

701 N Michigan Avenue, at E Huron Street, Near North, IL 60611 (1-800 621 8311/312 440 1500/ 312 440 1819/www.bristolhotels.com). CTA Chicago (Red). **Rates** *single/double* $169-$309; *suite* $189-$429. **Credit** AmEx, DC, Disc, MC, V. **Map** p306 J10.
It's déjà vu at this historic hotel, which reopened in the late 1990s after a $50 million restoration: vintage photographs and blueprints were used to restore the decorative brickwork and carved stone details of the northern Italian Renaissance exterior. The Allerton was built in 1924 as a men's 'club hotel' and was N Michigan Avenue's first high-rise. Since designated as a historic landmark, it was widely known for the Tip Top Tap (a sign for which now glows from atop the hotel's 25 storeys), a popular 1940s and '50s lounge, and for Don McNeill's *Breakfast Club* radio show of the 1950s. Taps on Two, a 130-seat signature restaurant with an adjoining 50-seat lounge, specialises in heartland cuisine.
Hotel services *Air-conditioning. Bar. Business services. Concierge. Disabled: adapted rooms. Gym. No-smoking floors. Parking. Restaurant.* **Room services** *Dataport. Mini-bar. Room service (24hrs). TV.*

Ambassador West

1300 N State Street, at W Goethe Street, Gold Coast, IL 60610 (1-800-996 3426/312 787 3700/fax 312 640 2967/www.wyndham.com). CTA Clark/Division. **Rates** *single* $159-$229; *double* $169-$249; *suite* $199-$800. **Credit** AmEx, DC, Disc, MC, V. **Map** p307 H7.
The two Ambassador hotels, East and West, face each other across the street like twins separated if not at birth, then at a tender age. Indeed, both now live with different parents. East is part of the Omni chain, while West has become 'A Wyndham Historic Hotel'. 'Historic' is right: this beautifully restored 12-storey classic dates back to 1920, when it opened as a residential hotel. While the more glamorous East, home of the fabled Pump Room, gets more attention, West quietly goes about its big banquet business.

A star hotel: the **House of Blues** (*p109*).

Regular guests enjoy its Old World charm, its concierge level with private lounge, and luxuries such as down comforters and plush bath robes.
Hotel services *Air-conditioning. Babysitting. Bars. Beauty salon. Business services. Concierge. Disabled: adapted rooms. Gym. No-smoking floors. Parking. Restaurants.* **Room services** *Dataport. Mini-bar. Room service. TV: cable.*

Chicago Marriott

540 N Michigan Avenue, at E Ohio Street, Near North, IL 60611 (1-800 228 9290/312 836 0100/ fax 312 836 6938/www.marriott.com). CTA Grand. **Rates** *single/double* $169-$229; *suite* $590-$1,145. **Credit** AmEx, DC, Disc, MC, V. **Map** p306 J10.
As the century turned, the jackhammers stopped and this Magnificent Mile hotel emerged from a cocoon of scaffolding sporting an elegant silver-grey sheaf of polished granite. This 46-storey, 1,176-room behemoth has acquired some stylish neighbours since its makeover, such as DisneyQuest and Nordstrom's. As it is, the hotel is quite self-sufficient with a pair of full-service restaurants, two lounges, Kinko's and a health club/sports centre that includes an indoor pool and an outdoor sports deck with basketball courts.
Hotel services *Air-conditioning. Bar. Beauty salon. Business services. Concierge. Disabled: adapted rooms. Gym. Limousine service. No-smoking floors. Parking. Restaurants. Swimming pool.*
Room services *Dataport. Room service (24hrs). TV: VCR/cable.*

Clarion Executive Plaza

71 E Wacker Drive, at N Wabash Avenue, The Loop, IL 60601 (1-800 252 7466/312 346 7100/fax 312 346 1721/www.clarionhotel.com). CTA Lake or State. **Rates** *single/double* $169-$229; *suite* $239-$259. **Credit** AmEx, DC, Disc, MC, V. **Map** p305 H11.
It's got a bit of a 1970s look and feel to it, but this high-rise is comfortable enough, with large rooms – the largest in the city, it claims – that are a legacy from the building's intended function: it was meant to be an apartment block but opened as a hotel. The location is great, too: just steps from Michigan Avenue and close to the Loop. The hotel restaurant is run-of-the-meal, but does at least sport a seasonal sidewalk café, while the bar has a funky Southwest motif that's left over from the eaterie's short stint as the Coyote Moon.
Hotel services *Air-conditioning. Bar. Business services. Concierge. Disabled: adapted rooms. Gym. No-smoking floors. Parking. Restaurant.* **Room services** *Dataport. Mini-bar. Room service (6.30am-10pm). TV: cable.*

Doubletree Guest Suites

198 E Delaware Place, at N Mies van der Rohe Way, Near North/Streeterville, IL 60611 (1-800 424 2900/ 312 664 1100/fax 312 664 9881/ www.doubletreehotels.com). CTA Chicago (Red). **Rates** *suite* $199-$369. **Credit** AmEx, DC, Disc, MC, V. **Map** p306 J9.
Climb out of the indoor pool on the 30th floor, and huge windows reveal a larger body of water – Lake Michigan – stretching toward the horizon. Located in the shadow of the John Hancock Center, this all-suites hotel is anchored by two excellent restaurants. Mrs Park's Tavern is full-service, upmarket and a cut above the typical hotel eaterie, while well-regarded Park Avenue Café is more formal and open only for dinner and a superb Sunday dim sum brunch. The comfortable suites feature a bedroom with separate parlour and convertible sofa, while a $7-million lobby refurbishment has created a spacious, pleasant area, where guests can drink coffee from the take-out coffee bar.
Hotel services *Air-conditioning. Bar. Business services. Concierge. Disabled: adapted rooms. Gym. No-smoking floors. Parking. Restaurant. Swimming pool.* **Room services** *Dataport. Mini-bar. Refrigerator. Room service (24hrs). TV: cable.*

Embassy Suites

600 N State Street, at W Ohio Street, Near North, IL 60610 (1-800 362 1779/312 943 3800/fax 312 943 7629/www.embassysuites.com). CTA Grand. **Rates** *suite* $229-$289. **Credit** AmEx, DC, Disc, MC, V. **Map** p306 H10.
This all-suites hotel is a travelling salesperson's nirvana. There's a two-hour 'manager's reception' daily from 5pm to 7pm daily with complimentary cocktails, and a full, cooked-to-order breakfast each morning: for the price of a room, then, you can also get bacon and eggs and Scotch and soda. For dinner, try the Papagus Greek Taverna Restaurant & Bar, which adjoins the hotel. If you plan to indulge

in all of this, you may want to work out: Embassy Suites is ready for you, with an indoor pool, sauna, whirlpool and fitness centre.
Hotel services *Air-conditioning. Bar. Business services. Concierge. Disabled: adapted rooms. Gym. No-smoking rooms. Parking. Restaurant. Swimming pool.* **Room services** *Dataport. Mini-bar. Refrigerator. Room service (9am-11pm). TV: VCR/cable.*

Hilton Garden Inn

10 E Grand Avenue, at N State Street, IL 60611 (1-800 445 8667/312 595 0000/fax 312 595 0955/ www.chicagodowntownnorth.gardeninn.com). CTA Grand. **Rates** *single/double* $119-$269; *suite* $359-$689. **Credit** AmEx, DC, Disc, MC, V. **Map** p306 H10.
Another brand-name spin-off arrived in downtown Chicago in November 1999. Although it's small compared to Hilton's Chicago flagship, it is nonetheless North America's largest Hilton Garden Inn and is in a prime location, just two blocks from the Mag Mile. The hotel has free fitness and business centres, but none of those added extras that you won't use but will end up paying for. As a result, this pleasant property, though in the shadow of Michigan Avenue's heavy hitters, is an attractive option, offering sleek rooms with high-tech workstations at trimmed prices. The guest rooms also have microwave ovens and a 24-hour pantry in the lobby stocks microwaveable cuisine.
Hotel services *Air-conditioning. Bar. Business services. Concierge. Disabled: adapted rooms. Gym. No-smoking rooms. Parking. Restaurant. Swimming pool.* **Room services** *Dataport. Refrigerator. Room service (6am-11pm). TV: cable.*

House of Blues

333 N Dearborn Street, at the Chicago River, Near North/River North, IL 60610 (1-800 235 6397/312 245 0333/fax 312 245 0504/www.loewshotels.com/ houseofblueshome.html). CTA Lake, Merchandise Mart or State. **Rates** *single/double* $119-$218; *suite* $350-$1,500. **Credit** AmEx, DC, Disc, MC, V. **Map** p306 H11.
No one's quite sure what exactly blues has to do with this burgeoning complex down near the river – aside from the free blue jelly bellies scattered across some of the tables – but there's no doubt that the House of Blues is an impressive hotel. It's not one for the faint-hearted, mind, a fact that's immediately apparent from the huge gold Buddha that guards the entrance to the hotel and the striking Moroccan-influenced lobby and bar. It doesn't get any more subdued in the 367 guestrooms and suites, either, but it somehow the gutsy, extravagant decor works rather well. The complex also holds a 36-lane AMC bowling alley and a Crunch fitness centre.
Hotel services *Air-conditioning. Bar. Business services. Concierge. Disabled: adapted rooms. Gym. No-smoking floors. Parking. Restaurant.* **Room services** *Dataport. Mini-bar. Refrigerator. Room service (24hrs). TV: cable.*

Hyatt on Printers Row

500 S Dearborn Street, at E Congress Parkway, The Loop, IL 60605 (1-800 233 1234/312 986 1234/fax 312 939 2468/ www.chicago.hyatt.com). CTA LaSalle, Harrison or Library. **Rates** *single* $119-$250; *double* $144-$275; *suite* $555-$650. **Credit** AmEx, DC, Disc, MC, V. **Map** p305 H13.

The **Hyatt Regency** holds the crown for biggest Hyatt in the world. *See page 109.*

Omnipresent elegance at the **Omni Ambassador East**.

Hotels are relatively scarce in the South Loop, but this one is a gem: historic, high-tech, comfortable and within walking distance from Grant Park, the Harold Washington Library Center, the revitalised Loop theatre district and State Street's shopping. The stylish 161-room hotel occupies the shell of two historic buildings, one of which was a printing plant; the design and decor are influenced by Frank Lloyd Wright. The rooms are sleek and equipped with high-tech electronics for work and play, while off the lobby is **Prairie**, known for its creative adaptations of heartland cooking (see p120).

The other main Hyatt in downtown Chicago, the **Hyatt Regency**, is altogether less characterful and aimed almost exclusively at the convention market, though with two mammoth towers holding over 2,000 rooms, it does hold the crown for the biggest Hyatt in the world. Prices at this vast hotel are slightly more expensive.

Branch: Hyatt Regency 151 E Wacker Drive, at N Michigan Avenue, The Loop, IL 60601 (1-800 233 1234/312 565 1234/fax 312 565 2966/ www.chicago.hyatt.com). **Map** p305 J11.
Hotel services *Air-conditioning. Business services. Concierge. Disabled: adapted rooms. Gym. No-smoking floors. Parking. Restaurant.*
Room services *Dataport (business rooms only). Fax (business rooms only). Mini-bar. Room service (6.30am-10pm). TV: cable.*

Midland

172 W Adams Street, at N LaSalle Street, The Loop, IL 60603 (1-800 621 2360/312 332 1200/fax 312 917 5771/www.midlandhotelchicago.com). CTA Quincy. **Rates** *single/double* $99-$259 (until spring 2001); $139-$299 (from spring 2001). **Credit** AmEx, DC, Disc, MC, V. **Map** p305 H12.

Since it began life in 1929 as a private men's club, this property has undergone major changes. In early 2000, it was in the throes of a full-scale renovation, converting it into one of Starwood's hip W Hotels. The new W Chicago City Center, due to open in 2001, will include the GiGi-A Paris Kitchen, offering contemporary French cuisine, and a bar, Whiskey Blue. Meanwhile, the old Midland offers a prime location in a stunning beaux-arts building in the heart of the financial district. The marble and mahogany lobby features vaulted arches and a gold-leaf ceiling.
Hotel services *Air-conditioning. Bar. Business services. Concierge. Disabled: adapted rooms. Gym. Limousine service. No-smoking floors. Restaurant.*
Room services *Dataport. Mini-bar. Refrigerator. Room service (6.30-10am, 11am-11pm). TV: cable.*

Omni Ambassador East

1301 N State Street, at E Goethe Street, Gold Coast, IL 60610 (1-800 843 6664/312 787 7200/fax 312 787 4760/www.omnihotels.com). CTA Clark/Division. **Rates** *single/double* $139-$199; *suite* $189-$549. **Credit** AmEx, DC, Disc, MC, V. **Map** p306 H8.

Consumer

A $22-million renovation programme has recently restored this landmark hotel to its former glory. Built in 1926 as a companion piece to what is now the Ambassador West across the street (they're now owned by separate companies, though an underground tunnel still connects the two), the hotel added the 'Omni' to its name in 1986. However, it still retains a genteel air. Popular with celebs (some of the well-appointed suites bear the names of Hollywood stars), it also offers a fine range of business services and the infamous Pump Room.

The **Omni Chicago**, meanwhile, is an all-suites property boasting an excellent Michigan Avenue location, though we found service to be poor.

Branch: Omni Chicago 676 N Michigan Avenue, at E Huron Street, Near North, IL 60611 (1-800 843 6664/312 944 6664/fax 312 266 3015/ www.omnihotels.com). **Map** p306 J10.

Hotel services *Air-conditioning. Bar. Beauty salon. Business services. Concierge. Disabled: adapted rooms. Gym. Limousine service. No-smoking floors. Parking. Restaurant.* **Room services** *Dataport. Mini-bar. Refrigerator (on request). Room service (6am-2am). TV: VCR (on request).*

Raphael

201 E Delaware Place, at N Mies van der Rohe Way, IL 60611 (312 943 5000/fax 312 943 5480). CTA Chicago (Red). **Rates** *single/double* $99-$209; *suite* $149-$259. **Credit** AmEx, DC, Disc, MC, V. **Map** p306 J9.

One of a plethora of hotels just east of the Magnificent Mile, the Raphael – twinned with the Tremont (*see below*) – is another perfectly pleasant place to stay for those seeking quasi-European lodgings in a central location. Opened as a hotel in 1978, the Raphael bills itself as 'Chicago's elegant "little" hotel'. Design-wise, there's something of a medieval thing going on in the lobby, though the comfortable rooms and suites are done out in more of a 19th-century fashion. Staff are able to assist in most business-related tasks.

Hotel services *Air-conditioning. Bar. Business services. Concierge. Disabled: adapted rooms. Gym. No-smoking rooms. Parking. Restaurant.* **Room services** *Dataport. Mini-bar. Room service (6am-11pm). TV: cable.*

Regal Knickerbocker Hotel

163 E Walton Street, at N Michigan Avenue, Gold Coast, IL 60611 (1-800 621 8140/312 751 8100/fax 312 751 9663/www.regal-hotels.com). CTA Chicago (Red). **Rates** *single* $149-$249; *suite* $205-$1,000. **Credit** AmEx, DC, Disc, MC, V. **Map** p306 J9.

Built in 1927, this 305-room landmark hotel has seen its share of comings and goings. Back when Hugh Heffner had his entertainment empire, it was a Playboy club and hotel. More recently, a $15-million refurb smartened guestrooms and reworked public spaces. In the companionable lobby, a horseshoe-shaped bar, which replicates a flapper-era model, dispenses around 50 varieties of martini to guests relaxing in club chairs and comfortable couches to listen to live jazz. Off the lobby is a pastry bar with truffles, cookies and other tempting desserts.

Hotel services *Air-conditioning. Babysitting. Bars. Business services. Concierge. Disabled: adapted rooms. Gym. No-smoking floors. Parking. Restaurants.* **Room services** *Dataport. Mini-bar. Room service (24hrs). TV: VCR/cable.*

Renaissance

1 W Wacker Drive, at N State Street, The Loop, IL 60601 (1-800 468 3571/312 372 7200/fax 312 372 0093/www.renaissancehotel.com). CTA Clark, Lake or State. **Rates** *single* $159-$259; *double* $169-$269; *suite* $310-$1,200. **Credit** AmEx, DC, Disc, MC, V. **Map** p305 H11.

For the person who likes to cover all the bases, this extremely comfortable hotel is ideal. It's large – but not too large, with 27 storeys and 553 rooms – and is equally well located for the Loop's Theatre District, the Mag Mile and the financial district. For those who prefer to eat in, the well-regarded **Cuisines** offers Mediterranean dishes (*see p135*), while the Great Street Restaurant features a contemporary American menu. All the guest rooms have bay windows, with views of the skyline, the river and (a distant) Lake Michigan.

Hotel services *Air-conditioning. Bar. Business services. Concierge. Disabled: adapted rooms. Gym. Limousine service. No-smoking floors. Parking. Restaurant. Swimming pool.* **Room services** *Dataport. Mini-bar. Refrigerator (suites only). Room service (24hrs). TV: VCR (on request)/cable.*

Silversmith

10 S Wabash Drive, at E Madison Street, The Loop, IL 60603 (1-800 227 6963/312 372 7696/fax 312 372 7320/www.crowneplaza.com/chi-silversmith). CTA Madison or Monroe (Blue, Red). **Rates** *single/double* $149-$249; *suite* $169-$289. **Credit** AmEx, DC, Disc, MC, V. **Map** p305 H12.

Tucked away under the El tracks, this boutique hotel has a definite and deliberate Frank Lloyd Wright flavour, including a wrought-iron accent piece in each room. Listed on the National Register of Historic Landmarks, the 1897 building is handsomely clad in dark green highly glazed terracotta, and was built to house silversmiths (hence the name) and jewellers. The lobby takes on a companionable air from 5-9pm with a cash bar, and from Monday through Thursday at 9pm, complimentary evening dessert is served: coffee, tea, gourmet cheesecake and fresh-baked cookies.

Hotel services *Air-conditioning. Babysitting. Bar. Business services. Concierge. Disabled: adapted rooms. Fitness room. Limousine service. No-smoking floors. Parking. Restaurant.* **Room services** *Dataport. Room service (6am-midnight). TV: VCR/cable.*

Tremont Hotel

100 E Chestnut Street, at N Michigan Avenue, Gold Coast, IL 60611 (1-800 621 8133/312 751 1900/ fax 312 751 8641). CTA Chicago (Red). **Rates** *single* $99-$319; *double* $119-$389; *suite* $375-$750. **Credit** AmEx, DC, Disc, MC, V. **Map** p306 J9.

Tucked away on Chestnut Street, the Tremont Hotel is twinned with the nearby **Raphael** (*see p110*). Both are small, European in flavour, nicely decorated – check out the architecturally themed pictures – and centrally situated. However, the Tremont offers a slightly leafier location and better amenities: each room contains both a VCR and a fax machine, for example. The adjoining **Iron Mike's Grille** (*see p119*), part-owned by former Bears coach Mike Ditka, provides room service, while Tremont House, on the other side of the hotel, contains 12 suites and is geared towards those staying in town for a while. **Hotel services** *Air-conditioning. Bar. Disabled: adapted rooms. Gym. Limousine service. No-smoking floors. Parking. Restaurant.* **Room services** *Dataport. Mini-bar. Refrigerator. Room service (7.30am-9.45pm). TV: VCR/cable.*

Wyndham Chicago

633 N St Clair Street, at E Huron Street, Near North/Streeterville, IL 60611 (312 573 0300/fax 312 274 0164/www.wyndham.com). CTA Chicago (Red). **Rates** *single/double* $179-$299; *suite* $214-399. **Credit** AmEx, DC, Disc, MC, V. **Map** p306 J10.
In 1999, Wyndham selected the Streeterville neighbourhood to establish its presence in downtown Chicago. This full-service flagship occupies the lion's share of a 28-storey multi-use tower just a block east of Michigan Avenue. Its casual, upscale restaurant, **Caliterra** (*see p127*), quickly made the top ten lists of local dining critics and has an attractive piano bar offering soft music and a light supper menu. Generous-sized guestrooms have nine-foot ceilings and offer high-speed Internet access. A welcome addition to Chicago's upper echelon.

Hotel services *Air-conditioning. Bar. Business services. Concierge. Disabled: adapted rooms. Gym. No-smoking floors. Parking. Restaurant. Swimming pool.* **Room services** *Dataport. Mini-bar (executive suites only). Refrigerator (on request). Room service (24hrs). TV: cable.*

Moderate

Best Western Inn of Chicago

162 E Ohio Street, at N Michigan Avenue, Near North/Streeterville, IL 60611 (1-800 557 2378/312 787 3100/fax 312 573 3180/www.bestwestern.com). CTA Grand. **Rates** *single* $99-$149; *double* $114-$164; *suite* $130-$325. **Credit** AmEx, DC, Disc, MC, V. **Map** p306 J10.
This modestly priced 358-room hotel provides a million-dollar location just a block east of Michigan Avenue. The standard rooms offer the amenities that you'd expect from this chain, but you also get the opportunity to live it up in a penthouse suite at an incredibly low price. Upping the ante to $250-$325 a night will buy a suite with a living room and access to a rooftop patio. Back down to earth, you'll find cheap eats at the Newsmaker Café, a basic all-purpose coffee shop with an interesting and unusual theme: more than 200 photos and artefacts chronicle the history of Chicago journalism.
Of the other Best Westerns in Chicago, the **Best Western River North** offers similarly excellent value for money (not least because it has a rooftop sundeck and offers free parking), while the **Best Western Grant Park** in the South Loop is both slightly cheaper and also slightly less appealing than its siblings.

Consumer

Hostels

Arlington International House

616 W Arlington Place, at N Larabee Street, Lincoln Park, IL60614 (773 929 5380/ 1-800 467 8355/fax 773 665 5485/ www.arlingtonhouse.com).CTA Fullerton. **Rates** *dormitory* from $17; *private room* from $36. **Credit** MC, V.

Chicago International Hostel

6318 N Winthrop Avenue, at W Rosemont Avenue, Far North, IL 60660 (773 262 1011/fax 773 262 3673/ chicagohostel@hotmail.com). CTA Loyola. **Rates** *dormitory* $15; *private room* $35-$48. **No credit cards.**

Garden Home Hostel

2822 W 38th Place, at S California Avenue, South Side, IL 60632 (773 254 0836/ www.hostels.com/fatjohnnies). CTA 94, 95 bus. **Rates** *dormitory* $10. **No credit cards.**

HI-Chicago

24 E Congress Parkway, at S State Street, The Loop, IL 60605 (312 360 0300/fax 312 360 0313/HIChicago2000@aol.com). CTA Harrison or LaSalle. **Open** from 15 June 2000. **Rates** from $17.50. **Credit** MC, V. **Map** p305 H13.

HI-Chicago Summer Hostel

731 S Plymouth Court, at W Polk Street, South Loop, IL 60605 (June-Sept 773 327 5350/Oct-May 312 360 0300/ HIChicago2000@aol.com). CTA Harrison. **Open** June-Sept only. **Rates** $19-$20. **Credit** MC, V. **Map** p304 H14.

International House of Chicago

1414 E 59th Street, at S Dorchester Avenue, Hyde Park, IL 60637 (773 753 2270). Metra 59th Street. **Rates** $37. **Credit** MC, V. **Map** p311 Y17.

Branches: Best Western River North 125 W
Ohio Street, at N LaSalle Street, Near North/River
North, IL 60610 (1-800 727 0800/312 467 0800/
fax 312 467 1665/www.bestwestern.com).
Map p306 H10.
Best Western Grant Park 1100 S Michigan
Avenue, at E 11th Street, South Loop, IL 60605
(1-800 528 1234/312 922 2900/fax 312 922 8812/
www.bestwestern.com). **Map** p304 J14.
Hotel services *Air-conditioning. Bar. Concierge.
Disabled: adapted rooms. Gym. No-smoking floors.
Restaurant.* **Room services** *Dataport. Refrigerator
(on request). Room service (6am-10pm). TV: cable.*

Claridge

*1244 N Dearborn Street, at W Goethe Street, Gold
Coast IL 60610 (1-800 245 1258/312 787 4980/
fax 312 266 0978/www.claridgehotel.com). CTA
Clark/Division.* **Rates** *single* $139-$169; *double* $149-
$225; *suite* $375-$475. **Credit** AmEx, DC, Disc, MC,
V. **Map** p307 H8.
The recently refurbished Claridge blends almost
seamlessly into the tree-lined surroundings of
Dearborn, offering serene classiness at decent prices.
The rooms vary considerably in size, but all are
clean, comfortable and unfussily decorated. The art
that lines the hotel's corridors, the eclectic Foreign
Affairs restaurant, the second-floor meeting rooms
and the morning limousine service – try getting a cab
on Dearborn and you'll appreciate it even more – all
add to the sophisticated effect, while the delicious
cookies, which are left at your bedside as part of the
turndown service with a card detailing the next day's
weather forecast, are a particularly nice touch.
Hotel services *Air-conditioning. Bar. Business
services. Concierge. Disabled: adapted rooms.
Limousine service. No-smoking floors. Parking.
Restaurant.* **Room services** *Dataport. Mini-bar.
Room service (6.30am-10pm). TV: VCR/cable.*

Congress Plaza

*520 S Michigan Avenue, at E Congress Parkway,
The Loop, IL 60605 (1-800 635 1666/312 427
3800/fax 312 427 7264/www.congresshotel.com).
CTA Harrison or Library.* **Rates** *single/double* $129-
$149; *suite* $275-$700. **Credit** AmEx, DC, Disc, MC,
V. **Map** p305 J10.
Although faded around the edges, this dowager is
alive and well and humming with activity. History
has been made in this hotel that was built in 1893 to
accommodate visitors to the World's Columbian
Exposition. Franklin D Roosevelt accepted the 1921
Democratic presidential nomination in the Gold
Room: peek inside to admire its intricate gold leaf
filigree and four oil paintings on the ceiling. The
lobby has original mosaics and a White House chair
said to have been a favourite of several presidents.
If you request an east-facing guestroom, you will
enjoy stunning views of Lake Michigan and
Buckingham Fountain.
Hotel services *Air-conditioning. Bar. Concierge.
Disabled: adapted rooms. Gym. No-smoking floors.
Parking. Restaurant.* **Room services** *Dataport.
Room service (6.30am-11pm). TV: cable.*

Courtyard By Marriott

*30 E Hubbard Street, at N State Street, Near North,
IL 60611 (1-800 321 2211/312 329 2500/fax 312
329 0293/www.marriott.com). CTA Grand.*
Rates *single/double* $139-$179; *suite* $159-$199.
Credit AmEx, DC, Disc, MC, V. **Map** p306 H11.
This chain property offers the unbeatable combination of comfortable lodgings, competitive prices and
a superb location. Just two blocks north of the river,
it's handy for the Loop's financial and theatre districts, yet is only a few minutes' walk from the Mag
Mile and is on the doorstep of some hugely popular
restaurants. If you have business to conduct, you'll
have a spacious desk and two-line phones with
voicemail. If you simply want to relax, head for the
gym, pool and sundeck.
Hotel services *Air-conditioning. Bar. Business
services. Concierge. Disabled: adapted rooms. Gym.
No-smoking floors. Parking. Restaurant. Swimming
pool.* **Room services** *Dataport. Room service (6am-
2am). TV: VCR/cable.*

Hampton Inn & Suites

*33 W Illinois Street, at N Dearborn Street, Near
North, IL 60610 (1-800 426 7866/312 832 0330/
fax 312 832 0333/www.hamptoninn-suites.com).
CTA Grand.* **Rates** *single* $109-$149; *double* $119-
$159; *suite* $159-$199. **Credit** AmEx, DC, Disc, MC,
V. **Map** p306 H11.
Most Chicago hotels of recent vintage are make-
overs, a tribute to the adaptive uses of classic architecture. This 230-room property opened in 1988 as
the first newly constructed hotel in Chicago in five
years. But it is mindful of Chicago's architectural
heritage: guests are treated to an exhibit of archaic
photographs and architectural artefacts from historic buildings, such as a stair stringer from Adler
and Sullivan's Chicago Stock Exchange building.
The rooms range from standard guestrooms to
apartment-style suites.
Hotel services *Air-conditioning. Bar. Business
services. Concierge. Disabled: adapted rooms. Gym.
Limousine service. No-smoking floors. Parking.
Restaurant. Swimming pool.* **Room services**
*Dataport. Refrigerator. Room service (10.30am-
11.30pm). TV: VCR/cable.*

Hotel Allegro

*171 W Randolph Street, at N LaSalle Street, The
Loop, IL 60601 (1-800 643 1500/312 236 0123/
fax 312 236 0917/www.allegrochicago.com). CTA
Clark or Washington (Blue, Red).* **Rates** *single/double*
$135-$250; *suite* $225-$395. **Credit** AmEx, DC, Disc,
MC, V. **Map** p305 H12.
With its love of whimsy, the California-based
Kimpton Hotel Group transformed the old Bismarck
Hotel (built around 1894) into a funky, colourful 483-
room art deco beauty that's pretty to look at and fun
to visit. The Allegro sports a showbiz theme, with
musical and theatrical icons throughout. Rooms are
decorated in vibrant colours, while the theatrically
themed suites include one decorated like the set of
Rent. Hotel staff are impossibly well-dressed and
convey a sense of camaraderie. The adjoining **312**

Accommodation

Chicago is independently operated by celebrity chef Dean Zanella and features creative Italian-American specialities (*see p133*), and the new bar, Encore, is well worth a visit. In another nice touch, all rooms have fax machines and CD players. **Hotel services** *Air-conditioning. Bar. Beauty salon. Business services. Concierge. Disabled: adapted rooms. Gym. Limousine service. No-smoking floors. Parking. Restaurant.* **Room services** *Dataport. Mini-bar. Room service (5am-1am). TV: VCR/cable.*

Hotel Burnham

1 W Washington Street, at N State Street, The Loop, IL 60602 (1-877 294 9712/312 782 1111/fax 312 782 0899/www.burnhamhotel.com). CTA Washington (Blue, Red). **Rates** *single/double* $155-$230; *suite* $250-$350. **Credit** AmEx, DC, Disc, MC, V. **Map** p305 H12.
One of Chicago's newest hotels is also one of its oldest: the Reliance Building, listed as a National Historic Landmark, was developed in 1894 by gifted architects Burnham and Root and is Chicago's first direct ancestor of the modern skyscraper. As a hotel, it offers 103 guestrooms and 19 suites, with rooms bearing the Kimpton Group's colourful trademark decor: here, it's indigo blue velvet, beige and gold fabrics mixed with harlequin design, velvet pillows and mischievous cherubs. The historic building, with its skin of cream-coloured glazed terracotta and wide expanses of broad, tall glass windows, is nestled among the shops on State Street. **Hotel services** *Air-conditioning. Bar. Business services. Concierge. Disabled: adapted rooms. Gym. No-smoking rooms. Parking. Restaurant.* **Room services** *Dataport. Mini-bar. Room service (24hrs). TV: cable.*

Hotel Monaco

225 N Wabash Avenue, at E Wacker Drive, The Loop, IL 60601 (1-800 397 7661/312 960 8500/fax 312 960 8538/www.monaco-chicago.com). CTA Lake or State. **Rates** *single/double* $145-$250; *suite* $425. **Credit** AmEx, DC, Disc, MC, V. **Map** p305 H11.
It looks as though the designer went wild decorating the lobby of this boutique hotel, but it works: velvet and damask, tiger stripes and red copper, gold, cream, and rich browns somehow are in harmony throughout. The lobby is a popular evening gathering place where complimentary wine is served around a limestone fireplace, while the 192 guestrooms pick up the colourful theme with bright red quilted headboards and warm greens and yellows; amenities include robes and mahogany writing desks. Off the lobby is **Mossant**, a large restaurant that serves what some claim are Chicago's best *pommes frites* (*see p129*). **Hotel services** *Air-conditioning. Bar. Business services. Concierge. Disabled: adapted rooms. Gym. No-smoking floors. Parking. Restaurant.* **Room services** *Dataport. Mini-bar. Refrigerator. Room service (24hrs). TV: VCR/cable.*

Lenox Suites

616 N Rush Street, at E Ontario Street, Near North, IL 60611 (1-800 445 3669/312 337 1000/fax 312 337 7217/www.lenoxsuites.com). CTA Grand. **Rates** *single/double* $109-$159; *suite* $229. **Credit** AmEx, DC, Disc, MC, V. **Map** p306 J10.
Long before Chicago became a major travel destination, the Lenox was a modest residential hotel, enjoying a great location a block west of the Mag Mile. Lately, the neighbourhood has become a hot

Seneca: suite accommodation at a sweet price. *See page 114.*

tourist destination with the installation of high-profile attractions such as DisneyQuest and ESPN Zone. These days, you can stretch the budget by eating in: rooms include kitchenettes, dishes and utensils, all guests get a daily basket of baked goods and there's both a coffee shop and a branch of Houston's on the premises. The rooms range from studios to one-bedroom suites.

Hotel services *Air-conditioning. Bar. Business services. Concierge. Disabled: adapted rooms. Gym. No-smoking floors. Parking. Restaurant.* **Room services** *Dataport. Mini-bar. Refrigerator. Room service (6am-11pm). TV: cable.*

Radisson Hotel & Suites

160 E Huron Street, at N Michigan Avenue, Near North/Streeterville, IL 60611 (1-800 333 3333/ 312 787 2900/fax 312 787 5158/ www.radissonchicago.com). CTA Chicago (Red). **Rates** *single* $109-$239; *double* $129-259; *suite* $149-$279. **Credit** AmEx, DC, Disc, MC, V. **Map** p306 J10.

A rare and treasured asset of this mid-range, mid-size (341-room) hotel is its rooftop outdoor pool: it's a favourite spot among sunseekers, who occupy chaise lounges sheltered by a glass windbreak and enjoy great views of sparkling Lake Michigan and the rooftops of Streeterville. The Radisson's location adjacent to the Mag Mile makes it extremely popular with tourists and airline flight crews. The guestrooms are cosy and well-equipped – the result of an early 1990s makeover – and include 96 suites. Off the lobby is the **Red Rock Grill**, which specialises in Tex-Mex cuisine and killer Margaritas (see *p140*).

Hotel services *Air-conditioning. Babysitting. Bar. Business services. Concierge. Disabled: adapted rooms. Gym. Limousine service. No-smoking floors. Parking. Restaurant. Swimming pool.* **Room services** *Room services (24 hours). TV: VCR/cable.*

Seneca

200 E Chestnut Street, at N Mies van der Rohe Way, Gold Coast, IL 60611 (1-800 800 6261/312 787 8900/fax 312 988 4438/ www.senecahotel.com). CTA Chicago (Red). **Rates** *single* $129-$189; *double* $129-$209; *suite* $149-$259. **Credit** AmEx, DC, Disc, MC, V. **Map** p306 J9.

The staff at the Seneca like to refer to the hotel as one of the city's best-kept secrets, and they're not wrong. Situated off Michigan Avenue, the Seneca is a pleasingly grand hotel offering luxury at prices that shame many of its competitors. The deluxe one-bedroom suites are just that, boasting spacious and tastefully decorated lounges and kitchens. They arguably represent the best value of the hotel's 66 rooms (all with kitchenette) and 57 suites. The three restaurants – Chalfin's Delicatessen, **The Saloon** steakhouse (see *p142*) and the new QP (upscale Greek) – are leased out rather than hotel-operated.

Hotel services *Air-conditioning. Bar. Beauty salon. Business services. Disabled: adapted rooms. Gym. No-smoking floors. Parking. Restaurant.* **Room services** *Dataport. Refrigerator. Room service (6.30am-10pm). TV: cable.*

Summerfield Suites

166 E Superior Street, at N Michigan Avenue, Near North/Streeterville, IL 60611 (1-800 833 4353/312 787 6000/fax 312 787 6133/ www.summerfieldsuites.com). CTA Chicago (Red). **Rates** *suite* $169-$269. **Credit** AmEx, DC, Disc, MC, V. **Map** p306 J10.

When this all-suites chain took over the old Barclay Hotel, it kept one of its finest assets (the rooftop pool), though it converted another (the private fine-dining club) into a comfortable space serving a complimentary buffet breakfast. Off the lobby is a branch of Benihana, the popular Japanese steak-house, while the Bookmark Lounge is a comfortable watering hole, which offers complimentary hors d'oeuvres with its drinks. All the suites have either fully equipped kitchenettes or microwave ovens and small refrigerators.

Hotel services *Air-conditioning. Bar. Beauty salon. Concierge. Disabled: adapted rooms. Gym. No-smoking rooms. Parking. Restaurant. Swimming pool.* **Room services** *Dataport. Mini-bar. Refrigerator. TV: VCR/cable.*

Budget

City Suites

933 W Belmont Avenue, at N Sheffield Avenue, Lake View, IL 60657 (1-800 248 9108/773 404 3400/ fax 773 404 3405/www.cityinns.com). CTA Belmont. **Rates** *single/double* $109-$169. **Credit** AmEx, DC, Disc, MC, V. **Map** p309 E3.

Admittedly, it's not downtown, but this 45-room boutique hotel is next to the Belmont El station, a hub that will get you downtown inside of 15 minutes and to Wrigley Field in less than half that. The Lake View East neighbourhood offers a lively mix of gentrified, bohemian and gay and lesbian lifestyles. The spotless suites all include a sleeper sofa, an armchair, a desk and a refrigerator.

Hotel services *Concierge. Limousine service. No-smoking rooms. Parking.* **Room services** *Dataport. Refrigerator. TV: cable.*

Comfort Inn Lincoln Park

601 W Diversey Parkway, at N Clark Street, Lincoln Park, IL 60614 (reservations 1-800 228 5150/ guests 773 348 2810/fax 773 348 1912/ www.comfortinn.com). CTA Diversey. **Rates** *single/double* $122-$135; *suite* $225. **Credit** AmEx, DC, Disc, MC, V. **Map** p308 G4.

Located in the heart of lively Lincoln Park, this budget hotel is housed in an attractive four-storey brick building accented with colourfully striped awnings. The cookie-cutter rooms are pretty basic, but clean, with added bonuses coming with the con-tinental breakfast served in the French provincial-style lounge and the off-street courtyard parking. For less than the price of a downtown room, you can upgrade to a suite with a jacuzzi and sauna.

Hotel services *Air-conditioning. Business services. No-smoking rooms. Parking.* **Room services** *Dataport. TV: cable.*

Radisson, and on, and on... *See p114.*

Days Inn Lincoln Park North

644 W Diversey Parkway, at N Clark Street, Lincoln Park, IL 60614 (1-888 576 3297/773 525 7010/fax 773 525 6998/www.lpndaysinn.com). CTA Diversey. **Rates** *single/double* $79-$170; *suites* $190-$235. **Credit** AmEx, DC, Disc, MC, V. **Map** p308 F4.
Located at the busy intersection of Broadway, Clark and Diversey, this decent budget option – the highest-rated Days Inn in Illinois, no less – offers basic rooms decorated in fresh, light colours. A complimentary continental breakfast is served in a comfortable sitting area off a lobby decorated with a showcase of collector plates, and there are complimentary passes available for the Bally's health club next door.

Also in Chicago are the **Days Inn Gold Coast** and the slightly pricier **Days Inn Lake Shore**, both of which offer similar amenities.
Branches: Days Inn Gold Coast 1816 N Clark Street, at W Menomenee Street, IL 60614 (1-800 325 2525/312 664 3040/fax 312 664 3048/ www.daysinn.com). **Map** p307 H7.
Days Inn Lake Shore 644 N Lake Shore Drive, at E Ontario Street, Near North/Streeterville, IL 60611 (1-800 329 7466/312 943 9200/fax 312 255 4411/ www.daysinn.com). **Map** p306 K10.
Hotel services *Air-conditioning. Bar. Limousine service. No-smoking rooms. Parking.* **Room services** *Dataport. Refrigerator (some rooms). TV: cable.*

Essex Inn

800 S Michigan Avenue, at E 8th Street, South Loop, IL 60605 (1-800 621 6909/312 939 2800/fax 312 939 0526). CTA Harrison. **Rates** *single/double* $69-$150; *suite* $200-$350. **Credit** AmEx, DC, Disc, MC, V. **Map** p306 J14.

This '70s-style hotel has been made over for the new millennium. As a result, you can get a comfortable suite with a million-dollar view of Lake Michigan, Museum Campus and Soldier Field for next to nothing. Parking, too, is a bargain at just $12 with in-and-out privileges. All 255 rooms have been redone and now include such amenities as dataports, voicemail, cable TV and fluffy towels that are seven times the thickness of those they replaced. The Savoy Bar & Grill also has been renovated and now offers a full-service menu. Located right alongside Hilton's flagship hotel, this definitely is in the 'best buy' category.
Hotel services *Air-conditioning. Bar. Business services. Concierge. Disabled: adapted rooms. No-smoking floors. Parking. Restaurant. Swimming pool.*
Room services *Dataport. Mini-bar. Refrigerator (on request). TV: cable.*

Howard Johnson Inn

720 N LaSalle Street, at W Superior Street, Near North/River North, IL 60610 (reservations 1-800 446 4656/guests 312 664 8100/fax 312 664 2365/ www.igohojo.com). CTA Chicago (Brown/ Purple, Red). **Rates** *single* $88-; *double* $103; *suite* $125-$150. **Credit** AmEx, DC, Disc, MC, V. **Map** p306 H10.
There's no pretense about this old-style, two-storey motor court: its sign says 'Ho Jo' and its prices are rock-bottom. An anachronism in the heart of trendy River North, the hotel's central courtyard provides free parking – a real cost-saver in a city where hotels charge upward of $20 a day to stash your motor.

There's no need to fret about a $20 breakfast from room service, as the hotel doesn't offer either. But attached to the hotel is a cheerful diner, and you'll be just steps away from the 'Su-Hu' galleries and within easy reach of River North's restaurants, bars and clubs.
Hotel services *Air-conditioning. No-smoking rooms. Parking. Restaurant.*
Room services *Dataport. TV: cable.*

Majestic

528 W Brompton Avenue, at N Lake Shore Drive, Lake View, IL 60657 (1-800 727 5108/773 404 3499/fax 773 404 3495/www.cityinns.com). CTA Addison (Purple/Red). **Rates** *single/double* $109-$169. **Credit** AmEx, DC, Disc, MC, V. **Map** p309 G1.
As with its sister properties City Suites and the Willows, this inn says good morning to guests with coffee and cinnamon rolls from **Ann Sather's** famous Swedish restaurant (*see p142*). Set on a quiet, tree-lined residential street within walking distance of the Lincoln Park Zoo, the recently refurbished and renamed hotel is housed in a building dating from the 1920s and offers 31 rooms and 22 suites. Buses along Lake Shore Drive, just half a block to the east, can get you to the Magnificent Mile in about 15 minutes.
Hotel services *Concierge. Limousine service. Non-smoking rooms. Parking.* **Room services** *Dataport. Refrigerator. TV: cable.*

Consumer

Cheap and cheerful, the **Ohio House** is a budget blessing.

Motel 6

162 E Ontario Street, at N St Clair Street, Near North/Streeterville, IL 60611 (reservations 1-800 466 8356/guests 312 787 3580/fax 312 787 1299/ www.motel6.com). CTA Grand. **Rates** *single $85-$106; double $95-$116; suite $99-$116.* **Credit** AmEx, DC, Disc, MC, V. **Map** p306 J10.

Usually, you'll look for this no-frills lodging chain along the nation's highways or in the far 'burbs. Here's one in the heart of the city, just a block east of fashionable North Michigan Avenue, on the site of a French-owned boutique hotel that went bust. This is surely one of the only Motel 6s in the whole country with chandeliers in the lobby – a reminder of its former life – though the rooms are more predictable: clean, comfortable and cheap. Adjoining the hotel is **Coco Pazzo Café**, a well-regarded Italian eaterie with a delightful sidewalk café (*see p132*). With this prime location, guests at Motel 6 really are getting champagne at beer prices.
Hotel services *Air-conditioning. Disabled: adapted rooms. Gym. No-smoking floors. Restaurant.*
Room services *Dataport. Mini-bar (suites only). TV: cable.*

Ohio House

600 N LaSalle Street, at W Ontario Street, Near North/River North, IL 60610 (312 943 6000/ fax 312 943 6063). CTA Grand. **Rates** *single/double $85; suite $137.* **Credit** AmEx, DC, Disc, MC, V. **Map** p306 H10.

This timeworn motel offers rooms at budget rates in a million-dollar River North location. The free parking is another big budget-stretcher, as is the coffeeshop that offers mammoth breakfasts for $3.35 and Friday night fish-and-chip dinners for $5.95. A large room above the office – management calls it a 'suite' – includes a refrigerator, a microwave and a sleeper sofa and could conceivably hold a family of five or six (it goes for $137). Other extras include free cable TV and a ten per cent discount for seniors.
Hotel services *Air-conditioning. Bar. No-smoking rooms. Parking.* **Room services** *TV: cable.*

Willows

555 W Surf Street, at N Broadway, Lincoln Park, IL 60657 (1-800 787 3108/773 528 8400/ fax 773 528 8483/www.cityinns.com). CTA Diversey. **Rates** *single/double $109-$169.* **Credit** AmEx, DC, Disc, MC, V. **Map** p309 F3.

A French Renaissance feel dominates at this cosy hotel up near the busy Clark/Diversey intersection. The entire hotel has just been refurbished and renovated and is looking much the better for it: the TVs even have the full 100-plus gamut of cable stations. Fans of minor hotel curiosities will enjoy riding in the original 1920s Otis elevator – creaks and all – while foodies will delight in the selections of Ann Sather goodies that are offered for breakfast.
Hotel services *Concierge. Limousine service. Non-smoking rooms. Parking.* **Room services** *Dataport. TV: cable.*

Restaurants

Watch out New York, heads up LA: Chicago has become a major player in the culinary stakes.

Tru style: top-flight American cuisine by Rick Tramonto and Gale Gand. *See page 121.*

For years, Chicago was regarded, somewhat scornfully, as a meat-and-potatoes kind of town. This isn't surprising in the one-time home of the stockyards, tagged by poet Carl Sandburg as the 'City of Big Shoulders'. Chicago also has long been a major convention city, and 'a good steak' was typically near the top of the 'don't miss' lists of the millions of meeting-goers who flocked to town. Few were disappointed: over the years, the city has spawned more than its share of top-flight steak joints and chophouses.

Many are still around, despite major setbacks. First came the closing of the stockyards. Then came the emphasis on healthier and lighter eating. For a while, beef became unfashionable and steakhouses looked as though they might become extinct. But beef has bounced right back and carnivores can be happy again, as steaks – like the similarly luxuriant cigars and swanky Martinis – are hip.

Meanwhile, the Chicago restaurant scene found itself in the throes of a quiet revolution. Tastes changed, the world became smaller, and restaurant diners became more demanding and more discerning. Ethnic restaurants flourished. Thai and Vietnamese, Mexican and Argentinian, Caribbean and Cuban, Russian and Ukrainian restaurants drew crowds. It became equally possible to find in that meat-and-potato town the likes of sushi and gumbo, delicate spring rolls and Asian noodles.

The city also began attracting legions of talented chefs who were soon flexing their culinary muscles and creating nouveau and fusion cuisine that attracts national attention and wide followings. Included in their ranks are many female chefs, some of whom rose to become top toques, while others opened their own restaurants. Home-grown culinary stars shining brightly include **Charlie Trotter** (*see page 119*), Suzy Crofton at **Crofton on Wells** (*see page 119*), Rick and Deanne Bayless at **Frontera Grill/Topolobampo** (*see page 134*) and Rick Tramonto and Gale Gand at **Tru** (*see page 121*).

At the same time, famous chefs and eateries from both coasts launched spin-offs in Chicago. Jean-Georges Vongerichten arrived with a

Consumer

green DOLPHIN street

Green Dolphin Street is Chicago's premiere supper-club. Under the culinary direction of Chef Rick Gresh Green Dolphin Street provides it's clientele with the finest ingredients available and the freshest jazz acts around. Come experience the combination
that has garnered such critical acclaim.

Three Stars: *Phil Vetell, Chicago Tribune*
Award of Excellence:*The Wine Spectator*
One of America's great wine friendly bars: *The Wine Enthusiast*

2200 North Ashland Avenue.
Ashland@Webster
Tel: 773.395.0066

cafe absinthe

Cafe Absinthe has been serving Chicago some of the finest American bistro cuisine since it's inception in 1993. Located at the epicenter of Wicker Park's thriving artistic and eclectic nightlife scene, Cafe Absinthe remains one of Chicago's great nights out. Chef Jim Hoban has been blazing new culinary trails with his combination of Midwestern ingredients and global flavors.

1954 West North Avenue. Enter in alley.Tel: 773.278.4488

version of the Thai-inspired French cuisine of **Vong** (*see page 123*), Wolfgang Puck introduced Chicagoans to his Cal-Asian cuisine with **Spago** (*see page 128*), and even **Smith & Wollensky** created a clone of its New York steakhouse. For every tried-and-true neighbourhood Italian eaterie and pizza palace, a new fashionable trattoria hit the scene. For every traditional French restaurant came a chic new bistro or brasserie.

As a result, Chicago now offers as diverse and enticing a dining scene as you'll find anywhere in America. The Windy City may not have as many restaurants as New York, but it may have as many good ones. In fact, with more than 6,000 restaurants, it's easily possible to find enough good ones to eat out every night of the year without repeating yourself. And you'll find dining out in Chicago considerably easier on the pocket than restaurant-hopping in Manhattan…

American

Charlie Trotter's

Wyndham Chicago Hotel, 816 W Armitage Avenue, at N Halsted Street, Old Town (773 248 6228/ www.charlietrotters.com). CTA Armitage. **Open** *with reservation only* from 6pm Tue-Sat; closed Mon. **Set menus** $100-$110. **Credit** AmEx, DC, Disc, MC, V. **Map** p307 F6.

Chicago's best-known chef never runs out of creative ideas for blending tastes and fresh, naturally raised ingredients, or for reinventing himself. This 1880s townhouse is the nerve centre for an Epicurean empire that includes a TV show and cookbook series. The restaurant is occasionally open on Monday; call ahead for dates. Reservations for weekend dining should be made up to 12 weeks in advance; four weeks' notice is required for dining during the week.

Crofton on Wells

535 N Wells Street, at W Grand Street, Near North/ River North (312 755 1790). CTA Grand. **Open** 11.30am-2.30pm, 5-10pm Mon-Thur; 11.30am-2.30pm, 5-11pm Fri, Sat; closed Sun. **Main courses** $15-$26. **Credit** DC, Disc, MC, V. **Map** p306 H10.

Amid the touristy hoopla of River North, this chef-owned restaurant provides an oasis of quiet as it showcases the considerable talents of Suzy Crofton. The minimalist, 70-seat storefront features delicious seasonal American cuisine prepared with a French flair. Start with grilled baby octopus with a spicy mushroom reduction and move on to pork loin with apple chutney.

Earth

738 N Wells Street, at W Superior Street, Near North/River North (312 335 5475). CTA Chicago (Brown/Purple). **Open** 11.30am-2.30pm, 5.30-9.30pm Mon-Sat; closed Sun. **Main courses** $15-$25. **Credit** AmEx, DC, MC, V. **Map** p306 H10.

Here's living proof that what is good for you can also both look good and taste good. Delicious organically produced food is served in an urban chic setting with white walls, a natural hickory floor and glass block vases filled with flowers. The eco-conscious haute cuisine includes grilled sirloin of free-range bison and roast loin of lamb with crayfish.

Fahrenheit

695 N Milwaukee Avenue, at W Grand Avenue, West Side (312 733 7400). CTA Chicago (Blue) or Clinton (Green). **Open** 5.30-10.30pm Mon-Thur, Sun; 5.30-11pm Fri, Sat. **Main courses** $14-$35. **Credit** AmEx, Disc, MC, V.

You might expect to find this sexy, hip space in Miami's trendy South Beach: it's hot, it's cool and it attracts a well-heeled, Gucci-clad crowd. Start with Tuscan-style scallops and move on to the roasted pheasant or braised lamb shank from young chef Patrick Concannon's menu.

Iron Mike's Grille

Tremont Hotel, 100 E Chestnut Street, at N Rush Street, Gold Coast (312 587 8989). CTA Chicago (Red). **Open** 7.30am-11pm Mon-Thur; 7.30am-midnight Fri, Sat; 7.30am-10pm Sun. **Main courses** $17-$32. **Credit** AmEx, DC, Disc, MC, V. **Map** p306 H9.

Although 'Da Coach' has long since departed the Bears, Iron Mike Ditka remains popular in Chicago, a fact evidenced by this eponymous eaterie. American Bistro cooking is exemplified by Ditka's favourite food – pork chops – accompanied here by grilled pancetta and a honey and green peppercorn sauce. You can also find pastas, steaks, chops and pot roasts at this memorabilia-packed restaurant.

Mashed Potato Club

316 W Erie Street, at N Orleans Street, Near North/ River North (312 255 8579). CTA Chicago (Brown/Purple). **Open** 5.30pm-midnight Mon-Thur; 5.30pm-2am Fri; 5.30pm-3am Sat; 5.30-11pm Sun. **Main courses** $16-$28. **Credit** AmEx, Disc, MC, V. **Map** p306 G10.

Spuds are king at this funky joint. Choose from more than 100 topping ingredients including asparagus, zucchini, beef gravy or crabmeat. Red potatoes are mashed, skin on, with garlic, butter and cream cheese. The decor blends inflatable pink flamingos, psychedelic colours and a huge mural of frolicking nudes. Triple Martinis reward the intrepid.

One Sixtyblue

160 N Loomis Street, at W Randolph Street, West Side (312 850 0303). CTA Ashland (Green). **Open** 5-10pm daily. **Main courses** $12-$25. **Credit** AmEx, DC, Disc, MC, V.

Michael Jordan has been spotted at this stylish restaurant; indeed, he's even rumoured to be a silent partner. The name incorporates the street number and colour of the gaudy blue exterior of the building, a former pickle factory whose sleek, contemporary interior features glasswork, a zinc bar and steel cables criss-crossing the high ceiling.

Consumer

Restaurants by area

Consumer

The Loop

312 Chicago (Italian p133); **Bacino's** (Pizza p136); **Berghoff** (German p129); **Cuisines** (Mediterranean p135); **Encore** (p137 The lunch bunch); **Everest** (French p129); **Italian Village Restaurants** (Italian p132); **Mossant** (French p129); **Mrs Levy's Delicatessen** (Jewish p134); **Nick & Tony's** (Italian:p132); **Plaza Tavern** (Continental p125); **Quincy Grille on the River** (American p120); **Regimental Grill** (p137 The lunch bunch); **Rhapsody** (French p129); **Rivers Euro-American Bistro** (American p120); **Robinson's No.1 Ribs** (Ribs p138); **Trattoria No.10** (Italian p134).

South Loop

Prairie (American p120).

Near North/River North

Al's Italian Beef (p133 Streetwise treats); **Bar Louie** (p136 The lunch bunch); **Club Creole** (Cajun, Creole & Southern p123); **Club Lago** (p136 The lunch bunch); **Coco Pazzo** (Italian p132); **Crofton on Wells** (American p119); **Earth** (American p119); **Frontera Grill/ Topolobampo** (Latin, Mexican & Spanish p134); **Grapes** (Mediterranean p135); **Kinzie Chop House** (Steak p141); **Klay Oven** (Indian p131); **Lou Malnati's Pizzeria** (Pizza p138); **Mambo Grill** (Latin, Mexican & Spanish p134); **Mashed Potato Club** (American p119); **Mr Beef on Orleans** (p137 The lunch bunch); **Original**

Gino's East (Pizza p138); **Savarin** (French p129); **Scoozi!** (p125 My kind of town).

Near North/Magnificent Mile

Ben Pao (Chinese p124); **Blue Crab Lounge** (p136 The lunch bunch); **Brasserie Jo** (French p128); **Brio** (Latin, Mexican & Spanish p134); **Corner Bakery** (p125 My kind of town); **Giordano's** (Pizza p137); **Gold Coast Dogs** (p133 Streetwise treats); **Harry Caray's** (Italian p132); **Heaven on Seven on Rush** (Cajun, Creole & Southern p123); **Lawry's the Prime Rib** (British p123); **Maggiano's Little Italy** (p125 My kind of town); **PF Chang's China Bistro** (Chinese p124); **Pizzeria Due** (Pizza p138); **Pizzeria Uno** (Pizza p138); **Redfish** (Cajun, Creole & Southern p124); **Spago** (Eclectic p128); **Star of Siam** (Thai p142); **Su Casa** (Latin, Mexican & Spanish p135); **Sullivan's Steakhouse** (Steak p142); **Vong** (Asian & pan-Asian p123); **Zinfandel** (American p121).

Near North/Streeterville

Bistro Pacific (Asian & pan-Asian p123); **Boston Blackie's** (p136 The lunch bunch); **Bubba Gump Shrimp Co** (Seafood p139); **Caliterra** (Eclectic p127); **Capital Grille** (Steak p141); **Joe's Be-bop Café & Jazz Emporium** (Cajun, Creole & Southern p124); **Nicolina's** (Mediterranean p136); **Red Rock Grill** (Southwestern p140); **Tru** (American p121).

Prairie

Hyatt at Printers Row, 500 S Dearborn Street, at W Congress Parkway, South Loop (312 663 1143). CTA LaSalle (Blue) or Library. **Open** 6.30-10am, 11.30am-2pm, 5-10pm daily. **Main courses** $18-$32. **Credit** AmEx, DC, Disc, MC, V. **Map** p305 H13.
Many of the recipes here are based on Midwest staples. But there is also a strong creative twist evident in such dishes as Iowa pork chop with barbecue butter, roasted buffalo with shallot sauce, and brandied duck-and-pheasant loaf. The decor is a take on Frank Lloyd Wright's Prairie School.

Quincy Grille on the River

200 S Wacker Drive, at W Adams Street, The Loop (312 627 1800/www.quincygrille.com). CTA Quincy. **Open** 11.30am-2pm, 5-7pm Mon-Fri; 5-7pm Sat, Sun. **Main courses** *lunch* $10.95-$21.95; *dinner* from $24.95. **Credit** AmEx, DC, Disc, MC, V. **Map** p305 G12.
Should you witness a mass exodus from this pleasant riverside restaurant, it will not be because

of the seafood-accented menu – which, in fact, is good reason to linger – but rather because curtain-up is approaching at the nearby Lyric Opera. Go for the pre-theatre dinner specials and enjoy the views of the river.

Rivers Euro-American Bistro

30 S Wacker Drive, at W Monroe Street, The Loop (312 559 1515). CTA Quincy or Washington (Brown/Orange/Purple). **Open** 11.15am-2.30pm, 5-9pm Mon-Thur; 11.15am-2.30pm, 5-10pm Fri; 5-10pm Sat; closed Sun. **Main courses** $15-$28. **Credit** AmEx, DC, Disc, MC, V. **Map** p305 G12.
On warm summer evenings, patrons at Rivers Bistro spill out onto the covered patio alongside the Chicago River, while during the season, the Lyric Opera crowd eats in the contemporary dining room surrounded by mahogany and etched-glass partitions and monumental Impressionist-style paintings. Rivers' quality signature dishes include pan-seared grouper, sautéd chicken with shrimp and spicy seafood stew.

Gold Coast

Bistrot Zinc (French p128); Café Luciano (Italian p131); Cape Cod Room (Seafood p140); CHIC Café (Culinary schools p127); Chicago Flat Sammies (p125 My kind of town); Fuzio (p137 The lunch bunch); Iron Mike's Grille (American p119); Le Colonial (Vietnamese p142); McCormick & Schmick's (Seafood p140); Mity Nice Grill (p125 My kind of town); Morton's of Chicago (Steak p141); The Saloon (Steak p142); Typhoon (Asian & pan-Asian p123).

Old Town

Bistrot Margot (French p128); Charlie Trotter's (American p119); Geja's Café (Fondue p128); ¡Salpicon! (Latin, Mexican & Spanish p135); Slicker Sam's (Italian p133); Trattoria Dinotto (Italian p134); Twin Anchors (Ribs p138).

Lincoln Park

Bacino's (p133 Streetwise treats); Blue Mesa (Southwestern p140); Byron's (p133 Streetwise treats); Earl of Loch Ness (British p123); Four Farthings Tavern (p136 The lunch bunch); Green Dolphin Street (French p129); RJ Grunts (p125 My kind of town); Shallots (Jewish/Kosher p134).

Lake View

Bacino's (p133 Streetwise treats); Bella Vista (Italian p131); Buca di Beppo (Italian p131); Byron's (p133 Streetwise treats).

Wicker Park/Bucktown

Coast (Eclectic p127); Mirai (Asian p123).

West Side

Al's Italian Beef (p133 Streetwise treats); Bluepoint Oyster Bar (Seafood p139); Byron's (p133 Streetwise treats); Costa's (Greek p131); Fahrenheit (American p119); Jim's Original (p133 Streetwise treats); Lou Mitchell's (p137 The lunch bunch); Mario's Italian Lemonade Stand (p133 Streetwise treats); Mas (Latin, Mexican & Spanish p134); One Sixtyblue (American p119); Pegasus (Greek p131); Vivo (p141 Shafted).

South Side

Emperor's Choice (Chinese p124); Three Happiness (Chinese p125).

Far North

Ann Sather (Swedish p142); Arun's (Thai p142); Carlucci (Italian p132); Chicago Brauhaus (German p131); Lutnia (Polish p138); Pasteur (Vietnamese p142); Red Apple (Polish p138); Svea (Swedish p142); Viceroy of India (Indian p131).

Suburbs & out of town

Crawdaddy Bayou (Cajun p123); Don's Fishmarket & Tavern (Seafood p140); Hecky's Barbecue (Ribs p138); Kendall College (Culinary schools p127); Le Français (French p129); Le Titi de Paris (French p129); White Fence Farm (American p121).

Tru

676 N St Clair Street, at E Huron Street, Near North/Streeterville (312 202 0001). CTA Chicago (Red). **Open** 5.30-10pm Mon-Thur; 5.30-11pm Fri, Sat; closed Sun. **Set menus** *prix fixe* $70; *dégustation* $75-$125. **Credit** AmEx, DC, Disc, MC, V. **Map** p306 J10.
Multi-course menus here showcase the creativity of chef-owners Rick Tramonto and Gale Gand. The stylish room is crisply minimalist – service tends to be overbearing – while the menu offers an incredible range of flavours: try the 'caviar staircase' (an elaborate serving dish, with a different type of caviar or accompaniment on each level), roasted monkfish with braised oxtail or langoustine ravioli with foie gras cream. Book weeks ahead.

White Fence Farm

S Joliet Road, Lemont (630 739 1720). Metra Lemont. **Open** 5-9pm Tue-Fri; 4-9pm Sat; noon-8pm Sun; closed Mon. **Main courses** $10-$18. **Credit** AmEx, DC, Disc, MC, V.

Northern Fried Chicken, anyone? Whatever you call it, the golden-brown chicken at this south-west suburban eatery is tops. Crisp on the outside, moist and meaty inside, it's been the speciality of the family-run restaurant for over 40 years. The meal includes a relish tray with bean salad, coleslaw, cottage cheese, pickled beets and sugar-dusted fritters.

Zinfandel

59 W Grand Avenue, at N Dearborn Street, Near North/Magnificent Mile (312 527 1818). CTA Grand. **Open** 11.30am-2.30pm, 5-10pm Mon-Thur; 11.30am-2.30pm, 5-11pm Fri; 10.30am-2.30pm, 5-11pm Sat; closed Sun. **Main courses** $20-$30. **Credit** AmEx, DC, MC, V. **Map** p306 H10.
American regional cooking at its best. A month-by-month culinary tour of the United States takes in the cuisines of Hawaii, Texas, the South Carolina Low Country and Pennsylvania Dutch country. Decor is 'funky rustic' with folk art and batiks; try the braised pot roast, devilled cod cakes or smoked barbecued spare ribs.

329 N DEARBORN
MARINA CITY, CHICAGO

312.923.2000
WWW.HOB.COM

RESTAURANT

The House of Blues Back Porch Restaurant serves the best in contemporary, Southern Delta—inspired cuisine, and the Second Stage presents the best of Chicago Blues

Gospel Brunch

Shout Hallelujah and say Yeah! What better way to start your Sunday than with our all you can eat brunch buffet and the best gospel choirs this side of the pearly gates. Seatings at 9: 30am, Noon, and 2:30pm

COMPANY STORE

You won't have to miss us if you take a piece of our "House" home with you. Our retail store offers the best of blues—inspired memorabilia.

MUSIC HALL

Our opera house inspired concert venue is known for celebrating music of all genres. House of Blues offers live shows 7 days a week.

Asian & pan-Asian

Bistro Pacific

680 N Lake Shore Drive, at E Erie Street, Near North/Streeterville (312 397 1800). CTA Grand. **Open** 11.30am-2.30pm, 5-10pm Mon-Thur; 11.30am-2.30pm, 5-11pm Fri; 5-11pm Sat; closed Sun. **Main courses** $9-$11. **Credit** AmEx, DC, Disc, MC, V. **Map** p306 K10.

Korean, Japanese, Chinese… you'll find a taste of each at this handsome eaterie in the old Furniture Mart building. It's great for romance on a budget, with dark, secluded, candlelit booths and a menu that offers main courses at great prices. Graze on the likes of steamed dumplings, Korean pancakes or pot stickers, or try the sushi, sashimi or maki.

Mirai

2020 W Division Street, at N Damen Avenue, Wicker Park/Bucktown (773 862 8500). CTA Damen (Blue). **Open** 5-10.30pm Mon-Thur, Sun; 5-11.30pm Fri, Sat. **Main courses** $9-$16. **Credit** AmEx, DC, Disc, MC, V. **Map** p310 B8.

This hip Wicker Park eaterie, with an imposing two-storey glass façade, offers fashionable sushi and sake. Six chefs work behind the sushi bar creating a flurry of sights and sounds. Upstairs, the lounge heats up as the evening wears on, with a DJ spinning a mix of lively beats.

Typhoon

Level Six, 900 N Michigan Avenue, at E Delaware Place, Gold Coast (312 642 5030). CTA Chicago (Red). **Open** 11.30am-9pm Mon-Thur; 11.30am-10pm Fri; noon-10pm Sat; noon-8pm Sun. **Main courses** $7-$17. **Credit** AmEx, DC, Disc, MC, V. **Map** p306 J9.

Typhoon has blown a fresh breeze into the tired restaurant scene at 900 N Michigan. Its modernistic, sharp-angled space features bright mosaic tiles, red and blue stained wooden floors and dramatic views of the city. A pan-Asian menu offers dishes (and beers) from Japan, China, Thailand and Vietnam.

Vong

6 W Hubbard Street, at N State Street, Near North/ Magnificent Mile (312 644 8664). CTA Grand. **Open** 5.30-10pm Mon-Thur; 5-11pm Fri, Sat; 5-10pm Sun. **Main courses** $18-$33. **Credit** AmEx, DC, Disc, MC, V. **Map** p306 H11.

Want to sample the famous Thai-inspired French cuisine of Jean-Georges Vongerichten? And do it inexpensively? Check out Vong's 'Bamboo Express', a three-course lunch designed to be enjoyed within 30 minutes. Vongerichten uses more than 150 herbs and spices to create his 'explosively flavourful food'.

British

Earl of Loch Ness

2350 N Clark Street, at W Fullerton Avenue, Lincoln Park (773 529 9879). CTA Fullerton. **Open** 11.30am-11pm Mon-Thur; 11.30am-3am Fri; 9am-3am Sat; 9am-2am Sun. **Main courses** $9-$15. **Credit** AmEx, DC, Disc, MC, V. **Map** p308 G5.

The basic pub fare at this Scottish-owned pub includes shepherd's pie, haggis, mince and tatties and, predictably, bangers, and there's imported beer to wash it all down. The weekend breakfast buffets include Irish ham and both black and white pudding. The Earl of Loch Ness also serves decent fish and chips, with succulent cod deep-fried in a light batter.

Lawry's the Prime Rib

100 E Ohio Street, at N Michigan Avenue, Near North/Magnificent Mile (312 787 5000). CTA Grand. **Open** 11.30am-2pm, 5-11pm Mon-Thur; 11.30am-2pm, 5pm-midnight Fri; 5pm-midnight Sat; 3-10pm Sun. **Main courses** $20-$30. **Credit** AmEx, DC, Disc, MC, V. **Map** p306 J10.

It's not really British, but it does serve the best roast beef in town and the setting – the century-old former McCormick mansion – is reminiscent of an English-style carvery. Moreover, it accompanies its excellent beef with authentic, light and fluffy Yorkshire pudding. The prime rib is served table-side with mashed or baked potato and whipped cream horseradish.

Cajun, Creole & Southern

Club Creole

226 W Kinzie Street, at N Franklin Street, Near North/River North (312 222 0300). CTA Merchandise Mart. **Open** 11am-9pm Mon-Fri; 5-10pm Sat; closed Sun. **Main courses** $7-$15. **Credit** AmEx, DC, Disc, MC, V. **Map** p306 G11.

'Laissez les bon temps rouler!' says the sign, and roll those good times do in this Deep South diner, a narrow, shotgun space decorated in New Orleans kitsch. Sample bayou beers and chow down on spicy gumbo, voodoo chicken, jambalaya or classic sandwiches such as oyster po-boys and Italian muffulettas, but whatever you eat, make sure you save room for the scrumptious sweet potato praline pie.

Crawdaddy Bayou

412 N Milwaukee Avenue, Wheeling (847 520 4800). Metra Wheeling. **Open** 11.30am-3pm, 5-10pm Tue-Thur; 4.30-10pm Fri; 4-10pm Sat, Sun; closed Mon. **Main courses** $7-$22. **Credit** Disc, MC, V.

This lively, noisy eaterie is out in the sticks but it is a great spot for live zydeco. Its menu celebrates southern Louisiana country cooking favourites such as jambalaya. Nightly seafood boils are prepared at the bar in a steam kettle. The Cajun General Store on the premises sells beignet mix, chilli pepper condiments and other Louisiana specialities, as well as themed souvenirs and T-shirts.

Heaven on Seven on Rush

Second Floor, 600 N Rush Street, at E Ohio Street, Near North/Magnificent Mile (312 280 7774). CTA Grand. **Open** 11am-10pm Mon-Thur, Sun; 11am-11pm Fri, Sat. **Main courses** $10-$20. **Credit** AmEx, DC, Disc, MC, V. **Map** p306 J10.

Consumer

A masochist's delight: chilli sauces galore at **Heaven on Seven**. *See page 123.*

Cajun cooking moved onto the Mag Mile when a wildly popular Loop lunch counter spawned this spin-off. Some complain it's too boisterous and full of tourists, but hey: that makes it just like the Big Easy, right? Specialities include gumbo, jambalaya, étouffée and po-boy sandwiches. Can't decide what to have? Say 'Jimmy feed me', and chef Bannos will gladly oblige.

Joe's Be-Bop Café & Jazz Emporium

Navy Pier, 600 E Grand Avenue, at Lake Michigan, Near North/Streeterville (312 595 5199). CTA Grand. **Open** 11am-11pm Mon-Thur, Sun; 11am-midnight Fri, Sat. **Main courses** $8-$15. **Credit** AmEx, DC, Disc, MC, V. **Map** p306 K10.

Head to Navy Pier for Southern-style Sunday brunch with a side of live jazz, blues and gospel music. Along with traditional brunch fare such as omelettes and French toast, Joe's offers barbecue bacon, cheese grits, red beans and rice and other Southern staples. Concoct your own Bloody Mary by choosing from more than 140 ingredients.

Redfish

400 N State Street, at W Kinzie Street, Near North/Magnificent Mile (312 467 1600). CTA Grand, Lake or State. **Open** 11am-11pm Mon-Thur; 11am-2pm Fri, Sat. **Main courses** $16-$28. **Credit** AmEx, DC, Disc, MC, V. **Map** p306 H11.

Chalk up another triumph for central casting. Here's another eatery that looks as though it belongs on a Louisiana bayou. It's festooned with Southern bric-a-brac and features a Bayou Grocery with a front stoop where good ol' boys entertain. The kitchen is deft with Cajun specialities.

Chinese

Ben Pao

52 W Illinois Street, at N Dearborn Street, Near North/Magnificent Mile (312 222 1888). CTA Grand. **Open** 11.30am-10pm Mon-Thur; 11.30am-11pm Fri; 5-11pm Sat; 4-9pm Sun. **Main courses** $9-$15. **Credit** AmEx, DC, Disc, MC, V. **Map** p307 H10.

With a sleek red and black interior, dramatic granite pillars and running water, Lettuce Entertain You's first venture into Chinese cuisine manages to combine harmony and balance with appealing food. A satay bar offers grilled-to-order skewered meats with sauces, while house specialities include shrimp dumplings and black pepper scallops. The bar serves Asian beers, microbrews and chilled sake.

Emperor's Choice

2238 S Wentworth Avenue, at W Cermak Road, South Side (312 225 8800). CTA Cermak/Chinatown. **Open** 11.30am-1am Mon-Sat; 11.30am-12.30am Sun. **Main courses** $7-$20. **Credit** AmEx, Disc, MC, V.

Unlike some of its cavernous tourist-trap neighbours, this Chinatown restaurant is a small, intimate store-front with soft lighting, fine art and delicate china. It offers some of the city's best Cantonese and other Chinese cooking, especially seafood: try Peking lobster, spicy Hunan shrimp or steamed oysters.

PF Chang's China Bistro

530 N Wabash Avenue, at E Grand Avenue, Near North/Magnificent Mile (312 828 9977). CTA Grand. **Open** 11am-11pm Mon-Thur, Sun; 11am-midnight Fri, Sat. **Main courses** $8-$14. **Credit** AmEx, DC, MC, V. **Map** p306 H10.

Find good food, a sleek, upscale setting and decent theatre at Chang's. There are dishes from Canton, Shanghai, Szechwan, Hunan and Mongolia, but the shrimp dumplings and orange peel beef stand out.

Three Happiness
2130 S Wentworth Street, at W Cermak Road, South Side (312 791 1228). CTA Cermak/Chinatown.
Open 10am-11pm Mon-Sat; 10am-10pm Sun.
Main courses $8-$9. **Credit** AmEx, MC, V.
One of the more popular restaurants in Chicago's small, bustling Chinatown, this huge eaterie is famous for its dim sum. Choose from a staggering spread:

steamed dumplings, deep-fried pastries, wrapped shrimp, spare ribs with black bean sauce and more.
Branch: 209 W Cermak Road, South Side (312 842 1964).

Continental

Plaza Tavern
70 W Monroe Street, at 1 First National Plaza, The Loop (312 977 1940). CTA Monroe (Blue, Red).
Open 11.30am-2pm, 5-11pm Mon-Fri; 5-11pm Sat.
Main courses $16-$34. **Credit** AmEx, DC, MC, V.
Map p305 H12.

My kind of town Richard Melman

Lawrence of Oregano. Jonathan Livingston Seafood. Now, we like our puns, but this is going too far. As, possibly, is RJ Grunts, and the ethnically incorrect Scoozi!. All these and plenty more are or were the names of Chicago eateries, and all are the brainchild of one Richard Melman.

There's no doubt that Melman has a penchant for whimsical names – he called his company Lettuce Entertain You Enterprises (LEYE), for Heaven's sake – as well as an advanced sense of the outrageous. Many of his restaurants, quite aside from offering fine food, also offer good theatre. Take **Scoozi!**, for example (410 W Huron Street, Near North/River North; 312 943 5900). Occupying a cavernous former commercial garage, it features strolling costumed accordion players, play-acting faux Italian waiters and taped *sotto voce* Italian conversations in the toilets.

But Melman is also a shrewd businessman. In the last 30 years, he has become one of America's most flourishing restaurateurs and a Chicago success story. LEYE now owns and licenses more than 75 restaurants in the States and in Japan. Very obviously, Melman has a way with food and concepts as well as with names.

The restaurant business has been Melman's life work, beginning with his early days in a family-owned restaurant and continuing throughout his teenage years, when he spent his time working in fast-food eateries, manning a soda fountain, and selling restaurant supplies. After realising he wasn't cut out to be a college student and failing to convince his father that he should be made a partner in the family business, Melman went into partnership with the late Jerry A Orzoff.

In 1971, the pair opened **RJ Grunts** (2056 N Lincoln Park West, Lincoln Park; 773 929 5363), a hip burger joint that soon became one of the hottest restaurants in Chicago. The pair wanted to present food differently – with a sense of humour, for a start – and created a youthful, fun restaurant that was a forerunner in the trend towards eating as entertainment that swept the US in the early 1970s. Although Lawrence of Oregano and Jonathan Livingston Seafood, two more early Melman operations, have long since passed from the scene, RJ Grunts remains popular.

Through his partnership with Orzoff, Melman formulated a philosophy based on the importance of partners, of sharing responsibilities and profits with them, and of developing and growing together. Melman now has 36 working partners. Some are celebrity chef-owners, but most are people who have risen through the organisation.

Today, LEYE restaurants range from fun, family-oriented eateries, such as the **Chicago Flat Sammies** (163 E Pearson Street, Gold Coast; 312 664 2733) or the **Mity Nice Grill** (Water Tower Place, 835 N Michigan Avenue, Gold Coast; 312 335 4745), to many of Chicago's top rooms, among them **Everest** (*see page 129*), **Tru** (*see page 121*) and **Vong** (*see page 123*). And then there's the wildly successful **Corner Bakery** chain, now in 19 Chicagoland locations (the original is at 516 N Clark Street, Near North; 312 644 8100), and the **Maggiano's Little Italy** restaurants, with four Chicago branches (including one at the same 516 N Clark Street address as the **Corner Bakery**; 312 644 7700) and six in other cities. Chicagoans consider themselves duly entertained, even if that pun is starting to wear a little thin.

Consumer

Continental sophistication at the **Plaza Tavern**. *See page 125.*

Want a little Johnny Mercer with your mignon? This 1940s-style supper club includes such standards as veal Oscar and châteaubriand, as well as a bandstand where a jazz trio and diva perform nightly. The sleek, sexy room features moody murals and overlooks the splashing fountain and Marc Chagall mosaic of First National Plaza.

Culinary schools

CHIC Café
361 W Chestnut Street, at N Orleans Street, Gold Coast (312 944 0882). CTA Chicago (Brown/Purple). **Open** *sittings* noon-1pm Mon-Fri, Sun; noon-1pm, 7-8pm Sat. **Set menus** *lunch* $12 (Mon-Sat); *brunch* $15 (Sun only); *dinner* $25 (Sat only). **Credit** MC, V. **Map** p306 G9.
Find tomorrow's superstar chefs today in the dining room of this cookery school (the name is an acronym for Cooking & Hospitality Institute of Chicago). The cuisine will please your palate, while the prices will ease your pocket: bring wine and enjoy excellent three-course lunches Monday to Saturday for $12, or four-course dinners (Saturday only) for $25. Chefs-in-training produce dishes like osso bucco with spring vegetables.

Kendall College
2408 Orrington Avenue, Evanston (847 866 1399/ www.kendall.edu). CTA Noyes. **Open** *term time only* noon-1.30pm Mon; noon-1.30pm, 6-8pm Tue-Fri; 6-8.30pm Sat; closed Sun. **Main courses** *lunch* $15 (prix fixe); *dinner* $25. **Credit** AmEx, Disc, MC, V.

You can also scout culinary-talent-in-the-making at the intimate student-operated restaurant of Evanston's well-regarded Kendall College. Meals are prepared by students enrolled in the culinary arts programme; lunch is $15, dinner starts at $25.

Eclectic

Caliterra
Wyndham Chicago Hotel, 633 N St Clair Street, at E Erie Street, Near North/Streeterville (312 274 4444). CTA Chicago (Red). **Open** 6.30am-11pm daily. **Main courses** $21-$35. **Credit** AmEx, DC, Disc, MC, V. **Map** p306 J10.
A stylish and rather excellent Streeterville eaterie offering John Coletta's northern California- and Tuscany-influenced menu. Specialities include veal chop with portobello fries and white bean relish, and five-spice seared duck breast. The adjoining lounge offers a light menu for late dining and live jazz.

Coast
2145 N Damen Avenue, at W Webster Avenue, Wicker Park/Bucktown (773 782 9700). CTA Damen (Blue). **Open** 5pm-2am Mon-Fri; 5pm-3am Sat; 11am-11pm Sun. **Main courses** $12-$19. **Credit** AmEx, DC, MC, V. **Map** p310 B6.
Although lacking a waterfront location, this hip café travels global coastal regions with its eclectic menu and the decor features oversized photos of ocean scenes. There's late-night dining and the large bar offers an extensive Martini list. Try duck jambalaya, wood-grilled calamari, or settle for a spicy burger or barbecued chicken sandwich with smoked Cheddar.

Spago

*520 N Dearborn Street, at W Grand Avenue, Near
North/Magnificent Mile (312 527 3700). CTA
Grand.* **Open** 11.30am-2pm, 5.30-10pm Mon-Thur;
11.30am-2pm, 5-10pm Fri; 5-10pm Sat; closed Sun.
Main courses $19-$32. **Credit** AmEx, DC, Disc,
MC, V. **Map** p306 H10.

With Hollywood-style fanfare, celeb chef Wolfgang
Puck has imported his inventive Cal-Asian cuisine
to Chicago (via chef Francois Kwaku-Dongo) and
gained a keen local following. The attractive but
noisy art-decorated dining rooms are the setting for
sophisticated cooking. Try Mediterranean fish soup,
smoked pork chop or seafood risotto. Alternatively,
visit the more casual Spago Bar & Grill (in the same
building) to sample Puck's celebrated meatloaf or
duck sausage pizza.

Fondue

Geja's Café

*340 W Armitage Avenue, at N Lincoln Avenue,
Old Town (773 281 9101). CTA Armitage.* **Open** 5-
10.30pm Mon-Thur; 5pm-midnight Fri; 5pm-12.30am
Sat; 4-10pm Sun. **Main courses** $20-$36.
Credit AmEx, DC, Disc, MC, V. **Map** p307 G6.

Isn't it romantic? Sharing a pot of gooey fondue in a
candlelit setting with a flamenco guitarist providing
background music. This restaurant is a stayer, a
long-standing favourite left over from the fondue
craze of the 1960s; its survival isn't surprising, given
the excellent cheese, beef, poultry, seafood and
chocolate fondues, and the superb wine list. And it
is *trés romantique*.

French

Bistrot Margot

*1437 N Wells Street, at W North Avenue, Old Town
(312 587 3660). CTA Sedgwick.* **Open** 5-9pm Mon,
Sun; 5-10pm Tue-Thur; 5-11pm Fri, Sat. **Main
courses** $12-$19. **Credit** MC, V. **Map** p307 H7.

If it's on the menu, go for the beef Wellington: it'll
perhaps be the best rendition you'll find anywhere.
With its high style, elegance and sense of folly, this
art nouveau eaterie in the Old Town neighbourhood
is like a Toulouse-Lautrec painting. A cosy bar and
open kitchen anchor two intimate dining rooms.

Bistrot Zinc

*1131 N State Street, at W Elm Street, Gold Coast
(312 337 1131). CTA Clark/Division.* **Open**
11.30am-3pm, 5-10pm Mon-Fri; 10am-3pm, 5-11pm
Sat; 10am-3pm, 5-9pm Sun. **Main courses** $12-$20.
Credit AmEx, DC, MC, V. **Map** p306 H9.

It's stretching the imagination to compare nightlife
along Chicago's Rush and State Streets with the
boisterous Pigalle district of Paris. But you could
almost get away with it at this neighbourhood café,
with its rattan café seating and French-made zinc
bar. Start with steamed mussels or onion and Brie
tart and move on to steak frites or bouillabaisse.

Brasserie Jo

*59 W Hubbard Street, at N Dearborn Street, Near
North/Magnificent Mile (312 595 0800). CTA
Grand.* **Open** 11.30am-4pm, 5-10.30pm Mon-Thur;
11.30am-4pm, 5-11.30pm Fri, Sat; 4-10pm Sun.
Main courses $10-$16. **Credit** AmEx, DC, Disc,
MC, V. **Map** p306 H11.

French formations at **Bistrot Zinc**.

As faux brasseries go, this one has a good pedigree. Created by Alsatian chef Jean Joho – of **Everest** fame (*see below*) – it's the best bet in town for a croque monsieur, but also features Alsatian specialities such as sausages with sauerkraut. Linger over a late-evening drink with recorded accordion music providing the background noise.

Everest

440 S LaSalle Street, at One Financial Place, The Loop (312 663 8920). CTA LaSalle (Brown/Orange/Purple). **Open** 5.30-9.30pm Tue-Thur; 5.30-10pm Fri, Sat; closed Mon, Sun. **Main courses** $30-$45. **Credit** AmEx, DC, Disc, MC, V. **Map** p305 H13.

Another of Chicago's top restaurants – figuratively and literally – sits atop the 40th floor of a building in the Loop, commanding a predictably spectacular view. It's a romantic spot – the sumptuous decor includes leopard-print rugs, fresh flowers and candlelight – while the contemporary French menu reveals the Alsatian roots of superchef Jean Joho. A *dégustation* menu is available.

Green Dolphin Street

2200 N Ashland Avenue, at N Clybourn Avenue, Lincoln Park (773 395 0066). CTA Division. **Open** 5.30-9pm Tue-Thur; 5.30-10.30pm Fri, Sat; closed Mon, Sun. **Main courses** $14-$30. **Credit** AmEx, DC, Disc, MC, V. **Map** p308 D5.

This retro supper club combines French-American fine dining, a riverside dining patio and a jazz club. With racy music and refined food, Green Dolphin Street represents an elegant $2-million makeover of a junkyard and auto-glass repair shop. Start with asparagus soup with crawfish tails, move on to roasted shallot-crusted rack of lamb and finish with indulgent chocolate soup. *See also p212.*

Le Français

269 S Milwaukee Avenue, Wheeling (847 541 7470). Metra Wheeling. **Open** *sittings* 6pm Mon-Thur; 6pm, 9pm Fri, Sat; closed Sun. **Main courses** $30. **Credit** AmEx, DC, MC, V.

Once tagged the best restaurant in America, Le Français still provides destination dining that attracts fly-ins to nearby Palwaukee airport. And now that master chef Jean Banchet has returned to the helm of the kitchen, its star is again on the rise. Think classic ingredients, classic presentation and classic cooking methods, all done in a simpler, cleaner, more contemporary spin.

Le Titi de Paris

1015 W Dundee Road, Arlington Heights (847 506 0222). Metra Arlington Heights. **Open** 11.30am-9.30pm Tue-Fri; 11.30am-10pm Sat; closed Mon, Sun. **Main courses** $26-$29. **Credit** AmEx, DC, Disc, MC, V.

Maître d' Marcel plays classical guitar and sings at this suburban eaterie, where the flower-filled dining rooms provide a complementary setting for classic French cuisine. The menu includes such delights as duck confit, lobster bisque, loin of veal and salmon with apples and cider sauce.

Mossant

Hotel Monaco, 225 N Wabash Avenue, at E Wacker Drive, The Loop (312 236 9300). CTA Lake or State. **Open** 7-10am, 11.30am-2.30pm, 5-10pm Mon-Thur; 7-10am, 11.30am-2.30pm, 5-11pm Fri; 8am-2pm, 5-11pm Sat; 8am-2pm, 5-10pm Sun. **Main courses** $15-$22. **Credit** AmEx, DC, Disc, MC, V. **Map** p305 H11.

Named after a Parisian milliner, Mossant tries hard to resemble a Parisian bistro. Certainly, the mussels steamed in Muscadet are authentic and the pommes frites that accompany them – with Dijon mayonnaise for dipping – may be the best fries in Chicago. Sink into a leather booth and admire the posters and artwork that play on the signature hat theme.

Rhapsody

65 E Adams Street, at N Wabash Avenue, The Loop (312 786 9911). CTA Adams or Monroe (Blue, Red). **Open** 11.30am-2pm, 5-8.45pm *or* 10.30pm Mon-Fri; 5-8.45pm *or* 10.30pm Sat, Sun. **Main courses** $19-$29. **Credit** AmEx, DC, Disc, MC, V. **Map** p305 H12.

Located in busy Symphony Center, this austere Loop restaurant – brick walls, white stucco ceiling – looks out onto a landscaped dining patio and, less attractively, an El station. It showcases the intricate flavours and artful presentation of Roland Liccioni, who served for a decade as chef de cuisine at the famous **Le Français** (*see above*). Try the signature tuna-smoked salmon terrine. The restaurant stays open until 10.30pm on concert evenings.

Savarin

713 N Wells Street, at Superior Street, Near North/River North (312 255 9520). CTA Chicago (Brown/Purple). **Open** 5-10pm daily. **Main courses** $15-$25. **Credit** AmEx, DC, Disc, MC, V. **Map** p306 H10.

Chef-owner John Hogan is poised for yet another restaurant success. The dazzling – but not flashy – interior of Savarin is a marriage of Empire and rustic styles, though foodies especially enjoy the upstairs 'chef gallery', hung with beautifully framed oils of culinary notables. Along with succulent braised meats and juicy roast fowl, the menu features classical coq au vin, steak frites, baked onion soup and salade Lyonnaise.

German

Berghoff

17 W Adams Street, at S State Street, The Loop (312 427 3170). CTA Adams or Monroe (Blue, Red). **Open** 11am-9pm Mon-Thur; 11am-9.30pm Fri; 11am-10pm Sat; closed Sun. **Main courses** $11-$19. **Credit** AmEx, MC, V. **Map** p305 H12.

You want old? Take a look at the liquor licence of this German-American favourite, the first issued after the repeal of Prohibition. Indeed, many of the waiters look as though they have been around that long. Go for plump Wurst, Sauerbraten, Strudel and other Teutonic staples, for house-brewed beer, and for sandwiches at the stand-up bar. *See also p144.*

Consumer

Chicago Brauhaus

4732 N Lincoln Avenue, at W Lawrence Avenue, Far North (773 784 4444). CTA Western (Brown). **Open** 11am-2am Mon, Wed-Sun; closed Tue. **Main courses** $8-$18. **Credit** AmEx, DC, Disc, MC, V.

You'll hear German spoken in this Lincoln Square neighbourhood and you'll likely hear it at this eaterie. The Chicago Brauhaus resembles nothing if not a Munich beer hall, and attracts many German patrons. Try schnitzel, smoked pork loin, Koenigsberger Klopse (meatballs in caper sauce) or other German specialities.

Greek

Costa's

340 S Halsted Street, at W Van Buren Street, West Side (312 263 9700). CTA UIC-Halsted. **Open** 11am-11pm Mon-Thur; 11am-midnight Fri, Sat; noon-11.30pm Sun. **Main courses** $10-$29. **Credit** AmEx, DC, Disc, MC, V.

You'll find all the old favourites at this good-looking Greektown eaterie, along with some unexpected and innovative twists. Start with taramasalata to pile onto crusty Greek bread, then look to moussaka, red snapper or lamb chops, kebabs and other excellent grilled meats. There's an authentically Aegean look to Costa's whitewashed walls and terracotta tiles.

Pegasus

130 S Halsted Street, at W Adams Street, West Side (312 226 3377). CTA UIC-Halsted. **Open** 11am-midnight Mon-Thur; 11am-1am Fri; noon-1am Sat; noon-midnight Sun. **Main courses** $5-$25. **Credit** AmEx, DC, Disc, MC, V.

A Greektown restaurant with whitewashed walls and Aegean murals, Pegasus proves that there's more to Greek food than gyros. Start with grilled octopus and move on to a delicious pasta dish made with morsels of beef or lamb braised with plum tomatoes, olive oil, wine, herbs and garlic. A rooftop deck provides one of Chicago's best alfresco dining spots and offers an unobstructed view of the city's stunning skyline.

Indian

Klay Oven

414 N Orleans Street, at W Hubbard Street, Near North/River North (312 527 3999). CTA Merchandise Mart. **Open** 11.30am-2.30pm, 5.30-10pm Mon-Fri; noon-3pm, 5.30-10pm Sat, Sun. **Main courses** $15-$18. **Credit** AmEx, DC, MC, V. **Map** p306 G11.

While Chicago can't compare with London in sheer number of good-quality Indian restaurants – few cities can – it does have a sizeable Indian population and some good Indian eateries. This one is located close to the Loop and specialises in tandoor oven cooking. The Klay Oven's charcoal-grilled lamb, chicken and prawns are all worth sampling, as are the wok-prepared stir fries.

Viceroy of India

2520 W Devon Avenue, at N Maplewood Avenue, Far North (773 743 4100). CTA 155 bus. **Open** noon-3.30pm, 5-10pm Mon-Thur, Sun; noon-3.30pm, 5-10.30pm Fri, Sat. **Main courses** $7-$13. **Credit** AmEx, DC, Disc, MC, V.

Chicago's 'Little Bombay', with its sari shops and spice emporia, is centred along a half-dozen blocks of W Devon Avenue. This atmospheric restaurant, with sitar music and Mughal-style carvings, specialises in North Indian cuisine but also offers some dishes from South India. The chicken tandoori and tender lamb shish kebab usually satisfy most western tastes.

Branch: 555 W Roosevelt Road, at Highland Road, Lombard (630 627 4411).

Italian

Bella Vista

1001 W Belmont Avenue, at N Sheffield Avenue, Lake View (773 404 0111). CTA Belmont. **Open** 11.30am-2.30pm, 4.30-10pm Mon-Fri; 4.30-11pm Sat, Sun. **Main courses** $13-$25. **Credit** AmEx, DC, Disc, MC, V. **Map** p309 E2.

This utterly romantic restaurant – the name means 'beautiful view' – is housed in a once-derelict bank. The 1929 Beaux Arts building has been transformed into a stunning neo-Italian restaurant with stencilling, hand-painted walls and wine-coloured wood imported from Africa. The Italian food is beautiful, too: pizza from wood-fired ovens, made-to-order pasta and steamed mussels.

Buca di Beppo

2941 N Clark Street, at W Wellington Avenue, Lake View (773 348 7673). CTA Belmont. **Open** 5-10pm Mon-Thur; 5-11pm Fri; 4-11pm Sat; noon-10pm Sun. **Main courses** $20-$25. **Credit** AmEx, Disc, MC, V. **Map** p309 F3.

Buca di Beppo is pure fun, from the sultry Sophia Loren photos to the irreverent displays relating to the papacy. Prices are reasonable and sharing essential for huge platters of immigrant Southern Italian food: almost everyone leaves with a brown carrier bag of extras. Spaghetti with meatballs as big as baseballs and wine from the chain's own vineyards make this an ideal spot for lively group gatherings.

Café Luciano

871 N Rush Street, at E Delaware Place, Gold Coast (312 266 1414). CTA Chicago (Red). **Open** 11.30am-10.30pm Mon-Thur, Sun; 11.30am-11.30pm Fri, Sat. **Main courses** $11-$20. **Credit** AmEx, DC, Disc, MC, V. **Map** p307 H9.

A window table here is a delightful spot for people watching, but Café Luciano is also a fine venue for live piano music and for decent Tuscan fare at reasonable prices. Try the escarole soup; it's swimming with chunks of sausage and white beans and flavoured with fennel. When coupled with crusty Italian bread and a salad, it makes for a tasty and satisfying meal.

Consumer

Holy cow! It's **Harry Caray's**.

Carlucci

6111 N River Road, Rosemont, Far North (847 518 0990). CTA Rosemont. **Open** 11.30am-2.30pm, 5-10pm Mon-Thur; 11.30am-2.30pm, 5-11pm Fri; 5-11pm Sat; 4.30-9pm Sun. **Main courses** $14-$24. **Credit** AmEx, DC, Disc, MC, V.

Convenient for O'Hare, Carlucci serves the cuisine of Tuscany in a setting reminiscent of a Tuscan country estate, with frescos, rich Persian rugs and decorative tiles. Try spit-roasted duck glazed with honey mustard.

Coco Pazzo

300 W Hubbard Street, at N Franklin Street, Near North/River North (312 836 0900). CTA Merchandise Mart. **Open** 11.30am-2.30pm Mon-Fri, 5.30-10.30pm Mon-Fri; 5.30-11pm Sat; 5-10pm Sun. **Main courses** $13-$30. **Credit** AmEx, DC, MC, V. **Map** p306 G11.

This New York import (with prices to match, though those in the café are cheaper) offers the flavours of Tuscany in a pretty setting. Its warm, earthy decor is enhanced by an exposed-beam ceiling, blue velvet drapes and a potato theme. Try grilled meat, pasta and thin-crust pizzas from the blue-tiled ovens. **Branch:** Coco Pazzo Café 636 N St Clair Street, at E Ontario Street, Magnificent Mile/Streeterville (312 664 2777).

Harry Caray's

33 W Kinzie Street, at N Dearborn Street, Near North/Magnificent Mile (312 828 0966). CTA Grand, Lake or State. **Open** 11.30am-2.30pm, 5-10.30pm Mon-Thur; 11.30am-2.30pm, 5-11pm Fri, Sat; 4-10pm Sun. **Main courses** $10-$30. **Credit** AmEx, DC, Disc, MC, V. **Map** p306 H11.

Named after the beloved Cubs broadcaster, this flamboyant restaurant offers a mix of standard Italian dishes and cuts of meat. Baseball fans enjoy the giant bat and 'Holy Cow!' sign outside and the uniforms, helmets and photographs inside. Stop by, if only for a beer and some home-made potato chips.

Italian Village Restaurants

71 W Monroe Street, at S Dearborn Street, The Loop (312 332 7005). CTA Monroe (Blue, Red). **Open** 11am-1am Mon-Thur; 11am-2am Fri, Sat; noon-midnight Sun. **Main courses** $11-$25. **Credit** AmEx, DC, MC, V. **Map** p305 H12.

Three restaurants under one roof offering distinct dining choices. Upscale **Vivere**, done out in post-industrial baroque, serves contemporary regional cuisine; the **Village** restaurant, decorated to resemble a village in Italy, offers standards such as chicken Vesuvio; folksy **La Cantina** focuses on seafood. Kitchens open early in the evening and close around midnight, ideal for pre- or post-theatre dining (call ahead for exact times).

Nick & Tony's

1 E Wacker Drive, at N State Street, The Loop (312 467 9449). CTA Lake or State. **Open** 11am-10pm Mon-Thur; 11am-11pm Fri; 5-11pm Sat; 5-10pm Sun. **Main courses** $10-$20. **Credit** AmEx, DC, Disc, MC, V. **Map** p305 H11.

This hard-working Loop eatery serves morning coffee, fresh baked goods and lunchtime sandwiches to office workers, moves on to pre-theatre menus, then welcomes its regular dinner crowd. Decorated as a take on a 1940s Italian chophouse, Nick & Tony's offers decent meat dishes and well-made pasta.

Slicker Sam's on Halsted

1723 N Halsted Street, at W North Avenue,
Old Town (312 397 9080). CTA North/Clybourn.
Open 4-11pm Tue-Thur; 4pm-midnight Fri, Sat;
1-9pm Sun; closed Mon. **Main courses** $12-$16.
Credit AmEx, DC, Disc, MC, V. **Map** p307 F7.
This neighbourhood Italian classic, famous for its
plastic grapes decor and excellent seafood, has
moved into yuppieland: the 'slicker' version of Sam's
offers new twists on old 'immigrant Italian' classics.

Baked clams, grilled octopus and osso bucco all
come highly recommended. Sadly, the original
Sam's on the West Side has recently closed down.

312 Chicago

Hotel Allegro, 136 N LaSalle Street, at W Randolph
Street, The Loop (312 696 2420). CTA Clark or
Washington (Blue, Red). **Open** 7am-noon, 5-10pm
Mon-Thur; 7am-noon, 5-11pm Fri, Sat; 8am-3pm,
5-10pm Sun. **Main courses** $10-$22. **Credit** AmEx,
DC, Disc, MC, V. **Map** p305 H12.

Streetwise treats

Start thanking your lucky stars round about
now. You won't find New York's convoys of
pushcart food vendors in Chicago. The city
has its own brand of street food, and it has
a definite Italian flavour.

High on the list of local favourites is the
Italian beef sandwich, a true Chicago original.
Its name stems from its popularity at Italian-
American weddings and religious feasts,
where serving thinly sliced beef in gravy
proved a tasty, economical way to feed a
crowd. Slices of roast beef are simmered in
well-seasoned juice and then plopped onto
chewy rolls, preferably with hot or sweet
peppers as garnish.

Most Italian beef stands also offer Italian
sausage sandwiches (also available in a
combination with beef). Ideally, these feature
all-pork sausages made without additives or
extenders. The Scala Packing Company, a
Chicago fixture since 1925, is a major
supplier of Italian beef and sausages.

Popular spots to sample Italian beef
sandwiches include **Al's Italian Beef** stand
along the stretch of Taylor Street known as
Little Italy (1079 W Taylor Street, between
Aberdeen and Carpenter Streets, West Side;
312 226 4017). Al's has another branch in
Near North/River North (169 W Ontario
Street, at Wells Street; 312 943 3222).
Also in River North is **Mr Beef** (*see page 137*
The lunch bunch), a media and celeb
hangout for the likes of Harrison Ford, Robert
DeNiro and George Wendt. Mr Beef himself
is Joe Zucchero, whose eaterie is one of the
last to slice and cook its own beef, using a
'secret' spice mix with five seasonings.

A light, refreshing dessert after a hefty
sandwich is Italian ice, a cup of shaved ice
drenched with syrup (usually lemon). And
Italian ice doesn't get much better than that
at **Mario's Italian Lemonade stand** (1070
W Taylor Street, West Side; no phone;
open from May to late October).

Hot dogs, Chicago-style, are all-beef
affairs and supplied, among others, by the
Vienna Sausage Co. Served on a bun that's
steamed until warm and airy – but without a
hint of evil sogginess – garnishes should
include one or all from pickle spears,
chopped onion, mustard, relish, hot peppers
and celery salt. *Never* ketchup. Most hot dog
stands also sell 'Polish'. Typically, these are
not ethnic sausages such as kielbasa, but
larger, plumper versions of hot dogs.

Gold Coast Dogs (418 N State Street, at W
Hubbard Street, Near North; 312 527 1222)
was named among the 'top dogs' in America
by *Money* magazine. Its franks should be
teamed with cheese fries made from Idaho
potatoes smothered with Wisconsin Cheddar.
Vienna All-Beef franks can also be found at
the three branches of **Byron's**: 1017 W Irving
Park Road, N Sheridan Road, Lake View/
Wrigleyville (773 281 7474); 1701 W
Lawrence Avenue, at N Paulina Street,
Far North (773 271 0900); 680 N Halsted
Street, at W Ancona Street, West Side
(312 738 0968).

Pizza by the slice is another popular walk-
away edible. **Bacino's** (*see page 136*) in Lake
View (3146 N Sheffield Avenue, at W Fletcher
Street; 773 404 8111) sells slices of stuffed
and thin-crust pizza to Cubs fans on their way
to Wrigley Field, and in summer, the Lincoln
Park branch (2204 N Lincoln Avenue, at W
Webster Avenue; 773 472 7400) also sells
pizza by the slice from an outdoor window.

Not too long ago, a visit to colourful
Maxwell Street Market and munching on a
pork chop sandwich were complimentary
Sunday morning experiences. Urban renewal
nudged out the grungy, colourful market (a
scaled-down, sanitised version now exists
nearby), but the pork chop stand remains.
Jim's Original, at the corner of W Maxwell
Street and S Halsted Street, West Side (312
666 0533), is almost worth the trip by itself.

Consumer

It's named after a Chicago area code, but that's the only thing phoney about this Italian-American eaterie. The room blends earth tones with sunny colours and features gilt mirrors, mica chandeliers, wall sconces, lots of fresh flowers and companionable booths to sit in. Signature dishes include the spit-roasted leg of lamb on parsnip purée with grappa-soaked grapes. This place is a popular pre-theatre dining spot.

Trattoria Dinotto
163 W North Avenue, at N Wells Street, Old Town (312 787 3345). CTA Sedgwick. **Open** noon-10pm Mon-Thur; noon-11pm Fri, Sat; 5-9pm Sun. **Main courses** $10-$16. **Credit** AmEx, DC, Disc, MC, V. **Map** p307 H7.
A neighbourhood favourite that looks and feels like a trattoria you'd find tucked away on a backstreet in Rome. It's run by Dino Lubbat, with his father George tending bar and mother Sue greeting guests. The pastas are well made, and you can't go wrong with veal marsala or scaloppine.

Trattoria No.10
10 N Dearborn Street, at W Madison Street, The Loop (312 984 1718). CTA Washington (Blue, Red). **Open** 11.30am-2pm, 5.30-9pm Mon-Thur; 11.30am-2pm, 5.30-10pm Fri; 5.30-10pm Sat; closed Sun. **Main courses** $15-$27. **Credit** AmEx, DC, Disc, MC, V. **Map** p305 H12.
This Loop favourite is in a basement, but what an elegant basement: with umber tones, terracotta floors, arched stucco walkways, murals and original art, it's as easy on the eye as the food – fresh risotto and handmade ravioli – is on the palate. Popular for business lunches and pre-theatre dinners.

Jewish/Kosher

Mrs Levy's Delicatessen
Second Floor, Sears Tower, 233 S Wacker Drive, at W Jackson Boulevard, The Loop (312 993 0530). CTA Quincy. **Open** 6.30am-3pm Mon-Fri; closed Sat, Sun. **Main courses** *sandwiches* $4.99-$7; *soups* $1.99-$2.59. **Credit** AmEx, DC, Disc, MC, V. **Map** p305 G12.
Just because it isn't particularly old doesn't mean this isn't a real deli. Sandwiches are piled high with lean pastrami and corned beef, and matzo ball soup and other soups are made from scratch daily, as are knishes and blintzes. There's even a real Mrs Levy, matriarch of the Levy group, who runs the place.

Shallots
2324 N Clark Street, at W Fullerton Avenue, Lincoln Park (773 755 5205). CTA Fullerton. **Open** 11.30am-1.30pm, 5.30-10pm Mon-Thur; hour after dusk-1am Sat; 5.30-10pm Sun; closed Fri. **Main courses** $17.50-$45. **Credit** MC, V. **Map** p308 F5.
There's more to Kosher cooking than chicken livers: this upmarket restaurant prepares superb Mediterranean-based food that also happens to be glatt (pure) Kosher. It almost defies belief that the

dazzling desserts such as baked Alaska and chocolate mousse cake contain no dairy products. The rich burgundy decor and tile mosaics are pretty, the food is impeccable.

Latin, Mexican & Spanish

Brio
10 W Hubbard Street, at N State Street, Near North/Magnificent Mile (312 467 1010). CTA Grand. **Open** 11.30am-2pm, 5.30-10pm Mon-Thur; 11.30am-2pm, 5.30-11pm Fri; 5.30-11pm Sat; closed Sun. **Main courses** $12-$20. **Credit** AmEx, DC, MC, V. **Map** p306 H11.
This Spanish restaurant is more than just a spot for tapas, though it does feature a handsome zinc tapas bar that sometimes offers midweek freebies accompanied by the sounds of a flamenco guitarist. Expect authentic Spanish cooking featuring the likes of garlic bread soup, thin-sliced Serrano ham and a bouillabaisse-like Catalonian stew.

Frontera Grill/Topolobampo
445 N Clark Street, at W Illinois Street, Near North/River North (312 661 1434). CTA Grand or Merchandise Mart. **Open** 11.30am-2.30pm, 5-10pm Tue-Thur; 11.30am-2.30pm, 5-11pm Fri; 10.30am-2.30pm, 5-11pm Sat; closed Sun. **Main courses** $16-$22. **Credit** AmEx, DC, Disc, MC, V. **Map** p306 H11.
Put aside notions of Tex-Mex grub: these adjoining restaurants serve authentic regional Mexican dishes – some say the best north of the border – created from recipes gathered by owners Rick and Deanne Bayless during extensive travels in Mexico. Upscale Topo accepts reservations, its sister restaurant does not (expect long waits at peak times). The chef's tasting dinner offers five courses for $52.

Mambo Grill
412 N Clark Street, at W Hubbard Street, Near North/River North (312 467 9797). CTA Grand or Merchandise Mart. **Open** 11am-9pm Mon, Tue; 11am-10pm Wed, Thur; 11am-11pm Fri; 5-11pm Sat; closed Sun. **Main courses** $13-$22. **Credit** AmEx, DC, Disc, MC, V. **Map** p306 H11.
Vibrant colours, a dark postmodern interior and hot South and Central American specialities make this a River North favourite. Unexpected twists and unusual sauces set off traditional Latin dishes: Cuban sandwiches are a good bet, as are spicy pork tamales. Potables include Margaritas and potent Brazilian cocktails.

Mas
1670 W Division Street, at N Paulina Street, West Side (773 276 8700). CTA Division. **Open** 5.30-10.30pm Mon-Thur; 5.30-11.30pm Fri, Sat; 11am-2pm, 5.30-10pm Sun. **Main courses** $15-$20. **Credit** AmEx, DC, MC, V.
The name – Spanish for 'more' – says it all at this bright storefront restaurant that was converted from an abandoned 1940s drugstore. The 'nuevo Latin' cuisine enjoys a loyal following from a fashionable

Mas has more than most. *See page 134.*

crowd that spills out into this still-grungy neighbourhood. Cocktails include Mojito, the classic
Cuban rum-mint drink.

¡Salpicon!

*1252 N Wells Street, at N Division Street,
Old Town (312 988 7811). CTA Clark or Division.*
Open 5-10pm Mon-Thur; 5-11pm Fri, Sat; 11am-
2.30pm, 5-10pm Sun. **Main courses** $15-$22.
Credit AmEx, DC, Disc, MC, V. **Map** p307 H8.
This colourful storefront showcases the stylish
Mexican regional cooking of Priscilla Satkoff, born
in Mexico City and apprenticed at the **Frontera
Grill** (*see p134*). Vivid colours and primitive folk art
set the stage for artfully prepared sophisticated
dishes. Sip Margaritas made with fresh limes.

Su Casa

*49 E Ontario Street, at N Rush Street, Near
North/Magnificent Mile (312 943 4041). CTA
Grand.* **Open** 11.30am-11pm Mon-Thur, Sun;
11.30am-midnight Fri, Sat. **Main courses** $10-$19.
Credit AmEx, DC, Disc, MC, V. **Map** p306 J10.
Though you could find more creative and better
Mexican food around, if you hanker for a simple
taco, burrito or combination platter – with rice and
refried beans, of course – this is several comfortable
cuts above a standard taco joint. Prices are friendly
and the Margaritas potent, and the whole lot is
served in an ambience of dark heavy wood within
olé range of the Mag Mile.

Mediterranean

Cuisines

*Renaissance Chicago Hotel, 1 W Wacker Drive,
at N State Street, The Loop (312 372 4459).
CTA Lake or State.* **Open** 11.30am-2pm, 5.30-9pm
Mon-Fri; 5.30-9pm Sat; closed Sun. **Main courses**
$8-$29. **Credit** AmEx, DC, Disc, MC, V.
Map p305 H11.
This is a romantic spot with comfortable uphol-
stered booths, dark panelling and soft lighting. An
open kitchen with a wood-burning grill produces
notable Mediterranean-style dishes: try the paella
or the lamb brochette with Moroccan spices. Loop
theatregoers can take advantage of the restaurant's
pre-theatre specials.

Grapes

*733 N Wells Street, at W Superior Street, Near
North/River North (312 943 4500). CTA Chicago
(Brown/Purple).* **Open** 11.30am-2pm, 5-11pm Mon-
Thur; 11.30am-2pm, 5-11.30pm Fri; 5-11.30pm Sat;
5-10pm Sun. **Main courses** $12-$24. **Credit** AmEx,
DC, Disc, MC, V. **Map** p306 H10.
This pretty River North storefront features a cobalt
blue tiled bar and hanging art lamps in purple, red,
amber and green. Expect Mediterranean/Southern
French dishes from the kitchen, such as seared
halibut with a sesame crust, eggplant purée and red
onion relish, and pork tenderloin with poached dates
and preserved lemons.

Nicolina's

NBC Towers, 455 N Cityfront Drive, at E North Water Street, Near North/Streeterville (312 832 2600). CTA Grand. **Open** 11.30am-2pm, 5-10pm Mon-Fri; 5-10pm Sat; 5-9pm Sun. **Main courses** $14-$22. **Credit** AmEx, DC, Disc, MC, V. **Map** p306 J11.
Warm and sunny decor and a creative menu that covers the Mediterranean waterfront from Spain, France and Italy to Greece, the Lebanon and North Africa. Try shrimp flamed with Ouzo, Portuguese stew, duck breast with apricots and figs, or one of the brick-oven pizzas. A takeaway section offers Mediterranean to go.

Pizza

Bacino's

75 E Wacker Drive, at N Michigan Avenue, The Loop (312 263 0070). CTA Lake or State. **Open** 11am-9pm Mon-Thur, Sun; 11am-10pm Fri, Sat. **Main courses** $10-$17. **Credit** AmEx, DC, Disc, MC, V. **Map** p305 J11.
A notable entry in the burgeoning Chicago-style stuffed pizza field, this mini-chain also offers what might seem like an oxymoron: heart-healthy pizza. Built to meet American Heart Association guidelines, this strange but healthy delicacy blends low-

The lunch bunch: where to go for

Bar Louie

226 W Chicago Avenue, at N Wells Street, Near North/River North (312 337 3313). CTA Chicago (Brown/Purple). **Open** 11am-4am Mon-Fri, Sun; 11am-5am Sat. **Main courses** $7-$10. **Credit** AmEx, DC, Disc, MC, V. **Map** p306 H10.
These neighbourhood eating/drinking spots are catching on faster than you can say 'Martini'. Though the formula is similar, each bar is a little different: some have outdoor seating, while some serve breakfast or brunch. The Italian-American assortment of appetisers, salads, sandwiches, pizzas and pasta is ideal for late-night dining.
Branches: 1704 N Damen Avenue, at W Wabansia Avenue, Wicker Park/Bucktown (773 645 7500); 1800 N Lincoln Avenue, at N Clark Avenue, Old Town (312 337 9800); 3545 N Clark Street, at W Addison Street, Lake View/Wrigleyville (773 296 2500); 123 N Halsted Street, at W Washington Boulevard, West Side (312 207 0500); 47 W Polk Street, at S Dearborn Street, South Loop (312 347 0000).

Blue Crab Lounge

21 E Hubbard Street, at N State Street, Near North/Magnificent Mile (312 527 2722). CTA Grand. **Open** 11.30am-10pm Mon-Thur; 11.30am-11pm Fri, Sat; 5-10pm Sun. **Main courses** $13-$18. **Credit** AmEx, DC, Disc, MC, V. **Map** p306 H11.
Head for the lounge of Shaw's Crab House for top-quality seafood, a strong line-up of jazz and blues and no cover charge. Patrons enjoy oysters on the half-shell, shrimp, clams, mussels, seafood gumbo, New England clam chowder and a variety of sandwiches, including pepper-crusted yellowfin tuna.

Boston Blackie's

164 E Grand Avenue, at N St Clair Street, Near North/Streeterville (312 938 8700). CTA Grand. **Open** 11am-11pm Mon-Sat; 11am-9pm Sun. **Main courses** $10. **Credit** AmEx, DC, Disc, MC, V. **Map** p306 J10.
This comfortable sports bar serves what arguably are Chicago's best burgers. The two-fisted juicy half-pounders are good with blue cheese or olives and a side of not-overly-greasy steak fries is large enough to share. It's busy – occasionally with staff from the *Jerry Springer Show*, filmed nearby – but super-fast.

Four Farthings Tavern

2060 N Cleveland Avenue, at W Dickens Avenue, Lincoln Park (773 935 2060). CTA Armitage. **Open** 11.30am-10.30pm Mon-Fri; 11.30am-11pm Sat; 10am-10pm Sun. **Main courses** $9-$26. **Credit** AmEx, DC, Disc, MC, V. **Map** p308 G6.
One side of this 1890s saloon is a lively bar where a youngish crowd shoot pool, watch TV sports and enjoy superior pub grub such as hamburgers, Cajun meatloaf and fish and chips. The 'bottled beer of the month' is $2 a pop. An adjoining dining room, with warm wood panelling and deep booths, serves prime beef, fresh seafood and specials such as roast duck.

Club Lago

331 W Superior Street, at N Orleans Street, Near North/River North (312 337 9444). CTA Chicago (Brown/Purple). **Open** 10.30am-8pm Mon-Fri; 11.30am-3pm Sat. **Main courses** $10. **Map** p306 G10.
'Club' is a misleading description of this gritty saloon that's a neighbourhood holdout in gentrified River North. Club Lago attracts a loyal lunch and early-dinner crowd who go for

fat cheeses, spinach, fresh mushrooms, herbs and spices. Still more amazing than the concept is that it actually tastes good, too.
Branch: 2204 N Lincoln Avenue, at Webster Avenue, Lincoln Park (773 472 7400).

Giordano's

730 N Rush Street, at E Superior Street, Near North/Magnificent Mile (312 951 0747/ www.giordanos.com). CTA Chicago (Red). **Open** 11am-midnight Mon-Thur, Sun; 11am-1am Fri, Sat. **Main courses** $10-$20. **Credit** AmEx, DC, MC, V. **Map** p306 J10.

Don't be tempted by the pasta or the other Italian specialities offered by this huge and successful chain: they're average at best. It's pizza you want at Giordano's, and specifically stuffed pizza, thick and crusty (try the spinach-and-mushroom stuffed version, though you can't really go wrong with any of them). This place is popular, so expect to wait at prime times.
Branches: 310 W Randolph Street, at N Franklin Street, The Loop (312 616 1200); 236 S Wabash Avenue, at E Adams Street, The Loop (312 939 4646); 2855 N Milwaukee Avenue, at N Dawson Avenue, Far North (312 862 4200).

the midday munchies

the signature green noodles al forno, oven-baked with a garlicky blend of three cheeses. Family-owned since 1952, the place seldom misses a trick with its delicious Italian-American standards.

Encore

Hotel Allegro, 171 W Randolph Street, at N LaSalle Street, The Loop (312 338 3788). CTA Clark or Washington (Blue, Red). **Open** 11am-midnight Mon-Fri; 4pm-midnight Sat; closed Sun. **Main courses** $7-$8. **Credit** AmEx, DC, Disc, MC, V. **Map** p305 H12.
There's a Jekyll and Hyde personality to this eaterie in the Loop Theatre District: lunch counter by day, hip lounge by night. For a casual lunch, try home-made soups and carved, slow-cooked beef brisket sandwiches with house-made barbecue sauce. At night, Encore offers its customers a light menu, accompanied by DJs and cocktails in an edgy lounge awash with hues of crimson, deep purple, moss green and gold.

Fuzio

1045 N Rush Street, at E Cedar Street, Gold Coast (312 988 4640). CTA Clark/Division. **Open** 11.30am-midnight Mon-Thur, Sun; 11.30am-2am Fri, Sat. **Main courses** $9-$19. **Credit** AmEx, DC, Disc, MC, V. **Map** p306 H9.
Along bustling, touristy (and often pricey) Rush Street, Fuzio offers style and value. Excellent, creative cuisine is served on handsome granite tabletops beneath cobalt blue sconces, with entrées priced under $10 and wines under $25. For a substantial lunch, start with semolina dumplings with tomato vinaigrette or Tuscan white bean salad with prosciutto, and then move on to one of the fine pastas.

Lou Mitchell's

565 W Jackson Boulevard, at S Jefferson Street, West Side (312 939 3111). CTA Clinton (Blue). **Open** 5.30am-3pm Mon-Sat; 7am-3pm Sun. **Main courses** $6-$8.
There's usually a long wait at this breakfast favourite, but bonuses include Milk Duds for waiting female patrons. Hearty breakfasts, served sizzling in iron skillets, come with double-yoke eggs and doorstep-sized Greek toast with home-made marmalade. Pancakes, waffles and omelettes are good, too.

Mr Beef on Orleans

666 N Orleans Street, at W Huron Street, Near North/River North (312 337 8500). CTA Chicago (Brown/Purple). **Open** 7am-4.45pm Mon-Fri; 10.30am-2pm Sat. **Main courses** $3-$5. **Map** p306 G10.
Italian beef sandwiches are done to perfection at this hole in the wall that's won rave notices from Jay Leno, Jim Belushi and others. Thin slices of juicy beef are garnished with sweet or hot peppers; Italian sausage sandwiches are also good. The 'dining room' has communal picnic tables.

Regimental Grill

10 S Riverside Plaza, at E Monroe Drive, The Loop (312 726 9347). CTA Madison or Monroe (Blue, Red). **Open** 6am-8pm Mon-Fri. **Main courses** $6-$14. **Credit** AmEx, MC, V. **Map** p305 K12.
Looking for an early breakfast prior to midweek Loop sightseeing? This is a comfortable spot – warm maple furniture, emerald plaids – for bacon and pancakes, as well as fancier fare such as eggs Benedict and frittata. It's also a popular luncheon venue with office workers: the London broil and the crabcake sandwich are both good choices.

Consumer

Lou Malnati's Pizzeria

*439 N Wells Street, at W Hubbard Street, Near
North/River North (312 828 9800). CTA
Merchandise Mart.* **Open** 11am-11pm Mon-Thur;
11am-11.30pm Fri, Sat; noon-10pm Sun. **Main
courses** $10-$20. **Credit** AmEx, DC, Disc, MC, V.
Map p306 H11.

Another contender for Chicago's 'best deep-dish
pizza' title is this family-operated River North pizzeria with suburban branches. It offers a low-fat cheese
version and, at the other end of the health spectrum,
addictive squares of breaded and deep-fried Cheddar
cheese. Malnati's bakes thin-crust pies, too, and
offers an excellent antipasto salad.
Branches: 958 W Wrightwood Avenue, at
N Sheffield Avenue Lincoln Park (773 832 4030);
and throughout the city.

Original Gino's East

*633 N Wells Street, at W Ontario Street, Near
North/River North (312 943 1124). CTA Chicago
(Brown, Purple).* **Open** 11am-11pm Mon-Thur, Sun;
11am-midnight Fri, Sat. **Main courses** *deep-dish
pizza* $14.85-$17.70. **Credit** AmEx, DC, Disc, MC, V.
Map p306 H10.

The location may have changed – Gino's recently
moved from its 'original' location into the premises
vacated by Planet Hollywood – but, as Led Zep
would say, the song remians the same. And the
song? Tourists, graffiti-scrawled walls and mammoth deep-dish pizza. Thin-crust pizza is available,
too, but that's hardly the point.
Branches: throughout the city.

Pizzeria Uno

*29 E Ohio Street, at N Wabash Avenue, Near North/
Magnificent Mile (312 321 1000). CTA Grand.*
Open 11.30am-1am Mon-Fri; 11.30am-2am Sat;
11.30am-11.30pm Sun. **Main courses** $10-$18.
Credit AmEx, DC, Disc, MC, V. **Map** p306 H10.

The birthplace, back in the 1940s, of Chicago's
famous deep-dish pizza. There are numerous franchise spin-offs around the world, but this original
delivers a superior product. The crust is thick but
not too doughy, the cheese satisfyingly gooey.
Expect tourist crowds and weekend waits at this
and its equally good sister restaurant Pizzeria Due
(located a block away).
Branch: **Pizzeria Due** 619 N Wabash Avenue,
at E Ontario Street, Near North/Magnificent Mile
(312 943 2400).

Polish

Lutnia

*5532 W Belmont Avenue, at N Central Avenue,
Far North (773 282 5335). CTA 77, 85 bus.* **Open**
11am-11pm Tue-Fri; 1-11pm Sat, Sun; closed Mon.
Main courses $10-$25. **Credit** MC, V.

In a city second only to Warsaw in Polish population, you must try some Polish cooking. Lutnia is
'posh Polish': in other words, not much of a culture
shock and far removed from the numerous Polish
storefronts along Milwaukee Avenue. Inside you'll

find candelabra, white napery and fresh roses. But
you'll also find a pierogi or two along with the
flambéed duck breast and stroganoff.

Red Apple

*3121 N Milwaukee Avenue, at W Belmont Avenue,
Far North (773 588 5781). CTA Belmont/56 bus.*
Open 11am-9.30pm daily. **Main courses** $5.
Credit Disc, MC, V.

Here's your basic 'pig-out Polish' with two locations
(both, of course, on Milwaukee Avenue, Chicago's
Little Warsaw). Both offer budget, all-you-can-eat
meals featuring hearty fare: dishes just like your
Grandma would have made if she had been Polish.
Tuck into pierogis with substantial fillings of meat,
cheese and vegetables, kielbasa (smoked sausage)
and stuffed cabbage, plus goulash and borscht.
Branch: 6474 N Milwaukee Avenue, at Devon Street,
Far North (773 763 3407).

Ribs

Hecky's Barbecue

*1902 Green Bay Road, Evanston (847 492 1182).
CTA Foster.* **Open** 11am-9pm Mon-Thur; 11am-
10pm Fri, Sat; 2-8pm Sun. **Main courses** $12-$15.
Credit AmEx, Disc, MC, V.

If you believe Chicago's only good ribs originate on
the southside, check out this Evanston storefront. A
bright yellow sign proclaims 'It's the sauce', which
comes in hot or mild versions. Hecky's does a huge
takeaway and delivery business, even to rib-hungry
travellers stuck in queues at O'Hare. Baked beans,
and red beans and rice are among available sides.

Robinson's No.1 Ribs

*940 W Madison Avenue, at N Clinton Street,
The Loop (708 383 8452). CTA Clinton (Green).*
Open 11am-10pm Mon-Thur; 11am-11pm Fri, Sat;
noon-9pm Sun. **Main courses** $9.95. **Credit** AmEx,
MC, V. **Map** p305 G12.

The 'No.1' originates from a win in the very first
annual rib cook-off championed by the late columnist Mike Royko. Charlie Robinson, a backyard chef,
took his title, recipe and fame and opened a small
rib joint. It's grown into a large restaurant that now
markets the secret sauce made with 17 herbs and
spices that accompanies fall-off-the-bone ribs.

Twin Anchors

*1655 N Sedgwick Street, at W Eugenie Street,
Old Town (312 266 1616). CTA Sedgwick.*
Open 5-11pm Mon-Thur; 5pm-midnight Fri; noon-
midnight Sat; noon-10.30pm Sun. **Main courses**
$10-$17. **Credit** AmEx, DC, Disc, MC, V.
Map p307 G7.

This neighbourhood tavern hosted Frank Sinatra on
occasion and now gets maximum mileage from it
with prominent photos of Ol' Blue Eyes and his
recordings on the jukebox. It's a grungy bar in a
neighbourhood of stylish brownstones and has been
around for more than half a century. And it still
draws big crowds because of its tender, meaty, slow-
cooked baby back ribs.

The supper crust

It's an undeniably great invention: all the classic ingredients of pizza, only more so. More cheese than a *Brady Bunch* retrospective. A crust so thick it makes French baguettes look like toothpicks. Artery-clogging amounts of meat. But Chicago-style pizza veterans, like tequila aficionados, all have a horror story: the story of the day they had 'one too many' slices with disastrous results. The worst result, of course, is that they didn't fancy Chicago-style pizza again for a very long, long time.

Don't miss out on this true Chicago institution, but please, please wait until you're so hungry, you can barely stand. Then go shopping at Marshall Field's, say, or go to see an exhibit at one of the museums until your eyes are crossing from hunger pangs. Then hang around for another hour. Only now will you be ready to appreciate Chicago-style pizza. Just don't be stupid about finishing every slice: listen to your stomach and your various heart valves. Remember, this is the Mount Everest of pizza, and the old climber's saying applies: the mountain doesn't care about your well-being.

Of course, the people who make the pizza do care, and have done ever since the late Ike Sewell invented this manhole-cover of a meal in the 1940s. It was during World War II that Sewell, a native Texan and all-American football player at the University of Texas, opened **Pizzeria Uno** (*see page 138*) with a partner in an old mansion in downtown Chicago. The story goes that Sewell wanted to run a Mexican joint, but his partner hated Mexican so they chose pizza instead. Sewell, though, baulked at the wimpy size of standard pizza, and opted instead to load up cheese in a deep dish inside a thick crust. Chicago-style pizza was born. In 1955, the deep-dish business boomed enough for Sewell to open **Pizzeria Due** on Wabash and Ontario Streets,

while he also served as a deep-dish pizza mentor of sorts: one of his early partners, Rudy Malnati, along with his son Lou, eventually broke away to open **Lou Malnati's Pizzeria** (*see page 138*), another standard bearer of deep-dish 'za in Chicago.

Sewell, of course, eventually licensed the name of his restaurant: hence, the Pizzeria Uno logo can be spied in towns across the globe. The original, however, still serves the best in town. To sample the true Sewell lineage, you'll have to go to either Pizzeria Uno or Due. But Lou Malnati's serves an impressive version that was learned at the feet of the master, while the **Original Gino's East** (*see page 138*) is as famous for its graffiti-scrawled walls as for its pizza. Just don't make plans for breakfast the next day. Or lunch.

Seafood

Bluepoint Oyster Bar
741 W Randolph Street, at N Halsted Street, West Side (312 207 1222). CTA Clinton (Green). **Open** 11.30am-10.30pm Mon-Thur; 11.30am-11pm Fri; 5-11pm Sat; 5-10.30pm Sun. **Main courses** $18-$27. **Credit** AmEx, DC, Disc, MC, V.
This Randolph Street newcomer quickly became one of Chicago's best seafood houses. Fresh fish and shellfish are flown in daily and the tiled raw bar

offers an incredible selection of oysters. The 'retro-cool' design – the whole place resembles an art deco/1940s fish house – includes bold terrazzo floors, potted palms, piscatorial prints, exposed ductwork and huge portholes.

Bubba Gump Shrimp Co
700 E Grand Avenue, at Navy Pier, Near North/Streeterville (312 595 5500). CTA Grand. **Open** 11am-10pm Mon-Thur; 11am-11pm Fri, Sat; 11am-9pm Sun. **Main courses** $8-$25. **Credit** AmEx, DC, Disc, MC, V. **Map** p306 K10.

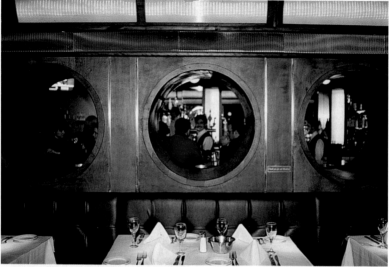

Bluepoint Oyster Bar: seafood through the round window. *See page 139.*

Sometimes you'll see Forrest Gump sitting on a bench outside this fun eaterie nursing a box of chocolates and waiting for Jenny. Despite the hokey Tom Hanks lookalike and the faux shrimp shack interior, you'll find excellent shrimp in many forms. You know: fried shrimp, shrimp kebab, shrimp steamed in beer, coconut-battered shrimp...

Cape Cod Room
Drake Hotel, 140 E Walton Street, at N Michigan Avenue, Gold Coast (312 440 8414). CTA Chicago (Red). **Open** noon-11pm daily. **Main courses** $20-$40. **Credit** AmEx, DC, Disc, MC, V. **Map** p306 J9.

If that trim, handsome man with intense blue eyes and snowy white hair looks familiar, well, Paul Newman is an occasional guest here, and partial to a nice bit of Dover sole. A fixture at the Drake since 1933, the Cape Cod Room restaurant serves fresh – and expensive – seafood. The cosy dining room features nautical trappings and cheery red and white gingham tablecloths.

Don's Fishmarket & Tavern
9335 Skokie Boulevard, Skokie (847 677 3424). Metra Morton Grove. **Open** 11.30am-11pm Mon-Thur; 11am-midnight Fri, Sat; 4-10pm Sun. **Main courses** $6-$10. **Credit** AmEx, DC, Disc, MC, V.

It's worth the trip to Skokie just for this eaterie. Don't be put off by the faux nautical decor, Don's is the place for perfectly prepared lobster, crab claws or simply grilled fresh fish. The wine list is easy on both the wallet and palate, too. Try and time your visit to Skokie to coincide with fun events such as Mardi Gras and the Lobsterfest.

McCormick & Schmick's
41 E Chestnut Street, at N Rush Street, Gold Coast (312 397 9500). CTA Chicago (Red). **Open** 11.30am-10pm Mon-Thur, Sun; 11.30am-11pm Fri, Sat. **Main courses** $16-$40. **Credit** AmEx, DC, Disc, MC, V. **Map** p306 H9.

This Portland, Oregon chain has anchored along Chicago's Gold Coast with a handsome dining room accented with mahogany, stained glass and brass. Booths for up to seven ('snugs') can be curtained off with velvet draperies. Fish is flown in daily, providing up to 35 fresh selections.

Southwestern

Blue Mesa
1729 N Halsted Street, at W Willow Street, Lincoln Park (312 944 5990). CTA North/Clybourn. **Open** 5-10pm Tue-Thur; 5-11pm Fri; 11.30am-11pm Sat; 11am-3pm, 4-10pm Sun. **Main courses** $12-$15. **Credit** AmEx, DC, Disc, MC, V. **Map** p307 F6.

Find the flavours of the South-west at this colourful restaurant that now sports a fresh, contemporary look. The Caesar salad features bold jalapeño-lime dressing; grilled marinated skirt steak is accompanied by roasted tomatillo sauce and there are over two dozen varieties of 100% blue agave tequilas. Yikes.

Red Rock Grill
Radisson Hotel, 160 E Huron Street, at N St Clair Street, Near North/Streeterville (312 255 1600). CTA Chicago (Red). **Open** 11am-10pm Mon-Thur, Sun; 11am-11pm Fri, Sat. **Main courses** $22-$27. **Credit** AmEx, DC, Disc, MC, V. **Map** p306 J10.

Consumer

Mamas, your sons may indeed grow up to be cowboys if they hang around this eaterie with its decor of pistols, spurs, steer horns and countless other trappings of the American South-west. The Red Rock's chilli is thick and spicy and the delicious barbecued pulled pork sandwiches well worth ordering. Even if you're not planning on eating anything, the companionable bar is a good spot in which to sip cold beer and watch sports on TV.

Steak

Capital Grille
633 N St Clair Street, at E Ontario Street, Near North/Streeterville (312 337 9400). CTA Grand. **Open** 11.30am-2.30pm Mon-Fri, 5-10pm Mon-Fri; 5-11pm Sat, Sun. **Main courses** $20-$30. **Credit** AmEx, DC, Disc, MC, V. **Map** p306 J10.
This high-end steakhouse in the Streeterville area is the kind of place where Michael Jordan has been known to put in some hang time. Capital Grille sports a locker packed with dry-aged beef. It also boasts an extensive wine cellar and offers a clubby ambience of polished leather and gilt-framed oil paintings. The tender beef steaks have plenty of heft (in size and price), but double-cut lamb chops are a good alternative.

Kinzie Chop House
400 N Wells Street, at W Kinzie Street, Near North/River North (312 822 0191). CTA Merchandise Mart. **Open** 11am-10pm Mon-Thur; 11am-11pm Fri; 4pm-11am Sat; closed Sun. **Main courses** $12-$45. **Credit** AmEx, DC, Disc, MC, V. **Map** p306 H11.
El trains rattle by this casual eaterie where seekers of comfort food enjoy meatloaf and chicken and dumplings. For carnivores, top steaks include a bone-in filet mignon. The staff bring a platter of raw meat to your table to demonstrate various cuts; sides include bacon-and-scallion mashed potatoes.

Morton's of Chicago
1050 N State Street, at W Maple Street, Gold Coast (312 266 4820). CTA Clark/Division. **Open** 5.30-11pm Mon-Sat; 5-10pm Sun. **Main courses** $30-$40. **Credit** AmEx, DC, Disc, MC, V. **Map** p306 H9.
A major destination for carnivores: raw steaks are presented at the table and cooked over a flaming grill in an open kitchen. Hash browns and asparagus are good sides for cooked-to-order prime beef. There's another branch of this national chain – and major expense-account restaurant – near O'Hare. **Branch:** 9525 W Bryn Mawr Avenue, Rosemont (847 678 5155).

Shafted

Celebrity diners frequently get the shaft at **Vivo**. For Madonna, Richard Gere, Cindy Crawford, Michelle Pfeiffer and other celebs, the only seat to have at this sleek Italian restaurant is the ultimate see-and-be-seen spot. It's a lone table perched on high atop a bricked-in elevator shaft, providing a commanding view of the chic room. This elevated table is often booked months ahead, though call ahead and you might just get lucky.

Vivo was the first eaterie to open up in the Randolph Street Market District back in 1991, when it redeveloped a former meat packing warehouse. Today, the neighbourhood is one of Chicago's hottest dining locales with a score or more of fashionable restaurants (and counting). The glitterati, though, are still drawn to Vivo.

With its high, black-painted ceiling, exposed brick walls stacked with wine bottles, dramatic pin lighting and futuristic metal seating, the restaurant is just about as good-looking as many of its punters. However, it's unlike most such celeb hangouts: its food is both tasty and pretty cheap. At lunch, for example, you can get a salad for $4-$6, pasta for $7-$12 and other mains for $9-$17. So, if you're a prudent

spender and a good actor – and wear all-black duds – you can see and be seen on a tight budget, and only your waiter will know for sure whether you're worth spying on.

During the summer, a few tables spill out onto the sidewalk and a not-to-be-missed piquant version of gazpacho swimming with tiny shrimp finds its way onto the menu. Vivo also has one of the best antipasto bars in the city, prettily arranged on slabs of marble and featuring a wonderful assortment of peppers, pickles and seasonal vegetables. Of the mains, try osso bucco, grilled chicken breast with lemon and garlic, or grilled veal tenderloin served with mushrooms and rosemary-scented potatoes, all preceded – in appropriately swanky fashion – with a cocktail from the bar. Going up...

Vivo
838 W Randolph Street, at N Peoria Street, West Side (312 733 3379). CTA Clinton (Green). **Open** 11.30am-2pm, 5.30-10pm Mon-Wed; 11.30am-2pm, 5.30-11pm Thur; 11.30am-2pm, 5.30pm-midnight Fri; 5.30pm-midnight Sat; 5-10pm Sun. **Main courses** $9-$17. **Credit** AmEx, DC, Disc, MC, V.

Have a bubbly time at **The Saloon**.

The Saloon

200 E Chestnut Street, at N Mies van der Rohe Way, Gold Coast (312 280 5454). CTA Chicago (Red). **Open** 11.30am-10pm Mon-Thur, Sun; 11.30am-11pm Fri, Sat. **Main courses** $12-$35. **Credit** AmEx, DC, Disc, MC, V. **Map** p306 J9.

The look and feel of a traditional New York steakhouse, but at Chicago prices. Select marbled, dry-aged cut of beef *au naturel* and have it prepared with a peppercorn crust, blackened, or al forno (with garlic, Parmesan and mushrooms), then settle back in the comfortable mahogany-panelled room and enjoy.

Sullivan's Steakhouse

415 N Dearborn Street, at W Hubbard Street, Near North/Magnificent Mile (312 527 3510). CTA Grand, Lake or State. **Open** 5.30-11pm Mon-Sat; closed Sun. **Main courses** $15-$25. **Credit** AmEx, DC, Disc, MC, V. **Map** p306 H11.

This retro 1940s chophouse is decorated with prizefight photos and a replica of John L Sullivan's championship belt. Prime beef is seared at high heat with a salt-and-pepper crust sealing in the juices. Sides, big enough to share, include creamed spinach, mushroom caps and horseradish mashed potatoes. A clubby bar features live jazz and chilled Martinis.

Swedish

Ann Sather

5207 N Clark Street, at W Foster Avenue, Far North (773 271 6677). CTA Berwyn. **Open** 7am-3.30pm Mon-Fri; 7am-5pm Sat, Sun. **Main courses** $7-$13. **Credit** AmEx, DC, Disc, MC, V.

Although Andersonville, once solidly Swedish, is yielding to other ethnic groups, some businesses remain. One is this Sunday breakfast fave, where thin Swedish pancakes with tart lingonberry sauce are de rigueur. For the original Ann Sather's, *see p203*.
Branch: 929 W Belmont Avenue, at Sheffield Street, Lake View (773 348 2378).

Svea

5236 N Clark Street, at W Foster Avenue, Far North (773 275 7738). CTA Berwyn. **Open** 7am-4pm Mon-Wed, Sat, Sun; 7am-10pm Thur, Fri. **Main courses** *breakfast* up to $8; *dinner* up to $12. **No credit cards.**

Another favourite Sunday morning Andersonville destination, Svea specialises in the 'Viking breakfast'. It's substantial enough to keep you going all day, and, anyway, don't all self-respecting pillagers start the day with a heaped plateful of eggs, Swedish bologna-like sausage, fried potatoes, pancakes and toast? You'll also find such staples as pea soup, meatballs and pickled herring.

Thai

Arun's

4156 N Kedzie Avenue, at W Berteau Avenue, Far North (773 539 1909). CTA 80 bus. **Open** 5-10pm Tue-Sun; closed Mon. **Main courses** *dégustation* $75. **Credit** AmEx, DC, Disc, MC, V.

The antithesis of the low prices and basic decor of storefront Thai restaurants, and both one of Chicago's top eateries and one of its prettiest. It offers only a *dégustation* menu, priced at $75. But for 14 courses, that's not too bad at all.

Star of Siam

11 E Illinois Street, at N State Street, Near North/Magnificent Mile (312 670 0100). CTA Grand. **Open** 11am-9.30pm Mon-Thur, Sun; 11am-10.30pm Fri, Sat. **Main courses** $5. **Credit** MC, V. **Map** p306 H11.

Though the decor is considerably more appealing than the usual Thai storefront, prices are just as affordable. Its contemporary look features exposed bricks and beams, light woods and plum-and-orange accents. Spices range from mild to super-hot.

Vietnamese

Le Colonial

937 N Rush Street, at E Oak Street, Gold Coast (312 255 0088). CTA Chicago (Red). **Open** noon-2.30pm, 5-11pm Mon-Fri; noon-2.30pm, 5pm-midnight Sat; 5-10pm Sun. **Main courses** $13-$23. **Credit** AmEx, DC, MC, V. **Map** p306 H9.

Revolving ceiling fans, louvred shutters, potted palms, sepia photos and lots of bamboo recall the French colonial era in Saigon during the 1920s. This trendy eaterie actually arrived on Chicago's Rush Street via New York. Recommended are the spicy beef salad, rich curried chicken, gingered roast duck and the chi-chi upstairs bar.

Pasteur

5525 N Broadway, at W Bryn Mawr Avenue, Far North (773 878 1061). CTA Bryn Mawr. **Open** noon-10pm Mon-Thur, Sun; noon-11pm Fri, Sat. **Main courses** $13-$23. **Credit** AmEx, DC, Disc, MC, V.

This handsome eaterie started life as a storefront in Chicago's Vietnamese enclave before a fire chased it north. The pretty new quarters recall French colonial days with palm trees, rattan furniture and murals of Vietnamese scenes. The restaurant is named after the Saigon street where the owners had their family home.

Bars & Pubs

You want to go where everybody knows your name? Well, they probably won't in Chicago's bars, but you'll still be glad you came.

You'll start upright, sure, but you may finish face down at **Cardozo's**. *See page 144.*

The architecture is stunning, the museums impressive, the restaurants exceptional. But the real character of Chicago comes alive in its bars. Whether swanky lounges (**Harry's Velvet Room**), trad Irish bars (too many to mention) or the just plain uncategorisable (**Weed's**), the city's imbiberies provide a perfect window on life here in its myriad forms, and provide a great reason to visit the city should the rest of its attractions not prove sufficient excuse.

It helps that Chicago is as friendly as a city of its size could be. In most neighbourhood bars, you can walk in alone and be telling your life story to someone at the bar almost before your beer's been poured. Speaking of beer, Chicago boasts a number of fine local microbreweries such as **Goose Island** – who have fine bars at 1800 N Clybourn Avenue (312 915 0071) and 3535 N Clark Street (773 832 9040) – Golden Prairie and the Chicago Brewing Company. Seek them out if you want a taste of the city without having to take a drink from the Chicago River.

Most bars, with the exception of those in the Loop, shut up shop around 2am, later on weekends. For other fine night-time imbiberies,

see chapters **Music** and **Nightlife**. And if you're under 35, be sure to always carry a photo ID that proves your age: the drinking age of 21 is strictly enforced by bartenders wary of getting busted by strict city enforcers, and you'll be carded often.

The Loop

As with most major financial districts, few people go out in the Loop: drinkers are mainly after-work unwinders and pre-theatre diners. Though the Theatre District is bringing custom back to the area, it can still feel rather deserted in the evening and on weekends, and most bars and pubs operate suitably limited hours.

Alcock's Inn

411 S Wells Street, at W Van Buren Street (312 922 1778). CTA LaSalle (Blue, Brown/Orange/Purple). **Open** 10am-late Mon-Fri; 11.30am-late Sat, Sun. **Credit** AmEx, MC, V. **Map** p305 H13.
This sports bar fills with traders after the market closes and attracts crowds before, during and after Bears games. The place can get rowdy, especially when the small but vocal groups of traders have hit it big.

Alumni Club

Stone Container Building, 150 N Michigan Avenue, at E Randolph Street (312 345 1400). CTA Randolph. **Open** 11am-8pm Mon-Fri; closed Sat, Sun. **Credit** AmEx, DC, Disc, MC, V. **Map** p305 J12.
A local chain with a reputation as a post-college pick-up bar, this Alumni serves a drastically different crowd than its Gold Coast and Lincoln Park counterparts: here, it's mainly white-collar professionals eating and enjoying a tame cocktail or two.

Berghoff

17 W Adams Street, at S State Street (312 427 3170). CTA Jackson (Blue, Red) or Monroe (Blue, Red). **Open** 11am-9pm Mon-Thur; 11am-9.30pm Fri; 11am-10pm Sat; closed Sun. **Credit** AmEx, MC, V. **Map** p305 H12.
Founded as an outdoor beer garden in 1893, the Berghoff holds City Liquor Licence No.1 and has been serving Berghoff beer since the end of Prohibition. Berghoff serves food (*see p129*), but for a less formal (and quicker) bite, try the Berghoff Café, a stand-up bar on the east end of the main floor.

Big Downtown

Palmer House Hilton, 124 S Wabash Avenue, at E Adams Street (312 917 7399). CTA Harrison. **Open** 11am-midnight daily. **Credit** AmEx, DC, MC, V. **Map** p305 H12.
The dark wood 1940s-style bar attracts a nice-sized after-work crowd on Fridays and a good share of guests from the hotel, one of the poshest in the city. The music is Sinatra and Ella, the clientele in suits and ties, the bar not worth making a special trip for.

Cactus

404 S Wells Street, at W Van Buren Street (312 922 3830). CTA LaSalle (Blue, Brown/Orange/Purple) or

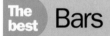

The best Bars

For lounge lizards
Zebra Lounge (page 148).

For professional drinkers
Tuman's Alcohol Abuse Center (page 159).

For cheezborgers, cheezborgers
Billy Goat Tavern (page 146).

For night owls
Old Town Ale House (page 150).

For homesick Brits
Red Lion Pub (page 155).

For underwear fetishists
Weed's (page 155).

For celeb-spotters
Booth one at the **Pump Room** (page 148).

Quincy. **Open** 11am-midnight Mon-Fri; closed Sat, Sun. **Credit** AmEx, DC, Disc, MC, V. **Map** p305 H13.
Another popular watering hole among the local traders, this Tex-Mex inspired joint serves a wide selection of beers (including many Mexican choices) and tequilas. A games room and several TVs give the place a sports bar feel; nachos and burgers are on the menu.

Cardozo's Pub

170 W Washington Street, at N LaSalle Street (312 236 1573). CTA Washington (Brown/Orange/Purple). **Open** 10.30am-9pm Mon-Thur; 10.30am-10pm Fri; closed Sat, Sun. **Credit** AmEx, DC, Disc, MC, V. **Map** p305 H12.
There's something of an everybody-knows-your-name-and-they're-all-glad-you-came atmosphere at this Loop bar. A mix of traders and locals huddle around the bar in the early evenings, shooting the shit and losing track of time in the cosy, window-less basement. The only drag is the early closing, though it's hardly uncommon in this part of town.

Cavanaugh's Bar & Restaurant

Monadnock Building, 53 W Jackson Boulevard, at S Dearborn Street (312 939 3125). CTA Jackson (Blue, Red) or Library. **Open** 11am-9pm Mon-Fri; closed Sat, Sun. **Credit** AmEx, DC, MC, V. **Map** p305 H13.
Grab a booth inside the Monadnock's six-foot-thick walls and chat about the building's unusual architecture (for which, *see page 25*), but don't get there too late: the place closes at 10pm. Pastas and sandwiches make up the menu.

Govnor's Pub

207 N State Street, at E Lake Street (312 236 3696). CTA Lake or State. **Open** 11am-1am Mon-Fri; 11.30am-midnight Sat; 11.30am-7pm Sun. **Credit** AmEx, Disc, MC, V. **Map** p305 H11.
Located in the city's Theatre District, this comfy English-style pub is popular before shows as well as with the typical lunch and after-work crowd. In the summer months, outdoor seating is available.

Metropole

Fairmont Hotel, 200 N Columbus Drive, at E Lake Street (312 565 7444). CTA Lake or State. **Open** 5-11pm Tue-Thur; 6pm-2am Fri, Sat; closed Mon, Sun. **Credit** AmEx, DC, Disc, MC, V. **Map** p305 J11.
The small dancefloor in front of the stage fills up quickly here, as hotel guests and music connoisseurs enjoy big-name local and national jazz, blues and swing acts in this hotel bar.

Miller's Pub

134 S Wabash Avenue, at E Adams Street (312 645 5377). CTA Adams. **Open** 11am-3am daily. **Credit** AmEx, DC, MC, V. **Map** p305 H12.
The walls of this boozer, founded in 1935, are covered with signed photos of Regis Philbin types who have visited over the years, though, in fairness, it was also a favourite of the genuinely legendary Bill Veeck. There's decent chophouse-style food, but most people come for the drinks and ambience.

As the El rattles overhead, take solace in a pint at **Miller's Pub**.

Monk's

203 W Lake Street, at N Wells Street (312 357 6665/368 0958). CTA Clark or Washington (Brown/ Orange/Purple). **Open** 10am-2am Mon-Fri; closed Sat, Sun. **Credit** AmEx, Disc, MC, V. **Map** p305 H11.
An Irish-ish pub, and a real spit-and-sawdust place: the floor is covered in peanut shells, and the lighting barely exists. Loud music cranks out of the well-stocked jukebox, as the bartender – Carla out of *Cheers*, or near enough – prowls about ominously. One of only a few late-opening bars in the neighbourhood, and something of a seedy treat.

South Loop

Buddy Guy's Legends

754 S Wabash Avenue, at E Balbo Drive (312 427 0333). CTA Harrison. **Open** 5pm-2am Mon-Fri, Sun; 5pm-3am Sat. **Credit** AmEx, Disc, MC, V. **Map** p305 H13.
Mr Guy shows up to play in this cavernous blues hall now and again, with national acts rounding out the calendar. Pool tables provide a pre- or post-music diversion for the eclectic crowd, which includes an even number of tourists and locals. *See also p211.*

Kitty O'Shea's

Chicago Hilton & Towers, 720 S Michigan Avenue, at E Balbo Drive (312 922 4400). CTA Harrison. **Open** 11am-2am daily. **Credit** AmEx, DC, MC, V. **Map** p305 J13.
An Irish pub that has somehow established a reputation as far more than your typical hotel bar. Most of the staff are Irish nationals – Guinness poured the proper way! Hurrah! – and frequent live Irish music gives the pub a vaguely authentic feel, even if the prices aren't exactly easy on the wallet.

South Loop Club

1 E Balbo Drive, at S State Street (312 427 2787). CTA Harrison. **Open** 11am-4am Mon-Fri, Sun; 11am-5am Sat. **Credit** AmEx, DC, Disc, MC, V. **Map** p305 H13.
It bills itself as a neighbourhood bar, but it's not in any sort of a neighbourhood. Still, the South Loop Club is a matey place that's often busy, in part due to the lack of other bars nearby. Bad news: the lights are usually way too bright. Good news: it's open very, very late.

Near North

As Near North and, in particular, River North have developed in recent years, new venues have popped up all over the place – some more garish than others, many nightclubs – while a few old joints have managed to stand the test of time. In the blocks along Michigan Avenue and in Streeterville, bars are a little more spread out, and tend towards the more mellow and upscale. In other words, this is the epitome of a 'something for everyone' scene.

Andy's

11 E Hubbard Street, at N State Street (312 642 6805). CTA Grand. **Open** 11am-1am Mon-Thur; 11am-2am Fri; 1pm-2am Sat; 6.30pm-midnight Sun. **Credit** AmEx, Disc, MC, V. **Map** p306 H11.

One of the only places in the city where you can hear live jazz at noon (there's music noon-2.30pm, plus at 5pm, 9.30pm and midnight), this river hangout is one of the city's busiest jazz venues. Once a hangout for local printers, the place has retained some of its grunge but now attracts a diverse, friendly crowd.

Billy Goat Tavern

Lower level, 430 N Michigan Avenue, at E Hubbard Street (312 222 1525). CTA Grand. **Open** 10am-3am daily. **Credit** MC, V. **Map** p306 J11.

The bar made famous by *Saturday Night Live* and frequented by newspaper folk is what you'd expect: Schlitz on tap, yellowing cuttings on the wall, cooks hollering 'cheezborger, cheezborger', regulars at the bar. If you're lucky, you'll see owner Sam Sianis, whose ancestor put a curse on the Cubs decades ago when his goat wasn't allowed into Wrigley Field.

Pippin's

806 N Rush Street, at W Chicago Avenue (312 787 5435). CTA Chicago (Red). **Open** 11am-4am Mon-Fri, Sun; 11am-5pm Sat. **Credit** AmEx, DC, MC, V. **Map** p306 J10.

This small pub is a toned-down version of its pick-up bar brother the **Lodge** (*see p148*). Rarely crowded, it's a good place to sit while dropping peanut shells on the floor and plugging the jukebox with change. The windows open onto the street in summer.

Red Head Piano Bar

16 W Ontario Street, at N State Street (312 640 1000). CTA Grand. **Open** 7pm-4am Mon-Fri, Sun; 7pm-5am Sat. **Credit** AmEx, DC, MC, V. **Map** p306 H10.

A piano bar with a 900-gallon, 50-ft long aquarium (it used to be called the Fish Head), the Red Head fills up quickly with an ageing though still-hip clientele. There's live piano-accompanied crooning most nights. However, be sure to dress up, otherwise you won't get past the admittedly splendid sign outside.

River North

Boss Bar

420 N Clark Street, at W Hubbard Street (312 527 1203). CTA Grand or Merchandise Mart. **Open** 10.30am-4am Mon-Fri, Sun; 10.30am-5am Sat. **Credit** AmEx, DC, MC, V. **Map** p306 H11.

Named for the late Mayor Richard J Daley, a huge mural of whom hangs inside this storefront bar. A jukebox blasts classic rock, and when the weather's nice, the garage door front is pulled wide open.

Brehon Pub

731 N Wells Street, at W Superior Street (312 642 1071). CTA Chicago (Brown/Purple). **Open** 11am-2am Mon-Fri; noon-3am Sat; noon-10pm Sun. **Credit** AmEx, DC, MC, V. **Map** p306 H10.

This homey Irish neighbourhood saloon found notoriety in 1978 during the 'Mirage Scandal', when a camera hidden here caught politicians on the take. These days, it's less eventful but no less charming.

After a dozen $2 Schlitzes, ample support is provided by the bar at the **Billy Goat Tavern**.

Consumer

The super-swanky **Harry's Velvet Room**.

ESPN Zone

43 E Ohio Street, at N Dearborn Street (312 644 3776). CTA Grand. **Open** 11.30am-midnight Mon-Thur; 11.30am-1am Fri; 10am-1am Sat; 10am-midnight Sun. **Credit** AmEx, Disc, MC, V. **Map** p306 H10.

The sports network's huge dining and entertainment complex opened in 1999, and is now a fixture for the city's sports nuts and overgrown kids, who tackle the climbing wall and virtual reality games with glee. On game days, get there early.

Fado

100 W Grand Avenue, at N Clark Street (312 836 0066). CTA Grand. **Open** 11.30am-2am daily. **Credit** AmEx, Disc, MC, V. **Map** p306 H10.

This three-storey Irish pub was built in Ireland and then shipped to the US, where it was assembled by Irish craftsmen. But while its six different bar themes appear authentic, it can't overcome its chain-restaurant feel. Contemporary Irish fare is served.

Green Door Tavern

678 N Orleans Street, at W Huron Street (312 664 5496). CTA Chicago (Brown/Purple). **Open** 11.30am-10pm Mon; 11.30am-midnight Tue-Thur; 11.30am-2am Fri, Sat; closed Sun. **Credit** MC, V. **Map** p306 G10.

Antiques and memorabilia hang from the ceiling of this building, one of the first to be built after the 1871 fire. It's been a bar since 1921 and still sports some of its original fixtures. A decent selection of beers and food draws an upscale River North crowd.

Harry's Velvet Room

56 W Illinois Street, at N Dearborn Street (312 527 5600). CTA Grand. **Open** 5pm-4am Mon-Fri, Sun; 7pm-5am Sat. **Credit** AmEx, DC, Disc, MC, V. **Map** p306 H11.

Sink down into one of the couches or lounge chairs in this dimly lit basement lounge, and enjoy a cigar and a Martini with everyone else. The bar is stocked with top-shelf liquor, wines and champagnes.

Streeterville

Dick's Last Resort

North Pier, 435 E Illinois Street (312 836 7870). CTA Grand. **Open** 10.30am-1.30am Mon-Thur, Sun;

10.30am-2.30am Fri, Sat. **Credit** AmEx, DC, Disc, MC, V. **Map** p306 K11.

If the name hasn't put you off already – and 'last resort' is perhaps being overly generous – then you'll find plenty here that'll send you packing before too long (OTT staff, poor food, worse music). Consider yourself duly warned.

Lizzie McNeil's

400 N McClurg Street, at E North Water Street (312 467 1992). CTA Grand. **Open** 3pm-1am Mon-Fri; 11.30am-2am Sat, Sun. **Credit** AmEx, MC, V. **Map** p306 J11.

A small Irish pub facing the river, with plenty of outdoor seating in warm weather. The fine selection of tap beer, the free popcorn and the jukebox with everything from Big Band to Elvis to top 40 all appeal (though the food is mediocre), but better yet, it rarely gets as packed as some of its neighbours.

O'Neill's Bar & Grill

152 E Ontario Street, at N Michigan Avenue (312 787 5269). CTA Chicago (Red). **Open** 11am-2am Mon-Fri; 11am-3am Sat; 11am-2am Sun. **Credit** AmEx, DC, Disc, MC, V. **Map** p306 J10.

An impossibly dark and narrow tavern just off Michigan Avenue, with reasonably priced burgers and beers. Walk through to the back to enjoy the rear patio, a kind of 'secret garden' in the middle of the madness of the downtown.

Streeters Tavern

Hotel St Benedict Flats (lower level), 50 E Chicago Avenue, at N Wabash Street (312 944 5206). CTA Chicago (Red). **Open** 11am-4am Mon-Fri, Sun; 11am-5am Sat. **Credit** AmEx, MC, V. **Map** p306 H10.

This underground space is popular with Loyola Law and Northwestern Medical school students, offering free hot dogs and chili at lunchtimes and top 40 tunes on the jukebox. Located in an 1883 brick-and-stone building that was saved from the wrecking ball when it acquired landmark status in 1990, it's now part of a charming nineteenth-century streetscape.

Gold Coast

There are basically two kinds of bars up around the Gold Coast: the swanky, higher-priced lounges on the periphery, and the post-college frat party pick-up bars along Division Street between Dearborn and State such as the **Alumni Club**, **Mother's** and **Shenanigans**. Either way, you'll want to be prepared: what's acceptable in one place won't be at another.

Up on Division, the atmosphere may change from bar to bar, but the clientele is pretty much the same: heavy drinkers looking for a good time even if they're past their prime. Locals generally don't frequent the area, though you may run into a few who've set out to prove they can still party all night with the best (and worst) of 'em. Chicago police shut this stretch to traffic on weekend nights to control the crowds.

Blue Agave

1050 N State Street, at W Maple Street (312 335 8900). CTA Clark/Division. **Open** 11.30am-midnight Mon-Thur, Sun; 11.30am-2am Fri, Sat. **Credit** AmEx, MC, V. **Map** p306 H9.

Stuffed burros, sombreros, serapes hanging from the ceiling, half a dozen varieties of Margaritas… yes, it's a Mexican bar, with the dozen or so Mexican beers a real bonus. Food can be had upstairs.

Butch McGuire's

20 W Division Street, at N State Street (312 337 9080). CTA Clark/Division. **Open** 10am-4am Mon-Fri; 8pm-5am Sat; 11am-4am Sun. **Credit** AmEx, Disc, MC, V. **Map** p307 H8.

One of the original singles bars (the place opened in 1961), the owner reckons Butch's has been responsible for thousands of marriages. It's a weak attempt at an Irish bar, but you gotta love 'em for trying.

Dublins

1050 N State Street, at W Maple Street (312 266 6340). CTA Clark/Division. **Open** 11am-4am Mon-Fri, Sun; 11am-5am Sat. **Credit** AmEx, DC, Disc, MC, V. **Map** p306 H9.

This little green pub nestled among the bustling Rush Street scene attracts a healthy after-work crowd, though weekend evenings are to be avoided. In the summer, the outdoor patio is a decent enough place to people-watch while enjoying a Guinness.

Hangge Uppe

14 W Elm Street, at N Rush Street (312 337 0561). CTA Clark/Division. **Open** 5pm-4am Mon-Fri, Sun; 5pm-5am Sat. **Credit** AmEx, DC, MC, V. **Map** p306 H9.

A long-time late-night Chicago club, the Hangge Uppe looks like a little hole in the wall from the outside. Walk down the stairs, though, and be greeted by rooms full of singles swilling beers, slamming shots and dancing like twats. A jukebox and an occasional DJ play dance music and classic rock.

Hotsie Totsie Yacht Club & Bait Shop

8 E Division Street, at N State Street (312 337 9128). CTA Clark/Division. **Open** 11am-4am Mon-Fri, Sun; 11am-5am Sat. **Map** p307 H8.

A rowboat hangs outside this neighbourhood bar, an oasis near Division Street. The nautical motif continues inside, but the true charms of this place are the regulars and the fact that it's rarely crowded. Harry Caray, Frankie Avalon and Sammy Davis Jr have all drunk here at one time or another.

Jilly's Bistro & Jilly's Retro Club

1007 N Rush Street, at W Oak Street (312 664 1001). CTA Chicago (Red). **Open** 3pm-2am Mon-Fri; 1pm-3am Sat; 5pm-2am Sun. **Credit** AmEx, DC, Disc, MC, V. **Map** p306 H9.

This is where the fat cats hang, so expect to be on your best behaviour – and maybe to shell out some cash – to get a seat inside. The club is for dancing, while the bistro is more casual.

Leg Room

7 W Division Street, at N State Street (312 337 2583). CTA Clark/Division. **Open** 7pm-4am Mon-Fri, Sun; 7pm-5am Sat. **Credit** AmEx, DC, Disc, MC, V. **Map** p307 H8.

The lone retro lounge among the beer-swilling Division Street crowd, where Martinis rule. Class? On Division Street? Why-I-oughtta…

The Lodge

21 W Division Street, at N State Street (312 642 4406). CTA Clark/Division. **Open** 2pm-4am Mon-Fri; noon-5am Sat; noon-4am Sun. **Credit** AmEx, DC, MC, V. **Map** p307 H8.

A mellow member of the Division Street family, the Lodge is still a bit of a singles bar, albeit for older drinkers. Peanuts are free, which explains why the floor is invariably covered in shells.

PJ Clarkes

1204 N State Street, at W Division Street (312 664 1650). CTA Clark/Division. **Open** 11.30am-2am Mon-Sat; 10.30am-2am Sun. **Credit** AmEx, DC, Disc, MC, V. **Map** p307 H8.

A casual, old-fashioned tavern, this is Chicago's take on the well-known New York club of the same name. The clientele has earned the place the title of 'the divorce bar'. 'Nuff said.

Pump Room

at Omni Ambassador East Hotel, 1301 N State Street, at E Goethe Street (312 266 0360). CTA Clark/Division. **Open** 3-10.30pm Mon-Fri; 3pm-1am Sat, Sun. **Credit** AmEx, Disc, MC, V. **Map** p307 H8.

If you can get in – there's a strict dress code – this is a whole bunch of swanky fun. Take one of the booths behind the bandstand, settle back with a cocktail and feel like a million dollars. Booth number one has been graced by almost every celeb you could care to mention. Service is atrocious, but that's hardly the point.

Underground Wonder Bar

10 E Walton Street, at N State Street (312 266 7761). CTA Chicago (Red). **Open** 4pm-4am Mon-Fri, Sun; 4pm-5am Sat. **Credit** AmEx, DC, MC, V. **Map** p306 H9.

A favourite celebrity haunt, the long narrow bar features live jazz nightly. Located in the lower level (as alluded to in the name), the place can be easy to miss. But a pretty eclectic, funky and friendly crowd manages to find it. You should, too.

Zebra Lounge

1220 N State Street, at W Division Street (312 642 5140). CTA Clark/Division. **Open** 4.30pm-2am Mon-Fri, Sun; 4.30pm-3am Sat. **Credit** AmEx, MC, V. **Map** p307 H8.

Practically everything is zebra-striped inside this Chicago landmark, open inside the Canterbury Court apartment block since 1933. There's piano music, bottled beer and singalongs, but mainly, it's the crowd that's most worth checking out: casts from nearby musicals occasionally join in and sometimes lead the impromptu performances inside this nearly hidden locale. An absolute treat.

Gardens of Eden

Perhaps it's the large German population in Lincoln Square. Or maybe it's the proximity to Milwaukee, the beer capital of America. Quite how beer gardens came to be so popular in Chicago isn't clear, but it's easy to understand the appeal. After a long, brutal winter spent huddling in a neighbourhood pub, there are few finer pleasures than stretching out beneath a shady tree and enjoying a beer in the warm sunshine of a Chicago summer.

The most visible beer garden is at the end of **Navy Pier**, and sidewalk establishments dot most big streets. But the best Chicago beer gardens are hidden off the beaten path, with the finest of all in the area around Germantown on the city's north side. **Resi's Bierstube** (*see Roscoe Village, page 158*) is the best of the bunch. Out the back door of this unassuming neighbourhood tavern are ten picnic tables, shaded by the leaves of two giant maple trees. The fence is lined with flower boxes and authentic German beer signs, a more than appropriate backdrop for Resi's 65 beers (including 24 weissbiers) and its menu of schnitzel and bratwurst. Try the extremely rare German Kuchlbauer, which apparently dates back to the year 1300.

Nearby is the hidden treasure of Chicago beer gardens, the aptly named **Great Beer Palace** (*see Far North, page 158*). A well-kept secret known only to fun-loving boozehounds, the Palace offers a wide selection of inexpensive German beers that are best enjoyed in the tree-lined garden out back. The atmosphere is pure Oktoberfest, and for sporting events they'll even bring a TV outside. Thirsty patrons are offered the option of drinking their suds from a giant glass boot, but only the heartiest souls will attempt the Viking Raid...

Elsewhere, beer gardens are just as popular, if slightly less authentic. Among the favourites is **Sheffield's Wine & Beer Garden** (*see Wrigleyville, page 157*), which offers an outdoor, sit-down bar and possibly the only outdoor pool table in the city. Large cottonwood trees and a host of microbrews add to the charm. Sheffield's packs them in

on weekend evenings, so those after tranquillity should visit during the day.

West of Wrigleyville is another hidden treasure. The **Village Tap** (*see Roscoe Village, see 158*) caters mainly to locals: young, casually dressed musicians, artists and slackers. But the beer garden is the true work of art. Almost completely shaded by trees, awnings and umbrellas, it too features a fountain, along with space heaters and an outdoor fireplace that renders it practically weatherproof. With 20 beers on tap and many more in the bottle, the Village Tap is a great option in any weather, and the best option in bad weather.

Another good bet is the rooftop beer garden at the **Red Lion Pub** (*see Lincoln Park, page 155*). This quasi-English imbiberie offers all sorts of authentic dishes (try the requisite fish and chips) and beers, which can then be carried upstairs and out the back to the multi-level deck. Partially shaded by an awning, the lower deck was built around a towering maple tree, which shoots up through the floor to shade the rest of the patrons. It's a pleasant and relaxing alternative to the bustle of Lincoln Avenue nightlife.

Go a few blocks south on Lincoln to Belden Avenue and you'll hit the **John Barleycorn Memorial Pub** (*see Lincoln Park, page 153*), which offers leaves, shade and a bubbling fountain in the beer garden adjoining this popular Lincoln Park tavern. One of the nicest places in the neighbourhood, the ample seating and piped-in classical music make it a good bet any time of day or night.

And we haven't really got room to go into much detail about the **Duke of Perth** (*see Lake View, page 156*), which boasts a huge outdoor garden along with 75 kinds of single malt Scotch; **Weed's** (*see Lincoln Park, page 155*), a quite bonkers neighbourhood haunt with a paved beer garden, a life-size bust of the bartender and hundreds of bras dangling from the ceiling; or any of the other 180-plus registered beer gardens in Chicago. The only rule of thumb is to arrive early: by law, all beer gardens in the city must close at midnight.

Old Town

With few exceptions, bars and pubs in Old Town are casual and laid-back, the kinds of places you might wander into during the day for a drink with old friends and walk out of 12 hours later with new friends in tow. Nightlife is mainly centred around the Wells Street and North Avenue entertainment areas, though there are a handful of other decent bars sprinkled close by about the neighbourhood.

Burton Place

1447 N Wells Street, at W Burton Place (312 664 4699). CTA Sedgwick. **Open** 11am-4am Mon-Fri, Sun; 11am-5am Sat. **Credit** AmEx, Disc, MC, V. **Map** p307 H8.

The quintessential corner tavern. Young regulars fill the seats at the bar early and, in the winter months, it's a battle for a spot beside the roaring fireplace. There's a party room upstairs that serves as an escape when the place gets too crowded.

Katacomb

1916 N Lincoln Park West, at W Wisconsin Street (312 337 4040). CTA Armitage or Sedgwick. **Open** 8pm-4am Wed-Fri; 8pm-5am Sat; closed Mon, Tue, Sun. **Map** p307 G6.

This newly reopened club has been the site of many a celebrity sighting. Somewhat exclusive, it heats up late at night; particularly so, as the bouncer has final say over who gets in and who gets left out in the cold.

Last Act

1615 N Wells Street, at W North Avenue (312 440 4915). CTA North/Clybourn. **Open** 3pm-2am Mon-Fri; noon-3am Sat; noon-2am Sun. **Credit** AmEx, DC, Disc, MC, V. **Map** p307 H7.

A **Second City** (*see p244*) haunt, with booths along the walls, pool tables and a pleasant beer garden. Popular with the after-show crowd, it sadly lacks the seedy character of near-neighbour the **Old Town Ale House**.

Marge's Pub

1758 N Sedgwick Street, at W Menomonee Street (312 787 3900). CTA Sedgwick. **Open** noon-2am Mon-Fri, Sun; noon-3am Sat. **Credit** MC, V. **Map** p307 G7.

Once a speakeasy, Marge's has stood the test of time as the rest of Old Town grew around it. Tucked on the corner of a residential block, it's now a favourite neighbourhood watering hole. Over the bar hang pictures of legendary Chicagoans, including the late Mayor Daley and Mike Ditka. The beer selection is weak, but you're coming here to drink Bud anyway.

Old Town Ale House

219 W North Avenue, at N Wieland Street (312 944 7020). CTA Sedgwick. **Open** noon-4am Mon-Fri, Sun; noon-5am Sat. **Map** p307 G7.

An Old Town staple, where **Second City** cast members (*see p244*) mingle with neighbourhood folk, yuppies and everyone in between. Inside, murals offer a glimpse at the cast of characters who've frequented the place over the years, while the jukebox out back has been voted the best in the city. Don't miss it.

Three foolhardy souls sup a Shark Bite at **Bamboo Bernie's** (*p151*). They'll regret it later.

River Shannon

425 W Armitage Avenue, at N Hudson Avenue (312 944 5087). CTA Fullerton. **Open** 4.30pm-2am Mon-Thur; 4.30pm-3am Fri; noon-3am Sat, Sun. **Credit** AmEx, Disc, MC, V. **Map** p307 G6.

Where older, wealthier people go to meet members of the opposite sex. A long, dark-wood bar fills most of the room, leaving little space to walk or talk, much less sit down. Decent beers help matters, as do the big windows looking out onto Armitage.

Sedgwicks

1935 N Sedgwick Street, at W Armitage Avenue (312 337 7900). CTA Fullerton. **Open** 10am-2am Mon-Fri, Sun; 9am-3am Sat. **Credit** AmEx, DC, Disc, MC, V. **Map** p307 G6.

Sedgwicks is where college grads go when they're nostalgic for the good old days. Good-looking guys in college sweatshirts and baseball caps drink beer, shoot pool and scream at whatever sport is on the TV, creating a frat house ambience.

Tequila Roadhouse

1653 N Wells Street, at W North Avenue (312 440 0535). CTA Sedgwick. **Open** 4pm-4am Mon-Fri, Sun; 4pm-5am Sat. **Credit** AmEx, MC, V. **Map** p307 H7.

The Roadhouse is one of the few places along this strip that gets downright crazy. Dirt-cheap drinks specials doubtless help, as do the late opening and the DJ who spins 'high octane' dance music on the weekends at 'the only place to dance in Old Town'.

Twin Anchors Inc

1655 N Sedgwick Street, at W North Avenue (312 266 1616). CTA Sedgwick. **Open** 5pm-midnight Mon-Thur; 5pm-midnight Fri; noon-midnight Sat; noon-10.15pm Sun. **Credit** AmEx, DC, Disc, MC, V. **Map** p307 G7.

For over 60 years, people have been flocking to Twin Anchors for its wood-baby back ribs, and the wood-panelled front bar offers them a warm welcome. Stop in for a beer, but beware the twin temptations of the noted barbecue and the fine jukebox.

Lincoln Park

Lincoln Park is packed with wealthy young professionals and college students, who fill the area's wide assortment of bars and nightclubs most nights. Nightlife in Lincoln Park is largely concentrated along two major strips, one on Halsted Street and another along Lincoln Avenue. However, drinks can usually be secured as close as the nearest street corner due to the preponderance of neighbourhood bars, one of Chicago's most endearing attractions.

Alumni Club

2251 N Lincoln Avenue, at W Webster Avenue (773 348 5100). CTA Fullerton. **Open** 4pm-1.30am Mon-Fri; 11am-2.30am Sat; 11am-1.30am Sun. **Credit** AmEx, DC, Disc, MC, V. **Map** p308 F5.

Far closer to the Gold Coast branch than to that in the Loop, this decidedly unappealing spot is a transplanted piece of the Division Street bar scene. Pissed office workers, girls' nights out and drunken Greek types act out a lairy routine each night to the insipid accompaniment of top 40 dance music.

Bamboo Bernie's

2247 N Lincoln Avenue, at W Webster Avenue (773 549 3900). CTA Fullerton. **Open** 7pm-4am Wed-Fri; 7pm-5am Sat; closed Mon, Tue. **Credit** MC, V. **Map** p308 F5.

With all the tacky splendour of Caribbean Night at a frat house, Bamboo Bernie's is a popular launching place for many a wild evening. Thatched huts provide the 'tropical' (ahem) setting for hordes of dazzlingly inebriated students who've come to guzzle the signature 90-oz $15 Shark Bite concoction.

Beaumont

2020 N Halsted Street, at W Armitage Avenue (773 281 0177). CTA Armitage. **Open** 5pm-4am Mon-Fri; 10am-5am Sat; 10am-4am Sun. **Credit** AmEx, DC, Disc, MC, V. **Map** p308 F6.

Beaumont is dance central for the strip of bars and restaurants that line Halsted from North Avenue up to Fullerton. The crowd is a mix of DePaul students and fun-minded Lincoln Park types finishing up a night of drinking and hoping not to go home alone. It's a kind of Bacchanalian chaos on weekends.

Burwood Tap

724 W Wrightwood Avenue, at N Burling Street (773 525 2593). CTA Fullerton. **Open** 11am-2am Mon-Fri, Sun; 11am-3am Sat. **Map** p308 F4.

The unassuming purple awning masks the bustling vibe of this surprisingly large neighbourhood favourite. The pool table and the conveniently situated TVs add to the attraction of the twin bars for the crowd of young professionals and college types.

Charlie's Ale House

1224 W Webster Avenue, at N Racine Avenue (773 871 1440). CTA Fullerton. **Open** 5pm-late Mon-Fri; 11am-late Sat, Sun. **Credit** AmEx, MC, V. **Map** p308 E5.

Most come to Charlie's for the selection of beers, and spend the evening discussing their Volvos and retirement plans. Almost offensively yuppie-ish, Charlie's is redeemed by the fact it's a beautiful bar: full of wood and polished brass, with a large, ivy-lined beer garden. Closing is hugely flexible: one night midnight, the next 2am.

Clark Bar

2116 N Clark Street, at W Dickens Avenue (773 327 3070). CTA Armitage, Fullerton or Sedgwick/22, 36 bus. **Open** 2.30pm-2am Mon-Fri; noon-2am Sat, Sun. **Credit** AmEx, Disc, MC, V. **Map** p308 G6.

The cosy and friendly Clark Bar fills up Thursdays through to Saturdays with locals munching on free pretzels and mustard (a nice touch, this). The grizzly back-wall photo offers a timely reminder that the St Valentine's Day Massacre took place across the street. Be warned: there's karaoke twice a week.

The missing links

There's a new drug in town. It's stronger than any Bacardi 151, any Martini, any slug of stout. It draws people to the bars like honey draws a bear. It is both addictive and ultimately unrewarding. It'll lose you your money, your friends and your sanity. It makes crack look like candy.

Peter Jacobsen's **Golden Tee Golf** is a stand-up video game, the single most popular in Chicago by a country mile. Machines first started popping up here and there in 1997, and a year later, more still began to appear. By 1999, the proliferation of the Golden Tee was getting out of hand... And 2000? It's hard to find a bar without the game. The game's creator, Incredible Technologies, is based in Rolling Meadows, Illinois, and as such, you'll see the greatest concentration of Golden Tee machines in the country. Well, you won't actually see it per se, but you'll see pieces and parts of it behind the three or four guys huddled around the machine, faces locked on the screen, nervously smoking cigarettes and drinking pints.

The game, like all the best ones, seems like it should be so easy. You can play 18 holes on one of three courses for just $2.50. The controls are not complex: a trackball, and that's about it. Move the trackball right to left, and it switches your club selection. Move the trackball back then forwards, and you'll swing the club. The marker on the screen tells you where the ball will land. Theoretically.

But once you've made that first backswing and sent that digital ball soaring, you're hooked and there's no turning back. Golden Tee is a game first and foremost, so the emphasis isn't so much on realism, but fun. Fun? Pshaw. Every course includes water hazards, sand traps and out-of-bounds areas, and even a great score through 17 holes can disappear after three straight water shots or a run-in with a tree or two.

And just to drive frustration levels higher, the game comments on your shots in a mocking Australian accent. Sometimes, the game compliments you: 'He's on

the dancefloor' means you've just put the ball on the green. 'What a drive!' means you've probably topped the 300-yard mark on your tee shot. At other times, you'll be tempted to hunt down Mr Jacobsen and belt the shit out of him with a four-iron. 'He's on the beach'? 'He's in the drink'? He's pushing his luck, frankly.

Golden Tee isn't just a money-eater. Certain machines are designated as Tournament Editions and are connected online to a central database, which tracks the best scores in the area. Five times a year, those with the best scores qualify for a Peter Jacobsen's Golden Tee Tournament, in which they compete against other mighty video game golfers in the area. Cash prizes are on hand, though the competition is tough: usually a mix of bar owners and managers, who have little else to do during the daytime but pump dollar after dollar into the machines, and Golden Tee junkies, who stopped going to bars for the alcohol long ago in favour of this most compelling of pub games.

And there's no sign of stopping the Golden Tee takeover. Incredible Technologies is already taking orders for the next edition, Golden Tee Fore!: with five courses, adjustable player angles and a 'shadow' golfing feature, which allows you to see how golfers from around the country got such low scores, it'll doubtless be a hit. Sadly, it doesn't allow you to smash your club against a nearby tree, scream at the greenskeeper or toss your golf bag into a lake when things go wrong. Which they will...

Well, it makes a change from the El: the **Red Lion Pub**. *See page 155.*

Gamekeepers

345 W Armitage Avenue, at N Lincoln Avenue (773 549 0400). CTA Armitage. **Open** 5pm-4am Mon-Fri; 11am-5am Sat; 11am-4am Sun. **Credit** AmEx, DC, Disc, MC, V. **Map** p308 G6.

If **Kincade's** (*see opposite*) is the sports bar of choice out west, Gamekeepers is its eastside match. Though located just a block from the park, drinkers here prefer to enjoy their sports either sat on a barstool or sat in the bleachers (always with beer in hand). In the evenings, the decibel level from the crowd and the multiple TVs can approach that of a Boeing jet.

Glascott's Groggery

2158 N Halsted Street, at W Webster Avenue (773 281 1205). CTA Fullerton. **Open** 11am-2am Mon-Fri; 11am-3am Sat. **Credit** AmEx, DC, Disc, MC, V. **Map** p308 F6.

A staple for local yuppies, this Irish bar been owned by the same family since 1937. The vibe is fun and the beer flows readily. Though the majority of patrons are neighbourhood regulars, college buddies and amateur athletic teams, Glascott's makes anyone feel welcome. If you like a drink, that is.

John Barleycorn Memorial Pub

658 W Belden Avenue, at N Lincoln Avenue (773 348 8899). CTA Fullerton. **Open** 4pm-2am Mon-Fri; 9am-3am Sat; 9am-2am Sun. **Credit** AmEx, MC, V. **Map** p308 F5.

A neighbourhood favourite, this, a comfortable and roomy tavern that dates back more than a century. Though it was forced into a stint as a Chinese laundry during Prohibition, Barleycorn's never stopped serving liquor (it also served as a speakeasy), and

the hard-drinking spirit remains firmly intact. Try a Bloody Mary and Guinness with Sunday brunch.

Kincade's

950 W Armitage Avenue, at N Sheffield Avenue (773 348 0010). CTA Armitage. **Open** 11am-2am daily. **Credit** AmEx, DC, MC, V. **Map** p308 E6.

Kincade's is the area's reigning sports bar. The many TVs and ample beer selection attract hordes of frat brothers decked out in the regalia of their alma mater: on Saturdays during college football season, Kincade's can have the feel (and smell) of university bleachers during a big game.

Local Option

1102 W Webster Avenue, at N Seminary Avenue (773 348 2008). CTA Armitage or Fullerton. **Open** 5pm-2am Mon-Fri; 3pm-3am Sat; 2pm-2am Sun. **Credit** AmEx, MC, V. **Map** p308 E5.

An unassuming neighbourhood hangout for DePaul students and other locals tired of the yuppie theme that predominates elsewhere in the locale. A pool table and several TVs offer diversions; cheap pitchers provide the beer.

McGee's

950 W Webster Avenue, at N Sheffield Avenue (773 549 8200). CTA Armitage. **Open** 11am-2am Mon-Fri, Sun; 10am-3am Sat. **Credit** AmEx, DC, Disc. **Map** p308 E5.

An attractive neighbourhood sports bar, McGee's is more low-key than **Kincade's** and lacks the locker-room smell of **Gamekeepers** (*see above*). On weekends, DePaul students and young Lincoln Park professionals pack in for burgers and football.

Screen test

Few things in Chicago bring people together en masse quite like the local sports teams, a ragtag bunch of loveable losers and streaking winners. The Blackhawks, Bears, White Sox and Cubs each have their own faithful, while the Bulls' run of success in the '90s created quite a few fans who were conspicuously absent during the team's pre-Jordan days. And despite the Cubs' 92-year Series drought, despite the White Sox's serial failure, despite the Blackhawks' inability to score goals, despite the Bears' relative lack of success over the course of the past 30 years, fans still love them. Grudgingly.

Just as some fans pour into Soldier Field, Comiskey Park, Wrigley Field and the United Center for games, so others simultaneously pour themselves into another Chicago sports tradition. More so than in most American cities, sports and bars in Chicago go together like hot dogs and mustard, like Michael Jordan and the number '23', like the words 'Cubs' and 'lose'. Of course, 'most every bar in Chicago will have the relevant games on TV, and every bar supports the Chicago teams unless you see another team's logo openly displayed. But that said, there are certain bars that, in the absence of a ticket for the game itself, are must-visits.

Though baseball isn't a sport that brings people to bars like football, there are still a few gems. And none more so than at Wrigley Field, the perimeter of which is surrounded by bars. Perhaps the most authentic Cubs experience comes at **Murphy's Bleachers**, which is packed before, during and after the game with wall-to-wall Cub fans.

It's not as easy to find a comparable White Sox bar, primarily because Comiskey Park is surrounded by rail yards, housing projects and concrete. But for a hardcore South Side Sox scene, head to **The Show**, where you'll often find some of the White Sox themselves enjoying a post-game pint. The spot for Blackhawks games – though hockey, like baseball, doesn't fill the bars – is **Cheli's Chili Bar**, owned by former Blackhawk Chris Chelios. Located close to the United Center, it's packed with Blackhawk memorabilia from as far back as the 1920s, hockey fans and, often, post-game Blackhawks.

The Bears are a lock to be on every television set in every bar in Chicago, but if just any old bar isn't good enough, head to

the bustling Rush Street area and plop yourself into the **Ultimate Sports Bar & Grill**. Sure it's modern, sure it's Rush Street, but you can bet there'll be a flock of Bears fans on Sundays; less surprising when you consider that the bar's ownership consists of Dan Hampton, Tom Waddle, Otis Wilson and Glen Kozlowski, all former Bears.

The once-proud Bulls are presently in a rebuilding phase – translation: they suck, and everyone knows it – but Chicago's diehards can still be found in the bars, watching the team of youngsters learn the game. One of the most popular bars for Bulls' games is **Spectrum**, a sports bar located in the centre of Greektown not far from the United Center. In addition to the requisite big-screen television and abundance of smaller screens, there's a 'Pop-A-Shot' basketball game, darts and pool. But remember, even if they are the worst team in the NBA, the Bulls always get priority on the big screen. Want another game? Don't even bother asking.

Cheli's Chili Bar

1137 W Madison Street, at S Racine Avenue, West Side (312 455 1237). Bus 20. **Open** *11am-8pm Mon-Fri, or until 2am on hockey nights; closed Sat, Sun.* **Credit** *AmEx, DC, Disc, MC, V.*

Murphy's Bleachers

3655 N Sheffield Avenue, at W Waveland Avenue, Lake View/Wrigleyville (no phone). CTA Addison (Red). **Open** *9am-2am Mon-Fri, Sun; 9am-3am Sat.* **Map** *p309 F1.*

The Show

3503 S Halsted Street, at W 35th Street, South Side (773 847 4711). CTA Sox/35th Street. **Open** *11am-2am Mon-Fri, Sun; 11am-3am Sat.*

Spectrum Bar & Grill

233 S Halsted Street, at W Jackson Boulevard, West Side (312 715 0770). CTA UIC-Halsted. **Open** *11am-4am Mon-Fri; 5pm-5am Sat; 5pm-4am Sun.* **Credit** *AmEx, Disc, MC, V.*

Ultimate Sports Bar & Grill

9 W Division Street, at N State Street, Gold Coast (312 654 0000). CTA Clark/Division. **Open** *11am-4am Mon-Fri, Sun; 11am-5am Sat.* **Credit** *AmEx, Disc, MC, V.* **Map** *p307 H8.*

Mickey's Snack Bar

2450 N Clark Street, at W Arlington Place (773 435 0007). CTA Fullerton. **Open** 11.30am-2am Mon-Fri; 10.30am-3am Sat; 10.30am-2am Sun. **Credit** AmEx, DC, MC, V. **Map** p308 G5.

As intimated in its name, Mickey's is actually a diner-themed restaurant with a full menu of basic burgers, sandwiches and appetisers. But its main attraction is its popular tree-shaded patio that overlooks Clark and caters to drinkers on warm summer afternoons and evenings.

O'Rourke's

1625 N Halsted Street, at W North Avenue (312 335 1806). CTA North/Clybourn. **Open** 8pm-2am Mon; 4.30pm-2am Tue-Fri; 5pm-3am Sat; 6pm-2am Sun. **Map** p307 F7.

You never know when an actor from **Steppenwolf** (*see p237*) is going to walk across the street and plop down next to you at this old standard on the edge of Old Town. Grab a Guinness, drop some change in the jukebox and be inspired by the huge posters of Irish greats like Joyce, Yeats and Wilde.

Parkway Tavern

748½ W Fullerton Avenue, at N Halsted Street (773 327 8164). CTA Fullerton. **Open** 3pm-2am Mon-Fri; noon-3am Sat; noon-2am Sun. **Credit** AmEx, MC, V. **Map** p308 F5.

A fun neighbourhood hangout just around the corner from the Lincoln Avenue strip. There's a satellite TV that screens all the major and minor sporting events, plus food from the Bourgeois Pig coffeehouse next door.

Red Lion Pub

2446 N Lincoln Avenue, at W Fullerton Avenue (773 348 2695). CTA Fullerton. **Open** noon-2am daily. **Credit** AmEx, DC, MC, V. **Map** p308 F5.

Authentic(-ish), British and rumoured to be haunted, the Red Lion is full of character, dark wood and heavy food. The downstairs bar and restaurant boast low ceilings and an excellent beer selection, while the cosier upstairs bar has a backroom and sizeable rooftop beer garden.

The Store

2002 N Halsted Street, at W Armitage Avenue (773 327 7766). CTA Armitage. **Open** 3pm-4am Mon-Fri; 11am-4am Sat; 11am-4am Sun. **Credit** Disc, MC, V. **Map** p308 F6.

Though the multiple TVs and pool table could pin it as a sports bar, the Store's principal attraction is its 4am closing time. The bar itself is long and narrow, and seating consists mainly of bar stools. A good last call bar if you're not willing to face the noise and crowd at the considerably more hectic **Beaumont** (*see p151*) up the road.

Twisted Lizard

1964 N Sheffield Avenue, at W Armitage Avenue (773 929 1414). CTA Armitage. **Open** noon-11pm Mon-Fri; noon-midnight Sat, Sun. **Credit** AmEx, DC, MC, V. **Map** p308 E6.

Principally a Mexican restaurant, Twisted Lizard merits mention if only for its pitchers of Margaritas. The food in this brightly-lit, subterranean lair is good, the atmosphere warm and friendly, and the Margaritas available in many flavours (the raspberry is great). Get there early, as the Lizard is a popular Thursday-Saturday starting point for many locals.

Waterloo Tavern

2270 N Lincoln Avenue, at W Belden Avenue (773 929 1300). CTA Armitage. **Open** 5pm-2am Mon-Fri, Sun; noon-3am Sat. **Credit** AmEx, Disc, MC, V. **Map** p308 F5.

This pleasantly straightforward bar is out of place on a block otherwise taken up with trendy, loud nightspots catering to bellowing fraternity alumni. The crowd of fresh-faced twentysomethings comes out to enjoy bar bands on Wednesdays, Fridays and Saturdays for a small cover charge.

Webster's Wine Bar

1480 W Webster Avenue, at N Clybourn Street (773 868 0608). CTA Fullerton. **Open** 5pm-2am Mon-Fri; 4pm-3am Sat; 4pm-2am Sun. **Credit** AmEx, DC, Disc, MC, V.

This quiet, stylish wine bar is tucked away at the far west end of Lincoln Park on the edge of the Chicago River's north branch (quite a hike from the nearest CTA stop). The knowledgeable staff offer an impressive selection of wine, which is complemented by a menu of appetisers and regular live jazz.

Weed's

1555 N Dayton Street, at W Weed Street (312 943 7815). CTA North/Clybourn. **Open** 3pm-2am Mon-Sat. **Credit** AmEx, DC, Disc, MC, V.

A truly peculiar spot in the middle of nowhere – west of Old Town, south of Lincoln Park – but well worth seeking out. The hundreds of bras hanging from the ceiling bear witness to both the power of the lubrication dished out by the perennially sunglassed bartender – a strangely lifelike bust of whom graces one corner of the dingy bar – and the lubriciousness of the clientele.

Lake View

While Lincoln Park is renowned as the epicentre of Chicago's bar scene, the nearby neighbourhood of Lake View, including **Wrigleyville** and **Roscoe Village**, gives it a pretty good run for its money. Hangouts here range from neighbourhood saloons to nightclubs and – around Wrigleyville, natch – sports bars.

The part of Lake View closest to the lakefront is commonly referred to as Boystown for its mostly gay population. If it's not your scene, check the windows for rainbow flags before entering any bar on Halsted or Broadway between Addison and Belmont, Boystown's main drags. But if it is, then *see chapters* **Gay & Lesbian** and **Nightlife** for more gay and lesbian hangouts.

Cubs lose. Again. The **Cubby Bear** (*p155*).

Lake View

Brother Jimmy's BBQ

2909 N Sheffield Avenue, at W Oakdale Avenue (773 528 0888). CTA Wellington. **Open** 5pm-1.30am Mon-Fri; 11am-2.30am Sat; 11am-midnight Sun. **Credit** AmEx, Disc, MC, V. **Map** p309 E3.

A bar dedicated to, of all things, the culture of North and South Carolina: barbecue, longneck beers and the Carolina Panthers. Put some South in yo' mouth on Sundays, when $18.95 buys you all the ribs and draft beer you can swallow. Donate a pig tchotchke and you'll get a free drink. No, really.

Club Eden

3407 N Clark Street, at W Roscoe Street (773 327 4646). CTA Belmont. **Open** 6pm-2am Mon-Fri, Sun; 6pm-3am Sat. **Credit** AmEx, MC, V. **Map** p309 E2.

Another popular destination before or after Cubs games, this bar and Mexican restaurant is a festive spot. The traditional Mexican fare is solid, but we suspect most people come for the lethal Margaritas, fortified with grain alcohol to provide an extra kick.

Duke of Perth

2913 N Clark Street, at W Oakdale Avenue (773 477 1741). CTA Wellington. **Open** 5pm-2am Mon; 11.30am-2am Tue-Fri; 11.30am-3am Sat; noon-2am Sun. **Credit** AmEx, MC, V. **Map** p309 F3.

Chicago goes Scottish at this Lake View staple. The food is fish 'n' chips, the drinks are whiskies (75 vari-

eties, no less) and the garden is a delight during summer. Homesick Scots may not, however, have their pangs for auld tradition entirely sated.

Elbo Room

2871 N Lincoln Avenue, at W George Street (773 549 5549). CTA Diversey. **Open** 7pm-2am Mon-Fri; 7pm-3am Sat; closed Sun. **Credit** AmEx, Disc, MC, V. **Map** p309 D3.

This bar and live music venue (*see p208*) has a funky, retro-ish atmosphere without trying too hard, unlike many latecomers to the '60s-kitsch scene. Have a drink in the smallish bar among the hip patrons, or pay the cover and head downstairs to the claustrophobic, cavelike underground music venue.

Schubas Tavern

3159 N Southport Avenue, at W Belmont Avenue (773 525 2508). CTA Belmont or Southport. **Open** 11am-2am Mon-Fri; 8am-3am Sat; 9am-2am Sun. **Credit** AmEx, DC, Disc, MC, V. **Map** p309 D3.

Housed in a 90-year-old building, Schubas is a typical vintage Chicago pub, with a 30-ft mahogany bar and tin ceilings. But it's the busy backroom that puts it on the map: there's music most nights, with a lean towards alt.country and rootsy rock (*see p210*).

Southport Lanes & Billiards

3325 N Southport Avenue, at W Aldine Avenue (773 472 6600). CTA Southport. **Open** 4pm-2am Mon-Fri; noon-3am Sat; noon-2am Sun. **Credit** AmEx, DC, Disc, MC, V. **Map** p309 D2.

When the conversation runs dry, you'll have plenty of distractions here: six billiards tables ($9 per hour on weekdays, $12 on weekends) and four bowling lanes ($14 per hour). However, the attraction is not the games, but the well-scrubbed clientele that comes to play them. The food is a little on the greasy side.

Star Bar/Pops for Champagne

2934 N Sheffield Avenue, at W Oakdale Avenue (773 472 7272/472 1000). CTA Belmont or Wellington. **Open** 5pm-2am Mon-Thur, Sun; 4pm-2am Fri; 5pm-3am Sat. **Credit** AmEx, DC, Disc, MC, V. **Map** p309 E3.

Because it's located in Lake View and not in the Gold Coast where it belongs, this pair goes out of its way to lord its upscale pretensions over the great unwashed. It's actually one bar with two themed rooms: the quiet, cosy and formal Star Bar, and the opulent wine bar Pops, which offers live jazz (there's a $10 cover Mon-Sat). Dress up.

Thurston's

1248 W George Street, at N Lincoln Avenue (773 472 6900). CTA Diversey or Wellington. **Open** 6pm-2am Mon-Fri, Sun; 6pm-3am Sat. **Credit** AmEx, MC, V. **Map** p309 D3.

Located across the street from the **Elbo Room**, this music venue/bar tries for a rock 'n' roll atmosphere. There's live music every night in the dark upstairs room, while downstairs offers comfy couches, loud music and food. There's a free buffet on Friday.

Will's Northwoods Inn

3030 N Racine Avenue, at W Nelson Street (773 528 4400). CTA Belmont. Open 11.30am-2am Mon-Fri, Sun; 11.30am-3am Sat. Credit AmEx, MC, V. Map p309 E3.

Decorated with stuffed pike and moose heads to suggest the quintessential Wisconsin tavern, Will's is a mecca for homesick Cheeseheads who come to watch Packers games and quaff a Leinenkugel. The Musky Fest, in late September, features a free buffet, a Wisconsin trivia contest and the rather tongue-in-cheek election of the Musky Queen.

Wrigleyville

Cubby Bear

1059 W Addison Street, at N Clark Street (773 327 1662). CTA Addison (Red). Open 4pm-2am Mon-Fri; 11am-3am Sat; 11am-2am Sun. Credit AmEx, DC, Disc, MC, V. Map p309 E1.

Located across from the Friendly Confines, this perpetually expanding bar is packed with sports fans on game days. In the off-season, the emphasis is on live music and dancing. Thursday nights offer 50¢ drafts and 75¢ cheeseburgers. Dude!

Ginger Man

3740 N Clark Street, at N Racine Avenue (773 549 2050). CTA Addison (Red). Open 3pm-2am Mon-Fri, Sun; 3pm-3am Sat. Credit AmEx, Disc, MC, V. Map p309 E1.

This edgy Wrigleyville institution has been known to blare classical music to keep Wrigley's gameday crowds at bay, preferring to cater to theatregoers heading to the area's alternative venues or hipsters looking for a drink after a show at the Metro a stone's throw away. There's a good selection of beers, and movie nuts may recognise the pool room from 1986's *The Color of Money.*

Hustlin' types head for the **Ginger Man**.

Hi Tops

3551 N Sheffield Avenue, at W Addison Street (773 348 0009). CTA Addison (Red). Open 5pm-2am Mon-Fri; 11am-3am Sat; 11am-10pm Sun. Credit AmEx, DC, Disc, MC, V. Map p309 E1.

Yet another garish temple to machismo by the ballpark. If you're here, you're watching sports on one of the 49 TVs, with other ambience provided by sports memorabilia. At night, things get wild when the tables and chairs are removed and a DJ starts up.

Irish Oak

3511 N Clark Street, at W Addison Street (773 935 6669). CTA Addison (Red). Open 11am-2am Mon-Fri, Sun; 11am-3am Sat. Credit AmEx, DC, Disc, MC, V. Map p309 E1.

Chicago is full of Irish-themed bars, but this one strikes the best balance between authenticity and tedious old-country kitsch. The usual Irish fare comes with a modern twist, including the prettiest, if not tastiest, fish and chips for miles. There's live music on Wednesdays and weekends.

Murphy's Bleachers

3655 N Sheffield Avenue, at W Waveland Avenue (no phone). CTA Addison (Red). Open 9am-2am Mon-Fri, Sun; 9am-3am Sat. Map p309 E1.

Located just behind Wrigley, Murphy's affords sports fans the rare opportunity to pay $4 for a can of Old Style. Most patrons amass on the sidewalk before or after Cubs games to bask in the sun, people-watch and take in the street theatre (a couple of industrious kids drumming on overturned plastic buckets for change). A tradition of sorts.

Sheffield's Wine & Beer Garden

3258 N Sheffield Avenue, at W Aldine Avenue (773 281 4989). CTA Belmont. Open 3pm-2am Mon-Fri; noon-3am Sat; noon-2am Sun. Credit AmEx, MC, V. Map p309 E2.

Just far enough away from Wrigley Field to elude most sports fans, Sheffield's is a great pre- or postgame hangout. There's the all-important beer garden, but the best seat in the house is on an elevated bench just inside the front door to the right: perched over the bouncer's shoulder, you can check out all the pretty folks who come through the door.

Sluggers World Class Sports Bar

3540 N Clark Street, at W Addison Street (773 248 0055). CTA Addison (Red). Open 3pm-2am Mon-Fri; 11am-3am Sat; 11am-2am Sun; Cubs home games opens at 10am. Credit AmEx, DC, Disc, MC, V. Map p309 E1.

This Wrigleyville landmark was voted the No.1 sports bar in Chicago and the third best in the country, and not without good reason. Downstairs, there's the typical array of pool tables and TVs; upstairs there are batting cages that throw balls and strikes up to 90mph – best avoided after a couple of drinks – basketball hoops, video games and Hi-Ball, a game that most closely resembles two-on-two basketball on a tiny trampoline.

Smart Bar

3730 N Clark Street, at N Racine Avenue (773 549 4140). CTA Addison (Red). **Open** 10pm-4am Mon-Fri, Sun; 10pm-5am Sat. **Map** p309 E1.

Once the epicentre of Chicago's punk scene, the **Metro**'s downstairs nightclub still attracts a punky crowd, with DJs spinning house, techno and the like. If dancing isn't your thing, then shoot some pool or grab a spot in the booths that surround the dance-floor and check out the goths. Failing that, then the excellent **Ginger Man** (*see p157*) is only a few doors down the street. *See also p222.*

Wild Hare

3530 N Clark Street, at W Addison Street (773 327 4273). CTA Addison (Red). **Open** 8pm-2am Mon-Fri, Sun; 8pm-3am Sat. **Map** p309 E1.

There's nothing fancy at all about this place, but that's OK: as the city's best reggae bar, the emphasis is on the music and the irie vibes created by the jubilant crowd. The bar attracts big names on weekends and showcases local talent during the week. *See also p211.*

Roscoe Village

Beat Kitchen

2100 W Belmont Avenue, at N Hoyne Avenue (773 281 4444). CTA Belmont. **Open** 11.30am-2am daily. **Credit** AmEx, Disc, MC, V.

There's a cosy bar area up front, packed with booths and lit by festive strings of Christmas lights. The menu offers mildly inventive bar food, and there's some form of live music seven nights a week in the backroom (though the management tends to make you pay a cover at the front door).

Resi's Bierstube

2034 W Irving Park Road, at N Damen Avenue (773 472 1749). CTA Ravenswood. **Open** 3pm-2am Mon-Fri, Sun; 3pm-3am Sat. **Credit** AmEx, DC, Disc, MC, V.

This German bar and restaurant in a blue-collar neighbourhood offers lots of hard-to-find imports on tap, served inside or in one of the city's best beer gardens. The menu offers the traditional schnitzels, plus, Mondays to Thursdays from 5pm, the cantankerous barmatron Edith making her delectable potato pancakes.

Village Tap

2055 W Roscoe Street, at N Hoyne Avenue (773 883 0817). CTA Paulina. **Open** 5pm-2am Mon-Fri; noon-3am Sat; noon-2am Sun. **Credit** AmEx, DC, Disc, MC, V.

This neighbourhood pub seems to be getting more and more crowded as affluent twentysomethings move further and further westward: the Starbucks that recently opened a few doors down could spell the end for what used to be one of the city's best-kept secret. The $3.50 microbrew pints and $11 pitchers appeal, as does the dressed-up pub grub and the spacious garden (heated in winter).

Far North

Great Beer Palace

4128 N Lincoln Avenue, at W Warner Avenue (773 525 4906). CTA Irving Park (Brown). **Open** 4pm-2am Mon-Fri; noon-3am Sat; noon-2am Sun. **Credit** AmEx, DC, Disc, MC, V.

This dingy standby offers a spacious beer garden, a raucous frat house atmosphere and 19 imported beers on tap, plus six or so seasonal brews. Cheap, greasy appetisers are all under $4, though it's notable for its Viking Raid: polish off six 8-oz glasses of German beer and win a plastic Viking hat. More fun than it sounds.

Green Mill Cocktail Lounge

4802 N Broadway, at W Lawrence Avenue (773 878 5552). CTA Lawrence. **Open** noon-4am Mon-Fri, Sun; noon-5am Sat. **Credit** AmEx.

Tucked away in a slightly seedy neighbourhood, this gem is just inconveniently located enough to elude the downtown crowd. A former Mob-run speakeasy, this late-night hotspot showcases live jazz music nightly. Get there early to snag a booth, but don't be surprised if you're asked to share when the place gets busy around 1am. Sunday's Uptown Poetry Slam is, in turns, haunting and hilarious.

Wicker Park & Bucktown

The area in and around Wicker Park and Bucktown wasn't handed its reputation as an enticingly hip neighbourhood: it had to work for it, and its nightlife played a huge part. Aside from the art galleries and music venues in the locale, there are plenty of terrific bars around the Damen-Milwaukee-North intersection: neighbourhood hangouts with a twist, most of 'em, the twist being that you won't find too many of Lincoln Park's yuppies or Wrigleyville's baseball nuts around here.

Lava Lounge

859 N Damen Avenue, at W Chicago Avenue (773 772 3355). CTA Damen (Blue). **Open** 5pm-2am Mon-Fri, Sun; 5pm-3am Sat.

The dark and cosy Lava Lounge attracts a smorgasbord of locals during the week and North Siders during the weekends. The three-room bar appears small, but the backrooms are full of nooks for small parties and booths for larger groups. There's a selection of microbrews on tap every month, and underground music on the hi-fi every night.

Lemmings

1850 N Damen Avenue, at W Moffat Street (773 862 1688). CTA Damen (Blue). **Open** 4pm-2am Mon-Fri; noon-3am Sat; noon-2am Sun. **Credit** AmEx, MC, V. **Map** p310 B6.

A quiet neighbourhood bar frequented by locals and often a getaway from the thumping bar scene up the street, Lemmings is a friendly Schlitz bar that still

A pair of very different friendly confines: Wrigley Field and **Sluggers**. *See page 157.*

serves the legendary quaff for $1.50 a pint. The crowd of regulars is a little older and quieter than is the norm around here.

Mad Bar
1640 N Damen Avenue, at W North Avenue (773 227 2277). CTA Damen (Blue). **Open** 5.30pm-2am Mon-Fri, Sun; 5.30pm-3am Sat. **Credit** AmEx, DC, Disc, MC, V. **Map** p310 B7.

Occupying a grey area between club and bar, the Mad Bar has a retro-lounge decor, helped mightily by furniture secured from JFK's TWA terminal from the '60s. The music is loud, imposing and often of the Chicago house variety, but Thursdays are reserved for the Latin sounds of Carnival Brazil.

Pontiac Café & Bar
1531 N Damen Avenue, at N Wicker Park Avenue (773 252 7767). CTA Damen (Blue). **Open** noon-2am Mon-Fri, Sun; noon-3am Sat. **Credit** MC, V. **Map** p310 B7.

With a full menu of submarine sandwiches, Italian snacks and panini, the Pontiac is one of Wicker Park's most visited bars, especially in summer. The full bar is stocked with both the very expensive and very cheap, as well as a full array of bottled and draft beers. Get there early, as it's pretty small.

Rainbo Club
1150 N Damen Avenue, at W Division Street (773 489 5999). CTA Damen (Blue). **Open** 4pm-2am Mon-Fri, Sun; 4pm-3am Sat. **Map** p310 B8.

Once a haunt of Nelson Algren, the Rainbo Club is a favourite of locals, artists, musos and writers. You'll catch some attitude if you're not one of the above, and the bartenders work as if their legs are made of lead. All the same, there's a genuinely artistic atmosphere here, and those in the know are likely to spot any number of semi-famous Chicago residents (members of Tortoise, for example), plus plenty more soon-to-bes and wannabes.

Silver Cloud Bar & Grill
1700 N Damen Avenue, at W Wabansia Avenue (773 489 6212). CTA Damen (Blue). **Open** 5pm-1am Mon; 11.30am-2am Tue-Fri; 10am-3am Sat; 10am-midnight Sun. **Credit** AmEx, DC, Disc, MC, V. **Map** p310 B7.

A midscale bar and restaurant that serves some of the best bar food in the city, the Silver Cloud has become a local favourite. There's a long bar for the drinkers, booths and tables for diners (try the incredible grilled cheese sandwiches) and a rotating selection of microbrews.

Tuman's Alcohol Abuse Center
2201 W Chicago Avenue, at N Leavitt Street (no phone). CTA 66 bus. **Open** 2pm-2am Mon-Fri, Sun; 2pm-3am Sat.

A bar for the pure-bred drinker. The crowd at this gem is one of the most diverse in the city: on any given night, it's crammed with bikers, businessmen, mohawked punks, hip hoppers and gang bangers, all co-existing in harmony thanks to Tuman's ultra-cheap booze. Prices tend to vary round by round, but it's cheaper than any other bar you'll find in the city.

Shops & Services

Credit cards at the ready: Chicago's shopping is among the world's best.

As miles go, it is pretty darn magnificent. But don't for one minute think that shopping in Chicago begins and ends on Michigan Avenue.

Of course, it is where everyone begins. And not without good reason, for the Magnificent Mile is a fine shopping spot. Many of the big names in fashion – whether high-end designer or populist streetwear – have homes on or very close by Michigan Avenue, as do all manner of other notable chains and three malls in the space of only six blocks. All this, and the enticing grandness of the street itself, mean that Michigan Avenue swarms with shoppers on weekends, an experience that can be suffocating.

But for genuinely unique shops, you'll have to head elsewhere. And luckily, elsewhere in Chicago has it well covered. Aside from the markets, there's State Street (that great street), where you'll find the world-renowned **Marshall Field's**; Lake View, home to dozens of esoteric and interesting shops, most found around Clark Street north of Diversey and on Halsted Street in Boystown; the Loop's **Jeweler's Center**; the bookstores of Hyde Park; Wicker Park, where you'll find an assortment of super-hip stores; and plenty more besides. Just remember to bring your credit cards, OK?

For toy shops, *see page 193* **Toy story**.

Antiques & auctions

More than two dozen antique shops cluster along **Belmont Avenue**, between Ashland Avenue and Western Avenue on the North Side, offering a range of periods and prices. Just south, on **Lincoln Avenue** are more individual shops and a pair of antiques malls.

Antiques Centre of Kinzie Square

220 W Kinzie Street, at N Wells Street, Near North/River North (312 464 1946). CTA Merchandise Mart. **Open** 10am-5pm Mon-Fri; noon-4pm Sat; closed Sun. **Credit** MC, V. **Map** p307 H11.
Look, don't touch at this upscale antiques centre for high-end furniture, jewellery, silver, porcelain and art from the 18th to the 20th centuries.

Broadway Antiques Market

6130 N Broadway, at W Hood Avenue, Far North (773 743 5444/www.bamchicago.com). CTA Granville. **Open** 11am-7pm Mon-Sat; noon-6pm Sun. **Credit** AmEx, Disc, MC, V.
Eighty-five dealers show off their wares at this two-level antiques mall in a former car dealership.

There's everything from Victorian pieces to '70s collectibles, with special emphasis on art deco, arts and crafts and modern. Worth the trek north.

Jay Robert's Antique Warehouse

149 W Kinzie Street, at N LaSalle Street, Near North/River North (312 222 0167). CTA Merchandise Mart. **Open** 10am-5pm Mon-Sat; closed Sun. **Credit** AmEx, MC, V. **Map** p307 H11.
A huge space in River North with a large inventory of fine antiques, including furnitures, fireplaces, antique clocks and stained glass.

Modern Times

1538 N Milwaukee Avenue, at W North Avenue, Wicker Park/Bucktown (773 772 8871). CTA Damen (Blue). **Open** 1-6pm Wed-Fri, noon-6pm Sat, Sun; closed Mon, Tue. **Credit** AmEx, MC, V. **Map** p310 C7.
This store is stuck in the '40s, '50s and '60s. Look for furniture, jewellery and vintage wear; rummage in the basement for some downmarket bargains.

Salvage One

*1524 S Sangamon Street, at W 16th Street, South
Side (312 733 0098). CTA Halsted (Orange).* **Open**
10am-5pm Mon-Sat; 11am-4pm Sun. **Credit** AmEx,
Disc, MC, V.

A humungous five-floor warehouse filled to the
rafters with beautiful and unusual furniture, fireplace mantels, claw-footed bathtubs, oak doors,
bathroom fixtures and other architectural artefacts.

Sotheby's

*215 W Ohio Street, at N Franklin Street, Near
North/River North (312 396 9599/www.sothebys.com).
CTA Merchandise Mart.* **Map** p306 G10.

The esteemed auction house has a Chicago presence with regular auctions of fine art, furniture,
jewellery, watches and wine. And something different: a new, annual sale of vintage motorcycles
and bicycles.

Art supplies

Aiko's Art Materials

*3347 N Clark Street, at W Roscoe Street, Lake
View/Wrigleyville (773 404 5600). CTA Addison
(Red).* **Open** 10am-5pm Tue-Sat; closed Mon, Sun.
Credit MC, V. **Map** p309 E2.

Many beautiful varieties of Japanese-made paper are
stocked at this Lake View delight.

Art Store

*1574 N Kingsbury Street, at W North Avenue,
Lincoln Park (312 573 0110). CTA North/Clybourn.*
Open 9am-9pm Mon-Fri; 9am-7pm Sat; 11am-6pm
Sun. **Credit** AmEx, Disc, MC, V.

This clean, well-lit warehouse-size art store has a little bit of everything and parking to boot.

Paper Source

*232 W Chicago Avenue, at N Franklin Street, Near
North/River North (312 337 0798). CTA Chicago
(Brown/Purple).* **Open** 10am-7pm Mon-Fri; 10am-
5pm Sat; noon-5pm Sun. **Credit** AmEx, Disc, MC, V.
Map p306 G10.

Look over hundreds of papers for writing, wrapping
and binding, plus rubber stamps, wedding supplies
and other creative gift items.

Pearl Art & Craft Supplies

*225 W Chicago Avenue, at N Franklin Street,
Near North/River North (312 915 0200). CTA
Chicago (Brown/Purple).* **Open** 9am-7pm Mon-Sat;
noon-5pm Sun. **Credit** AmEx, Disc, MC, V.
Map p306 G10.

This rather roomy art department store – conveniently located across from **Paper Source** – is
crammed to the hilt with a wide range of art and
craft supplies to satisfy the suburban hobbyist as
well as the serious artiste.

Consumer

Michigan Avenue: magnificent indeed.

Books

General

Barbara's Bookstore

1350 N Wells Street, at W Schiller Street, Old Town (312 642 5044). CTA Clark/Division. **Open** 9am-10pm Mon-Sat; 10am-9pm Sun. **Credit** AmEx, Disc, MC, V. **Map** p307 H8.

Barbara's is a cosy hangout with all the bustle of a superstore but none of the bureaucracy. The chain has strong politics and current events sections, as well as a great selection of art books.
Branches: throughout the city.

Barnes & Noble

1130 N State Street, at W Cedar Street, Gold Coast (312 280 8155). CTA Clark/Division. **Open** 9am-11pm Mon-Sat; 10am-10pm Sun. **Credit** AmEx, Disc, MC, V. **Map** p306 H9.

This wood-panelled readery is a chain store of the more refined sort. Though sprawling, B&N claims excellent customer service.
Branches: 659 W Diversey Parkway, at N Clark Street, Lake View (773 871 9004); 1441 W Webster Avenue, at N Clybourn Avenue, Lincoln Park (773 871 3610).

Borders Books & Music

830 N Michigan Avenue, at N Pearson Street, Near North/Magnificent Mile (312 573 0564). CTA Chicago (Red). **Open** 8am-11pm Mon-Sat; 9am-9pm Sun. **Credit** AmEx, DC, Disc, MC, V. **Map** p306 J9.

A book/music/coffee empire of the sort spoofed in *You've Got Mail*, the four-storey Borders on the Mag Mile does have something to offer beyond its brand names and tourist throngs: 200,000 titles, in fact.
Branch: 2817 N Clark Street, at W Diversey Parkway, Lake View (773 935 3909).

Brent's Books

309 W Washington Boulevard, at N Franklin Street, The Loop (312 364 0126). CTA Randolph. **Open** 8am-7pm Mon-Fri; 10am-4pm Sat; closed Sun. **Credit** AmEx, Disc, MC, V. **Map** p305 G12.

This cosy shop has many strengths, but it's especially outstanding in the psychology department.
Branch: 316 N Michigan Avenue, at W Wacker Drive, The Loop (312 920 0940).

Lincoln Park Bookshop

2423 N Clark Street, at W Fullerton Avenue, Lincoln Park (773 477 7087). CTA Fullerton. **Open** 9am-10pm daily. **Credit** AmEx, MC, V. **Map** p308 G5.

'All we lack is a potbellied stove and a cracker barrel,' says owner Joel Jacobson of this neighbourhood hangout. In addition to a number of comfy chairs, the store features a knowledgeable and opinionated staff who will steer you to the right tomes.

Seminary Cooperative Bookstore Inc

5757 S University Avenue, at E 58th Street, Hyde Park (773 752 4381). Metra 59th Street. **Open**
8.30am-9pm Mon-Fri; 10am-6pm Sat; noon-6pm Sun. **Credit** AmEx, Disc, MC, V. **Map** p311 X12.

At the hub of Hyde Park's dazzling array of bookstores, this shop is a mecca for scholars. If you're seeking obscure texts, you'll most likely leave happy. The 57th Street location is a more general bookstore.
Branch: 1301 E 57th Street, at S Kimbark Avenue, Hyde Park (773 684 1300).

Unabridged Bookstore

3251 N Broadway, at W Belmont Avenue, Lake View (773 883 9119). CTA Belmont. **Open** 10am-10pm Mon-Fri; 10am-8pm Sat, Sun. **Credit** AmEx, Disc, MC, V. **Map** p309 F2.

This general bookstore reflects the neighbourhood folk who shop there: thus, it has a sizeable children's section, a large travel department and prominent gay and lesbian selections.

University of Chicago Bookstore

970 E 58th Street, at S Ellis Avenue, Hyde Park (773 702 8729). CTA 4 bus. **Open** 8am-6.30pm Mon-Fri; 10am-5pm Sat; closed Sun. **Credit** AmEx, Disc, MC, V. **Map** p311 X17.

Managed by Barnes & Noble college bookstores, this campus outlet draws students, faculty staff, neighbourhood folk and scrubs-clad medical types from the hospital next door. It's laid-back enough for you to swig your Starbucks in the stacks.

Specialist

For **Women & Children First**, *see page 205.*

Abraham Lincoln Book Shop

357 W Chicago Avenue, at N Orleans Street, Near North/River North (312 944 3085). CTA Chicago (Brown/Purple). **Open** 9am-5pm Mon-Sat; closed Sun. **Credit** MC, V. **Map** p306 G10.

This 60-year-old shop devoted to Abraham Lincoln and Civil War lore is also the founding site of the Civil War Round Table, a discussion group that keeps stories of the blue and the grey alive.

Afrocentric Bookstore

Chicago Music Mart, DePaul Center, 333 S State Street, at E Jackson Boulevard, The Loop (312 939 1956). CTA Jackson (Red). **Open** 9.30am-6pm Mon-Fri; 10am-4.30pm Sat; closed Sun. **Credit** AmEx, Disc, MC, V. **Map** p305 H13.

The Afrocentric, the first bookstore of its kind in downtown Chicago, has over 7,000 titles devoted to the African-American experience, as well as that of the African diaspora.

Chicago Comics

3244 N Clark Street, at W Belmont Avenue, Lake View (773 528 1983). CTA Belmont. **Open** noon-8pm Mon-Fri; 11am-8pm Sat; noon-6pm Sun. **Credit** AmEx, Disc, MC, V. **Map** p309 F2.

A haven for compulsive comic devotees, Chicago Comics has a sprawling selection of underground comics and 'zines, foreign imports, alternative and small-press comics, toys and enough knick-knacks to keep any R Crumb-types happy.

Keep one eye on the sparky art at **Chicago Comics**. *See page 162.*

Children in Paradise Bookstore

909 N Rush Street, at E Chestnut Street, Gold Coast (312 951 5437). CTA Chicago (Red). **Open** 10am-7pm Mon-Thur; 10am-8pm Fri, Sat; noon-5pm Sun. **Credit** AmEx, MC, V. **Map** p306 H9.

The city's **Barnes & Noble** and **Borders** superstores have fine kiddie-lit sections, but this place is solely focused on young readers. There are story hours on Tuesdays and Wednesdays and occasional parties and puppet shows.

Occult Bookstore

1561 N Milwaukee Avenue, at N Damen Avenue, Wicker Park/Bucktown (773 292 0995). CTA Damen (Blue). **Open** 11am-7pm Mon-Thur; 11am-9pm Fri, Sat; noon-6pm Sun. **Credit** MC, V. **Map** p301 C7.

In 2000, the Occult Bookstore turned 80, making the term 'New Age' a bit off-base. Instead, the Occult deals in 'astrology, yoga, UFOs and psychic phenomena'. Psychic Lucy Saxman gives readings on Friday and Saturday afternoons. Other on-site wares and services include computerised horoscopes, incense, herbs, tarot cards and essential oils.

Prairie Avenue Bookshop

418 S Wabash Avenue, at E Van Buren Street, The Loop (312 922 8311). CTA Jackson (Red). **Open** 10am-6pm Mon-Fri; 10am-4pm Sat; closed Sun. **Credit** AmEx, Disc, MC, V. **Map** p305 H13.

One of the US's most impressive architectural bookstores, with 15,000 titles on architecture, design, interiors, city planning and graphic design, not to mention sit-around furniture by Frank Lloyd Wright, Mies van der Rohe and Le Corbusier.

Rand McNally

444 N Michigan Avenue, at E Illinois Street, Near North/Magnificent Mile (312 321 1751). CTA Grand. **Open** 9am-8pm Mon-Sat; 11am-6pm Sun. **Credit** AmEx, Disc, MC, V. **Map** p306 J11.

Travellers in need of new maps, atlases, travel accessories, a geography lesson or just some expert advice need only stop at Rand McNally to find it all. **Branch**: 150 S Wacker Drive, at E Adams Street, The Loop (312 332 2009).

Transitions Bookplace

1000 W North Avenue, at N Sheffield Avenue, Lincoln Park (312 951 7323). CTA North/Clybourn. **Open** 8am-10pm Mon-Thur, Sun; 8am-11pm Fri, Sat. **Credit** AmEx, DC, Disc, MC, V.

At 6,000 sq ft (558 sq m), this 'personal growth' bookstore has grown to quite a size. You can browse among books, incense and gifts to the burbling of fountains and the scent of burning candles.

Second-hand & antiquarian

Afterwords New & Used Books

23 E Illinois Street, at N State Street, Near North/Magnificent Mile (312 464 1110). CTA Grand. **Open** 9am-9pm Mon-Thur; 9am-11pm Fri; 10am-11pm Sat; noon-7pm Sun. **Credit** AmEx, MC, V. **Map** p306 H11.

'We'll get any book at any time,' promises the manager of Afterwords, which specialises in ferreting out obscure books and out-of-print tomes. Customers can also access the Internet from store computers and order customised stationery there.

Shops & Services

O'Gara & Wilson Booksellers Ltd

1448 E 57th Street, at S Blackstone Avenue, Hyde Park (773 363 0993). CTA 6 bus. **Open** 9am-10pm Mon-Sat; noon-8pm Sun. **Credit** Disc, MC, V. **Map** p311 Y17.

Humanities 'R' Us: academic books on history, theology, philosophy and more. The antiquarian section offers 16th-century tomes with four-figure prices; sale stock includes paperback mysteries for a buck.

Powells

1501 E 57th Street, at S Harper Avenue, Hyde Park (773 955 7780). CTA 6 bus. **Open** 9am-11pm daily. **Credit** MC, V. **Map** p311 Y17.

Powells processes hundreds of remainders a day. The South Side stores have strong academic sections, particularly in medieval history, philosophy and lit crit, while the North Side branch has a large art and photography selection and a rare book room. **Branches:** 828 S Wabash Avenue, at S 8th Street, South Loop (312 341 0748); 2850 N Lincoln Avenue, at W Diversey Parkway, Lake View (773 248 1444).

Department stores

Barney's New York

25 E Oak Street, at N Rush Street, Gold Coast (312 587 1700). CTA Clark/Division. **Open** 11am-7pm Mon-Sat; noon-6pm Sun. **Credit** AmEx, Disc, MC, V. **Map** p306 H9.

This sleek, urban department store is where no-nonsense professionals and socialites come to shop. Barney's has transferred its NYC sophistication to Chicago lock, stock and barrel: 'tude included.

Bloomingdale's

900 N Michigan Avenue, at E Walton Street, Near North/Magnificent Mile (312 440 4460). CTA Chicago (Red). **Open** 10am-8pm Mon-Sat; noon-7pm Sun. **Credit** AmEx, MC, V. **Map** p309 J9.

This classic harkens from the trendier side of the New York state of mind. On a Mag Mile chock full of haute hot spots and staid tradition, Bloomies is all about fun. A must for the younger shopper.

Carson Pirie Scott

1 S State Street, at E Madison Street, The Loop (312 641 7000). CTA Madison. **Open** 9.45am-7pm Mon-Fri; 9.45am-6pm Sat; 11am-6pm Sun. **Credit** AmEx, Disc, MC, V. **Map** p305 H12.

A conservative mainstay, CPS is known for its practical (and practically priced) goods and its fabulous Louis Sullivan design, particularly the iron embellishments on the north-west door.

JC Penney

Ford City Mall, 7601 S Cicero Avenue, at W 78th Street, South Side (773 581 6600). CTA 54 bus. **Open** 10am-9pm Mon-Fri; 10am-8pm Sat; 11am-6pm Sun. **Credit** AmEx, Disc, MC, V.

This department store is an innocuous bargain-hunter's dream. It has little of the glitz of its Michigan Avenue counterparts, but all the comforts of a suburban shopping experience.

A Chicago staple: Marshall Field's.

Lord & Taylor

Water Tower Place, 835 N Michigan Avenue, at E Chestnut Street, Near North/Magnificent Mile (312 787 7400). CTA Chicago (Red). **Open** 10am-9pm Mon-Thur; 9am-9pm Fri; 10am-8pm Sat; 11am-7pm Sun. **Credit** AmEx, Disc, MC, V. **Map** p306 J9.

One of the more staid of the Mile's upscale shopping experiences, but also a classic one, known for its good sales.

Marshall Field's

111 N State Street, at E Randolph Street, The Loop (312 781 1000). CTA Randolph (Red). **Open** 9.45am-7pm Mon-Wed; 9.45am-8pm Thur; 9.45am-7pm Fri, Sat; 11am-6pm Sun. **Credit** AmEx, Disc, MC, V. **Map** p305 H12.

As Chicago as it gets, Marshall Field's is where the city's sons and daughters have congregated for generations, whether they're lunching under the Christmas tree in the Walnut Room, sampling the famous chocolate Frango mints or buying essentials on one of the store's nine levels. At Field's, you can find anything from stationery to hosiery, fine china to bridal gowns. Adding to the nostalgia factor is architectural grandeur: perhaps most notably, a mosaic-topped, domed atrium. A visit to Chicago without buying a box of Field's Frangos is like going to the Louvre and skipping the *Mona Lisa. See also page 48.*
Branch: Water Tower Place, 835 N Michigan Avenue, at E Chestnut Street, Near North/ Magnificent Mile (312 335 7700).

Time Out Chicago Guide **165**

Montgomery Ward

4620 S Damen Avenue, at W 47th Street, South Side (773 650 1090). CTA Western (Orange). **Open** 10am-9pm Mon-Fri; 10am-7pm Sat; 11am-6pm Sun. **Credit** AmEx, Disc, MC, V.

A utilitarian stalwart, this Chicago-based company's store presses on despite some financial troubles in its recent history. It has a reliable selection of electronics, automotive appliances and housewares. **Branches:** 7601 S Cicero Avenue, at W 78th Street, South Side (773 284 4800); and throughout the city.

Neiman Marcus

737 N Michigan Avenue, at E Chicago Avenue, Near North/Magnificent Mile (312 642 5900). CTA Chicago (Red). **Open** 10am-7pm Mon-Sat; noon-5pm Sun. **Credit** AmEx, DC, MC, V. **Map** p306 J10.

Though very pricey, this speciality store woos shoppers with its airy interior and haute fashions, accessories and food. Designer salons dominate: you'll find a reliable Chanel suit here and also encounter the latest and greatest in fashion.

Saks Fifth Avenue

Chicago Place, 700 N Michigan Avenue, at E Superior Street, Near North/Magnificent Mile (312 944 6500). CTA Chicago (Red). **Open** 10am-7pm Mon-Sat; noon-6pm Sun. **Credit** AmEx, DC, MC, V. **Map** p306 J10.

The upper crust feel at home among Saks' trad offerings. You'll find more classic fashions than wild trends, and a strong children's department. Menswear is now located in a new store across the street.

Sears Roebuck & Co

1601 N Harlem Avenue, at W North Avenue, West Side (773 836 4100/www.sears.com). CTA 72 bus. **Open** 9.30am-9pm Mon-Fri; 9am-8pm Sat; 10am-6pm Sun. **Credit** AmEx, Disc, MC, V.

Sears' advertising campaign, inviting shoppers to 'come see the softer side of Sears', touts its fun fashions and homey housewares. But devotees still come here for the more manly wares, too.

Target

2656 N Elston Avenue, at W Logan Boulevard, West Side (773 252 1994). CTA Western, then 49 bus. **Open** 8am-10pm daily. **Credit** AmEx, Disc, MC, V.

Once merely another discount superstore, Target has jacked up the cool factor on its inexpensive clothes and housewares. Now it's a trendy destination for twentysomething apartment renters and well-heeled homeowners. **Branches:** throughout the suburbs.

Electronics

Bang & Olufsen

15 E Oak Street, at N Rush Street, Gold Coast (312 787 6006). CTA Chicago(Red). **Open** 10am-6pm Mon-Thur; 10am-7pm Fri; 10am-6pm Sat; noon-5pm Sun. **Credit** AmEx, DC, Disc, MC, V. **Map** p306 H9.

Aurally sublime and astronomically priced stereos from the highly regarded Danish maker.

Best Buy

1000 W North Avenue, at N Sheffield Avenue, Lincoln Park (312 988 4067). CTA North/Clybourn. **Open** 10am-9pm Mon-Sat; 11am-6pm Sun. **Credit** AmEx, Disc, MC, V.

This electronics superstore offers a dizzying array of stereos, telephones, TVs, PCs, VCRs and DVDs. **Branches:** throughout the city.

Sony Gallery

663 N Michigan Avenue, at E Erie Street, Near North/Magnificent Mile (312 943 3334). CTA Grand. **Open** 10am-7pm Mon-Fri; 10am-6pm Sat; noon-5pm Sun. **Credit** AmEx, Disc, MC, V. **Map** p306 J10.

Look at and listen to all the latest high-tech electronics, from camcorders to boomboxes, in this stylish two-level salon; just don't expect the teens to let you anywhere near the Playstations. It's worth stopping in, however, to see the cool diorama of Chicago.

United Audio Centers

900 N Michigan Avenue., at E Walton Street, Near North/Magnificent Mile (312 664 3100). CTA Chicago (Red). **Open** 10am-7pm Mon-Thur; 10am-8pm Fri; 10am-6pm Sat; noon-6pm Sun. **Credit** AmEx, Disc, MC, V. **Map** p306 J9.

An audio and video store with a wide selection of brands and prices. **Branch:** Century Mall, 2828 N Clark Street, at W Diversey Parkway, Lake View (773 525 7005).

Fabrics & trimmings

Fishman's Fabrics

1101 S Desplaines Street, at E Roosevelt Street, South Side (312 922 7250). CTA Clinton (Blue). **Open** 9am-5.30pm Mon-Sat; 9.30am-5pm Sun. **Credit** AmEx, Disc, MC, V. **Map** p304 F14.

Three floors of cottons, wools, linens and laces at this long-time Chicago fabric merchant off Roosevelt Road on the near South Side.

Loomcraft

640 N LaSalle Street, at W Erie Street, Near North/River North (312 587 0055). CTA Chicago (Red). **Open** 10am-9pm Mon, Thur; 10am-6pm Tue, Wed, Fri, Sat; closed Sun. **Credit** Disc, MC, V. **Map** p306 H10.

At this River North staple, you pick the fabric, but they make the custom-designed draperies, bedspreads, chair/couch upholstery and the like.

Tender Buttons

946 N Rush Street, at E Oak Street, Gold Coast (312 337 7033). CTA Chicago (Red). **Open** 10am-6pm Mon-Fri; 10am-5.30pm Sat; closed Sun. **Credit** MC, V. **Map** p306 H9.

A tiny museum-like boutique, with hundreds of buttons from antique to modern, plus cufflinks and studs.

Vogue Fabrics

Water Tower Place, 835 N Michigan Avenue, at E Chestnut Street, Near North/Magnificent Mile (312 787 2521). CTA Chicago (Red). **Open** 10am-7pm Mon-Thur; 10am-8pm Fri; 10am-6pm Sat; noon-6pm Sun. **Credit** AmEx, Disc, MC, V. **Map** p306 J9.

A great variety of sewing materials is available at this local chain's location in Water Tower Place. **Branch**: 623 W Roosevelt Road, at S Desplaines Street, West Side (312 829 2505).

Fashion

Children

Active Kids

1967 N Fremont Street, at W Armitage Avenue, Lincoln Park (773 281 2002). CTA Armitage. **Open** 10am-6pm Mon-Sat; noon-5pm Sun. **Credit** AmEx, MC, V. **Map** p308 F6.
Outdoor apparel, shoes and accessories for the little camper. *See page 181* for the grown-up store.

All Our Children

2217 N Halsted Street, at W Webster Avenue (773 327 1868). CTA Armitage. **Open** 10am-6pm Mon-Fri; 10am-5pm Sat; noon-5pm Sun. **Credit** AmEx, Disc, MC, V. **Map** p308 F5.
A Lincoln Park boutique with handsome children's clothing from toddler up to age ten.

Madison & Friends

1003 N Rush Street, at E Oak Street, Gold Coast (312 642 6403). CTA Clark/Division. **Open** 10am-6pm Mon-Wed; 10am-7pm Thur; 10am-6pm Fri, Sat; noon-5pm Sun. **Credit** AmEx, MC, V. **Map** p306 H9.
A hip store with clothes, shoes and a manicure bar where girls can get their nails done. The owners also run a baby store across the street.
Branch: 11 E Oak Street, at N State Street, Gold Coast (312 642 6403).

Oilily

900 N Michigan Avenue, at E Walton Street, Near North/Magnificent Mile (312 642 1166). CTA Chicago (Red). **Open** 10am-7pm Mon-Thur; 10am-8pm Fri; 10am-6pm Sat; noon-6pm Sun. **Credit** AmEx, DC, Disc, MC, V. **Map** p306 J9.
Mod clothes from the Dutch designer for kids and mothers who are definitely not afraid of colour.

Clubwear

The Alley

858 W Belmont Avenue, at N Clark Street, Lake View (773 525 3180). CTA Belmont. **Open** 10am-10pm Mon-Thur; 10am-midnight Fri, Sat; noon-8pm Sun. **Credit** MC, V. **Map** p309 F2.
This alternative emporium in Lake View – look for the hearse parked in the Dunkin' Donuts lot – has everything a young goth or punker needs.

Diesel

923 N Rush Street, at E Walton Street, Gold Coast (312 255 0157). CTA Chicago (Red). **Open** 11am-8pm Mon-Sat; 11am-6pm Sun. **Credit** AmEx, Disc, MC, V. **Map** p306 H9.
Jeans and other body-conscious duds for the fast crowd from the Italian clothing chain.

Flashy Trash

3524 N Halsted Street, at W Addison Street, Lake View/Wrigleyville (773 327 6900). CTA Addison (Red). **Open** 11am-8pm Mon-Sat; noon-6pm Sun. **Credit** AmEx, Disc, MC, V. **Map** p309 F1.
Vintage gear and designer goods are mixed with aplomb at this fun, funky shop. There's plenty to

Flashy Trash.

Consumer

inspire on the tightly packed racks, including bowling shirts, cocktail dresses and kimonos, plus new designs from Storm of London, Verge, Tom of Finland and Diesel.

Untitled/Aero
2707 N Clark Street, at W Schubert Avenue, Lincoln Park (773 404 0650). CTA Diversey. **Open** 11am-8pm Mon-Thur; 11am-8.30pm Fri, Sat; noon-6pm Sun. **Credit** AmEx, Disc, MC, V. **Map** p308 F4.
Two trendy shops owned by the same person, Untitled stocks clothes and shoes for the baggy-panted skater set (both men and women), while Aero aims for older but still trendy guys.

Designer

A stroll down Oak Street offers a roll call of all the biggies in fashion. Many are ensconced in converted townhomes, including Giorgio Armani, Jill Sander and Sonia Rykiel.

Agnès B
46 E Walton Street, at N Rush Street, Gold Coast (312 642 7483). CTA Chicago (Red). **Open** 10am-6pm Mon-Sat; noon-6pm Sun. **Credit** AmEx, MC, V. **Map** p306 H9.
Simple, chic women's basics from the French label.

Betsy Johnson
72 E Oak Street, at N Michigan Avenue, Near North/Magnificent Mile (312 664 5901). CTA Chicago (Red). **Open** 10am-6pm Mon-Sat; noon-5pm Sun. **Credit** AmEx. MC, V. **Map** p306 J9.
Youthful, feminine clothing for skinny minnies.

Blake
2448 N Lincoln Avenue, at W Fullerton Avenue, Lincoln Park (773 477 3364). CTA Fullerton. **Open** 10.30am-7pm Mon-Fri; 10.30am-6.30pm Sat; noon-6pm Sun. **Credit** AmEx, Disc, MC, V. **Map** p308 F5.
A severely minimalist shop in Lincoln Park – is there even a sign? – specialising in hot international designers such as Ann Demeulemeester and Dries Van Noten. It's mostly women's clothing, but there are usually some items for men, too.

Gucci
900 N Michigan Avenue, at E Walton Street, Near North/Magnificent Mile (312 664 5504). CTA Chicago (Red). **Open** 10am-7pm Mon-Thur; 10am-8pm Fri; 10am-6pm Sat; noon-6pm Sun. **Credit** AmEx, DC, MC, V. **Map** p306 J9.
Cutting-edge clothing, shoes and accessories from the high-priced, high-fashion house.

June Blaker
200 W Superior Street, at N Wells Street, Near North/River North (312 751 9220). CTA Chicago (Brown/Purple). **Open** 10am-6pm Mon-Sat; closed Sun. **Credit** AmEx, DC, Disc, MC, V. **Map** p306 G10.
Fashionistas peruse this boutique for the latest from edgy Euro and Japanese designers such as Comme des Garçons and Yohji Yamamoto. There are also selections of jewellery and accessories.

The super-chic **Agnès B**.

Polo Ralph Lauren
750 N Michigan Avenue, at E Chicago Avenue, Near North/Magnificent Mile (312 280 1655). CTA Chicago (Red). **Open** 10am-7pm Mon-Sat; noon-5pm Sun. **Credit** AmEx, Disc, MC, V. **Map** p306 J10.
RL's fantasy manse on Michigan Avenue is the largest Polo shop in the world, and offers men's, women's and children's clothing and housewares.

Prada
30 E Oak Street, at N State Street, Gold Coast (312 951 1113). CTA Chicago (Red). **Open** 10am-6pm Mon-Sat; noon-6pm Sun. **Credit** AmEx, DC, MC, V. **Map** p306 H9.
An understated three-level store offering clothing, shoes and bags from the Italian designer.

Cynthia Rowley
808 W Armitage Avenue, at N Halsted Street, Lincoln Park (773 528 6160). CTA Armitage. **Open** 11am-7pm Mon-Fri; 10am-6pm Sat; noon-5pm Sun. **Credit** AmEx, MC, V. **Map** p308 F6.
A hometown girl made good, Rowley's shop sells her own affordable line of playful women's clothing.

Sulka
55 E Oak Street, at N Rush Street, Near North/Magnificent Mile (312 951 9500). CTA Chicago (Red). **Open** 10am-6pm Mon-Sat; closed Sun. **Credit** AmEx, DC, MC, V. **Map** p306 H9.
The height of luxury from the conservative haberdasher: elegantly tailored men's suits, cashmere sweaters, leather outerwear, silk robes and pyjamas, and custom-made shirts.

Ultimo
114 E Oak Street, at N Michigan Avenue, Near North/Magnificent Mile (312 787 1171). CTA Chicago (Red). **Open** 10am-6pm Mon-Sat; noon-5pm Sun. **Credit** AmEx, DC, Disc, MC, V. **Map** p306 J9.
High fashion ground zero. This rarefied multi-level boutique for men and women has been a trailblazer in Chicago. It can be a thoroughly intimidating experience, unless you smell of money and expect to be pampered.

Dry cleaning

Gibson Couture Cleaners

3432 N Southport Avenue, at W Roscoe Street, Lake View (773 248 0937). CTA Addison (Red). **Open** 7am-7pm Mon-Fri; 7am-5.30pm Sat; closed Sun. **Credit** AmEx, Disc, MC, V. **Map** p309 D2.
Gibson specialises in special care for your special clothes. Get alterations done by the Jamaican tailor upstairs, Tailor Mon.

Erotic & fetish

Cupid's Treasures

3519 N Halsted Street, at W Addison Street, Lake View/Wrigleyville (773 348 3884). CTA Addison (Red). **Open** 11am-midnight Mon-Thur, Sun; 11am-1am Fri, Sat. **Credit** AmEx, DC, Disc, MC, V. **Map** p309 F1.
A dimly lit sex-toy emporium dealing in costumes, props and other helpful devices. Don't miss the in-store dildo boutique.

House of Whacks

3514 N Pulaski Road., at W Cornelia Avenue, Far North (773 725 9132). CTA Addison (Blue). **Open** *by appointment only.* **Credit** AmEx, Disc, MC, V.
The city's premier fashion house for latex clothing is open only by appointment to weed out the gawkers from the aficionados. The 100-plus designs were created by owner Cindy DeMarco.

Leather Sport

3505 N Halsted Street, at W Addison Street, Lake View/Wrigleyville (773 868 0914). CTA Addison (Red). **Open** 11am-midnight daily. **Credit** MC, V. **Map** p309 F1.
The name says it all, really; leather wear for men and women, plus rubber and PVC accessories.

Male Hide Leathers

2816 N Lincoln Avenue, at W Diversey Parkway, Lake View (773 929 0069). CTA Diversey. **Open** noon-8pm Tue-Sat; 1-5pm Sun; closed Mon. **Credit** AmEx, MC, V. **Map** p308 E4.
Leather with a decidedly gay twist, including jackets, pants, boots and more.

Hats

A few women's shops carry hats, including **Krivoy** (1145 W Webster Avenue, at N Clifton Avenue, Lincoln Park; 773 248 1466), **Pentimento** (1629 N Milwaukee Avenue, at W North Avenue, Wicker Park/Bucktown; 773 227 0576) and **Art Effect** (651 W Armitage Avenue, at N Howe Street, Lincoln Park; 312 664 0997). The **Millinery Arts Alliance** displays its wares every Thursday at Brasserie Jo (59 W Hubbard Street, at N Clark Street, Near North/River North (312 595 0800). The hand-made hats are *très cher* (from $100); diners get a free dessert if they show up to dine *au chapeau*.

Clothes, not mints with holes, are sold at **Polo Ralph Lauren**.

Linda Campisano Millinery

900 N Michigan Avenue, at E Walton Street, Near North/Magnificent Mile (312 337 1004). CTA Chicago (Red). **Open** 10am-6pm Mon-Thur, Sat; 10am-8pm Fri; noon-6pm Sun. **Credit** AmEx, Disc, MC, V. **Map** p306 J9.

Located on the sixth floor of the **Bloomingdale's** building, Campisano uses century-old wooden hat blocks to create original hats for both men and women, plus bridal veils and headpieces.

Hats Plus

4706 W Irving Park Road, at N Milwaukee Avenue, Far North (773 286 5577). CTA Irving Park (Blue). **Open** 10am-6pm Mon-Wed, Fri, Sat; 10am-8pm Thur; 11am-5pm Sun. **Credit** AmEx, Disc, MC, V.

It's a big hike to this Far North location, but men who take their headgear seriously will want to make the effort for the city's largest selection of 'fur, felt, wool, straw and more' and an expert staff.

Jewellery & accessories

Coach Store

900 N Michigan Avenue, at E Walton Street, Near North/Magnificent Mile (312 440 1777). CTA Chicago (Red). **Open** 10am-8pm Mon-Fri; 9am-6pm Sat; 10am-6pm Sun. **Credit** AmEx, DC, Disc, MC, V. **Map** p306 J9.

Fine leather goods, including handbags, wallets, briefcases and accessories.

Jeweler's Center

5 S Wabash Avenue, at E Madison Street, The Loop (312 853 2057). CTA Madison. **Open** 8am-6pm Mon-Fri; 8am-5.30pm Sat; closed Sun. **Credit** varies by jeweller. **Map** p305 H12.

Blocks of Wabash Avenue used to be known as Jeweler's Row because of all the jewellery merchants grouped there. There are still more than 150 jewellers concentrated over 13 floors in the Mallers Building, including appraisers, watch dealers and repairers.

Tiffany & Co

730 N Michigan Avenue, at E Superior Street, Near North/Magnificent Mile (312 944 7500). CTA Chicago (Red). **Open** 10am-6pm Mon-Wed, Fri, Sat; 10am-7pm Thur; noon-5pm Sun. **Credit** AmEx, DC, Disc, MC, V. **Map** p306 J10.

Not as grand as the original on Fifth Avenue, but still a magnificent store. If you can't afford any of the sparkling baubles here, think of it as a museum.

Lingerie

Victoria's Secret

Water Tower, 835 N Michigan Avenue, at E Chestnut Street, Near North/Magnificent Mile (312 440 1169). CTA Chicago (Red). **Open** 10am-8pm Mon-Fri; 10am-7pm Sat; noon-6pm Sun. **Credit** AmEx, Disc, MC, V. **Map** p306 J9.

Slinky sex-you-up wear for the masses at this chain's downtown boudoir.

Rings 'n' things at the **Jeweler's Center**.

Local designers

Fitigues

939 N Rush Street, at E Walton Place, Gold Coast (312 943 8676). CTA Chicago (Red). **Open** 10am-6pm Mon-Sat; noon-5pm Sun. **Credit** AmEx, Disc, MC, V. **Map** p306 H9.

Upscale everyday wear from a husband-and-wife team, with an emphasis on comfy custom-made fabrics for women, men and children.
Branches: 2130 N Halsted Street, at W Webster Avenue, Lincoln Park (773 404 9696); *outlet* 1535 N Dayton Street, at W Weed Street, Lincoln Park (312 255 0095).

Hino & Malee

50 E Oak Street, at N Rush Street, Gold Coast (312 664 7475). CTA Chicago (Red). **Open** 10am-6pm Mon-Sat; closed Sun. **Credit** AmEx, Disc, MC, V. **Map** p306 H9.

This highly regarded husband and wife design team offer women's ready-to-wear and couture clothing.

p45

1643 N Damen Avenue, at W North Avenue, Wicker Park/Bucktown (773 862 4523). CTA Damen (Blue). **Open** 11am-7pm Mon-Sat; noon-6pm Sun. **Credit** AmEx, Disc, MC, V. **Map** p310 B7.

This super-hip shop, frequented by model types, is typical of the designer boutiques that have sprung up in Wicker Park of late. The young proprietress-es of the industrial-chic space have got exclusives on both local and New York up-and-comers.

Shoes

The new branch of **Nordstrom's**, famed for its women's shoes, is located off Michigan Avenue. If you've got cash to burn, boutiques such as **Donald J Pliner** (106 E Oak St, at N Rush Street, Gold Coast; 312 202 9600) and **Salvatore Ferragamo** (645 N Michigan Avenue, at E Erie Street, Near North/ Magnificent Mile; 312 397 0464) can dress up your tootsies a treat.

Alternatives

942 N Rush Street, at E Walton Place, Gold Coast (312 266 1545). CTA Chicago (Red). **Open** 11am-7pm Mon-Fri; 10am-7pm Sat; noon-5pm Sun. **Credit** AmEx, MC, V. **Map** p306 H9.
Urban designer footwear for guys and gals.
Branch: 1969 N Halsted Street, at W Armitage Avenue, Lincoln Park (773 943 1591)

Harry's Gold Coast Shoe Repair

1 W Chestnut Street, at N State Street, Gold Coast (312 337 3742). CTA Chicago (Red). **Open** 8am-6.30pm Mon-Fri, 8am-5pm Sat; closed Sun. **Credit** AmEx. **Map** p306 H9.
Centrally located, super-speedy shoe repairs.

John Fleuvog

1539-41 N Milwaukee Avenue, at N Damen Avenue, Wicker Park (773 772 1983). CTA Damen (Blue). **Open** 11am-7pm Mon-Sat; noon-5pm Sun. **Credit** AmEx, Disc, MC, V. **Map** p310 C7.
Chicago outpost for trendy Canadian urban cobbler.

Kenneth Cole

540 N Michigan Avenue, at E Grand Avenue, Near North/Magnificent Mile (312 644 1163). CTA Grand. **Open** 10am-8pm Mon-Sat; noon-6pm Sun. **Credit** AmEx, MC, V. **Map** p306 J10.
Sophisticated shoes for your urban uniform.

Walk on by **Harry's Gold Coast Shoe Repair** if your peds are ailing.

G'Bani

949 N State Street, at E Walton Place, Gold Coast (312 440 1718). CTA Chicago (Red). **Open** 10am-7pm Mon-Sat; noon-5pm Sun. **Credit** AmEx, DC, Disc, MC, V. **Map** p306 H9.
Fashion-forward Gold Coast boutique with stylish selections for women and men.

Lori's Discount Designer Shoes

824 W Armitage Avenue, at N Dayton Street, Lincoln Park (773 281 5655). CTA Armitage. **Open** 11am-7pm Mon-Thur; 11am-6pm Fri; 10am-6pm Sat; noon-5pm Sun. **Credit** AmEx, Disc, MC, V. **Map** p308 F6.
A fave of shoe-crazed Chicago women, this institution has one of the largest selections of American and European designer shoes in the city at 10-30% below department store prices.

Sole Junkies

3176 N Clark Street, at W Belmont Avenue, Lake View/Wrigleyville (773 348 8935). CTA Belmont. **Open** 11am-8pm Mon-Sat; noon-6pm Sun. **Credit** AmEx, Disc, MC, V. **Map** p309 F3.
Pushing new frontiers in footwear, this groovy shoe shop has all the biggest and most outlandish platforms and other shoes for making the scene, plus casual sneakers and chunky street shoes.

Speciality

Alcala's Western Wear

1733 W Chicago Avenue, at N Ashland Avenue, West Side (312 226 0152). CTA 66 bus. **Open** 10am-8pm Mon, Thur, Fri; 10am-7pm Tue, Wed, Sat; 10am-5pm Sun. **Credit** AmEx, DC, Disc, MC, V.
Let's rodeo! Jeans, hats and 10,000 pairs of cowboy boots are corraled at this store.

Rochester Big & Tall Men's Clothing

840 N Michigan Avenue, at E Chestnut Street, Near North/Magnificent Mile (312 337 8877). CTA Chicago (Red). **Open** 9.30am-6.30pm Mon-Wed, Fri; 9.30am-6pm Sat; noon-5pm Sun. **Credit** AmEx, DC, Disc, MC, V. **Map** p306 J9.
A range of clothing, from fine tailored to sportswear and shoes, in sizes that range from large to mammoth.

Translucere

2147 W Belmont Avenue, at N Hoyne Avenue, Far North West (773 477 6006). CTA Paulina. **Open** noon-7pm Tue-Sat; closed Mon, Sun. **Credit** AmEx, Disc, MC, V.
The one-stop shop for men who like to dress in women's clothing (and 'Rubenesque women', as it advertises) offers big sizes, high heels, breast forms, corsets, wigs, make-up and more.

Vintage & second-hand

Lake View is fertile ground for thrift shopping. To begin, walk west from the Belmont El station and explore the two-level shop at 812 W

Mall talk

Downtown, the main shopping malls are on the Magnificent Mile: **900 N Michigan**, (picturd)**Chicago Place** and the huge **Water Tower Place** all have a range decent stores. However, if you're feeling adventurous – and have some credit card bills to accumulate – there are plenty of malls out of town, among them **Northbrook Court**, **Woodfield Mall** and **Oakbrook Center**, the latter perhaps the most impressive of the lot. However, be warned: all the out-of-town malls are best reached by car.

900 N Michigan Avenue

900 N Michigan Avenue, at E Walton Street, Near North/ Magnificent Mile (312 915 3916). CTA Chicago (Red). **Open** 10am-7pm Mon-Thur; 10am-8pm Fri; 10am-6pm Sat; 12am-6pm Sun. Map p306 J9.

Century Shopping Center

2828 N Clark Street, at W Diversey Parkway, Lake View (773 929 8100). CTA Diversey. **Open** 10.30am-9pm Mon-Fri; 10.30am-6pm Sat; noon-6pm Sun. Map p308 F4.

Chicago Place

700 N Michigan Avenue, at E Superior Street, Near North/Magnificent Mile (312 642 4811). CTA Chicago (Red). **Open** 10am-7pm Mon-Fri; 10am-6pm Sat; noon-5pm Sun. Map p306 J10.

Gurnee Mills

6170 W Grand Avenue, Off I-94/I-294 (exit at Route 132 W/Grand Avenue), Gurnee (847 263 7500). **Open** 10am-9pm Mon-Sat; 11am-6pm Sun.

Northbrook Court

2171 Northbrook Court, Off Route 41 (via I-94), Northbrook (847 498 1770). **Open** 10am-9pm Mon-Fri; 10am-7pm Sat; 11am-6pm Sun.

Oakbrook Center

Off I-88 (Cermax Road exit), Oak Brook (630 573 0700). **Open** 10am-9pm Mon-Sat; 11am-6pm Sun.

Water Tower Place

835 N Michigan Avenue, at E Chestnut Street, Near North/Magnificent Mile (312 440 3166). CTA Chicago (Red). **Open** 10am-7pm Mon-Thur; 10am-8pm Fri; 10am-6pm Sat; noon-6pm Sun. Map p306 J9.

Woodfield Mall

Off Route 53 S (Woodfield Road exit), via I-90, Schaumburg (847 330 1537). **Open** 10am-9pm Mon-Sat; 11am-6pm Sun.

Belmont Avenue, at N Halsted Street, Lake View: **Hollywood Mirror** (773 665 8790) on the ground level, **Ragstock** (773 868 9263) upstairs, with an entrance on the alley.

Beatnix

3400 N Halsted Street, at W Roscoe Street, Lake View (773 281 6933). CTA Belmont. **Open** 11am-10pm Mon-Thur; 11am-midnight Fri, Sat; noon-9pm Sun. **Credit** MC, V. **Map** p309 F2.
This colourful, multi-room shop has the outfits and accessories, both new and used, to keep club kids, drag queens and muscle boys looking their best.

Brown Elephant Resale Store

3651 N Halsted Street, at W Addison Street, Lake View/Wrigleyville (773 549 5943). CTA Addison *(Red).* **Open** 11am-6pm daily. **Credit** AmEx, MC, V. **Map** p309 F1.
One of the biggest resale shops in the city, the Brown Elephant directs all its profits to the **Howard Brown Health Center** (*see p282*). The huge space offers tons of clothing (it's often high quality, thanks to the well-heeled gay men who donate their garb), plus furniture, books, kitchenware and other bric-a-brac. **Branch**: 3939 N Ashland Avenue, at W Byron Street, Lake View (773 244 2930).

Daisy Shop

67 E Oak Street, at N Michigan Avenue, Near North/Magnificent Mile (312 943 8880/ www.daisyshop.com). CTA Chicago (Red). **Open** 11am-6pm Mon-Sat; noon-5pm Sun. **Credit** AmEx, Disc, MC, V. **Map** p306 J9.
A discreet location on the sixth floor offers cover to rich Gold Coast doyennes who don't want their neighbours to know they shop for used… sorry, 'gently worn' clothing. One of several resales shop for women's couture, it offers swanky cast-offs at 50-80% off the regular outrageous prices.

Strange Cargo

3448 N Clark Street, at N Sheffield Avenue, Lake View/Wrigleyville (773 327 8090). CTA Addison *(Red).* **Open** 11.30am-6.45pm Mon-Sat; 11.30am-5pm Sun. **Credit** MC, V. **Map** p309 E2.
A fun, prototypical thrift shop, with dresses, jeans, shirts, hats, coats, shoes and assorted kitschy toys.

US#1 Vintage Clothing & Denim

1509 N Milwaukee Avenue, at N Damen Avenue, Wicker Park (773 489 9428). CTA Damen (Blue). **Open** 11am-7pm daily. **Credit** AmEx, MC, V.
Racks of recycled jeans and jackets in suede, leather, denim and faux fur.

Flower Bucket Shop

158 W Washington Boulevard, at N LaSalle Street, The Loop (312 346 9773). CTA Washington. **Open** 8am-5pm Mon-Fri; closed Sat, Sun. **Credit** AmEx, Disc, MC, V. **Map** p305 H12.

The Flower Bucket offers all its blooms at wholesale prices and has made its reputation on incredibly low-priced roses: a dozen red ones, cash and carry, can be had for a mere $9.99.

Branches: 1100 W Belmont Avenue, at N Southport Avenue, Lake View (773 935 9773); 1164 N LaSalle Street, at W Division Street, Gold Coast (312 943 9773); 1375 E 53rd Street, at S Dorchester Avenue, Hyde Park (773 955 5700).

Green Inc

1718 N Wells Street, at W St Paul Avenue, Old Town (312 266 2806). CTA Sedgwick. **Open** 9am-7pm Mon-Sat; 11am-6pm Sun. **Credit** MC, V. **Map** p307 H7.

This Old Town oasis doesn't just sell orchids, tropical plants and other flowering fronds: it's also a source for antique Chinese porcelain and ethnographic art from Africa, Southeast Asia and South America.

Urban Gardener

1006 W Armitage Avenue, at N Sheffield Avenue, Lincoln Park (773 477 2070). CTA Armitage. **Open** 10am-7pm Mon-Fri; 10am-8pm Sat; 11am-5pm Sun. **Credit** AmEx, Disc, MC, V. **Map** p308 E6.

Garden Design magazine selected this dazzling store as one of the ten best shops in America. It specialises in outdoor furniture, plant containers and other unique garden decorations.

Wisteria

3715 N Southport Avenue, at W Grace Street, Lake View/Wrigleyville (773 880 5868). CTA Southport. **Open** 4-9pm Thur, Fri; noon-9pm Sat; noon-5pm Sun; closed Mon-Wed. **Credit** MC, V. **Map** p309 D1.

Rather like stepping into your eccentric aunt's walk-in closet, this vintage salon has wonderful heirlooms and period clothing for men and women (mostly '40s and '50s), plus an assortment of old suitcases, vintage ashtrays and kitchenware.

Florists & garden suppliers

Fertile Delta

2764 N Lincoln Avenue, at W Diversey Parkway, Lincoln Park (1-877 533 7845/773 929 0333). CTA Diversey. **Open** 9am-6pm Mon-Sat; closed Sun. **Credit** AmEx, Disc, MC, V. **Map** p308 E4.

This mammoth store up in Lincoln Park – there's a florist and separate garden centre, both of which draw green-fingered locals with equal enthusiasm – will track down whatever rarefied bloom you request. In winter, it's a favourite haunt for fresh Christmas trees; in spring, gardeners flock here for primo plantables.

Food & drink

Bread, cakes & pastries

Lutz Continental Café & Pastry Shop

2458 W Montrose Avenue, at N Western Avenue, Far North (773 478 7785). CTA Montrose (Brown). **Open** *shop* 7am-8pm Tue-Thur, Sun; 7am-10pm. Fri, Sat; closed Mon; *café* 11am-8pm Tue-Thur, Sun; 11am-10pm Fri, Sat; closed Mon. **Credit** MC, V.

A sophisticated 52-year-old patisserie, Lutz is most famous for its German delicacies such as Black Forest gateau, strawberry whipped cream and marzipan. If you feel like something stronger, there are also a number of rum- and liqueur-soaked cakes.

Swedish Bakery

5348 N Clark Street, at W Summerdale Avenue, Far North (773 561 8919). CTA Berwyn. **Open** 6.30am-6.30pm Mon-Thur; 6.30am-8pm Fri; 6.30am-5pm Sat; closed Sun. **Credit** AmEx, DC, Disc, MC, V.

This 70-year-old Andersonville classic is massive and incredibly popular. You'll always have to fight a throng to get to the bakery's tantalising array of cookies, breads and pastries, which is why there's always free coffee on tap while you wait.

Consumer

Coffee & tea

Intelligentsia

3123 N Broadway, at W Barry Avenue, Lake View (773 348 8058). CTA Belmont. **Open** 6am-10pm Mon-Thur; 6am-11pm Fri; 7am-11pm Sat; 7am-10pm Sun. **Credit** AmEx, Disc, MC, V. **Map** p309 F3.

With its fireplace and communal tables, Intelligentsia is a nice antidote to Broadway's chain coffeehouses. It serves its own blend of beans and an array of teas. **Branches**: throughout the city.

Ten Ren Tea & Ginseng Company of Chicago

2247 S Wentworth Avenue, at W 22nd Street, South Side (312 842 1171). CTA Cermak-Chinatown. **Open** 9.30am-7pm daily. **Credit** AmEx, MC, V.

This Chinatown find sells Asian teas, from Jasmine to Chinese black and green teas to a rare Mountain Green Oolong Tea, which sells for $127.40/lb. Ginseng is also available, in its myriad forms.

Confectionery

Blommer's Chocolate Factory

600 W Kinzie Street, at N Desplaines Street, West Side (312 492 1336). CTA Grand. **Open** 9am-5pm Mon-Fri; closed Sat, Sun. **Credit** DC, Disc, MC, V. **Map** p306 F11.

The factory provides cocoa powder, chocolate and cocoa butter to candy manufacturers, whose wares it then sells in its store. Check out the World's Largest Chocolate Bar, which weighs in at ten pounds (4.5 kg).

FAO Schweetz

Water Tower Place, 835 N Michigan Avenue, at E Chestnut Street, Near North/Magnificent Mile (312 787 3773). CTA Chicago (Red). **Open** 11am-8pm Mon-Fri; 10am-8pm Sat; 11am-7pm Sun. **Credit** AmEx, DC, MC, V. **Map** p306 J9.

A sweet-centred spin-off from FAO Schwarz, this garish store boasts a bevy of succulent and super-sweet candy selections.

Garrett's Popcorn Shop

670 N Michigan Avenue, at W Erie Street, Near North/Magnificent Mile (312 944 2630). CTA Grand. **Open** 9.30am-9pm Mon-Sat; closed Sun. **Credit** AmEx, DC, Disc, MC, V. **Map** p306 J9.

At almost any time of the day, customers craving Garrett's cult caramel corn form a line outside its small storefronts, lured by the sugary aroma that wafts down the block.

Branches: 2 W Jackson Boulevard, at N State Street, The Loop (312 360 1108); 26 E Randolph Street, at N State Street, The Loop (312 630 0127); 18 E Adams Street, at N State Street, The Loop (312 263 8234).

Superior Nut & Candy

4038 N Nashville Avenue, at W Irving Park Road, Far North (773 282 3930). CTA Irving Park/ 81 bus. **Open** 9am-5pm Mon-Sat; closed Sun. **Credit** MC. V.

I want candy! **FAO Schweetz**.

Superior roasts its nuts in a nearby factory, making the offerings as fresh as can be. Keep an eye out for their weekly sales.

Fruit & vegetables

Stanley's Fruits & Vegetables

1558 N Elston Avenue, at W North Avenue, West Side (773 276 8050). CTA North/Clybourn. **Open** *Oct-Mar* 6am-9pm Mon-Sat; 6am-8pm Sun; *Apr-Sept* 6am-10pm Mon-Sat; 6am-9pm Sun. **Credit** MC, V.

Home chefs are devoted to the high-quality and inexpensive produce at Stanley's, which is worth the extra stop on your shopping jaunt.

Health food

Sherwyn's Health Food Stores

645 W Diversey Parkway, at N Clark Street, Lincoln Park (773 477 1934). CTA Diversey. **Open** 9am-8pm Mon-Fri; 9am-7pm Sat; 11am-7pm Sun. **Credit** Disc, MC, V. **Map** p308 F4.

An earthy health-food store with a mind-boggling array of vitamins and herbs, Sherwyn's also carries a range of cruelty-free cosmetics, juicers and other appliances, as well as imports such as Earth and Sky Italian pastas.

Meat & fish

Burhops

Father & Son Plaza, 609 W North Avenue, at N Larrabee Street, Old Town (312 642 8600). CTA Sedgwick. **Open** 9.30am-6.30pm Mon-Fri; 10am-6pm Sat; 10am-5pm Sun. **Credit** MC, V. **Map** p307 F7.

The vendors at Burhops know that buying fish can be a dicey business, so they walk nervous customers through the process, helping them select the right cuts and even offering preparation suggestions.

Old Towne Butcher Shop

*1547 N Wells Street, at W North Avenue, Old Town
(312 640 0256). CTA Sedgwick.* **Open** 11am-7pm
Tue-Fri; 10am-6pm Sat; 11am-5pm Sun; closed Mon.
Credit AmEx, DC, Disc, MC, V. **Map** p307 H7.
For the busy professionals of the Old Town neighbourhood, this butcher is invaluable, offering plain,
prime cuts of meat as well as pre-prepared goodies
such as veggie patties, meat loaves, marinated
steaks, shish-kebabs and four varieties of home-
made Italian sausage.

Specialist food shops

Conte-di-Savoia
European Specialties

*1438 W Taylor Street, at N Ashland Avenue, West
Side (312 666 3471). CTA Polk.* **Open** 9am-6pm
Mon-Sat; 9am-4pm Sun. **Credit** AmEx, Disc, MC, V.
Foodies go out of their way for Conte-di-Savoia's
Italian luxuries, from rare olive oils to spicy cuts of
meat to rich cheeses. Don't leave without sampling
the store's home-made pasta toppers, particularly
the creamy, tomato-based Romano sauce.

Supermarkets

Dominick's Finer Foods

*1340 S Canal Street, at W Maxwell Street, West Side
(312 850 3915). CTA Clinton (Blue).* **Open** 24hrs
daily. **Credit** AmEx, Disc, MC, V. **Map** p304 G15.
A Chicago favourite, Dominick's prides itself on its
freshness. Some locations, such as the one near the
Fullerton El stop, pair a posh deli with a serviceable
supermarket. Not all branches are open 24 hours.
Branches: throughout the city.

Jewel Food Stores

*1210 N Clark Street, at W Division Street, Gold
Coast (312 944 6950). CTA Clark/Division.* **Open**
24hrs Mon-Sat; closed midnight Sun-6am Mon.
Credit AmEx, DC, Disc, MC, V. **Map** p307 H8.
Almost as ubiquitous as Starbucks, Jewel is a pleas-
ant, sprawling workhorse of a supermarket.
Branches: throughout the city.

Treasure Island

*75 W Elm Street, at N Clark Street, Gold Coast (312
440 1144). CTA Clark/Division.* **Open** 7am-10pm
Mon-Fri; 7am-8pm Sat; 8am-8pm Sun. **Credit** Disc,
MC, V. **Map** p307 H8.
Billed as a European supermarket, Treasure Island
sells exotic foodstuffs and dainties next to your
run-of-the-mill laundry detergent and potato chips.
It's *the* destination for those hard-to-find, unusual
cooking ingredients.
Branches: five branches in downtown Chicago.

Whole Foods Market

*3300 N Ashland Avenue, at W Henderson Street,
Lake View (773 244 4200). CTA Paulina.* **Open**
8am-10pm daily. **Credit** AmEx, Disc, MC, V.
Map p309 D2.

Wildly popular and sometimes wildly expensive,
this crunchy mart specialises in organic produce,
bulk seeds, nuts and grains, as well as fun items like
honey on tap, vegetarian sushi and home-made
salad dressings.
Branch: 1000 W North Avenue, at N Sheffield
Avenue, Lincoln Park (312 587 0648).

Wine, beer & spirits

Bin 36

*339 N Dearborn Street, at W Kinzie Street, Near
North/River North (312 755 9463). CTA Grand.*
Open 6.30am-10pm Mon-Thur, Sun; 6.30am-11pm
Fri, Sat. **Credit** AmEx, DC, Disc, MC, V.
Map p306 H11.
This wine store aims to teach the novice the fine art
of wine purchasing. A three-tiered operation, Bin 36
has a tavern, which offers 50 wines by the glass and
the half-glass, an upscale eaterie in the cellar, and a
wine shop where wine tastings and demonstrations
are held.

Casey's

*1444 W Chicago Avenue, at N Bishop Street, West
Side (1-800 213 2337). CTA 66 bus.* **Open** 11am-
9pm Mon-Thur; 11am-10pm Fri, Sat; 12.30-8.30pm
Sun. **Credit** AmEx, DC, Disc, MC, V.
Though Casey's has a fine wine and liquor selection,
it's known for its beers: over 400 different varieties,
ranging from fruity Belgian imports to quirky
Illinois microbrews. The staff will help the stymied
sort through the selection.

House of Glunz

*1206 N Wells Street, at W Division Street, Gold
Coast (312 642 3000). CTA Clark/Division.* **Open**
10am-7pm Mon-Sat; closed Sun. **Credit** AmEx, MC,
V. **Map** p307 H8.
The city's oldest wine shop harbours some of the
world's oldest wines: its 25,000-bottle collection
includes several that date back to the early 1800s.

Furniture & home accessories

Container Store

*908 W North Avenue, at N Clybourn Avenue,
Lincoln Park (312 654 8450). CTA North/Clybourn.*
Open 9am-9pm Mon-Sat; 11am-6pm Sun.
Credit AmEx, Disc, MC, V. **Map** p307 F7.
Stylish neatniks quickly become addicted to the
groovy Container Store, and because the attractive
catch-alls and organisers are a cut above throwaway
plastic bins, the CS habit can prove to be quite a
pricey one.

Crate & Barrel

*850 W North Avenue, at N Clybourn Avenue,
Lincoln Park (312 573 9800). CTA North/Clybourn.*
Open 10am-9pm Mon-Fri; 10am-7pm Sat; 11am-6pm
Sun. **Credit** AmEx, Disc, MC, V. **Map** p307 F7.

Consumer

Chicago to go

Accent Chicago

875 N Michigan Avenue, at E Delaware Place, Near North/Magnificent Mile (312 654 8125). CTA Chicago (Red). **Open** 9am-11.30pm daily. **Credit** AmEx, Disc, MC, V. **Map** p306 J9.

A basic souvenir shop that fits the bill when you need to prove you were here: T-shirts, sweatshirts, toys, photographs, mugs and sports team memorabilia.

Branches: Chicago Hilton & Towers, 720 S Michigan Avenue, at E Balbo Drive, South Loop (312 360 0115); Sears Tower, 233 S Wacker Drive, at W Jackson Boulevard, The Loop (312 993 0499).

Art Institute of Chicago Museum Shop

111 S Michigan Avenue, at W Adams Street, The Loop (312 443 3583). CTA Adams or Jackson (Red). **Open** 10.30am-4.30pm Mon, Wed-Fri; 10.30am-7.30pm Tue; 10am-5pm Sat, Sun. **Credit** AmEx, Disc, MC, V. **Map** p305 J12.

It always requires a little discipline to avoid sneaking into this enormous gift shop before a proper visit to the galleries. There's a vast library of art books, racks of postcards, stationery, jewellery, and assorted gift items adapted from the Art Institute's collection.

Branch: Fifth floor, Bloomingdale's Building, 900 N Michigan Avenue, at E Walton Street, Near North/Magnificent Mile (312 482 8275).

Chicago Architecture Foundation Shop & Tour Center

224 S Michigan Avenue, at E Jackson Boulevard, The Loop (312 922 3432). CTA Adams. **Open** 9am-7pm Mon-Sat; 9.30am-6pm Sun. **Credit** AmEx, Disc, MC, V. **Map** p305 J12.

A shop with a fine selection of architectural books and other printed matter, jewellery, toys and art objects inspired by Frank Lloyd Wright (Prairie-style shower curtains, anyone?) and other architectural masters. *See also p53.*

Sleek yet affordable, hip yet comfy, C&B is the blond-wood-and-chrome answer to your decorating needs. This mammoth store – just check out the looming, white architectural wonder that is its Lincoln Park location – is great for dishes, cooking utensils and glasses.

A low-priced spin-off, **CB2**, opened on Lincoln Avenue in early 2000, selling everything from trendy travel alarm clocks to neon-coloured power strips and super-hip brooms.

Branch: 646 N Michigan Avenue, between E Ontario & E Erie Streets, Near North/Magnificent Mile (312 787 5900); **CB2** 3757 N Lincoln Avenue, at W Grace Street, Far North (773 755 3900).

Elizabeth Marie

3453 N Southport Avenue, at W Cornelia Avenue, Lake View (773 525 4100). CTA Southport. **Open** 10.30am-6pm Tue-Sat; closed Mon, Sun. **Credit** MC, V. **Map** p309 D2.

This children's store features the most cunning new and antique children's furniture in town, as well as a room devoted to custom linens. Though the selection at Elizabeth Marie is small, the cuteness factor is mammoth.

Green Acres

1464 N Milwaukee Avenue, at N Wolcott Avenue, Wicker Park/Bucktown (773 292 1998). CTA Division. **Open** noon-6pm Wed-Fri; 11am-5pm Sat, Sun; closed Mon, Tue. **Credit** AmEx, Disc, MC, V. **Map** p310 C8.

Green Acres stocks its shelves by scavenging the heartland's old houses. These out-of-the-attic wares are very now and very eclectic, from old pie safes to an elephant-leg pool table.

Mig & Tig

549 N Wells Street, at W Ohio Street, Near North/River North (312 644 8277). CTA Merchandise Mart. **Open** 10am-7pm Mon-Sat; closed Sun. **Credit** AmEx, MC, V. **Map** p306 H10.

Homeowners addicted to the redo are devoted to Mig & Tig. The designers will help you furnish a room with their famous cutting-edge wares.

Pottery Barn

734 N Michigan Avenue, at E Superior Street, Near North/Magnificent Mile (312 587 9602). CTA Chicago (Red). **Open** 10am-7pm Mon-Sat; 11am-6pm Sun. **Credit** AmEx, Disc, MC, V. **Map** p306 J10.

All jewel tones and warm ochres, this high-end furniture and housewares store is all about cosy, posh goods to curl up with on a cold day. Browsing the store on the Magnificent Mile is a sumptuous experience in itself.

Branch: 865 W North Avenue, at N Clybourn Avenue, Lincoln Park (312 587 9837).

Restoration Hardware

938 W North Avenue, at N Sheffield Avenue, Lincoln Park (312 475 9116). CTA North/Clybourn. **Open** 10am-9pm Mon-Fri; 10am-7pm Sat; 11am-6pm Sun. **Credit** AmEx, MC, V.

Branch: John Hancock Center, 875 N Michigan Avenue, at E Delaware Place, Near North/ Magnificent Mile (312 751 1380).

City of Chicago Store

163 E Pearson Street, at N Michigan Avenue, Near North/Magnificent Mile (312 742 8811). CTA Chicago (Red). **Open** 10am-5pm daily. **Credit** AmEx, MC, V. **Map** p306 J9.
Want to take a piece of Chicago back home with you? Out-of-service Chicago street signs and parking meters are among the city's cast-offs sold at this unique gift shop. More conventional souvenirs include ceramics, books, posters, T-shirts and CDs.

NBC Tower Gift Shop

454 N Columbus Drive, at E Illinois Street, Near North/Streeterville (312 832 0484). CTA Grand. **Open** 9.30am-6pm Mon-Fri; closed Sat, Sun. **Credit** AmEx, DC, Disc, MC, V. **Map** p306 J11.
The place to go when you *simply* must have that Jerry Springer T-shirt. There are also

coffee mugs and the like from *Friends* and other NBC shows.

Sports World

3555 N Clark Street, at W Addison Street, Wrigleyville (773 472 7701). CTA Addison (Red). **Open** 9am-6pm daily; later on Cubs night games. **Credit** AmEx, DC, Disc, MC, V. **Map** p309 E1.
This baseball paradise does most of its trade on the 81 days of the year that the Cubs play: it's located right by Wrigley Field. Come here for shirts, caps, sweats and other goodies.

Symphony Store

220 S Michigan Avenue, at E Adams Street, The Loop (312 294 3345). CTA Adams. **Open** 9.30am-6.30pm Mon-Sat; 11am-6pm Sun; later on concert nights. **Credit** AmEx, DC, Disc, MC, V. **Map** p305 J12.
Impress the folks back home with some high-culture souvenirs from the world-renowned Chicago Symphony Orchestra, including a full range of recordings, posters, books and gifts.

The masterminds behind this nostalgic hardware chain have dug up classic thermoses, old doorknobs, even erasers from your fondest childhood memories. Now, these once-homely items cost an arm and a leg. But memories are priceless. Aren't they?

Shabby Chic

46 E Superior Street, at N Rush Street, Near North/ Magnificent Mile (312 649 0080). CTA Chicago (Red). **Open** 10am-6pm Mon-Sat; noon-5pm Sun. **Credit** AmEx, DC, MC, V. **Map** p306 J10.
The idea is casual elegance, the furniture is custom-made and every item is machine-washable.

Gifts

For Chicago-themed souvenirs, *see above* **Chicago to go**.

Elements

102 E Oak Street, at N Michigan Avenue, Near North/Michigan Avenue (312 642 6574). CTA Chicago (Red). **Open** 10am-6pm Mon-Sat; noon-5pm Sun. **Credit** AmEx, MC, V. **Map** p306 J9.
This upscale gift and home design store has a fine selection of one-of-a-kind artisan-made jewellery.

Gallery 37 Store

66 E Randolph Street, at N Wabash Avenue, The Loop (312 744 7274). CTA Randolph. **Open** 10am-6pm Mon-Sat; closed Sun. **Credit** AmEx, Disc, MC, V. **Map** p305 H12.

This gift shop displays one-of-a-kind paintings, sculptures, ceramics and other art objects created by young apprentice artists. All the proceeds of this city-run programme go to non-profit organisations.

Museum of Contemporary Art Store

220 E Chicago Avenue, at N Mies van der Rohe Way, Near North/Streeterville (312 397 4000). CTA Chicago (Red). **Open** 10am-8pm Tue; 10am-6pm Wed-Sun; closed Mon. **Credit** AmEx, DC, Disc, MC, V. **Map** p306 J9.
The MCA's store sells books, high-design home furnishings and jewellery in the same spirit as the forward-looking art in its galleries.

Paper Boy

1351 W Belmont Avenue, at N Southport Avenue, Lake View (773 388 8811). CTA Southport. **Open** noon-7pm Tue-Fri; 11am-7pm Sat; 11am-5pm Sun; closed Mon. **Credit** MC, V. **Map** p309 D3
Hallmark? Schmallmark. This creative shop has one of the best selections of cards in the city, plus stationery, wedding invites and other funky impulse items. Be sure to skip across the street to see the owner's twisted toy store, **Uncle Fun** (*see p193*).

Poster Plus

200 S Michigan Avenue, at E Adams Street, The Loop (312 461 9277). CTA Adams. **Open** 10am-6pm Mon, Wed, Fri; 10am-8pm Tue, Thur; 9.30am-6pm Sat; 11am-6pm Sun. **Credit** AmEx, Disc, MC, V. **Map** p305 J12.

Consumer

Across from the Art Institute, this poster shop displays a beautiful collection of vintage and reproduction artwork, plus Chicago-themed posters from the '20s and '30s. There a framing service on site.

Health & beauty

Beauty products

Auroma

1007 W Webster Avenue, at N Sheffield Avenue, Lincoln Park (773 248 1173). CTA Armitage. **Open** 10am-7pm Mon-Fri; 10am-6pm Sat; 11am-5pm Sun. **Credit** Disc, MC, V. **Map** p308 E5.
A feast for the nose: this Australian-based beauty company sells scented everything, from therapeutic oils to shampoos, conditioners and facial products.

Aveda

John Hancock Center, 875 N Michigan Avenue, at E Delaware Place, Near North/Streeterville (312 664 0417). CTA Chicago (Red). **Open** 10am-7pm Mon-Sat; 11am-6pm Sun. **Credit** AmEx, MC, V. **Map** p306 J9.
Lotions, potions and 'purefumes', including such unusual items as the mugwort-infused Tourmaline-Charged Hydrating Cream, which creates a protective electrical field around your face.

Bath & Body Works

Water Tower Place, 835 N Michigan Avenue, at E Chestnut Street, Near North/Magnificent Mile (312 751 1880). CTA Chicago (Red). **Open** 10am-7pm Mon-Thur; 10am-8pm Fri; 10am-7pm Sat; noon-6pm Sun. **Credit** AmEx, DC, Disc, MC, V. **Map** p306 J9.
This affordable source of fruity and flowery products is changing its image and going all sleek and urban. Its body smoothers and air fresheners, though, will remain just as yummy.
Branches: Citicorp Building, 500 W Madison Street, at S Canal Street, the Loop (312 466 8837); 29 S Wabash Avenue, at E Madison Street, The Loop (312 263 6780).

Les Perfums Shoppe Century

Century Mall, 2828 N Clark Street, at W Diversey Parkway, Lincoln Park (773 525 9077). CTA Diversey. **Open** 10.30am-9pm Mon-Fri; 10.30am-6pm Sat; noon-6pm Sun. **Credit** AmEx, Disc, MC, V. **Map** p308 F4.
Looking for your grandmother's long-lost scent? Try Les Perfums, which imports hard-to-find perfumes from secret sources in Paris. Among their wares are obscure scents from Dior and Laura Biagiotti.

Ulta 3 Cosmetics

3015 N Clark Street, at W Wellington Avenue, Lake View (773 348 7315). CTA Belmont. **Open** 10am-9pm Mon-Fri; 10am-7pm Sat; 11am-6pm Sun. **Credit** AmEx, Disc, MC, V. **Map** p309 F3.
This cosmetics superstore can keep a girl happy for hours with perfumes, aisles and aisles of make-up, tons of hair products and accessories and any other beautifiers you could imagine.

Branch: 1000 W North Avenue, at N Sheffield Avenue, Lincoln Park (312 664 0230).

Beauty services

Kiva

196 E Pearson Street, at N Mies van der Rohe Way, Near North/Streeterville (312 840 8120). CTA Chicago (Red). **Open** 10am-5pm Mon; 10am-8pm Tue, Wed; 9am-9pm Thur; 9am-8pm Fri; 9am-6pm Sat; 10am-5pm Sun. **Credit** AmEx, Disc, MC, V. **Map** p306 J9.
One of the most luxurious spas in the city, Kiva's offerings include the Milk Paraffin Cocoon, an hour-long, head-to-toe heat and moisture treatment, and heavenly Ayurvedic treatments.

Nail Bar

3228 N Broadway, at W Belmont Avenue, Lake View (773 935 7700). CTA Belmont. **Open** 9am-8pm Mon-Sat; 10am-6pm Sun. **Credit** MC, V. **Map** p309 F2.
This hip new storefront in Boystown invites you to belly up to the bar to have your cuticles massaged or your tootsies painted. Body and facial waxing is also offered.

Salon & Spa Blue

2915 N Sheffield Avenue, at W George Street, Lake View (773 525 2583/www.salonblue.com). CTA Diversey. **Open** *Salon* 9am-7.30pm Tue, Wed; noon-7pm Thur; 10am-5pm Fri; 9am-6pm Sat; noon-6pm Sun. *Spa* call for details. **Credit** MC, V. **Map** p309 E3.
Hipsters, celebrities and edgy socialites go to Salon Blue. In addition to the latest hair cuts on the block, the spa offers feel-good packages, which include scalp treatments, rejuvenation massages and hand and foot wraps.

Sister Skincare & Waxing

Suite 964W, 845 N Michigan Avenue, at E Pearson Street, Near North/Magnificent Mile (312 943 8800). CTA Chicago (Red). **Open** 9am-6pm Mon, Tue, Sun; 9am-7pm Wed, Thur; 9am-6pm Fri, Sat. **No credit cards**. **Map** p306 J9.
Sisters Jeanette Abou-Mourad and Elaine Youhanna practise the painful art of facial and body waxing. In addition to zipping the hair off every body part you can imagine (*except* men's bikini lines, Abou-Mourad cautions), the sisters do lash and brow tinting and facials.

Urban Oasis

12 W Maple Street, at N State Street, Gold Coast (312 587 3500/www.urban-oasis.com). CTA Clark/Division. **Open** 3-8pm Mon; 10am-8pm Tue-Thur; 9am-7pm Fri; 9am-5pm Sat; noon-5pm Sun. **Credit** AmEx, Disc, MC, V. **Map** p306 H9.
Every massage on the map is offered at Urban Oasis, including reflexology, deep tissue, sport, incense, hot stone and pregnancy massages. The Oasis salon also offers aromatherapy wraps and yoga classes.

Vinyl junkies dig the plastic fantastic at **Dr Wax**.

Hairdressers

Heidi's Salon & Spa

110 E Delaware Place, at N Michigan Avenue, Near North/Magnificent Mile (312 337 6411). CTA Chicago (Red). **Open** 9am-8pm Mon-Fri; 9am-6pm Sat; 10am-5pm Sun. **Credit** Disc, MC, V. **Map** p306 J9.
This all-purpose salon is a prime site for celebrity-spotting thanks to clipper to the stars, Jeri Delgado, who joined Heidi's staff after moving to Chi-town from LA. Though Delgado's reservation book is usually packed tight, the salon's other stylists can also help you get ready for your close-up.

Truefitt & Hill

900 N Michigan Avenue, at E Walton Street, Near North/Magnificent Mile (312 337 2525). CTA Chicago (Red). **Open** 7.30am-7pm Mon-Thur; 7.30am-8pm Fri; 7.30am-6pm Sat; noon-6pm Sun. **Credit** AmEx, Disc, MC, V. **Map** p306 J9.
A Brit classic whose barbers wield straight razors. In addition to haircuts and close shaves, men can get manicures, pedicures, beard trims, steam facials and of course, shoe shines. The only thing that's no longer old-fashioned about this joint is the prices.

Visionaries

357 W Chicago Avenue, at N Orleans Street, Near North/River North (312 337 4700). CTA Chicago (Brown/Purple). **Open** 10am-5pm Mon, Tue; 11am-7pm Wed; 10am-7pm Thur, Fri; 9am-5pm Sat, Sun. **Credit** AmEx, MC, V. **Map** p306 G10.
A downtown mecca for African-American clients, Visionaries does it all, from natural styles, braids and locks to traditional relaxed 'dos or spiral cuts. Spa offerings include salt scrubs, customised facials and mega-moisturising manicures and pedicures.

Markets

For **Maxwell Street Market**, *see page 180* **To the max**.

Antiques & flea markets

Get out of town to peruse the goodies on sale at the antiques and flea markets in the semi-rural counties west of the city. One of the very best in the country is **Sandwich Antiques Market** (773 227 4464), held on the third or fourth Sunday of the month.

From May to October it attracts about 600 dealers and hundreds of collectors and bargain-hunters to the town of Sandwich, about 60 miles (97 kilometres) west of Chicago. Less prestigious but still fun for the itinerant junker is the indoor **Kane County Flea Market** (630 377 2252), held year-round on the first weekend of the month in the town of St Charles.

Farmers' markets

Selling produce, canned jams, honey, bread and flowers, about two dozen city-sponsored farmers' markets are held in parks and school and church parking lots from June to October. Downtown, markets are set up in **Federal Plaza** (Tuesday) and **Daley Plaza** (Thursday). The **Green City Market**, which specialises in organic produce, is held on Fridays in an alley off State Street, directly south of the Chicago Theatre. Call 312 744 9187 for further information.

Music

For aisles full of CDs, as well as books, mags, videos and other pop matter, head to the **Virgin Megastore**, (540 N Michigan Avenue, at E Grand Avenue, Near North/Magnificent Mile; 312 645 9300) or **Tower Records** (214 S Wabash Avenue, at E Adams Street, the Loop; 312 663 0660; 2301 N Clark Street, at W Belden Avenue, Lincoln Park; 773 477 5994). You might also want to check out the **Chicago Music Mart** in the basement of the DePaul Centre in the Loop (333 S State Street, at E Jackson Boulevard), where you can browse in a dozen stores selling pianos, drums, sheet music and other musical goods or just listen to one of the free noon-time concerts.

Dr Wax

1203 N State Street, at E Division Street, Gold Coast (312 255 0123). CTA Clark/Division. **Open** 11.30am-8pm Mon-Thur; 11.30am-9pm Fri, Sat; noon-6pm Sun. **Credit** Disc, MC, V. **Map** p307 H8.
A good, general-interest shop with a selection of alternative, jazz, soul and imports in CD and record format, both new and used.
Branch: 2523 N Clark Street, at W Deming Place, Lincoln Park (773 549 3377).

Consumer

Evil Clown

3418 N Halsted Street, at W Roscoe Street, Lake View (773 472 4761). CTA Addison (Red). **Open** noon-10pm Mon-Fri; 11am-9pm Sat; noon-7pm Sun. **Credit** AmEx, MC, V. **Map** p309 F2.

Listen on headphones before you buy at this tidy little indie-rock shop in Lake View. It stocks CDs only, both new and second-hand.

Gramophone Records

2663 N Clark Street, at W Drummond Place, Lincoln Park (773 472 3683). CTA Diversey. **Open** 11am-9pm Mon-Fri; 10.30am-8.30pm Sat; noon-6pm Sun. **Credit** AmEx, Disc, MC, V. **Map** p308 F4.

Club DJs shop this legendary Lincoln Park store for what's hot on vinyl. There are also mix cassettes and some CDs.

Hear Music

932 N Rush Street, at E Walton Place, Gold Coast (312 951 0242). CTA Chicago (Red). **Open** 10am-10pm daily. **Credit** AmEx, DC, MC, V. **Map** p306 H9.

The selection at this sophisticated shop is oh so tastefully edited that it seems nearly impossible to leave without picking up a few CDs. The music covers a sweep of genres from country and western (the cool stuff) to world music and all of it can be previewed before you buy. The store's 'Artist Choice' selections allow customers to survey the favourite tunes of hipsters such as Lucinda Williams or Tom Waits.

Jazz Record Mart

444 N Wabash Street, at E Illinois Street, Near North/Magnificent Mile (312 222 1467). CTA Grand. **Open** 10am-8pm Mon-Sat; noon-5pm Sun. **Credit** AmEx, Disc, MC, V. **Map** p306 H10.

The knowledgeable staff at this store lead shoppers through what is claimed to be the largest inventory of jazz and blues records in the world. The selection includes gospel, R&B and world music, from the latest issues on Delmark Records (owned by the store's proprietor) to old stuff on 45s and 78s dating right back to the '20s.

The Quaker Goes Deaf

1937 W North Avenue, at N Damen Avenue, Wicker Park/Bucktown (773 252 9334). CTA Damen (Blue). **Open** 11am-10pm Mon-Thur; 11am-midnight Fri, Sat; noon-10pm Sun. **Credit** AmEx, Disc, MC, V. **Map** p310 B7.

To the max

The city's oldest market, **Maxwell Street**, is a rather pale version of its former self since the city and the University of Illinois evicted it from its namesake street in the mid 1990s. The market began in what was then the city's immigrant ghetto and over the years has launched the careers of Jewish haberdashers and blues musicians; the latter still occasionally perform impromptu jam sessions in the market.

For people whose tastes run to sifting through interesting junk, the market used to provide a fine opportunity for sharpening one's scavenging skills, but these days the wares for sale – old TVs, random auto parts, salsa tapes, T-shirts – are less than inspiring. However, it's still a vestige of the city's past and always draws a colourful crowd. In recent years, the city's growing Mexican population has added its own layer to the historic market, with a variety of vendors selling tamales, churrascos and other street-fair food. The market is open year-round and is located a few blocks west of the Field Museum. *See also page 79.*

Maxwell Street Market

On S Canal Street & W Roosevelt Road, West Side (312 922 3100). **Open** 7am-3pm Sun only. **Map** p304 G14.

The legendary **Merz Apothecary**.

There must be some story behind the loopy name of this eclectic shop. New and used, indie and import – including ambient, experimental, stoner rock and hard-to-find represses – videos, books, posters and magazines are all on sale, and it's open 'til midnight at the weekend.

Record Roundup

2034 W Montrose Avenue, at N Damen Avenue, Far North (773 271 5330). CTA Montrose (Brown). **Open** noon-7pm Tue-Sat; noon-6pm Sun; closed Mon. **No credit cards**.

An idiosyncratic hodge-podge shop in Lincoln Square owned by cartoonist and filmmaker Heather McAdams and her husband. It's crammed full of country music records and other obscure vinyl, plus old comic books, board games, paperbacks and random curiosities.

Opticians

Both **Marshall Field's** (312 781 3573) and **Carson Pirie Scott** (312 641 7393) have their own optical counters.

Lens Crafters

Information 1-800 522 5367.
Full-service optical chain with numerous branches. **Branches**: throughout the city.

Pearle Vision

Wrigley Building, 410 N Michigan Avenue, at E Hubbard Street (1-800 937 3937/312 644 0885). CTA Grand. **Open** 10am-6pm Mon-Sat; closed Sun. **Credit** AmEx, Disc, MC, V. **Map** p306 J11.

A full line of eyewear, on-site exams and a good place for a pit stop when your glasses are not well. **Branches**: throughout the city.

Sun King

44 E Chicago Avenue, at N Wabash Avenue, Gold Coast (312 649 9110). CTA Chicago (Red). **Open** 11am-7pm Mon-Thur; 11am-6pm Fri; 10am-6pm Sat; noon-5pm Sun. **Credit** AmEx, MC, V. **Map** p306 H10.

Prescription glasses, designer sunglasses, contact lenses and eye examinations are all available at this central store.
Branch: 826 W Armitage Avenue, at N Dayton Street, Lincoln Park (773 975 7867).

Pharmacies

Merz Apothecary

4716 N Lincoln Avenue, between W Leland & W Lawrence Avenue, Far North (773 989 0900). CTA Western (Brown). **Open** 9am-6pm Mon-Sat; closed Sun. **Credit** AmEx, Disc, MC, V.

Definitely worth the trek north even if nothing is ailing you. One of the city's real gems, Merz is a century-old establishment that specialises in allo-pathic and homeopathic medicines, as well as herbal treatments, vitamins and soaps, many of them European imports and good for you and the planet. The Indian pharmacist has carried on the tradition begun by previous owners (and even manages to speak German to the old ladies who still shop here).

Osco Drug

3101 N Clark Street, at W Barry Avenue, Lake View (1-888 443 5701/773 477 1967). CTA Belmont. **Open** 24hrs daily. **Credit** AmEx, Disc, MC, V. **Map** p309 F3.

One of the city's big pharmacy chains (**Walgreens**, *see below*, is the other), Osco Drug is often paired with **Jewel** grocery stores (*see p175*). The other vaguely central 24-hour Osco Drug is at 2940 N Ashland Avenue, at W Wellington Avenue, Lake View (773 348 4156).
Branches: throughout the city.

Solomon-Cooper Drugs

1051 N Rush Street, at E Cedar Street, Gold Coast (312 944 3577). CTA Clark/Division. **Open** 8am-8pm Mon-Fri; 9am-6pm Sat; 9am-3pm Sun. **Credit** AmEx, Disc, MC, V. **Map** p306 H9.

A rare beast: an independently owned pharmacy, with a central location on the Gold Coast.

Walgreens

757 N Michigan Avenue, at E Chicago Avenue, Near North/Magnificent Mile (1-800 925 4733/312 664 8686). CTA Chicago (Red). **Open** 24hrs daily. **Credit** AmEx, Disc, MC, V. **Map** p304 J10.

This chain has dozens of Chicago area locations. Downtown, there is another 24-hour store at 641 N Clark Street, at W Ontario Street, Near North/River North (312 587 1416).
Branches: throughout the city.

Sport

See also chapter **Sport & Fitness**.

Active Endeavors

935 W Armitage Avenue, at N Sheffield Avenue, Lincoln Park (773 281 8100). CTA Armitage. **Open** 10am-6pm Mon-Fri; 10am-5pm Sat; noon-5pm Sun. **Credit** AmEx, Disc, MC, V. **Map** p308 E6.

Outdoor apparel from Patagonia, the North Face, Moonstone, Columbia and others, including tents, climbing gear, travel books, even canoes and kayaks. It plans to open on Michigan Avenue in late 2000.
Branch: 1527 Chicago Avenue, Evanston (847 869 7070).

Bats, balls and stupendous sneakers: such is the way at **Sportmart**.

Niketown

669 N Michigan Avenue, at E Huron Street, Near North/Magnificent Mile (312 642 6363). CTA Chicago (Red). **Open** 10am-7pm Mon-Fri; 9.30am-6pm Sat; 11am-6pm Sun. **Credit** AmEx, DC, MC, V. **Map** p306 J10.

Besides all the sports shoes and clothes, this multi-storey temple to the swooshed shoemaker has a basketball half-court, an aquarium, a video theatre for the latest commercials and souvenirs of his Airness and other Nike pitchpeople.

North Face

875 N Michigan Avenue, at E Delaware Place, Near North/Magnificent Mile (312 337 7200). CTA Chicago (Red). **Open** 10am-7pm Mon-Sat; 11am-5pm Sun. **Credit** AmEx, Disc, MC, V. **Map** p306 J9.

A spacious store in the Hancock Center for adventurers and wannabes who have turned camping and outdoorsy gear into a kind of fetish wear.

Push

40 E Chicago Avenue, at N Wabash Avenue, Near North (312 573 9996). CTA Chicago (Red). **Open** 2-7pm Tue; 11am-7pm Wed-Sat; noon-5pm Sun; closed Mon. **Credit** AmEx, DC, MC, V. **Map** p306 H10.

Sure to please those tweenaged skate rats, this subterranean store stocks boards, T-shirts and has, like, some totally cool stickers.

Sportmart

620 N LaSalle Street, at W Ontario Street, Near North/River North (312 337 6151). CTA Grand. **Open** 9.30am-9.30pm Mon-Fri; 9am-9pm Sat; 10am-7pm Sun. **Credit** AmEx, Disc, MC, V. **Map** p306 H10.

This eight-storey flagship store has entire floors given over to every possible athletic pursuit (except fishing). Busloads of tourists create a frenzy for the pro sports memorabilia.

Branch: 3134 N Clark Street, at W Fletcher Street, Lake View (773 871 8501); and suburban locations.

Vertel's Authentic Running & Fitness

24 S Michigan Avenue, at E Madison Street, The Loop (312 683 9600). CTA Madison. **Open** 8.30am-7pm Mon-Fri; 10am-6pm Sat; noon-5pm Sun. **Credit** AmEx, MC, V. **Map** p305 J12.

This well-established store caters for runners and other athletes, with shoes and other apparel (the staff are not fans of Nike, so don't look for it here). The expert shoe-fitters send customers outside for a lap on the sidewalk to test out the footwear. Weekly fun runs depart from the downtown store.

Branch: 2001 N Clybourn Avenue, at W Armitage Avenue, Lincoln Park (773 248 7400).

Travel agents

Council Travel

1160 N State Street, at W Division Street, Gold Coast (312 951 0585). CTA Clark/Division. **Open** 9.30am-5.30pm Mon, Tue, Thur; Fri; 10.30am-5.30pm Wed; 11am-4pm Sat; closed Sun. **Credit** AmEx, MC, V. **Map** p307 H8.

This international travel agency is geared to students but is a good resource for people of all ages who need help with air fares, rail passes, youth hostels and other essentials for travelling on the cheap.

Arts & Entertainment

Art Galleries

Who needs SoHo when you can have SuHu? Chicago is a minefield of great artists and thrilling galleries.

After decades at the margins, Chicago has, in the past 20 years or so, become one of the leading gallery centres in America. Focused loosely around four districts – Michigan Avenue, River North, Wicker Park & Bucktown and, increasingly, the near-West Side – Chicago's gallery scene is an emerging powerhouse with neither the pretension nor the high prices of SoHo's.

The rise of Chicago's art scene can be traced to the gentrification the River North area in the '70s and '80s, when galleries moved into the neighbourhood, supplanting the small factories that originally occupied these buildings. A devastating fire in 1989, which displaced nine River North galleries, only temporarily slowed the scene's inexorable rise, and the area surrounding Superior and Huron Streets (aka SuHu) now boasts around 75 galleries.

As River North has grown more sedate and touristy, the late 1980s and early '90s saw the rise of Wicker Park and the near-West Side scenes: the current hotbed of gallery activity is an area roughly bound by Grand, Halsted, Randolph and May, known as the West Loop Gate and home to the likes of **Fassbender** and **Vedanta**. This general move westwards in hipdom has created a seismic shift in the gallery scene. To their credit, most Chicago galleries try hard to be appealing to the public. In River North, free wine and snacks are served on Friday-night openings, and there are massive openings on the first Friday after Labor Day.

Though the breadth and quality of the Chicago gallery scene is such that just about any kind of art can be found in any part of town, several broad generalisations can be made. Michigan Avenue galleries are the most traditional and upscale (the best place to find, say, old and modern masters); River North galleries are the most aggressively contemporary (head here for Calder mobiles, in other words); and West Side galleries are the funkiest (glue sculptures and the like).

Chicago Gallery News, a free guide with comprehensive listings of exhibits and detailed maps, can be found in many hotels and galleries. Visitors may well find it essential for navigating the artistic world. The *Chicago Reader* is also a must-have for information on openings at the myriad spaces in the city.

In addition to the galleries listed below, be sure to visit the **Art Institute of Chicago**, a wonderful treasure trove of a museum (*see page 51*). The Institute's notable collections include a world-renowned selection of Impressionist and post-Impressionist pieces. For details of the **Museum of Contemporary Art**, *see page 65*.

The Loop

School of the Art Institute of Chicago, Betty Rymer Gallery
280 S Columbus Drive, at E Jackson Drive (312 443 3703). CTA Adams or Jackson (Red). **Open** 10am-5pm Mon-Wed, Fri, Sat; 10am-8pm Thur; closed Sun. **Map** p305 J12.
Open since 1989, this space is dedicated to the work of students both past and present, to exhibits from the school's various departments and programmes, and to the works of emerging and established international artists such as Ed Paschke. Look out for its excellent series of guest lectures.

South Loop

Hothouse
31 E Balbo Drive, at S Wabash Avenue (312 362 9707/www.hothouse.net). **Open** 6pm-1am Mon-Fri, Sun; 6pm-2am Sat (hours change often, so call ahead). **Map** p305 H13.
An eclectic gallery/performing space, the non-profit Hothouse is one of the city's most beloved bohemian institutions. Besides national and international jazz, indie and world music acts, this South Loop cultural anchor features performance art, outsider and folk art, paintings and photography.

Near North

River North
Look into the **Douglas Dawson Gallery** (222 W Huron Street, at N Franklin Street; 312 751 1961) for fascinating non-Western art, including African ceramics and textiles and Far Eastern furniture. On N Wells Street at no.740, the **Carl Hammer Gallery** (312 266 8512; www.hammergallery.com) displays contemporary, outsider and folk art by American and European artists. Across the street at no.739, the contemporary abstract art at the **Roy Boyd Gallery** (312 642 1606) is also well worth a look.

Ancient and modern come together at the **Art Institute of Chicago**.

Ann Nathan Gallery

218 W Superior Street, at N Franklin Street (312 664 6622). CTA Chicago (Brown/Purple). **Open** *10am-5.30pm Tue-Fri; 11am-5pm Sat; closed Mon, Sun.* **Map** *p306 G10.*

Now in a lovely space on the city's most art-intensive block, the smart, offbeat Ann Nathan Gallery has gone through several incarnations and name changes. The pieces displayed here range from works in wood and clay to more traditional painting, sculpture and multimedia, from artists both near and far.

Gruen Galleries

226 W Superior Street, at N Franklin Street (312 337 6262). CTA Chicago (Brown/Purple). **Open** *11am-4.30pm Mon-Sat; closed Sun.* **Map** *p306 G10.*

One of the oldest galleries in River North, Gruen has hosted exhibitions by painters such as Tom Parish and Joe Burnett, but is most noted for its West African artefacts and for works in iron, forged by Erwin Gruen himself in the gallery's basement.

Judy A Saslow Gallery

300 W Superior Street, at N Franklin Street (312 943 0530/www.jsaslowgallery.com). CTA Chicago (Brown/Purple). **Open** *10am-6pm Tue-Sat, or by appointment.* **Map** *p306 G10.*

One of several galleries in the 300 W Superior building, the Judy A Saslow gallery has showcased the works of painters such as Tom Schneider and collage artist Troy Campbell.

Kass/Meridian

215 W Superior Street, at N Franklin Street (312 266 5999/www.kassmeridian.com). CTA Chicago (Brown/Purple). **Open** *11am-5pm Tue-Fri; 11am-4pm Sat; closed Mon, Sun.* **Map** *p306 G10.*

A Chicago fixture for close to 20 years, this specialist in contemporary prints, paintings and sculpture has featured work by the likes of Haring and Warhol. It's best known for pieces by influential and high-end American and Western European artists.

Lydon Fine Art

309 W Superior Street, at N Franklin Street (312 943 1133). CTA Chicago (Brown/Purple). **Open** *9am-5pm Tue-Sat; closed Mon, Sun.* **Map** *p306 G10.*

Best known for its work curating corporate and personal art collections, Lydon nonetheless has a distinguished collection of landscape and abstract art. Most of its featured artists are established and reliable, if not necessarily spectacular.

LyonsWier Packer Gallery

300 W Superior Street, at N Franklin Street (312 654 0600/www.aronpacker.com). CTA Chicago (Brown/Purple). **Open** *10am-5pm Tue-Sat; closed Mon, Sun.* **Map** *p306 G10.*

In autumn 1999, venerable local galleries Lyons Wier and Aron Packer joined forces to open this powerhouse gallery at art-centric 300 W Superior Street. The realism-heavy collection gives prominence to both established and developing local artists.

Photography

Anchor Graphics

Fifth Floor, 119 W Hubbard Street, at N Clark Street, Near North/River North (312 595 9598/www.anchorgraphics.org). CTA Grand or Merchandise Mart. **Open** 9am-5pm Mon-Fri; noon-5pm Sat; closed Sun. **Map** p306 H11

This graphic facility and gallery is a state-of-the-art, not-for-profit printshop that also sells works by artists like Paul Sierra and Ed Paschke. A great and instructive find for anyone curious about how prints get made.

Carol Ehlers Gallery

Suite 303, 750 N Orleans Street, at W Chicago Avenue, Near North/River North (312 642 8611). CTA Chicago (Brown/Purple). **Open** 10am-5pm Tue-Fri; 11am-5pm Sat; closed Mon, Sun. **Map** p306 G10.

One of the city's finest and friendliest galleries, the Carol Ehlers Gallery exhibits everything from turn-of-the-century to post-postmodern photography. Walker Evans and William Wegman are just two of the many prominent photographers who have had work represented by Ehlers.

Perimeter Gallery Incorporated

210 W Superior Street, at N Wells Street (312 266 9473). CTA Chicago (Brown/Purple). **Open** 10.30am-5.30pm Tue-Sat; closed Mon, Sun. **Map** p306 G10.

Understated and minimalist, Perimeter is as much about the staging as about the art, but does offer one of the town's finest ceramics collections.

Sonia Zaks Gallery

311 W Superior Street, at N Orleans Street (312 943 8440). CTA Chicago (Brown/Purple). **Open** 11am-5.30pm Tue-Fri; noon-5pm Sat; closed Mon, Sun. **Map** p306 G10.

One of the mainstays of River North, Zaks has represented established and emerging artists including Doug Shelton, Ben Mahmoud and Guy Benson.

Zolla/Lieberman

325 W Huron Street, at N Franklin Street (312 944 1990/www.zollaliebermangallery.com). CTA Chicago (Brown/Purple). **Open** 10am-5.30pm Tue-Sat; closed Mon, Sun. **Map** p306 G10.

Specialising in contemporary paintings, sculptures, drawings and photography, the influential Zolla/Lieberman moved into its current space in the late 1980s. It's a more than worthy showcase for artists such as Deborah Butterfield and John Buck.

Catherine Edelman Gallery

300 W Superior Street, at N Franklin Street, Near North/River North (312 266 2350/www.edelmangallery.com). CTA Chicago (Brown/Purple). **Open** 10am-5.30pm Tue-Sat; closed Mon, Sun. **Map** p306 G10.

One of the most high-profile photographic galleries in town, this gallery was established by photographer Edelman to help further the careers of other contemporary photographers. Annie Leibovitz, Dan Estabrook and Sally Mann are among those who have had their works spotlighted here.

City Gallery

Water Tower, 806 N Michigan Avenue, at E Pearson Street, Near North/Magnificent Mile (312 742 0808/www.chicagointheyear2000. org). CTA Chicago (Red). **Open** 10am-6.30pm Mon-Sat; 10am-5pm Sun. **Map** p306 J9.

The Historic Water Tower, one of the sole survivors of the Chicago Fire of 1871, now houses City Gallery, a city-run showcase of photographs of Chicago by local artists. The gallery's exhibitions have included a series of photographs documenting Chicago's 176 neighbourhoods during the millennium year.

Magnificent Mile

Kenneth Probst

46 E Superior Street, at N Wabash Avenue (312 440 1991). CTA Chicago (Red). **Open** 11am-6pm Tue-Sat; closed Mon, Sun. **Map** p306 H10.

This Impressionist-heavy gallery specialises in works from 1840 to 1940, as well as in pieces from both rising and established Chicago artists. Pieces from both the Hudson River School and the Chicago School have been particularly excellent.

Kenyon Oppenheimer

410 N Michigan Avenue, at the Chicago River (312 642 5300/www.audobonart.com). CTA Grand. **Open** 10am-6pm Mon-Sat; closed Sun. **Map** p306 J11.

One of the city's leading purveyors of Audubon prints, including the rare *Birds of America* and *Viviparous Animals of North America*, the gallery recently moved to a sprawling space in the Wrigley Building. A leader in custom framing and paper conservation.

R H Love

40 E Erie Street, at N Wabash Avenue (312 640 1300). CTA Chicago (Red). **Open** 9am-5pm Mon-Sat; closed Sun. **Map** p306 H10.

Located in the sweeping and gorgeous Nickerson Mansion (worth the trip in itself), Love's gallery

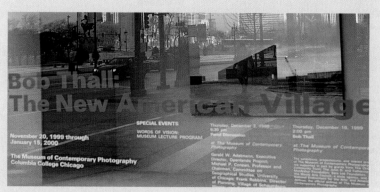

Museum of Contemporary Photography

Columbia College Chicago, 600 S Michigan Avenue, at E Harrison Street, South Loop (312 663 5554/www.colum.edu/museum/mocp). CTA Harrison. **Open** 10am-5pm Mon-Wed, Fri; 10am-8pm Thur; noon-5pm Sat; closed Sun. **Map** p305 J13.

The alternative arts-driven Columbia College opened this space in 1967 to showcase some of the finest photography from around the world, with an eye towards documenting the medium's changing role in society.

Printworks

311 W Superior Street, at N Franklin Street, Near North/River North (312 664 9407). CTA Chicago (Brown/Purple). **Open** 11am-5pm Tue-Sat, or by appointment. **Map** p306 G10.

The tiny but mighty Printworks is one of the best places in which to find works by names like Hollis Sigler and Michiko Itatani, as well as any number of up-and-coming artists. The owners are affable and erudite, and the photography and range of books are equally impressive.

features a fine collection of pieces from colonial to present times. Past artists have included Cassatt, Butler and Albert Bierstadt.

Streeterville

Arts Club of Chicago

201 E Ontario Street, at N St Clair Street (312 787 3997). CTA Grand. **Open** 11am-6pm Mon-Fri; 11am-4pm Sat; closed Sun. **Map** p306 J10.

Now the *grande dame* of the Chicago art scene, the Arts Club was once a cutting-edge space, showing works by Picasso as early as 1916. The Arts Club is now located in a lovely space off the Magnificent Mile, though it still retains the Mies van der Rohe staircase from its old location as well as a series of Byzantine rules governing admission. Non-members are welcome to enjoy lunch in the dining room, guest lectures and an impressive series of free exhibits.

Gold Coast

Atlas

Sixth Floor, 900 N Michigan Avenue, at E Walton Street (1-800 545 2929). CTA Chicago (Red). **Open** 10am-7pm Mon-Thur; 10am-8pm Fri; 10am-6pm Sat; noon-6pm Sun. **Map** p306 J9.

The always-bustling Atlas features everything from Old World prints to contemporary serigraphs, as well as an impressive series of guest lectures. The sister branch has slightly different opening hours.

Branch: 535 N Michigan Avenue, at E Grand Avenue, Near North/Magnificent Mile (312 329 9330).

Richard Gray

Room 2503, John Hancock Center, 875 N Michigan Avenue, at E Delaware Place (312 642 8877/www.richardgraygallery.com). CTA Chicago (Red). **Open** 10am-5.30pm Tue-Sat; closed Mon, Sun. **Map** p306 J9.

Perhaps the city's most distinguished gallery, the Richard Gray is nicely situated on the 25th floor of the Hancock Center, where it displays works by contemporary superstars such as Calder, Picasso, Miró, Dubuffet and Matisse.

Wally Findlay

188 E Walton Place, at N Michigan Avenue (312 649 1500). CTA Chicago (Red). **Open** 10am-6pm Mon-Fri; 10am-5pm Sat; closed Sun. **Map** p306 J9.

One of the oldest galleries in the country, Findlay's began in Kansas City in 1870 and moved to Chicago in 1932. It features impressive Impressionist and post-Impressionist collections, prominent contemporary artists and 19th- and 20th-century masters.

Old Town

Gallery 1756
1756 N Sedgwick Street, at W Menomonee Street, Old Town (312 642 6900). CTA Sedgwick. **Open** noon-6pm Wed-Sat. **Map** p307 G7.
This townhouse-cum-art-space has a stunning photography collection, as well as an impressive array of Impressionist work, antiques, furniture, found art, textiles, architectural work and pieces by local artists. The Turkish owners have been known to serve home-cooked Turkish food during openings.

West Side

While you're in the West Loop Gate area, seek out **Rhona Hoffman** (Suite 104, 312 N May Street, at W Fulton Street; 312 455 1990/ www.artnet.com/rhoffman.html) for art by contemporary American and European artists.

ARC Gallery
1040 W Huron Street, at N Carpenter Street (312 733 2787/www.icsp.net/arc). CTA Chicago (Blue). **Open** 11am-5pm Tue-Sat; closed Mon, Sun.
This energetic, experimental non-profit women's co-operative gives space and support to emerging artists in general, and female artists in particular.

Donald Young Gallery
933 W Washington Street, at N Sangamon Street (312 455 0100/www.donaldyoung.com). CTA Clinton (Green) or UIC-Halsted. **Open** 10am-5.30pm Tue-Fri; 11am-5.30pm Sat; closed Mon, Sun.
After seven years on the West Coast, Donald Young returned to Chicago in 1999 to jump-start this space on the up-and-coming near-West Side. Featuring everything from video to sculpture to paintings, this outstanding gallery has handled the work of Bruce Nauman, Cristina Iglesias and Robert Mangold.

Fassbender Gallery
835 W Washington Boulevard, at N Halsted Street (312 666 4302/www.fassbendergallery.com). CTA Halsted (Green). **Open** 10am-5.30pm Tue-Fri; 11am-5.30pm Sat; closed Mon, Sun.
Fassbender's deals predominantly in German art, though artists from the US and the rest of Europe are also well represented, as is a variety of media ranging from sculpture to painting to work on paper. The gallery moved into this building in March 2000.

Klein Artworks
400 N Morgan Street, at W Hubbard Street (312 243 0400/www.kleinart.com). CTA Clinton (Green). **Open** by appointment only Mon, Sun; 10am-5.30pm Tue-Sat.
According to owner Paul Klein, the gallery's aesthetic is 'contemporary abstraction'. Exemplifying this is the work of Japanese artist, Jun Kaneko, a regular exhibitor, whose unique ceramic sculptures (some of which are 12-feet high) are beginning to gain him an international reputation.

Sixspace
1851 W Chicago Avenue, at N Wolcott Street (312 563 0097/www.sixspace.com). CTA Chicago (Blue) or 66, 147 bus. **Open** 6-10pm Fri; 11am-6pm Sat, Sun; closed Mon-Thur.
Located in the increasingly funky East Village and operating on the premise that 'art shouldn't be exclusive', this new-ish, egalitarian gallery caters to all segments of the community, including students, the elderly and the underprivileged.

Vedanta Gallery
110 N Peoria Street, at W Washington Street (312 432 0708/www.vedantagallery.com). CTA Clinton (Green). **Open** 10am-6pm Tue-Fri; 11am-5pm Sat; closed Mon, Sun.
Specialising in both up-and-coming and established artists, Vedanta offers everything from painting and sculpture, photography, paper and video works. Along with its sister location, it's rapidly becoming one of the city's destination art galleries.
Branch: V2 835 W Washington Boulevard, at N Halsted Street; 312 432 0221.

Wicker Park & Bucktown

Idao
Suite 3W, 1616 N Damen Avenue, at N Milwaukee Avenue (773 235 4724/www.idaogallery.com). CTA Damen (Blue). **Open** noon-7pm Thur-Sat, or by appointment. **Map** p306 B7.
Run by artist Kara Hughes – a vivid personality even by art world standards – this influential, one-room gallery has sculpture, abstract art, mixed media and found art. Its emphasis on up-and-coming artists means bargains can often be found, but it's worth a visit just for a local artist's rendering of Hughes as *The Queen of Bucktown*, with a crown and a cigarette.

Wood Street Gallery
1239 N Wood Street, at W Division Street (773 227 3306). CTA Damen (Blue). **Open** 11am-5.30pm Tue-Fri; 10am-5pm Sat (or by appointment); closed Mon, Sun.
An important gallery in the Wicker Park area, Wood Street focuses on contemporary artworks by local and national artists. Paintings, drawings and manipulated photography are on show inside, while a new garden area displays large-scale sculptures.

South Side

Woman Made Gallery
1900 S Prairie Avenue, at E Cullerton Street (312 328 0038/www.womanmade.org). CTA Cermak-Chinatown. **Open** noon-7pm Mon-Fri; noon-4pm Sat, Sun. **Map** p304 J16.
This not-for-profit gallery was founded in 1992 to support women artists and promote awareness of the role of women in the arts. In addition to monthly exhibitions and a series of fine workshops, the gallery's location in the Keith Mansion, part of the Prairie Avenue group, makes it an irresistible draw.

Children

Keeping the kiddies amused is child's play in Chicago, though be sure to wrap 'em up nice and warm.

Heck, even getting around the city on the elevated train will strike most kids as having a rollercoaster feel to it. The downtown area is especially kid-conducive with lots of shops, restaurants and museums catering to *les petites*. And once the young 'uns have exhausted those possibilities, there's plenty going on in the Windy City to keep them occupied.

Given Chicago's ethnic diversity, kids can get a dose of culture from practically every part of the world just by taking a tour of the city's neighbourhoods. During the summer, almost all of the neighbourhoods play host to a festival that usually offers up something for kids. The city's parks are another good option: whatever the 'hood, there's usually some sort of tot lot to be found in it. And there's always the lakefront, where the kiddies can hang on the beach, take a dip in the lake, pedal down the bike path or Rollerblade their little legs off. Bless.

Of course, part of the challenge is entertaining the darlings once Chicago's infamous frigid weather sets in. Along with the museums and a new wave of indoor amusement parks, there's a slew of playhouses and dance companies that host special events for children. The city also boasts a mess of movie theatres and plays host to the **Chicago International Children's Film Festival** (*see page 196 Festivals*). Held at Facets Multimedia each autumn, the event features a mix of indie flicks from around the world. Just think of it as a sort of Sundance for the schoolyard set.

So whether a kid is into the latest Japanese anime or prefers to investigate the world's largest T-Rex, parents should be spared the dreaded 'What are we doing to do noooowww?' whine. Keep your fingers crossed.

Animals & parks

Lincoln Park Zoo
2150 N Cannon Drive, at W Webster Avenue, Lincoln Park (312 742 2000/www.chicagoparkdistrict.com). CTA Fullerton. **Open** 9am-4.30pm daily. **Admission** free. **Map** p308 H5.
It's free, and while that's a perfectly fine reason to visit, this zoo also happens to be located in one of the city's most gorgeous parks. Along with the usual animal attractions, there's a Children's Zoo that gives kids an up-close-and-personal view of animals while they're still bambinos and throws in a crash

The **Children's Museum.** *See page 190.*

course on conservation, too. And don't miss the Farm in the Zoo, a five-acre working replica of a typical Midwestern farm complete with red barns housing cows, sheep and horses. *See also p73.*

Oz Park
2021 N Burling Street, at W Webster Avenue, Lincoln Park (312 742 7898/www.chicagoparkdistrict.com). CTA Fullerton. **Open** dawn-dusk daily. **Admission** free. **Map** p308 F6.
Easily recognisable thanks to the silver statue of the Tin Man from *The Wizard of Oz* – whose author, L Frank Baum, lived and worked in Chicago – the park has courts for basketball, volleyball and tennis. There's also a bike path, a play area for the tots and – of course – a yellow brick road.

Shedd Aquarium
1200 S Lake Shore Drive, at McFetridge Drive, Museum Campus (312 939 2438/www.sheddnet.org). CTA Roosevelt/State or Roosevelt/Wabash. **Open** *Sept-May* 9am-5pm Mon-Fri; 9am-6pm Sat, Sun; *June-Aug* 9am-6pm daily. **Admission** *aquarium & oceanarium* $11; $9 3-11s, over-65s; free under-3s; *aquarium only* $6; $5 3-11s; free under-3s. **Credit** AmEx, DC, MC, V. **Map** p304 K14.
There's something fishy about a kid who doesn't like this place. The oceanarium features a recreation of the Pacific Northwest coastline where visitors can spot whales, dolphins, sea otters and harbour seals. Plan it right and the children can even catch a poolside feeding session, though the daily hand-feeding of fish by divers – with underwater commentary, no less – is just as popular. A new permanent exhibit, which opened in summer 2000, simulates the banks of the Amazon River during the rainy season. Visitors are encouraged to buy tickets in advance from Ticketmaster (312 559 0200). *See also p58.*

Out of town

Bronzeville Children's Museum

9500 S Western Avenue, Evergreen Plaza, South Side (708 636 9504). CTA 95th Street/Dan Ryan. **Open** 10am-5pm Tue-Sat; closed Mon, Sun. **Admission** $3; $2 children.
Aimed at African-American children, but appealing to kids of all colours, this is the only museum of its type in the country. First-year themes included educator and agriculturist George Washington Carver, African-Americans in aviation and how blacks built the West.

Brookfield Zoo

8400 W 31st Street, at First Avenue, Brookfield (708 485 0263). Metra Hollywood. **Open** 10am-5pm daily. **Admission** $7; $3.50 concessions, 3-12s; free under-3s. **Credit** MC, V.
This 216-acre (88-ha) zoo boasts 20 displays that successfully recreate the animals' natural habitats. It also has a children's zoo, where kids can get their hands on turtles, iguanas, armadillos and other creatures, while the walk-in farmyard brings visitors 'nose-to-muzzle' with calves and goats.

Gameworks

601 N Martingale Road, Schaumburg (847 330 9675). Metra Schaumburg. **Open** 11am-midnight Mon-Wed; 11am-1am Thur; 11am-2am Fri; 10am-2am Sat; 10am-midnight Sun. **Admission** free.
Offerings here range from classic video games to Star Wars simulators. Under-21s must be accompanied by an adult after 6pm and are banished completely at 10pm.

Kiddieland

8400 North Avenue, Melrose Park (708 343 8000/www.kiddieland.com). Bus 318 Pace. **Open** Apr, May, Sept, Oct Fri-Sun only; June-Aug daily; times vary, phone for details. **Admission** $17.50 ($14.50 after 5pm); $14.50 ($11.50 after 5pm) under-6s; $10.50 seniors; free under-3s. **Credit** Disc, MC, V.
Unlike most of its competitors, the godfather of amusement parks focuses on the under-54in crowd, with a mini choo-choo train and an old-fashioned carousel. Admission includes entrance to the park, unlimited rides and free soft drinks. The park sometimes closes in bad weather.

Babysitting & childcare

American Childcare Services

312 644 7300/www.americanchildcare.com. **Credit** AmEx, DC, MC, V.
A large staff of sitters provides childcare services to hotel guests looking for some time away from the kiddies. Citing frequent changes, the agency does not release rates, but there is a four-hour minimum and clients should book 24 hours ahead. The agency also provides group childcare for conventioneers.

North Shore Nannies

847 864 2424. **Credit** MC, V.
This agency offers a 'temp nanny service' covering both the city and 'burbs. Rates are $10 per hour with a four-hour minimum paid directly to the nanny by cash or cheque, plus an additional agency fee of $18 for up to six hours, $30 for six to 12 hours and $40 for 12 to 24 hours. Advance booking is recommended, particularly at the weekend.

Museums

Almost all of the city's museums include a little something for the kids, but the following tend to be the best bets in terms of entertainment. For details of the others, *see* chapter **Sightseeing**.

Children's Museum

700 E Grand Avenue, at Navy Pier, Near North/ Streeterville (312 527 1000/www.chichildrens museum.org). CTA Grand. **Open** 10am-5pm Tue, Wed, Fri-Sun; 10am-8pm Thur; closed Mon, except school holidays 10am-5pm. **Admission** $6.50; $5.50 concessions; free families 5-8pm Thur. **Credit** AmEx, D, MC, V. **Map** p306 K10.
Not only will kids have a blast here, but they might learn something, too. A quick lesson in gravity, for example, is provided by a long conveyor belt that carries the kids' creations up to the ceiling and then hurls them down. Alternatively, children can opt to dig for dino bones in a replica excavation pit or host a mock TV show. Wee ones will probably opt for the play area with a bakery, gas station, bus and construction zone. Be warned, though: the exit leads directly into a well-stocked gift shop. *See also p66*.

Children's Museum of Immigrant History

6500 S Pulaski Road, at W 65th Street, South Side (773 582 6500). CTA Pulaski (Orange). **Open** 10am-4pm daily. **Admission** $3; $2 concessions; $1 under-12s. **Credit** AmEx, MC, V.
Designed to teach kids about ethnic diversity, the museum features exhibits, workshops, live demonstrations and performances highlighting the arts, history and culture introduced to the US by various

Kohl's Children's Museum

165 Green Bay Road, Wilmette (847 256 6056). Bus 213 Pace. **Open** 9am-noon Mon; 9am-5pm Tue-Sun. **Admission** $5; $4 concessions. **Credit** AmEx, MC, V.
Emphasising a hands-on approach, this museum not only has a room full of Duplo blocks but has covered the tables and walls with them, too. Kids can build a bird's nest, create a giant spider's web or paint their very own masterpiece in the artist's studio.

Santa's Village, Racing Rapids & Polar Dome Ice Arena

Routes 25 & 72, East Dundee (847 426 6751/www.santasvillageil.com). **Open** *Santa's Village & Racing Rapids* May, Sep 11am-dusk Sat, Sun; June-Aug 10am-dusk Mon-Fri; 11am-dusk Sat, Sun. *Polar Dome* Sept-Apr 11.30am-1pm Tue; 8.30-10.30pm Fri; 1.30-3.30pm, 8.30-10.30pm Sat; 1.30-4pm Sun.
Admission *Santa's Village* $15.95-$17.95; free under-2s; *Racing Rapids* $12.95; free under-2s; *Combined ticket* $22.95-$24.95; *Polar Dome* $5; skate hire $2. **Credit** MC, V.

This place is downright trippy when the sun is beating down and you're standing next to a towering frozen North Pole as Christmas carols float through the air. The park has a petting zoo, kiddies' rides and rollercoasters. Next door is Racing Rapids, an action park with a water slide and a water tube ride. From September until April the Polar Dome Ice Arena is open for public skating and lessons.

Six Flags Great America Theme Park

542 N Route 21, Gurnee (847 249 1776/ information 847 249 4636). Metra Union Pacific North. **Open** *late Apr-late Aug* daily; *early Sept* Sat, Sun only; times vary, phone for details. **Admission** $39; $19.50 children under 48ins, seniors; free under-2s.
Credit AmEx, DC, MC, V.
The place is huge, but among the highlights are Raging Bull, a 'hypertwister coaster' that travels at up to 70 miles per hour and Escape from Dino Island, a motion simulator adventure. Younger tots can enjoy the fun at Camp Cartoon Network and Looney Tunes National Park.

immigrant groups. Part of the Balzekas Museum of Lithuanian Culture, the kids section includes an exhibition where kids can try out ancient Lithuanian folk instruments or dress up in traditional costumes.

Field Museum

1400 S Lake Shore Drive, at E Roosevelt Road, Museum Campus (312 922 9410/www.fmnh.org). CTA Roosevelt/State or Roosevelt/Wabash.
Open 9am-5pm daily. **Admission** $7; $4 3-11s, concessions; free Wed. **Credit** AmEx, DC, MC, V. **Map** p304 J14.
The fact that this is the home of Sue, a truly huge T-Rex, is probably enough to pull in the kids. Still, there's plenty of other stuff worth checking out. In particular, the cool mummies and tombs in the Ancient Egyptian display. *See also p57.*

Museum of Science & Industry

5700 S Lake Shore Drive, at E 57th Street, Hyde Park (773 684 1414/www.msichicago.org). Metra 59th Street. **Open** 9.30am-4pm Mon-Fri; 9.30am-5.30pm Sat, Sun. **Admission** $7; $6 concessions; $3.50 3-11s; free under-3s. **Credit** AmEx, DC, MC, V. **Map** p311 Z17.
This museum has mass appeal, but some displays are especially fascinating to children. Adults might not be overly impressed with the walk-through heart, but kids seem to find it highly entertaining, and the U505 submarine captured in battle

during World War II is another fave, attracting 23 million visitors since 1954. Wee ones are usually charmed by the chick incubator, where you can watch as chicks break out of their shells. There's also Colleen Moore's fairy castle, a miniature masterwork, and a new collection of 500 fast-food toys dating back to the practically prehistoric 1970s. *See also p88.*

Recreation

Dave & Buster's

1030 N Clark Street, at W Oak Street, Gold Coast (312 943 5151). CTA Clark/Division. **Open** 11.30am-1am Mon-Thur; 11.30am-2am Fri, Sat; 11.30am-midnight Sun. **Admission** $5 from 10pm Fri, Sat; free all other times. **Credit** AmEx, DC, MC, V. **Map** p306 H9.
Though the main focus here is on arcade games, Dave & Buster's offers everything from shuffleboard to high-tech virtual reality games. And unlike rival indoor amusement venues, this place offers frazzled adults the opportunity to take the edge off with a cocktail.

Different Strummer

909 W Armitage Avenue, at N Bissell Street, Lincoln Park (773 525 6165). CTA Armitage. **Open** 10am-9pm Mon-Thur; 10am-5pm Fri-Sun. **Credit** AmEx, MC, V. **Map** p308 E6.

Part of the Old Town School of Folk Music Children's Center, this shop offers plenty for the budding musician. There are CDs, videos and toy instruments, as well as real ones made especially for younger players. This is the ideal place for the little rocker who is demanding a mini Les Paul.

DisneyQuest

55 E Ohio Street, at N Rush Street, Near North (312 222 1300/http://disney.go.com/disneyquest). CTA Grand. **Open** 11am-10pm Mon-Wed; 11am-midnight Thur, Fri; 10am-midnight Sat; 10am-10pm Sun. **Admission** $34 all-day pass; $16 pay-to-play. **Credit** AmEx, MC, V. **Map** p306 J10.
Billed as 'the ultimate interactive adventure', this five-floor indoor amusement park offers several virtual rides. Visitors can shoot jungle rapids on a virtual cruise or put on some funky-looking goggles and battle virtual comic-book villains with a laser sword. Adventurous kids can even take a spin on their very own cybercoaster.

Navy Pier

600 E Grand Avenue, Near North/River North (312 595 7437/www.navypier.com). CTA Grand. **Open** 10am-8pm Mon-Thur; 10am-10pm Fri, Sat; 10am-7pm Sun. **Admission** free. **Map** p306 K10.
The newly glammed-up Navy Pier offers plenty for the young 'uns. Inside, there's a botanical garden, an IMAX theatre and the Children's Museum. Outside, the most visible attraction is the 150-ft (46-m) Ferris wheel that offers a boffo view of the skyline and lakefront. There's also a musical carousel. Weather permitting, both rides operate daily. During the winter, Navy Pier has a free outdoor ice-skating rink. *See also p65.*

Restaurants

Although Chicago is chock-a-block with places for the tykes to eat, some are especially suitable for children's discriminating taste buds.

Caesarland

7300 W Foster Avenue, at N Harlem Avenue, Far North (773 774 1585). CTA Harlem (Blue). **Open** 11am-9pm Mon-Thur, Sun; 10.30am-10pm Fri, Sat. **Credit** MC, V.
Part of the ubiquitous Little Caesar's pizza chain, this outlet adds some fun and games to the recipe. In between scarfing down the mediocre pizza, kids can get their hands on a choice of interactive play equipment, video games and rides. Admission is free, though some games require tokens.

Ed Debevic's

640 N Wells Street, at E Erie Street, Near North/River North (312 664 1707). CTA Chicago (Red). **Open** 11am-10pm Mon-Thur, Sun; 11am-11.30pm Fri, Sat. **Credit** AmEx, DC, MC, V. **Map** p306 H10.
The burgers and shakes are pretty dang tasty in this ersatz '50s diner. But the real attraction is the gumsnapping, beehive-wearing waitresses who just loooooove to insult unsuspecting patrons. The staff

have also been known to jump up on the counters for a musical number and/or dance party. Customers can expect long waits, but there are pinball machines and a DJ spinning '60s and '70s tunes to help pass the time.

Rock 'n' Roll McDonald's

600 N Clark Street, at E Huron Street, Near North/River North (312 664 7940). CTA Grand (Red). **Open** 24hrs daily. **Map** p306 H10.
Hardly your average Golden Arches outlet, this Macky D's pays homage to rock 'n' roll with cut-outs of the Supremes and the Doors gracing the outside. Inside there are platinum Elvis records, life-size replicas of the Beatles, and a candy-apple red '59 Corvette. Hey, at least you know the kids will eat.

Theatre

In addition to those listed below, it's worth checking out the **Puppet Parlor** (1922 W Montrose Avenue; 773 774 2919), which stages splendid marionette entertainments.

Chicago Playworks for Families & Young Audiences

DePaul's Merle Ruskin Theatre, 60 E Balbo Drive, at S Wabash Avenue, South Loop (773 325 7900/box office 312 922 1999/http://theatreschool.depaul.edu/perform/). CTA Harrison. **Tickets** $7; $2 under-18mths. **Credit** Disc, MC, V. **Map** p305 H13.
Founded as the Goodman Children's Theater in 1925, Chicago Playworks, run by the Theater School at DePaul University, is one of the oldest continuously running kiddie companies. The playhouse presents three productions each season and offers post-show discussions, ice-cream socials with the cast and backstage tours.

Emerald City Theatre

shows at Old Town School of Folk Music Children's Center, 909 W Armitage Avenue, at N Bissell Street, Lincoln Park (Emerald City Theatre 773 529 2690/www.emeraldcitytheatre.com). CTA Armitage. **Open** *shows* usually two matinees Sat, Sun. **Tickets** $10; $8 children. **Credit** MC, V. **Map** p308 E6.
Jolly kids' fare, such as Dr Seuss stories and *The Wizard of Oz*, is offered by this fine establishment. The season at the Old Town School runs September to June, though the theatre usually run a special summer production in another venue.

Children's Theatre Fantasy Orchard

750 W Wellington Avenue, at N Halsted Street, Lake View (773 539 4211). CTA Wellington. **Open** *box office* 8am-5pm Mon-Fri. *Shows* dates & times vary. **Tickets** $9; $7 children. **Credit** AmEx, MC, V. **Map** p309 F3.
Kids can catch dramatisations of fairy tales and folk tales from around the world at the Fantasy Orchard. There's also an annual presentation of *African Cinderella*. Based on an African folk tale, this version doesn't have a glass slipper, but makes some of the same points.

Toy story

If all else fails to entertain the kids, some parental units have been known to use a little bribery. And what better place for that than a toy shop? (For children's clothes and books, see chapter **Shops & Services**).

American Girl Place

111 E Chicago Avenue, at N Rush Street, Near North (312 255 9876). CTA Chicago (Red). **Open** *10am-7pm Mon-Wed, Sun; 10am-9pm Thur-Sat.* **Credit** *AmEx, DC, MC, V.* **Map** *p306 J10.*

A one-stop source for all things American Girl, this surreal three-floor store offers outfits, accessories and furniture for the beloved dolls, plus goodies for the owner ranging from a $5 computer mouse pad to a $110 jacket. There's even a 'Dress Like Your Doll' boutique, where girls can pick up a $160 Scandinavian outfit, get all decked out like Kirsten and have their picture on a souvenir cover of *American Girl* magazine. And because that shopping can build up an appetite, there's a café where girls— and their dolls – can sample the $16 American Girl's Tea and nibble some of Kirsten's Minnesota Cranberry Bread or Josefina's Cinnamon Bizochito. If that's not enough action for one day, they can catch the musical, *The American Girl's Revue*: tickets cost $25 and reservations are accepted for visitors aged six and up.

FAO Schwarz

840 N Michigan Avenue, at E Pearson Street, Gold Coast (312 587 5000). CTA Chicago (Red). **Open** *10am-6pm daily.* **Credit** *AmEx, DC, MC, V.* **Map** *p306 J9.*

The Chicago branch of this venerable New York store can get ridiculously crowded and the FAO theme song incessantly playing in the background doesn't help one's sanity. But the selection of toys is amazing, including those created specially for FAO. A menagerie of stuffed animals, including an impressive Steiff stash, takes up most of the first floor. The other two floors contain everything from Madame Alexander dolls to the latest *Star Wars* swag. There's also a Barbie boutique all done out in hot pink, with an entrance suitably framed by two fountains filled with those tiny pointy plastic shoes she likes so much.

Quake

3759 N Southport Avenue, at W Grace Avenue, Lake View/Wrigleyville (773 404 0607). CTA Southport. **Open** *1-6pm Wed-Fri; noon-6pm Sat; noon-5pm Sun; closed Mon, Tue.* **Credit** *Disc, V.* **Map** *p309 D1.*

Aimed at kids and collectors with a penchant for toys from the last 30 or so years, Quake is the place to find that elusive Mystery Date game or the talking Pee-Wee Herman doll you've been longing for. Vintage lunch boxes, *Star Wars* action figures and board games from the '60s and '70s can all be snagged for a reasonable price.

Toys R Us

10 S State Street, at W Madison Street, The Loop (312 857 0667). CTA Madison, Monroe (Blue/Red) or Washington (Blue/Red). **Open** *9.30am-7pm Mon-Wed, Fri-Sun; 9.30am-8pm Thur.* **Credit** *AmEx, D, MC, V.* **Map** *p305 H12.*

A location right in the heart of downtown helps make this branch of the toy chain a good bet on a rainy day. It also has a Kids R Us clothing shop on the lower level.

Uncle Fun

1338 W Belmont Avenue, at N Southport Avenue, Lake View (773 477 8223). CTA Belmont or Southport. **Open** *noon-7pm Wed-Fri; 11am-7pm Sat; noon-5pm Sun; closed Mon, Tue.* **Credit** *MC, V.* **Map** *p309 D2.*

This is probably the only store around where shoppers can find entire drawers full of such delights as inflatable rats, 'super-colossal jumbo plastic olives', tiny trolls and whoopee cushions. Pop fans young and old can choose from a dizzying array of licensed goods, ranging from Spice Girls keychains to Johnny Quest pens. And old-timers might enjoy the stockpile of tin toys.

Film

Chaplin filmed here, but so did Macauley Culkin. Still, Chicago's movie scene has recovered, and now offers something for 'most every taste. Roll 'em...

Chicago was once the setting for an opulent and majestic array of cinemas. On the heels of the Great Restoration, architects and businessmen rushed to erect theatres, each competing in their lavishness and scale. Towering marquees screened the latest in celluloid fare to spellbound crowds, in picture palaces worthy of the name. Serpentine stairways spilled marble into cavernous lobbies; exotic oriental and Moorish adornments garnished the interiors; massive drapes were hung from the mezzanine walls; and string quartets, perched on the balcony, serenaded the arriving crowds. These cinemas were houses of splendour, built with an imagination that rivalled the creativity behind the films that flickered inside them. Many were also on the vaudeville circuit, and hosted big-name performers such as Jack Benny, Sid Caesar and Will Rogers.

By the late 1920s, all the prominent Hollywood film studios had been formed, and they poured their works into the city with fervour. The town was fascinated with the new diversion, but the fixation would not last: the Great Depression put paid to most legal forms of frivolity, and many of the cinemas fell claim to the wrecker's ball. Some were spared and found new life as apartment complexes, shopping malls, churches or office buildings, while others – such as the **Esquire** and **Biograph** – were divided up into several smaller theatres, with lacklustre results. A select few, such as the **Vic Theatre** (originally the Victoria and now home to **Brew & View**) and the **Music Box Theatre**, were able to maintain their original design; some even still boast organs that rise up and play from their vaudevillian stages. Others still have been painstakingly restored to their exquisite state: the Chicago and Oriental, say, which are now part of the Loop's revitalised Theatre District.

The modern-day multiplex has also experienced difficulties while trying to find a home in metropolitan Chicago. Availability of space is, of course, a major obstacle, and many corporations have been forced to stack their theatres on new grounds or squeeze them into existing shopping and office complexes. As a result, a diverse range of cinemas exists in Chicago, and the quality of the movie experience is unpredictable. This chapter lists those within reach of downtown.

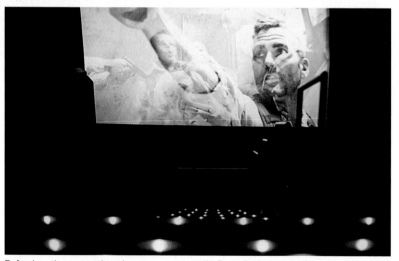

Refreshes the parts other cinemas cannot reach: **Brew & View at the Vic**. *See page 196.*

TICKETS & INFORMATION

Cinema tickets and information on screenings can be obtained from the cinema box offices, as well as from publications such as *Newcity* and the *Chicago Reader*. The most convenient way to obtain tickets for most cinemas is to purchase them in advance by phone or via the internet from **Moviefone** (312 444 3456/ www.moviefone.com), which accepts all major credit cards. Mainstream cinemas charge around $8-$8.50 for an adult ticket, with concessions for children and seniors. Most also operate substantial discounts for screenings before 6pm, and for the first screening on Saturday and Sunday – like the discounts for children and seniors, these typically are priced at $5-$5.50. Tickets for second-run, repertory and arthouse cinemas may be up to $4 cheaper (we have given individual credit card details for these cinemas as tickets are often only available through the cinema box office). Parents should note that many cinemas won't admit children under six years old after 6pm: if you've got a kiddie in tow, always call ahead to check.

Mainstream & first-run

Biograph

2433 N Lincoln Avenue, at W Fullerton Avenue, Lincoln Park (773 348 4123). CTA Fullerton. **Map** p308 F5.

The Biograph is famous as the site where the notorious bank robber John L Dillinger fled before being gunned down by FBI agents (*see p14* **Crime & the city**); indeed, bullet holes reputedly still exist in the telephone poles and alley walls beneath the art deco façade. Among locals, however, the place is considered a worthy venue for first-run feature films, with three moderately sized screens and lots of seating.

Broadway

3175 N Broadway, at W Belmont Avenue, Lake View (773 327 4114). CTA Belmont. **Map** p309 F3.

This Lake View cinema features a single screen with Dolby sound and plentiful seating. It shows first-run movies, but new features are slow to replace the incumbent flicks.

Burnham Plaza

826 S Wabash Avenue, at E 9th Street, South Loop (312 922 1090). CTA Harrison, Roosevelt/State or Roosevelt/Wabash. **Map** p304 H14.

A spacious multiplex located on the south side of the Loop, offering new releases over five large screens, each with DTS sound.

Esquire

58 E Oak Street, at N Michigan Avenue, Gold Coast (312 280 0101/280 1205). CTA Chicago (Red). **Credit** AmEx, Disc, MC, V. **Map** p306 J9.

This multi-levelled cinema is located in a strip of Gold Coast stores and chic boutiques just north of

the Magnificent Mile. The Esquire, an art deco landmark, was once a splendid cinema but has since been parcelled up into five smaller screens. First run-Hollywood movies are shown daily.

Hyde Park

5238 S Harper Avenue, at E 53rd Street, Hyde Park (773 288 4900). Metra 53rd Street. **Map** p311 Y16.

The three screens on the ground floor of this multiplex have Dolby sound, while the larger upstairs screen boasts digital sound. Hyde Park also guarantees the cheapest popcorn-and-drink deal in town.

McClurg Court

330 E Ohio Street, at N McClurg Court, Near North/Streeterville (312 642 0723). CTA Grand. **Map** p306 J10.

The McClurg claims to be the 'best and biggest theater in the Midwest', and it's hard to disagree. The three-piece cinema has become a hotspot for Hollywood's technically dazzling blockbusters, since its screens boast truly sophisticated sound systems. All three are designed with stadium seating.

900 N Michigan Theaters

900 N Michigan Avenue (lower level of Bloomingdale's mall), at E Delaware Street, Gold Coast (312 787 1988/787 9048). CTA Chicago (Red). **Map** p306 J9.

The two screens of this cinema are located in the lower level of the upmarket mall. The amenities are standard, though both screens are equipped with digital sound. Parking is available in the mall garage, with entrances on Walton or Rush Streets; further discounts are given with valid parking tickets.

Pipers Alley

1608 N Wells Street, at W North Avenue, Old Town (312 642 7500/642 6275). CTA Sedgwick. **Map** p307 H7.

This recently remodelled Old Town multiplex is one of the few cinemas to showcase first-run independent and offbeat movies. It was once part of a bohemian neighbourhood – you could even get pizza and beer along with the film – but has adopted a more commercial image and now sells $4 tubs of popcorn and outsized fizzy drinks. Considering the price of the tickets, the surroundings are a bit dishevelled, and the foyer can get very congested.

600 N Michigan Theaters

600 N Michigan Avenue, entrance at N Rush Street & E Ohio Street, Near North/Magnificent Mile (312 255 9340). CTA Grand. **Map** p306 J10.

This three-tiered facility, actually located on Rush Street near the south end of the Magnificent Mile, showcases first-run films on nine screens. The screens vary in size, and seating can be awkward, as some provide aisles only at the ends of long rows.

Water Tower

845 N Michigan Avenue, at E Chestnut Street, Gold Coast (screens 1-4 312 649 5792/screens 5-7 312 440 1554). CTA Chicago (Red). **Map** p306 J9.

The seven small screens showing first-run releases here are located on two entirely different levels of a shopping mall. If you arrive in a group, buy your tickets together to avoid being split up between concurrent showings.

Webster Place

1471 W Webster Avenue, at N Clybourn Avenue, Lincoln Park (773 327 3100). CTA Fullerton. **Map** p308 D5.

A multiplex popular with the Lincoln Park crowd, this shopping mall complex features a respectable variety of first-run Hollywood movies and offers concurrent screenings for the top box-office grossers. The screens are large, the seats have cup-holders and the parking is free with a validated ticket. Arrive early or book tickets in advance on opening weekends, as seats tend to sell out quickly.

Second-run & repertory

Brew & View at the Vic Theatre

3145 N Sheffield Avenue, at W Belmont Avenue, Lake View (312 618 8439/773 929 6713/ www.brewview.com/www.victheatre.com). CTA Belmont. **No credit cards. Map** p309 E3.

Brew & View is the alter ego of the Vic Theatre, a once opulent five-storey theatre originally designed as a vaudeville house and now host of weekend rock concerts and screenings of second-run films during the week. Tickets range from $4 to $6. Three bars stay open during the nightly sprees of comic classics and action-adventure flicks, and the bursts of commentary from the post-college crowd who attend the nightly showings is often more entertaining than the celluloid fare. Nightly drink specials fuel the critiques.

Three Penny Cinema

2424 N Lincoln Avenue, at W Fullerton Avenue, Lincoln Park (773 935 5744/935 6416). CTA Fullerton. **No credit cards. Map** p308 F5.

This humble two-screen cinema is nearly eclipsed by the neighbouring **Biograph** (*see p195*), but the second-run selection is sound – the Three Penny snatches out-of-prime movies just before they're introduced to the rest of the second-tier venues – and the tickets are cheap. New seats, complete with cup-holders, fill the two small cinemas, and popcorn tubs can be refilled for 25¢ at the concession stand.

Festivals

Chicago's film festival community is as diverse as the city's cultural composition. Over a dozen film festivals showcase works throughout the year, including Latino, Polish and Russian festivals, the nation's largest underground film festival and its second oldest lesbian and gay film festival. The pick of the fests are listed in date order below.

Chicago Latino Film Festival

(312 431 1330/www.chicagolatinocinema.org). **Date** early Apr.

Award-winning feature-length and short films from Spain, Portugal, the US and Latin America are celebrated during this 13-day festival hosted by the International Latino Cultural Center of Chicago. The 100 or so submissions are screened at the cultural centre and theatres in the Water Tower. Numerous directors, actors and cast members attend to exhibit their works and moderate post-screening discussions in what is usually an interesting event.

Chicago Underground Film Festival

(773 327 3456/866 8660/www.cuff.org). **Dates** early Aug.

This week-long film festival is as much of a success story as the independent movies showcased could hope for. In six years, the event has evolved from a season of local works held in downtown hotel conference rooms into the largest underground film festival in the country. The programme includes a medley of national and international submissions, all hoping to be acquired by corporate studios and distributors (or, at least, be viewed by an audience). Styles range from sobering documentary to Dadaist experimentalism, and the quality is equally varied.

Chicago International Children's Film Festival

(773 281 9075/www.cicff.org). **Dates** Oct.

Hundreds of acclaimed films for kids from around the world compete at this

Village Theatre

1548 N Clark Street, at W North Avenue, Old Town (312 642 2403/www.villagetheatres.com). CTA Sedgwick. **Credit** MC, V. **Map** p307 H7.

The four small cinemas that comprise the Village offer a colourful blend of art, foreign and mainstream releases. The venue has won over fans of cult classics by offering midnight screenings of their favourite films on weekends, as well as through its role as host of the **Chicago Underground Film Festival** (*see p196* **Festivals**). Free refills are offered on all sizes of soda and popcorn.

Arthouse & speciality

Chicago Filmmakers

5243 N Clark Street, at W Berwyn Avenue, Andersonville (773 293 1447/www.chicago filmmakers.org). CTA Berwyn. **Credit** MC, V.

A crucial resource for filmmakers and cinephiles, this non-profit exhibitor provides equipment, offers production classes and rents out over 600 films to local cinemas and galleries. It is also constructing a 75-seat screening room for experimental filmmakers to present their work. Screenings are currently held at **Columbia College** (600 S Michigan Avenue; 312 663 1600) and the **Chicago Cultural Center** (78 E Washington Street; 312 346 3278; *see p53*); tickets for non-members cost $6. The group also sponsors the **Chicago Lesbian & Gay International Film Festival** each November (*see below* **Festivals**).

Facets Multimedia Center

1517 W Fullerton Avenue, at N Ashland Avenue, Lincoln Park (information 773 281 4114/office 773 281 9075/www.facets.org). CTA Fullerton. **Credit** AmEx, Disc, MC, V. **Map** p308 D5.

Facets caters to audiences on the wayside of the blockbuster crowds. The two theatres are stark and stifling, but the quality and selection of art films offered is exquisite. The main theatre showcases vintage classics and works by contemporary foreign and independent filmmakers, while the second is dedicated to documentary and experimental projects made for video. Tickets for both cost $5-$7 (there are no discounts). An exhaustive library of over 40,000 videos is available for sale and rental, either over the counter or by mail. The non-profit organisation hosts the **Chicago International Children's Film Festival** (*see p196* **Festivals**) each October, and offers film classes throughout the year.

Film Center

School of the Art Institute of Chicago, S Columbus Drive & E Jackson Boulevard, The Loop (312 443 3737/www.artic.edu/saic/art/filmcntr). CTA Adams or Jackson (Red). **Credit** AmEx, MC, V. **Map** p305 J12.

The screening room at the Art Institute is plain, but the films shown are unique. The Film Center's calendar is filled with everything from experimental student works to contemporary foreign flicks, and premières by some of the world's most recognised directors are not uncommon. The centre runs a lecture series on Tuesdays in which filmmakers and

world-class festival organised by **Facets Multimedia** (*see above*). A feast of independent works, with both animated and live-action shorts on the agenda, it's enjoyed by children and parents for ten days each October. Filmmakers, animators and celebrity cast members participate in workshops, and there's also a week-long media arts camp.

Chicago International Film Festival

(*312 425 9400/www.chicago.ddbn.com/ filmfest*). **Dates** Oct.

Both distinguished and fledgling directors offer up their latest works for scrutiny by the critical jury of this competitive film festival, which is the oldest in North America. Screenings are scheduled throughout the city's arthouses, along with assorted première parties, tributes and other special presentations. Directors, stars and other movie industry folk are generally on hand to introduce the films and hold

question-and-answer sessions after the viewing. All events are open to the public, but seating is obviously limited. Both tickets for individual events and multi-movie deals are available.

Chicago Lesbian & Gay International Film Festival

(*773 2931447/ www.chicagofilmmakers.org*). **Dates** Nov.

The Chicago Lesbian & Gay International Film Festival was first organised by **Chicago Filmmakers** (*see above*) in 1981, making it the second oldest film festival of its kind in the world. The festival spreads a critically acclaimed blend of gay and lesbian feature films, documentaries and shorts across 14 days each November. Films are screened at the **Music Box Theatre** (*see p198*) and the **Village Theatre** (*see above*), with various gay bars and clubs hosting opening night, post-screening and closing-night parties to jolly the festivities along. *See also p203* **The queer year**.

The way it used to be. Enjoy vintage cinema at the **Music Box Theatre**.

cast appear to provide insight into their movies (invariably screened as part of the event). Advance previews of first-run movies are regularly offered to members. Tickets for non-members cost $7 (no discounts) and cannot be purchased in advance.

Fine Arts

418 S Michigan Avenue, at E Van Buren Street, The Loop (312 939 3700/office 312 939 3495). CTA Jackson (Red) or Library. **Credit** AmEx, Disc, MC, V. **Map** p305 J13.

This four-screen movie house offers the most conservative selection of all Chicago's arthouse cinemas, but benefits from its convenient location and association with the **Art Institute of Chicago** (*see p51*). The largest theatre boasts a grand two-tier balcony and huge screen, the second has a single balcony and smaller screen, and the remaining pair are stark and small. The Fine Arts recently celebrated its centenary and is showing its age. Carpets are frayed, seats are ropy and the façade has seen better days. Still, many see all this as integral to its charm.

Music Box Theatre

3733 N Southport Avenue, at W Waveland Avenue, Lake View (773 871 6604/871 6607/ www.musicboxtheatre.com). CTA Southport. **No credit cards. Map** 309 D1.

The Music Box is a cherished and important outlet for independent, foreign, classic and cult films. The restored venue is one of the few vintage relics that's avoided being divided into smaller screens over the years, and the effect is delightfully rewarding. Mechanical clouds drift listlessly across the ceiling, twinkling stars illuminate pixillated Moorish adornments, and a vintage organ is still played to fortunate patrons during silent films and the occasional intermission. A smaller 100-seat screen, once a neighbouring shop, shows more avant-garde films; but sightlines are obscured when it's crowded.

Tickets cost $8, or $6 for the classic film matinees at the weekend (no discounts). The Music Box also hosts the **Chicago International Film Festival** and the **Chicago Lesbian & Gay International Film Festival** (*for both, see p197* **Festivals**).

Navy Pier IMAX

600 E Grand Avenue, at Lake Michigan, Near North/ Streeterville (312 595 0090/www.navypier.com). CTA Grand. **Credit** MC, V. **Map** p306 K10.

This six-storey hulk of a cinema offers long-running selections of educational and scientific visual adventures. The theatre is also equipped for 3D movies that require the viewer to don a goofy headset in order to experience the full, dizzying effect; arrive early to avoid being placed in the motion sickness-inducing seats at the sides. Popular 35mm films are shown on Friday, Saturday and Sunday nights on the giant screen, as part of the 'Late Night at the Max' series. Tickets cost $11 for adults and $9 for children (no discounts). For the **Omnimax Cinema** at the Museum of Science & Industry, which offers a similarly spectacular cinematic experience, *see p88*.

University of Chicago Doc Films

Ida Noyes Hall, 1212 E 59th Street, at S Woodlawn Avenue, Hyde Park (information 773 702 8574/ hotline 773 702 8575/www.docfilms.uchicago.edu). Metra 59th Street. **No credit cards. Map** p311 Y18.

Home to the longest-running student film society in the country. Screenings of 'socially relevant' movies are held daily throughout the academic year (and four nights a week during the summer) in the university's Max Palevsky Cinema, a 490-seat auditorium with a DTS/Dolby surround sound system and high quality projectors. Movies are typically presented in thematic series over the ten-week term. There are three showings of features at the weekends, with student films and festivals for speciality groups offered from time to time. Tickets cost $3-$4 (no discounts).

Gay & Lesbian

Chicago's gay community is out and proud in Boystown and Andersonville, so you can be both scene *and* heard in the Windy City.

Clickety-click, two fat ladies and all that bollocks at **Disco Bingo**. *See page 200.*

You can't miss them. They stand erect on Halsted Street, undeniably phallic, ringed in rainbow colours, reaching into the sky like homo rockets poised for lift-off.

These, er, sculptures stand as testament to the respect the city of Chicago has for its gay community. Mayor Daley gave the green light to a streetscape project to show appreciation for all of the effort local gays have made to gentrify – that is, chase out the riff-raff, pretty up the area and construct bland cookie-cutter condos – what was once known as 'the gay ghetto'. Sure, this new-found respect grew out of an increase in revenue and tourist dollars, but hey, we'll take respect any way we can get it. All along Halsted Street in Lake View, popularly known as **Boystown**, the streets were widened, trees were planted and the homo rockets found their place, along with circular planters that indicate the names of cross-streets.

Chicago has come a long way from the era of police raids and cowering in the closet. But fear not: this is the gay community, after all, and seediness and kitsch still abound. For every

chic eaterie, there's a darkened club with a backroom; for every upmarket hair salon, there's a dive bar filled with lecherous men.

If Halsted Street is Boystown's main nightlife artery, lined with most of the city's gay bars and clubs, then **Broadway** is the locale of daytime hustle and bustle. Running almost parallel to Halsted, Broadway is where you'll find boys coming back from pumping up at the gym, browsing for books or chatting and cruising at the coffeeshop. Groups stop to chat on the street bound by an undeniable intimacy. Chicago may be America's third largest city, but the visual element of its gay community, who frequent the partyboy hangouts, is quite small. And like any scene filled with raging libidos, it tends to get a bit incestuous.

There's something to do every night: often too much to do, in fact. Check the listings in the fag rags (*see* **Read all about it**, *page 204*) for mentions of special theme nights. The only real gap in the Chicago gay clubbing calendar is on Tuesdays, which makes it as a good time as any to have a laid-back evening at any of the bars.

The streets of Boystown are safe and are perhaps the only ones in the city where a same-sex couple holding hands won't raise eyebrows. However, there have been a few gay-bashing incidents in the past, most notoriously (and ironically) right across the street from the police station at Addison and Halsted. As always, it's best to be on guard.

The other local homo hotspot is **Andersonville**, north of Lake View. Settled by Swedish immigrants, the locale is popular with lesbians and mellowed-out gay men. With a smattering of bathhouses and bars, a feminist-minded bookstore and some of Chicago's best restaurants, you won't be short of things to do. The residents are easy-going – in contrast to the frenzied pace of life in Boystown – and fiercely opposed to the idea of their homo sweet home becoming yuppified and homogenised like the neighbourhoods to the south.

For gay helplines, resource centres and other services, *see chapter* **Directory**.

LESBIAN INTEREST
Girlbar and **Star Gaze** are the only predominantly female drinking and dancing spots in the city, though lesbians can also always be found at the **Closet**. Your best bet is to take the El up Berwyn and head towards Clark Street in Andersonville.

The nightclub **Berlin** (*see page 219*) now offers Women's Obsession every Wednesday, while its night Prince Sundays – guess when it's held – is similarly popular with the gals. Twice a month the **Mountain Moving Coffee House** is held in the Ebenezer Lutheran Church (1650 W Foster Street, at Ashland Avenue; 312 409 0276), an event for lesbian comics and singers that is strictly for women and children only. Phone ahead for dates and performers.

CRUISING
There are still areas in Chicago where men can go for clandestine sexual encounters with strangers. Though prostitution is illegal and getting caught soliciting sex could carry a jail sentence, there are hustlers on Halsted, particularly north of Addison, and drag queen prostitutes on Broadway north of Addison.

Sex in public is also a punishable offence. Belmont Rocks on the lakefront was once an infamous cruising ground, but lost its notoriety in the late 1990s. Montrose Harbor is still popular, though, especially with those in cars: drive along the circuitous route and you'll see solitary men sitting in their vehicles, tapping brake lights and flashing brights as a signal for sex. The website **www.cruisingforsex.com** contains a comprehensive list of popular spots, including a number of downtown bathrooms.

Entertainment

About Face Theatre
3212 N Broadway, at W Belmont Avenue, Lake View (773 549 7943/www.aboutfacetheatre.com). CTA Belmont. **Open** *box office times and dates vary; shows usually 8pm Thur-Sun.* **Credit** MC, V. **Map** p309 F2.
Consistency and quality rule the city's pre-eminent gay theatre troupe, whose productions are always of a high calibre. *See also p235.*

Bailiwick Repertory
1229 W Belmont Avenue, at N Racine Avenue, Lake View (773 883 1090/www.bailiwick.org). CTA Belmont. **Open** *box office 11am-showtime daily; shows times vary Thur-Sun.* **Credit** AmEx, Disc, MC. **Map** p309 E2.
Less serious than About Face, Bailiwick stages what can generously be described as progressive theatre: what the productions lack in engaging dialogue, they make up for in male nudity. It also hosts the Pride Fest series of plays. *See also p235.*

Baton Lounge
436 N Clark Street, at E Illinois Street, Near North/River North (312 644 5269). CTA Grand or Merchandise Mart. **Open** *shows 8.30pm, 10.30pm, 12.30am Wed-Sun; closed Mon, Tue.* **Admission** $8-$10. **Credit** AmEx, DC, Disc, MC, V. **Map** p306 H10.
Chicago's premier drag venue only allows pre-ops to perform, but these drag queens are so convincing, straight men have been known to fall for them. Look out for Mimi Marks, a stunning Marilyn Monroe-esque bombshell who's worked the circuit for years, and the Miss Continental Pageant in October. Chances are you'll be seated near a tittering bachelorette party.

Disco Bingo
Rehab, 3641 N Halsted Street, at W Addison Street, Lake View/Wrigleyville (773 325 2233). CTA Addison (Red). **Open** *Rehab 4pm-2am Mon-Thur; 4pm-4am Fri, Sun; 4pm-5am Sat; Disco Bingo from 9pm Mon.* **Credit** Disc, MC, V. **Map** p309 F1.
This twisted version of the old favourite, held at the bar attached to **Circuit** (*see p202*), ain't no church hall gambling for the octogenarian set. Hostess Daisy Mae is a sarcastic sourpuss with a razor-sharp wit and a big heart. Rounds are themed: Cheerleader Bingo, for example, in which wigs and pompons are passed around and half the bar tries to out-chant (and out-cuss) the other.

Gentry
440 N State Street, at E Illinois Street, Near North (312 836 0933). CTA Grand. **Open** 4pm-2am Mon-Fri, Sun; 4pm-3am Sat. **Credit** AmEx, DC, Disc, MC, V. **Map** p306 H10.
Two well-known local drag crooners belt out songs at the two branches of this mellow piano bar: Honey West, who also hosts a Sunday brunch at **Cucina Bella** (543 W Diversey Avenue; 773 868 1119), and

Alexandra Billings, a legendary comedic thespian who still performs plays. The Boystown location is open until 3am on Fridays.
Branch: 3320 N Halsted Street, at W Buckingham Place (773 348 1053).

Lolita's
4400 N Clark Street, at W Montrose Avenue, Far North (773 561 3356). CTA Montrose. **Open** 5pm-2am Mon-Fri, Sun; 5pm-3am Sat. **Admission** $5. **No credit cards.**
The throbbing strobe and swirling lights can be a bit disconcerting as you try to find your burrito in the dark, but Lolita's – on the fringes of Uptown – is definitely a one-of-a-kind spot: part Mexican restaurant, part drag queen performing space. Latino (Latina?) stars take to the stage to lip-sync tunes.

Bars

Big Chicks
5024 N Sheridan Road, at W Foster Avenue, Far North (773 728 5511/www.bigchicks.com). CTA Argyle. **Open** 3pm-2am Mon-Fri, Sun; 2pm-3am Sat. **No credit cards.**
This fun Andersonville hangout could almost be considered an art gallery: owner Michelle Fire displays her eclectic collection of paintings and photographs. The predominantly male crowd enjoys the midnight special, 50¢ shots. Michelle also cooks up a mean barbecue/buffet on Sunday afternoons.

Roscoe's (*see p202*). How very civilised.

Cell Block
3702 N Halsted Street, at W Waveland Avenue, Lake View/Wrigleyville (773 665 8064/www.cellblock-chicago.com). CTA Addison (Red). **Open** 4pm-2am Mon-Fri; 2pm-3am Sat; 2pm-2am Sun. **Admission** free Mon-Fri, Sun; $5 Sat. **No credit cards. Map** p309 F1.
A prison motif dominates this appropriately seedy bar. The leather dress code is strictly enforced for entry into the backroom, the Holding Cell. Venture into the Yard, with a chain web and a narrow cage, for S&M sexploits.

Chicago Eagle
5015 N Clark Street, at W Winnemac Avenue, Far North (773 728 0050). CTA Argyle. **Open** 8pm-4am Mon-Fri, Sun; 8pm-5am Sat. **No credit cards.**
Entering through the back of a semi truck sets the rough-and-tumble mood at this Andersonville leather bar. Get your boots spit-shined upstairs at the cruisey bar, while in the Pit, there's a chain-link fence cage for holding 'prisoners' and plenty of dark corners.

The Closet
3325 N Broadway, at W Buckingham Place, Lake View (773 477 8533). CTA Belmont. **Open** 2pm-4am Mon-Fri; noon-5am Sat; noon-4am Sun. **No credit cards. Map** p309 F2.
Lesbian-owned and operated, this tiny bar offers a laid-back locale in which to watch divas on video. It's also a popular late-night option, becoming packed with gay boys once the other bars close.

Cocktail
3359 N Halsted Street, at W Roscoe Street, Lake View (773 477 1420). CTA Belmont. **Open** 4pm-2am Mon-Fri; 2pm-3am Sat; 2pm-2am Sun. **Credit** AmEx, MC, V. **Map** p309 F2.
Small but swank, hip but unpretentious, this glammed-up bar offers an extensive Martini menu. Check out the go-go boys gyrating away at Spank, the Thursday-night staple.

Girlbar
2625 N Halsted Street, at W Wrightwood Avenue, Lincoln Park (773 871 4210). CTA Fullerton. **Open** 7pm-2am Tue-Fri; 7pm-3am Sat; 6pm-2am Sun. **Admission** free-$5. **No credit cards. Map** p308 F4.
If you're a lesbian looking for some lovin', this is your best bet in the city. There's a small dancefloor, two patios and pool tables, and though it's mellow on most nights, weekends can be jumping.

Lucky Horseshoe Lounge
3169 N Halsted Street, at W Belmont Avenue, Lake View (773 404 3169). CTA Belmont. **Open** 2pm-2am Mon-Fri; noon-3am Sat; noon-2am Sun. **No credit cards. Map** p309 F3.
A decidedly seedy haunt frequented mostly by older gents who like to gawk at the low-rent strippers on one of the two platforms. The amiable bar staff ensure that your time here will be interesting, if a bit creepy.

Arts & Entertainment

Melrose is open all hours. *See p204.*

Roscoe's

3354 N Halsted Street, at W Roscoe Street, Lake View (773 281 3355). CTA Addison (Red). **Open** 2pm-2am Mon-Thur; 1pm-2am Fri; noon-3am Sat; noon-2am Sun. **Admission** $3 Sat only. **Credit** MC, V. **Map** p309 F2.

The Bar That Ate Halsted Street, locals joke. With two pool table rooms, multiple bars, a dancefloor and a patio, Chicago's legendary guppie bar is now frequented mostly by suburbanites and out-of-towners.

Sidetrack

3349 N Halsted Street, at W Roscoe Street, Lake View (773 477 9189). CTA Addison (Red). **Open** 3pm-2am Mon-Fri; 2pm-3am Sat; 2pm-2am Sun. **Credit** AmEx, DC, Disc, MC, V. **Map** p309 F2.

You can tell how people feel about this video bar by whether they call it Sidesnacks or Sidetrash. No matter how much it expands, the place is still eternally crowded with cruising Gap-clad boys.

Clubs

In addition to the venues listed here, many straight or mixed clubs host gay events on designated nights of the week. For complete club listings, *see pages 218-223* **Nightlife**.

Berlin (*see page 219*) is popular with people of all sexual persuasions. Weekends get packed and tend to be a pan-sexual free-for-all – it's just as common to see two breeders mashing to electronica as it is to see two gays going at it – but Thursday nights after 2am are when the boys flock in for **Men in Motion**, and Wednesday's **Women's Obsession** is the night for lesbo party gals.

Boom Boom Room at Red Dog

1958 W North Avenue, at N Damen Avenue, Wicker Park/Bucktown (773 278 1009). CTA Damen (Blue). **Open** 10pm-4am Mon-Fri; 10pm-5am Sat. **Admission** $5-$15. **Credit** AmEx, DC, MC, V. **Map** p310 B7.

A diverse crowd – a mix of Hispanics, blacks, whites, males, females, gays and straights – makes this club perhaps the best in the city. Wacky Jojo greets guests at the door to this loft party, where most of the space is set aside for boogieing. *See also p223.*

Charlie's

3726 N Broadway, at W Waveland Avenue, Lake View/Wrigleyville (773 871 8887). CTA Addison (Red). **Open** 3pm-2am Mon, Tue; 3pm-4am Wed-Fri, Sun; 3pm-5am Sat. **Admission** free-$3. **Credit** AmEx, DC, Disc, MC, V. **Map** p309 F1.

Yee-haw! The dancefloor is corralled off, and gay men move in unison under the cowboy boot-shaped disco ball. If you don't know the two-step dances, you won't be able to join the party until late, when the music shifts from country to pop dance. The bar is awash with genteel Southern gents with awshucks attitudes that'll charm your pants off.

Circuit

3641 N Halsted Street, at W Addison Street, Lake View/Wrigleyville (773 325 2233). CTA Addison (Red). **Open** 9pm-2am Wed, Thur; 9pm-4am Fri, Sun; 9pm-5am Sat; closed Mon, Tue. **Admission** $4-$8. **Credit** Disc, MC, V. **Map** p309 F1.

Once the premier spot for Latino queers, this dolled-up warehouse space has been taken over by shirtless boys still mourning the closure of Fusion down the street. Expect smooth and sculpted überfags writhing about half-naked on their alphabet cocktails to salsa and Latin stuff during the week, and slightly poppier and housier tunes at the weekends.

Manhole

3458 N Halsted Street, at W Cornelia Avenue, Lake View (773 975 9244). CTA Addison (Red). **Open** 9pm-4am Mon-Fri, Sun; 9pm-5am Sat. **Admission** $2-$8 (after midnight). **No credit cards. Map** p309 F2.

'Stop moping and start groping', the sign at the front of this sewer-like setting for libidinous gay men once read. Pornos play throughout at this stroke and poke orgy, and there's often an (un)dress code for the backroom dancefloor: you can't go in without taking off your shirt.

Star Gaze

5419 N Clark Street, at Foster Avenue, Far North (773 561 7363/http://members.aol.com/stargazeclub). CTA Berwyn. **Open** 6pm-2am Tue-Thur; 5pm-2am Fri; 11am-3am Sat; noon-2am Sun. **Admission** *Fri, Sat* $5-$10. **Credit** AmEx, DC, Disc, MC, V.

This attitude-free lesbian hangout on the edge of Andersonville has all the right stuff: a super-friendly bartender, pool tables and a dancefloor.

Bathhouses & boothstores

Bijou Theatre

1349 N Wells Street, at W Evergreen Avenue, Old Town (312 943 5397/Bijou Boys Hotline 312 409 8100/www.bijouworld.com). CTA Clark/Division or Sedgwick. **Open** 24hrs daily; *shows* 8.30pm, 10.30pm Mon, Thur; 2pm, 4pm, 8.30pm, 10.30pm Wed; 8pm, 10pm, midnight Fri, Sat. **Admission** *shows* $19 members; $20 non-members. **Map** p307 H8.

Don't let the quaint Victorian townhouse exterior fool you – this theatre at the very southernmost tip of Old Town showcases hardcore flicks and exotic dancers.

Man's Country

5015 N Clark Street, at W Argyle Street, Far North (773 878 2069). CTA Argyle. **Open** 24hrs daily. **Admission** $10-$40. **No credit cards.**
A popular bathhouse among the 30-plus crowd on the fringes of Andersonville, with nude pornstar dancers at weekends. The overpowering bleach smell assures good, clean fun in a dingy locale.

The Ram

3511 N Halsted Street, at W Cornelia Avenue, Lake View (773 525 9528). CTA Addison (Red). **Open** 24hrs daily. **Credit** AmEx, MC, V. **Map** p309 F2.
Porno movies and sexual devices are sold up front. Pay for entry to the back, where men can wander the narrow hallway, hang out in booths or watch movies to get them in the mood.

Steamworks

3246 N Halsted Street, at W Belmont Avenue, Lake View (773 929 6080). CTA Belmont. **Open** 24hrs daily. **Admission** *membership* $6; *room rentals* $13-$25. **Credit** MC, V. **Map** p309 F2.

Choose whether you want a locker or a room, wrap a towel around yourself and wander to your heart's content. A jacuzzi, showers and a video area are some of the locations in this renowned den, arguably the most pleasant of the city's bathhouses.

Restaurants

For Mexican food with drag shows on the side – or vice versa, depending on your priorities – *see page 201* **Lolita's**.

Ann Sather Restaurant

929 W Belmont Avenue, at N Sheffield Avenue, Lake View (773 348 2378). CTA Belmont. **Open** 7am-10pm daily. **Main courses** $7-$13. **Credit** AmEx, DC, MC, V. **Map** p309 E2.
This gay-owned Swedish eatery in Lake View has been serving up hearty meals and ace cinnamon rolls for years, and still impresses. The owners are regular contributors to local gay charities, and are higly regarded in the community. For their Andersonville branch, *see p142.*

The queer year

One of two circuit parties held in Chicago, the **Fireball** – formerly known as the Hearts Party – is a Valentine's Day weekend event that draws party boys from around the world, even though it's in the middle of winter. As with any large event in Chicago, various activities take place all weekend, with proceeds benefiting AIDS charities. Pick up one of the free gay weeklies for listings, or check its website at www.thefireball.com.

Memorial Day weekend in May brings with it **International Mr Leather** (773 878 6360). Head to the Congress Hotel to see the bizarre leather bazaar that leaves shellshocked out-of-towners slack-jawed. With the last Sunday in June comes the fun-filled **Pride Parade** (773 348 8243), which runs along Halsted Street and Broadway. Fill water bottles with celebratory Mimosas to kickstart the festivities, find a spot to cheer the floats as they cruise by, and head to Diversey Harbor for the rally that follows the parade. As a protest against the cat calls and boob-grabbing that have taken place at the Pride Parade, a hard-core local group called the Lesbian Avengers has started an alternative parade called the **Dyke March** (312 409 3705).

Mid-August finds locals flocking to the largest of the city's summer street fairs, **North Halsted Market Days**. Mill about in the sunshine, browsing through the various

booths, dehydrate yourself with alcohol and dance outside. The fair runs between Belmont and Grace, and you'll find yourself wandering back and forth all day. A month later, show your support for increased research by joining the **AIDS Walk** (312 422 8200), usually held on the last Sunday in September.

In November, the **Chicago Lesbian & Gay International Film Festival** (773 293 1447; www.chicagofilmmakers.org/~reeling) hits the Windy City. Traditionally, the first-week flicks are shown at the venerable Music Box Theatre, and elsewhere in the second week. Opening night is always a big shebang. *See also page 197.*

The second circuit party hosted in Chicago is **Pumpkinhead**, held on Hallowe'en weekend. In 1999, the big night was held at **Green Dolphin Street**, a club/restaurant at Ashland and Clybourn with a patio overlooking the river (*see page 212*). Also around Hallowe'en is the **Night of 100 Drag Queens** at Sidetrack, an event that lives up to its name. There are two stages, featuring quick shots of wannabes having their brief moments of stardom. It can be a bit overwhelming, but a good time is more or less guaranteed. Tickets cost $10, or $25 including the pre-event reception. For more on other seasonal events in Chicago, *see chapter* **Chicago by Season**.

Caribou Coffee

*3300 N Broadway, at W Aldine Avenue, Lake View
(773 477 3695). CTA Belmont.* **Open** 6am-11pm
Mon-Thur, Sun; 6am-midnight Fri, Sat. **Credit**
AmEx, MC, V. **Map** p309 F2.
Believe it or not, there are some gay men who temporarily give their livers a break. This cosy coffeeshop is where they sip their mocha skim lattes,
no whipped cream.

Dellwood Pickle

*1475 W Balmoral Avenue, at N Clark Street, Far
North (773 271 7728). CTA Berwyn.* **Open** 4-10pm
Tue-Thur; 4-11pm Fri, Sat; 9am-9pm Sun; closed
Mon. **Main courses** $8.25-$10.25. **Credit** AmEx,
DC, Disc, MC, V.
This no-frills Andersonville favourite offers great
food (especially if you like Gorgonzola and artichoke
entrées) at surprisingly affordable prices.

Melrose

*3233 N Broadway, at W Melrose Street, Lake View
(773 327 2060). CTA Belmont.* **Open** 24hrs daily.
Main courses $7.95-$16.95. **Credit** MC, V.
Map p309 F2.
The place to see and be seen, the morning after: how
else will you find out who went home with who? The
diner fare is mediocre, but it is open round the clock.

Nookies Tree

*3334 N Halsted Street, at W Buckingham Place, Lake
View (773 248 9888). CTA Belmont.* **Open** 7am-
midnight Mon-Thur, Sun; 24hrs Fri, Sat. **Main
courses** $5-$12. **No credit cards. Map** p309 F2.
A cosy Lake View diner with a sidewalk café mural
and pleasingly salubrious opening hours on the

weekends. Congenial staff, excellent soups and
extensive breakfast and burger selections usually
quell the after-hours munchies.

Oo-La-La!

*3335 N Halsted Street, at W Buckingham Place,
Lake View (773 935 7708). CTA Belmont.* **Open**
5.30-11pm Mon-Sat; 10am-3pm, 5.30-10pm Sun.
Main courses $15-21. **Credit** AmEx, MC, V.
Map p309 F2.
A posh bistro right along Boystown's main drag
that serves up delectable Italian and French cuisine.
There are daily specials and a full bar.

Shops

Barbara's Bookstore

*1350 N Wells Street, at W Evergreen Avenue, Old
Town (312 642 5044). CTA Clark/Division.* **Open**
9am-10pm Mon-Sat; 10am-9pm Sun. **Credit** AmEx,
Disc, MC, V. **Map** p307 H8.
A cheery lesbian-owned store on the southern
fringes of Old Town with a great array of titles,
including photography, children's books, fiction and
biographies.

Batteries Not Included

*3420 N Halsted Street, at W Roscoe Street,
Lake View (773 935 9900). CTA Belmont.*
Open noon-midnight daily. **Credit** AmEx, MC, V.
Map p309 F2.
Run out of lube in the middle of the night? Head to
this sex shop, where the fun, queeny owner will let
you test his favourite variety. You can indulge your
libido in the knowledge that half of the profits go to
charity. The window displays are always a hoot.

Read all about it

Perhaps the first thing you should do when
you arrive in Chicago is head to Halsted
Street or Broadway in the heart of Boystown,
stop in at one of the many restaurants or
shops and pick up one of the free gay and
lesbian weeklies. News-wise, pick from the
Windy City Times and a recent upstart, the
Chicago Free Press, which developed from
most of the *Windy City Times* staff got fed up
with working conditions and jumped ship.
Animosity between the two titles has kept the
lawsuits flying, though the *Free Press* has
proven itself the better of the papers.

A family of newspapers, **Lambda
Publications** (www.outlineschicago.com)
pitches its products at lesbians and racial
minorities. *Outlines* comes out weekly and
features a column by Tracy Baim that
does a nice job of summing up news
and local events. The minuscule *Nightlines*

focuses on entertainment, while
Blacklines and *En La Vida* are both
monthly publications.

For bar and events listings along with
frivolous filler editorial – 'Gotcha', Billy
Masters' gossip column, is one of the only
things inside worth reading – flip through the
ads in **Gay Chicago**. Be sure to pick up the
ever-irreverent **Gab**, an endless source of
bitchy humour, bar and club listings and, on
its back page entitled 'The Skinny', gossip
from the local gay scene.

Away from traditional print media,
www.snapsaint.com offers the dirty dish on
the local underground scene, featuring
photos and sordid stories of drag queens, fag
divas, drug dealers, hustlers and other
überfags. Alternatively, tune into the Lesbigay
radio show on 1240 and 1470 AM, which
runs 5-7pm from Monday to Friday.

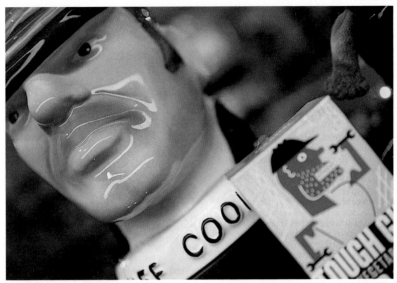

'My friend went to Chicago and all I got was this simply *dahling* china bloke.' **Gay Mart.**

Beatnix

3400 N Halsted Street, at W Roscoe Street, Lake View (773 281 6933). CTA Addison (Red). **Open** 11am-10pm Mon-Thur; 11am-midnight Fri, Sat; noon-9am Sun. **Credit** MC, V. **Map** p309 F2.

The naughty window displays at this trendy thrift-store upset neighbours and prompted a local alderman to complain, so Beatnix responded by making the mannequins even more scandalous. A good place to snazz up your wardrobe on a limited budget; this is the drag queen wig and dress headquarters.

Gay Mart

3457 N Halsted Street, at W Cornelia Avenue, Lake View/Wrigleyville (773 929 4272). CTA Addison (Red). **Open** 11am-7pm Mon-Thur, Sun; 11am-9pm Fri, Sat. **Credit** AmEx, Disc, MC, V. **Map** p309 F2.

An expansive kitsch-fest jam-packed with Betty Boop, Curious George, *South Park* and *Star Wars* memorabilia. Giggle over the anatomically gifted Billy dolls: they'd make Barbie and Ken blush.

Specialty Video

3221 N Broadway, at W Belmont Avenue, Lake View (773 248 3434). CTA Belmont. **Open** 10am-10pm Mon-Thur, Sun; 10am-11pm Fri, Sat. **Credit** AmEx, Disc, MC, V. **Map** p309 F2.

Most Boystown video stores offer some adult titles, but this spot has an extensive non-porn selection, too.

Unabridged Bookstore

3251 N Broadway, at W Belmont Avenue, Lake View (773 883 9119). CTA Belmont. **Open** 10am-10pm Mon-Fri; 10am-8pm Sat, Sun. **Credit** AmEx, Disc, MC, V. **Map** p309 F2.

The Borders/Barnes & Noble/Crown triumvirate hasn't closed down this independent store, which stocks great selections of mags and books. The staff tape little cards with their recommendations all along the shelves. Sex advice columnist Dan Savage once said this was the first place he shoplifted porn.

Universal Gear

3153 N Broadway, at W Belmont Avenue, Lake View (773 296 1090). CTA Belmont. **Open** 11am-10pm Mon-Thur, Sun; 11am-11pm Fri, Sat. **Credit** AmEx, Disc, MC, V. **Map** p309 F3.

Dubbed Universal Queer, this is where the fashionable 'mos shop 'til they drop. It sells contemporary Euro chic duds for men.

We're Everywhere

3434 N Halsted Street, at W Newport Avenue, Lake View (773 404 0590). CTA Addison (Red). **Open** noon-9pm Mon-Fri; 11am-8pm Sat, Sun. **Credit** AmEx, Disc, MC, V. **Map** p309 F2.

Where else would you buy your Boystown T-shirt? This gay gift shop is filled with homo-themed clothes and rainbow jewellery.

Women & Children First

5233 N Clark Street, at W Foster Avenue, Far North (773 769 9299/www.womenandchildrenfirst.com). CTA Berwyn. **Open** 11am-7pm Mon, Tue; 11am-9pm Wed-Fri; 10am-7pm Sat; 11am-6pm Sun. **Credit** AmEx, Disc, MC, V.

Dykes and Tykes, as some call it, is a must for feminist and child-oriented literature, specialising in lesbian and gay titles, music, videos and magazines all the way up in Andersonville.

Music

They got it good, and that ain't bad, but Chicago's music scene is far more than just getting the blues.

Rock, Roots & Jazz

When people think Chicago music, they inevitably envision the Chicago blues. After World War II, a migration of black people from the South brought an adulterated version of traditional, Delta blues. By upping the tempo and plugging in their guitars, electric blues – or Chicago blues – emerged to take the music world by storm. You couldn't walk down the old Maxwell Street market area without hearing a world-famous musician playing on the street corner. Men like Muddy Waters, Buddy Guy and Howlin' Wolf not only brought fame to the city, but also to record labels such as Chess, Aristocrat and Argonaut.

That, of course, was a long time ago. Though today the blues fan is presented with at least ten performers in ten different places on any given night, audiences tend to be touristy and over 30, the young, black blues audience having pledged allegiance to hip hop long ago. In fact, there is arguably a larger blues scene in, say, Germany than there is in Chicago.

But as the largest city in the Midwest, Chicago is on the itinerary for every touring band worth its salt, and also enjoys one of the richest local music scenes in the country. Thanks to its status as a stronghold of internationally acclaimed independent record labels (Touch & Go, Drag City, Thrill Jockey, Victory), the city also attracts an abundance of indie and underground rock bands, which makes the city's small club scene both popular and close-knit.

The Chicago industrial sound, cultivated in the 1980s by bands like Big Black and Ministry, replaced by heavy interest in post-rock (Chicago is, after all, Tortoise's hometown), garage rock and, a little surprisingly, country music. For in addition to serving as base for Smashing Pumpkins, R Kelly, Tortoise and Liz Phair, the city is also the home of insurgent country, an indie-country music scene spearheaded by local record label Bloodshot Records (*see page 213*).

It's worth mentioning that music clubs remain relatively static in Chicago, and new clubs or venues open rarely. For this, we have Mayor Daley to thank: his strict regulation of liquor licences and bans on loud music in certain areas of the city haven't really helped the scene to flourish. But while the occasional small club does close, most of the venues listed below are cornerstones of the scene and here to stay.

TICKETS & INFORMATION

The vast array of weekly music can best be found in *Newcity* and the *Chicago Reader*. *Newcity*, the smaller of the two, doesn't list absolutely every event in the city, but the listings are fairly extensive and its format makes for easy sifting. The *Chicago Reader* is murderously extensive and full-to-bursting with listings of every event.

With only a few exceptions, tickets for club shows are available only at the door, though even popular bands playing small clubs rarely sell out before the day of the show. Buy tickets for large shows at the venues' box offices or over the phone or internet through Ticketmaster. Most blues and jazz clubs don't sell advance tickets unless the act is huge.

Weekday shows in smaller clubs (up to **Double Door** or even **House of Blues** size) usually start at about 9pm and finish at 1am. On Fridays and Saturdays, shows run from 10pm to 2am. In the giant venues (the likes of the **Aragon** and the **United Center**), shows start and finish much earlier: usually from 7.30pm to 10.30pm (at the latest) on any night of the week.

The best Venues

For blues the way God intended
The **Checkerboard Lounge** (page 212).

For fat ladies singing
The **Civic Opera House** (page 215).

For acts about to make it big
The **Metro** (page 210).

For arse-shaking basslines
The **Wild Hare** (page 211).

For lazing on a sunny afternoon
The **Ravinia Festival** (page 217).

For anything but the blues
The **House of Blues** (page 209).

Delilah's: Samson couldn't resist. Can you?

Smaller bars and clubs rarely charge more than $8, perhaps up to $12 if the act is very well known. For concerts at the **House of Blues** and other, bigger venues, tickets could go for anything from $20 to $75. And for the clubs and bars, at least, anything not designated as an all-ages show is only open to those over the age of 21. Be sure to always carry a photo ID.

Ticketmaster

(312 559 1212/www.ticketmaster.com). **Open** 8am-9pm Mon-Fri; 8am-8pm Sat; 8am-6pm Sun. **Credit** AmEx, DC, Disc, MC, V.

General & rock clubs

Allstate Arena

6920 N Mannheim Road, at W Higgins Road, Rosemont (847 635 6601). CTA Rosemont. **Open** *box office* 11am-7pm Mon-Fri; noon-5pm Sat; 3hrs before performance Sun. **Credit** AmEx, Disc, MC, V.
Formerly called the Rosemont Horizon and also the home of International Hockey League franchise the Chicago Wolves, this super-venue is reserved for bands too small to merit the **United Center** *(see p211)*. It usually offers massive programme tours featuring six or more bands. The arena has decent sound, but its northern location (in Rosemont, closer to O'Hare than downtown) makes it more attractive to suburbanites than city dwellers.

Aragon Ballroom

1106 W Lawrence Avenue, at N Broadway, Far North (773 561 9500). CTA Lawrence. **Credit** AmEx, Disc, V. **Open** hours vary.
Built more than 70 years ago, the Aragon Ballroom (or 'Brawlroom', as it's unlovingly dubbed) was constructed for ballroom dancing and hit its peak in the late 1950s and '60s. These days, the 4,500-seater Uptown venue is the place to hear bands such as Primus, Megadeth and Alanis Morissette pre-superstardom. Unfortunately, the stately surroundings, with high ceilings and an expansive surface area, make for terrible sound: unless you're one of the lucky ones up front, you'll just catch echoes.

Cubby Bear

1059 W Addison Street, at N Clark Street, Lake View/Wrigleyville (773 327 1662). CTA Addison (Red). **Open** *during Cubs games* 10am-2am Mon-Fri, Sun; 10am-3am Sat; *otherwise* 4pm-2am Mon-Fri; 11am-3am Sat; 11am-2am Sun; *live music* Sat, some Thur. **Credit** AmEx, DC, Disc, MC, V. **Map** p309 E1.
A long-time, catch-all venue that's changed names more often than the Cubs change managers, the Cubby Bear offers anything from Digital Underground to Lee 'Scratch' Perry or Grateful Dead cover bands. Its location by Wrigley Field means it's a favourite spot for post-Cubs games revelry, so during the season it's crammed with people who couldn't care less about music. *See also p157.*

Delilah's

2771 N Lincoln Avenue, at W Diversey Parkway, Lincoln Park (773 472 2771). CTA Diversey. **Open** 4pm-2am Mon-Fri, Sun; 4pm-3am Sat. **No credit cards.** **Map** p308 E4.
A bit of a cheat: this little bar doesn't actually offer live music (entry, too, is free), but it is a full-on rock'n'roll bar, the only one of its kind in the city. The atmosphere is great, the crowd a mix of regulars, curious barhoppers and underground denizens, and it's not unusual for bands to put in an appearance after a gig. DJs are on hand from Sunday to Wednesday: Monday is usually a punk rock night, with Wednesday devoted to insurgent country. Delilah's also boasts the largest selection of whiskies in the Midwest, and its imported beer selection is unparalleled (owner Mike Miller spends a lot of time in Belgium). Not to be missed.

Double Door

1572 N Milwaukee Avenue, at N Damen Avenue, Wicker Park/Bucktown (773 489 3160/ www.doubledoor.com). CTA Damen (Blue). **Open** 8pm-2am Mon-Fri, Sun; 8pm-3am Sat. **Credit** *bar only* AmEx, MC, V. **Map** p310 B7.
The **Metro**'s younger brother *(see p210)*, the Double Door is a large room that fits 500, smaller than the Metro but larger than a small club. It hosts rock as well as weekly hip hop and DJ events. Downstairs there's a place to get away from the music, with pool tables, video games and a second full-service bar.

Have twice the fun at the **Double Door**. *See page 207.*

Elbo Room

2871 N Lincoln Avenue, at W George Street, Lake View (773 549 5549). CTA Diversey. **Open** 7pm-2am Mon-Fri, Sun; 7pm-3am Sat. **Credit** AmEx, Disc, MC, V. **Map** p309 D3.

A two-floored venue in the Lake View area, the Elbo Room books an eclectic range of acts: everything from straight rock to acid jazz, hip hop and funk. The ground floor room is a good but hardly enormous space, though its low ceiling and intimate confines mean that brass instruments can sound a bit too loud when blown into a microphone. Should you need it, the dimly lit upstairs bar offers sanctuary from the music. *See also p156.*

Empty Bottle

1035 N Western Avenue, at W Cortez Street, Wicker Park/Bucktown (773 276 3600/ www.emptybottle.com). CTA Damen (Blue). **Open** 3pm-2am Mon-Fri; noon-3am Sat; noon-2am Sun. **No credit cards. Map** p310 A9.

One of the city's premier club-sized venues, the nine-year-old Empty Bottle, situated on the edge of Ukrainian Village and Humboldt Park, hosts alternative, rock, punk, metal and pop shows. A slew of cheap beers and liquors ensures that the Bottle always gets business from a loyal group of regulars, regardless of the music. Owner Bruce Finkleman has a good ear for music, however, so the Bottle is usually jammed on Friday and Saturday nights, while Tuesday nights are usually held open for the Ken Vandermark Trio. Wednesdays have traditionally become the night for jazz and improvised and experimental music, and have succeeded in pulling international acts like Mats Gustafsson and Peter Brötzmann.

Fireside Bowl

2648 W Fullerton Avenue, at N Talman Avenue, Wicker Park/Bucktown (773 486 2700). CTA California (Blue (NW)). **No credit cards. Open** 6pm-2am daily.

The Fireside Bowl, an all-ages music venue, is located on the northern edge of Bucktown inside a converted bowling alley, hence the name. Indeed, the lanes and pins are still in residence, but bowling is only allowed infrequently due to the punk and hardcore shows, plus the occasional experimental and metal gigs that now take place here. Though the Fireside can fit 800 people, even the most crowded shows rarely pull more than 300. The Fireside's status as the only full-time, all-ages venue in the city means that it attracts a very young, lively and up-for-it crowd. There is, however, a bar for those gig-goers old enough to imbibe, though it is manned by the slowest bartender in the western world.

FitzGerald's

6615 W Roosevelt Road, Berwyn (708 788 2118/ www.fitzgeraldsnightclub.com). CTA Oak Park (Blue). **Open** 7pm-1am Tue-Thur; 7pm-3am Fri, Sat; 5pm-1am Sun; closed Mon. **Credit** AmEx, DC, Disc, MC, V.

A long-standing suburban staple, FitzGerald's is the only small music venue/bar in Chicago decorated with warm wood panelling and mounted deer heads. It hosts mostly country, rock and blues between Thursday and Saturday, with Sundays reserved for big band jazz. Poetry-reading events are held on Tuesdays. FitzGerald's is occasionally closed on Sunday evenings as well as Mondays for private events, so phone ahead to check it's open before heading over there.

Grant Park Petrillo Music Shell

*235 S Columbus Drive, at E Jackson Drive, The Loop
(312 742 4763). CTA Adams or Jackson (Blue, Red).*
Open *mid-June-Aug* concerts usually Wed-Sat.
Map p305 J12.
A large space for free concerts in the expansive
Grant Park, the Petrillo Music Shell is the site of
many large music festivals (Blues Fest, Jazz Fest,
Celtic Fest; *see p90* **The sounds of summer**). If
there's a concert going on in Grant Park, expect huge
crowds, slow lines and baby carriages by the dozen.

Hideout

*1354 W Wabansia Avenue, at N Ada Street,
Wicker Park/Bucktown (773 227 4433/
www.hideoutchicago.com). CTA 9, 72 bus.* **Open**
3pm-2am Tue-Fri; 7pm-3am Sat; closed Mon, Sun. **No
credit cards.**
An out-of-the-way bar located in an industrial corridor on the fringe of Wicker Park off North Avenue,
the Hideout is Chicago's most beloved country and
roots bar, and a hangout for those who are part of
the city's country music scene. Tuesday nights are
reserved for Devil in a Woodpile, an authentic country blues act that often packs the Hideout on a night
when few other bars are occupied. Owners Katie and
Tim Tuten go out of their way to ensure the staff
are friendly, one of the reasons the Hideout has so
many regulars.

HotHouse

*31 E Balbo Drive, at S Wabash Avenue, South Loop
(312 362 9707/www.hothouse.net). CTA Harrison.*
Open 5pm-2am Mon-Fri, Sun; 5pm-3am Sat. **Credit**
AmEx, MC, V. **Map** p305 H13.
The HotHouse was a floating operation until only a
few years ago, when it settled into its current, near-
South Side home and became the city's premier
venue for world music and jazz. It incorporates two
performance spaces which fit roughly 200 people
each, though they're rarely in use simultaneously.
You might catch the Congo's Sam Mangwana on one
night, the Chicago Samba School the next and
Native American poetry readings the night after,
which should give you some idea of the eclecticism
on offer.

House of Blues

*329 N Dearborn Street, at W Kinzie Street, Near
North/River North (312 923 2000/www.hob.com).
CTA Grand, Lake or State.* **Open** *restaurant*
11.30am-10pm daily; *music* hours vary. **Credit**
AmEx, DC, Disc, MC, V. **Map** p306 H11.
Chicago's branch of the nationwide chain is worth
visiting even if only to see the gaudy art inside: a
combination of outsider art and rural folk art, it
places the ambience somewhere between juke joint
and opera house. The House of Blues also presents
some of the best national and international acts,
though rarely the blues. A four-level hangout with
opera boxes and an elevating stage, it also boasts
one of the city's best sound systems. The first-floor
restaurant serves authentic Southern cooking and
hosts occasional blues events, with Sunday brunch
featuring gospel groups from C hicago's South Side).
Though purists scorn the place, its strength lies not
in the blues it books, but in its eclecticism: any place
that runs the gamut from skinhead hardcore to LTJ
Bukem must have something going for it.

Punk and metal fire up the youth of Chicago at the **Fireside Bowl**. *See page 208.*

Arts & Entertainment

Metro & Smart Bar

3730 N Clark Street, at N Racine Avenue, Lake View/ Wrigleyville (773 549 0203/www.metrochicago.com). CTA Addison (Red). **Open** *Metro hours vary; Smart Bar* 10pm-4am Mon-Fri, Sun; 10pm-5am Sat. **Credit** AmEx, V. **Map** p309 E1.

A medium-sized venue and former theatre, the **Metro** has a great reputation and attracts well-known national and international bands to its intimate space. Well-regarded long-time owner Joe Shanahan's attention has helped bring notoriety to well-known local bands such as Smashing Pumpkins, though perhaps we shouldn't hold him entirely responsible. The main floor is standing-room only, and there are a limited number of tables and chairs on the balcony. The sound is great and the sightlines better, and the Metro remains one of the best venues in the city, if not the country. Downstairs, the **Smart Bar** (*see p158*) features DJs nightly, spinning anything from Chicago house to jazz or punk; major touring DJs like Smith & Mighty regularly put in an appearance here. The neighbourhood crowd is an interesting mix of clubhoppers, alternative hipsters, gig-goers and frat kids.

Old Town School of Folk Music

4544 N Lincoln Avenue, at W Montrose Avenue, Far North (773 728 6000). CTA Western. **Open** *box office* 9.30am-10pm Mon-Thur; 9.30am-5pm Fri-Sun. **Credit** AmEx, MC, V.

The 42-year-old Old Town School of Folk Music recently moved from its digs in, um, Old Town to this more modern, spacious facility on the edge of Ravenswood. Opened in 1957 by Midwest folk hero

Win Stracke, the place is primarily a music school, but on most weekends, concerts by folk, bluegrass and country artists are held in its 420-seater theatre.

Park West

322 W Armitage Avenue, at N Clark Street, Lincoln Park (773 929 5959). CTA Armitage. **Open** *box office* 11am-5pm Mon-Fri; closed Sat, Sun. **No credit cards. Map** p308 G6.

This upmarket venue usually caters to an older audience. Acts ranging from jazz to light rock are the order of the day, with occasional visits by the Dark Star Orchestra, a Grateful Dead cover band who pull in legions of idiots. A semicircle of booths and chairs surrounds the stage (phone ahead to reserve), and it usually operates a non-smoking policy.

Riviera Theatre

4746 N Racine Avenue, at W Lawrence Avenue, Far North (773 275 6800). CTA Lawrence. **Open** hours vary. **Credit** AmEx, Disc, V.

Part of the Uptown triumvirate (with the **Aragon Ballroom**, *see p207* and the **Green Mill**, *see p212*), the Riviera is larger than the **Metro** (*see above*) but smaller than the Aragon and pulls in acts accordingly. You're not likely to find anything above and beyond radio fare here on a bill that might range from the Offspring to Yes.

Schubas Tavern & Harmony Grill

3159 N Southport Avenue, at W Belmont Avenue, Lake View (773 525 2508/www.schubas.com). CTA Belmont or Southport. **Open** 11am-2am Mon-Fri; 8am-3am Sat; 9am-2am Sun. **Credit** AmEx, DC, Disc, MC, V. **Map** p309 D3.

Enjoy great gigs in the shadow of Marina City at the **House of Blues**. *See page 209.*

Aragon Ballroom: old-school splendour and new-school rock. *See page 207.*

The backroom of **Schubas Tavern** is a catch-all venue for just about every type of music you could hope to find or avoid. In the late 1990s, Schubas put itself on the map as a venue for insurgent country, but has since expanded its booking policy to include pop, jazz, blues, world music and funk. While the front bar is an established neighbourhood hangout, the back attracts all types of crowds depending on the concert (*see p156*). The adjacent **Harmony Grill** features gourmet sandwiches; it's an easy and cheap place in which to grab a meal before the show.

United Center

1901 W Madison Street, at N Damen Avenue, West Side (312 559 1212). CTA Ashland (Green) or Medical Center. **Open** hours vary. **Credit** AmEx, Disc, MC, V.
A monstrous venue home to the Chicago Bulls, the Chicago Blackhawks and, from time to time, concerts by mammoth touring artists both national and international. The Center comes with all the cavernous acoustics and terrible sightlines that you'd expect from such a place, not to mention the prohibitively expensive concessions.

Wild Hare

3530 N Clark Street, at W Newport Avenue, Lake View/Wrigleyville (773 327 4273). CTA Addison (Red). **Open** 7pm-2am Mon-Fri, Sun; 7pm-3am Sat. **No credit cards. Map** p309 E2.
Essentially the city's only reggae bar, the Wild Hare pulls international acts as well as those from the healthy local stable of artists. There's reggae seven nights a week, with an occasional ska or Jamaican soul act thrown in once a month. As close to a dancehall as you'll get in Chicago. *See also p158.*

Blues clubs

Blue Chicago

736 N Clark Street, at W Superior Street, Near North (312 642 6261/www.bluechicago.com). CTA Chicago (Brown/Purple, Red). **Open** 8pm-2am Mon-Fri; 8pm-3am Sat; closed Sun. **Credit** AmEx, MC, V. **Map** p306 H10.
This pair of four-year-old blues clubs, located in the heart of Chicago's tourist belt, do a good job of recreating a juke joint feel, though both are generally filled with wall-to-wall out-of-towners. Blue Chicago at Superior is the larger of the two, with the Ohio location built in the long tavern style. Acts are local, and often feature female vocalists such as Grana Louise, Big Time Sarah and Patricia Scott. While aficionados will cringe at even the first two notes of *Sweet Home Chicago*, the venues' penchant for catering to tourists ensures that you'll hear it, and every other tired old standard, at least once a night. **Branch**: 536 N Clark Street, at Ohio Street, River North (312 661 0100).

Buddy Guy's Legends

754 S Wabash Avenue, at E Balbo Drive, South Loop (312 427 0333/www.buddyguys.com). CTA Harrison. **Open** 5pm-2am Mon-Fri, Sun; 5pm-3am Sat. **Credit** AmEx, Disc, MC, V. **Map** p305 H13.
Buddy Guy *is* Chicago blues, and his club, despite the heavy presence of tourists lured by the name, is one of the city's most dynamic, offering an equal sampling of new and old blues artists. Unlike the juke joints it attempts to recall, Buddy's is quite large, but don't let that put you off. There's live blues every night of the

week, plus a free acoustic show for the after-work crowd on Fridays. The restaurant serves soul food and Southern cooking, and there's a barbecue that would smoke the glitter off the **House of Blues**' walls. A tourist trap, but one with substance. *See also p145.*

Checkerboard Lounge
428 E 43rd Street, at S Martin Luther King Drive, South Side (773 624 3240). CTA 4 bus. **Open** 11am-2am Mon-Fri, Sun; 11am-3am Sat. **No credit cards**.
The one-time home-from-home for Buddy Guy and Junior Wells, the Checkerboard is one of the few blues clubs that's more than 25 years old. A little run-down and, thanks to King Drive renovations, in danger of closing, the place remains among the most authentic blues clubs in the city, its heritage all the more realistic due to its South Side location (it's easiest reached by cab, incidentally). An authentic alternative to the plain-Jane downtown blues clubs.

Kingston Mines
2548 N Halsted Street, at W Wrightwood Avenue, Lincoln Park (773 477 4646/www.kingston-mines.com). CTA Fullerton. **Open** 8pm-4am Mon-Fri, Sun; 8pm-5am Sat. **Credit** AmEx, DC, Disc, MC, V. **Map** p308 F4.
Another veteran of Chicago's blues scene, Kingston Mines has been bringing the city solid electric blues for more than 30 years. Its location at the edge of Lincoln Park attracts a fair number of tourists but not to the extent of the downtown clubs, and its 4am/5am licence also brings in a huge after-hours crowd. With two stages in adjoining rooms, the venue boasts non-stop blues from 9.30pm until last call. Like most blues clubs in the city, there's a restaurant attached.

Lee's Unleaded Blues
7401 S Chicago Avenue, at 74th Street, South Side (773 493 3477). CTA 30 bus. **Open** noon-2am Mon-Fri, Sun; noon-3am Sat. **No credit cards**.
An authentic juke joint inhabited mainly by long-time regulars, Lee's has been one of the South Side's favourite blues clubs since the early 1980s. Though the acts here aren't big names, the intimate confines encourage call-and-response interaction between the performers and crowds. A gritty club in the Chicago tradition, and much the better for it.

Lilly's
2513 N Lincoln Avenue, at W Altgeld Street, Lincoln Park (773 525 2422). CTA Fullerton. **Open** 4pm-2am Wed-Fri; 4pm-3am Sat; closed Mon, Tue, Sun. **No credit cards**. **Map** p308 F5.
A cosy two-floor blues spot that keeps things cheap despite its location in expensive Lincoln Park. What sets it apart is the dizzying array of beers (both bottled and on tap) and the piano, an instrument few Chicago clubs want to bother with. Acts draw on the local talent pool, with Eddy Clearwater and Howling Wolf, Jr often featured on the weekends. It's a small club, but it rarely gets too crowded. Oh yeah, and then there's Lilly herself: don't mess with her or you'll be positively flayed by her razor-sharp tongue.

Rosa's
3420 W Armitage Avenue, at N Kimball Avenue, West Side (773 342 0452/www.rosaslounge.com). CTA 73, 82 bus. **Open** 8pm-3am Tue-Fri; 8pm-4am Sat; closed Mon, Sun. **Credit** AmEx, Disc, MC, V.
While not necessarily the most authentic blues club in the city, this far-West Side hangout is generally considered by Chicagoans in the know to be the best. Owners Tony and Rosa book 100% authentic blues – some from the Mississippi Delta, some country blues, some Chicago blues – and whatever's on offer, the crowd knows how to appreciate it. Rosa's even pushes the bubble by booking near-jazz players like Melvin Taylor (who has a regular gig) and the Ruby Harris Electric Violin Blues Band.

Smoke Daddy
1804 W Division Street, at N Wood Street, Wicker Park/Bucktown (773 772 6656). CTA Division. **Open** 11am-1am Mon, Fri-Sun; 5pm-1am Tue-Thur. **Credit** AmEx, Disc, MC, V. **Map** p310 C8.
Attempting to mimic a vintage roadhouse/diner joint, Smoke Daddy serves up a fiery barbecue in the TexArkana style and features free music every night. Jazz and rockabilly both find a home here, but the weekend slant is definitely towards the blues. Granted, Smokedaddy is as much about the food as the music, but it's an excellent excuse to enjoy barbecued pork, listen to the blues and explore this edge of Wicker Park.

Jazz clubs

For **Andy's**, *see page 146.*

Green Dolphin Street
2200 N Ashland Avenue, at N Clybourn Avenue, Lincoln Park (773 395 0066.www.jazzitup.com). CTA 6, 70 bus. **Open** 5.30-10pm Tue-Thur, Sun; 5.30-11pm Fri, Sat; closed Mon. **Credit** AmEx, DC, MC, V. **Map** p308 D5.
A high-end restaurant/jazz venue aimed at and patronised by the well-paid 30- to 50-year-old crowd. Light jazz is the general fare, though Tuesdays feature Latin and world jazz. An evening at Green Dolphin Street is more about the exclusive atmosphere than the music: there's a humidor boasting expensive cigars and a ceiling-high liquor cabinet filled with expensive selections.

Green Mill
4802 N Broadway, at W Lawrence Avenue, Far North (773 878 5552). CTA Lawrence. **Open** noon-4am Mon-Fri; noon-5am Sat; 11am-4am Sun. **Credit** AmEx.
A visit to the Green Mill is an absolute must for any visitor to Chicago. This venerable club, situated in the heart of old Uptown, dates back to the days of Al Capone, who, legend has it, used to sit in the booth facing the door so no one could get in without him seeing. The Green Mill is small and fills extremely fast on the weekends: if you want to sit, you'll likely have to wait. Acts range from soft jazz

Urban cowboys

Chicago. The Windy City. Home of the electric blues, Sears Tower, Al Capone, the Black Sox and… country music?

Yes, really. Comparable to any small music scene in Chicago, whether post-rock, punk, free jazz or freestyle, the city has an oddly large country music scene, especially when compared to more obvious cities such as Denver, Tucson or Los Angeles. The source behind it is Bloodshot Records, the self-professed home of insurgent country, an underground brand of cowboy music that flared in the early 1990s and has burned steadily since.

Formed by a trio of punk-rock-gone-country old schoolers – Nan Warshaw, Eric Babcock and Rob Miller – Bloodshot debuted in 1993 with *For a Life of Sin: A Compilation of Insurgent Chicago Country*. Since then, and despite the departure of Babcock in 1997, the label has seen steady growth, especially of its nationwide profile.

This isn't, of course, your dad's country music. No Garth Brooks, no Shania Twain. In fact, insurgent country is far closer to your grandfather's country music: the young bands share more ground with Hank Williams and George Jones than with line-dancing and hee-haw. Insurgent country is essentially roots country, applied with independent-minded cynicism and the tuneful aggression of punk. National bands like Whiskeytown, the Old 97s and BR5-49 anchor the scene's mass appeal, while in Chicago, the likes of the Blacks, Anna Fermin and Trigger Gospel, and the Waco Brothers (fronted by former Mekon and British expat Jon Langford) keep up a local presence.

And then there's Bloodshot Records' most lauded name, Robbie Fulks, who rocketed to indie music heights with his first two Bloodshot records, *South Mouth* and *Country Love Songs*. His blend of classic two-step country blended with a pure hillbilly nasal twang, in addition to his gift for writing a snappy song with a sense of humour, earned him a deal with Geffen, though despite the move from indie to major label, Fulks still lives and often plays in Chicago.

Currently, the Bloodshot roster includes bands from around the country, though it's likely that outside Chicago, the bands are little more than diversions. Alejandro Escovedo, the Sadies, Neko Case and Her Boyfriends, Andre Williams and Trailer Bride,

for example, have all released well-received CDs on the Bloodshot label.

Venue-wise, while **Schubas Tavern** (page 210) featured a veritable who's who of insurgent country bands three years ago, the club has recently eased back on the amount of country it books, paving a straight road for the **Hideout** (page 209). By virtue of its pally bar staff and the constant country bands on the stage, Hideout has become the new, unofficial home of country in Chicago. In addition, Bloodshot bands can be seen on a weekly basis at the **Empty Bottle** (page 208), the **Double Door** (page 207), the **Metro** (page 210) and **FitzGerald's** (page 208).

Bloodshot owners Nan Warshaw and Rob Campbell have DJed the insurgent country night on Wednesdays at **Delilah's** (page 207) for more than five years, and the weekly event is still running strong. If you're in town on a Wednesday night, you could do a lot worse than heading down to Delilah's and trying out the scene for yourself. Why? For one, the folks in the bar are about the friendliest in the whole city. And for two, you'll be in a room with a lot of folk who never thought they'd like country music either, but do.

Arts & Entertainment

to jump blues to cutting-edge modern-day experimental jazz, with Sundays reserved for the Uptown Poetry Slam, a contest that pulls in a consistently raucous crowd. Wednesdays are usually held open for Kurt Elling, though his touring schedule often sends him out of town; call ahead to check. *See also p158.*

Jazz Showcase
59 W Grand Avenue, at N Clark Street, Near North/River North (312 670 2473). CTA Grand. **Open** *shows* 8pm, 10pm Tue-Thur; 9pm, 11pm Fri, Sat; 4pm, 8pm, 10pm Sun; closed Mon. **Credit** AmEx, MC, V. **Map** p306 H10.
Jazz Showcase owner Joe Segal has been promoting shows for more than 50 years, and almost always sticks to what he knows best: bebop, hard bop and just plain old bop. Segal has serious credibility in the jazz community, so the Showcase tends to be the venue of choice for internationally acclaimed artists such as Jacky Terrasson and Milt Jackson, who usually play five-day runs. The club is smoke-free, has a one-drink minimum and isn't the friendliest of places: it stops short of a dress code, but you'll feel the eyes if you show up in jeans and a T-shirt.

The Note
1565 N Milwaukee Avenue, at N Damen Avenue, Wicker Park/Bucktown (773 489 0011). CTA Damen (Blue). **Open** 8pm-4am Mon-Fri, Sun; 4pm-5am Sat. **Credit** AmEx, Disc, MC, V. **Map** p310 B7.
This hipster venue in Wicker Park – designated on the outside by a solitary, neon blue note – offers everything from salsa to R&B, but the emphasis is on jazz, acid jazz and hip hop. Weekends here are a veritable flurry of Martinis and blended drinks, well-dressed jazz fans, intelligent punks and anyone else bored with standard rock: an equal swathe of all ages, cultures and colours, and one of the friendliest crowds in the city. There's a pool table and bar in the front room, with the music going off in the long, table-filled back room.

Pops For Champagne
2934 N Sheffield Avenue, at W Wellington Avenue, Lake View (773 472 1000). CTA Wellington. **Open** 5pm-2am Mon-Thur, Sun; 4pm-2am Fri; 5pm-3am Sat. **Credit** AmEx, DC, Disc, MC, V. **Map** p309 E3.
A bar with more than 100 kinds of champagne, Pops features smooth piano jazz (yikes) and a very high degree of sophistication: there's a fireplace, minimal lighting and very professional waiting and bar staff. The jazz isn't the most dynamic. And neither is the venue, come to think of it. *See also p156.*

Velvet Lounge
2128½ S Indiana Avenue, at E 21st Street, South Side (312 791 9050/www.velvetlounge.net). CTA Cermak/Chinatown. **Open** 9pm-1.30am Wed-Fri; 9pm-2am Sat; 6-10.30pm Sun; closed Mon, Tue. **No credit cards. Map** p304 J16.
Just south of McCormick Place, the Velvet Lounge is an insider jazz venue, attracting members (both in the audience and on stage) of the local avant-garde jazz scene. It's a smallish room with good acoustics and a heart of bop.

Hitting the high note: a cool crowd enjoy hot jazz at **The Note**.

Classical & Opera

Full orchestral and classical music are woefully under-represented in Chicago. That's not to say it doesn't exist, but outside the **Chicago Symphony Orchestra** and the university ensembles, few orchestras have their own performance haunts, and so are doomed to play a rotating schedule of churches, catch-all concert spaces, outdoor events and college campuses. But despite a comparatively small amount of interest from young people, not to mention a lack of the public arts funding that's so common in Canada and Europe, Chicago does boast two of the world's premier classical music groups in the form of the Chicago Symphony Orchestra and the **Lyric Opera**.

Now in its 109th year, the Chicago Symphony Orchestra regained world renown by hiring **Daniel Barenboim** as its musical director (*see page 216* **My kind of town**), and has since cemented its reputation among the world's elite. In addition to classic works, the CSO presents new pieces by international and local composers throughout its season, which runs from September to May. It's also one of the world's most efficiently run orchestras, posting surplus budget numbers for 13 of the last 14 years.

Additionally, the CSO also boasts the only training orchestra association in America, the **Civic Orchestra of Chicago**, for which young musicians are recruited to learn the vitals behind playing in a major orchestra. The Civic Orchestra, founded in 1920, presents eight to ten concerts every year, all of which are free. Concerts are vigorous if not perfectly polished, but at the very least offer a chance of seeing tomorrow's classical music stars at a young age.

The Lyric Opera, meanwhile, is headed by William Mason, who succeeded general director Ardis Krainik in 1997, and who has worked for the Lyric throughout most of his 30-year career. Under the rule of artistic director Bruno Bartoletti, who retired in April 2000 to be replaced by Matthew A Epstein, the Lyric has pulled international talent like Luciano Pavarotti, Dmitri Hvorostovsky and Samuel Ramey, which perhaps explains its incredible local support: the company boasted more than 37,000 season-ticket holders for the September 1998 to March 1999 period.

In addition, the city is also home to a vibrant chamber music scene. On top of regular chamber performances by various members of the CSO, smaller companies such as the **Chicago Chamber Musicians**, **Chicago Sinfonietta**, **Concertante di Chicago**, **Pacifica String Quartet**, **Vermeer Quartet** and **Music of the Baroque** also play throughout the course of the classical music season (essentially, September to May). During the summer months, two main venues open up for classical music: **Ravinia** and **Grant Park**, the latter of which doesn't charge for entry unless you want to sit in the really posh bit.

TICKETS

Tickets for the CSO, Lyric Opera and Ravinia are available through their respective offices, as well as through the all-powerful **Ticketmaster** (*see page 207*). Tickets are rarely sold in advance for smaller chamber music concerts; in any case, many are free. Concerts in churches are free, though the prices in other venues vary wildly: the Civic Opera charges from $28 to $120, for example, while Symphony Center shows cost $11-$175 and Ravinia events $8-$60. For information on concerts, pick up the *Chicago Reader*, whose classical listings are extremely comprehensive.

Leaving aside the Symphony Center, the Lyric Opera, Ravinia and Grant Park, performances are held throughout the city and suburbs with little consistency. Listed below are the venues used most frequently for classical events, though the specific companies that play each venue vary from year to year.

Venues

Anderson Chapel at North Park University
3225 W Foster Avenue, at N Sawyer Avenue, Far North (773 244 5743). CTA 92 bus. **Open** hours vary.
Anderson Chapel is home to the Chamber Music at North Park series. Weekends also occasionally feature gospel, symphonic choirs and symphony orchestras. As you'd expect, it's church seating here, but it is surprisingly comfortable.

Chapel of St James Quigley Preparatory Seminary
831 N Rush Street, at E Pearson Street, Gold Coast (312 787 8625). CTA Chicago (Red). **Open** hours vary. **Map** p306 J9.
Built in 1919 and patterned after Paris' Sainte-Chapelle, this building, in the National Register of Historic Places, features mostly smaller-scale performers. Soloists in recital, choirs such as His Majestie's Clerkes, the Chicago Baroque Ensemble and the Chicago Sinfonietta play, usually for free, inside the chapel on a regular-ish basis. During the warmer months, concerts are held in the courtyard.

Civic Opera House
20 N Wacker Drive, at E Madison Street, The Loop (312 332 2244/www.lyricopera.com). CTA Washington (Brown/Orange/Purple). **Open** box office noon-6pm Mon-Sat; closed Sun. **Credit** AmEx, DC, Disc, MC, V. **Map** p305 G12.

Arts & Entertainment

A full-on art deco motif dominates this recently refurbished space, which functions as home to the Lyric Opera. The Lyric generally runs two productions in rotation, five days a week. Despite its size – the capacity here is more than 3,500 – the acoustics are the best in the city and sightlines allow the kids to watch the opera instead of the backs of heads. The lobby features a full bar during the intermissions, so non-opera fans can ease their pain without undue difficulty.

DePaul University Concert Hall
800 W Belden Avenue, at N Halsted Street, Lincoln Park (773 325 7260). CTA Fullerton. **Open** hours vary. **Map** p308 F5.

A former chapel with pew seating and arching, vaulted ceilings, the DePaul University Concert Hall – also known as Belden Hall – hosts university-based recitals as well as smaller chamber acts such as the Chicago Chamber Musicians, the Vermeer Quartet and the Pacifica String Quartet.

Fourth Presbyterian Church
126 E Chestnut Street, at N Michigan Avenue, Gold Coast (312 787 4570). CTA Chicago (Red). **Open** *performances* noon-1pm Mon-Fri. **Map** p306 J9.
The Gothic-styled Fourth Presbyterian Church has hosted the Noonday Music series for more than two years, providing a daily dose of solo recitals and chamber music away from the hustle and bustle of

My kind of town Daniel Barenboim

Though their city is often pinned as a poor cultural second to New York, Chicagoans can boast one asset that puts them ahead of their New York rivals. That asset is Daniel Barenboim, the ninth musical director of the Chicago Symphony Orchestra.

Born in Buenos Aires in 1942 to piano teacher parents, the young Barenboim played his first piano concerto in front of a large audience at the age of seven. It was the beginning of a very busy career for a young man in an old geezer's profession. Barenboim later attended Igor Markevich's conducting classes in Salzburg, worked as a pianist on Klemperer's complete Beethoven piano concertos in the 1960s, played Brahms with Barbirolli, performed Mozart with the English Chamber Orchestra and married Jacqueline Du Pré. He then went on to found the Orchestre de Paris and act as its musical director, resigning in 1989 in order to take over the reins of the Opéra de Paris. But Barenboim quit the opera before even taking over, allegedly due to an argument over creative freedom with the opera's theatre director.

And so, to Chicago, when Barenboim was anointed as the hand-picked successor to legendary Sir Georg Solti at the helm of the CSO. And it's been onwards and upwards ever since. Since arriving a decade ago, Barenboim has increased the profile of the already internationally renowned orchestra, and spearheaded the development of classical music in Chicago. He was the impetus behind a $110-million renovation of the old Orchestra Hall, now a block-sized musical centre for the city, and founded the country's sole Apprentice Conductor's Program. The appreciative CSO signed Barenboim to a contract extension that will see him through the 2005-6 season.

But though his tangible influences are felt in the Symphony Center and various programmes peripheral to the CSO, it is Barenboim's artistic vision that has brought the CSO greater acclaim. In addition to presenting a mix of hoary classics and new works, Barenboim's love of opera has resulted in the CSO's performances of Strauss's *Elektra*, all three Mozart/DaPointe operas and Beethoven's *Fidelio*. Barenboim builds the Orchestra's seasons thematically. In autumn 2000, it's 'Mahler and Modernism'; spring 2001 will celebrate the Verdi anniversary; and autumn of the same year continues with the light and airy 'Wagner and Modernism'. Somehow, he manages all this while still maintaining his posts as artistic and general music director of the Deutsche Staatsoper Berlin and conductor of the Civic Orchestra. Oh, and giving piano concerts around the world. As if he wasn't busy enough already.

In 2000, New York's Carnegie Hall will bow to the master and present 'Perspectives: Daniel Barenboim', a 15-concert series commemorating his 50 years of professional performance. It's a series that promises to bring the man's genius to even greater attention. A genius about which Chicagoans already know a great deal.

Mag Mile shopping. The church also occasionally hosts other classical and chamber music concerts.

Ganz Hall at Roosevelt University

430 S Michigan Avenue, at E Van Buren Street, The Loop (312 341 3780). CTA Jackson (Red) or Library. **Open** hours vary. **Map** p305 J13.
Formerly part of the Sullivan Hotel, Ganz Hall is now part of the Roosevelt University's music school. In addition to various student recitals and soloists, the likes of the Chicago Chamber Musicians and the Contemporary Music Ensemble often play here.

Grant Park Petrillo Music Shell

235 S Columbus Drive, at E Jackson Drive, The Loop (312 742 4763/www.chicagoparkdistrict.com). CTA Adams or Jackson (Blue, Red). **Open** *mid-June-Aug* concerts usually Wed-Sat. **Map** p305 J12.
The sweeping Grant Park serves as host to all manner of free music events during the summer, of which the biggest is the classically-minded Grant Park Music Festival (*see p90* **The sounds of summer**). Regular performers include the Chicago Symphony Orchestra – though often without Daniel Barenboim, who usually tours in the summer – the Ravinia Festival Orchestra, the Civic Orchestra of Chicago and, most often, the Grant Park Festival Orchestra. Short-season concerts are usually based around a theme: 'American Weekend' around 4 July, for example, or the self-explanatory 'Opera Week'.

Mandel Hall at the University of Chicago

1131 E 57th Street, at S University Avenue, Hyde Park (773 702 8069). Metra 55th-57th Street. **Open** hours vary. **Map** p311 X17.
Home to many University of Chicago-sponsored events, the Hall is also the venue for the Howard Mayer Brown International Early Music Series and the University of Chicago Chamber Music Series.

Old St Patrick's Church

700 W Adams Street, at S Desplaines Street, West Side (312 648 1021). **Open** hours vary.
One of the few downtown survivors of the Chicago Fire, the city's oldest church (it was built in 1856) features a stunning panorama of 12 stained-glass windows. Though the concert schedules are erratic, Old St Pat's has hosted concerts by the likes of the Metropolis Symphony and Music of the Baroque.

Preston-Bradley Hall at the Chicago Cultural Center

78 E Washington Boulevard, at N Michigan Avenue, The Loop (312 744 6630). CTA Randolph or Washington (Blue, Red). **Open** 10am-7pm Mon-Wed; 10am-9pm Thur; 10am-6pm Fri; 10am-5pm Sat; 11am-5pm Sun; *performances* hours vary. **Map** p305 J12.
Part of the Chicago Cultural Center, Preston-Bradley Hall – the original site of Chicago's public library, incidentally – hosts concerts under the world's largest Tiffany stained-glass dome. Any number of classical music events can be seen here, from small chamber performances to choral symphonies.

Dan's the man at the **Symphony Center**.

Ravinia Festival

Ravinia Park, Green Bay Road, Highland Park (847 266 5100/www.ravinia.com). Metra Ravinia Park. **Open** hours vary. **Credit** AmEx, DC, Disc, MC, V.
The Ravinia is a trio of music spaces. The Pavilion is a gigantic lawn space, open for concerts ranging from classical to folk to pop, while smaller jazz and classical ensembles play the Bennett-Gordon Hall or the Martin Theatre. During the warm months, there are concerts almost every day at the Pavilion. Lawn chairs are available for rent: $8 gets you two chairs and a side table.

Symphony Center

220 S Michigan Avenue, at E Adams Street, The Loop (312 294 3000/www.chicagosymphony.org). CTA Adams or Jackson (Blue, Red). **Open** *box office* 10am-6pm Mon-Sat; 11am-4pm Sun. **Credit** AmEx, DC, MC, V. **Map** p305 J12.
A multi-million-dollar renovation in 1997 turned the Symphony Center from run-down home of the Chicago Symphony Orchestra into a veritable music mall. In addition to functioning as the CSO's home, the Symphony Center houses the Civic Orchestra of Chicago, the Chicago Youth Symphony, a learning centre for music and the Chicago chapter of the National Academy of Recording Arts and Sciences (the folks who vote for the Grammys). In addition, the Center runs a monthly jazz programme and hosts touring international orchestras, chamber groups and choral ensembles. The interior of the Center also finds space for a restaurant, **Rhapsody** (*see p129*), which fills up fast on the nights of CSO performances. Children's concerts are frequently held on Saturday mornings.

Arts & Entertainment

Nightlife

Chicago's club scene holds many delights for discerning disco dicks and divas. But first, you'll have to get past the bouncers...

If there's one thing that local club owners can't get into their brains, it's that while Chicago may transcend the Midwest, it's not, and never will be, New York. And yet they try, oh so very hard, to recreate that snooty Manhattan vibe. Even if a club is empty, you may find yourself waiting in line so the management can assume the pretension of high demand. And even if you're wearing the hippest of Airwalk sneakers, they just might turn you away for not meeting the strict dress code (whatever *that* is). If you're a male by yourself or in a group, be prepared to wait an extra 15 minutes before being allowed to enter (club owners and clubgoers alike fear the dreaded male-dominated 'sausage fests'). And once you're at the door, you still might have to drop $20 on the cover charge.

And yet Chicagoans play along with this ludicrous game, despite the fact that the city lacks a little glamour: the only celebrities that tend to grace the town's hip hotspots are merely passing through the Windy City while filming a movie here. As a result, local scenesters succumb to the illusion of glitz and sophistication.

The latest trends in club concepts reflect this desire to be as invigorating and exciting as NYC. Clubs have become cosy, swanky hideouts, covered in plush velvet and leopard prints, filled with organic shapes and comfy booths. In the wake of the movie *Swingers* a few years back, a wave of Vegas chic swept the city: suddenly, a bunch of clubs and restaurants started offering humidors and designated rooms for cigar-sucking, Martini-sipping high-class players. Annoying cigar smoke aside, this loungey trend has been a welcome one in a city overrun by sports bars.

Now, though, in a bid to outlive the average club life expectancy of a mere year and a half, it seems that no club is complete without a theme. **Biology Bar**, with its scientific beakers and test tubes, and **Circus**, with its tightrope walkers and fire-breathing jugglers on stilts, exemplify this trend. Other owners choose to rape and pillage an entire culture and plaster it all over their interiors. The most popular choices are Asian (**Hell**, **Dragon Room**) and Middle Eastern (**Zentra**, **Karma**).

The tragedy of all this, though, is that the club spaces have invariably been purchased from previous owners and then gutted for a

Berlin will take your breath away.

multi-million-dollar renovation project. The layouts are redesigned and one uniquely luxurious decor replaces another. Often, so much money is spent on this process that owners get themselves in over their heads and cannot afford to promote the new club. They go out of business in a year, and so become part of a vicious cycle of unnecessary scrapping and rebuilding.

Owners also cannot seem to decide whether they want to open a nightclub, a bar or a restaurant. As a result, they incorporate elements of all three, leaving Chicago nightlife haunts with identity crises. What to call this new breed of venue in which to dance and drink and nibble on overpriced hors d'oeuvres? Clubstaurants? Restaclubs? Anyway, for the listings in this section, only those that incorporate dancing and/or have music as an essential element have been included. Because otherwise, they'd be... well, bars or restaurants, right?

INFORMATION

Aside from checking out the clubbing section in *Newcity*, the best way to find out what's on is to pick up flyers and inappropriately named VIP passes. Head to Chicago's answer to the Village – the intersection of Clark and Belmont, and Hipster Central – and you'll find piles of flyers for clubs and rave parties in trendy shoestores (**Sole Junkies**, **Shop 913**), thrift stores (**Ragstock**, **Hollywood Mirror**) and used CD and record stores (**Disco Go Round**, **Record Exchange**); for all, *see chapter* **Shops & Services**. Go further and check out the club's website, and you'll often be rewarded a printable pass offering free or discounted entry.

You'll need an ID that says you're at least 21 to get into clubs. This is a strict city: bouncers will card you as you walk in the door, and there's no way of getting around it. Many clubs close at 2am, though it's always possible to find some that remain open until 4am. For whatever reason, establishments are allowed to stay open an extra hour on Saturday nights. So, the 2ams become 3ams and the 4ams remain open until 5am. Don't be surprised to step out of the darkness after a lengthy night of clubbing to be assaulted by blinding sunlight and the incessant chirping of early-morning birds. Assuming you've got past the bouncers in the first place, that is…

Finally, be sure to call ahead before venturing out. Clubs constantly evolve, change music policies and – should the worst come to the worst – go under, DJs hop from one establishment to another and cover charges vary wildly (though as a general rule, it'll be cheaper – perhaps even free – earlier in the week, and you'll never have to pay more than $20). It's for this reason that we've largely steered clear of listing specific club nights, though *Newcity* runs details of what's on in any given week. After all, there's nothing as tenuous as the element of cool that big-city nightclubs try to grasp and retain. But, of course, that's all part of the excitement. Isn't it?

Venues

For information on specifically gay clubs, *see pages 200-202*.

Aqua

820 W Lake Street, at N Green Street, West Side (312 942 9999). CTA Clinton (Green). **Open** 8pm-3am Thur-Sat; closed Mon-Wed, Sun. **Credit** AmEx, DC, Disc, MC, V.
Everything about The Bar Formerly Known As Mint (it changed its name in early 2000) screams upscale: tuxedoed bartenders, coin-shaped kaleidoscopes and even a cigar area. DJs spin techno, house and underground below the main floor.

Artful Dodger

1734 W Wabansia Avenue, at N Hermitage Avenue, Wicker Park/Bucktown (312 227 6859). CTA Damen (Blue). **Open** 5pm-2am Mon-Fri; 8pm-3am Sat; 8pm-2am Sun. **Credit** MC, V. **Map** p310 C7.
One of the only spots in which to boogie in Wicker Park, a neighbourhood known for its hipster bars. The predominantly local crowd hang out and guzzle from a choice of 30 beers, though some choose the bright blue Margarita-esque aquavelva, a house

speciality. The back room has a small dancefloor and dismal booths. DJs play hip hop, house and pop. It's a paltry two bucks to get in on Friday and Saturday, and free the rest of the time.

Aura

640 N Dearborn Street, at W Erie Street, Near North (312 266 2114/773 774 1919/www.aceplaces.com/aura). CTA Chicago (Red). **Open** 10pm-4am Thur, Fri; 10pm-5am Sat; 10pm-4am Sun; closed Mon-Wed. **Credit** AmEx, DC, MC, V. **Map** p306 H10.
An open, multi-storeyed space on the edge of River North with a balcony encircling the club and a heavenly painting on the dome. If you're a sucker, you'll try out the latest fad and pay for pure oxygen, on sale here. Stand by the window that looks down into the garish **Excalibur** (*see p221*) and laugh haughtily at the dorks below. The musical mix usually features trance and house.

Berlin

954 W Belmont Avenue, at N Sheffield Avenue, Lake View (773 348 4975). CTA Belmont. **Open** 8pm-4am Mon, Sun; 5pm-4am Tue-Fri; 5pm-5am Sat. **No credit cards. Map** p309 E2.
Anything goes at this long-time staple of Chicago nightlife, a libidinous free-for-all with a healthy mixture of gays and straights. It's easy to get caught up in the swirl: thrust yourself onto the crowded dancefloor, then thrust yourself at the cutie next to you. The music can be anything from house to big beat, though Thursday's Men in Motion gay night, complete with go-go boys and DJ Michael Serafini is among the most popular evenings (*see p202*).

Big Wig

1551 W Division Street, at N Ashland Avenue, West Side (773 235 9100). CTA Division (Blue). **Open** 8pm-2am Mon-Fri, Sun; 8pm-3am Sat. **Credit** AmEx, MC, V.
As the name implies, this club, located a half-mile south-east of Wicker Park, took the hairdresser theme and ran with it. The owner's mother used to own a salon, and this chic joint has the relics: hairdryer lightshades above the bar, mannequin heads with wigs, and clever but creepy disinfectant Barbosol jars holding olives and cherries. Music is dance stuff, ranging from house to drum 'n' bass.

Biology Bar

1520 N Fremont Street, at W North Avenue, Lincoln Park (312 266 1234). CTA North/Clybourn. **Open** 9pm-4am Wed-Fri; 9pm-5am Sat; closed Mon, Tue, Sun. **Credit** AmEx, MC, V.
Taking its cue from London's Pharmacy, this newest theme on the block serves up cocktails in test tubes and beakers. A tornado light fixture welcomes clubgoers, the bars and tabletops are covered in papyrus, and everything is awash in a bright neon blue-green. The owners claim the ionisation air filtration system removes the smell of smoke from your clothes as pop Latin songs blast forth from the speakers.

Arts & Entertainment

Social chemistry and physical interaction: it can only be the **Biology Bar**. *See page 219.*

Circus

901 W Weed Street, at N Fremont Street, Lincoln Park (312 266 1200/www.circuschicago.com). CTA North/Clybourn. **Open** 9pm-4am Wed-Fri; 9pm-5am Sat; closed Mon, Tue, Sun. **Credit** AmEx, MC, V.
A three-room big-top spectacle in the clubby corridor found south of Lincoln Park and west of Old Town, beginning with a psychotic oversized ringmaster leering from the ceiling in the funked-out, whimsical front lounge. Tightrope walkers and firejugglers on stilts entertain the crowds on the spacious, circular dancefloor.

Club Inta's

157 W Ontario Street, at N Wells Street, Near North/River North (312 664 6880). CTA Chicago (Brown/Purple). **Open** 9pm-4am Mon; 6.30pm-4am Tue; 7pm-4am Wed, Thur, Sun; 5pm-4am Fri; 8pm-5am Sat.* **Credit** AmEx, Disc, V. **Map** p306 H10.
Alas, you've missed your chance to see Dennis Rodman's wedding dress: his club, Illusions, has faded away, and has since been replaced by this black-and-gold gilded salsa and merengue nightspot. Chandeliers and a marble bar set the glitzy mood, and there's live music on Saturdays.

Club 720

720 N Wells Street, at W Superior Street, Near North/River North (312 397 0600/www.club720.com). CTA Chicago (Brown/Purple). **Open** 7pm-4am Tue-Fri; 10pm-5am Sat. **Credit** AmEx, DC, Disc, MC, V. **Map** p310 H10.
Four storeys, three of which have dancefloors, await you at this salsa/merengue hotspot. A lively crowd dirty dances in the ultra-posh setting, but be warned: 720 boasts some of the steepest covers in the city, and groups of men will more than likely have to wait a while before they're allowed in. Saturday, predictably, is the most popular night.

Crobar

1543 N Kingsbury Street, at W Weed Street, Lincoln Park (312 413 7000). CTA North/Clybourn. **Open** 10pm-4am Wed, Thur, Sun; 9pm-4am Fri; 10pm-5am Sat; closed Mon, Tue. **Credit** AmEx, MC, V.
The pinnacle of the city's club scene – west of Old Town, south of Lincoln Park – is still a pure adrenaline rush: at weekends, the place gets jumping and is absolutely packed. Go-go cages hang above the dancefloor, a stained-glass church window is positioned at the back, a catwalk winds along near the DJ booth, and the mezzanine holds a chill-out space.

Dragon Room

809 W Evergreen Avenue, at N Halsted Street, Lincoln Park (312 751 2900/ www.dragonroomchicago.com). CTA North/Clybourn. **Open** 10pm-4am Thur, Fri, Sun; closed Mon-Wed. **Credit** AmEx, MC, V. **Map** p307 F8.
Sip sake and nibble on sushi at this three-tiered nightclub in the middle of nowhere south of Lincoln Park. To construct the decor, the owners must have ransacked Chinatown, though the city is as much of a celeb-magnet as is possible in Chicago. The music runs the gamut from alternarock to hip hop to jazz, though house is a regular feature.

Drink

702 W Fulton Street, at N Desplaines Street, West Side (312 733 7800). CTA Clinton (Green). **Open** 5.30pm-3am Thur; 5.30pm-4am Fri; 6pm-5am Sat; closed Mon-Wed, Sun. **Credit** AmEx, DC, MC, V. **Map** p305 F11.
This massive orange, green and yellow infused club has a huge puzzle piece dancefloor, where mainstreamers shake their thangs to not-so-alternative alternative tunes. Drunkenness is encouraged, so why not order a bucket full of your choice? There's a cigar room, plus separate vodka and tequila bars.

Excalibur

632 N Dearborn Street, at W Ontario Street,
Near North (312 266 1944/www.aceplaces.com/x/).
CTA Grand. **Open** 5pm-4am Mon-Fri; 5pm-5am
Sat; 6pm-4am Sun. **Credit** AmEx, DC, Disc, MC, V.
Map p306 H10.

This unappealing hangout is always jam-packed
with suburbanites. The Cabaret, the main room,
hosts cheesy butt-shakin' contests, while upstairs is
Club X, full of balconies and go-go gals, sometimes
with an extra cover. But if the people here seem
foolish, who cares? They surely don't. And at least
there's a Ms Pac-Man machine in the basement.

Exit

1315 W North Avenue, at N Elston Avenue,
Lincoln Park (773 395 2700/www.exitchicago.com).
CTA North/Clybourn (Red) or Damen (Blue).
Open 8pm-4am Mon-Fri, Sun; 8pm-5am Sat. **No**
credit cards.

Motorcycle men mix riotously with babes in black
leather at this practically legendary punk club way
out in the sticks. The theme here is S&M-inspired,
and the dancefloor is essentially a cage in which a
rowdy crowd can cavort to hardcore industrial music,
low-down-and-dirty punk and other deafening treats.
Girls get in free; guys never pay more than $5.

House parties

'In the beginning there was
Jack. And Jack had a groove.
And from this groove came
the groove of all grooves. And
while one day viciously
throwing down on his box,
Jack boldly declared, "Let
there be house".'

At the beginning of the
1980s, disco was declared
dead, but black gay Chicago
refused to read the obituary.
On the dancefloor of a club
called the Warehouse, they
kept on dancing with
abandon – 'jacking' – to a mix
of old Philadelphia disco classics and
pumping synth funk from Europe. Keeping
disco alive in the Windy City was a DJ from
New York, Frankie Knuckles (pictured), who
would chop up old songs on a tape recorder
to make them more repetitive and play a
drum machine under the beat to make the
rhythm harder and heavier.

Such DJ skills were commonplace in the
underground clubs of NYC, but here in the
corn-fed Midwest, it blew their minds. In
Frankie's honour, they named the music
'house', after his club. Other DJs were key to
this sound, particularly a frenzied drug-driven
crazy called Ron Hardy at a club called the
Music Box, and a fast-mixing team of radio
DJs called the Hot Mix Five. But what really
started to drive house music was the
clubbers themselves.

By about 1983, a style of DJing had
evolved in Chicago in which the DJs drove
their dancers into states of drum-hypnotised
fury with endless, repetitive rhythm tracks.
Then, when they'd pumped them long
enough, they'd give them the orgasmic
release of a great vocal song. This style

demanded a steady supply of
simple drum tracks, and as
studio equipment had just
become small and affordable,
clubbers as well as DJs could
get in on the act.

Here was music with no
experience necessary. All you
had to do was cook up a
rhythm on a drum machine,
add a bassline ripped off from
your favourite disco track and
played on a cheap Casio
keyboard, and voila: instant
local fame and free entry into
all the clubs. Suddenly, everybody in Chicago
became a producer, eagerly pushing tapes
under DJs' noses: Steve Hurley, Marshall
Jefferson, Jesse Saunders, Farley Jackmaster
Funk, Chip E, Adonis, DJ Pierre and many more.

Eventually, some of these kids figured out
how to turn these tapes into real records and
some local music biz mobsters figured out
how to rip off all these eager young non-
musicians. When people in the UK got
excited about this radical new music –
especially the bleepy variant known as acid
house – its future was secured.

Although most of the original producers still
live here, there isn't much of a house scene
left in Chicago, especially now that hip hop
has (belatedly) swept the city. But there are
still some old school house nights if you're
prepared to look for them. Check out the
flyers in **Gramophone Records** for the
lowdown and you may find yourself in a club
with some former legend playing classics in
the back room.

And now that house and its musical offspring
have swept the world, Frankie Knuckles, the
music's 'godfather', can just smile and say: 'I
view house as disco's revenge.'

Funky Buddha Lounge

728 W Grand Avenue, at N Halsted Street, West Side (312 666 1695/www.tribads.com/funkybuddha). CTA Chicago (Blue). **Open** 9pm-2am Mon-Fri, Sun; 9pm-3am Sat. **Credit** AmEx, MC, V. **Map** p306 F10.

A large metal replica of a buddha greets patrons willing to spend so much they'll be financially forced to take a vow of abstinence after a night out here. A super-chic international crowd mingles in this intimate club: candles and chandeliers light the darkened room, while funky house and tribal tunes waft through the air. Expect anything from soul and world rhythms to flat-out funk on various nights of the week.

Glow

1615 N Clybourn Street, at W North Avenue, Lincoln Park (312 587 8469). CTA North/Clybourn. **Open** 10pm-4am Tue, Wed; 8pm-4am Thur, Fri; 8pm-5am Sat; closed Mon, Sun. **Credit** AmEx, MC, V. **Map** p307 F7.

Another offering from Big Time Productions, the duo behind **Crobar** (*see opposite*). Contemptuous model-wannabes strut their stuff on the catwalk and nibble on exotic cuisine at this la-di-da restaurant/club, which also offers an extensive wine and champagne list. Downtempo drum 'n' bass pumps through the crowd, while house dominates at the club nights.

Hell

1115 N Branch Street, at W Division Street, West Side (312 280 7997). CTA Chicago (Blue). **Open** 11pm-4am Thur, Fri, Sun; 11pm-5am Sat; closed Mon-Wed. **Credit** AmEx, Disc, MC, V.

Asian-inspired sinfulness. Act naughty in the lounge near the funky silver flower light slowly swirling over a small well-pond. The dancefloor takes up most of the space, sectioned off by a wavy metal mesh. Fear not: the people with horns and leather face masks are just the waiting staff and doormen. Expect techno tunes and a devilish good time, and all for no cover charge.

Karma

318 W Grand Avenue, at N Orleans Street, Near North/River North (312 321 1331/www.karmachicago.com). CTA Merchandise Mart. **Open** 10pm-4am Thur, Fri; 10pm-5am Sat; closed Mon-Wed, Sun. **Credit** AmEx, DC, Disc, MC, V. **Map** p306 G10.

Giving **Crobar** (*see p220*) a run for its money as Chicago's favourite nightclub, this expansive venue offers two dancefloors, clubkid host(esses), fortune tellers and Hindu sculptures. Most importantly, it's the primary stopover for touring DJs looking to guest-spin. The Temple holds the main dancefloor; kids chill out in the basement Serpentine Room.

Liar's Club

1665 W Fullerton Street, at N Ashland Avenue, Lincoln Park (773 665 1110). CTA Fullerton. **Open** 8pm-2am Mon-Fri, Sun; 8pm-3am Sat. **Credit** AmEx, DC, Disc, MC, V. **Map** p308 D5.

Unique 'dancing' at **Circus**. *See page 220.*

A basement hangout for the low-maintenance rock 'n' roll crowd. Make your way to the dancefloor, which is small and slanted but does come with trippy lights. Entry is free, except Friday and Saturday nights.

Liquid

1997 N Clybourn Street, at N Racine Avenue, Lincoln Park (773 528 3400). CTA Armitage. **Open** 6pm-2am Wed-Fri; 7pm-3am Sat; closed Mon, Tue, Sun. **Credit** AmEx, DC, Disc, MC, V. **Map** p308 E6.

Itching to show off the swinging moves you picked up from slow-mo-ing the legendary Gap commercial? Here you can jitterbug and skitter your way around the large wooden dancefloor while live bands play on Thursday, Friday and Saturday nights. And if you don't know the moves, fear not: get there early and they'll give you lessons.

Mad Bar

1640 N Damen Avenue, at W North Avenue, Wicker Park/Bucktown (773 227 2277). CTA Damen (Blue). **Open** 6pm-2am Mon-Fri, Sun; 6pm-3am Sat. **Credit** AmEx, Disc, MC, V. **Map** p310 B7.

This space is so small that every inch is taken up with tables. Still, the Mad Bar is too often overlooked on the Chicago club scene, though it gets by with a loyal following. Expect anything from drum 'n' bass to house and funk on various nights of the week.

Neo

2350 N Clark Street, at W Fullerton Avenue, Lincoln Park (773 528 2622). CTA Fullerton. **Open** 10pm-4am Tue, Thur; 9pm-4am Fri; 9pm-5am Sat; closed Mon, Wed, Sun. **No credit cards. Map** p308 F5.

Rumours persist that this goth club is closing, though it was still here in early 2000. Perhaps it's undead, like its clientele: these pale-faced, black-clad kids still haven't gotten over their '80s angst. Odd, then, that they're as friendly as hell.

NV

5 W Division Street, at N State Street, Gold Coast (312 664 9000). CTA Clark/Division. **Open** 10pm-4am Tue-Fri; 10pm-5am Sat; closed Mon, Sun. **Credit** AmEx, Disc, MC, V. **Map** p307 H8.

Another upscale lounge in which to while away the after-dark hours. Acid jazz and downtempo beats put you in the mood: suck down a Martini and make your way to the positively miniscule dancefloor.

Polly Esther's

213 W Institute Place, at N Franklin Street, Near North/River North (312 664 0777/ www.polyesthers.com). CTA Chicago (Brown/Purple). **Open** 8pm-3am Thur; 8pm-4am Fri; 8pm-5am Sat; closed Mon-Wed, Sun. **Credit** AmEx, MC, V. **Map** p306 G9.

Part of a national chain of goofy, nostalgia-inducing retro clubs: downstairs is the Culture Club, while drinks include the Brady Punch (ouch). If only more of the people flailing wildly about on the *Saturday Night Fever*-esque lit-up dancefloor took the '70s theme seriously.

Red Dog

1958 W North Avenue, at N Damen Avenue, Wicker Park/Bucktown (773 278 1009). CTA Damen (Blue). **Open** 10pm-4am Mon, Fri; 10pm-5am Sat; closed Sun. **No credit cards. Map** p310 B7.

This dance party starts right as you walk in the door: one step in posits you right in the middle of the pulsating dancefloor. The Red Dog draws a supremely diverse crowd – gays and straights, blacks, Hispanics and whites, males and females – and you won't find anything else like it in the city. There's a mellower area upstairs, but anywhere else, you're practically forced to join the energetic crowd grooving away to house music. *See also p220.*

rednofive

440 N Halsted Street, at W Hubbard Street, West Side (312 733 6699). CTA Chicago (Blue) or Clinton (Green). **Open** 10pm-4am Thur, Fri; 10pm-5am Sat; closed Mon-Wed, Sun. **Credit** AmEx, Disc, MC, V. **Map** p306 F11.

This new start-up has already impressed local club-goers with its guest DJ line-up, which has included Derrick Carter. Head down the stairs for a descent into hipness: lights beam and flash, slicing the darkness and raising the energy. Tuesdays are Jazzid, an industry night (frequented by people who work in nightclubs), while house parties dominate the big nights later in the week.

Smart Bar

3730 N Clark Street, at W Addison Street, Lake View/Wrigleyville (773 549 0203). CTA Addison (Red). **Open** 10pm-4am Mon-Fri, Sun; 10pm-5am Sat. **Credit** AmEx, V. **Map** p309 E1.

A tiny cavern below the concert venue **Metro** (*see p210*). Intimate and back-to-basics – what more do you need in a nightclub other than comfy booths, two candlelit bars, a pool table in the corner and a small dancefloor? – the music here is a wild mix: hip hop one night, ska and punk the next, house the next. Something for everyone, then.

Spin

800 W Belmont Avenue, at N Halsted Street, Lake View (773 327 7711/www.spin-nightclub.com). CTA Belmont. **Open** 4pm-2am Mon, Tue, Thur, Fri, Sun; 8pm-2am Wed; 4pm-3am Sat. **No credit cards. Map** p309 F2.

Make your way through the front bar area and slip behind the curtains to be transported into another world. Up front, it's a video bar; out back, there's darkness and dancing, flashing lights and glowsticks. The crowd leans toward gay males and their straight female companions, and you'd be advised to check your 'tude at the door. Cover is never more than $5.

Spy Bar

646 N Franklin Street, at W Erie Street, Near North (312 587 8779). CTA Chicago (Brown/Purple). **Open** 10.30pm-4am Fri; 10.30pm-5am Sat. **Credit** AmEx, MC, V. **Map** p306 G10.

Yet another ultra-glam lounge, this one is at least underground and surprisingly low on attitude. Sink into fluffy couches and admire the finer touches, such as the fur on the bathroom doors (it's faux). Fridays and Saturdays see DJs Jason Christopher and Maurice Joshua spinning sophisticated house.

Voyeur

151½ W Ohio Street, at N LaSalle Street, Near North/River North (312 832 1717). CTA Grand. **Open** 10pm-4am Thur, Fri, Sun; 10pm-5am Sat; closed Mon-Wed. **Credit** MC, V. **Map** p306 G11.

Keep watch! Hidden cameras film clubgoers at this gimmick-laden establishment, but the power lies with the women in the bathroom: they have the prime viewing spot. Curvy booths, four bars and a steel-plated dancefloor make up the decor; the music is generally hip hoppy or housey. No denim.

Zentra

923 W Weed Street, at N Sheffield Avenue, Lincoln Park (312 787 0400). CTA North/Clybourn. **Open** 10.30pm-4.30am Thur, Fri; 10.30pm-5pm Sat; closed Mon-Wed, Sun. **Credit** AmEx, DC, Disc, MC, V.

Jumping on the Eastern Zen trip bandwagon, Zentra comes with an opium den motif, including hookah girls offering flavoured tobacco. There are grass patches in the middle of the floor, a precarious too-dark stairwell and progressive dance music on the large dancefloor. Watch out for the camels at the door: they've been known to spit.

Arts & Entertainment

Sport & Fitness

The pro teams may suck, but there's plenty for participatory types in Chicago.

Most big American cities love their sports. Chicago, though, obsesses over them. The hoop-shooting Bulls surely need no introduction, but neither do the rough-and-tumble Bears or the gloriously inept Cubs. Despite the lack of success enjoyed by the city's sports teams in the last few years, locals still take what can, if understatement is your particular thing, be described as a keen interest in the progress of their teams. Or, more often, the lack of it.

Many, too, choose to have a go themselves, at anything from fishing to sledding. As befits a city of its size, Chicago boasts some excellent sporting facilities, which visiting health nuts will doubtless devour with glee.

Spectator sports

American football

Nothing captures the essence of Chicago quite like the **Chicago Bears**. One of the National Football League's oldest franchises, the tough, gritty play that historically distinguishes the team is beloved by locals. The Bears won the Super Bowl at their first – and, so far, only – attempt in 1986 under the guidance of Mike Ditka, an irascible and amusingly volatile old school loudmouth who still enjoys God-like status among Bears faithful despite the fact that he left the team in January 1993. Often referred to affectionately as simply 'Da Coach', Ditka's presence still looms large in the city, and fans flock to his restaurant (*see page 119*) on game days.

Unfortunately, fans have had little to cheer about since '86. Ditka moved on to coach the New Orleans Saints with even less success than his old team have since enjoyed: indeed, he was fired after the 1999 season. The Bears' former running back and local legend Walter Payton died of cancer in late 1999. And, of course, the Bears are still losing. There is some good news, though: the Bears' lack of success has made it easier to get a ticket. And with a promising new coach (Dick Jauron) and quarterback (Cade McNown) in place, the future is if not bright, then slightly less dim than it's been for a while.

Though it can get bone-chillingly cold by the time December rolls around – both the weather and the fans' enthusiasm for watching another losing team, that is – the 66,944-capacity Soldier Field remains a Chicago institution. Whatever the weather and the result, a Bears game is still a tremendous experience; just remember to wear about five sweaters and come armed with a dictionary of profanities with which to translate some of the barbs lobbed at opposing players by the hardier Bears fans. Tickets for one of the team's eight annual home games can be pricey, but if the weather is bad or the opponent isn't a hated rival – Green Bay, say – scalped tickets can be purchased at face value or less from outside the west side of the stadium. Get there early to witness the scary pre-game tailgate parties.

Chicago Bears
Soldier Field, 425 E McFetridge Place, at S Lake Shore Drive, Museum Campus (information 847 615 2327/ tickets 312 559 1212/www.chicagobears.com). CTA Roosevelt/State or Roosevelt/Wabash. **Season** Aug-Dec. **Tickets** $37. **Credit** AmEx, DC, Disc, MC, V. **Map** p304 J15.

Baseball

Along with the similarly hard done-by Boston Red Sox (whose fans are more self-pitying), the **Chicago Cubs** are the nation's favourite baseball underdogs. They're much-loved in the city, despite – or perhaps because of – the fact they haven't won a World Series since 1908. Their tale is a long and torrid one, which really deserves a box to itself (*see page 226* **The ivy leagues**)...

The **Chicago White Sox** have a similarly dismal record, though 1999 saw them at least better their crosstown neighbours, while the policy of youth ahead of overpriced veterans may yield some rewards in a few years' time. However, the Sox have never really garnered the same sort of affection that's bestowed on the Cubs, and so don't enjoy nearly the fan support of their North Side rivals.

The Sox play at Comiskey Park, a 44,321-capacity stadium down south at 35th Street. What it lacks in character it makes up for in... well, not much, to be honest. The neighbourhood's ugly, the team's ugly, but, perhaps worst of all, the stadium itself is ugly. Completed in time for the 1991 season with pots of city cash – the team had threatened to leave town if they didn't get a new stadium – the park now looks horrendously dated, thanks to the construction of homelier parks such as Baltimore's Camden Yards and Cleveland's Jacobs Field. Still, a decent seat is usually easy to come by, while those with things to do during the day will be pleased to note that, unlike the Cubs, the Sox play most games at night.

Chicago Cubs

Wrigley Field, 1060 W Addison Street, at N Clark Street, Lake View/Wrigleyville (information 773 404 2827/tickets from within Illinois 312 831 2827/tickets from outside Illinois 1-800 347 2827/www.cubs.com). CTA Addison (Purple, Red). **Season** Mar-Oct. **Tickets** $4-$25. **Credit** AmEx, DC, Disc, MC, V. **Map** p309 E1.

Chicago White Sox

Comiskey Park, 333 W 35th Street, at S Shields Avenue, South Side (information 312 674 1000/ tickets 312 831 1769/www.chisox.com). CTA Sox/35th Street. **Season** Mar-Oct. **Tickets** $13-$22. **Credit** AmEx, DC, Disc, MC, V.

Basketball

Led by Michael Jordan (*see page 232* **My kind of town**), the **Chicago Bulls** dominated the National Basketball Association in the 1990s. En route to winning six titles, they also became the hottest ticket in town, with courtside seats selling for thousands of dollars apiece. Jordan, though, retired after the 1997 season, and the nucleus of the championship team has left. Neither the fans nor the team has recovered.

The Bulls have played truly dismal ball in the seasons following Jordan's departure, which, when coupled with the antipathy created by the NBA strike in the late 1990s, has made tickets far easier to come by. Inexplicably, the team still tries to get away with charging Jordan-era prices, which spiral up to $85 a seat. However, season-ticket holders who bought during the good years and haven't completely given up hope often sell single-game tickets cheaply, either outside the arena or in *Chicago Tribune* and *Chicago Reader* classified ads.

Chicago Bulls

United Center Arena, 1901 W Madison Street, at N Damen Avenue, West Side (information 312 455 4000/tickets 312 559 1212/www.nba.com/bulls). CTA Ashland or Medical Center. **Season** Nov-Apr. **Tickets** $10-$85. **Credit** AmEx, DC, Disc, MC, V.

Hockey

Another once-proud franchise (can you spot a theme developing here?), the **Chicago Blackhawks** have suffered declining fortunes of late, and have spent the past few seasons mired in or near last place. Add to their dismal record the departure in 1999 of team captain

The **Chicago Bears** try to avoid another loss.

Chris Chelios to the hated Detroit Red Wings, and it's obvious that hockey fans in Chicago have had little to cheer about. The exception – and it's a big one – is when the aforementioned Red Wings come to town. The rivalry still draws large and passionate crowds, and tickets, which are usually easy to get hold of, suddenly become scarce. It may be some time, though, before the Blackhawks turn themselves into challengers for anything but last place.

Chicago Blackhawks

United Center Arena, 1901 W Madison Street, at N Damen Avenue, West Side (information 312 455 7000/tickets 312 559 1212/www.chiblackhawks.com). CTA Ashland or Medical Center. **Season** Oct-Apr. **Admission** $15-$75. **Credit** AmEx, DC, Disc, MC, V.

Soccer

The **Chicago Fire**, the city's sole Major League Soccer team, is perhaps the one sports franchise in the city that can boast a growing local fanbase. MLS champions in 1998, the team's appeal has spread beyond diehard soccer fans to include children and other Chicago sports nuts who are disenchanted by the other teams' losing records. Visitors expecting, say, the standard of soccer played in the English Premiership may go away disappointed, but for

The ivy leagues

Losers don't get much more loveable than the Chicago Cubs. They also don't get much more inept. Founded in 1870, the Cubs haven't won a World Series since 1908, have reached the playoffs only once in the last decade (they got swept in the first round), and finished the 1999 season with a 67-95 record, good enough for last place in a division that also includes such high-powered baseball giants as the Milwaukee Brewers and the Pittsburgh Pirates.

Yet despite all this, the fans continue to flock to the corner of Clark and Addison, and getting a ticket for a Cubs game is harder than it's ever been. On the surface, this inverse correlation between uselessness and popularity is tricky to figure out. Until, that is, you actually go to a game at Wrigley Field. And then it all becomes crystal clear.

Now that Fenway Park – home of those other glorious losers, the Boston Red Sox – looks certain to be bulldozed, Wrigley Field will soon have no rivals to the claim of

greatest ballpark in the land. Intimate, cosy and all but untarnished by the modern world (it was built in 1914 and looks its age, though in a good way), it's a wonderful place to catch a game. The crowd, too, is a delight, from the grizzled veterans in the box seats, to the notorious Bleacher Bums who bake daily beyond the ivy, to the ticketless funseekers who congregate out on Waveland Avenue, just beyond the bleachers, in the hope of catching a home run ball tattooed by the mighty Sammy Sosa (pictured; 66 homers in 1998, 63 the following year).

Couple the park with those that fill it on a daily basis, then, and you have the recipe for the perfect afternoon out. Yes, afternoon, for the Cubs are famously the only major league team who play the vast majority of their games during the day (lights were only installed in 1988, decades after everyone else had caught on to the idea of playing after dark). The time of day makes a Cubs home game a pleasingly naughty experience, akin to hanging out with 35,000 teenagers who've been given the afternoon off school and can't believe their luck.

Afternoon baseball is just one of many traditions that the Cubs cling on to: from the communal seventh-inning rendition of *Take Me Out to the Ballgame* to the ivy on the walls (planted in 1937 by the legendary Bill Veeck, who also built the ancient scoreboard) and the jolly organist, an afternoon at Wrigley is a pleasantly old-fashioned affair. In fact, the atmosphere is arguably as much as – if not more of – an attraction than the team itself.

Tickets, of course, are usually scarce, though you may get lucky if the visiting team isn't someone like the Mets, the Cardinals or the Braves. Scalpers are

plentiful, though by law they have to stand across the street from the stadium. If you can bear to wait a couple of innings, the price will drop.

Sadly, as far as the team is concerned, it's pretty much all bad news. Sammy Sosa's entertaining penchant for smacking the living crap out of a baseball was about the only thing that went right in 1999. The hitting sucked, the defence sucked, and the pitching... you guessed it. The only redeeming feature of the season is that the Cubs didn't cave in to the demands of free agent Steve 'Human Rain Delay' Trachsel, who had the gall to ask for around $20 million over three years after losing 18 games in 1999.

Some of the players who helped make the last year of the 20th century such a grim one for the Cubbies have been let go: fan favourite Mickey Morandini, perennially injured lead-off hitter Lance Johnson, pensionable infielder Gary Gaetti and the spectacularly overpaid Jeff Blauser chief among them. But despite the acquisition of fine Dodgers pitcher Ismael Valdes and the probable return of pitching phenom Kerry Wood, the future looks bleak. If new manager Don Baylor can manage to lead the team to anything other than fifth or last place in the NL Central, it will have been a decent achievement; a .500 record will be near enough miraculous.

Not that the locals will care, mind: they'll still head up to the Friendly Confines on a sunny afternoon, kick back with a few plastic beakers of Old Style, root-root-root for the home team (especially Sammy), and raise a resigned smile when, three hours later, their heroes have been thoroughly hammered by any one of 15 other major league teams. Winners, after all, are so much harder to relate to.

most non-Americans who visit town and can't go a week without a dose of the Beautiful Game, plus an increasing number of locals, the Fire plugs the soccer void rather nicely.

Chicago Fire
Soldier Field, 425 E McFetridge Place, at S Lake Shore Drive, Museum Campus (312 705 7200/tickets 312 559 1212/www.chicago-fire.com). CTA Roosevelt/ State or Roosevelt/Wabash. **Season** Apr-Sept. **Tickets** $12-$23. **Credit** AmEx, DC, Disc, MC, V. **Map** p304 J15.

Active sports

Call it the Winded City. A recent survey in *Men's Fitness* magazine rated Chicago sixth worst in the country in fitness terms. Pure and simple sloth is undoubtedly a factor in the city's shameful health and fitness ranking, but it's also a result of the long, brutal winters that drive folks into bars and restaurants for months at a time. Well, that's their excuse, anyway.

However, this is one instance where the saying 'When in Rome, do as the Romans' should not apply. As boaters, bikers or runners of the mid-October **Chicago Marathon** (*see page 95*) will attest, many outdoor sports open up whole new vistas (literally) on Chicago. A jog on the Lakefront Trail is arguably the best sightseeing bargain in town: you get lighter, your wallet doesn't. So don't let Chicago's dismal fitness ranking fool you: there are recreation opportunities galore in Chicago, whatever the season. Don't blame your waistline on the weather.

Before you start donning your lycra tights or Michael Jordan jersey, pick up the invaluable monthly **Windy City Sports** magazine (773 992 2140/www.windycitysportsmag.com), which details upcoming events and provides information on just about every amateur sport in the Chicago metropolitan area. Look for it, gratis, in the vestibules of most sporting goods stores, in book and record stores and at many health clubs, or check its website for information, directions and even online registration.

Finally, what's the point of playing sports if you can't make friends? One social/sports club, **Chicago Sports Monster** (773 866 2955), hosts leagues in various team sports, while the aptly named **Chicago Sports & Social Club** (773 883 9596) runs matey leagues year-round in everything from volleyball to touch football.

Basketball

The Chicago Park District boasts more than 1,000 courts around the city. Many are in fine condition, some are in disrepair, but most are packed on a sunny day, a legacy of Mr Jordan

Arts & Entertainment

and his dominant Bulls teams of a few years back. Call the **Chicago Park District** on 312 742 7529 or see www.chicagoparkdistrict.com for details of your nearest outdoor court.

If you're in Chicago during the summer and have a competitive streak to sate, the city holds a three-on-three tournament in Grant Park. If you do OK, give the Bulls a call: they need your help. For more courts, *see pages 229-30*

Fitness clubs: some have basketball facilities, but you'll either have to join or pay a visitor's fee – usually from $10 up – to use the courts.

Hoops the Gym

1380 W Randolph Street, at N Racine Avenue, West Side (312 850 4667). CTA Ashland (Green). **Open** 24hrs daily. **Rates** $110 per hr. **Credit** MC, V.
If you're willing to pay to play, the two excellently maintained Hoops are where Jordan wannabes congregate to see who's got game. The hefty fee becomes reasonable if split between a big group. **Branch**: 1001 W Washington Street, at N Morgan Street, Greektown (312 850 9496).

Boating

You don't have to be Donald Trump to enjoy Lake Michigan up close and personal. Several organisations offer sailing lessons, including the **Chicago Park District** (312 747 0737) and the **Chicago Sailing Club**, which also offers rentals and charters (Belmont Avenue, at Lake Michigan; 773 871 7245). If you have your own boat, phone the Park District to find out about leasing space in Chicago harbours.

Bowling

A full list of bowling alleys can be gleaned from the *Yellow Pages*. Listed below are our picks of where to play the sport in which getting three strikes doesn't mean you're out. Apart from **AMF**, rates refer to the cost of lane hire.

AMF Marina City Lanes

330 N State Street, at W Kinzie Street, Near North (312 644 0300). CTA Grand. **Open** 10am-midnight Mon-Thur, Sun; 10am-2am Fri; 10am-3am Sat. **Rates** $5 per person, per game. **Credit** MC, V. **Map** p306 H11.
A hugely high-tech operation just by the **House of Blues** (*see p209*), with a laser light show, fog machine and DJs on the weekends.

Diversey River Bowl

2211 W Diversey Parkway, at N Logan Boulevard, Bucktown (773 227 5800). CTA Western (Blue (NW)). **Open** noon-2am Mon-Fri, Sun; noon-3am Sat. **Rates** $18 per hr. **Credit** MC, V.
Rolling along to Saturday night's Rock 'n' Bowl north of Bucktown is a rite of passage at this Chicago standby. There are 36 lanes.

Southport Lanes

3325 N Southport Avenue, at W Aldine Avenue, Lake View (773 472 6600). CTA Southport. **Open** 4pm-2am Mon-Fri; noon-3am Sat; noon-2am Sun. **Rates** $14 per hr. **Credit** AmEx, DC, Disc, MC, V. **Map** p309 D2.
Pin boys reset the pins on four hard-to-book alleys, while a young, hip crowd packs the popular adjoining bar sipping the drink *du jour*.

Waveland Bowl

3700 N Western Avenue, at W Waveland Avenue, Far North (773 472 5900). CTA Western (Brown). **Open** 24hrs daily. **Credit** MC, V.
Insomniac bowlers have recourse to Waveland's 40 lanes every waking hour.

Cycling

Be warned: cycling in Chicago is a contact sport. Always wear a helmet, and be extra-vigilant for erratic drivers or car doors that open suddenly in your path. That said, many city streets now have bike lanes that help to reduce the danger somewhat, though many cars remain heedless. But even on the car-free stretch down by the lake, the traffic of inline skaters, walkers, joggers and other cyclists poses a serious threat if you're not wary.

There's also an incredibly bad bike theft problem in Chicago, so always lock your bike. Look for one of the city-installed bike racks, use a U-lock, and be sure to secure both wheels. Take any removable parts, too: seats, odometers or gear bags. If you don't, someone else might. The best solution is to take the bike indoors with you if at all possible.

Cyclists in Chicago – indeed, in the US as a whole – are required to obey all traffic laws, such as stopping at stop signs and red lights and not cutting in and out of traffic. For more information, contact the **Chicago Bicycle Federation** (Suite 1000, 417 S Dearborn Street, at W Congress Parkway; 312 427 3325), which publishes an excellent seven-county map of bike trails ($6.95 for non-members) as well as riders' picks of the best city routes. It can also hook riders up with bike rentals, though several decent rental outlets are listed below.

If you're new in town, the 15-mile **Lakefront Trail** is a good place to start. Stretching south of the University of Chicago and north to Evanston, the path is clearly marked and offers majestic views of the skyline, Navy Pier, Soldier Field, Museum Campus, and, of course, Lake Michigan. Keep your eye on the road if you don't want to spend part of your stay in one of Chicago's fine hospitals. Finding the path is as easy as riding a bike: head for the lake (east of wherever you are, unless you're already swimming in it), and look for the yellow lines.

Bike Chicago

*Navy Pier, at E Grand Avenue, Near North/
Streeterville (312 755 0488/1-800 915 2453/
fax 312 755 1220/www.bikechicago.com). CTA
Grand.* **Open** *1 Apr-31 Oct* 8am-10pm daily; *tours*
11.30am, 1.30pm daily. **Bike hire** from $8 per hr;
Mon-Thur from $10 per day; *Fri-Sun* $30 per day.
Credit AmEx, MC, V. **Map** p306 K10.
Bike Chicago also arranges free tours for all levels
of fitness and ability to Lincoln Park, the Baha'i
Temple or Grant Park; the sightseeing tour lasts two
hours and takes in six leisurely miles. Rates include
locks, helmets and maps.
Branch: North Avenue Beach, at N Lake Shore
Drive, Lincoln Park (773 327 2706).

Bike Stop

*1034 W Belmont Avenue, at N Kenmore Avenue,
Lake View (773 868 6800). CTA Belmont.* **Open**
summer 10am-7pm Mon, Tue, Thur; 10am-6pm Sat;
10am-5pm Sun; closed Wed, Fri; *winter* 10am-7pm
Mon, Tue, Thur; 10am-6pm Sat; noon-5pm Sun;
closed Wed, Fri. **Closed** Wed, Fri. **Rates** $7 per
hr; $30 per day. **Credit** AmEx, Disc, MC, V.
Map p309 E2.

On the Route

*3146 N Lincoln Avenue, at N Ashland Avenue, Lake
View (773 477 5066/www.ontheroute.com). CTA
Southport.* **Open** noon-8pm Mon-Thur; noon-7pm
Fri; noon-4pm Sat, Sun. **Rates** $35 per day. **Credit**
AmEx, Disc, MC, V. **Map** p309 D3.

Tee off at **Metrogolf**. *See page 230.*

Fishing

The easiest fish to catch in Lake Michigan are
alewives, which float up to the shore in early
summer, silvery bodies bobbing. Dead. A whiff
of that 'dead alewive' aroma, and you'll know
it's best to leave them to their watery grave.

Thankfully, though, the alewives are now not
too much of a problem, most have been eaten by
the Pacific salmon that were bizarrely imported
into the lake in the 1960s and which have since
spawned a huge charter fishing industry. Lake
Michigan also boasts many other live fish:
perch are the most sought-after catch among
pier anglers, while the annual smelt-fishing
season is a sight to behold.

You'll need a licence to fish legally in Illinois;
they're available to over-16s at bait stores
(check the *Yellow Pages* for your nearest), major
sporting goods stores, currency exchanges or
the City Clerk's office, though this latter option
is only to be taken if you want to spend more
time standing in line than casting lines.

The **Illinois Department of Natural
Resources** (312 814 2070) offers guidebooks on
where to fish. For starters, try Chicago's parks
(the **Chicago Park District** offer information
on 312 742 7529); **Cook County Forest
Preserve** (1-800 870 3666); and, of course,
Lake Michigan. Indeed, you can cast right off
the shore at harbours including the popular
Belmont Harbor (Lake Michigan, at 3200
North; 312 742 7673), **Diversey Harbor** (Lake
Michigan, at 2800 South; 312 742 7762);
Burnham Park Harbor (Lake Michigan, at
1200 South; 312 742 7009), and **Monroe
Harbor** (Lake Michigan, at 100 South; 312 742
7643). Laws forbid casting within 100 feet of a
moored vessel or a vessel under way; harbours
may allow fishing only in certain areas.

Fitness clubs

Check with your hotel to see if it has a club on
the premises or offers temporary membership
at a nearby club. But if your lodgings don't
offer free Stairmasters on demand, Chicago has
more than enough fitness clubs: check the
Yellow Pages for a full list, and try to take a tour
and get a free workout before signing up.

Bally Total Fitness

*820 N Orleans Street, at W Chicago Avenue, Near
North/River North (312 573 4300). CTA Chicago
(Brown).* **Open** 5am-10pm Mon-Fri; 8am-6pm Sat,
Sun. **Rates** $63 per mth. **Credit** AmEx, DC, Disc,
MC, V. **Map** p306 G10.
As with any chain – there are two dozen branches
in Chicago – the quality varies wildly, but rates are
reasonable. Visitors are often permitted to use the
club for a day for a small fee.

Arts & Entertainment

Ice ice baby: you can skate on State at, um, **Skate on State**. *See page 232.*

Lakeshore Athletic Clubs

441 N Wabash Avenue, at E Illinois Street, Near North (312 644 4880). CTA Grand. **Open** 5.30am-10pm Mon-Fri; 6.45am-8pm Sat, Sun. **Rates** $15 per day with hotel room key. **Credit** AmEx, Disc, MC, V. **Map** p306 H11.

These fitness clubs are aimed at, and almost invariably patronised by, the beautiful people.

Lehmann Sports Club

2700 N Lehmann Court, at W Diversey Parkway, Lincoln Park (773 871 8300/ www.lehmansportsclub.com). CTA Diversey. **Open** 5am-11pm Mon-Thur; 5am-10pm Fri; 7am-8.30pm Sat, Sun. **Rates** $15 per day. **Credit** AmEx, MC, V. **Map** p308 G4.

A young, go-get-'em clientele packs this well-appointed Lincoln Park gym.

McClurg Court Sports Center

333 E Ontario Street, at N Fairbanks Court, Near North/Streeterville (312 944 4546). CTA Grand. **Open** 5.30am-10pm Mon-Fri; 8am-9pm Sat; 8am-8pm Sun. **Rates** $12 per day. **Credit** AmEx, MC, V. **Map** p306 J10.

The main Streeterville sports centre has facilities for swimming, basketball, racquetball and tennis.

Women's Workout World

1031 N Clark Street, at W Maple Street, Gold Coast (312 664 2106). CTA Clark/Division. **Open** 6am-9.30pm Mon-Thur; 6am-9pm Fri; 8am-4pm Sat, Sun. **Rates** $10 per day. **Credit** AmEx, Disc, MC, V. **Map** p306 H9.

WWW offers several locations for females who want to avoid the leerers.

Golf

The Chicago Park District maintains several public courses; for the one nearest you, call 312 245 0909. Outside the city, the options are as big as a Tiger Woods tee shot. Check the *Yellow Pages* for detailed listings, or call **Chicagoland Golf** (630 719 1000) for specific information on the hundreds of courses in the Chicago area.

Cog Hill Golf & Country Club

12294 Archer Avenue, Lemont (630 257 5872). Metra Lemont. **Open** *winter* 6am-5pm daily; *summer* 6am-9pm daily. **Rates** $31-$115. **Credit** Disc, MC, V.

Cog Hill is home to the Western Open each July, and Tiger Woods dominates the course. Most likely, it will dominate you.

Jackson Park

S Hayes Drive, at E 63rd Street, South Side (312 245 0909). Metra 63rd Street. **Open** sunrise-sunset daily. **Rates** *residents* Mon-Fri $15.50, $7.50 concessions; Sat, Sun $16.50, $8.50 concessions; *non-residents* Mon-Fri $17.50, $9.50 concessions; Sat, Sun $18.50, $10.50 concessions. **Map** p311 Z18.

The Chicago Park District's one 18-hole course should challenge even low-handicappers.

Metrogolf Illinois

221 N Columbus Avenue, at E Wacker Drive, The Loop (312 616 1234). CTA Lake or State. **Open** 10am-7pm daily. **Rates** $15 for 9 holes; $10 for 100 balls. **Map** p305 J11.

A strange but endearing little nine-hole course down by the river, north-east of The Loop. Be sure to book.

Horse riding

Believe it or not, you can ride a horse within
city limits, though there are plenty more equine
facilities out in the suburbs (check the *Yellow
Pages* under 'Stables').

Noble Horse Equestrian Center

*1410 N Orleans Street, at W North Avenue, Old
Town (312 266 7878). CTA Sedgwick.* **Open** 10am-
9pm daily. **Rates** $30 per 30min lesson; $50 per hr.
Credit MC, V. **Map** p307 G7.
An indoor riding arena offering lessons in riding,
dressage and jumping.

Inline skating

As with cycling, skating in the Chicago streets
is done at your own risk. Chicago drivers are
still getting used to sharing the road with bikes,
and have a tendency not even to notice skaters
until one is slammed up against the hood of
their car. Still, the Lakefront Trail (*see page
228*) is usually a pleasant way to while away an
afternoon, while adventurous types may prefer
to join a pickup game of roller hockey at
Diversey Harbor (2800 N Lake Shore Drive,
south of W Diversey Parkway). Skates can be
hired from the places listed below (prepare to
pay a hefty deposit), as well as from **Bike
Chicago** (*see page 229*).

City Sweats

*2467 N Clark Street, at W Fullerton Avenue,
Lincoln Park (773 348 2489). CTA Fullerton.*
Open 11am-8pm Mon-Fri; 10am-6pm Sat; 11am-5pm
Sun. **Rates** $7 per hr; $19 per day. **Credit** AmEx,
MC, V. **Map** p308 G5.

Londo Mondo

*1100 N Dearborn Street, at W Maple Street, Gold
Coast (312 751 2794). CTA Clark/Division.* **Open**
10am-7pm Mon-Fri; 10am-6pm Sat; 11am-6pm Sun.
Rates $7 per hr; $20 per day. **Credit** AmEx, Disc,
MC, V. **Map** p306 H9.

Windward Sports

*3317 N Clark Street, at W Belmont Avenue, Lake
View (773 472 6868). CTA Belmont.* **Open** 10am-
5pm Mon, Tue, Sat, Sun; 11am-8pm Wed-Fri.
Rates $10-$20 per day. **Credit** AmEx, Disc, MC,
V. **Map** p309 F2.

Pool

The question is not where you can but where
you *can't* play pool in Chicago. Many bars have
tables, and if you know chalk from a cue ball,
you might get to play a few games. Bear in
mind that the winner keeps the table, so if
you're just learning, a bar might not be the
place to hone your game. Chicago's standout
pool halls, though, are listed below.

Chris's Billiards

*4637 N Milwaukee Avenue, at W Lawrence Avenue,
Far North (773 286 4714). CTA Jefferson Park.*
Open 9am-2am daily. **Rates** *9am-5pm* $2.55 per
hr; *5pm-2am* $2.95 per hr.
Some 45 pool tables, plus billiards and snooker, tournaments for the true hustler and lessons for the true
hack. *The Color of Money* was part-filmed here.

Marie's Golden Cue

*3241 W Montrose Avenue, at N Kedzie Avenue, Far
North (773 478 2555). CTA Kedzie (Brown).* **Open**
noon-2am daily. **Rates** *noon-6pm* $3.50 per hr; *6pm-
2am* $6.50 per hr. **Credit** MC, V.
19 pool tables, one billiards table, plus lessons and
regular tournaments at this Irving Park hangout.

Rock climbing

Unless you want to tackle the Sears Tower,
world-class climbing is out of reach in Chicago.
But indoor climbing gyms offer a scaled down
version, for beginners or seasoned spidermen.

ESPN Zone

*43 E Ohio Street, at N Wabash Avenue, Near North
(312 644 3776). CTA Grand.* **Open** 11.30am-11pm
Mon-Thur, Sun; 11am-midnight Fri, Sat. **Credit**
AmEx, Disc, MC, V. **Map** p306 H10.
A revolving wall simulates an ascent, so would-be
climbers can practise while staying on terra firma.

Hidden Peak

*Lakeshore Academy of Gymnastics, 937 W Chestnut
Street, at N Sangamon Street, West Side (312
563 9400). CTA Chicago (Blue).* **Open** noon-2pm,
5-9pm Mon-Fri; noon-6pm Sat; 11am-4pm Sun.
Credit MC, V.
Hidden Peak offers a beginners' class ($35) on the
basics; seasoned climbers must do a safety check.

Running

The **Chicago Area Runners Association**
(203 N Wabash Avenue; 312 666 9836) gives
information on everything from upcoming races
to ideal running routes, of which the Lakefront
Trail (*see page 228*) is a popular choice. The
Chicago Marathon (information on 312 904
8000) is ideal for beginners, at least insofar as
any marathon is ideal for beginners: the flat,
fast 26.2-mile course weaves through some of
the city's coolest neighbourhoods, and drew
24,000-odd hardy runners in 1999.

Skating & sledding

Wintertime visitors can also sled courtesy of the
Chicago Park District, who maintain a number
ultra-fast toboggan runs with wooden chutes;
call 312 742 7529 for full details. In addition to
Skate on State, there's also a rink at **Navy
Pier** during the winter.

Skate on State

N State Street, at W Randolph Street, The Loop (312 744 3315). CTA Lake or State. **Open** *Nov 27-Feb 28* 9am-7.15pm Mon-Wed, Fri-Sun; 9am-9.45pm Thur. **Rates** *free; skate hire* $3; $2 children. **Map** p305 H12.
A temporary rink is set up on State during the winter, drawing in some 300,000 locals and visitors each year for fun and frolics on the ice.

Skiing

The best entree into Midwest skiing is through one of Chicago's skiing clubs. For cross-country and downhill flavours, try the well-organised 1,200-member **Lake Shore Ski Club** (312 777 1200), whose members tend to be 30 or older; non-members are welcome on day trips. The **Lincoln Park Ski Club** skews younger in age (20s to 40s), but you must pay the $30 fee in order to join (312 337 2582).

Viking Ski Shop

3422 W Fullerton Avenue, at N Kimball Street, Far North (773 276 1222). CTA Logan Square. **Open** 10.30am-9pm Mon, Tue, Thur, Fri; 11am-6pm Wed; 10am-5pm Sat; 11am-5pm Sun. **Credit** AmEx, Disc, MC, V.
Ski-gear rental, and information on skiing in the Midwest over in Logan Square (north of Bucktown).

Soccer

With its large Latin American and Polish population, it's no surprise the world's game is popular in Chicago. Some of the liveliest pickup

My kind of town Michael Jordan

First of all, we know what you're thinking. 'He retired a few years ago, right? So why the hell write about him now?' The answer's a simple one: Chicago sports still haven't really got over it. By Easter 2000, only one of Chicago's sports teams (the 1998 Cubs) had enjoyed so much as a winning season, let alone a championship year, since our hero went out at the top. Only one local athlete (Cubs slugger Sammy Sosa) has captured the

public's imagination in anything approaching the same way. Living legend doesn't even come close.

Chicago is not only Michael Jordan's kind of town, it practically *was* his town during the 1990s. His accomplishments are well known, but to recap: six NBA championships, five league MVPs, more records than the National Sound Archive and a domination of his game like no other athlete in recent times.

It all started quietly enough, mind. Indeed, he was cut by his high school varsity team as a sophomore before making his name as a University of North Carolina freshman in 1982. After that, there wasn't much stopping him. Drafted in 1984 by the Bulls, Jordan was elected to the All-Star team the following year; in 1987, he started a streak during which he was the league's leading scorer for seven straight seasons. But in 1991, it went not just national, but global. That year, and for the two years afterwards, Jordan led the Bulls to the NBA title, becoming the most famous and most marketable athlete in the world in the process.

In Chicago, it was like the Second Coming. Years of underachieving had hardened the sports-mad locals to defeat, not just in basketball but in everything else. Jordan, though, made them believe again. When he took time out, maintaining that he'd nothing left to prove, and made an ill-advised move into baseball, the Bulls fell away again.

But after spending the summer of 1994 with the White Sox's Double-A team, Jordan decided he'd had enough (he hit an anorexic .204, as if to prove he was actually human).

and league action happens just off the lake at Montrose Avenue. For further information, contact the **Illinois Soccer Association** (5306 W Lawrence Avenue; 773 283 2800) or the **National Soccer League of Chicago** (4534 N Lincoln Avenue; 773 275 2850).

Swimming

Since Lake Michigan is about as warm as a Russian winter most days of the year, don't count on taking a quick freshwater dip unless it's at least 85 degrees out in July. Still, during nice weather, thick-skinned aquanauts swim laps from Navy Pier north toward the Oak Street Beach, and buoys theoretically protect swimmers from passing boats (still, be careful).

Deciding he'd like another crack at the NBA, he returned to the Bulls in time for the 1995 playoffs, though no title would be forthcoming. Until the following year, that is, when Jordan steered perhaps the greatest team in NBA history to the title. And again in 1997. And 1998. And then...

To say grown men wept openly on the streets of Chicago is perhaps overstating the issue. But the retirement of number 23 spelt the end for a halcyon period for sport in Chicago. A period during which the town rediscovered the winning habit. A habit it's since misplaced. Again.

Though he's gone from the courts, he's not been forgotten. Jordan swapped one ball for another and took up golf, reputedly playing at least 36 holes every day of the week. For a while, there was even talk of him turning pro, though all such frivolity fell by the wayside in 1999 when Jordan missed the cut by a mile in his first pro tournament, a tiny local event in Chicago. 'At last,' thought hackers everywhere, 'I can be like Mike.'

However, it looks like the book may finally be closing on Jordan's Chicago presence. In January 2000, he bought a stake in the faltering Washington Wizards NBA franchise, intending to turn the franchise around in much the same way he once did on the court with the Bulls. Given the present state of his old team, there are locals who wish he'd stayed a little closer to home. But for the time being, Chicagoans will have to bid a fond farewell to the man who brought them the one thing they thought they'd never see again. Victory.

The lake is officially open for swimming from Memorial Day to Labor Day.

The **Chicago Park District** (312 747 7529/ www.chicagoparkdistrict.com) has numerous indoor pools that are both free and, generally, well-maintained, though don't expect a barcalounger at poolside. Among the best is **Welles Park**, a full-size pool in a great Lincoln Square building (2333 W Sunnyside Avenue, at N Western Avenue; 312 742 7515). Otherwise, try some of the city's fitness clubs or check the *Yellow Pages*.

Tennis

With over 600 tennis courts around Chicago, it's easier to find a court than a partner. Fees vary, with some public courts charging a nominal fee; for park district lessons, call 312 742 7821. If you prefer to play indoors, there are courts at health clubs such as the W Fullerton branch of the **Lakeshore Athletic Club** (*see page 230*), and at the **Midtown Tennis Club** (2020 W Fullerton Avenue, at N Damen Avenue; 773 235 2300). Some of the finest public courts are listed below, though for details of others, check with the **Chicago Park District** (312 742 7529/www.chicagoparkdistrict.com).

Daley Bicentennial Plaza

337 E Randolph Street, at N Columbus Drive, The Loop (312 742 7648). CTA Randolph. **Open** 7am-10pm Mon-Fri; 9am-5pm Sat, Sun. **Rates** $5 per hr. **Map** p305 J12.
Rally beneath the skyscrapers, but you'll have to pay a nominal fee.

Diversey

138 W Diversey Parkway, at N Lake Shore Drive, Lincoln Park (773 348 9533). CTA Randolph. **Open** 7am-10pm Mon-Fri; 9am-5pm Sat, Sun. **Rates** $5 per hr. **Map** p308 G4.
If you've got a game similar to Pete Sampras (except, like, much worse), try out the only four remaining clay courts in the city.

Oz Park

2021 N Burling Street, at W Webster Avenue, Lincoln Park (312 742 7898). CTA Fullerton. **Open** dawn-dusk daily. **Rates** $5 per hr. **Map** p308 F6.
As the Tin Man looks on, follow the yellow felt ball.

Volleyball

Along the lake, it's the same wherever you go: pickup games galore, especially at **Foster Beach** (Foster Avenue, at the lake) and the **North Avenue** Beach (North Avenue, at the lake), the Centre Court of Chicago beach volleyball. In bad weather, check with nearby health clubs or the YMCA for a court near you.

Theatre, Dance & Comedy

All plays and no work. Oh, and both movement and laughs, too.

Theatre

Widely admired for its guts, integrity and unpretentious good humour, Chicago's diverse theatre scene is one of the biggest and most important in North America. Though the numbers (and the names) are constantly changing, the city is a willing home to some 200 professional and semi-professional theatre companies, ranging from celebrated international ensembles performing in plush downtown auditoria to impoverished, short-lived troupes specialising in basement experimentation on a budget of $49.99 or less.

Thanks to Chicago's reputation as a kind of postgraduate finishing school for American actors and directors, theatre here is rather like an ongoing Edinburgh Festival, only with the fringe out front. On a typical weekend night in Chicago, there will be more than 100 shows of all stripes from which the visitor can choose.

The theatrical landscape can be broken down into several categories. The biggest companies, such as the **Goodman** and **Steppenwolf**, have subscription seasons and their own dedicated spaces that they occasionally permit others to use. Some long-standing and highly regarded locals prefer the lower-cost option of itinerancy, though, occupying one of the city's diverse collection of rental houses only when they have a show in production. At the experimental end, you can find tiny Chicago theatres permanently occupying a funeral home, a former ballroom, old factories and any other place where they can put up a light and a few folding chairs. And one of the great Chicago theatrical traditions involves improv, on which more later.

The city has recently invested millions of dollars in renovating its magnificent stock of downtown theatres and surrounding them with new state-of-the-art performance spaces. But though touring productions of big musicals usually play downtown, most of the best Chicago theatres are still found in the residential neighbourhoods, especially to the north of the city in Lincoln Park and Lake View. It's here you'll find the qualities that make Chicago theatre distinctive: youth, vitality, honesty and a scrappy willingness to pursue creative goals without worrying much about financial reward.

With all this theatrical activity taking place, it's inevitable that shows vary drastically in quality. Some of the smaller companies are little more than a group of twentysomething friends with drama degrees, a few bucks and a couple of half-baked ideas. But these are also often the very places where you'll find the most exciting work. Unlike snootier and less inclusive New York or LA, almost every show in Chicago gets covered in the local papers. Check the reviews before heading into the theatrical jungle: there are Midwestern riches just waiting to be mined.

TICKETS & INFORMATION

Strong coverage of Chicago theatre is found in the *Reader* (which has the best listings) and in the *Tribune*'s Friday pullout (which carries most of the theatre advertising). Archived reviews of shows currently playing can be found at **www.metromix.com**.

In addition, the **League of Chicago Theatres** (312 554 9800) publishes a generally accurate quarterly guide that can be ordered over the phone or picked up for free in most hotels and tourist centres. The League's website (www.theatrechicago.org) provides links to the many homepages of Chicago theatres. Though most touring shows and some resident companies sell tickets through the ubiquitous **Ticketmaster** phone line (*see opposite*), it's generally best to buy direct from the theatre box offices and avoid surcharges. Tickets for most shows can be had for between $15 and $25, though some – the Goodman and Steppenwolf, for example – charge more in the $30-$45 range, while others let punters in for a little less (tickets for the **Trap Door**, for example, range from $8 to $12).

For half-price tickets on the day of a performance, go in person to one of the League's three **Hot Tix** booths (*see opposite*). The helpful booths, which can additionally be found at some branches of Tower Records, also sell full-price advance tickets. Phone information about the day's shows is updated at 10am; calls cost $1 per minute.

Note that many Chicago theatres, especially the small ones, perform from Thursday to Sunday only. On Fridays and Saturdays, late-night shows begin at around 11pm.

Hot Tix

Information 1-900 225 2225. **Open** 10am-6pm Tue-Sat; noon-5pm Sun; closed Mon. **Credit** AmEx, MC, V. **Branches**: 108 N State Street, at W Washington Boulevard, The Loop; Waterworks Visitor Center, 163 E Pearson Street, at N Michigan Avenue, Near North/Magnificent Mile; 1616 Sherman Avenue, Evanston.

Ticketmaster

(312 902 1500/www.ticketmaster.com). **Open** 8am-9pm Mon-Fri; 8am-7pm Sat; 8am-6pm Sun. **Credit** AmEx, DC, MC, V.

Major companies

There are so many theatres in Chicago that what follows is a necessarily selective list. Since local actors and other creative types work all over the place, it's a smart idea to pick shows based on what's getting good reviews. But here, at least, are the most important troupes.

About Face Theatre

3212 N Broadway, at W Belmont Avenue, Lake View (773 549 7943/www.aboutfacetheatre.com). CTA Belmont. **Open** *box office* times and dates vary; *shows* usually 8pm Thur-Sun. **Credit** MC, V. **Map** p309 F2.

This Lake View troupe calls itself Chicago's 'serious gay theatre', though it occasionally lets its hair down with more campy fare. But as a rule, About Face offers original adaptations of gay-themed novels, new plays by gay authors and revivals of seminal works such as *The Boys in the Band.* The pervasive sensibility is young, hip, intellectual and politically involved, and artistic standards are generally high.

American Theater Company

1909 W Byron Street, at N Lincoln Avenue, Far North (773 929 1031/www.atcweb.org). CTA Irving Park. **Open** *box office* noon-showtime Thur-Sun; hours vary Mon-Wed; *shows* season runs Sept-May, usually Thur-Sun. **Credit** AmEx, MC, V.

Get your hot tickets at, um, **Hot Tix**.

An Irving Park theatre that proudly declares its blue-collar origins and working class sensibility, this North Side troupe specialises in classic and more contemporary American fare performed with bigger energy than budgets. A good place to find gutsy Chicago acting, ATC offers an authentic kind of local experience where the actors would be happy to go drinking with you after the show.

Bailiwick Repertory

1229 W Belmont Avenue, at N Racine Avenue, Lake View (773 883 1090/www.bailiwick.org). CTA Belmont. **Open** *box office* 11am-showtime daily; *shows* times vary Thur-Sun. **Credit** AmEx, Disc, MC. **Map** p309 E2.

One of Chicago's most eclectic and daring theatres with two frantically busy stages, the Bailiwick also features plenty of progressive and gay programming, even if it takes itself a bit less seriously than **About Face**. There's always something going on at the Bailiwick, which is the kind of wacky arts centre where naked monologues are billed alongside new musicals and political dramas share a space (and often a set) with revivals of Noel Coward plays. Bailiwick also rents its stages to other troupes.

Chicago Shakespeare Theater

800 E Grand Avenue, at Navy Pier, Near North/Streeterville (312 595 5600/ www.chicagoshakes.com). CTA 65, 66 bus. **Open** *box office* 10am-4pm Tue-Sat; *shows* 7.30pm Tue-Thur; 8pm Fri; 4pm, 8.30pm Sat; 3pm Sun. **Credit** AmEx, Disc, MC, V. **Map** p306 K10.

Formerly the Shakespeare Repertory Theater, this 'all-Bard-all-the-time' troupe changed its name in 1999 after it moved to an opulent new home (modelled on the Swan Theatre in Stratford-Upon-Avon) on Navy Pier. An evening combining Chicago-style hot dogs and rhyming couplets may seem bizarre, but the theatre not only offers stunning views from its lobbies but is surrounded by numerous restaurants and bars in which to spend the rest of the night (or the second act). The diet here is RSC redux, though edgier stuff appears in the attached studio theatre and there are also outdoor performances in summer. Standards have been rising since the move to the new theatre.

Chicago Theatre Company

500 E 67th Street, at S Rhodes Avenue, South Side (773 493 0901). CTA 3 bus. **Open** *box office* 6.30-9pm Fri, Sat; 1-5pm Sun; *shows* 8pm Fri, Sat; 3pm Sun. **Credit** MC, V.

Chicago has several theatres whose work is aimed at African-American audiences, but the Chicago Theatre Company consistently upholds the highest standards. Offering a mix of original works and revivals, this South Side troupe is based in a tiny basement theatre where the audience feels part of the action. A proud part of a highly supportive community, work at the CTC invariably has something worthwhile to say about the human condition. If you should get the opportunity to check out this group in the heart of the South Side, try and take it.

Drama as you like it at the **Chicago Shakespeare Theater** on Navy Pier. *See page 235.*

Court Theatre

5535 S Ellis Avenue, at E 55th Street, Hyde Park (773 753 4472/www.uchicago.edu/aff/court_theatre). CTA 55 bus. **Open** *box office* noon-5pm Mon, Tue; noon-showtime Wed-Sun; *shows* times and dates vary. **Credit** AmEx, Disc, MC, V. **Map** p311 X17.
The upmarket Court specialises in revivals of classic plays: if your tastes run to Greek drama, the Spanish Golden Age or Molière, head here to see productions executed to a consistently high standard by a troupe of resident and guest actors under the leadership of artistic director Charles Newell. It's not generally a place to kick back with escapist fare, but guest directors like Jo Anne Akalitis offer plenty of intellectual stimulation and experimentation.

Goodman Theatre

Until Nov 2000: 200 S Columbus Drive, at E Monroe Street, The Loop (312 443 3800/www.goodman-theatre.org). CTA Adams or Monroe (Red). *From Nov 2000: 170 N Dearborn Street, at W Randolph Street, The Loop.* CTA Randolph or Washington (Blue, Red). **Open** *box office* 10am-7pm daily; *shows* 7.30pm Mon-Fri; 8pm Sat, Sun. **Credit** AmEx, Disc, MC, V. **Map** p305 J12 (Columbus Drive) and H11 (Dearborn Street).
The audience may tend to be a little older than at the **Steppenwolf** (*see p237*), but the Goodman has for many years been the most prestigious theatre in the city. Established in 1925, this is the high priest of the city's theatrical establishment, though the work on its two stages has been far from stuffy under the exemplary stewardship of artistic director Robert Falls. The season here is a top-drawer mix of classical and contemporary: many of David Mamet and August Wilson's plays have premièred here, for

example. At the end of 2000, the Goodman moves to a splendiferous new home on Randolph Street: with two state-of-the-art theatres in the heart of the Loop, the Goodman is likely to continue its dominance.

Lifeline Theatre

6912 N Glenwood Street, at W Farwell Avenue, Far North (773 761 4477/www.lifelinetheatre.com). CTA Morse. **Open** *box office* 2-6pm Thur; 2-6pm Fri, Sat; 2-3.30pm Sun; *shows* 8pm Thur-Sat; 3.30pm Sun. **Credit** V.
Chicago has a growing tradition of supporting original adaptations of novels and poems, and the Lifeline Theatre is one of the best places in town in which to find drama that goes beyond the usual scripted cannon. With a long-standing commitment to shows suitable for families, Lifeline is an intimate but literate theatre with great integrity.

Next Theatre

927 Noyes Street, at Ridge Avenue, Evanston (847 475 1875/www.nexttheatre.org). CTA Noyes. **Open** *box office* noon-6pm Mon-Fri, or noon-showtime on performance days; *shows* 7.30pm Thur; 8pm Fri, Sat; 3pm Sun. **Credit** AmEx, Disc, MC, V.
Located in the Noyes Cultural Arts Center (also the home of the impressive Piven Theatre Workshop), this small but reliable company offers a progressive season of shows with an emphasis on the new and the unconventional. Next, which turns 20 years old in 2001, has more maturity than some of its scrappier competitors but has never settled for the stodgy. Since its founding by Harriet Spizziri and Brian Finn, the company has established a tradition of producing shows that promote social awareness.

Steppenwolf Theatre Company

1650 N Halsted Street, at W North Avenue,
Lincoln Park (312 335 1650/www.steppenwolf.org).
CTA North/Clybourn. **Open** *box office* 11am-5pm
daily, or 11am-5pm Tue-Sun during performance
runs; *shows* usually 7.30pm Tue-Sun, plus some
matinées and late shows. **Credit** AmEx, DC, Disc,
MC, V. **Map** p307 F7.

The actor-centred Steppenwolf first gained fame as
the blue-collar brand leader in macho acting, typified
by John Malkovich's famously insane performance
in the acclaimed 1982 production of Sam Shepard's
True West. But thanks to the extraordinary accomplishments of its star-laden ensemble of actors –
which also includes co-founder Gary Sinise, Joan
Allen, Martha Plimpton and Kevin Anderson – the
rough-and-ready house style is now played out in a
very posh, high-tech house at the southern end of
Lincoln Park where Chicago hipsters work the lobby
crowds. Since attendance suggests street-cred among
locals, tickets are perennially hard to snag (you may
get lucky with returns). The bill can be esoteric, but
standards are reliably high.

Strawdog Theatre Company

3829 N Broadway, at W Grace Street, Lake
View (773 528 9696/www.strawdog.org). CTA
Sheridan (Red). **Open** *shows* 8pm Fri, Sat; 7pm Sun.
Map p309 F1.

The surroundings are rough at this Lake View
theatre – it's located above a shop and up a long
flight of stairs – but Strawdog is a long-established

Being John Malkovich

When it comes to pizza and hot dogs,
Chicago has its own unsubtle but juicy style.
And as with these fat-laden comestibles, the
city has lent its name to a distinctive style of
acting. If an actor of either sex walks into an
audition anywhere in America with Chicago
theatre credits on his or her resumé, the
auditor won't be expecting a
training in the effete
subtleties of a Royal Academy
or a familiarity with the
societal comedies born on
New York's Upper East Side.

In acting circles, Chicago
style means aggression,
energy, blue-collar grit and,
where possible, a healthy
dose of macho swagger. Like
drama degrees, trust funds or
fancy ways of speaking, pretty
faces are not required or
much admired here. In fact, a
decent beer gut on an actor
might be a clue that they
started their career in off-Loop
theatre. The preferred pedigree is a few years
of industrial labour, a dysfunctional family
background and a long-cultivated disdain for
the pretensions of traditional theatrical
methodology. Any actor motivated only by
money or fame is likely to be thrown into
Lake Michigan.

The derivation of this archetype is the
Steppenwolf Theatre Company (*see above*), a
justly vaunted troupe famous for inventing
what is ignobly but widely known as 'balls-out
acting'. The stories may be apocryphal, but
veteran Chicago theatre-goers love to recount
how they feared for their very lives watching

young and frighteningly intense versions of
Gary Sinise and John Malkovich trample over
the boundaries between art and life as they
bashed away at each other in the suburban
church basement where Steppenwolf started
out in the mid-1970s.

In the early stages of their careers, Dennis
Franz and Joe Mantegna
continued building the
Chicago mystique at Stuart
Gordon's old Organic Theatre,
a troupe that did original work
mainly because no one had
enough money to pay
royalties. Ensemble-devised
shows such as *Bleachers*
Bums, a funny 1977 piece
about a miserable day in the
generally miserable life of a
Cubs fan, cemented
Chicago's reputation as the
only theatre city where actors
and writers were no different
from regular folks; except,
perhaps, in their considerable
propensity for alcohol. But even though
tastes and styles have diversified over the
past decade, local actors still most love to
get their chops around the work of the city's
most famous native playwright.

From *Sexual Perversity in Chicago* to
Glengarry Glen Ross, David Mamet's caustic
plays capture the harsh vitality of the city of
his birth. His expletive-laden style of
dialogue was memorably described by one
New York critic as 'a crossfire of
scatological buckshot'. But then only a
Chicago actor really knows what Mamet is
talking about.

Arts & Entertainment

company with a tradition of edgy, interesting work. Based on the desires of an ensemble of resident actors and directors, it's big on new work and cutting-edge American fare. The theatre is so intimate that you can see the actors sweat. And on a hot summer night, you'll probably be sweating yourself.

Trap Door Productions

1655 W Cortland Street, at N Paulina Street, Wicker Park/Bucktown (773 384 0494). CTA 73 bus. **Open** *shows* times and dates vary. **Map** p310 C6.

Uninterested in money or conventional success, the Trap specialises in out-there productions of obscure works by such maverick European writers as Ionesco and Witkiewicz. The space itself seats only about 50 people in not much comfort, and if you venture out here, be aware that the quality of the work can be widely uneven. But if nihilism, neo-absurdism and wacky experimentation are your bag, you won't be bored here.

Victory Gardens Theater

2257 N Lincoln Avenue, at W Webster Avenue, Lincoln Park (773 871 3000/www.victorygardens.org). CTA Fullerton. **Open** *box office* noon-8pm Tue-Sat; 10am-4pm Sun; *shows* 8pm Tue-Fri; 5pm, 8.30pm Sat; 3pm Sun. **Credit** AmEx, Disc, MC, V. **Map** p308 F5.

The Chicago citadel of new work, this long-established but informal theatre offers an exclusive diet of world premières, most penned by the members of its generally talented ensemble of affiliated writers. Located in a busy strip of bars and restaurants in Lincoln Park, the much-loved Victory Gardens boasts an intimate theatre where the playwright and the words always have the principal focus. There are four stages in the complex, three of which are rented out to carefully picked tenants.

The winning **Victory Gardens Theater**.

Itinerant companies

Defiant Theatre

Information 312 409 0585/www.defianttheatre.org

The boys and girls at Defiant like to think of themselves as 'Chicago's most dangerous theatre company', which generally means an incendiary mix of physical acting, profanity and sex. Luckily, they're a talented bunch, and most Defiant productions are full of invention. There's a special interest here in puppetry, Kabuki and other non-realistic theatrical traditions. Since the company likes to fit the space to the show, Defiant frequently moves around.

Famous Door Theatre Company

Information 773 404 8283/ www.famousdoortheatre.org

With an eclectic repertoire covering everything from Harold Pinter to Joshua Sobol, Famous Door has become one of Chicago's most beloved and reliable mid-sized theatre companies. Run by a group of regular folks who have scraped and saved for years to keep their dream going, Famous Door savvily hires the best directors in town. Its favoured venue is the **Theatre Building** (*see p240*).

Lookingglass Theatre Company

Information 773 477 9257/ www.lookingglasstheatre.org

Since founding member David Schwimmer found fame as one of the *Friends*, this trendy troupe has taken on a slightly Hollywood dimension. But it built its reputation through inventive adaptations of classical myths and contemporary novels, and has always placed an emphasis on a highly physical style of acting. Youthful, smart and compelling, this is one of Chicago's best itinerant companies.

Roadworks Productions

Information 312 492 7150/www.roadworks.org

Roadworks speciality lies in articulating the angst of disenfranchised youth by focusing on British and American playwrights who capture the daily grit of life for those poor, misunderstood kiddies. A lively ensemble of actors specialises in hyper-realistic work.

Teatro Vista

Information 773 568 7871/www.teatrovista.org

Given the size of Chicago's Latino population, the city should support more companies dedicated to concerns of this sector of the community. But Teatro Vista ('theatre with a point of view') does a pretty superb job of filling the void by bringing to Chicago work by playwrights from south of the border, as well as new plays that dramatise the concerns of all Chicagoans. Standards are reliably high and performances are almost always in English.

Venues

Theatre District

Chicago has an enviable collection of big downtown theatres and has recently seen the benefit of salvaging and marketing them as a 'new' district centred on Randolph Street. The Loop will never be Broadway, but many of these former movie palaces and vaudeville houses are architectural gems with interiors so spectacular that any stage set has a hard time competing with the walls and ceiling.

If you love old theatres, you'll enjoy strolling around the area and visiting the over-the-top **Oriental Theatre** (24 W Randolph Street) and the neighbouring, more dignified **Cadillac Palace** (151 W Randolph Street), the outer lobbies of which are open all day. The sites of touring Broadway shows and occasional long-running productions, both of these theatres were meticulously restored to their former glories in the late 1990s and now offer a steady diet of musicals and other Broadway-style fare.

As its stage is too small for huge musicals, the **Chicago Theatre** (175 N State Street) instead offers a blend of concerts, dance and theatre, and also features a lush interior. Meanwhile, the enormous **Auditorium Theatre** (50 E Congress Parkway) boasts 4,000 seats and a stunning Louis Sullivan interior, while the less overwhelming **Shubert Theatre** (22 W Monroe Street) remains the best place in Chicago to see Broadway plays and smaller musicals. Future plans for the district include a new (and badly needed) music and dance theatre that will have around 1,000 seats.

Tickets for all the venues listed above and below are available from **Ticketmaster**. Prices start from $10 at the **Ivanhoe**, spiralling to $49 at the **Briar Street Theatre** and occasionally beyond in the Theatre District.

Other theatres

For **Theatre on the Lake**, *see chapter* **Chicago by Season**.

Briar Street Theatre

3133 N Halsted Street, at W Belmont Avenue, Lake View (773 348 4000). CTA Belmont. **Open** *box office* 9am-10pm Mon-Sat; noon-7pm Sun; *shows* 8pm Wed, Thur; 7pm, 10pm Fri; 4pm, 7pm, 10pm Sat; 3pm, 6pm Sun. **Credit** AmEx, Disc, MC, V. **Map** p309 F3.
The Briar Street Theatre is a mid-sized rental house that was gutted in 1998 to make way for a long-running production of *Blue Man Group*, the hugely successful high-tech piece of performance art that was still going strong in early 2000. Located in a great neighbourhood just south of Boystown, it attracts a young and decidedly hip crowd.

Ivanhoe Theater

750 W Wellington Avenue, at N Clark Street, Lake View (773 975 7171). CTA Wellington. **Open** *box office by phone* 10am-9pm daily; *shows* times vary Fri-Sun. **Credit** AmEx, MC, V. **Map** p309 F3.
The Ivanhoe is a three-stage complex in Lake View with an eclectic range of offerings. In the basement is improv troupe the **Free Associates** (*see p243*); in the mid-sized space is the long-running *Hellcab*, an extremely funny show about life driving a Chicago cab. Offerings on the main stage change constantly, though you'll probably find owner Doug Bragan, a true Chicago eccentric, selling tickets in his own box office.

Royal George Theatre

1641 N Halsted Street, at W North Avenue, Lincoln Park (312 988 9000). CTA North/Clybourn. **Open** *box office* 10am-7pm Mon-Sat; noon-6pm Sun; *shows* usually 8pm daily. **Credit** AmEx, MC, V. **Map** p307 F7.
This commercial theatre on the outermost fringe of Old Town generally hosts recent hits from the Off-Broadway season, as well as productions transferring from Chicago's resident theatres. Located directly opposite the **Steppenwolf** (*see p237*), the Royal George's cabaret has long been the home of the harmonising musical, *Forever Plaid*, which has been running, incredibly, for years.

No parking at the **Cadillac Palace**.

Theatre Building

*1225 W Belmont Avenue, at N Southport Avenue,
Lake View (773 327 5252). CTA Belmont.* **Open**
*box office noon-6pm Wed; noon-showtime Thur-Sun;
shows times and dates vary.* **Credit** AmEx, Disc,
MC, V. **Map** p309 D3.

A pioneer of Chicago's off-Loop scene, the Theatre
Building includes three black-box theatres located
in a former industrial space. The quality and type
of fare varies, but there are usually several shows
on offer in an arts centre that is the preferred home
of several of Chicago's itinerant companies. The
Theatre Building sponsors one resident company,
New Tuners, an incubator for new musicals.

Dance

Dance in Chicago is often overshadowed by the
other arts, partly because the local dance
community has long lacked collective
leadership and marketing skills. But though the
dance community in Chicago is relatively
young, a proud tradition has emerged in the last
30 years. Today, the city supports two world-
famous companies and a host of smaller troupes
and independent choreographers. Perhaps
unsurprisingly, the traditions of jazz and
theatrical dance are well represented, and
Chicago plays host to many visiting companies
each year.

TICKETS & INFORMATION

The *Reader*, the *Tribune* and the *Sun-Times*
have extensive dance listings and reviews. Some
dance events are available at the half-price **Hot
Tix** booths (*see page 235*), depending on their
venues. The **Ticketmaster** arts line (*see page
235*) also has information on dance events.

Although its infrastructure has been shaky of
late, the **Chicago Dance Coalition** (312 419
8384) is a good source for information on
Chicago dance. Tickets are usually in the $10-
$25 range, though the **Joffrey** offers seats for
as much as $75.

Major dance companies

Hubbard Street Dance Chicago

*1147 W Jackson Boulevard, at S Racine Avenue, West
Side (312 850 9744/www.hubbardstreetdance.com).
CTA Racine.*

The city was delighted when Hubbard Street Dance
added the suffix 'Chicago' to its name, reflecting the
close relationship between the city and its premier
dance company. Founded in 1977 by choreographer
Lou Conte (still artistic director), Hubbard Street
offers an eclectic mix of modern, tap and classical
with a repertoire that has frequently drawn on the
work of Bob Fosse and Twyla Tharp. In March 1988,
Hubbard Street moved into a renovated building in

the West Loop. Visitors are welcome at the spacious
dance centre, the venue for classes and rehearsals but
not shows. The troupe is often on tour, but give annual performances at the **Auditorium Theatre** (*see
p239*) and, each summer, at the **Ravinia Festival**
(*see p90*).

Joffrey Ballet of Chicago

*Auditorium Theatre, 50 E Congress Parkway, at S
Michigan Avenue, The Loop (312 739 0120/
www.joffrey.com). CTA Harrison.* **Map** p305 J13.

Founded by Gerald Arpino and the late Robert
Joffrey in 1956, the Joffrey has long been one of the
leading smaller American ballet companies, and has
presented more than 235 ballets by some 85 different choreographers. In 1995, Arpino moved the company's HQ to Chicago, and though it remains a
touring company, its local engagements include an
annual *Nutcracker* and a summer stand at the
Ravinia Festival (*see p90*).

Muntu Dance Company of Chicago

*Kennedy King College, 6800 S Wentworth Avenue,
at W 67th Street, South Side (773 602 1135/
www.muntu.com). CTA 69th Street.*

'Muntu' means 'the essence of humanity', and this
troupe is continually exploring its roots through contemporary and ancient African and African-
American dance, music and folklore. Much of its
work features the synthesis of dance, rhythm and
song, and audiences generally find it hard to stay in
their seats. Founded in 1972, the troupe uses authentic masks and costumes and prides itself on
researching the cultural and social significance of
the dances it performs. There are frequent performances at the **Athenaeum Theatre** (*see below*).

River North Dance Company

Information 312 944 2888.

Now over a decade old, this hip and lively touring
troupe's trademark is a breezy style with an emphasis on accessibility; most of the choreography comes
from Chicago-based artists. Co-artistic director
Sherry Zunker Dow often describes River North as
'the dance company for the MTV generation'.

Best of the rest

Other dance companies of interest include the
youth-oriented **Ballet Chicago** (312 251 8838);
the **Chicago Moving Company** (773 880 5402);
Hedwig Dances (773 871 0872); **Jan Eckert
& Dancers** (773 883 8620); and the celebrated
Trinity Irish Dancers (773 594 4434).

Major dance venues

Athenaeum Theatre

*2936 N Southport Avenue, at N Lincoln Avenue,
Lake View (773 935 6860). CTA Wellington.* **Open**
*box office noon-5pm Mon-Fri; until showtime and Sat,
Sun on performance days; shows usually Thur-Sun,
times vary.* **Credit** AmEx, MC, V. **Map** p309 D3.

The annual Next Dance Festival takes place over three winter weekends at this 900-seat spot, showcasing small Chicago troupes and solo artists. The theatre presents other dance events during the year.

Dance Center

Columbia College, 4730 N Sheridan Road, at W Lawrence Avenue, Far North (773 989 3310). CTA Lawrence. **Open** *box office times and dates vary; shows 8pm, days vary.* **Admission** $16-$20. **Credit** AmEx, Disc, MC, V.
An offshoot of one of the area's best college dance programmes, Uptown's Dance Center presents modern events of both local and national significance.

Museum of Contemporary Art

220 E Chicago Avenue, at N Mies van der Rohe Way, Near North/Streeterville (312 280 2660/ *www.mcachicago.org). CTA Chicago (Red).* **Open** 10am-8pm Tue; 10am-5pm Wed-Sun. **Admission** $7; $4.50 concessions; free under-12s. **Credit** AmEx, DC, Disc, MC, V. **Map** p306 J10.
The multi-disciplinary MCA has emerged as one of Chicago's most important presenters of international dance companies, as well as performance artists and other non-commercial touring performers who need the support of a large museum.

Ruth Page Auditorium

1016 N Dearborn Street, at W Oak Street, Gold Coast (312 337 6543). CTA Clark/Division. **Open** 10am-9pm Mon-Thur; 10am-7.30pm Fri; 9am-4.30pm Sat. **Admission** prices vary. **Map** p306 H9.
The spiritual heart of Chicago's dance community, the intimate and dance-oriented Ruth Page hosts a variety of classes and events throughout the year.

My kind of town Bill Murray

There have been plenty of Chicagoans to hit the comedy big time: you could pin **Second City** (*see page 244*) as the Triple-A version of *Saturday Night Live* (only Second City is funnier). Some of *SNL*'s best have passed through Chicago – from Belushi to Farley – and they keep on coming: current *SNL*ers Tim Meadows and Horatio Sandz are Second City vets.

But the love for Bill Murray among Chicagoans is special. For starters, he was born here: in 1950, to be precise, into a large Irish-Catholic family with long-planted Chicago roots. He grew up in Wilmette, where he spent his time being cut from his high school's basketball team and caddying (of course). He tried college but quit after being busted for pot possession at O'Hare. And then it was off to join his older brother Brian in the Second City.

The *National Lampoon Radio Hour* came next, then Howard Cosell's short-lived Saturday night variety show and, in 1977, *Saturday Night Live*. 1979's *Meatballs* made him a screen star, and the rest – from *Stripes* to *Groundhog Day* to the more recent *The Cradle Will Rock* – is history. With 1998's *Rushmore*, Murray solidified his Steve Martin-like transition from goofball to venerable comic actor. As he once memorably said, 'I'm a nut, but not just a nut.'

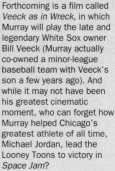

Murray lives in New York now, but his ties to Chicago remain strong. A lifelong Cubs fan, Murray drops in on the Cubs TV announcer's box from time to time, and even led the Wrigley Field crowd in *Take Me Out to the Ballgame* shortly after Harry Caray died.

Forthcoming is a film called *Veeck as in Wreck*, in which Murray will play the late and legendary White Sox owner Bill Veeck (Murray actually co-owned a minor-league baseball team with Veeck's son a few years ago). And while it may not have been his greatest cinematic moment, who can forget how Murray helped Chicago's greatest athlete of all time, Michael Jordan, lead the Looney Toons to victory in *Space Jam*?

He can be slyly ironic, even deadly sarcastic. But bitter or excessively cynical he is not. Even in his early movies, his face proclaimed a world-weariness, but this shell is constantly betrayed by a sweetness, a vulnerability and a childlike penchant for goofing off. He's a consummate entertainer, but a deeply private man. And all of this – what he chooses to show the world – reflects the mood of the city in which he was born and raised. They may not be as funny, but you can bet there's a version of Bill Murray in every Chicago neighbourhood bar.

Comedy

Bill Murray, Mike Myers, Jerry Stiller, Chris Farley… and the list goes on. Name a North American comic talent, and chances are they have spent time honing their skills in Chicago. It's no great mystery why, for though a small stand-up scene does exist, when it comes to finding late-night laughs and innovative, taboo-breaking comedy, improvisational theatre – or shows created out of improv jam sessions – is the name of the game in town.

And improv did literally begin as a game. Viola Spolin, dubbed the 'High Priestess of Improvisation', probably never imagined that John Belushi would someday be yelling 'Cheezborger! Cheezborger!' on national TV when she introduced 'games' that relied on instinct and group co-operation to teach theatre to Chicago children during the Depression. But in the hands of Spolin's son, Paul Sills, and his University of Chicago pals (including Mike Nichols and Elaine May), these games became the basis for theatre itself with the legendary improvisational group the Compass Players in the 1950s. Nichols and May went on to Broadway, but Sills stuck around Chicago to co-found the **Second City**. What began on a shoestring in 1959 has become an institution.

With new venues and troupes consistently springing up, improv is now a major and respected component of the city's theatre scene. After Chicago improv guru Del Close died in 1999, for example, his skull was given to the prestigious **Goodman Theatre** to be used in the role of Yorick in a future production of *Hamlet*. A night of improv can take place in a packed space where waiters bring you high-priced drinks, or in a tiny BYOB room with fewer members in the audience than there are improvisers on stage.

It's almost impossible to keep track of all the improv troupes in the city. Some are based in one theatre, while others roam from stage to stage. Recently, minority troupes have begun to form (the African-American Oui Be Negroes, the homosexual GayCo, the all-women Sirens and the Latino Salsation), but it's impossible to neatly define improv and how it is used here.

Some theatres use improv as a brainstorming technique: their revues, all scripted, grow out of improvised jam sessions. Improvisers who use improv as an end in itself are further divided: some prefer long-form improvisation where one suggestion from the audience can set off the improvisers for the duration of a show, while others engage in short-form improvisation, relying on games and audience participation.

Rules are always broken, and which style is best is a matter of personal taste. There are no

guarantees, either: a group can be fantastic one night and lousy the next. But when it's good, there's no comedy as exhilarating.

TICKETS & INFORMATION

The *Chicago Reader* and *Newcity* both offer listings for almost every venue in Chicago. Tickets can be bought directly from theatre box offices, and range in price from $5 to $15 in just about all of the venues listed below. Many improv troupes don't perform in a set location: check listings, or log on to the **Chicago Improv Page** (http://amasis.com/improv) for more details on their movements.

Improv

Annoyance Theatre

3747 N Clark Street, at N Racine Avenue, Lake View/Wrigleyville (773 929 6200/www.annoyance.com). CTA Addison (Red). **Open** *box office* from 7.30pm Fri, Sat; *shows: Co-ed Prison Sluts* 10.30pm Fri, Sat; *Screw Puppies* 12.30am Sat; check local listings for additional shows. **Map** p309 E1.

Home to the long-running profane jailhouse musical *Co-ed Prison Sluts*, the Annoyance, founded in 1987, uses improv in rehearsals to create its shows. And the shows – with titles like *After School Special Gone Bad, Manson: the Musical* and *Portrait of a Virgin* – have rightfully earned the theatre a reputation for pushing boundaries, knocking down sacred cows and making you laugh despite yourself. The smoky space, which features a bare stage, brick walls covered in graffiti and audience members who know all the lines, has an underground, clubhouse feel. It's a bring-your-own-booze joint.

ComedySportz

TurnAround Theatre, 3209 N Halsted Street, at W Belmont Avenue, Lake View (773 549 8080/www.comedysportz.com). CTA Belmont. **Open** *box office* 30min before showtime; *shows* 8pm, 10.30pm Fri, Sat; *Student Show* 8pm Wed; *The Hot Karl* midnight Sat. **Credit** Disc, MC, V. **Map** p309 F2.

With venues all over the US, ComedySportz is the Starbucks of improv, though it's no surprise that Chicago hosts one of the stronger franchises. Two teams battle each other in improv games, complete with a scoreboard and a wiseacre referee. The performers are talented and spirited, but many of the games play like derivatives of Charades. This is, however, the only venue in the city geared towards families, since swear words and raunchy material are frowned on. Improvisers get to let loose once a week with an adult-oriented show, *The Hot Karl*.

Free Associates

Ivanhoe Theater, 750 W Wellington Avenue, at N Clark Street, Lake View (773 975 7171). CTA Wellington. **Open** *box office by phone* 10am-9pm daily; *shows* 8.15pm, 10.30pm Fri, Sat.. **Credit** AmEx, MC, V. **Map** p309 F3.

Improv-based parodies are the niche this group has carved for itself. *Cast on Hot Tin Roof, As We Like It: Shakespeare in Your Face, Blithering Heights?* You get the picture. For the last few years the Free Associates have packed their 60-seat dungeon-like space with *BS*, a parody of TV show *ER*. Audience members, usually fairly intoxicated, shout out the crass suggestions and the cast, with varying degrees of success, try to turn it all into intelligent parody.

Low Sodium Entertainment

Stage Left Theater, 3408 N Sheffield Avenue, at N Clark Street, Lake View (773 549 3250/ www.lowsodiumonline.com). CTA Addison (Red). **Open** *box office from 30min before show; shows: Gorilla Theater* 11pm Fri, Sat; *Gameshow!* 1am Sat; *The Evil Show* 1am Sun. **Credit** *online only* AmEx, MC, V. **Map** p309 E2.

This ensemble has tons of energy and isn't afraid to break the rules, but the shows are too messy and uninspired to be entertaining. That said, the potential is there, but the group could eventually find a respectable place in the Chicago scene with its unique three-way competition, short-form improv style. Stay away from *Gameshow!*, an awful, late-night audience-participatory parody of a TV quiz. Another bring-your-own-booze venue. In addition, a Low Sodium stand-up group performs at 11.15pm and 12.45am on Friday and Saturday at Links Hall (3435 N Sheffield Street, at W Newport Avenue).

ImprovOlympic

3541 N Clark Street, at W Addison Street, Lake View/Wrigleyville (773 880 0199/ www.improvolymp.com). CTA Addison (Red). **Open** *shows* daily, times vary. **Credit** Disc, MC, V. **Map** p309 E1.

This two-stage venue is where improv is probably most self-consciously regarded as an art form. The speciality of the house is a long-form improv style called the Harold. Created by Del Close, it features improvising teams creating fluid acts loosely revolving around one audience suggestion. For an awe-inspiring performance, drop in on Mondays at 8.30pm when veterans show off their skills in *The Armando Diaz Experience, Theatrical Movement & Hootenanny*. Alumni include Andy Richter, Mike Myers and the Upright Citizens Brigade.

Playground

3341 N Lincoln Avenue, at W Roscoe Street, Lake View (773 871 3793/www.the-playground.com). CTA Southport. **Open** *shows* 8pm Thur-Sat. **Credit** Disc, MC, V.

Graduates of the Second City and ImprovOlympic training programmes can find a place to perform here, a 40-seat, BYOB shopfront space just west of Lake View featuring plenty of nascent troupes. It even hosts something called the 'Improv Incubator', where lonely improvisers pay a small fee to meet each other. As entertainment, the result is a little hit and miss, but in a typical night, four troupes each perform 30-minute long-form acts, one of which is bound to be funny. Thankfully, tickets are cheap at $5-$7.

Schadenfreude

Heartland Studio Theater, 7016 N Glenwood Avenue, Far North (773 293 0024/ www.schadenfreude.net). CTA Morse. **Shows** usually 10pm Fri, Sat.

In a narrow space where you're encouraged to take a free can of cheap beer from a cooler on your way in, six actors put on a hilarious one-hour revue of

Base camp Chicago

Over the past decade, Chicago has emerged as the live parody capital of America, turning Hollywood icons and television kitsch into cheap and profitable theatrical fodder designed to appeal to audiences who delight in seeing their childhood gods reduced to howling fools.

The trend turned hot after the **Annoyance Theatre** had the inspired idea of simply reading the original teleplays to *The Brady Bunch* in a public forum. Since no modern satirist could have conceived of such unintentional hilarity, the show was a huge hit. Since then, we've had live versions of *Plan 9 From Outer Space, Night of the Living Dead* and *The Twilight Zone*; dramatisations of the novels of Judy Blume; and the movie *Carrie* becoming *sCarrie*, a full-blown musical replete with flowing menstrual blood.

How do they get the rights to this stuff? In most cases, they don't bother asking, causing consternation and threatened lawsuits when a hit show garners a little too much publicity. But if the producer has a sense of humour, they sometimes approve the whole tawdry affair, as with the recent *Xena Live!*. A swashbuckling tribute to the TV show, it came with one important difference: the lesbian subtext was thrust front and centre.

Check the *Chicago Reader* listings for the current late-night playlist, but the leading proponents of the genre are the **Annoyance Theatre, Sweetback Productions, Factory Theatre, About Face Theatre** and the **Bailiwick Arts Center**. Be sure you know enough about the source that you'll get the jokes, have several cocktails first, and prepare to sweat in a tiny space. High art awaits.

rotating sketches every Friday and Saturday night. Scripted but based on improv jams and with props and costumes, the aptly named Schadenfreude is exciting theatre, both absurd and pointed. Just waiting to be discovered, these guys are what *Saturday Night Live* should be and may be today's version of Chicago's legendary Compass Players. Get there early to ensure seats (it's only $5 to get in, after all).

Second City

1616 N Wells Street, at W North Avenue, Old Town (312 337 3992/www.secondcity.com). CTA Sedgwick. **Open** *box office* 10.30am-9pm Mon-Thur; 10.30am-11pm Fri, Sat; noon-9pm Sun; *shows: main stage* 8pm Mon; 8.30pm Tue-Thur; 8pm, 11pm Fri, Sat; 8pm Sun; *ETC stage* 8.30pm Thur; 8pm, 11pm Fri, Sat; 8pm Sun. **Credit** AmEx, DC, Disc, MC, V. **Map** p307 H7.
The grandaddy of all improv theatres, Second City doesn't perform improv in the strictest sense. Revues, with titles like *The Psychopath Not Taken*, are mostly scripted, but based on improvisations that take place after the shows and in rehearsals. Now over 40 years old, Second City is a well-polished machine and a top tourist attraction. And unlike so many Chicago comedy venues, it doesn't feel underground or as if it's struggling to make ends meet.

The city's top comic actors perform here, just waiting to be snatched away by *Saturday Night Live* or *Mad TV*, but the humour is still cutting-edge, often topical and even satirical despite the fact that this is, in many ways, the comedy establishment. Another revue plays in Second City ETC, the second stage, from Thursday to Sunday. Tickets for both stages are $15. In addition, students and experimental acts perform in Donny's Skybox Studio from time to time.

Stand-up

At the Crib

Inta's, 157 W Ontario Street, at N LaSalle Street, Near North/River North (312 664 6880). CTA Grand. **Open** *shows* 8.30pm Wed; 8pm Sun. **Map** p306 H10.
At the Crib comedy showcase runs two nights a week, featuring local comics as well as performers from Black Entertainment Television's show *Comic View* (tickets $10).

The Elevated

The Philosophers, 2833 N Sheffield Avenue, at W Diversey Parkway, Lake View (773 477 3661). CTA Diversey. **Open** *show* 8.30pm Wed. **Map** p308 E4.
Located in a bar and billiard club, this showcase is hosted by local comic Cayne Collier and geared towards more alternative (but less experienced) hipster performers (tickets $4).

Zanies

1548 N Wells Street, at W North Avenue, Old Town (312 337 4027). CTA Sedgwick. **Open** *shows* 8.30pm Tue-Thur, Sun; 8.30pm, 10.30pm Fri; 7pm, 9pm, 11.15pm Sat. **Credit** MC, V. **Map** p307 H7.
Though the one major stand-up club in downtown Chicago to survive the post-'80s boom doesn't really

ImprovOlympic. No, we don't know what they're up to either. But we're sure it's very, very funny.

create much of a buzz, it's a reliable place to see seasoned local comics you've never heard of, as well as national touring acts like Bobcat Goldthwait and Anthony Clark. A typical night features an MC, an opening comic and a headliner for around $15 with a two-drink minimum.

Festivals

Chicago Comedy Festival

www.comedytown.com **Date** May/June.
The Chicago Comedy Festival attempts to encompass all that is funny: sketches, films, one-man shows and, of course, stand-up. Based at around a dozen venues in the Old Town and Near North/River North neighbourhoods, the week-long festival has grown quickly and is already attracting attention in the comedy industry. And that means more big-name performers alongside unknowns waiting to be signed by HBO and network reps. Tickets for the comedy festival are available in advance from the festival website, **Ticketmaster** (*see p235*) and the venues themselves.

Chicago Improv Festival

(Information 773 862 5082/www.cif.com). **Date** late Apr.
This week-long festival combines local talent with national names to celebrate improvisational theatre: indeed, each year the festival hosts an *Improv 'Til Dawn.* The rapidly expanding fest is held at different locations across the city and has featured such acts as Upright Citizen's Brigade, the Groundlings and Colin Mochrie of *Whose Line is it Anyway?.*

Trips Out of Town

Getting Started

Chicago may be a great city, but there's a whole world on its doorstep that's well worth exploring.

Within an easy drive of the skyscrapers and concrete canyons of Chicago are the towering pines of pristine North Woods and the rolling sand dunes of Lake Michigan's shore. Poet Carl Sandburg, while impressed by Chicago's 'Big Shoulders', was also an admirer of those magnificent sand dunes, saying that they are to the Midwest what the Grand Canyon is to Arizona and Yosemite is to California.

Diversity – of both the land and its people – is part of the lure of the Midwest. Standing in contrast to its famous flat prairies are craggy, unglaciated regions of hills and valleys that escaped the mighty Ice Age glaciers that rolled over the land 15,000 years ago.

In a south-west region of Wisconsin, appropriately dubbed 'Hidden Valleys', are valleys so much like those in Switzerland that they drew a settlement of immigrants who, to this day, maintain Swiss customs and traditions at the town of **New Glarus**. In that same region are the tiny communities of **Mount Horeb**, settled by Norwegians, and **Spring Green**, which carries the legacy of Welsh immigrants and which has since found fame of sorts as the boyhood home and later the headquarters of architect Frank Lloyd Wright, himself of Welsh heritage (*see page 30* **The Wright stuff**). Nearby is the town of **Mineral Point**, settled by lead miners from Cornwall in south-west England and still known for the stone houses they built and the Cornish pasties (meat-and-vegetable filled pastry turnovers) that they left as part of their culinary legacy.

Another factor that makes Chicago an ideal centre for touring the Midwest is its geography. Drive east from downtown Chicago and within half an hour you're in Indiana; in little more than an hour you're in Michigan. Wisconsin is only an hour's drive north, and you can reach the Mississippi River and neighbouring Iowa in less than three hours. **Milwaukee**, meanwhile, is a mere 90-minute drive, while **St Louis** can be reached by road in about five hours. In fact, it is estimated that about 20 per cent of the nation's population lies within a comfortable one-day drive of the Windy City.

To enjoy most of the destinations described in this chapter, you'll need to drive. Long-distance bus services are spotty, and train services to many communities are non-existent.

There are exceptions, of course, such as travelling from Chicago to **Springfield** or **Milwaukee** by train: both cities are connected to Chicago by a decent Amtrak service. Conversely, some resort areas, such as **Mackinac Island**, are so far from Chicago that it's more feasible to fly in than burn the best part of a couple of days on the round-trip drive. Southern Illinois and neighbouring Kentucky are accessible by flying into St Louis and renting a car there. For more on car hire firms and train travel, *see chapter* **Directory**.

But wherever you go, however you get there, you'll usually receive a warm welcome. Folk in America's heartland are generally genuinely friendly to strangers.

On yer bike! **Mackinac Island**.

Illinois

Tread in Abraham Lincoln's footsteps through the historic town of Springfield or relive Ronald Reagan's earliest years at his boyhood home in Dixon.

Galena

Picturesque Galena is a time-warp town. Established in the 1820s during a lead-mining boom, it's tucked away in Illinois's north-west corner, where Iowa, Wisconsin and Illinois converge near the Mississippi. Today, more than 85 per cent of Galena's buildings appear on the National Register of Historic Places; many of them are now occupied by the town's more than 100 shops.

Housed in an 1858 Italianate mansion, the **Galena/Joe Davies' County History Museum** is a good spot to start a visit. An hourly audio-visual presentation chronicles how the town became what it is today, with permanent exhibitions including a Civil War exhibit. Check into another piece of history by visiting the **Ulysses S Grant Home**. The building is a reminder of the day (18 August 1865) when, with a jubilant procession, speeches and fireworks, the proud citizens of Galena welcomed home their returning Civil War hero.

Before going off to war, Grant had worked at a Galena store owned by his father and managed by his younger brothers. Upon his return, townsfolk presented General Grant with a handsome, two-storey brick mansion. The house, built in 1860 in the Italianate bracketed style, has been restored to the way it appeared in drawings published in the 14 November 1868 edition of Frank Leslie's *Illustrated Newspaper*. The house contains original furnishings of the Grant family, as well as memorabilia of the 18th president, including china and silver from the White House.

Be sure to visit the tasting room and gift shop of **Galena Cellars Winery**, housed in a restored 1840s granary. The winery produces more than two dozen varieties of grape and fruit wines, including an award-winning Pinot Noir and a cranberry wine that took a double gold medal against stiff competition. Its vineyards, planted with around four acres of grapes, lie a ten-minute drive from town through beautiful countryside along the historic **Stagecoach Trail**. Views from this region, which contains the highest point in what is otherwise a monotonously flat state, are spectacular. **Platteville**, Wisconsin, home of the Chicago Bears' summer training camp, lies about 22 miles (35 kilometres) north.

The wide variety of lodgings run the gamut from basic motels, historic hotels and Victorian B&Bs to accommodation at two major resorts, **Chestnut Mountain Resort** and **Eagle Ridge Inn & Resort**. Indeed, stay at a comfortable rental house at the latter, a 6,800-acre (2,754-hectare) resort spread out among rolling hills six miles (ten kilometres) east of Galena, and you may not even get around to exploring the town. For if you enjoy outdoor activities, there's plenty to do year-round without leaving the resort property, with activities including hayrides, hiking, fishing and canoeing. A trail system, known for its flora and fauna, including native prairie and wild ginger, muskrat and wild turkey, winds around Lake Galena and into rolling hills and woodland.

If you happen to be visiting Eagle Ridge on a winter weekend when there is no snow and you're a not-to-be-thwarted downhill skier, you can get a taste of winter sports at **Chestnut Mountain Resort**, which makes its own snow and often has a good base. Located eight miles (13 kilometres) south-east of Galena on a wooded palisade overlooking the Mississippi, it offers downhill skiing and snowboarding.

Galena Cellars Winery

515 S Main Street, Galena (1-800 397 9463/815 777 3330/www.galenacellars.com). **Open** *Jan-Memorial Day* 9am-5pm Mon-Thur; 9am-8pm Fri, Sat; 9am-6pm Sun; *Memorial Day-Dec* 9am-8pm Mon-Sat; 9am-6pm Sun. **Admission** free. **Credit** AmEx, Disc, MC, V.

Galena/Joe Davies' County History Museum

211 S Bench Street, Galena (815 777 9129). **Open** 9am-4.30pm daily. **Admission** $3.50; $2.50 10-18s; free under-10s. **Credit** MC, V.

Ulysses S Grant Home State Historic Site

500 Bouthillier Street, Galena (815 777 3310). **Open** 9am-5pm daily. **Admission** *suggested donation* $3; $1 under-17s.

Getting there

By car

Galena is approximately 165 miles (265km) north-west of Chicago. Take the I-90 (Northwest Tollway) to Rockford, then take US 20.

Getting around

This is definitely a walking town: most of the shops and restaurants are packed into two parallel streets. **Brill's Trolley Tours Inc** offers one-hour narrated tours (815 777 3121).

Tourist information

Galena/Jo Davies' County Convention & Visitors' Bureau

Old Train Depot, 101 Bouthillier Street, Galena (1-888 777 4099). **Open** 9am-5pm daily.
There is also a visitors' centre at Old Market House, 121 N Commerce Street (815 777 1448).

Where to stay

Eagle Ridge Inn & Resort

444 Eagle Ridge Drive, Galena (1-800 892 2269/fax 815 777 4502/www.eagleridge.com). **Rates** $120-$239. **Credit** AmEx, DC, Disc, MC, V.
These 300-plus secluded, privately owned homes with one to four bedrooms are ideal for families or groups of friends. There is also an 80-room inn perched on a wooded bluff overlooking Lake Galena.

Galena Cellars Vineyard

4746 N Ford Road, Galena (815 777 3330/fax 777 3335/www.galenacellars.com). **Rates** $125. **Credit** AmEx, DC, Disc, MC, V.
Snuggled amid some of the highest and prettiest country in Illinois, this vineyard offers two suites converted from the upstairs of a farmhouse.

Chestnut Mountain Resort

8700 W Chestnut Road, Galena (1-800 397 1320/ 815 777 3120/fax 777 1068/www.chestnutmtn.com). **Rates** *single* $89-$129. **Credit** AmEx, DC, Disc, MC, V.
In winter, ski down slopes that plunge toward the Mississippi River; in summer, ride the chairlift down the same slopes to the river's edge. This property offers 119 rooms, a pool, a restaurant and a lounge.

Where to eat

Galena is especially well endowed with good restaurants and eating is a major pastime.

Eldorado Grill

219 N Main Street, Galena (815 777 1224). **Open** 5-9pm Mon, Thur-Sun; *summer* also 5-9pm Wed; closed Tue. **Main courses** $12-$32. **Credit** AmEx, Disc, MC, V.
Naturally raised meats and other fresh ingredients, home-made sauces and superb Margaritas.

Fried Green Tomatoes

1301 N Irish Hollow Road, Galena (815 777 3938). **Open** 5-9.30pm Mon-Thur, Sun; 5-10pm Fri; 4.30-10.30pm Sat. **Main courses** $12-$24. **Credit** Disc, MC, V.

Set in the rolling countryside just outside town, this Italian restaurant occupies handsome quarters in an historic brick farmstead. Stop for a drink by the fireplace of the comfortable piano bar and order the eponymous fried green tomatoes; for something more substantial, try the pasta or veal dishes.

Vinny Vanucchi's Little Italy

201 S Main Street, Galena (815 777 8100). **Open** 11am-10pm daily. **Main courses** $9-$15. **Credit** AmEx, DC, Disc, MC, V.
Enter through a deli to try the traditional Italian fare at this basic eaterie. It's not fancy: the red and white tablecloths are vinyl, the vines are plastic and even some – but not all – of the sepia photos of turn-of-the-19th-century family scenes came via job lots. The food, though, is genuine and well executed.

Rockford & the Rock River

The stretch of the Rock River between Rockford and Dixon is picturesque to a fault. Along one especially pretty two-mile stretch – just south of Castle Rock State Park – the road is canopied by leafy branches dappled with sunlight. Though scenic Route 2 parallels much of the river's course along its west bank, the river twists and turns so much that you find yourself crossing it.

A major landmark on the east bank of the river near Oregon is the monolithic 50-foot (15-metre) statue of a Native American built on a towering bluff in Lowden State Park. Sculptor Lorado Taft created the statue known as **Black Hawk**, after the warrior chief who for so long valiantly resisted efforts to drive his people from their valley.

But you'd do well to start a Rock River road tour at **Rockford**, the second-largest city in Illinois. It has numerous diversions, including an excellent theatre, a symphony orchestra and a dance company, comfortable lodgings, top-rate restaurants and, grouped together in what is known as the **Riverfront Museum Park**, a trio of excellent museums: the **Discovery Center Museum**, a hands-on children's museum with a planetarium and outdoor science park; **Rockford Art Museum**, downstate Illinois's largest art museum, which offers a permanent collection of 19th- and 20th-century American art; and the splendid **Burpee Museum of Natural History**, with its subject-matter mix of dinosaurs and Native American history. The latter's signature exhibit is a coal forest with simulated thunderstorms, two-storey-high trees and an 85-foot (26-metre) long mural that sets the stage for a full-size adult Tyrannosaurus Rex skeletal cast.

Rockford's strong Swedish heritage dates back to a period in the nineteenth century when every sixth person in Sweden left for America.

Make an odyssey to the **Ulysses S Grant Home**. *See page 247.*

Many of these immigrants settled in Rockford, creating one of the largest Swedish settlements in the Midwest and establishing Rockford's pre-eminence in furniture manufacturing through their skilled craftsmanship.

During its heyday, for example, there were 93 furniture companies in Rockford. Many one-of-a-kind pieces made by Swedish craftsmen can be seen with a guided tour of the Italianate brick mansion owned by furniture magnate John Erlander and now the **Erlander Home Museum**. This Victorian home in Haight Village, a National Historic District, was built by Swedish craftsmen in 1871. A display of artefacts brought to America by Swedish settlers includes the trunk used by the Erlanders in 1854, the tools of Swedish craftsmen, handmade farm implements, wood carvings and Swedish copper, pewter and glass.

Another sight of sorts is, in the main, a shop. Housed in the rambling rooms of three buildings, **Toad Hall Books & Records** has incredible collections of records, cookbooks, Oz and Tarzan collectibles, political buttons, baseball cards and thousands of magazines dating back to 1870. Movie fans will find posters, lobby cards, stills and press books; jazz enthusiasts will spend hours with the books, photographs, autographs, sheet music, mags and 50,000 records. And the shop somehow finds room for over 50,000 comics and pulp magazines, too.

Follow the river south to learn the story of the 'Plow that won the West'. **Grand Detour** is as pretty now as it was when French explorers named it for the bend in the river. But Native Americans have the most lyrical description for this sweeping oxbow bend: they say the river is so pretty that it doubles back to take another look at itself.

Grand Detour's most famous citizen was John Deere, a brawny young blacksmith from the hills of Vermont who stepped off a riverboat to begin a new life. Deere discovered that the ploughs that farmers had brought west were unsuitable for the gumbo-like rich black soil of the prairies: every few steps, the farmer would have to stop the team and clean the plough. The ingenious blacksmith found fame and fortune by creating a steel plough with a highly polished surface that scoured itself clean, an achievement commemorated at the **John Deere Historic Site**. The original blacksmith shop has been excavated and an archaeological exhibition building now covers the site. Informative tours include a demonstration by a working blacksmith.

Nearby, **White Pines Forest State Park** is threaded with hiking trails that wind through the last stands of virgin white pines in Illinois. You can drive through a large section of the park, splashing through unique fords across a stream. The park lodge provides rustic lodging and home-cooked meals.

Trips Out of Town

Where it all began: **Ronald Reagan's Boyhood Home**.

Dixon, meanwhile, is a river town, the family home of Ronald Wilson Reagan, who moved here with his parents in 1920, aged nine. The **Ronald Reagan Boyhood Home** is now a museum and visitors' centre chronicling the formative years of the 40th president. The house has been restored to the way it looked when the Reagans lived there, furnished with pieces typical of the period. Ronald and his older brother Neil shared one of three upstairs bedrooms; Mrs Reagan, who supplemented the family's income by taking in mending, used another as a sewing room.

Burpee Museum of Natural History
737 N Main Street, Rockford (815 965 3433).
Open 10am-5pm Tue-Sat; noon-5pm Sun; closed Mon. **Admission** $4; $3 children; free under-3s. **Credit** MC, V.

Discovery Center Museum
711 N Main Street, Rockford (815 963 6769).
Open 10am-5pm Tue-Sat; noon-5pm Sun; closed Mon. **Admission** $4; $3 children; free under-2s. **Credit** MC, V.

Erlander Home Museum
404 S Third Street, Rockford (815 963 5559).
Open 2-4pm Sun; closed Mon-Sat.

John Deere Historic Site
8393 S Main Street, Grand Detour (815 652 4551).
Open *Apr-Oct* 9am-5pm daily. **Admission** $3; free under-12s.

Rockford Art Museum
711 N Main Street, Rockford (815 968 2787/ www.rockfordartmuseum.com). **Open** 11am-5pm Tue-Fri; 10am-5pm Sat; noon-5pm Sun; closed Mon.

Ronald Reagan Boyhood Home
816 S Hennepin Avenue, Dixon (815 288 3404).
Open *Feb-Mar* 10am-4pm Sat; 1-4pm Sun; *Apr-Sept* 10am-4pm Mon-Sat; 1-4pm Sun; closed Jan, Dec. **Admission** free.

Toad Hall Books & Records
2106 Broadway, Rockford (815 226 1259).
Open noon-7pm Mon, Wed, Thur; 10am-7pm Fri, Sat; noon-6pm Sun; closed Tue. **Credit** AmEx, Disc, MC, V.

Getting there

By car
Rockford is about 85 miles (137km) north-west of Chicago. Take the I-90 (Northwest Tollway) to Rockford. Follow US 2 along the Rock River between Rockford and Dixon.

Tourist information

Blackhawk Waterways Convention & Visitors' Bureau
201 N Franklin Street, Polo (1-800 678 2108/ 815 946 2108). **Open** 8.30am-4.30pm Mon-Fri; closed Sat, Sun.

Rockford Area Convention & Visitors' Bureau
211 N Main Street, Rockford (1-800 521 0849/815 963 8111/www.gorockford.com). **Open** 8.30am-5pm Mon-Fri; closed Sat, Sun.

Where to stay

Cliffbreakers Comfort Suites & Conference Center
700 W Riverside Boulevard, Rockford (1-800 478 9395/815 282 4965/fax 815 637 4704). **Rates** *suite* $89-$198. **Credit** AmEx, DC, Disc, MC, V.
A comfortable all-suite hotel along the Rock River, Cliffbreakers has an indoor pool, a whirlpool, a Swedish hot-rock sauna, a fitness centre, a restaurant and a lounge. Of the 104 suites, 87 offer river views, while some are bi-level suites with fireplaces and loft sleeping quarters.

Colonial Rose Inn

8230 S Green Street, Grand Detour (815 652 4422/ fax 652 3594/www.essex1.com/people/roseinn). **Rates** $85. **Credit** MC, V.
Built between 1855 and 1857, this inn is reminiscent of a New England hostelry. The five rooms each have private baths, and lodging includes full breakfast. The inn is a noted fine-dining destination.

White Pines Forest State Park Inn

6712 W Pines Road, Mount Morris (815 946 3817/ fax 946 3006). **Rates** $68. **Credit** Disc, MC, V.
Rustic is the prevailing theme at this state park lodge, offering 25 one-room log cabins with gas-operated fires and large bathrooms.

Where to eat

Stockholm Inn

2420 Charles Street, Rockford (815 397 3534). **Open** 6am-8pm Mon-Fri; 6am-12.30pm Sat; 7am-1pm Sun. **Main courses** $6-$10. **Credit** Disc, MC, V.
A family-style eaterie known for Swedish dishes such as thin pancakes, meatballs and pea soup. Try *flaskpannkaka*, a baked egg and pork breakfast dish: singer and TV hostess Dinah Shore enjoyed it so much that she included it in her cookbook.

Trattoria Fantini

1313 Auburn Street, Rockford (815 961 3674). **Open** 5-9.30pm Mon, Wed-Sat; 11.30am-2pm, 5-9.30pm Tue; closed Sun. **Main courses** $8-$20. **Credit** AmEx, DC, Disc, MC, V.
This restaurant provides a romantic setting for fine Italian dining. Main courses include roasted veal shank and wood-grilled duck breast. Breads and desserts are made on the premises.

White Pines Inn

6712 W Pines Road, Mount Morris (815 946 3817). **Open** 8am-2pm, 5-8pm Mon-Thur; 8am-2pm, 5-9pm Fri; 8am-9pm Sat; closed Sun. **Main courses** $8-$20. **Credit** Disc, MC, V.
This lodge was built by the Civilian Conservation Corps in the 1930s. Its specialities include chicken pot pie, prime rib and red raspberry pie.

Springfield

It's for good reason that the Illinois capital is affectionately known as 'Mr Lincoln's Home Town'. In and around Springfield, the presence of the 16th president is inescapable. In many instances, the careful restoration of some of the historic sites creates the impression that 'Honest Abe' has only just left the building.

The **Lincoln's Home National Historic Site** is operated by the National Park Service, and offers daily guided tours given by park rangers. Lincoln occupied the modest, two-storey frame home, which he purchased for $1,200, for 17 years (1844-61). It sits in a leafy neighbourhood with brick-and-plank sidewalks, immaculate lawns and handsome gas street lamps (now converted to electricity).

It's the only home the great man ever owned, and has been restored to its Lincoln-era glories. Visit the parlour where Lincoln was asked to run for president and where he spread papers out on the floor to read, since he was unable to find a comfortable chair to fit his lanky frame. Hanging on a peg in the hall is a tall hat such as Lincoln wore, suggesting, perhaps, that the bootstrap lawyer has simply slipped out to tend the garden or play with the kids.

The **Old State Capitol** is a fine example of Greek revival architecture. Built in 1837, it's been painstakingly restored and its Hall of Representatives and Senate Chamber appear as if the legislators of the day had just left for a temporary adjournment. It was here in 1858 that Lincoln made his 'house divided' speech on slavery. A scant seven years later, the body of the slain president lay in state in the same building. Tours of the Capitol and costumed interpretive programmes are offered year round.

Across from the Old State Capitol are the **Lincoln-Herndon Law Offices**, where Lincoln practised law. Cases were tried in the federal court below the law offices; sometimes, Lincoln would lie on the office floor and observe the proceedings in the courtroom below through a peephole in the floorboards. Another must-see is the **Lincoln Depot**, from where he delivered his famous farewell address – which some say ranks with the Gettysburg Address – on 11 February 1861 before departing to Washington, DC to assume the Presidency. 'Here I have lived a quarter of a century and have passed from a young to an old man,' he said, his voice trembling. 'I now leave, not knowing whether ever I may return, with a task before me greater than that which rested upon Washington.' Inside the restored depot are waiting rooms, a ticket seller's cage and a lively audio-visual re-creation of Lincoln's 12-day journey to his inauguration.

Springfield's most moving site, though, is undoubtedly **Lincoln's Tomb**. Each Tuesday evening between June and August, a retreat ceremony is held in front of the tomb with drill, musket firing and the haunting sound of the *Retreat and Taps* played by a bugler. Captured in an inscription on the north window are the poignant words spoken by Secretary of War Edwin M Stanton at Lincoln's death: 'Now he belongs to the ages.'

If you've had enough of Lincoln, Springfield also boasts the **Dana-Thomas House State Historical Site**, considered to be one of the best-preserved and most complete of Frank Lloyd Wright's early Prairie School houses.

Trips Out of Town

Dana-Thomas House State Historical Site

301 E Lawrence Avenue, at 4th Street, Springfield (217 782 6776). **Open** 9am-4pm Wed-Sun; closed Mon, Tue. **Admission** $3; $1 children; free under-3s.

Lincoln's Home National Historic Site

8th Street, at Jackson Street, Springfield (217 492 4241). **Open** 8.30am-5pm daily; later in summer.

Lincoln–Herndon Law Offices State Historic Site

6th Street, at Adams Street, Springfield (217 785 7289). **Open** *Mar-Oct* 9am-5pm daily; *Nov-Feb* 9am-4pm daily. **Admission** *suggested donation* $2; $1 children.

Lincoln Tomb State Historic Site

Oak Ridge Cemetery, off N Grand Avenue or Walnut Street, Springfield (217 782 2717). **Open** 9am-5pm daily. **Admission** free.

Old State Capitol State Historic Site

Downtown Mall, 1 Old State Capitol Plaza, at Adams, Washington, 5th & 6th Streets, Springfield (217 785 7960). **Open** 9am-5pm daily.

Getting there

By car

Springfield is 200 miles (322km) south-west of Chicago. Take I-55 from Chicago to Springfield, exit 98-B (Clearlake).

By train

Amtrak provides a Chicago–Springfield service with three trains daily in each direction. Travel time is about 3½ hours.

Tourist information

Springfield Illinois Convention & Visitors' Bureau

109 N 7th Street, Springfield (1-800 545 7300/217 789 2360). **Open** 8am-5pm Mon-Fri; closed Sat, Sun.

Where to stay

Crowne Plaza Hotel

3000 S Dirksen Parkway, Springfield (217 529 7777/fax 217 529 6666). **Rates** $60-$350. **Credit** AmEx, DC, Disc, MC, V.

This deluxe 288-room, sleek hotel is well endowed with such amenities as concierge floors, an indoor pool, a fitness centre and a rooftop garden.

Hilton Springfield

7th Street, at Adams Street, Springfield (217 789 1530). **Rates** *single* $104-$172. **Credit** AmEx, DC, Disc, MC, V.

This downtown high-rise is within walking distance of the Lincoln Historic Sites. And, for guests who need

to relax after all that sightseeing, the hotel has 367 rooms, a fitness centre, pool and a good-quality Cajun restaurant, **Gumbo Ya Ya's**.

The Inn at 835

835 S 2nd Street, at Canedy Street, Springfield (1-888 217 4835/217 523 4466/www.innat835.com). **Rates** *single* $98; *double* $159. **Credit** AmEx, DC, Disc, MC, V.

Built in 1909 as Springfield's first modern apartment house, this ten-room inn is listed on the National Register of Historic Places. Included in the room rates is a cooked-to-order breakfast; complimentary wines are also served each evening.

Where to eat

Café Brio

524 E Monroe Street, at 6th Street, Springfield (217 544 0574). **Open** 11am-10pm Mon-Thur; 11am-11pm Fri; 11am-3pm Sat, Sun. **Main courses** $10-$18. **Credit** AmEx, DC, MC, V.

Specialities here include pork tenderloin with Caribbean spices, filet mignon with a spicy sauce, and a range of enchiladas, tacos and chimichangas. Margaritas are made from freshly squeezed fruit juice. The café is housed in a loud, open, friendly space, with earth tones and distressed-wood tables.

Cozy Dog Drive-In

2935 S 6th Street, Springfield (217 525 1992). **Open** 8am-8pm Mon-Sat; closed Sun. **Main courses** $3-$7.

Fans of Route 66 head directly to this diner – owner Buz Waldmire calls it 'a greasy spoon with a personality' – for memorabilia, tall stories, donuts and dogs.

Feed Store

516 E Adams Street, at 6th Street, Springfield (217 528 3355). **Open** 11am-3pm Mon-Sat; closed Sun. **Main courses** $5. **Credit** AmEx, MC, V.

You want soup? You got soup. The Feed Store serves up to 250 quarts of fresh home-made soup every day, with a list that runs from beef barley and cream of broccoli to Wisconsin cheese and zucchini chowder.

Gumbo Ya Ya's

Hilton Springfield, 7th Street, at Adams Street, Springfield (217 789 1530). **Open** 5-10pm. Mon-Sat; closed Sun. **Main courses** $9-$22.50. **Credit** AmEx, DC, Disc, MC, V.

This Cajun restaurant atop the Hilton (30th floor) offers great views of the city and excellent live jazz. Best bet: sip on a Dixie beer and munch on 'mud bugs' – deep-fried, battered crawfish tails.

Robbie's

4 Old State Capitol Plaza, Springfield (217 528 1901). **Open** 11am-7pm Mon-Fri; 11am-3pm Sat; closed Sun. **Main courses** $5-$6. **Credit** AmEx, MC, V.

This downtown saloon is popular for lunchtime soups, salads and sandwiches. Don't miss the home-made pies, especially seasonal pies such as pumpkin (banana cream and pecan are also good).

Indiana

Stunning architecture, dead gangsters and covered bridges await as you head south-east from the Windy City.

Columbus

Everyone loves an underdog, and tiny Columbus, Indiana, with a population of only 37,000, is a veritable David among architectural Goliaths.

This Hoosier town, surrounded by stubby cornfields, has more distinguished architecture than cities 50 times its size. When the American Institute of Architects asked members to rank US cities based on design quality and innovation, diminutive Columbus came in sixth. It was exceeded only by (in order) Chicago, New York, San Francisco, Boston and Washington. Pretty heady company.

The town has nearly 60 buildings designed by world-renowned architects. The list reads like a who's who of modern architecture: Eliel Saarinen, Harry Weese, Alexander Girard, IM Pei, Robert Venturi, Richard Meir and Kevin Roche (the last four winners of the Pritzker Prize, architecture's equivalent of the Nobel). In fact, when an up-and-coming architect is invited to design a building in Columbus, that architect knows that he or she has arrived.

In 1957, the **Cummins Engine Company**, a Fortune 500 company that makes diesel engines and is the town's major employer, offered to pay the architectural fees for sorely needed new schools, stipulating that distinguished national architects be asked to design them. As a result, J Irwin Miller, chairman of Cummins, has become to Columbus what the Medici family was to Renaissance Florence. In fact, he has been dubbed the 'Medici of the Midwest'.

In order to get the most out of Columbus's architectural gems, stop first at the **Columbus Area Visitors' Center** built in 1864 and expanded and redesigned by Kevin Roche. It is a showcase for the *Yellow Neon Chandelier and Persian Window*, an installation by glass artist Dale Chihuly, and also offers one- and two-hour architectural bus tours, as well as maps and self-guided tours.

One of the highlights of the tour is the **First Christian Church**, a geometric building of bluff brick and limestone designed by Eliel Saarinen and dedicated in 1941. Its bold simplicity influenced the subsequent design of contemporary churches in America and signalled the beginning of modern architecture

in Columbus. Among many other delights are: Eero Saarinen's (son and partner of Eliel Saarinen) **North Christian Church**, irreverently dubbed the 'Oil Can Church' because of its cone-shaped roof and 192-foot (58.5-metre) spire, and **Fire Station No.1**, an example of a seamless 1990s addition to a 1941 building that is an eclectic blend of art nouveau and art deco styles. The bank, post office and numerous schools are all tour stops, as is the steel, glass and concrete Cummins Engine Company corporate headquarters. There's also the two-block long **Commons Mall**, a skylighted shopping centre with exhibits halls and a play area dominated by *Chaos I*, a 30-foot (nine-metre), seven-ton moving sculpture by Jean Tinguely of Switzerland. A bizarre, fascinating Rube Goldberg-like contraption, it resembles an animated scrap heap.

Columbus is the antithesis of dull and provincial. Innovative and culturally rich, invitingly clean and well-scrubbed, 'It is,' observed architectural writer Blair Kamen, 'a textbook case of what a small town should be.' But it is not just the architecture. It is the spirit, too: grade-school kids take architecture classes; factories have bubbling fountains and landscaped gardens where workers take their lunch; there are outdoor symphony concerts; and the public art includes sculptures by Henry Moore, J Seward Johnson, Jr, Jean Tinguely and Dale Chihuly. The annual **Popfest**, held in June, attracts 7,000 people with lawn chairs, blankets and coolers to the public library plaza to listen to music in the shadow of a Henry Moore.

Columbus is not only a nice place to visit: one can't help thinking it wouldn't be bad living there, either. It has two symphony orchestras, a city band, a dance company, theatrical groups and the only branch of the **Indianapolis Museum of Art**. There are two universities, an exemplary school system, 15 public parks covering nearly 500 acres (202 hectares) and an enclosed ice rink. Columbus's **Otter Creek Golf Course**, designed by Robert Trent Jones, was rated at four and a half stars (Pebble Beach got five) by *Golf Digest*. For shoppers, **Prime Outlets** is a large factory-outlet mall located just north of town.

And then there's all that architecture...

Columbus Architectural Tour

812 372 1954. **Tours** *Mar-Nov* 10am Mon-Fri;
10am, 2pm Sat; 11am Sun. **Rates** $9.50; $3-$9
concessions; free under-3s.

Indianapolis Museum of Art

*390 The Commons, Columbus (812 376 2597/
www.ima-art.org).* **Open** 10am-5pm Tue-Thur, Sat;
10am-8pm Fri; noon-4pm Sun; closed Mon.

Getting there

By car

Columbus is about 45 miles (72km) south of
Indianapolis and about 225 miles (362km) south-east
of Chicago. It's off I-65, the major north–south artery
through Indiana that begins at Gary, east of Chicago.

Getting around

Columbus is a good walking town: the 9½-mile
(15.3km) 'People's Trail' links the city parks,
while the bus system will take you anywhere
around town for 25¢.

Tourist information

Columbus Area Visitors' Center

506 5th Street, Columbus (1-800 468 6564). **Open**
9am-5pm Mon-Sat; 10am-4pm Sun.
The Kevin Roche-designed centre houses an exhibit
on architecture in Columbus and a gift shop.

Where to stay

Columbus Inn

*445 5th Street, at Franklin Street, Columbus
(812 378 4289).* **Rates** *single* $99; *double* $109.
Credit AmEx, DC, Disc, MC, V.
The former City Hall, built in 1895 and listed on the
National Register of Historic Places, has been reno-
vated as a B&B inn with 29 rooms and five suites.

Holiday Inn & Conference Center

*2480 Jonathan Moore Pike, Columbus (812 372
1541/fax 379 2729).* **Rates** *single* $79; *double* $89.
Credit AmEx, DC, Disc, MC, V.
An indoor pool, a Jacuzzi, a dining room, a bakery,
a gift shop, a games room and an exercise centre.

Ramada Inn

*2485 Jonathan Moore Pike, Columbus (812 376
3051/fax 376 0949).* **Rates** *single* $85; *double* $95.
Credit AmEx, DC, Disc, MC, V.
This 166-room property has pools, an exercise room,
tennis courts, a restaurant and lounges.

Where to eat

Zaharako's Confectionery

*329 Washington Street, at 4th Street, Columbus
(812 379 9329).* **Open** 10am-3.30pm Mon-Sat;
closed Sun. **Main courses** $1-$3.

A turn-of-the-century soda fountain and confec-
tionery full of mahogany and Italian marble. Locals
go for home-made potato soup and chilli and a
Zaharako creation: 'cheese-BR-GER', essentially
grilled cheese sandwiches slathered with meat sauce.

Lake & Porter Counties

Just a few miles from the cookie-cutter
commercialism of Merrillville, Indiana, where
every chain that ever sold a franchise appears
to be represented, is a working gristmill built in
1876. Nestled against a still millpond, it
provides a setting so picturesque that on
virtually every weekend during warm-weather
months, several weddings are held there.

Pretty **Deep River County Park** is one
of the many surprises to be found in Lake
County, Indiana, Chicago's backdoor neighbour.
Though flames still leap into the sky from the
steel mills and urban blight is still in evidence,
Indiana's north-western corner is emerging as a
nearby playground with some bright new
offerings to attract visitors.

Just as Easterners cherish a trip to 'the shore',
thousands of Chicagoans grew up looking
forward to visiting 'the dunes'. For family fun,
this magnificent beach playground offers
swimming, body-surfing and the exhilaration of
a tumbling, careening romp down steep sandy
slopes after a leg-wearing climb to the summit.
On a clear day, the Chicago skyline is clearly
visible, shimmering on the horizon of sparkling
Lake Michigan.

Natural beauty is a large part of the charm
of Lake and Porter counties. The sloping white
expanses of the **Indiana Dunes National
Lakeshore**, which covers 13,000 acres (5,265
hectares), encompass a state park and a state
nature preserve. Here, you can camp, swim,
hike, bicycle and look for orchids, irises and
prickly-pear cactus. Of course, with four
casinos, gaming remains a major draw for
visitors to north-western Indiana. Even if
you're not into gambling, don't overlook these
casinos as good dining destinations.

Though its past as a former gas station is
still apparent, the **Lake Michigan Winery**
at Whiting has had an interesting makeover.
Grease pits have been filled in and the concrete
floors now bear a vintage Wurlitzer jukebox,
a turn-of-the-19th-century barrel piano and café
tables where cheese and sausage trays are
served. A full calendar of events includes a
lecture series, a succession of brunch buffets
and a popular grape stomp and steak fry. A
major festival held on Father's Day includes
tastings of more than 100 wines from across
the state (Indiana now boasts more than a
score of wineries).

Public Enemy Number One

In 1934, the sleepy little town of Crown Point, Indiana, made national headlines when the FBI's 'Public Enemy Number One', John Dillinger, escaped from the 'secure, escape-proof' local jail while waiting to stand trial for the murder of an East Chicago policeman. Dillinger made his escape by brandishing a fake gun, made either from wood blackened with shoe polish, or from soap. However, he didn't last long: Dillinger was soon gunned down by federal agents with real guns outside Chicago's **Biograph Theatre** (*see page 195*).

People are fascinated with Prohibition-era gangsters and Lake County, Indiana feeds that fascination with the **John Dillinger Museum**, part of a glittering new visitors' centre opened in Hammond in 1999. It exhibits a collection of artefacts relating to the bank robber and his crime sprees, including the Dillinger death mask. Exhibits, including clips of newsreel footage, depict life during the Depression.

Some think it glorifies criminals, though the Lake County CVB argues that, on the contrary, the museum promotes the theme that 'crime doesn't pay'. There is, for example, a tribute to East Chicago policeman

Patrick O'Malley, whom Dillinger killed following a bank robbery and a wall commemorating Lake County police officers who have given their lives in the line of duty.

The displays throughout the museum's 12 galleries focus on criminal investigation techniques, and many feature interactive elements. Visitors can try on a bulletproof vest to get an idea of its weight and bulk; identify 'terror gang' members from descriptions and photos; witness a bank robbery and answer questions about what they observed; and step into a c1920s jail cell to experience the dark, cramped quarters of a state penitentiary prisoner. They'll also examine evidence and respond as jurors; learn about gangster rap (*screw* = prison guard; *moll* = girlfriend, etc); match suspect fingerprints with samples in a 1930s FBI lab and put together a Bertillion description card using component tiles.

John Dillinger Museum

Lake County Convention & Visitors' Bureau, I-80/94, at Kennedy Avenue, Hammond (1-800 255 5253). **Open** *9am-5pm daily.* **Admission** *$4; $3 concessions.* **Credit** *AmEx, MC, V.*

The Lake County seat at **Crown Point** was once a marriage mill where Rudolph Valentino and his new bride circled the courthouse in a touring car, and where Ronald Reagan and Muhammad Ali were wed (not to each other). It was here that John Dillinger bluffed his way out of jail with a fake gun (*see above* **Public Enemy Number One**). Today, the imposing red-brick courthouse, built in 1878 in a combination of Romanesque and Georgian styles, houses shops, boutiques and a historical museum.

In contrast, Deep River County Park, just a few miles north-east in Hobart, is a 1,000-acre (405-hectare) preserve that has canoeing, hiking trails and unique events such as after-dark 'owl walks'. In a meadow, the Deep River Grinders, a baseball team who play according to 1858 rules, take on teams from around the Midwest. The

park also incorporates the **Deep River Water Park**, an aquatic theme park with fast waterslides, cool pools and a lazy river.

In 1837, as Chicago was incorporating as a city, John Wood, who had travelled west from Massachusetts, was building a sawmill and wooden gristmill alongside the Deep River. In 1876, at about the time that Custer was leading the Seventh Cavalry into the Battle of the Little Bighorn, John's son, Nathan, built the brick gristmill. Today, visitors can watch the miller grind corn, wheat and rye using 4,000-pound (1,812-kilogram) stones. Visitors can buy sacks of flour to take home and visit an upstairs museum and art gallery. Photographers may wish to time a visit around 1 May, peak bloom time for about 5,000 tulips planted alongside a gazebo near the photogenic mill.

Deep River County Park & Woods Historic Gristmill

9410 Old Lincoln Highway, Hobart (219 947 1958).
Open *May-Oct* 10am-5pm daily.

Deep River Water Park

US 30, east of I-65, Hobart (1-800 928 7275/219 947 7850). **Open** *late May-mid-June, mid-late Aug* 10am-6pm daily; *mid June-mid-Aug* 10am-6pm Mon, Wed-Sun; 10am-9.30pm Tue; *late Aug-Labor Day weekend* 10am-6pm Sat, Sun. **Admission** $12; $5.25 children under 46in. **Credit** Disc, MC, V.

Historic Lake County Courthouse

Courthouse Square, Crown Point (219 663 0660). **Open** 10am-5pm Mon-Thur; 10am-6pm Fri; 10am-5pm Sat; closed Sun.

Indiana Dunes National Lakeshore

off Highway 12, Chesterton (219 926 7561). **Open** 6am-sunset; varies from beach to beach: call ahead.

Lake Michigan Winery

816 119th Street, at Calumet Avenue, Whiting (219 659 9463). **Open** 1-7pm daily.

Getting there

By car

These two counties, Chicago's neighbours to the east, are accessible via the Chicago Skyway and I-80-90-94.

By train

The Chicago South Shore & South Bend Railroad follows the curve of the Lake Michigan shoreline into Indiana and makes several stops in Lake and Porter counties. The trains are used by commuters who travel to Chicago from Indiana and Michigan and by day trippers heading for the Dunes. Trains leave from the **Randolph Street RTA station** on Randolph Street, at Michigan Avenue (312 836 7000).

Tourist information

Lake County Convention & Visitors' Bureau

I-80/I-94, at Kennedy Avenue, Hammond (1-800 255 5253). **Open** *summer* 8am-8pm daily; *other times* 9am-6pm daily.
In addition to picking up maps and brochures, you can watch videos about local attractions and visit the **John Dillinger Museum**.

Where to stay

Radisson Hotel at Star Plaza

800 E 81st Avenue, Merrillville (219 769 6311/fax 769 1462). **Rates** $99-$1,200. **Credit** AmEx, DC, Disc, MC, V.
This 347-room hotel houses J Ginger's Steakhouse along with other eateries and lounges. The Star Plaza Theater next door has 3,400 seats, excellent acoustics and, usually, big-name performers.

Spring House Inn

303 N Mineral Springs Road, Porter (1-800 366 4661/219 929 4600/fax 219 926 8258). **Rates** $69-$169. **Credit** AmEx, DC, Disc, MC, V.
Nestled alongside wildflower-carpeted woodlands on the banks of the Little Calumet River, the Spring House Inn has 50 rooms, all with either a balcony or a patio.

Where to eat

In addition to those eateries listed below, north-western Indiana's casinos provide excellent dining options. The **Empress Casino** (825 Empress Drive, Hammond; 1-888 436 7737/219 473 7000) has a 24-hour deli and offers fine dining at the Harborside Steakhouse, while the French Quarter Room at **Harrah's East Chicago Casino** (1 Showboat Place, East Chicago; 1-800 427 7247/219 378 3000) has a cosy, rustic feel and a decent wine cellar.

Miller Bakery Café

555 S Lake Street, Miller Beach (219 938 2229). **Open** 11.30am-2pm, 5-9pm Tue-Fri; 11.30am-2pm, 5-10pm Fri; 5-10pm Sat; 4-8pm Sun; closed Mon. **Main courses** $13-$28. **Credit** AmEx, DC, Disc, MC, V.
This stylish restaurant occupies a one-time bakery; the food and ambience are as chic as at some of Chicago's trendiest eateries, and offered at bargain Indiana prices.

Phil Smidt's

1205 N Calumet Avenue, at Indianapolis Boulevard, Hammond (1-800 376 4534/219 659 0025). **Open** 11.15am-9pm Tue-Thur; 11.15am-9.30pm Fri, Sat; 1-7.30pm Sun; closed Mon. **Main courses** $12-$25. **Credit** AmEx, MC, V.
This 450-seat restaurant evolved from a small bar and grill that opened in 1910, and is now a favourite stop for firm, sweet and buttery pan-fried perch and for tender sautéd frog legs.

Valentino's Café & Ice Cream Parlor

Old Courthouse Square, Crown Point (219 663 4812). **Open** 11am-4pm Mon-Thur; 11am-5pm Fri, Sat; closed Sun. **Main courses** $3-$6.
Salads, sandwiches, soups, ice-cream and sundaes are on the menu here. The decor features a collection of movie stills of Rudolph Valentino, whose marriage licence is displayed by the cash register.

Louis's Bon Appetit

302 S Main Street, Crown Point (219 663 6363). **Open** 5.30-11pm Tue-Sat; 11am-2pm Sun; closed Mon. **Main courses** $13-$19. **Credit** AmEx, DC, Disc, MC, V.
Louis's occupies an 1897 Romanesque mansion with cupolas, rotundas, beautiful woodwork and stained-glass windows. The speciality here is cuisine from the Armagnac region of France, the origin of owner Louis Retailleau. Bastille Day celebrations in July attract 3,000 revellers for cabaret and street dancing.

Parke & Montgomery Counties

As rural as a *rutabaga*, neighbouring Montgomery and Parke Counties are places in which to find banjo pickers and chicken dumpling dinners, folk crafts and country stores, twisting country roads and meandering streams. You'll also find superb canoeing waters and covered bridges. Lots of them.

Covered bridges are practical as well as picturesque. Early in the 19th century, it was found that roofed bridges, with their protected superstructures, long outlasted open-trestle wooden bridges. In Parke County, no fewer than 32 remain: creaking, rustic structures that attract tourists, artists and photographers, and that are the focus of a mammoth ten-day festival every autumn.

Rockville is a good spot to begin a tour. Wander the square, with its beautifully restored historic brick buildings sporting immaculate tuckpointing. Across from the gingerbread 1879 courthouse are quaint shops and restaurants.

As you follow the covered-bridge trails, you'll see a Clydesdale farm at Tangier, a one-room schoolhouse at Mecca and the bed of the famed Wabash and Erie Canal at Montezuma. **Mansfield** and **Bridgeton** are mill towns, with double-span bridges, rushing waters and working gristmills: buy some cornmeal or buckwheat to take home.

Billie Creek Village, meanwhile, is a recreated turn-of-the-19th-century settlement with a tree-lined creek and three covered bridges. Included among 30 buildings are two churches, a schoolhouse and a general store that is one of the Midwest's largest handmade crafts consignment shops. Visitors can ride in a horse-drawn wagon and visit a broom factory and farmhouse where a coal range is used for cooking and baking. Designed to be a working village, this crossroads hamlet features

costumed artisans working their trades at a newspaper handpress, the blacksmith's anvil, the foot-powered loom and the potter's wheel.

Watch for bald eagles along the **Wabash River** and **Sugar Creek**, a spectacularly scenic river that cuts though deep gorges and past towering sandstone bluffs. Popular with canoeists, it offers exciting but manageable rapids as well as quiet, secluded stretches ideal for swimming and fishing. It also provides a different perspective on the covered bridges: it flows under two of them.

The river runs through **Turkey Run State Park**, which has rock canyons to explore, 14 miles (22.5 kilometres) of hiking trails and stands of virgin wood, with sycamore, tulip poplar and huge black walnut trees. Down-home cooking and accommodation is provided at a comfortable inn.

Clements Canoes, near Crawfordsville, offers a number of trips ranging from a 30-mile (48-kilometre) journey through the pristine wilderness corridor of Sugar Creek (with overnight camping) to a mini-trip that can be accomplished in a few hours with stops for picnicking and swimming. It also offers a four-to-six-hour whitewater trip that takes paddlers alongside shale bluffs, through narrow channels and around large rocks on the upper stretch of Sugar Creek.

Diversions in **Crawfordsville** include the **Ben-Hur Museum**, housed in a handsome building that served as General Lew Wallace's studio. Wallace served in the Mexican and Civil Wars, acted as vice-president of the Lincoln assassination trial, was president of the Andersonville trial, became governor of the Territory of New Mexico, and was made US Minister to Turkey. He was also the author of *Ben-Hur*, published in 1880. The book was the best-selling novel of the 19th century, outsold only by the Bible, and was subsequently made into several Hollywood movies (including one starring Charlton Heston, a recent visitor to the

Troubled bridge over water.

Up **Sugar Creek** with a paddle.

museum) and a Broadway play. Wallace, a true Renaissance man, even designed the building that now houses the museum and personally supervised its construction.

Another Crawfordsville museum, the **Old Jail Museum**, houses one of only seven known rotary jails and is the last in fully working order. Built in 1882, the rotary cell block consists of a two-tiered turntable divided into pie-shaped wedges, with a total of 16 cells. The jail rotates and provides only one opening per storey. The design was intended to control prisoners with few guards and without personal contact between prisoners and jailer. Toy handcuffs are popular souvenirs with young visitors. And who knows who else…

Ben-Hur Museum
501 W Pike Street, Crawfordsville (765 362 5769). **Open** *Apr-Oct* 1-4.30pm Tue-Sun; expanded hours June-Aug. **Admission** $2; 50¢ under-12s.

Billie Creek Village
US 36, 1 mile east of Rockville (765 569 3430). **Open** 9am-4pm daily. **Admission** *summer only* $3.50. **Credit** AmEx, Disc, MC, V.

Clements Canoes
613 Lafayette Avenue, Crawfordsville (765 362 2781/www.clementscanoes.com). **Open** *Apr-Sept* daily. **Rates** $23-$54 per two-person canoe. **Credit** MC, V.

Old Jail Museum
225 N Washington Street, Crawfordsville (765 362 5222). **Open** *June-Aug* 1-4.30pm Tue, Sun; 10am-4.30pm Wed-Sat; closed Mon; *Apr, May, Sept, Oct* 1-4.30pm Wed-Sun; closed Mon, Tue. **Admission** free groups of 15 or fewer; otherwise $2; 50¢ children.

Turkey Run State Park
State Road 47, Marshall (765 597 2635). **Open** dawn-11pm. **Admission** *Apr-Oct* $2 Indiana vehicle; $5 out-of-state vehicle.

Getting there

By car
Crawfordsville is approximately 150 miles (241km) south of Chicago. Take I-80-90-94 east to I-65 south. About 10 miles (16km) south of Lafayette, take IN158 west, then US 231 south into Crawfordsville.

Getting around
In Rockville, pick up a map detailing five tour loops, each beginning and ending at the 1883 depot that serves as Parke County's tourist centre. Routes range in length from 25 to 42 miles (40-68km), each offering a sampling of four to six covered bridges, a dozen of which date back to the 19th century.

Tourist information

Montgomery County Visitors' & Convention Bureau
218 E Pike Street, Crawfordsville (765 362 5200). **Open** 8am-5pm Mon-Fri; 10am-4pm Sat.

Parke County Tourist Center
Highway 36, 3 blocks east of Rockville Square, Rockville (765 569 5226). **Open** 8am-4pm daily.

Where to stay

Billie Creek Inn
Rural Route 2, Box 27, Rockville (765 569 3430). **Rates** *rooms* $49-$79; *suites* $69-$119. **Credit** AmEx, Disc, MC, V
Staff wear 19th-century garb, but amenities at this 31-room inn are modern despite the Indiana-made cherry furniture, brass lamps and original artwork.

Old Maple Inn
Rural Route 1, Box 207, Carbon (765 548 0228). **Rates** $65-$125.
Occupying a century-old farmhouse, this B&B offers comfortable quarters, home cooking and friendly hosts, Darren and Cindy Chadd. Departing guests leave with a souvenir gift of a little brown jug of maple syrup tapped at a nearby farm. During your stay, walk to the picturesque 1907 covered bridge over Conley's Ford.

Turkey Run Inn
Rural Route 1, Box 44, Turkey Run State Park (765 597 2211). **Rates** *single* $65; *double* $76. **Credit** AmEx, Disc, MC, V.
This rustic inn has 61 rooms in the main lodge as well as 21 sleeping cabins, plus pools and horseback riding. Book ahead, as it gets busy in high season. The restaurant offers hearty home cooking and full dining-room service.

Where to eat

Long Horn Tavern & Restaurant
Rural Route 1, Box 98, Coxville (765 548 9282). **Open** 10am-9pm Mon-Thur; 10am-10pm Fri, Sat; noon-6.30pm Sun. **Main courses** $9-$17. **Credit** AmEx, Disc, MC, V.
A former grocery store, gas station and tavern built in 1923 and expanded with lumber salvaged from old barns, the Long Horn Tavern is a good spot for steaks and for excellent fried chicken (but avoid the fatty ribs).

Weber's Family Restaurant
105 S Jefferson Street, Rockville (765 569 6153). **Open** 6am-8pm Mon-Thur; 6am-9pm Fri, Sat; 7am-3pm Sun. **Main courses** $7. **Credit** MC, V.
Weber's is a popular eatery that features all-you-can-eat evening specials. Steaks, catfish and shrimp are all good, reliable choices, as are fruit cobblers and home-made pies.

Michigan

Fudge, fishing and fun await across the water in Chicago's lakefront neighbour.

Mackinac Island

Along the Straits of Mackinac, the 50-mile (80-kilometre) long passage linking Lake Huron and Lake Michigan, the early-morning sun glints off steel spans of one of the world's longest suspension bridges. Silhouetted against the merging blue of sky and water is the distinctive low-slung superstructure of a Great Lakes freighter steaming eastwards with a cargo of iron ore from Minnesota.

On **Mackinac Island** (pronounced 'Mack-in-aw'), the sun creeps over the Grand Hotel's famous porch, which stretches for more than twice the length of a football field. Guests taking the fresh morning air settle with newspapers into white wicker rockers; others sip their morning coffee and admire the riot of wildflowers on a hillside garden sloping down to immaculate lawns. Horse-drawn carriages clip-clop up to the hotel to shuttle departing guests to the ferry dock, their drivers calling, 'Taxi downtown.'

'Downtown' on Mackinac Island is a cluster of gift shops, boutiques, inns, tourist homes, lively bars, restaurants and more than a dozen fudge shops selling about one million pounds (454 tonnes) a year of the island's favourite confection. The aroma of fudge cooking in gleaming copper pots and cooling on marble slabs is inescapable. Created to satisfy the sweet craving of Victorian-era visitors, fudge is the island's only export and popular with day visitors, known to locals as 'Fudgies'. Cinnamon rolls are another island goodie; try them both at **Martha's Sweet Shop**.

The **Mustang Lounge**, an island fixture since 1948, is a popular beer and hamburger joint, the only eaterie open year round. It has a vintage jukebox and a pool table that is moved out in summer to make room for tourists. Other notable stops include shops offering scrimshaw, Michigan-made products and British imports. **Doud's**, dating back to the 1840s, is the oldest family grocery store in the state.

The **Grand Hotel**, more than 100 years old, is set on 200 acres (81 hectares) and is an attraction in itself (indeed, it charges non-guests a visitors' fee of $10, which may be applied to the luncheon buffet). Stepping beyond the classic Grecian columns into the cool of the

antique-filled interior is to enter a genteel world (there is a dress code after 6pm) where you'll find high tea, chamber music, ballroom dancing, afternoon concerts, distinguished shops and sumptuous, multi-course dinners (there's no tipping: an 18 per cent charge is added automatically).

The 343-room hotel offers numerous bars and dining rooms as well as an incredible variety of recreational opportunities: a serpentine swimming pool, a challenging 18-hole golf course, and such esoteric pastimes as croquet and lawn bowling. Enjoy an aperitif and hors d'oeuvres in the balloon-like interior of the rooftop Cupola Bar, with windows that offer views of the bridge and hydro-jet ferries throwing up high rooster tails of spray.

A tour by horse and carriage takes you past brightly coloured Victorian houses built from white pine (slid across the ice from the mainland). You'll journey down narrow, climbing streets flanked by white picket fences enclosing 200-year-old lilac trees bought by the French, to magnificent turn-of-the-19th-century summer homes built by lumber barons. Scenery includes high bluffs, woodlands, towering prehistoric limestone formations, myrtle-covered hills and meadows where wild raspberries grow.

The British built **Fort Mackinac** during the American Revolution on a limestone bluff. It passed back and forth as a pawn in Anglo-American conflicts until it was held by the US following the war of 1812. Frozen in time as a garrison of the 1880s, the fort is populated by costumed interpreters who provide colourful historical re-enactments with thundering cannons and smoking musket. Perched at the edge of the bluff, the **Fort Mackinac Tea Room** (operated by the Grand Hotel) is a pleasant spot to linger.

Fort Mackinac

Mackinac Island (906 847 3328/ www.mackinac.com). **Open** 8 May-16 June 9.30am-4pm daily; 17 June-20 Aug 9.30am-6.30pm daily; 21 Aug-24 Sep 10am-6pm daily; 25 Sep-8 Oct 10am-4pm daily. **Admission** $7.50; $4.50 6-12s.

Mackinac Island State Park

Mackinac Island (906 847 3328/www.mackinac.com). More than 80% of the island is state park land. Find information at a park visitors' centre and nature exhibits at the **British Landing Nature Center**.

Getting there

By car

Mackinac Island is about 390 miles (628km) north-east of Chicago. Take I-94 east to Benton Harbor, I-196 north to Grand Rapids, MI 131-31 north to Mackinaw City or St Ignace.

Reach the island via ferry from either Mackinaw City or St Ignace (connected by a five-mile (8-km) long bridge). Several ferry lines provide a service, with crossing times ranging from around 15 minutes aboard a high-speed catamaran to up to 40 minutes on traditional ferries. You can park your car at the docks.

Driving the soaring suspension bridge is an experience worth the toll. By tradition, the Michigan governor leads a Labor Day walk across the bridge that attracts about 60,000 participants.

By air

Northwest Airlines serves Pellston airport, 12 miles (19km) south of Mackinaw City, with air taxi service to the island airport or taxi service to the docks.

Tourist information

Mackinac Island Chamber of Commerce

Mackinac Island (1-800 454 5227/906 847 3783/847 6418). **Open** 10am-5pm Mon-Fri; 10am-1pm Sat, Sun. The information office on Main Street across from the Arnold Line ferry dock is open 365 days a year.

Getting around

Motorised traffic is prohibited on the island. Horse-drawn carriages meet the ferry arrivals at the docks. The island, about 3½ miles (5.5km) long and eight miles (13 km) around, is ideal for hikers, cyclers and riders. There are island tours by horse-drawn carriages, as well as horses and buggies available for rent that you can drive yourself.

Where to stay

Grand Hotel

Mackinac Island (1-800 334 7263). **Rates** $485-$685. **Credit** AmEx, Disc, MC, V. This century-old, 319-room vacation retreat is undoubtedly the grandest place on the island to stay.

Mission Point Resort

Mackinac Island (1-800 833 7711/fax 248 488 3222). **Rates** *summer* $189-$469; *other times* $119-$399. **Credit** AmEx, Disc, MC, V. This 236-room resort is within easy walking distance of the ferry dock. Amenities include tennis courts, heated pool and hot tubs, while the dining room offers spectacular views of the Straits of Mackinac.

Where to eat

Grand Hotel and **Mission Point Resort** (*see above*) both have excellent dining rooms. For variation, try the following:

Mustang Lounge

Astor Street, Mackinac Island (906 847 9916). **Open** 10am-midnight daily. **Main courses** $5-$10. A friendly watering hole for beer, burgers and pizza.

South Haven

Chicago-area residents have a long history of vacation getaways to South Haven, across the lake in Van Buren County in south-west Michigan. Early last century, 'resorting' in South Haven was such a major pastime that, in 1925, 250,000 visitors descended upon the town by steamship. Even earlier, schooners were used to ship lumber and fruit from South Haven to Chicago and other lake cities.

The stylish resort community remains closely tied to the rhythms of Lake Michigan. It also remains a big draw for Illinois vacationers and weekend travellers, offering excellent beaches, fine restaurants and a good choice of accommodation. These days, though, most Chicagoans arrive by car. Charter fishing for trout and salmon is a major attraction, as are 'party boats' that go in search of schools of perch and canoe trips on the Black River.

One of South Haven's most photographed structures is the pink-hued lighthouse that dates back to 1872 when a wooden tower was built. The present steel tower was constructed in 1903. Tours are offered during some of the community's annual festivals.

The **South Haven Center for the Arts** showcases the work of local, regional and nationally known artists and hosts many touring exhibits. Also in South Haven, the **Michigan Maritime Museum** chronicles the use of boats on Michigan's Great Lakes. There are exhibits devoted to Native Americans, fur traders and settlers, as well as the boatbuilders who created schooners and steamers, plus an exhibit of marine art that shows how artists recorded maritime history and a 500-foot (152-metre) long boardwalk on the Black River that offers views of harbour traffic.

One of the region's newer attractions is the **GingerMan Raceway**, a two-mile (3.2-kilometre), 36-foot (11-metre) wide road course with 13 turns. The annual calendar includes events for the Sports Car Club America (for production, GT and formula racecars), super-speedway racing karts, vintage sports-racing cars, historic sports car racing and super-speedway motorcycles.

Pony and trap: summer on **Mackinac Island**.

Close to South Haven is the trailhead of the multi-use, 34-mile (55-kilometre) **Kal-Haven Trail**, which stretches eastward to Kalamazoo. Originally a railroad completed in 1870, the railbed has been converted to a trail with a limestone/slag surface for hikers, cyclists, equestrians, cross-country skiers and – when there is a four-inch snow base – snowmobilers. The trail passes through small towns and villages, across seven bridges that were originally railway trestles, and past many points of historical interest.

Trail highlights include a covered bridge across the Black River, a hilly area full of wildflowers, wetlands with pretty blue irises and the community of **Mentha**, once the world's largest producer of mint. At **Bloomingdale**, there is a restored depot and caboose that now serves as a museum; near **Mattawan** is the Michigan Fisheries Interpretive Center, site of a fish hatchery. If you wish to rent equipment or need a shuttle, both are available from **CyclePath Adventures** (616 372 2404).

Also to the east of South Haven, about 25 miles (40 kilometres) away, is the **St Julian Winery**. Founded in 1921, this is the oldest and largest winery in the state. Visitors can tour the site, do a tasting and buy some award-winning wines to take home. **HawksHead Links**, meanwhile, is a golfing challenge: swept by winds off Lake Michigan, it resembles a classic seaside links. Accommodation is offered by the Inn at HawksHead, which has nine guestrooms set in a restored faux English Tudor manor.

One of South Haven's most popular attractions comes at the end of the day. Because the resort community is located on the eastern shore of Lake Michigan, it enjoys dramatic sunsets. One of the most enjoyable ways to witness these pretty pink spectacles is from the decks of the **White Rose**, a 50-foot (15-metre) long excursion boat that also offers moonlight cruises and a dinner cruise on the Black River and Lake Michigan.

GingerMan Raceway
61414 Phoenix Road, South Haven (616 253 4445/ www.gingermanraceway.com). **Open** varies. **Admission** varies.

HawksHead Links
6959 105th Avenue, South Haven (616 639 2121/www.hawksheadlinks.com). **Open** 7am-9pm daily. **Rates** $45-$60. **Credit** AmEx, Disc, MC, V.

Kal-Haven Trail
Trail head at Wells Street, South Haven (616 637 2788). **Admission** $2.

Michigan Maritime Museum
260 Dyckman Avenue, South Haven (616 637 8078). **Open** 10am-5pm Tue-Sat; noon-5pm Sun; closed Mon. **Admission** $2.50; $1.50 concessions. **Credit** Disc, MC, V.

St Julian Winery
716 Kalamazoo Street, Paw Paw (616 657 5568). **Open** 9am-5pm Mon-Sat; noon-5pm Sun.

South Haven Center for the Arts
602 Phoenix Street, South Haven (616 637 1041). **Open** 10am-5pm Tue-Thur; 10am-4pm Fri; 1-4pm Sat, Sun.

White Rose
815 E Wells Street, South Haven (1-888 828 7673/616 639 8404). **Cruises** *dinner cruise* 5-7pm Thur-Sat; *sunset cruise* sunset Tue-Sun; *afternoon cruise* 1.30pm Fri, Sat. **Rates** *dinner* $37.50; *sunset, afternoon* $15. **Credit** MC, V.

Mackinac Island: once a British fort, now a genteel bastion of the finer things in life.

Getting there

By car

South Haven is approximately 120 miles (193km) north-east of Chicago. Take I-94 east to Benton Harbor, then I-196 north.

Tourist information

South Haven/Van Buren County Lakeshore Convention & Visitors' Bureau

415 Phoenix Street, South Haven (616 637 5252). **Open** 9am-5pm Mon-Fri; *summer* also 9am-5pm Sat; closed Sun.

Southwestern Michigan Tourist Council

2300 Pipestone Road, Benton Harbor (616 925 6301). **Open** 8.30am-5pm Mon-Fri; *summer* also 8.30am-5pm Sat; closed Sun.

Where to stay

Old Harbor Inn

515 Williams Street, South Haven (616 637 8480/ fax 616 637 9496). **Rates** $75-$190. **Credit** AmEx, Disc, MC, V.
On the banks of the Black River, this 37-room inn is part of a complex of shops and boutiques designed to resemble a New England fishing village. Moored alongside is the *Idler*, an attractive century-old New Orleans riverboat offering pleasant opportunities for alfresco drinking and dining.

Yelton Manor

140 North Shore Drive, South Haven (616 637 5220). **Rates** $90-$225. **Credit** AmEx, MC, V.
Yelton Manor occupies a pair of Victorian mansions and offers a total of 17 rooms. It incorporates a traditional B&B (featuring a full breakfast each morning and evening hors d'oeuvres) and a more private guesthouse, where continental breakfast is delivered to the door of each guestroom. Here's where the traveller will find whirlpools, fireplaces and balconies with views of Lake Michigan.

Where to eat

Clementine's

500 Phoenix Street, South Haven (616 637 4755). **Open** 11am-10.30pm Mon-Thur; 11am-11.30pm Fri, Sat; noon-10pm Sun. **Main courses** $9-$14. **Credit** AmEx, Disc, MC, V.
This popular downtown eaterie incorporates the 1897 Citizens Bank Building, including its original tin ceilings and brickwork. Favourites on the menu include honey mustard chicken salad and a tasty concoction called 'Bandito Fettuccine' (basically, egg fettuccine gone Mexican).

Tello's Trattoria & Cabaret

7379 North Shore Drive, South Haven (616 639 9898). **Open** 11.30am-2am daily. **Main courses** $6-$19. **Credit** AmEx, Disc, MC, V.
Wine bottles filled with lamp oil glow on the tables at this upscale roadhouse. Tello's Trattoria has a tempting menu: you ought to try crab cakes, grilled pork tenderloin with tomato fritters or grilled salmon with citrus-caper sauce.

Wisconsin

Cheese, beer and mustard are all on the menu in Wisconsin, which boasts
a strong European heritage.

Madison

Come Saturday morning in Madison,
Wisconsin, the term 'Wake up and smell the
coffee' has a literal meaning. This is when
locals and tourists – some 18,000 of them each
week – converge on the **Dane County
Farmers' Market**. It's held every Saturday
between 6am and 2pm from May to October in
the square around Wisconsin's **Capitol**, a
striking neo-classical building dating from 1917
and featuring the only granite dome in the US.

However, it's neither history nor architecture
but more sensual pleasures that draw this
Saturday-morning crowd. The aroma of freshly
brewed coffee and the sweet scent of basil. The
taste of fresh bakery and handmade cheeses.
And the prospect of shopping for farm-fresh
produce: free-range eggs, fat, pungent onions,
sweet-scented impatiens, fuschias and begonias,
plump, spicy sausages, and home-made bread,
jam, jelly and honey. Bring along shopping
bags – or, if you have one, a little red pull-
wagon (these are very popular) – for there is
plenty to buy by way of crafts as well as
produce. When you're ready for a break, rest on
the lawn or on the Capitol steps where there is
usually a concert going on.

Even aside from this delightful Saturday-
morning ritual, it's easy to see why Madison
is not only a fun place to visit but also on
everyone's shortlist for best, healthiest and
safest place to live. It's one of the best bicycling
cities, a top-ten canoe town and number one
best city for women. It's built on an isthmus
bordered by Lake Monona and Lake Mendota:
with five area lakes, 13 public beaches and
more than 200 parks, outdoor recreation focuses
on biking, hiking, fishing and canoeing.
Culturally, Madison offers a resident orchestra,
opera, theatre and a full performing arts
schedule at the University of Wisconsin.

Downtown's 'Museum Mile' includes the
State Historical Museum, **Madison
Children's Museum**, **Madison Art Center**,
the university's **Elvehjem Art Museum**, and
the **Wisconsin Veteran's Museum**. The
latter uses dioramas to chronicle American
military activities from the Civil War through to
the Persian Gulf conflict. But undoubtedly, the
most exciting – and most publicised – new

attraction in town is the **Monona Terrace
Community & Convention Center**.
Conceived by Frank Lloyd Wright more than 60
years ago, it opened in 1997 after decades of
architectural and civic controversy.

With curving, geometric forms, this stunning
250,000-square-foot (23,250-square-metre)
building links the Lake Monona shoreline with
the State Capitol two blocks away. There are
tours of the building every day, and on
Saturday mornings, Michael Feldman's
nationally syndicated public radio programme,
Whad'Ya Know?, is broadcast live from the
Lecture Hall at Monona Terrace (for free tickets,
call 1-800 942 5669).

Wander around the coffeeshops and stores of
downtown Madison. In particular, the clusters
of boutiques and speciality shops on **Monroe
Street** and the used and antiquarian bookstores on and around **State Street**, which

Dane County Farmers Market in Madison.

draw collectors from Chicago and further afield in search of rare first editions. One don't-miss stop is the **Canterbury Booksellers Café Inn**, a wonderful bookstore that is also a great place to stay (*see below*).

Elvehjem's Museum of Art
800 University Avenue, at Lake Street, Madison (608 263 2246). **Open** 9am-5pm Tue-Fri; 11am-5pm Sat, Sun; closed Mon. **Admission** free. **Credit** *shop only* MC, V.

Madison Art Center
211 State Street, at Johnson Street, Madison (608 257 0158/www.madisonartcenter.org). **Open** 11am-5pm Tue-Thur; 11am-9pm Fri; 10am-9pm Sat; 1-5pm Sun. **Admission** free. **Credit** *shop only* AmEx, Disc, MC, V.

Madison Children's Museum
100 State Street, at E Washington Street, Madison (608 256 6445/www.kidskiosk.org). **Open** 9am-4pm Tue-Sun. **Admission** $4. **Credit** MC, V.

Monona Terrace Community & Convention Center
1 John Nolen Drive, at Martin Luther King Boulevard, Madison (608 261 4000). **Open** 9am-5pm daily. **Admission** *tours* $3.

State Historical Museum
30 N Carroll Street, at State Street (608 264 6565/www.shsw.wisc.edu). **Open** 10am-5pm Tue-Sun; closed Mon. **Admission** *suggested donation* $2. **Credit** AmEx, MC, V.

Wisconsin Veteran's Museum
30 W Mifflin Street, at N Carroll Street, Madison (608 267 1799/http://museum.dva.state.wi.us). **Open** 9am-4.30pm Mon-Sat; *Apr-Sept* also noon-4pm Sun. **Admission** free. **Credit** *shop only* AmEx, MC, V.

Getting there

By car
Madison is approximately 145 miles (233km) north-west of Chicago. Take I-90 to Beltline Highway (US 12/18), then follow signs to downtown (look for the Capitol dome symbol).

Getting around
Madison is pedestrian-friendly and walking is a good way to get to know the town. There is also a bus service, however, that offers all-day passes for $3.

Tourist information

Greater Madison Convention & Visitors' Bureau
613 E Washington Avenue, Madison (1-800 373 6376/608 255 2537/www.visitmadison.com). **Open** 8am-5pm Mon-Fri; closed Sat, Sun.

Wright on: the **Monona Terrace Center**.

Where to stay

Canterbury Booksellers Café Inn
315 W Gorham Street, Madison (608 258 8899). **Rates** $150-$260. **Credit** AmEx, MC, V.
This inn-cum-bookstore-cum-café lives up to its unusual name: guestrooms are identified by Chaucerian characters, while whimsical murals depicting scenes from *The Canterbury Tales* cover each door.

Edgewater
666 Wisconsin Avenue, Madison (1-800 922 5512/fax 608 256 0910). **Rates** $109-$399. **Credit** AmEx, DC, MC, V.
Since it was built in 1948, this 111-room landmark hotel has hosted all manner of luminaries. Elvis took over an entire floor but was reclusive; Elton John was more visible, playing the piano for the other patrons. A photo gallery in the Cove Lounge draws current guests into a game of 'who was who': when you get stuck, ask for a booklet identifying more than 100 celebs.

Madison Concourse Hotel
1 W Dayton Street, Madison (1-800 356 8293). **Rates** $99-$169. **Credit** AmEx, DC, Disc, MC, V.
This is the city's major downtown convention hotel, within easy walking distance of most attractions. It offers 390 rooms, an indoor pool, fitness centre, restaurants and lounges.

Where to eat

Don't leave town without a stop at the **UW student union** (800 Langdon Street) or **UW Babcock Hall** (1605 Lindon Street) for legendary ice-cream that has been produced by the UW School of Agriculture since the early 1900s. Using a formula that's hardly changed over the years, it is deliciously creamy (with a 12 per cent butterfat content). For something more substantial, try one of the following.

Admiralty Room

at Edgewater Hotel, 666 Wisconsin Avenue, Madison (1-800 922 5512/608 256 9071/fax 608 256 0910). **Open** 6.30-10am, 11.30am-2pm, 5.30-10pm Mon-Fri; 7.30-10am, 11.30am-2pm, 5.30-10pm Sat; 7.30-10am, 11am-2pm, 5.30-10pm Sun. **Main courses** *dinner* $20-$25. **Credit** AmEx, DC, MC, V.

Watching the sunset is a ritual at this historic room. When the big red ball is set to kiss the horizon along the far shore of Lake Mendota, staff ceremoniously raise mesh blinds that cover big picture windows. The room perpetuates the dying art of tableside cooking with the likes of steak Diane.

Great Dane Pub & Brewing Company

123 E Doty Street, Madison (608 284 0000/ www.greatdanepub.com). **Open** 11am-2am daily. **Main courses** $10. **Credit** AmEx, MC, V.

Casual dining on well-made burgers and hot sandwiches, as well as fish and chips, brats and mash and chicken potpie. The microbrewery offers about a dozen handcrafted brews made on the premises.

Mariner's Inn

5339 Lighthouse Bay Drive, Madison (608 246 3120). **Open** 5-9.30pm Mon-Thur; 4.30-10pm Fri, Sat; 4.30-9pm Sun. **Main courses** $15-$40. **Credit** MC, V.

The flavourful steaks here match those of many big-city steakhouses, but at thoroughly modest prices. The building, a former speakeasy, dates back to 1863 and is tucked into a harbour on Lake Mendota. Boaters pull up for drinks at tables shaded by tall trees on a lawn that sweeps down to the water's edge.

Milwaukee

Much as viola players and rock drummers are the butt of jokes among musicians the world over, so Milwaukee comes in for a regular comedic battering at the hands of Chicagoans. Two hours by train from Chicago's Union Station, the city is all too readily sneered at by Chicagoans overused to the big-city atmosphere and attitude that permeates their town.

Of course, every which way you look at Milwaukee, Chicago it ain't. The few comparison points between the two cities – for Cubs, see Brewers; for Chicago River, see Milwaukee River; for John Wayne Gacy, see Jeffrey Dahmer – reveal nary a shared trait between them, aside from a lakeside location and some desperately cold weather. However, while the attractions of Chicago are obvious, Milwaukee is by no means without its charms.

Like Chicago, Milwaukee was settled by the Native American Potawatomie tribe, before being overrun by white speculators in the 1830s. Milwaukee, though, comes with even more Native American heritage than its Illinois neighbour: aside from the Potawatomies, at least half a dozen other Native American tribes were resident in the area known as Millocki before most were evacuated in 1838.

It was around this time that the Germans arrived in force, an influx that was to have a huge effect on both the character and the economy of the city. For with the Germans came beer, and the economic foundations on which Milwaukee would be built. Pabst, Schlitz and – most famously – Miller all started in Milwaukee from German families, and all went on to huge economic success.

The beer remains, with the megabreweries complemented nicely by several microbreweries that have started up over the last decade or so. And though the post-war period hasn't always been a tale of unbridled economic joy, the city is back on the rise. Swathes of the admittedly small downtown area have been redeveloped to pleasing effect – most notably the Historic Third Ward, which has been developed from dilapidated warehouses into a lovely, boutiquey shopping and dining district – and new businesses seem to be springing up all over.

Much of this prosperity is mirrored in a new downtown development that the city hopes will bring more visitors to the town each year. Perhaps influenced by the economic rewards reaped by Chicago from McCormick Place, Milwaukee built its own model: the **Midwest Express Center**, a multimillon-dollar convention venue boasting 28 meeting rooms and a 189,000-square-foot (17,577-square-metre) exhibition space.

Perhaps the crown jewels of Milwaukee's attractions can be found at **Milwaukee Public Museum**. An all-encompassing three-floor natural history museum with a stock of some six million exhibits, it's a fun place that is, above all else, a great place to take the kids. On the first floor, there's a cute little evocation of the old streets of Milwaukee, while across the hall are exhibits detailing the rain forest's dinosaur life (including the world's largest dinosaur skull). The best stuff, though, is on the second floor, with the North American Indians exhibit a particular winner (compiled, incidentally, with the help of some of Wisconsin's tribes).

The high-tech museum trend appears to have passed the place by – interactivity is limited to

Milwaukee County Historical Society.

Tall but perfectly formed: the **County Zoo**.

a few videos and some pick-up flaps – but it's to the museum's credit that it's still a charming and culturally educative place. Be sure to visit the butterfly garden: a delightful and, assuming you don't get stuck in there with a coach party of schoolkids, peaceful exhibit. The garden was previewed in 1999 and was scheduled to open permanently in spring 2000.

The area around the Public Museum is home to a couple of the city's other main attractions, and is known informally as Museum Center. There's **Discovery World: The James Lovell Museum of Science, Economics & Technology**, whose high-tech interactive exhibits make a nice contrast with its neighbour. And there's the **Humphrey IMAX Dome Theater**, which boasts a six-storey-high screen and a 12,000-watt sound system.

However, if you're only in town briefly, and if the weather isn't too horrific, you should make **Milwaukee County Zoo** your first port of call. One of the largest zoos in the country – 3,000 animals, 200 acres (81 hectares), 250 staff – Milwaukee County Zoo is also one of the best. Founded in 1892 as a tiny display in Washington Park, the zoo moved to its present parkland site in 1958. Since then, the zoo has grown and grown, and is now an extremely impressive attraction.

Every conceivable animal is included, and presented – if that's the right word – sympathetically and informatively in a peaceful setting that's a delight just to walk around on a sunny summer's day. It'll take you upwards of three hours to see everything, but it's well worth it for the colourful aviary, the flamingos, the petting mandrills, the mischievous golden lion tamarin, the gazelle-like bongo, the emus, the bats and – our favourite – the springhaas, which look like rabbits and jump like kangaroos but which are actually rodents. Many of the displays place emphasis on the role of the zoo in conservation and breeding programmes, and the zoo is a member of the Special Survival Plan.

While slightly less culturally educative, the **Miller Brewing Co** does at least offer free (if self-aggrandising) tours. Learn how Frederic Miller started at a tiny Plank Street property (a replica of which sits outside the main plant); how the brewery churns out six gazillion bottles of Miller Lite a minute (or something); and that Miller has five of the top ten selling beers in the US, one of which – Milwaukee's Best – isn't cheap, merely 'popularily priced'. This last piece of alcoholic revisionism was, at least, relayed with a knowing smile by the chatty guide, while the gratis beers at the end are just what the doctor ordered after the brisk tour.

Back in central Milwaukee, you'll find several other smaller museums that are well worth a look, plus one that art-lovers will want to make a beeline for at the earliest opportunity. The **Milwaukee Art Museum**, situated right on the lake, boasts some 20,000 works of art including a large collection of works by Milwaukee native Georgia O'Keefe. The proposed $50-million extension, designed by architect Santiago Calatrava, will make the vista over the lake even more stunning: a magnificent white building with wings – no, really – it's scheduled to open in 2001. Close by is the **Betty Brinn Children's Museum**, an interactive place designed for under-10s and parents.

Of the others, there's **America's Black Holocaust Museum**, the only museum of its type in the US and highly educative to boot. Down by the charming River Walk is the **Milwaukee County Historical Society**, another educative museum set in a lovely old building. And, perhaps most bizarrely, there's the **International Clown Hall of Fame**, which currently finds its home in the basement of a shopping mall (though it does have plans to move). Here you can learn about how Lou Jacobs 'started in showbiz as the rear end of a stunt alligator', and that Hall of Famer Mark Anthony is 'perhaps the foremost sculptor of foam props in the world'. Fans of comically gargantuan shoes will find much to admire.

It's not all museums in Milwaukee, of course. Shoppers will be charmed by the lovely Historic Third Ward, and specifically by stores such as **Marlene's A Touch of Class** (249 N Water Street; 414 272 2470), a great two-floor used clothing outlet; **Artasia** (159 N Broadway; 414 220 4292), a would-be Boho shop chock-full of eastern and Asian artefacts; **Broadway Paper** (181 N Broadway; 414 277 7699), a charming store entirely dedicated to the art of giftwrapping; and the mammoth **Water Street Antique Market** (318 N Water Street; 414 278 7008). Elsewhere, the **Grand Avenue Mall** on the main Wisconsin Street drag should fill most people's corporate chain-shopping needs, while bookworms will find solace poring over a tome in the fabulously musty **Renaissance Book Shop** (834 N Plankinton Street; 414 271 6850).

There are also a fair few nice bars and eateries in the Third Ward, too, among them the pleasingly airy gay bar the **M&M Club** (124 N Water Street; 414 347 1962) and the **Milwaukee Ale House** (*see page 269*). Decent watering holes can also be found around Walker's Point to the south of downtown, among them **Steny's Tavern** (800 S 2nd Street; 414 672 7139) and **Fritz's on 2nd** (814 S 2nd Street; 414 383 3211). However, most of central Milwaukee's nightlife is centred around Water Street, where you'll find around a dozen bars. Be sure to stop by the excellent **Water Street Brewery** (1101 N Water Street; 414 272 1195), a great microbrewery whose bar food is a cut above the norm. There is also a rash of fine bars and eateries further north-east on Brady Street, including the **Jo-Cat Pub** (1311 E Brady Street; 414 765 9955) and the **Nomad World Pub** (1401 E Brady Street; 414 224 8111).

And then there's the unique **Safe House** (779 N Front Street; 414 271 2007), a James Bond-themed bar-restaurant that's been wheeling out its cheeky line in spy schtick for years. To be honest, it's looking a little tired these days, but there's still fun to be had in its multi-roomed layout. It even takes its furtive theme to the front door, which is labelled not 'Safe House' (otherwise it wouldn't be a safe house, would it?), but 'International Exports, Ltd'. And no, we're not telling you the password.

Culturally, too, Milwaukee's on the up and up. Quite aside from the myriad festivals – the biggest of which is the all-conquering music **Summerfest**, which takes place from late June to early July (1-800 273 3378) – there's the fine **Milwaukee Symphony Orchestra**, which performs regularly in the city, and a plethora of theatre groups. Incidentally, make sure you don't get the **Marcus Center for the**

Performing Arts (929 N Water Street; 313 273 7121), downtown's main entertainment venue, confused with Art's Performing Center, a superbly named strip joint a few blocks away.

America's Black Holocaust Museum

2233 N 4th Street, at North Avenue, Milwaukee (414 264 2500). **Open** 9am-5pm Mon, Tue, Thur, Fri; noon-3pm Sun. **Admission** $5; $3-$4 concessions. **Credit** AmEx, Disc, MC, V.

Betty Brinn Children's Museum

929 E Wisconsin Avenue, at Lincoln Memorial Drive, Milwaukee (414 390 5437/www.bbcmkids.org). **Open** 9am-5pm Tue-Sat; noon-5pm Sun; *June-Aug* also 9am-5pm Mon. **Admission** $4. **Credit** Disc, MC, V.

Discovery World

815 N James Lovell Street, at Wells Street, Milwaukee (414 765 9966/www.discoveryworld.org). **Open** 9am-5pm daily. **Admission** $5.50; $4-$4.50 concessions. **Credit** Disc, MC, V.

Humphrey IMAX Dome Theater

800 W Wells Street, at Museum Center, Milwaukee (414 319 4629/www.humphreyimax.com). **Tickets** $6.50; $5-$5.50 concessions; *matinee performances* Mon-Fri $4.50. **Credit** AmEx, Disc. MC, V.

International Clown Hall of Fame

Suite LL700, Grand Avenue Mall, 161 W Wisconsin Avenue, at N 2nd Street, Milwaukee (414 319 0848/www.webdom.com/chof). **Open** 10am-4pm Mon-Fri. **Admission** $2; free under-6s.

Milwaukee Art Museum

750 N Lincoln Memorial Drive, at Lake Michigan, Milwaukee (414 224 3200/www.mam.org). **Open** 10am-5pm Tue, Wed, Fri, Sat; noon-9pm Thur; noon-5pm Sun; closed Mon. **Admission** $5; $3 concessions.

Milwaukee County Historical Society Library & Museum

910 N Old World 3rd Street, at Kilbourn Avenue, Milwaukee (414 273 8288/www.milwaukeecounty histsoc.org). **Open** *Museum* 9.30am-5pm Mon-Fri; 10am-5pm Sat; 1-5pm Sun. **Admission** free.

Milwaukee County Zoo

10001 W Bluemound Road, Milwaukee (414 771 3040/www.milwaukeezoo.org). **Open** *Nov-Mar* 9am-4.30pm daily; *Apr-Oct* 9am-5.30pm daily. **Admission** $6.50-$8; $4.50-$7 concessions. **Credit** MC, V.

Milwaukee Public Museum

800 W Wells Street, at Museum Center, Milwaukee (414 278 2702). **Open** 9am-5pm daily; closed 4 July, 23 Nov, 25 Dec. **Admission** $6.50; $4-$5 concessions. **Credit** AmEx, Disc, MC, V.

Getting there

By car

Milwaukee is approximately 90 miles (145km) north of Chicago on the I-94.

Trips Out of Town

Milwaukee

W RESERVOIR AVE
W PLEASANT ST
W GALENA ST
W CHERRY ST
W VLIET ST
W HIGHLAND AVE
W STATE ST
W KILBOURN AVE
W WISCONSIN AVE
W MICHIGAN ST
W CLYBOURN ST
W ST PAUL AVE
W HINMAN ST
W PITTSBURGH AVE
W OREGON ST
W FLORIDA ST
W VIRGINIA ST

E VINE ST
E LAND PL
E HAMILTON ST
E PEARSON ST
E BRADY ST
E KEWAUNEE ST
E PLEASANT ST
E LYON ST
E OGDEN AVE
E KNAPP ST
E JUNEAU AVE
E HIGHLAND AVE
E STATE ST
E KILBOURN AVE
E WELLS ST
E MASON ST
E WISCONSIN AVE
E MICHIGAN ST
E CLYBOURN ST
E ST PAUL AVE
E BUFFALO ST
E ERIE ST
E CORCORAN ST

EAST TOWN

Veterans Park

Milwaukee County Historical Society
Discovery World
Milwaukee Public Museum
Midwest Express Center
Grand Avenue Mall
Betty Brinn Children's Museum
Milwaukee Art Museum
Milwaukee Union Station

HISTORIC THIRD WARD

Lake Michigan

Menomonee River

0   0.5 mile
0   800 metres
© Copyright Time Out Group 2000

Marcus Ampitheater

By rail

Milwaukee is a 90-minute train ride from Chicago's Union Station; services are frequent.

Getting around

Milwaukee is best explored on foot, though bus and trolley services serve outlaying areas.

Tourist information

Greater Milwaukee Convention & Visitors' Bureau

510 W Kilbourn Avenue, at N 6th Street, Milwaukee (1-800 231 0903/414 273 7222/www.milwaukee.org). **Open** 8am-5pm Mon-Fri.

Where to stay

In addition, several chains have branches in Milwaukee, including the **Holiday Inn** (611 W Wisconsin Street; 414 273 2950), the **Hyatt Regency** (333 W Kilburn Avenue; 1-800 233 1234/414 276 1234) and the **Hilton** (509 W Wisconsin Avenue; 414 271 7250).

Astor Hotel

924 E Juneau Avenue, between Astor & N Marshall Street, Milwaukee (1-800 558 0200/414 271 4220/ fax 414 271 6370). **Rates** $69-$119. **Credit** AmEx, Disc, MC, V.

A mid-range hotel close to Lake Michigan. It's traditionally furnished and has a decent eaterie.

Hotel Wisconsin

720 N Old World 3rd Street, at W Wisconsin Avenue, Milwaukee (414 271 4900/fax 271 9998). **Rates** $59-$89. **Credit** AmEx, DC, Disc, MC, V.

One of the best budget options in the city, thanks to its central location and free parking.

Pfister Hotel

424 E Wisconin Street, at N Jefferson Street, Milwaukee (1-800 558 8222/414 273 8222/fax 414

273 5025/www.pfister-hotel.com). **Rates** $264-$1,050. **Credit** AmEx, DC, Disc, MC, V.
Over 100 years old, the characterful, charming and handily located Pfister is perhaps *the* hotel in which to stay when in town.

Where to eat

African Hut
1107 N Old World 3rd Street, at E Juneau Street, Milwaukee (414 765 1110). **Open** 11.30am-10pm Mon-Thur; 11.30am-11pm Fri, Sat; closed Sun. **Main courses** $7.95-$17.95. **Credit** AmEx, DC, Disc, MC, V.
An absolute treat, this, offering a range of delectable dishes from assorted African countries. The peanut stew banfi is astonishing, though you'd do well with just about everything on the menu. Don't miss.

Café Vecchio Mondo
1137 N Old World 3rd Street, at E Juneau Avenue, Milwaukee (414 273 5700). **Open** 11am-2am Mon-Fri; 5pm-2am Sat, Sun. **Main courses** $6-$15. **Credit** AmEx, MC, V.
Splendid sandwiches, fine fondues, wicked wines and magnificent Martinis. A lovely spot.

Lake Park Bistro
3133 E Newberry Boulevard, Lake Park, Milwaukee (414 962 6300/www.foodspot.com). **Open** 11.30am-2pm, 5.30-9pm Mon-Thur; 11.30am-2pm, 5.30-10pm Fri; 5-10pm Sat; 10.30am-2pm, 5-8pm Sun. **Main courses** $7.95-$28.95. **Credit** AmEx, DC, Disc, MC, V.
Its lakeside location is a real boon for this French restaurant, whose owners usually specialise in Italian. The food is tasty French fare, with the desserts especially heavenly.

Mader's
1037-41 N Old World 3rd Street, at W State Street, Milwaukee (414 271 3377). **Open** 11.30am-9pm Mon; 11.30am-10pm Tue-Thur; 11.30am-11pm Fri, Sat; 10.30am-9pm Sun. **Main courses** $14-$25. **Credit** AmEx, DC, Disc, MC, V.
About as German as you could hope to find – and about as touristy, too – Mader's offers implausibly sturdy Teutonic fare in a traditional setting.

Milwaukee Ale House
233 N Water Street, at E Buffalo Street, Milwaukee (414 226 2337/www.ale-house.com). **Open** 11am-2am Mon-Sat; noon-10pm Sun. **Main courses** $6.50-$14. **Credit** AmEx, Disc, MC, V.
This microbrewery has been spinning its own twist on beertown since the late 1990s. Try its $5.50 beer sampler before tucking into the great bar food.

Mount Horeb

Mount Horeb lies within the unglaciated area of south-western Wisconsin that slipped through the icy fingers of the great glaciers that covered much of the region during the Ice Age. As a

result, the land retained its rugged, craggy topography of high ridges and steep-sided valleys. This is picture-book country, perfect for hiking, cycling and just plain exploring, where soaring, wooded hillsides etched with intricate rocky outcrops overlook sparkling brooks, and prize dairy herds graze in ridiculously green pastures.

With its pleated and wrinkled terrain, this area drew early Norwegian settlers because of its similarity to their homeland, and the quaint town of Mount Horeb reflects the heritage of the immigrants who settled the area in the 1870s: Main Street is decorated with carved wooden trolls carved by local artist Michael Feeney and dubbed 'The Trollway', while shops offer a variety of Scandinavian imports.

Nordic heritage is preserved in even greater detail at **Little Norway**, located three miles (4.8 kilometres) west of Mount Horeb, where insights into pioneer history are provided by costumed guides. The property portrays life on an 1856 Norwegian pioneer farmstead and is furnished with one of the largest privately owned collections of Norwegian antiques in the United States. When Norway's King Harald (then crown prince) visited Little Norway in 1965, he remarked how much the settlement resembled its namesake.

The first settler here, though, was Osten Olson Haugen from Tinn Telemarken, Norway. In 1856, he bought 40 acres (16.2 hectares) of land and made the area his home, building a farm in which his family worked until they moved away from the area in 1920. For the next five years, although the fields were rented and the hillsides pastured, the buildings themselves remained unoccupied. When Isak Dahle purchased the property in 1927, he named it Nissedahle, after Nissedal, Norway, where his grandparents had been born. The name translates to 'Valley of the Elves.'

Since Dahle's great nephew Scott Winner took over Little Norway in 1982 – his family homesteaded the area in the 1840s – he has spent countless hours personally doing the carpentry to restore and maintain the historic settlement. It is a labour of love that becomes apparent when Scott dons native Norwegian costume to conduct a tour and whistle a few bars of Grieg's *Peer Gynt*.

One of the tour highlights is a visit to a replica of a 12th-century *stavekirke*, or **stave church**, built in Norway for the Norwegian government and used as its pavilion at the Chicago Columbian Exposition of 1893. After the Exposition, the building was moved to Lake Geneva, Wisconsin, and was later sold to the prominent Wrigley family, who moved it to grace their summer estate. In

Trips Out of Town

1936 the *stavekirke* found a home at Little Norway, which is where it's remained from that day to this.

The ornate building is made of hewn pine and has a high-peaked roof and gingerbread decorations. Dragons breathing flame from the gables watch in vigilance against evil spirits, and the faces of pagan Norwegian kings and queens peer down from beam-ends. Before World War II there were more than 900 such churches in Norway, dating back to the 11th and 12th centuries. Today, fewer than 30 remain.

The former Exposition pavilion is now once again home to Norwegian crafts and culture. There are dozens of beautiful chests and fine embroidered wall hangings, and exquisite pieces of furniture include a large spice cabinet with secret compartments, fireside benches with intricately carved dragonheads, handsome sideboards, looms, cabinets and cupboards.

Back in town, don't miss a stop at the bizarre **Mount Horeb Mustard Museum** (*see opposite* **Captain Mustard to the rescue**). Nearby, the **Cave of the Mounds** is a significant underground cavern filled with stalactites, stalagmites and other formations, first discovered in 1939.

Cave of the Mounds
Brighma Farm, Blue Mounds, 3 miles west of Mount Horeb (608 437 3038). **Open** *Sept-May* 10am-4pm Mon-Fri; 9am-5pm Sat, Sun; *June-Aug* 9am-7pm daily. **Admission** $10; $5 5-12s. **Credit** AmEx, MC, V.

Little Norway
3576 County Highway JG, Blue Mounds, 3 miles west of Mount Horeb (608 437 8211). **Open** *May, June, Sept, Oct* 9am-5pm daily; *July, Aug* 9am-7pm daily. **Admission** $8; $3-$7 concessions. **Credit** MC, V.

Getting there

By car
Mount Horeb is about 165 miles (265km) north-west of Chicago. Follow I-90 to Madison, then travel west on Highway 18 for 20 miles (32km).

Tourist information

Mount Horeb Area Chamber of Commerce
Main Street, Mount Horeb (608 437 5914). **Open** *summer* 10am-3pm daily.
The Chamber of Commerce can provide information about Mount Horeb and the surrounding region.

New Glarus

From Berne, the capital of Switzerland, to the town of Glarus, it is about 80 miles (129 kilometres). From Madison, the capital of

Mount Horeb: because I'm worth it.

Wisconsin, to the community of New Glarus – as Swiss as an unnumbered bank account – it is less than 25 miles (40 kilometres).

The new was settled by the old. In 1845, 108 immigrants from the Swiss canton (state) of Glarus travelled to America, hoping to escape the poverty prevalent in their homeland. The arduous journey involved a trip to Holland by canal and Rhine riverboat, a 49-day voyage to Baltimore and a trip by rail, canal and riverboat to Galena, Illinois, via Pittsburgh, Pennsylvania and St Louis, Missouri. The immigrants walked the last 60 miles (97 kilometres) to their new home in south-west Wisconsin and settled on 1,280 acres (518 hectares) of land purchased at $1.25 an acre.

The Swiss immigrants sought a landscape resembling the one they had left behind, and found it cradled in the Little Sugar River valley of Green County. Cresting one of the surrounding hills and sighting the valley where the pretty Swiss village is snuggled, it would not be startling to hear a yodel echo across the valley. In fact, on the first Sunday in August, yodellers, alphornists and folk dancers meet here and celebrate **Swiss Independence Day**.

With a population of 1,900, the village resembles a Swiss mountain town. Chalet-style buildings feature carved balconies decorated by colourful coats of arms, Swiss flags and banners and window boxes spilling with bright red geraniums. The clank of cowbells welcomes you to shops selling lace, embroidery, cheese, baked goods (including rich, dense *stollen*) and a variety of *wurst*, including *landjäger*, a dried sausage favoured by Swiss hunters that makes a great munchie. The microbrewery even produces handcrafted European-style beers, including lager, pilsner, bock and seasonal specialities such as *weiss* (wheat beer).

The **Swiss Historical Village Museum** is a replica pioneer village with log cabins, a log church and a one-room schoolhouse. Operated by the local historical society, it preserves the history and records of New Glarus and tells the story of Swiss immigration and colonisation as well as early colonial life in the town. Its 14 buildings include a traditional Swiss bee house, a replica cheese factory, a blacksmith's shop, a general store and a print shop that displays equipment used to print the *New Glarus Post* from 1897 to 1967. Meanwhile, the **Chalet of the Golden Fleece Museum** is an authentic copy of a Swiss-Bernese mountain chalet, characterised by a white plaster foundation and brown-stained wood walls. The museum houses a collection of more than 3,000 Swiss items from dolls to kitchenware, as well as other antiques and artefacts from around the world.

Over the Labor Day weekend, the **Wilhelm Tell Festival** celebrates Switzerland's most endearing folk hero with an outdoor performance of Friedrich Schiller's *Wilhelm Tell*. Staged in a wooded glen, it has a cast of more than 200 area residents, many on horseback, in authentic 13th-century costume. The festival also includes musical events and a candlelit parade.

Chalet of the Golden Fleece Museum
618 2nd Street, New Glarus (608 527 2614). **Open** *May-Oct* 10am-4pm daily.

Swiss Historical Village
612 7th Avenue, New Glarus (608 527 2317). **Open** *May, Sept, Oct* 10am-4pm daily; *June-Aug* 9am-4.30pm daily. **Admission** $6; $2 6-13s.

Swiss Independence Day Festival
New Glarus (information 1-800 527 6838/608 527 2095). **Date** 1st Sun in Aug.

Wilhelm Tell Festival
New Glarus (1-800 527 6838/608 527 2095). **Date** Labor Day weekend.

Getting there

By car
New Glarus is 150 miles (241km) north-west of Chicago. Take I-90 (Northwest Tollway) to Rockford, then US 20 west to Freeport, where Highway 26 will take you across the stateline to join Highway 69. It's then only about 30 miles (48km) to New Glarus via Monroe, known for its production of Swiss cheese.

Captain Mustard to the rescue

The couple took their mustard purchases to the counter. She was wearing a Chicago Cubs sweatshirt, he a Chicago White Sox jacket. She had chosen a raspberry mustard that she planned to spread on turkey sandwiches. He had plumped for horseradish mustard (categorised as a 'sinus buster') and chilli pepper mustard that he thought would taste great with squeaky Wisconsin cheese curds. Cubs and Sox, sweet and hot... perhaps opposites do attract.

'This guy's a hoot,' said Ms Cubbie, referring not to Mr Sox but to Barry Levenson, proprietor of the **Mount Horeb Mustard Museum**. A former Wisconsin assistant state's attorney, his claim to fame is his 'passionate appreciation for fine mustards and a perpetual blank look on his face'. He's full of quips and gags about his favourite condiment: there are 'Mustard happens' T-shirts and a phony scratch-and-sniff patch in his catalogue. He even appears in tights and cape as comic-book hero Captain Mustard.

Levenson, who grew up in New England, seems at home in this small Midwestern town. His museum-cum-shop houses the world's largest collection of prepared mustards – over 3,100 – which range from excruciatingly hot to tantalising sweet. His window is decorated with collegiate pennants and sweatshirts lauding good old Poupon U, for which he devised a fight song. Visitors to the museum can also relax in the Mustard Piece Theatre to watch a 25-minute video that visits the mustard fields of Canada, the sausage carts of Germany and the restaurants of Dijon, France.

Mount Horeb Mustard Museum
109 E Main Street, Mount Horeb (1-800 438 6878/www.mustardmuseum.com). **Open** 10am-5pm daily.

Trips Out of Town

Getting around

New Glarus is so tiny that it is easily navigable
on foot. The surrounding countryside is ideal
for cycling and hiking: in particular, the 23-mile
(37-kilometre) **Sugar River Trail**, which runs
from New Glarus to Brodhead. Tracing an
abandoned railroad right-of-way, the trail
passes through rolling hills and state wildlife
refuges, past dairy farms, across old planked
trestle bridges and under a covered bridge.

Tourist information

New Glarus Tourism & Chamber of Commerce

*112 6th Avenue, New Glarus (1-800 527 6838/608
527 2095).* **Open** *late May-late Oct* 10am-5pm daily;
otherwise 9am-4.30pm Mon-Fri.

Where to stay

New Glarus is small, so accommodation options
are limited. The New Glarus Hotel (*see page
273*) has a number of rooms and the hotels of
Madison (*see page 263*) are within easy reach.

Chalet Landhaus Inn

*801 Highway 69, New Glarus
(1-800 944 1716/608 527 5234/fax 608 527 2365/
www.chaletlandhaus.com).* **Rates** $76-$145.
Credit AmEx, DC, Disc, MC, V.
This 67-room motel, built in traditional Swiss-chalet
style, is fully equipped with modern conveniences
(and also has a courtyard with umbrella tables).

Where to eat

New Glarus Hotel

*1st Street, at 6th Avenue, New Glarus (608 527
5244).* **Open** 11am-8pm Mon-Thur, Sun; 11am-10pm
Fri, Sat; *Nov-Apr* closed Tue. **Main courses** $10-
$18. **Credit** AmEx, Disc, MC, V.
Owner Hans Lenzlinger, who learned to cook during a stint in the Swiss Army, offers many traditional favourites at this hotel-restaurant, whose
enclosed upper balcony has picture windows looking out on the picturesque shops of Main Street
and over rooftops to the green hills that surround
the village.

Wisconsin Dells

Call it brash and noisy, but there is no doubt
that the Wisconsin Dells, with its Vegas-like
theme hotels and array of adventure parks,
giant waterparks and video arcades, is one of
the greatest kid-pleasers in the whole of the
Midwest. It's a place for hotdogs, frozen custard
and freshly made fudge. It's where you go to
buy moccasins, ride in helicopters, plunge from

New Glarus. It's like punk never happened.

a bungee jump, catch the skilful, daredevil acts
at the famous **Tommy Bartlett Thrill Show**,
or check out magician Rick Wilcox at the **Rick
Wilcox Theater**. It's where you go when the
kids tire of pretty countryside and want
something to *do*.

Once strictly seasonal, the Dells is emerging
as a year-round destination thanks in part to
the advent of indoor waterparks, such as those
at **Wilderness Hotel**, **Black Wolf Lodge**
and the **Wintergreen Resort**. But despite the
many entertainments, the Dells also are scenic.
The towering sandstone cliffs and cool, fern-
filled gullies remain unspoiled, and a tour of the
upper and lower rivers by boat or aboard a
careening amphibious duck – a World War II
landing craft – are enjoyable outings.

Another good way to spend the day is to take
a tour of the **Nanchas Elk Ranch**, a working
ranch set on 160 acres (65 hectares) of rolling
hills that maintains a herd of up to 125 elk.
Each season there is something new to see: in
spring, new calves are born; in early summer,
visitors can watch as mothers and calves
develop bonds and bulls start their antler
growth; and late summer/fall marks the start of
the breeding season.

For a fun family horseback riding adventure,
head for the **OK Corral Riding Stable** on
Highway 16E, a mile east of the Dells (608 254
2811). The mounts are gentle enough for
children – smaller kids can ride double with an
adult – and the trail runs through scenic terrain.
Hour-long rides follow a trail into **Devil's
Canyon**, a 100-foot (30-metre) deep sandstone
canyon formed at the same time as the famous
rock formations along the Wisconsin River. The
trail dips into a fern-filled glen where it can be
up to 20°F cooler. White-tailed deer are
common; red foxes, sandhill cranes and wild
turkeys can sometimes be spotted, too.

And if that's not enough wildlife for you,
visit the 80-acre (32.4-hectare) reserve of the
International Crane Foundation at

Baraboo. There are 15 species of cranes throughout the world, 11 of which are considered endangered. Baraboo is the only place in the world that's home to all 15, including the whooping crane, one of the world's most endangered birds and the tallest bird in North America (the adult stands up to five feet (1.5 metres) high). Its name was inspired by its loud, distinctive call, audible up to two miles (3.2 kilometres) away.

Nearby, you can ride a steam train through the Baraboo Hills from the **Mid-Continent Railway Museum** at North Freedom. It operates steam trains such as the Chicago & North Western No.1385, built in 1907. The one-hour excursions depart four times daily, passing through the ghost town of **LaRue**, a former iron-mining community. Exhibits of railroading memorabilia, including a rare steam-powered rotary snowplow, are housed in an 1894 depot and in train and coach sheds.

International Crane Foundation
E11376 Shady Lane Road, Baraboo (608 356 9462). **Open** *May-Oct* 9am-5pm daily. **Admission** $12; $3.50-$6 concessions. **Credit** MC, V.

Mid-Continent Railway Museum
Walnut Street West, North Freedom (1-800 930 1385/608 522 4261/www.mcrwy.com). **Trains** *mid-late May, Labor Day-end Sept* 10.30am, 12.30pm, 2pm, 3.30pm Sat, Sun; *late May-Labor Day* 10.30am, 12.30pm, 2pm, 3.30pm daily. **Admission** $9-$11; $4.50-$8 concessions; free under-3s. **Credit** AmEx, Disc, MC, V.

Nanchas Elk Ranch Tours
County Highway H, 9 miles west of Wisconsin Dells (608 524 4355). **Open** *June-Oct* 10am-5.30pm daily. **Admission** $8; $6 children. **Credit** MC, V.

Original Wisconsin Ducks
1890 Wisconsin Dells Parkway, Wisconsin Dells (608 254 8751). **Open** *summer* 8am-7pm daily. **Admission** $14.50; $8.75 6-11s. **Credit** MC, V.

Roll up, roll up

The midday sun beats down relentlessly as a family of five African elephants frolic in the watering hole, stirring up the muddy brown water. They spend about 20 minutes cooling off, splashing themselves, squirting water over each other with their trunks and sitting in the refreshing pool.

It's appropriate that the scene, while far from the Serengeti Plain, is set at the Baraboo River in south-central Wisconsin. Since the tiny town of Baraboo is only about a dozen miles south of the tourist hoopla of Wisconsin Dells, why not a water park for pachyderms? In fact, this cooling dip in the river is a part of the daily warm-weather ritual at the **Circus World Museum**.

The museum, operated by the State Historical Society of Wisconsin, is living proof that museums are not simply informative and educational: they can also be fascinating, funky and downright fun. It is as a museum should be: rich with history and packed with informative exhibits and rare artefacts, from glittering costumes to gilded rolling calliopes. But it also has acrobats, elephants, clowns and music. Visitors can take a course called Juggling 101, learn how to apply clown make-up and enjoy a single-ring circus performance under a Big Top.

The Circus World Museum collects, preserves and presents American circus history at the original winter quarters of the Ringling Brothers' Circus (1886-1918), an area designated a National Historic Landmark. On a 60-acre (24.3-hectare) site, the museum keeps eight historic Ringling buildings and barns that once housed giraffes, camels, elephants and other exotic animals, along with performance and baggage horses, office operations and train cars.

'There's a sucker born every minute' was part of the doctrine of PT Barnum, the legendary circus entrepreneur. Barnum, who promoted 28-inch (71-cm) tall Tom Thumb and catapulted singer Jenny Lind to fame as the 'Swedish Nightingale,' is among the famous circus figures featured in 'The World's Greatest Showmen', a lively and colourful audio-visual programme.

Perennially popular with youngsters are rides on elephants and ponies, a petting menagerie and a giant merry-go-round that rotates to the tunes of an old-time band organ. Look out, too, for the presentations of circus music, especially those on the Gavioli band organ: it somehow replicates the sound of an 80-piece orchestra.

Circus World Museum
426 Water Street, Baraboo (608 356 0800). **Open** *Nov-May* 10am-4pm Mon-Sat; 11am-4pm Sun. **Admission** $5; $2.50-$4 concessions. **Credit** AmEx, Disc, MC, V.

Trips Out of Town

Talk to the buffalo at **Black Wolf Lodge**.

Steaming through the **Baraboo Hills** (*p273*).

Rick Wilcox Theater

1666 Wisconsin Dells Parkway, Wisconsin Dells (608 254 5511). **Open** varies. **Admission** $12-$21. **Credit** MC, V.

Tommy Bartlett Thrill Show

560 Wisconsin Dells Parkway, Wisconsin Dells (608 254 2525). **Open** *shows summer* 1pm, 4.30pm, 8.30pm. **Admission** $12-$19. **Credit** Disc, MC, V.

Getting there

By car

Wisconsin Dells is 188 miles (303km) north-west of Chicago. Follow I-90 from Chicago to Dells exits 92, 89, 87, 85 (the best for downtown is exit 87).

Tourist information

Wisconsin Dells Visitor & Convention Bureau

701 Superior Street, Wisconsin Dells (1-800 223 3557). **Open** 8am-5pm daily.
Stop by this downtown office to make your lodging reservations and to pick up maps, brochures and other information.

Where to stay

Black Wolf Lodge & Conference Center

I-90/94 & Highway 12, at exit 92 (1-800 559 9653/608 253 2222/fax 253 2224). **Rates** $139-$339. **Credit** MC, V.
Youngsters delight at a stuffed buffalo head that slowly moves and talks on command at this 309-room resort. The indoor waterpark includes a four-storey treehouse with more than 60 sprays and geysers; outside, there's a further four-storey, two-flume waterslide and swimming pools.

Treasure Island Waterpark Resort

1701 Wisconsin Dells Parkway, Wisconsin Dells (1-800 800 4997/608 254 8560/fax 608 253 9960). **Rates** $149-$239. **Credit** AmEx, Disc, MC, V.

This 239-room property is another Dells resort with large indoor and outdoor waterparks. Treasure Island's Bay of Dreams is a 50,000-sq-ft (4,650-sq-m) indoor water complex that includes speedy, splashy waterslides, a lazy river, a leisure pool and a fun but safe kiddy pool.

Wilderness Hotel & Golf Resort

511 E Adams Street, Wisconsin Dells (1-800 867 9453/608 253 9729/fax 608 254 4982). **Rates** $125-$209. **Credit** AmEx, Disc, MC, V.
Another mega-resort, the Wilderness also boasts an 18-hole golf course to complement its indoor and outdoor waterparks. The indoor version even claims to be the nation's largest.

Where to eat

Cheese Factory

521 Wisconsin Dells Parkway South, Lake Delton (608 253 6065). **Open** 9am-9pm Thur-Sat; 9am-3pm Sun. **Main courses** $7-$12. **Credit** AmEx, MC, V.
Housed in a handsome wood-and-brick building that was formerly a cheese factory, this fun restaurant specialises in appetising vegetarian dishes. Shakes and sundaes are available from an old-fashioned soda fountain.

Culver's

312 Broadway, Wisconsin Dells (608 253 9080). **Open** 10.30am-9pm Mon-Thur, Sun; 10.30am-10pm Fri, Sat.
Frozen custard, rich and creamy, is synonymous with Wisconsin, and this chain does it better than most. While you're at it, try and save room for a Culver burger and/or a shake.

Sand County Café

138 1st Street, Baraboo (608 356 5880). **Open** 11am-2pm, 5-9pm Tue-Sat. **Main courses** $8-$16. **Credit** MC, V.
This eaterie is housed in a large 1880s mansion and offers an eclectic mix of international and local favourites on its tempting menu. Why not try the apple ginger pork stir-fry or a spicy South-western version of the Cornish pasty and finish with one of the home-made fruit pies.

Directory

Directory

Getting Around

Arriving by air

Chicago is served by two airports: **O'Hare International** (ORD) and **Chicago Midway** (MID).

O'Hare is one of the largest and busiest airports in the world, and a suitably daunting place. All domestic flights and international departures by domestic airlines use Terminals 1, 2 and 3; non-US international airlines use Terminal 5 (except for Lufthansa departures, which leave from Terminal 1). The terminals are linked by a people-carrier system that runs 24 hours daily. Midway Airport, meanwhile, is considerably smaller, slightly closer to downtown Chicago, and mostly receives flights by lower-cost airlines.

For further information on both airports, including maps and a full list of airline contact numbers, head to: **www.cityofchicago.org/aviation**

Chicago O'Hare International Airport
I-190 West (773 686 2200).

Chicago Midway Airport
5700 S Cicero Avenue (773 838 0600).

Major airlines

In addition to the following, Chicago is served by many international carriers, including Air France, Swissair and SAS.

American Airlines
UK: 0345 789 789
US: 1-800 433 7300
website: www.aa.com

British Airways
UK: 0845 773 3377
US: 1-800 247 9297
website: www.britishairways.com

Northwest Airlines
UK: 0870 556 1000
US: 1-800 225 2525
website: www.nwa.com

United Airlines
UK: 0845 844 4777
US: 1-800 241 6522
website: www.unitedairlines.com

Virgin Atlantic
UK: 01293 747 747
US: 1-800 862 8621
website: www.virginatlantic.com

To & from O'Hare Int'l Airport

By El

The Chicago Transit Authority (CTA) provides a 24-hour service on its Blue line between O'Hare and downtown Chicago. The journey takes around 45 minutes, at least once you've found the station. At the airport, follow signs marked 'Trains to the city': pedestrian passageways link the airport's CTA station (deep under a vast car park) with the terminals. If you're still confused, pick up a map of the airport, available from stands scattered around at regular intervals. Like all CTA fares, it'll cost $1.50.

By taxi

There's a taxi rank outside the baggage reclaim area of each terminal. The fare to downtown Chicago should come to about $30 plus tip, though the traffic on I-90 can extend the usual 30-minute travel time – and the fare – at busy times. Money can be saved by partaking in the Shared Ride scheme: up to four passengers can share a cab from O'Hare to downtown

Chicago (designated by the authorities to be as far north as Fullerton Avenue, and as far south as McCormick Place) for a flat fee of $15 per person, though you may have to wait a little longer than usual.

By shuttle

Airport Express (312 454 7799) charge $17.50 single/$30 return for the journey downtown. Their booth is located in the baggage reclaim area.

By bus

Buses to outlying regions arrive at and depart from the Bus/Shuttle Center under the central car park.

To & from Midway Airport

By El

The Orange line links downtown Chicago and Midway Airport. The journey time will be around 35 minutes, and the fare will be the standard $1.50.

By shuttle

Airport Express (312 454 7799) charges $12 single/$22 return for the journey downtown. Their booth is located in the baggage reclaim area.

By taxi

The fare to downtown Chicago from Midway should be around $20 plus tip, with the ride taking 20-25 minutes. The Shared Ride scheme (*see above* **To & from O'Hare**

International Airport)
allows for a flat fee of $10
per person.

Arriving by train

Amtrak trains (1-800 872
7245/www.amtrak.com) arrive
and depart from **Union
Station** (210 S Canal Street, at
E Adams Street; 312 655 2385)
in the West Loop.

Arriving by bus

Greyhound buses (1-800 229
9424; www.greyhound.com) run
routes to Chicago from
innumerable towns and cities.
Services arrive at the **main
bus station** at 630 W Harrison
Street, at S Desplaines Street,
West Loop (312 408 5980).

Public transport in Chicago

The **Regional
Transportation Authority
(RTA)** oversees transport in
the Chicago metropolitan area.
Service is divided between the
**Chicago Transit Authority
(CTA)**, which operates buses
and elevated/subway trains in
Chicago and 38 surrounding
suburbs; the **Metra**, a
suburban rail system; and
Pace, a suburban bus system.

RTA Travel Center

*11 S Wells Street, at W Madison
Street, The Loop (312 836
7000/www.rtachicago.com).* **Open**
5am-1am daily. **Map** p305 H12.
The RTA Travel Center provides
information on Chicago's buses and
trains. Maps and timetables can also
be ordered on the above number.

CTA trains

The CTA's elevated/subway
train system – or 'El', as it is
known to just about everyone
in the city – consists of seven
colour-coded lines (Red, Blue,
Purple, Brown, Green, Orange
and Yellow) that serve vast
swathes of the Chicago area.
The service is, in the main,

extremely reliable and speedy,
if a little creaky in parts.

Most lines run every five to
15 minutes until late at night,
with both the Red and Blue
lines running around the clock
(between 1.30am and 4.30am,
Red line trains are scheduled
every 15 minutes, Blue line
trains once an hour). Care
should obviously be taken
when riding the trains late at
night. Train routes and
destinations are shown on the
platform and on the front and
side of trains. For more on
fares and ticketing, *see page
278* **CTA fares & passes**.

It's worth noting that
several stations on the El
system confusingly share the
same name: Chicago, for
example, is the name of a
station on the Red line (at
Chicago Avenue and State
Street), on the Brown and
Purple lines (the junction of
Chicago Avenue and Franklin
Street in the River North
neighbourhood) and the Blue
line (the junction of Chicago
Avenue and Milwaukee
Avenue, in the middle of
nowhere). Where such a
dilemma occurs during this
book, we've listed the line(s)
being referred to in brackets
after the station's name.

It's also worth noting that
there are plenty of El stations
in the Loop: in the area
bounded by Wells to the west,
Wacker to the north, Michigan
to the east and Van Buren to
the south – a range of six
blocks east to west, eight
blocks north to south – there
are no less than 16 El stations.
We've listed the nearest one or
two to each listed place
throughout this book, but the
chances are that if you're in the
Loop and want to get to
somewhere else in the Loop,
it'll be just as quick to walk as
it is to catch the El.

For a full map of the El
system, plus an El and bus
map for downtown Chicago,
see pages 312-13.

Chicago Transit Authority

*CTA Customer Assistance, 7th
Floor, Merchandise Mart, at N Wells
Street & E Kinzie Street, Near
North/River North (1-888 968 7282/
www.transitchicago.com).* **Open**
7am-8pm Mon-Fri; closed Sat, Sun.
Map p306 G11.

CTA buses

CTA bus stops are marked by
white and blue signs listing the
names and numbers of the
routes followed by the
destination. The same
information is shown on the
front of the buses themselves.
Most bus routes run every ten
to 15 minutes from dawn until
at least 10.30pm daily. Routes
10, 130 and 157 do not run
daily. Night buses, known as
Night Owls, run every 30
minutes on some routes and
are indicated by a picture of an
owl. In order to transfer
between buses or from bus to
El (or vice versa) you require a
transfer card (*see page 278*).

Below are some of the more
popular and/or useful routes:

22: Clark

Southbound, the 22 runs on Clark
Street between the far North Side
and Polk Street in the Loop. The
northbound route runs up Dearborn
Street from Polk Street until
Washington Square, where it joins
Clark Street and continues north.

29: State

The 29 runs up State Street from the
far South Side to Illinois Street just
north of the Chicago River, where it
turns east and heads to Navy Pier.
The return journey follows the same
route, but leaves Navy Pier along
Grand Avenue until State Street
before heading south.

36: Broadway

Southbound, the 36 runs from the far
North Side down Broadway to
Diversey Parkway, then heads south
on Clark Street before joining State
Street at Division Street and
continuing south to Polk Street in the
Loop. The northbound service begins
at Polk Street, heading up Dearborn
Street as far as Illinois Street where it
joins State Street. At Division Street,
it joins Clark Street, and at Diversey
Parkway, it joins Broadway and
continues to the far North Side.

66: Chicago

Runs east along Chicago Avenue between the far West Side and Fairbanks Court in Streeterville, whereupon it heads south on Fairbanks to Illinois Street and then east to Navy Pier. The westbound route is identical but for the fact it leaves Navy Pier along Grand Avenue instead of Fairbanks.

72: North

Runs along North Avenue between Lincoln Park and the far West Side.

151: Sheridan

Runs in a slightly circuitous fashion around parts of the Loop, taking in Union Station and then heading along Jackson Boulevard, turning north on State Street, then east on Washington Boulevard and north again on Michigan Avenue. It then joins Lake Shore Drive at Oak Street, passing directly through Lincoln Park (stopping by the Zoo) and eventually picking up Sheridan Road at Diversey Parkway. After turning left on Byron Street, it rejoins Sheridan Road north of Wrigley Field and continues to the far North Side.

CTA fares & passes

El stations do not have manned ticket booths. In order to enter the CTA system, passengers must buy a Transit Card from a machine situated by the turnstiles. This card is then swiped through a slot on the turnstile – or through the fare box on a bus – to permit travel, with the relevant fare deducted automatically.

Transit Cards are valid on CTA buses and El trains. They can be purchased from machines at CTA stations for as little as $1.50 (the standard fare for a ride on the El or bus services) and recharged up to a maximum value of $100 as required: the customer decides how much they want to spend. It's a good idea to pay more than the minimum when you buy, for two reasons. Firstly, if you take up to two El or bus journeys within two hours of taking your initial ride, you will only be billed a transfer fee of 30¢ or 15¢ for concessions (though when you're simply changing from one line to

another at the same station, you won't be billed a transfer fee). And secondly, each $10 spent equates to $11 of travel; each $20 to $22 of travel, etc.

The correct amount for each journey is deducted automatically as the card passes through the turnstile or fare box. The card can be shared by up to seven people at once as long as it is inserted the correct number of times. Ready-charged cards can be purchased for $10 or $20 from currency exchanges, certain shops or from the internet.

A **single CTA fare** costs $1.50, or 75¢ for children aged seven to 11. Senior citizens and disabled travellers can also apply for reduced fares by phone (312 836 7000). Children under six travel for free if accompanied by a fare-paying adult. If you're buying a single fare only, be sure to ask for a transfer if you need one.

The main alternative to a Transit Card is a CTA **Visitor Pass**, which allows unlimited travel on CTA buses and trains for the designated number of days. The one-day pass is known, rather quaintly, as a **Fun Pass**, and costs $5. Other Visitor Passes are available for two ($9), three ($12) and five ($18) days. They are available from Visitors' Centres, Union Station, O'Hare and Midway Airports, some CTA stations, Hot Tix booths and some museums. They can also be booked in advance by phone (1-888 968 7282) or from the CTA's informative website (www.transitchicago.com). CTA visitor passes also entitle the bearer to discounts at selected museums and theatres.

Metra rail

The Metra is a 12-line commuter rail system that serves 245 stations in north-east Illinois, as well as parts of Indiana. The Metra's Chicago termini are **LaSalle Street**

Station (414 S LaSalle Street, at E Congress Parkway, The Loop); **Randolph Street Station** (E Randolph Street, at N Michigan Avenue, The Loop); the **Richard B Ogilvie Transportation Center** (500 W Madison Street, at S Canal Street); and **Union Station** (*see page 277*). Metra offers a variety of fares, from simple single-route fares to ten-route tickets – which save 15 per cent on the equivalent fares if purchased separately – and a $5 pass for unlimited travel on Saturdays and Sundays.

Metra

Metra Passenger Services, 547 W Jackson Boulevard, at S Clinton Street, The Loop (312 322 6777/ www.metrarail.com). **Open** 8am-5pm daily. **Map** p305 G12.

Pace

Pace buses serve Chicago's outlying suburbs. **Single fare** prices vary according to the route from $1.10 (local fare) to $1.25 (regular fare) to $2.75 (premium fare). Reduced price tickets are available for children under 12, and others on application to the RTA. The CTA Transit Card (*see above*) is valid on Pace routes. Pace also offers a number of reduced rate passes including the **10-ride ticket**, which offers 11 rides for the price of ten and can be shared by multiple travellers.

Pace

Pace Passenger Services (847 364 7223/www.pacebus.com). **Open** 8am-5pm Mon-Fri; closed Sat, Sun.

Taxis

Taxis are prevalent in the Loop and surrounding areas and can be hailed from the street. Further out, you'd be better off booking a taxi by telephoning one of the major cab companies on the numbers below.

Meters start at $1.60, then increase $1.40 for every mile, or 20¢ for every 45 seconds of waiting time. Additional

Directory

passengers over the age of 12 and under the age of 65 are charged 50¢. There is no charge for baggage. Tipping is optional, but usually expected. For longer journeys, drivers may be willing to charge a flat fee, which should be agreed in advance. The Shared Ride scheme offers flat rates per person to and from the airports and from McCormick Place ($5 per person) when more than one person is travelling in the cab (*see page 276*).

Registered taxis in Chicago are usually safe and reliable. However, if you have a complaint, contact the **Department of Consumer Services** (312 744 9400), who will issue you with a complaint form.

Cab companies

Checker Cabs 312 243 2537.
Flash Cabs 773 561 1444.
Jiffy Cab Company 773 487 9000.
Yellow Cabs 312 829 4222.

Driving

As in most major cities, driving in Chicago is not recommended, and shouldn't be undertaken by those with faint hearts. The city's grid system makes it relatively easy to negotiate and cars can prove useful if you're planning on spending time out in the suburbs. But, otherwise, it's not really worth the hassle to hire a car for the duration of your stay. If you're arriving in the city in your own car, then you're best off leaving it

parked at your hotel (though many charge a prohibitive amount for parking) and using the CTA or cabs.

Car rental

In most cases, you'll need to be 25 or over to rent a car – some firms, though, will rent to over-21s – and a credit card is essential. Rental rates should include insurance and unlimited mileage but will be subject to a special city and state tax of 18 per cent. Remember to fill the car up with petrol before returning it so as not to incur refuelling charges.

The best time to rent is at the weekends when there are fewer business travellers in the city. All the major companies have outlets at O'Hare and, in most cases, in the city itself and at Midway.

Rental companies

Alamo 1-800 327 9633
http://alamo.com
Avis 1-800 831 2847
http://avis.com
Budget 1-800 686 6800
http://budget.com
Dollar 1-800 800 4000
http://dollar.com
Hertz 1-800 654 3131
www.hertz.com
National 1-800 227 7368
www.nationalcar.com
Thrifty 1-800 367 2277
http://thrifty.com

Parking

Parking in Chicago is prohibitively expensive. Car parks charge upwards of $15

per day and hotel garages can cost even more. Street parking is limited and most of it is controlled by meters. Be careful not to park in a towing area otherwise you could end up paying not only a parking fine, but also the cost of retrieving your car from the pound. If you do get towed for illegal parking, call the Chicago Police Department (312 744 6000).

Cycling

For general information on cycling in Chicago and details of hiring bikes, *see page 228*. The main guidelines for cycling in Chicago include wearing a protective helmet at all times and locking your bike as securely as possible. The CTA allows bicycles on trains on Saturdays and Sundays during the summer from Memorial Day Weekend (late May) until Labor Day (first Mon in Sept). Riders under 18 must be accompanied by an adult.

Boat services

For sightseeing cruises on the Chicago River and Lake Michigan, *see page 82* **Tours**.

Shoreline Water Taxi

(information 312 222 9328/ www.shorelinesightseeing.com). CTA Grand. **Open** *Memorial Day-Labor Day* 10am-6pm daily. **Tickets** *single* $6; $3-$5 concessions; *all-day pass* $12; $6-$10 concessions. **Map** p306 K10. Fast and frequent connections between Navy Pier and the Shedd Aquarium or Sears Tower.

Resources A-Z

Business

Give the city of Chicago credit: back in the bad old days before the city attracted a great many tourists, it found itself a niche and it has stuck with it ever since. That niche, of course, is conventions. And what started

off as a relatively humble enterprise has spiralled into a behemoth: Chicago now hosts an astonishing four million-plus visitors each year whose sole purpose for being in Chicago is to attend a trade fair or convention. Out of control? Not quite.

But it sure as hell feels like it sometimes.

The bulk of the convention action (if those two words are not mutually exclusive) occurs down at **McCormick Place**. You may have been told McCormick Place is big. Huge, even. Well, that's not even

Major conventions

National Restaurant Hotel-Motel Show 20-23 May 2000 *105,000 delegates*
NPE Plastics Expo 19-23 June 2000 *75,000 delegates*
International Hardware Week 13-16 August 2000 *70,000 delegates*
International Manufacturing Technology Show 6-14 September 2000 *125,000 delegates*
Graph Expo & Converting Expo 24-27 September 2000 *45,000 delegates*
Pack Expo 5-9 November 2000 *80,000 delegates*
Radiological Society Scientific Assembly 26 November-1 December 2000 *61,000 delegates*
International Housewares Show 14-17 January 2001 *60,000 delegates*
Promat 12-15 February 2001 *40,000 delegates*
National Manufacturing Week 5-8 March 2001 *60,000 delegates*
National Restaurant Hotel-Motel Show 19-22 May 2001 *105,000 delegates*
World's Trade Fair 18-20 June 2001 *60,000 delegates*
International Hardware Week 12-15 August 2001 *72,000 delegates*
Print & Converting Expo 6-13 September 2001 *100,000 delegates*
Radiological Society Scientific Assembly 25-30 November 2001 *60,000 delegates*
International Housewares Show 13-16 January 2002 *65,000 delegates*
National Manufacturing Week 18-21 March 2002 *61,000 delegates*
Kitchen & Bath Industry Annual Show 5-7 April 2002 *40,000 delegates*
Spring & Windows World 22-25 April 2002 *86,000 delegates*

close. It's practically its own planet. Try this on for size: 2.2 million square feet of exhibition space, a further 170,000 square feet of banquet, ballroom and meeting room space, all spread over three separate buildings (named North, South and East) that cover a total of 27 acres.

Once you get there, it'll take you five minutes short of forever to find where you're supposed to be. And once you've got where you're supposed to be, don't expect to find your way out in a hurry. Bring a compass, tinned goods and other essential supplies, and – as a precaution – a sleeping bag. However, the facilities are as dazzlingly modern as you could hope to find, though please be warned that there is absolutely nothing to do within several blocks of the centre. In for a penny, in for the proverbial pound.

The other main convention centre in Chicago is a relatively new operation, and sits proudly on Navy Pier. There are a mere 170,000 square feet of exhibition space here in **Festival Hall**, and it's for

that reason that conventions held here tend to be smaller than those at McCormick. However, the facilities are equally modern, while Navy Pier itself boasts plenty of attractions and eateries at which you can while away your lunch hour.

Further out – close to O'Hare International Airport, which explains the plethora of business-oriented hotels in the area – is yet another monster meeting place. The **Rosemont Convention Center** benefits from its location space-wise – there are 600,000 square feet of exhibition space here – but also suffers for it: while McCormick is slightly set apart from the downtown action, Rosemont is a long way away from it.

In addition, conventions and trade fairs are held at other locations, such as Orchestra Hall at the Symphony Center, Merchandise Mart and an array of downtown hotels.

The majority of hotels in downtown Chicago offer some form of business facilities, though the **Chicago Hilton & Towers** (*see page 101*), the

Chicago Marriott (*see page 106*) and the **Hyatt Regency** (*see page 109*; there's also a Hyatt Regency at McCormick Place itself) are particularly geared towards business travellers. If you're here on business, you may well find that your hotel offers all the business services you require. However, it's a good idea to always call ahead and check if you're after something specific. We've also listed a short selection of other business services below.

Business libraries

Harold Washington Public Library

Business/Science/Technology Division, 400 S State Street, at W Van Buren Street, The Loop (312 747 4400/www.chipublib.org). CTA Library. **Open** 9am-7pm Mon; 11am-7pm Tue, Thur; 9am-5pm Wed, Fri, Sat; 1-5pm Sun. **Map** p305 H13.

Loyola Graduate Business School

25 E Pearson Street, at N State Street, Gold Coast (312 915 6625). CTA Chicago (Red). **Open** 8am-10pm Mon-Thur; 8am-6pm Fri; 10am-6pm Sat; noon-6pm Sun. **Map** p306 H9. Non-Loyola students can't check anything out from this library.

Directory

Convention centres

McCormick Place Convention Complex

2301 S Lake Shore Drive, at E 23rd Street, South Side (312 791 7000/ www.mccormickplace.com). Metra 23rd Street.

Festival Hall

Navy Pier, 600 E Grand Avenue, at Lake Michigan, Near North/ Streeterville (312 595 5300). CTA Grand/bus 65, 66. **Map** p306 K10.

Rosemont Convention Center

5555 N River Road (near O'Hare Airport, off I-190), Rosemont (847 692 2220).

Courier services

Apex Courier

448 N Halsted Street, at W Grand Avenue, West Side (312 666 4400). CTA Clinton (Green). **Open** 24 hours daily. **Credit** AmEx, MC, V.

Arrow Messenger Service

1322 W Walton Street, at N Milwaukee Avenue, West Side (773 489 6688). CTA Chicago (Blue). **Open** 24 hours daily. **Credit** AmEx, MC, V.

Federal Express

233 S Wacker Drive, at W Adams Street, The Loop (1-800 463 3339). CTA Quincy. **Open** 9am-7pm Mon-Fri. **Credit** AmEx, Disc, MC, V. **Map** p395 G12.

United Parcel Service

1500 S Jefferson Street, at W 15th Street, West Side (1-800 742 5877). CTA Roosevelt/State or Roosevelt/ Wabash. **Open** 8am-6pm Mon-Fri. **Credit** AmEx, DC, MC, V. **Map** p304 G15.

Office services

Acme

218 S. Wabash Avenue, at E Adams Street, The Loop (312 922 1155). CTA Adams or Jackson (Red). **Open** 8am-5pm Mon-Fri. **Credit** MC, V. **Map** p305 H12.
Offers on demand digital printing, layout and desktop design, laminating, photo reproductions, mounting and drafting supplies.

Alphagraphics

645 N Michigan Avenue, at E Erie Street, Near North/Magnificent Mile (312 266 9266). CTA Chicago (Red).
Open 8am-9pm Mon-Thur; 8am-6pm Fri; 9am-2pm Sat. **Credit** AmEx, DC, Disc, MC, V. **Map** p306 J10.
Copying central, basically.
Branch: 208 S LaSalle Street, at E Adams Street, The Loop (312 368 4507).

Kinko's

55 E Monroe Street, at S Dearborn Street, The Loop (312 701 0730). CTA Monroe (Blue, Red). **Open** 24 hours daily. **Rates** computer hire $12/hour (PC); $24/hour (Mac). **Credit** AmEx, DC, Disc, MC, V. **Map** p305 H12.
All the usual Kinko's services.
Branches: 1201 N Dearborn Street, at W Division Street, Gold Coast (312 640 6100); 444 N Wells Street, at W Illinois Street, Near North/River North (312 670 4460); and throughout the city.

Sir Speedy

226 E Ontario Street, at N St Clair Street, Near North/Streeterville (312 280 4781). CTA Grand. **Open** 8.30am-5.30pm Mon-Fri. **Credit** AmEx. **Map** p306 J10.
Printing and copying services.

Secretarial services

Alliance Business Centers

225 W Washington Boulevard, at N Franklin Street, The Loop (312 419 7150). CTA Washington (Brown/ Orange/Purple). **Open** 8.30am-5pm Mon-Fri. **Credit** AmEx, DC, V. **Map** p305 G12.
Full office support services.
Branch: 203 N LaSalle Street, at W Lake Street, The Loop (312 346 2030).

Translation services

Inligua

200 W Madison Street, at N Wells Street, The Loop (312 641 0488). CTA Washington (Brown/Orange/ Purple). **Open** 8am-7.30pm Mon-Fri. **Credit** MC, V. **Map** p305 H12.

TransPerfect Translations

333 W Wacker Drive, at W Lake Street, The Loop (312 444 2044). CTA Washington (Brown/ Orange/Purple). **Open** 9am-5pm Mon-Fri. **Credit** AmEx, MC, V. **Map** p305 G11.

Climate

Weather in Chicago is, to put it mildy, changeable. Summer can be pleasant, with temperatures in June, July and August regularly in the 80s. However, it also rains a fair amount during this time, and can get uncomfortably humid.

Winter, however, is a different story: though recent winters have had their mild moments, January's average temperature is below freezing, and the city gets close to 40 inches of snow a year. And all year round, there's the wind to contend with. In short, then, whatever the season, prepare for anything.

Consulates

All foreign embassies are located in Washington, DC, although many countries also have a consulate or consulate general in Chicago; the official Chicago city website (**www.ci.chi.il.us**) has a complete list.

Canadian Consulate General

Suite 2400, 180 N Stetson Avenue, at E Lake Street, The Loop (312 616 1860). CTA Lake or State. **Open** 8.30am-4.30pm Mon-Fri. **Map** p305 J11.

Republic of Ireland Consulate

Suite 911, Wrigley Building, 400 N Michigan Avenue, at E Hubbard Street, Near North/Magnificent Mile (312 337 1868). CTA Grand. **Open** 10am-noon, 2-4pm Mon-Fri. **Map** p306 J11.

United Kingdom Consulate General

Suite 1300, Wrigley Building, 400 N Michigan Avenue, at E Hubbard Street, Near North/Magnificent Mile (312 346 1810/fax 312 464 0661). CTA Grand. **Open** 8.30am-5.30pm Mon-Fri. **Map** p306 J11.

Customs & immigration

During your flight, you will be handed an immigration form and a customs declaration form to be presented when you land at the airport. Expect to explain the nature of your visit (business and/or pleasure). If

Directory

you don't have a return ticket and are planning a long visit, you will be questioned closely about your intentions while in the country. For more details, *see page 290* **Visas**.

US customs regulations allow foreign visitors to import the following, duty-free: 200 cigarettes or 50 cigars (not Cuban; over-18s only) or 2kg of smoking tobacco; one litre (1.05 US quart) of wine or spirits (over-21s only); and up to $100 in gifts ($400 for returning Americans). Note that as of 2000 the importation of previously exported US-made cigarettes and other tobacco products is banned. You can take up to $10,000 in cash, travellers' cheques or endorsed bank drafts in or out of the country tax-free. Amounts above that must be declared, or you risk forfeiting the lot. You may also need to declare any foodstuffs or plants: many are prohibited entirely; plants, plant products, fruits and vegetables must be declared and canned or processed items are restricted. Check with the US Customs Service in Washington (202 927 6724; www.customs.gov/travel/travel.htm) to be sure.

UK Customs & Excise allows returning travellers to bring in £145 worth of gifts and goods and an unlimited amount of money, as long as you can prove it's yours.

Disabled visitors

While Chicago is reasonably accessible to disabled visitors (a lot of the buses have lifts, there are elevators on elevated CTA platforms and the sidewalks have ramps), it is wise to call ahead to check accessibility.

Accessible Journeys
(1-800 846 4537/
www.disabilitytravel.com).
An organisation dedicated to providing safe and accessible travel opportunities for disabled people. It has offices around the world and publishes an electronic newsletter.

Mayor's Office for People with Disabilities
(312 744 7050/hearing impaired 312 744 4964).
Good source of general information about all aspects of disabled and handicapped access in the city. Best to call them before you come to town.

Getting around

303 Medi Cab
847 259 5555.
Decent way of getting around in handicapped-accessible vehicles with trained personnel. Rates are $2.40 for the first mile, then 20¢ for each additional 1/8 mile.

RTA Travel Center
Ground Floor, 11 S Wells Street, at W Madison Street, The Loop (312 836 7000/hearing impaired 312 836 4949). **Open** 5am-1am daily.
Map p305 H12.
The RTA can provide information on which public train platforms and buses are wheelchair accessible.

Taxi Access Program
7th Floor, Merchandise Mart, at N Wells Street & E Kinzie Street, Near North/River North (312 432 7025/hearing impaired 432 7116). CTA Merchandise Mart. **Open** 7am-6pm Mon-Fri. **Map** p306 J11.
This is a programme run by the city and the CTA that gives some disabled people discounted taxi ride fares. Contact the centre two or three weeks before arriving in the city. If you qualify, you can buy vouchers worth up to $10 each for about $1.50 for discounted rides with participating taxi companies.

Electricity

Rather than the 220-240V, 50-cycle AC used in Europe, Chicago (and the US as a whole) uses a 110-120V, 60-cycle AC voltage. Except for dual-voltage, flat-pin plug shavers, most foreign visitors will need to run any small appliances brought with them via an adaptor, available at airport shops.

Bear in mind, too, that most US videos and TVs use a different frequency from those in Europe: you will not be able to play back camcorder footage during your trip. However, you can buy and use blank tapes.

Emergencies

If it's an absolute emergency, call **911** (ambulance, police or fire). However, anything less than absolutely critical should rather be directed to the following numbers:
Chicago Police Department
312 746 6000.
Chicago Fire Department
312 744 6666.
FBI
312 431 1333.
Illinois State Police – Chicago District 847 294 4400.
Illinois Poison Control
1-800 942 5969/TDD 312 942 2214.

Gay

Health

Howard Brown Health Center
4025 N Sheridan Road, at W Irving Park Road, Far North (773 388 1600/www.howardbrown.org). CTA Sheridan. **Open** 8.30am-7.30pm Mon-Thur; 8.30am-4.30pm Fri; closed Sat, Sun.
The centre provides comprehensive health services for the gay community, including primary care, anonymous HIV testing, support groups and research.

North Side Prevention Program
3651 N Halsted Street, at W Waveland Avenue, Lake View/Wrigleyville (773 871 3300). CTA Addison (Red). **Open** call ahead.
Map p309 F1.
Pop in to this Howard Brown-affiliated centre and the goofy staff might just demonstrate the strength of their free condoms by blowing them up and pulling them over their heads. You'll walk out loaded up with a variety of rubbers, lube samples and educational literature, though you may also run into the staff on your travels, as they often pop into local bars, bathhouses and the like to spread the word.

Resources

Chicago Area Gay & Lesbian Chamber of Commerce
3713 N Halsted Street, at W Waveland Street, Lake View (1-888 452 4262/773 871 4190/www.glchamber.org. **Open** 11am-

6pm Mon-Sat; 11am-3pm Sun.
Map p309 F1.
A great place to start a homo
exploration in Chicago.

Gerber-Hart Library
*1127 W Granville Avenue, at N
Broadway, Far North (773 381
8030). CTA Granville.* **Open**
6-9pm Wed, Thur; noon-4pm Fri-Sun;
closed Mon, Tue. **Admission** free;
annual membership $35. **Credit**
AmEx, MC, V.
The Midwest's largest lesbigay
library, archive and resource centre.
Membership is required to check
out books, but anyone is welcome
to browse.

Horizons Community Services
*961 W Montana Street, at N
Sheffield Avenue, Lake View
(773 929 4357). CTA Fullerton.*
Open 6-10pm Mon-Fri; closed Sat,
Sun. **Map** p305 E5.
Education and support groups
provided in a wonderful
environment. A great spot for gay
youths to hang out and feel accepted.

Health

See also above **Emergencies** .

Contraception, abortion & STDs

Planned Parenthood
*10th Floor, 14 E Jackson Boulevard, at
N State Street, The Loop (312 427
2270/www.plannedparenthood.org).
CTA Jackson.* **Open** 9am-6pm Mon,
Thur; 8am-5pm Tue; 10am-7pm Wed;
8am-1pm Fri; 9.30am-2pm Sat; closed
Sun. **Map** p305 H13.
A non-profit organisation that can
supply contraception, treat STDs and
perform abortions.
Branches: 1200 N LaSalle Street,
at W Division Street, Gold Coast
(312 266 1033); 1152 N Milwaukee
Avenue, at W Division Street, West
Side (773 252 2240).

Clinics & hospitals

There is no national health care
system in the United States, so
if you are treated in a health
care facility you will be
required to either show proof of
insurance or pay in full. If
possible, get hold of your
insurance company first and it
will let you know which
hospital you should go to.
Make sure that you have ID and

insurance details on you at all
times, so that in case of an
emergency, you have them at
the ready. Waits in the
emergency room tend to be long
and prices are high, so don't
take a trip there unnecessarily.
   On the plus side, Chicago is
home to several world-class
hospitals (though they're not
quite as exciting as they look
on *ER* and *Chicago Hope*) and
you're more or less guaranteed
to receive the best possible
service from the local staff.
   For general information call
Advocate Health (1-800 323
8622), a central phone number
that can connect you to eight
hospitals in the metropolitan
area. Emergency rooms at the
following hospitals are open 24
hours daily.

Children's Memorial Hospital
*700 W Fullerton Avenue, at N
Lincoln Avenue, Lincoln Park
(773 880 4000/
www.childrensmemorial.org).
CTA Fullerton.* **Map** p308 F5.
A full range of pediatric speciality
services.

Cook County Hospital
*1835 W Harrison Street, at S Wood
Street, West Side (312 633 6000).
CTA Medical Center.*

Northwestern Memorial Hospital
*250 E Superior Street, at N Fairbanks
Court, Near North/River North (312
908 2000/www.nmh.org). CTA
Chicago (Red).* **Map** p306 J10.
New, state-of-the-art facility, with
luxury hotel-like furniture, soaring
atriums and food so good that non-
sick locals have been known to stop
in for a bite.

Rush-Presbyterian-St Luke's Medical Center
*1653 W Congress Parkway, at S
Ashland Avenue, West Side (312 942
5000/www.rush.edu). CTA Medical
Center/7, 26 buses.*
Probably the most technologically
advanced hospital in the city and one
of the most renowned in the world.

University of Chicago Hospital
*5841 S Maryland Avenue, at E 58th
Street, Hyde Park (773 702
1000/www.uchospitals.edu). Metra
59th Street.*

Dentists

Chicago Dental
312 726 4321.
Dental referrals.

Pharmacies

The following pharmacies are
open 24 hours; call the 1-800
and 1-888 numbers for
information on other 24-hour
locations in Chicago.

Osco
*3101 N Clark Street, at W Barry
Avenue, Lake View (1-888 443
5701/773 477 1967). CTA Belmont.*
Open 24hrs daily. **Credit** AmEx,
Disc, MC, V. **Map** p309 F3.

Walgreens
*757 N Michigan Avenue, at E
Chicago Avenue, Near North/
Magnificent Mile (1-800 925
4733/312 664 8686). CTA Chicago
(Red).* **Open** 24hrs daily. **Credit**
AmEx, Disc, MC, V. **Map** p304 J10.

Helplines

Alcoholics Anonymous
312 346 1475.

Illinois AIDS/HIV & STD Hotline
1-800 243 2437.

Narcotics Anonymous
708 848 4884.

Insurance

Non-nationals should arrange
baggage, trip-cancellation and
medical insurance before they
leave home. Medical centres
will ask for details of your
insurance company and your
policy number if you require
treatment; keep this
information with you.

Internet access

Chicago has few real
cybercafés but dozens of
places offering free Internet
access. One of the main
providers of Internet access
is the **Chicago Public
Library**, which has numerous
branches throughout the city

Directory

(*see below* **Libraries**). Each offers 30 minutes of free access, although specific facilities vary from branch to branch and many are a bit out of the way for most travellers. Point your browser to **www.chipublib.org** for a complete listing of locations, with phone numbers, hours of operation and directions.

Screenz

2717 N Clark Street, at W Diversey Parkway, Lake View (773 348 9300/www.screenz.com). CTA Diversey-Brown. **Open** 9am-midnight Mon-Thur, Sun; 9am-1am Fri, Sat. **Terminals** 42. **Rates** $9.60 per hour. **Credit** AmEx, Disc, MC, V. **Map** p308 F4.
This is the only notable cybercafé in the city. Browsing rates are reasonable – though you will have to buy a $10 card to get started and then top it up with cash – and though it gouges you a bit on printing fees at 30¢ per page, there are 42 terminals, so there's rarely a wait.

Libraries

In addition to the **Harold Washington Library Center** in the Loop, branches of the Chicago Public Library include the **Lincoln Park Library** (1150 W Fullerton Avenue, at N Racine Avenue, Lincoln Park; 312 744 1926); **Near North Library** (310 W Division Street, at N Wells Street, Gold Coast; 312 744 0991) and the **John Merlo Library** (644 W Belmont Avenue, at Broadway, Lake View; 312 744 1139). All are open from 9am to 9pm Monday to Thursday and from 9am to 5pm on Friday and Saturday.

Harold Washington Library Center

400 S State Street, at W Congress Parkway, The Loop (312 747 4999/www.chipublib.org). CTA Library. **Open** 9am-7pm Mon, Tue; 11am-7pm Wed; 9am-5pm Thur; 11am-7pm Fri, Sat; 1-5pm Sun. **Map** p305 H13.
Located in a state-of-the-art building on the southern edge of the Loop, the main branch of the Chicago Public Library is the second largest in the world. It houses two million volumes, plus an auditorium theatre, the

Chicago Blues Archives and the Jazz, Blues and Gospel Hall of Fame. There are also 30 terminals available for free Internet access, though you'll often have to wait in line to use one and the 30-minute time limit is strictly enforced.

Liquor laws

The legal drinking age in Chicago is 21. It is against Illinois law to sell or distribute alcoholic beverages to individuals under 21 years of age. Even if you're over 21, you'll be carded regularly by bar staff if there's even the remotest possibility that you're under 21. Always carry a photo ID that gives your age and, preferably, date of birth.

Lost property

If you lose something on a bus or train, call the CTA's lost and found department. It's divided into numerous different regions, depending on the train or bus line you were using when you lost the item.

Bus

For items left on a bus, call 312 664 7200 or 312 744 2900 during business hours and ask for 'lost and found'.

El

The telephone lines are open 6am to 7pm from Monday to Saturday.
Blue 773 686 0785.
Purple/Red/Yellow 773 262 4163.
Brown 773 539 3434.
Green 708 366 0083.
Orange 773 581 9281.

Taxi

If you lose something in a cab, call the city's **Department of Consumer Services Lost & Found Division** (312 744 2900).

Money

Each dollar ($) is divided into 100 cents (¢). Coins range from copper pennies (1¢) to silver nickels (5¢), dimes (10¢) and quarters (25¢), plus rarer half-dollar (50¢) and one dollar coins. A new 'golden' $1 coin was launched in early 2000.
Currency notes come in six denominations: $1, $5, $10,

$20, $50 and $100, though the $100 is not accepted by all businesses.

ATMs

Automated Teller Machines (ATMs) or cashpoints are easy to find. Most machines will accept American Express, MasterCard and Visa credit cards and selected debit cards provided you know your Personal Identification Number (PIN), but you will be charged interest for drawing out cash. Check with your credit card company or bank for details of charges before leaving home.
If you want to find out the location of the nearest ATM, phone **Plus ATM Location Service** (1-800 843 7587) and follow the recorded instruction, or try **Cirrus** (1-800 424 7787).

Banks

American National Bank

120 S LaSalle Street, at W Monroe Street, The Loop (312 661 5000). CTA Quincy or Monroe (Blue). **Open** 8.30am-4pm Mon-Fri; closed Sat, Sun. **Map** p305 H12.

Bank of America

231 S LaSalle Street, at W Adams Street, The Loop (312 828 2345). CTA Quincy. **Open** 8.30am-4pm Mon-Fri; closed Sat, Sun. **Map** p305 H12.

Citibank

69 W Washington Boulevard, at N Dearborn Street, The Loop (312 263 6660). **Open** *counter service* 8.30am-4.30pm Mon-Fri; closed Sat, Sun; *telephone enquiries* 24hrs daily. **Map** p305 H12.

First Chicago

35 W Wacker Drive, at N Dearborn Street, The Loop (312 732 1000). CTA Clark. **Open** 8am-5pm Mon-Fri. **Map** p305 H11.

Bureaux de change

A word of warning: stores that bill themselves as currency exchanges in Chicago will not help you exchange your currency. Currency exchanges

Websites

Bars Online Chicago
www.barsonline.com/chicago
A handy portal in its own right, this site collects the surprisingly wide array of Chicago nightspots that have an Internet presence. In addition to bar locations, photographs and assorted other oddities (click on the Monkey Bar for an interesting example), the best feature on this site is the guide to college and pro football bars, which explains where fans congregate to root for their alma mater or hometown team.

Chicago Metromix
www.metromix.com
Metromix is the *Chicago Tribune*'s web-based entertainment guide and the best Chicago resource on the Internet. Part of the reason for its excellence is the presence of the *Trib*'s arts writers, who are infinitely better that most net scribes. Reviews also often appear in Metromix before they show up in the paper. What really makes this site so valuable, however, is its full use of the Internet's potential. Dependable reviews of practically every nightclub, bar and restaurant in the city are easy to find, while concert and museum listings are available and ticket bookings can be handled online. A must-visit.

Chicago Reader
www.chicagoreader.com
The *Reader*'s website doesn't offer too much of the weekly newspaper's media and arts coverage. Locally, it's used mainly for apartment-hunting: the *Reader*'s apartment listings go online on Tuesday evening, two days before it hits the streets. Best of all is the Restaurant Finder, which allows you to search for eateries by neighbourhood, cuisine, price and distance from more than 200 theatres, clubs, cinemas and buildings.

Chicago Tribune
www.chicagotribune.com
The city's flagship newspaper also boasts its best news website. In recent years, the *Trib* has poured money into its web operations (which include **Metromix** and **Digital City Chicago**) and the results have more than justified the investment. This website has won numerous national awards and remains on the cutting edge of Internet news: most of the regular paper's content is posted online, along with up-to-the-minute news and sports.

City of Chicago
www.ci.chi.il.us
The city itself operates a homepage that's surprisingly helpful and easy-to-navigate. It includes a seasonal guide to Chicago festivals, a downloadable interactive city map, handy links to O'Hare and Midway airports and a list of special events. If you can get past the cloying tone of civic pride, click on the 'Fun and Sundry Facts' section, where you'll learn that Chicago has the only river in the world that runs backwards (the Chicago River's flow was reversed by engineers in 1900 for sanitary purposes).

CTA
www.transitchicago.com
Everything you ever wanted to know about the Chicago Transit Authority, including downloadable system maps (in PDF format), details of fares and passes and information on timetables for trains and buses.

Digital City Chicago
www.chicago.digitalcity.com
Part of the *Chicago Tribune*'s comprehensive web effort, Digital City Chicago is sort of a clearing house for links and information, with lightweight columnists, entertainment and sports features and plenty of links to other *Trib* sites. Its purpose is never made exactly clear, but at least it's easy to navigate.

4Chicago
www.4chicago.com
Like any web portal, this one clearly wants you to buy, buy, buy. But it's better than most because, in addition to the countless come-ons, it posts a thorough Chicago guide to everything you can think of on its main page.

Newcity
www.newcitychicago.com
An online version of the weekly freesheet, with plenty of sparky comment and listings content to get your teeth into. There's also a free web-based email service on the site.

Yahoo!
chi.yahoo.com
A fine directory of Chicago information and links, including direct links to the online *Yellow Pages* and Mapquest's online maps of the city, terrifically useful for finding cross-streets and exact locations of addresses.

Directory

in Chicago are basically cheque-cashing services and don't accept or change foreign currency. To exchange your foreign currency for US dollars, try one of the banks on page 284 or the following bureaux de change.

American Express

625 N Michigan Avenue, at E Ohio Street, Near North/Magnificent Mile (312 435 2570). CTA Chicago (Red). **Open** 8.30am-6pm Mon-Fri; 9am-5pm Sat. **Map** p306 J10.
Branch: 122 S Michigan Avenue, at E Adams Street, The Loop (312 435 2595). CTA Adams.

Thomas Cook

9 S LaSalle Street, at W Madison Street, The Loop (312 649 0288). CTA Monroe (Blue, Red). **Open** 9am-5.30pm Mon-Fri. **Map** p305 H12.

Credit cards

Most establishments in Chicago, whether they be restaurants, shops or theatres, will take at least one and usually more credit cards (this is the US, after all). The most widely accepted cards, in order, are Visa, Mastercard, American Express, Discover and Diners Club. The following is a list of numbers to call if you lose your credit cards and/or travellers' cheques:

American Express
1-800 528 4800.
AmEx travellers' cheques
1-800 221 7282.
Diners Club 1-800 234 6377.
Discover 1-800 347 2683.
Mastercard 1-800 307 7309.
Thomas Cook travellers' cheques 1-800 223 7373.
Visa 1-800 336 8472.

Tax

Visitors from, say, the UK may wonder why, when they take an item to the counter in a shop, they get charged for more than the price listed for the product. Don't worry: they're not trying to rip you off (well, probably not, anyway). It's simply that unlike in the UK, sales tax is not included in the price listed and is only added at the till, so be sure to

adjust your calculations accordingly before you find yourself caught short of cash at the counter.

In Chicago, sales tax on the vast majority of goods is 8.75 per cent. The main exceptions are newspapers (tax-free) and central restaurants (9.75 per cent). For hotel rooms and services, though, tax rises to a nasty 14.9 per cent, while car rental is billed at a tax rate of 18 per cent.

Travellers' cheques

The majority of establishments in Chicago do accept travellers' cheques, including restaurants, bars, shops and hotels.

Opening hours

Listed below are some general guidelines on opening hours. However, the key word here is 'guidelines': hours are extremely variable in all cases. If you're after the opening hours for a specific establishment, see the chapter in question.

Banks 8.30am-4pm Mon-Fri.
Bars 11am-2am daily.
Businesses 9am-5pm Mon-Fri.
Convenience stores 9am-11pm daily; many stores open 24hrs.
Post offices 8am-5pm Mon-Fri, plus Sat am.
Shops 10am-6pm Mon-Sat; some stores open shorter hours Sun.

Postal services

Post office opening hours in Chicago are usually 8am to 5pm Monday to Friday, with many branches also open on Saturday mornings. The city's main post office is open 24 hours.

If you have no fixed address while travelling and want to receive post when you are away, you can have it sent poste restante 'c/o General Delivery' to any post office with a zip code. You will need proof of identity (passport) in order to collect it.

Stamps for standard letters weighing up to 1 ounce cost 33¢ within the US, 55¢ to Canada and $1 to all other countries. Post cards cost 22¢ (domestic) or 55¢ (international). US mailboxes are red, white and blue with the US Mail bald eagle logo on the front and side. Due to increases in terrorism, mailings exceeding a maximum weight must be taken directly to a post office counter employee. There is usually a schedule of pick-ups and a list of restrictions inside the lid. Make sure you don't put mail into FedEx or other couriers' boxes.

For more information on the **US Postal Service**, head to www.usps.com.

Main Post Office

433 W Harrison Street, at S Canal Street, Chicago, IL 60607 (312 654 3895). CTA Clinton (Blue). **Open** 24hrs daily. **Map** p305 G13.

Fort Dearborn

540 N Dearborn Street, at W Grand Avenue, Near North/River North (312 644 7528). CTA Grand. **Open** 7.30am-5pm daily. **Map** p307 H10.

Loop Station

211 S Clark Street, at W Adams Street, The Loop (312 427 4225). CTA Jackson (Blue, Red). **Open** 7am-6pm Mon-Fri. **Map** p305 H12.

Ontario

227 E Ontario Street, at N St Clair Street, Near North/Streeterville (312 642 7698). CTA Grand. **Open** 8am-6pm Mon-Fri. **Map** p306 J10.

Religion

Devout travellers are in luck in Chicago. There are places of worship just about everywhere you turn, in almost every denomination you can imagine (and a few you can't).

Baptist

Unity Fellowship Baptist Church

211 N Cicero Avenue, at W Maypole Avenue, West Side (773 287 0267). CTA Cicero (Green). **Services** 8.15am, 11.15am, 5pm Sun.

Catholic

Holy Name Cathedral

735 N State Street, at E Superior Street, Near North (312 787 8040). CTA Chicago (Red). **Services** 6am, 7am, 8am, 12.10pm, 5.15pm Mon-Fri; 5.15pm, 7.30pm Sat; 7am, 8.15am, 9.30am, 11am, 12.30pm, 5.15pm Sun. **Map** p306 H10.

Old St Mary's Church

23 E Van Buren Street, at S State Street, The Loop (312 922 3444). CTA Library. **Services** 7.15am, 12.10pm Mon-Fri; noon, 5pm Sat; 8am, 10.30am, noon Sun. **Map** p305 H13.

Eastern Orthodox

St George Orthodox Cathedral

917 N Wood Street, at W Iowa Street, West Side (312 666 5179). CTA Chicago (Blue). **Services** 9.30am Sun.

Episcopal

Grace Episcopal Church

637 S Dearborn Street, at W Harrison Street, South Loop (312 922 1426). CTA Harrison. **Services** 12.15pm Wed; 8am, 11am Sun. **Map** p305 H13.

Episcopal Church of St James

65 E Huron Street, at N Wabash Avenue, Near North/Magnificent Mile (312 787 7360). CTA Chicago (Red). **Services** 12.10pm Mon, Tue, Thur, Fri; 12.10pm, 5.30pm Wed; 9am Sat; 8am, 9am, 11am Sun. **Map** p306 H10.

Jewish

Chicago Loop Synagogue

15 S Clark Street, at W Madison Street, The Loop (312 346 7370). CTA Monroe (Blue/Red). **Services** 8.05am Mon-Fri. **Map** p305 H12.

Chicago Sinai Congregation (Reform)

15 W Delaware Place, at N State Street, Gold Coast (312 867 7000). CTA Chicago (Red). **Services** 6.15pm Fri; 11am Sun. **Map** p306 H9.

Lutheran

First St Paul's Evangelical Lutheran Church

1301 N LaSalle Street, at W Goether Street, Gold Coast (312 642 7172). CTA Clark/Division. **Services** 7am, 7pm Wed; 9.15am, 11am Sun. **Map** p307 H8.

Methodist

Chicago Temple First United Methodist Church

77 W Washington Boulevard, at N Clark Street, The Loop (312 236 4548). CTA Washington (Brown/Orange/Purple). **Services** 5pm Sat; 8.30, 11am Sun. **Map** p305 H12.

Muslim

Downtown Islamic Center

218 S Wabash Avenue, at E Jackson Boulevard, The Loop (312 787 9095). CTA Adams or Jackson (Red). **Services** 1.30pm, 5.20pm Mon-Thur; noon Fri. **Map** p305 H12.

Presbyterian

Fourth Presbyterian Church

126 E Chestnut Street, at N Michigan Avenue, Near North/Magnificent Mile (312 787 4570). CTA Chicago (Red). **Services** 8am, 11am, 6.30pm Sun. **Map** p306 J9.

Quaker

Fellowship of Friends

515 W Oak Street, at N Mohawk Street (312 944 4493). CTA Chicago (Brown/Purple). **Services** 11am Sun. **Map** p306 G9.

Safety

Safety in Chicago is pretty much a matter of common sense. Among the dos and don'ts are:

● Don't draw attention to yourself by unfolding a huge map and looking lost.
● Don't leave your purse, pocketbook or wallet in a place where you could easily be pickpocketed (for example, in your back pocket, or in an undone bag).
● Do beware of hustlers: while one person is disturbing you from the front, another could already be half a block away with your cash and credit cards.
● Do leave valuables in a hotel safe if at all possible.
● Don't carry too much cash at any one time, and if you have multiple credit cards, leave one or more at the hotel in case of emergencies.
● Do avoid deserted areas late at night: the West Loop, for example.

In addition, there are some parts of town that are no-go areas for tourists. Among them are the Cabrini-Green housing complex (south of Division Street and west of Orleans); some parts of the West Side, especially around Little Italy; and parts of the South Side.

Students

While never considered a great collegiate city, Chicago has a large and active student population as well as a number of excellent universities. Indeed, it's probably only a matter of time before some marketing genius in the mayor's office comes up with a slogan like 'City of Big Learners'. This prevalence of excellent educational establishments is of obvious benefit to the city: not least because there are a lot of students who want a lot of places in which to drink and dance, which brings a boost to the local economy. Though there are plenty of clubs and bars in the downtown area, those are mostly for locals; for the most part, students tend to hang out closer to their schools.

DePaul University

2320 N Kenmore Avenue, at W Fullerton Street, Lincoln Park (773 325 7000/www.depaul.edu). CTA Fullerton. **Map** p308 E5.

Directory

Useful numbers

Emergency services 911
Local directory enquiries 411
National directory enquiries 1 + [area code] + 555 1212
Operator O
International operator OO
US international access code 011
International country codes UK 44; Australia 61; Japan 81

While not the most prestigious school in the city, DePaul University has it made when it comes to nightlife thanks to its Lincoln Park location. There are clubs, bars, and storefront theatres just littering the place. The natives – frat boys, many of 'em – can get restless at times, but there's usually another, quieter spot just around the corner that you can nip off to if you like. The **John Barleycorn Memorial Pub** (*see p153*) and the **Red Lion Pub** (*see p155*) are both classic DePaul watering holes.

Loyola University Chicago

6525 N Sheridan Road, at W Devon Avenue, Far North (773 274 3000/ www.luc.edu). CTA Loyola.
The Chicago branch of Loyola University has about 14,000 students on its two campuses. The Water Tower campus is near the Gold Coast, but there's not much in the way of student housing down there and so there's very little campus life (though law students tend to throng across the street to **Flapjaws Saloon**, 22 E Pearson Street, at N State Street; 312 642 4848). The main campus is on the North Side lakeshore in Rogers Park. It's a diverse neighbourhood with a good selection of unpretentious bars such as **Hamilton's Pub** (6341 N Broadway, at W Rosemont Avenue, Far North; 773 764 8133).

Northwestern University

1999 Sheridan Road, at Foster Street, Evanston (847 491 3741/ www.northwestern.edu). CTA Foster.
Like Loyola, Northwestern Univeristy is split between a north lakeshore and a downtown campus. Of the almost 18,000 students, most of them reside on or near the school's Edenic, tree-lined main campus in Evanston. The most common complaint of students is the lack of serious nightlife up there, though **Pete Miller's Steakhouse** (1557 Sherman Avenue; 847 328 0399) is a great, though expensive, place for a

martini, a steak and some live jazz. Northwestern's Magnificent Mile campus has some lakeshore housing, and students there (mostly business and medical students) tend to head up to the Rush and Division bars a few minutes' walk away.

University of Chicago

5801 S Ellis Avenue, at E 58th Street, Hyde Park (773 702 1234/ www.uchicago.edu). Metra 59th Street. **Map** p311 X17.
One of the most renowned educational institutions in the world, the University of Chicago is located in beautiful Hyde Park. The neighbourhood is known more for its museums and amazing array of bookstores than its nightlife, though **Jimmy's Woodlawn Tap** (1172 E 55th Street, at S Woodlawn Avenue; 773 643 5516) is one of the few notable bars here, not least because it keeps an encyclopedia and a compete set of Shakespeare plays on hand with which to settle disputes.

University of Illinois-Chicago

1200 W Harrison Street, at S Halsted Street, West Side (312 996 3000/www.uic.edu). CTA UIC-Halsted.
The University of Illinois-Chicago was built a little to the west of the Loop in 1965 by Mayor Daley. Boasting some 25,000 students, it's now the largest school in the city. Unfortunately, Daley bulldozed a formerly vibrant community to make way for the school, and it's taken it a while to recover. Fortunately, just a few blocks north is the West Loop neighbourhood with a thriving bar and restaurant scene.

Language schools

Berlitz Language Center

2 N LaSalle Street, at E Madison Street, The Loop (312 943 4262). CTA Washington (Brown/Orange/ Purple. **Credit** AmEx, MC, V. **Map** p305 H12.

International Language Communication School

333 N Michigan Avenue, at the Chicago River, Near North/ Magnificent Mile (773 549 6441). CTA Grand. **Credit** MC, V. **Map** p306 J11.

Telephones

Dialling & codes

There are five area codes in the Chicago metropolitan area. Area code 312 covers downtown Chicago (roughly as far north, west and south as 1600 on the street grid); 773 covers the rest of the city; the northern suburbs are area code 847; the southern and western suburbs are 708; and the areas to the far west are 630. If you are calling locally, you don't need to dial the area code. Otherwise, you should dial 1, followed by the appropriate area code, followed by a seven-digit number (this applies to all US and Canada numbers).

When calling Chicago from abroad, dial the international access code of the country from which you are calling (00 from the UK), followed by the US country code (1), followed by the area code and number (as before). Numbers prefaced by 1-800, 1-888 and 1-877 are toll-free. Numbers prefaced with 1-900 are charged at a premium rate.

If you encounter voicemail, note that the 'pound' key is the one marked # and the 'star' key *. On automated answering systems, '0' often gets you straight to an operator without having to endure the usual Dantean nightmare.

To call abroad from Chicago (or anywhere else in the States), dial the international access code (011), followed by the country code (44 for the UK; 64 New Zealand; 61 Australia; 49 Germany; 81 Japan – see the phone book for others) and then the area code and number.

If you want to make a collect (reverse charges) call, dial '0' for the operator before dialling the number you are trying to reach.

Mobile phones

Pretty much everywhere in the Chicago metropolitan area is well covered for cellular phone service. If you're leaving town, you might experience some service difficulties in downstate Illinois or central Wisconsin. Check with your carrier before leaving the area. Foreign visitors should also note that Chicago's cellular phone network is not GSM-compatible, and you'll need to contact your phone service provider before you leave for Chicago if you're with a GSM-based network at home.

If you want to get cellular service while you're in town, check the *Yellow Pages* for dealers, or try either of the dealers listed below.

AT&T Wireless Service

235 W Monroe Street, at N Franklin Street, The Loop (1-888 383 4727). CTA Quincy. **Open** 8am-6pm Mon-Fri. **Map** p305 G12.

Cellular One

170 W Ontario Street, at N LaSalle Street, Near North/Streeterville (312 642 7800). CTA Grand. **Open** 9am-6pm Mon-Fri; 10am-4pm Sat. **Map** p306 H10.

Public phones

To use a public phone, pick up the receiver, listen for a dialling tone and feed it change (35¢ for a local call); some phones ask you to dial first and then assess the cost. Operator, directory and emergency calls are free. It is not advisable to use a payphone for long-distance or international calls, as a quarter is the highest denomination a payphone will accept. A recorded voice will tell you how much change you need to put in to complete the call.

It's worth remembering that in Chicago, calling a number that's only several blocks away can sometimes mean using an entirely different area code, which can cost at least $1. Depending upon the length of your visit, you may be better off buying a phone card.

Phone cards

European-style prepaid phone cards that you insert directly into public phones instead of change are not available in the United States. However, in their absence, several rival telecommunications companies provide charge cards linked to an account, which are available from supermarkets, drugstores and convenience stores in various denominations.

Shop around for the longest talk-time for the lowest price. Examples include **AT&T** (1-800 225 5288), **MCI** (1-800 888 8000) and **Sprint** (1-800 366 2255), though there are plenty of smaller companies touting for custom in what is an extremely competitive field. When looking for the best deal, don't just look at the price per minute to the area you think you'll be calling most: also pay attention to the small print that details connection charges. Though a card may offer 5¢ a minute to the UK, say, the connection charges may be up to $1 more per call than with those cards that offer rates of 6¢ or 7¢ per minute; the same goes for long-distance calls within the US.

A phone card is also a must-have if you're staying in a hotel and expect to make a few calls. Many high-end hotels – and more than a few low-end ones – charge absurd rates for phone calls made from guestrooms, with charges getting more ludicrous the further away you're calling (international calls, for example, are impossibly dear).

Chicago operates under US Central Standard Time (CST), six hours behind Greenwich Mean Time (GMT) and one hour behind Eastern Standard Time (EST). The border between Eastern and Central Standard Times is just to the east of Chicago: Michigan and most of Indiana are in the EST zone. From the first Sunday in April until the last Sunday in October 'Daylight Saving Time' means the clocks in Chicago are one hour ahead of CST.

Tipping

First rule of tipping: don't forget to do it. Waiters, bartenders, bellhops and the like are often paid a menial wage and many depend on tips to get by. Don't be a tightwad.

In general, tip bartenders and waiters 15 per cent or thereabouts. Cab drivers should also get around 15 per cent. Hotel staff also expect – and deserve – tipping. Bellhops should be given a buck a bag, while doormen, valet parkers and chambermaids merit a dollar or two (for the latter, leave it on the pillow each morning as you leave the room).

Tourist information

Chicago Office of Tourism

Chicago Cultural Center, 78 E Washington Boulevard, at N Michigan Avenue, The Loop (1-800 226 6632/312 744 2400/fax 312 744 2359/www.ci.chi.il.us/tourism). CTA Randolph or Washington (Blue). **Open** *telephone enquiries* 9am-5pm Mon-Fri. **Map** p305 J12. Contact the Office of Tourism for a free visitor information pack on Chicago's events and attractions.

Chicago Water Works Visitors' Center

163 E Pearson Street, at N Michigan Avenue, Near North/Magnificent Mile. CTA Chicago (Red). **Open**

Directory

information booth 7.30am-7pm daily; *Hot Tix* 10am-6pm Tue-Sat; 11am-5pm Sun; closed Mon; *City of Chicago Store* 9.30am-5pm Mon-Sat; 11am-5pm Sun; *Flat Sammies* 7.30am-5pm daily. **Map** p306 J9.
Located in a 19th-century Pumping Station, the recently renovated visitors' centre includes a tourist information booth; the City of Chicago Store, which sells souvenirs and collectibles; Hot Tix, which offers half-price tickets for over 125 theatres in the Chicago area (*see p235* **Theatre, Dance & Comedy**), and a restaurant, Flat Sammies.

Chicago Cultural Center Visitors' Information Center

77 E Randolph Street, at Michigan Avenue. CTA Randolph or Washington (Blue). **Open** 10am-6pm Mon-Fri; 10am-5pm Sat, Sun. **Map** p305 J12.
An essential stop for all visitors to Chicago, the Cultural Center was built as the city's first public library in 1897. Come here for tourist information, free leaflets and maps, and to join one of several tours of the city. Art exhibitions and live shows are also often held here.

Illinois Market Place Visitors' Information Center

Navy Pier, 700 E Grand Avenue, Near North/Streeterville. CTA 65, 66 bus. **Open** 10am-8pm Mon-Thur; 10am-10pm Fri, Sat; 10am-8pm Sun. **Map** p306 K10.
An information booth with leaflets about attractions in Chicago and further afield.

Chicago Convention & Tourism Bureau

McCormick Place, 2301 S Lake Shore Drive, at Lake Michigan, South Side (312 567 8500/fax 312 567 8533/www.chicago.il.org). **Open** 8am-5pm Mon-Fri.
Information on conventions and, to a lesser extent, tourism in the city.

Illinois Bureau of Tourism

Suite 3400, James R Thompson Center, 100 W Randolph Street, at N LaSalle Street (1-800 226 6632/312 814 4732/www.enjoyillinois.com). CTA Washington (Brown/Orange/Purple). **Open** *1-800 number* 24hrs daily; *office & 312 number* 8.30am-5pm Mon-Fri. **Map** p305 H11.
Staff here can supply visitors with details on tourism and attractions in the state of Illinois.

Tours

For details of sightseeing tours of Chicago, *see page 82* **Tours**.

Visas

Under the Visa Waiver Programme, citizens of the UK, Japan, Australia, New Zealand and all west European countries (except for Portugal, Greece and the Vatican City) do not need a visa for stays in the US of less than 90 days – business or pleasure – if they have a passport that is valid for the full 90-day period and a return ticket. An open standby ticket is acceptable.
    Canadians and Mexicans do not need visas but must have legal proof of their residency. All other travellers must have visas. Full information and visa application forms can be obtained from your nearest US embassy or consulate.
    In general, send in your application at least three weeks before you plan to travel. Visas required more urgently should be applied for via the travel agent booking your ticket.

US Embassy Visa Information (UK only)

Recorded information 0891 200 290 (50p per minute)/advice & appointments 0991 500 590 (£1.50 per minute)/fax 020 7495 5012.

Women

In so far as Chicago is a safe city, it's a safe city for women: that is, there are places into which you shouldn't venture late at night, though this is the case whether you're male or female (*see page 287* **Safety**). However, when walking the streets at night – especially alone, which is not ideal – you'd do well to take as much care as you'd take in any big city: avoid unlit and deserted streets

and be alert for people trailing you. When travelling on trains late at night, seek out the busiest carriage.

CCHR Advisory Council on Women

Information: 312 744 4113.
An equal opportunities advocate overseen by the City's Commission on Human Relations.

Chicago Rape Crisis Hotline

1-888 293 2080. **Open** 24hrs daily.
Rape crisis counselling, and referrals to other organisations.

Greenhouse Shelter

Chicago Abused Women Coalition, PO Box 477916, Chicago, IL 60647 (shelter hotline 773 278 4566). **Open** *hotline* 24hrs daily.
Emergency accommodation, food and clothing for abused women and their children, plus counselling, advocacy and information on a range of issues.

National Organization for Women (NOW)

30 E Adams Street, at N State Street, The Loop (312 578 9351/www.chicagonow.org). CTA Adams. **Map** p305 H12.
A group devoted to furthering feminist issues and causes.

Rape Victim Advocates of Chicago

Suite 240, 228 S Wabash Avenue, at E Jackson Boulevard, The Loop (312 663 6303). CTA Adams. **Open** *office* 9am-5pm Mon-Fri. **Map** p305 H12.
Counselling and advocacy for victims of sexual assault.

YWCA Chicago

180 N Wabash Avenue, E Lake Street, The Loop (312 372 6600). CTA Lake or State. **Open** 8.30am-5pm. **Map** p305 H11.
Counselling and childcare.

Working in Chicago

Foreigners seeking work in the US must enlist a US company to sponsor them for an H-1 visa, which permits the holder to work in the US for five years. It will also have to convince the Immigration department that no American is qualified to do the job. Contact your American embassy for full details.

Further Reading

Fiction

Nelson Algren
The Neon Wilderness
This collection of short stories made Algren's name when it was published in 1947, and set the scene for novels including *Never Come Morning* and *The Man with the Golden Arm*.
Saul Bellow *The Adventures of Augie March*
A coming-of-age tale of sorts, and one of several Chicago novels by the mighty Bellow; also worth investigating is the magisterial *Humboldt's Gift*.
Theodore Dreiser
Sister Carrie
Perhaps the first great Chicago novel, a tale of the corruption of a young woman in the big bad city.
James T Farrell
Studs Lonigan
Farrell's three Studs Lonigan books – *Young Lonigan*, *The Young Manhood Of Studs Lonigan* and *Judgment Day* – tell of the coming of age of an Irish-American in Chicago in the early 20th century, and are available in one University of Illinois-published paperback.
Eugene Izzi *The Criminalist*
Eugene Izzi was found hanging outside the window of his Loop office in 1996. A situation which would, were he still alive, have made a great premise for one of his gritty city crime novels.
Sara Paretsky
VI Warshawski
A three-novel volume featuring Paretsky's 'tec creation, containing *Indemnity Only*, *Deadlock* and *Killing Orders*. Warshawski appears in innumerable Paretsky novels, though this offers as good a crash-course as any.
Upton Sinclair *The Jungle*
Sinclair's masterpiece, which caused a major sensation when published in 1906, is set in the Chicago stockyards at the turn of the century.

Scott Turow
The Laws of Our Fathers
One of many blockbusting page-turners from the Chicago lawyer turned author; others include *Presumed Innocent* and *Guilty as Charged*.

Non-fiction

Jane Addams *20 Years at Hull House*
An autobiography of sorts from the pioneering social reformer.
Simone de Beauvoir
Beloved Chicago Man
The French writer's letters to one-time beau Nelson Algren make for fascinating reading.
Gwendolyn Brooks
Selected Poems
An excellent collection of poetry from the first African-American winner of the Pulitzer Prize.
Sandra Cisneros
Loose Woman
A collection of poems by the author of the excellent *A House on Mango Street*.
Robert Cromie *The Great Chicago Fire*
How the city lost its innocence. And most of its buildings, too.
Peter Golenbock *Wrigleyville*
The sorry story of the Chicago Cubs, entertainingly told.
Ben Hecht and Charles MacArthur *The Front Page*
Classic stage work co-authored by a notable local hack.
LeAlan Jones and Lloyd Newman *Our America*
Subtitled 'Life and Death on Chicago's South Side', *Our America* tells of life in Chicago's ghettos as seen through the eyes of two teenaged residents.
Richard Lindberg
To Serve and Collect
Splendidly-titled survey of police corruption in Chicago between 1855 and 1960.
David Mamet *Mamet Plays 1*
A selection of Mamet's stage works, including *Sexual Perversity in Chicago*.

Mike Royko *One More Time*
A collection of articles by the grand old man of Chicago journalism. Also worth a look is his biography of former mayor Richard J Daley, *Boss*.
Carl Sandburg *Selected Poems*
As edited by George and Willene Hendrick, this collection of Sandburg's oeuvre includes the classic *Chicago Poems*.
Richard Schneirov et al (eds) *The Pullman Strike and the Crisis of the 1890s*
One of the defining moments in Chicago's history gets the essay treatment.
Alice Sinkevitch (ed)
AIA Guide to Chicago
'AIA' stands for the American Institute of Architects, who, with the Chicago Architecture Foundation, are behind this excellent survey of the city's notable buildings.
David Starkey, Richard Guzman (eds) *Smokestacks and Skyscrapers*
Chicago Writing 101, with extracts from works by over 70 Chicago writers (including many on this list). Useful.
Studs Terkel
Division Street: America
One of many hugely worthwhile books from the country's premier social historian: others include *Coming of Age* and *Working*.
Bill Veeck with Ed Linn
Veeck As In Wreck
The autobiography of the legendary baseball executive who planted the ivy at Wrigley Field before later buying the White Sox. One of the most entertaining sports books ever written; sadly, it's out of print.
Lynne Warren et al (ed)
Art in Chicago 1945-1995
Exactly what you'd expect: a survey of over 100 artists who worked in Chicago during the 50 years following World War II.
Richard Wright *Native Son*
A prescient tale of murder and racial issues in Chicago.

Directory

Advertisers' Index

Please refer to the relevant sections for
addresses/telephone numbers

Maps

Place of interest and/or entertainment	☐
Railway stations	☐
Parks	☐
Hospitals/universities	☐
Neighbourhood	LOOP
Metra station	Ⓜ
CTA station (colour designates line)	Clark ✥

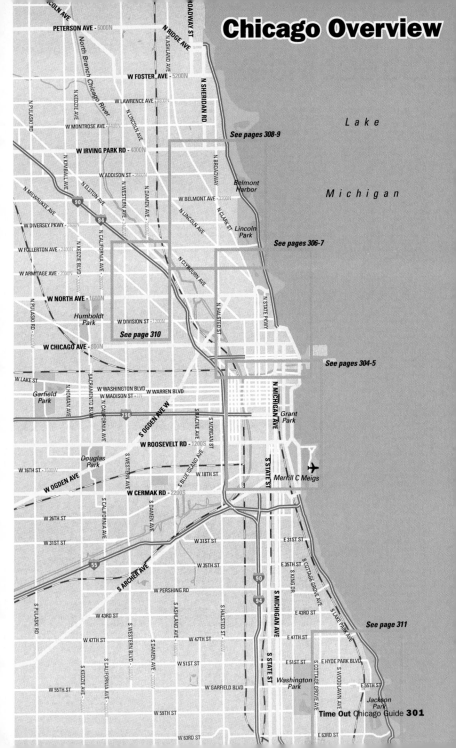

PETERSON AVE - 6000N

North Branch Chicago River

W FOSTER AVE - 5200N

W LAWRENCE AVE - 4800N

W MONTROSE AVE - 4400N

W IRVING PARK RD - 4000N

W ADDISON ST - 3600N

W BELMONT AVE - 3200N

Lake

Michigan

Belmont Harbor

See pages 308-9

W DIVERSEY PKWY - 2800N

W FULLERTON AVE - 2400N

W ARMITAGE AVE - 2000N

Lincoln Park

See pages 306-7

W NORTH AVE - 1600N

Humboldt Park

W DIVISION ST - 1200N

See page 310

W CHICAGO AVE - 800N

See pages 304-5

W LAKE ST

Garfield Park

W WASHINGTON BLVD

W WARREN BLVD

W MADISON ST - 1N

Grant Park

S OGDEN AVE W

W ROOSEVELT RD - 1200S

Douglas Park

W 16TH ST - 1600W

W 18TH ST

Merrill C Meigs

W OGDEN AVE

W CERMAK RD - 2200S

W 26TH ST

W 31ST ST

W 31ST ST

E 31ST ST

W 35TH ST

E 35TH ST

W PERSHING RD

W 43RD ST

E 43RD ST

See page 311

W 47TH ST

W 47TH ST

E 47TH ST

W 51ST ST

E 51ST ST

E HYDE PARK BLVD

Washington Park

W GARFIELD BLVD

E 55TH ST

Jackson Park

W 55TH ST

W 59TH ST

W 63RD ST

E 63RD ST

Street Index

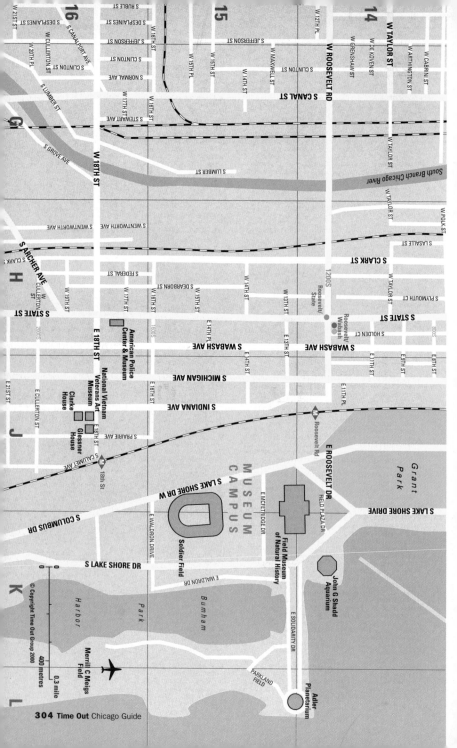

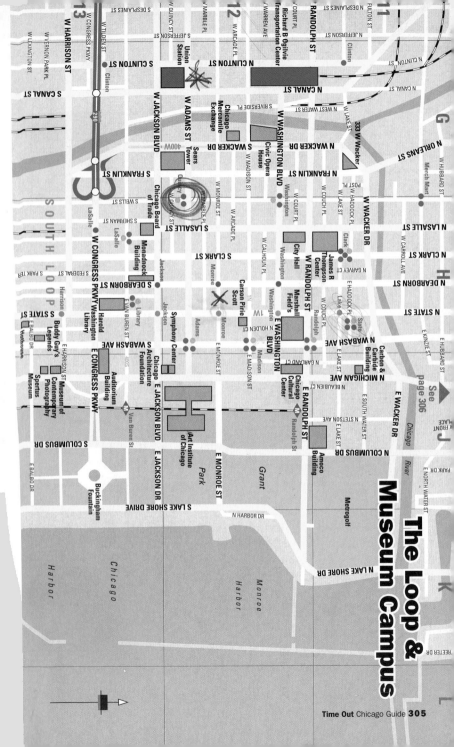

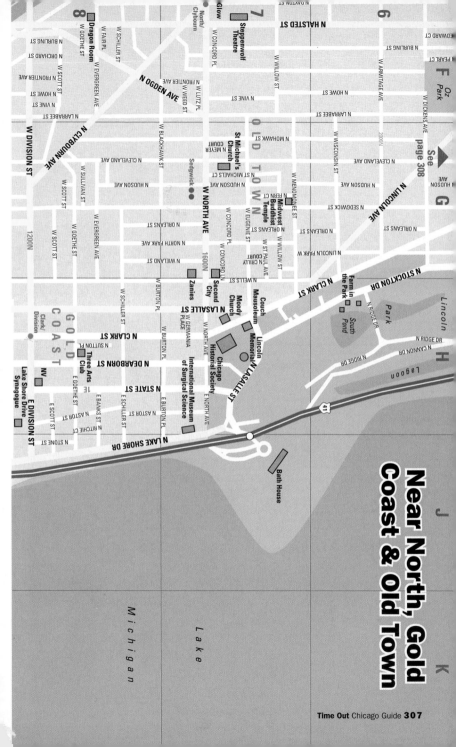

Near North, Gold Coast & Old Town

8 Dragon Room
W GOETHE ST
W FAIR PL
W BURLING ST
N ORCHARD ST
W BURTON ST
N HALSTED ST
Glow
North/Clybourn
7 Steppenwolf Theatre
W CONCORD PL
W SCHILLER ST
N HOWE ST
W SCOTT ST
N LARRABEE ST
W EVERGREEN AVE
N CLYBOURN AVE
N OGDEN AVE
N FRONTIER AVE
W WEED ST
N LUTZ PL
W VINE ST
W WILLOW ST
N HOWE ST
W ARMITAGE AVE
N LARRABEE ST
W DICKENS AVE
EDWARD CT
PEARL CT
Oz Park
F
W DIVISION ST
N CLYBOURN AVE
W SULLIVAN ST
W BLACKHAWK ST
N CLEVELAND AVE
Sedgwick
St Michael's Church
N MEYER CT
N ST MICHAELS CT
N MOHAWK ST
O L D   T O W N
W WISCONSIN ST
N CLEVELAND AVE
N HUDSON AVE
N SEDGWICK ST
N LINCOLN AVE
See page 308
2000N
G
1200N
W SCOTT ST
W GOETHE ST
W EVERGREEN AVE
W HUDSON AVE
N ORLEANS ST
Midwest Buddhist Temple
N FERN CT
W NORTH AVE
W EUGENIE ST
W MENOMONEE ST
N HUDSON AVE
N ORLEANS ST
N ORLEANS ST
1600N
N WIELAND ST
N NORTH PARK AVE
W CONCORD PL
W CONCORD PL
N CRILLY CT
W ST PAUL AVE
W WILLOW ST
W CONCORD PL
N SEDGWICK ST
N LINCOLN PARK W
W BURTON PL
W BURTON PL
Zanies
Second City
N LASALLE ST
N WELLS ST
Moody Church
Couch Mausoleum
N CLARK ST
N STOCKTON DR
Farm in the Park
N RIDGE DR
South Pond
Lincoln Park
H
W SCHILLER ST
W GERMANIA PLACE
Chicago Historical Society
W NORTH AVE
N LASALLE ST
Lincoln Memorial
N RIDGE DR
N CANNON DR
Clark/Division
G O L D   C O A S T
Three Arts Club
N SUTTON PL
N DEARBORN ST
International Museum of Surgical Science
1E
E GOETHE ST
E BANKS ST
E BURTON PL
Lake
N STATE ST
NV
Lake Shore Drive Synagogue
E DIVISION ST
E SCOTT ST
N RITCHIE CT
N ASTOR ST
E SCHILLER ST
E BANKS ST
N STONE ST
N LAKE SHORE DR
Bath House
L a g o o n
J
M i c h i g a n
L a k e
M i c h i g a n
K

Lincoln Park & Lake View

1 N ASHLAND AVE

2 1600W

3

W OAKDALE AVE
W NELSON ST
W BARRY AVE
W OAKDALE AVE

W MELROSE ST
W FLETCHER ST

W BELMONT AVE

Athenaeum Theatre

Elbo Room

Pops for Champagne

W GEORGE ST

W WELLINGTON AVE

Wellington

Vic Theatre

W BELMONT AVE

Berlin

Belmont

W FLETCHER ST

Briar Street Theatre

Spin

Ivanhoe Theatre

N CLARK ST

Comedy Sportz

3200N

About Face Theatre

N BOSWORTH AVE
N GREENVIEW AVE
N JANSSEN AVE
N SOUTHPORT AVE
N WAYNE AVE

Music Box Theatre

D

Schubas Tavern

Southport Lanes

Ballwick Repertory/ Theatre Building

W BELMONT AVE

W HENDERSON ST
W ROSCOE ST
W CORNELIA AVE

Shell Park

Southport

W LAKEWOOD AVE
W MAGNOLIA AVE
N RACINE AVE
N CLIFTON AVE
N SEMINARY AVE
N KENMORE AVE
N SHEFFIELD AVE
N WILTON AVE

W ADDISON ST

Wild Hare

W EDDY ST

Improv Olympic

Wrigley Field

Addison

3600N

W PATTERSON AVE
W WAVELAND AVE
N CLIFTON AVE
N SEMINARY AVE
N KENMORE AVE

Metro

Annoyance Theatre

CLARK ST

ALTA VISTA TER

WRIGLEYVILLE

N WILTON AVE

W BRADLEY PL

Strawdog Theatre

Park

E

N GRACE ST

N JANSSEN AVE

W NEWPORT AVE
W CORNELIA AVE

W BUCKINGHAM PL
W ALDINE AVE

N RETA AVE
N FREMONT ST
N HALSTED ST

W PATTERSON AVE

F

W BROMPTON AVE

N ELAINE PL

800W

W PINE GROVE AVE

W ROSCOE ST
W MELROSE ST
W ALDINE AVE
W HAWTHORNE PL
W STRATFORD PL
W ADDISON ST
W BROMPTON AVE

N LAKE SHORE DR

41

W BELMONT HARBOR DR

Belmont Harbor

Lake Michigan

G

H

N MILDRED AVE
N WILTON AVE
N NELSON ST
N SEMINARY AVE
W FLETCHER ST
N DAYTON ST
N CALIFORNIA TER
W ORCHARD ST
W BARRY AVE
N WATERLOO CT
N BRIAR PL

W SURF ST
W OAKDALE AVE
W BURLING S

N BROADWAY
N CAMBRIDGE AVE
N HUDSON AVE
N PINE GROVE AVE

W PINE GROVE AVE
W BRIAR PL
W BARRY AVE
W SURF ST

N SHERIDAN RD
N COMMONWEALTH AV

Wicker Park
& Bucktown

© Copyright Time Out Group 2000

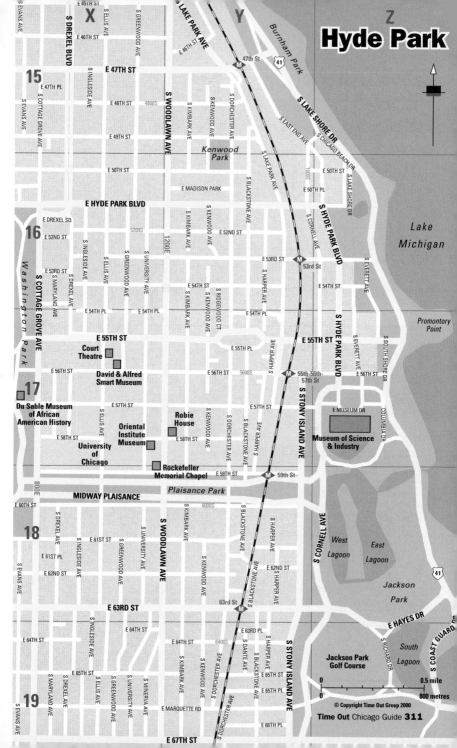

Hyde Park

Downtown Travel

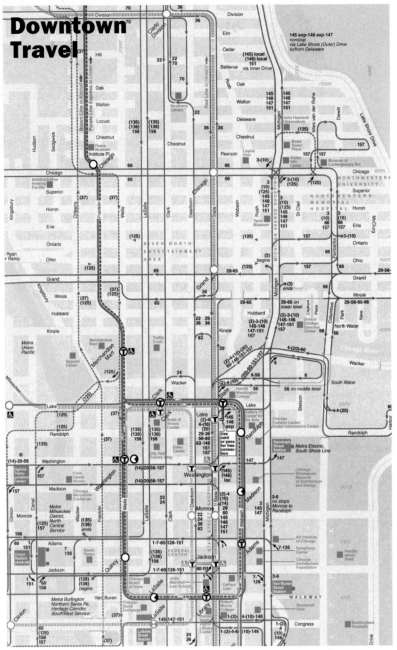

Trips Out of Town

© Copyright Time Out Group 2000

0   150 km
0   100 miles

WISCONSIN

Stevens Point

Green Bay

Appleton

Oshkosh

Wisconsin Dells

Baraboo

Madison

Mount Horeb

New Glarus

Galena

Rockford

Waukesha

Milwaukee

Arlington Heights

CHICAGO
See Overview Map

Aurora

Moline

ILLINOIS

Peoria

Bloomington

Champaign

Decatur

Springfield

Green Bay

Washington Island

Beaver Island

Lake Michigan

Traverse City

Cadillac

MICHIGAN

Grand Rapids

Holland

Lansing

South Haven

Kalamazoo

Gary

Hobart

South Bend

Fort Wayne

INDIANA

Kokomo

Anderson

Crawfordsville

Rockville

Indianapolis

Terre Haute

Columbus

Mackinac Island

Lake Huron

Mackinaw City

CTA Rail System

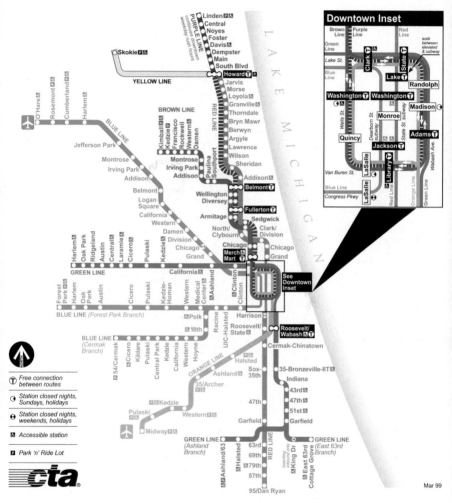

CHICAGO

FOR THE TIME OF YOUR LIFE.

GETAWAY TO CHICAGO FOR WORLD-CLASS MUSEUMS AND ATTRACTIONS AND PLENTY OF YEAR-ROUND EVENTS AND ACTIVITIES.

CHICAGO FESTIVALS AND EVENTS:

CHICAGO WINTERBREAK–
JANUARY-MARCH

GREAT CHICAGO PLACES
& SPACES–MAY

CHICAGO GOSPEL MUSIC
FESTIVAL–JUNE

CHICAGO BLUES
FESTIVAL–JUNE

CHICAGO COUNTRY
MUSIC FESTIVAL–
JUNE-JULY

TASTE OF CHICAGO–
JUNE-JULY

VENETIAN NIGHT–JULY

CHICAGO AIR & WATER
SHOW–AUGUST

VIVA! CHICAGO–AUGUST

CHICAGO JAZZ FESTIVAL–
AUGUST-SEPTEMBER

CELTIC FEST CHICAGO–
SEPTEMBER

WORLD MUSIC FESTIVAL
CHICAGO–SEPTEMBER

CHICAGOWEEN–OCTOBER

CHICAGO HOLIDAY FUN–
OCTOBER-JANUARY 1

CITY OF CHICAGO
RICHARD M. DALEY
MAYOR

FOR MORE INFORMATION ABOUT CHICAGO SPECIAL EVENTS VISIT THE MAYOR'S OFFICE OF SPECIAL EVENTS WEBSITE AT WWW.CITYOFCHICAGO.ORG/SPECIALEVENTS OR CALL (312) 744-3315

FOR MORE INFORMATION ABOUT CHICAGO, VISIT THE CHICAGO OFFICE OF TOURISM'S WEBSITE AT WWW.CITYOFCHICAGO.ORG/TOURISM OR CALL (312) 744-2400

Illinois 2000
The celebration of a lifetime

Time Out

Chicago

From the top of the Sears Tower to the bottom of Lake
Michigan, the first edition of the *Time Out Chicago Guide*
has the Windy City well and truly covered. Written and
researched by a team of resident writers and with colour
photographs throughout, it's the definitive guide to
America's most underrated city.

The Chicago Guide includes:

- the lowdown on the world-renowned architecture of the Loop
- enough great restaurants, bars and entertainment venues to fill
your every evening for 12 months or more
- Wrigley Field, Soldier Field and the full scoop on local sports
- the blues and Barenboim: Chicago's music scene in full
- the Magnificent Mile and beyond in a detailed shopping section
- comprehensive, full-colour maps of the city, and map references
for every venue featured in the guide

... all with full details of opening times, prices and transport.

'Time Out's guides have become standards'
The Times

'The most hip and culturally savvy I've used'
The New York Times

First Edition

PENGUIN
Reference

ISBN 0-14-029078-8

U.K.	£10.99
CAN	$20.99
U.S.	$14.95

9 780140 290783